PROMISE AND PERFORMANCE OF AMERICAN DEMOCRACY

THIRD EDITION

JOHN WILEY & SONS, INC.

NEW YORK   LONDON   SYDNEY   TORONTO

PROMISE AND PERFORMANCE OF AMERICAN DEMOCRACY

Richard A. Watson
UNIVERSITY OF MISSOURI-COLUMBIA

with
Michael Fitzgerald
UNIVERSITY OF MISSOURI-COLUMBIA

This book was designed by Angie Lee.
Photo research by Rosemary Eakins and Peggy Allen.
Photo Editor, Stella Kupferberg.
Depth Editor, Arthur Vergara.
Production was supervised by Debra Schwartz.

Library of Congress Cataloging in Publication Data:

Watson, Richard Abernathy, 1923–
    Promise and performance of American government, state and local edition.

    Enl. version of F. A. Watson's Promise and performance of American democracy, 3d ed.
    Includes bibliographies and index.
    1. United States—Politics and government—Handbooks, manuals, etc. I. Fitzgerald, Michael R., 1947–   joint author. II. Title.
JK274.W33   1977b   320.4'73   77-20869
ISBN 0-471-02916-5

Printed in the United States of America.

10 9 8 7 6 5 4 3 2 1

To George A. Peek, Jr.
who first stimulated my interest in the basic course

And to my students
who have sustained it.

The essential purpose of this edition of the text remains the same as that of previous editions, namely, to provide basic factual information about American government, concepts around which to organize that information, and a critical evaluation of the American political system. I have also retained the basic organizational approach that is a distinguishing feature of this book and that both teachers and students say works so well in the classroom: comparing the actual performance of American democracy with its theoretical promises.

However, unlike so many new editions of textbooks, this is a genuine *revision* and not just an updating of previous material. Many of the ideas for the revision came from a survey of users of the second edition undertaken by the Wiley organization in early 1976. In addition, Robert Kvavik of the University of Minnesota and Norman Thomas of the University of Cincinnati did in-depth, chapter-by-chapter analyses of the second edition and offered many helpful suggestions for the book's improvement. I appreciate the constructive criticisms I received from all these sources and have included most of their suggestions for needed changes in this third edition.

The most basic organizational change in this edition consists in the incorporation of material on public policy making *throughout* the text instead of an isolated inclusion of the material in a separate section. There are two reasons for this. The first is the very practical one that over half the respondents in the user survey said that constraints of time did not permit them to get to the last three chapters of the previous editions; and these chapters dealt specifically with public policy. The second reason is the greater soundness of relating policy to process so that a student can see how major decisions on matters of public policy are shaped by the kinds of people who participate in the political process, by the structures and procedures utilized by the Congress, the executive branch, and the courts in their decision making, and by the ways in which the officials of the three branches supplement, modify, or nullify one another's actions.

Analyses of public policy making thus appear in various sections of the book. Energy policy is discussed in the chapter on Congress, foreign and military policy in the chapter on the presidency, the regulation of cigarette advertising in the chapter on bureaucracy, and school desegregation in the chapter dealing with the courts. Public policy matters are also discussed in other chapters besides those dealing with the formal branches of government—for example, government decisions affecting blacks and women appear in the chapter on interest groups, recent campaign finance laws and their effect on political contests are

PREFACE TO THE THIRD EDITION

analyzed in the chapter on elections and campaigns, and the obscenity and abortion controversies are incorporated in the chapter on civil liberties.

I have also written two entirely new chapters for this edition. The chapter on *bureaucracy* treats all aspects of the subject, including the composition of the federal bureaucracy, executive branch reorganization, budgeting, impoundment, and presidential and congressional attempts to control the bureaucracy. A new chapter on *voting behavior* analyzes the change from the importance of party affiliation as the major factor in voters' decisions in the 1950s to the increased importance of issues and candidate personality in the 1960s and 1970s; also included is an in-depth analysis of voting in the 1976 presidential election based on information from Gallup and other polls.

In addition to these entirely new chapters, major changes have been made in the others. For example, chapters 8 and 9 have been rewritten to detail the factors involved in the nomination and election of Jimmy Carter. The chapter on the contemporary presidency contains new material on Carter's innovative methods in communicating with the American public and his increased emphasis on human rights in foreign policy. And the chapter on Congress covers the current controversy over congressional ethics and the major changes that have occurred in the last few years in the power structure of the House of Representatives.

This edition has also been greatly improved by the numerous contributions of my colleague, Michael Fitzgerald. He has written an excellent chapter on State and Local Government for the National-State-Local edition of the text, developed the list of political novels that appears in the Selected Readings at the end of each chapter of the text, and prepared an Instructor's Manual that not only contains far more questions than typically appear in such publications but also includes innovative classroom aids such as suggested films, games, class projects, and the like.

Finally, this third edition benefits from the inclusion of a large glossary of terms—some of them technical, some of them the particular vocabulary of political science, some of them familiar terms with unfamiliar meanings—to which the student can make ready reference in the course of his reading.

Thus this edition is in many ways a new book with basic organizational changes, additional chapters and material, and added pedagogical features designed to make the text more useful to both students and faculty.

As with previous editions, I continue to be indebted to many persons for their considerable assistance. Included are my colleagues at the University of Missouri who share their awareness and insights concerning new developments and literature in various areas of American politics; the excellent Wiley team— Wayne Anderson, an editor with ideas, Arthur Vergara, a master of the proper turn of phrase, and Stella Kupferberg, who has a sixth sense for just the right picture, cartoon, or headline to illustrate a point; and my colleague, Robert Karsch, whose fine eye for detail is reflected in the index of this edition and the previous one.

As always, I am grateful for the support I receive from my wife, Joan, who typed and helped edit the manuscript, and from my children, Tom, Suzy and little John, who think that their dad is "always writing."

August 17, 1977   Richard A. Watson

CONTENTS

ix

PROMISE AND PERFORMANCE OF AMERICAN DEMOCRACY

Waiting to field the public's questions.

Chapter 1

On a balmy Saturday afternoon in Washington, D.C. in early March 1977, the nation's newly elected President, Jimmy Carter (together with Walter Cronkite, C.B.S. anchorman), sat in the White House Oval Office and for two hours answered questions called in by citizens from all parts of the United States. First suggested by CBS News President Richard Salant and approved by Carter's aides, the "Ask President Carter" program was carried by more than 260 radio stations and filmed for television as well. Also contributing its technical expertise to the program was the American Telephone and Telegraph Company (AT&T), which activated a special "900" area-code for the toll-free calls that were funneled electronically from 16,000 exchanges to a room in the Executive Office Building where 32 CBS staffers checked the identities of the successful callers and transferred them across the street to the White House. Thus the new Chief Executive and two of the nation's corporate giants, CBS and AT&T, joined efforts in the first "Dial-a-President" venture for the American people.

The questions called into the White House indicated that Americans had a number of matters on their minds. Some were concerned with major issues in domestic and foreign policy. Peter Belloni of Denver, Colorado asked if the federal tax on gasoline would soon be raised by 25 cents a gallon; the President assured the caller that despite rumors to that effect, he had never proposed such a thing or even insinuated to anyone that he was going to raise federal gas taxes by that amount. Joseph Willman of Sterling Heights, Michigan wanted to know what the President would do if Uganda's Idi Amin detained Americans; Carter replied that he intended to "keep cool" and informed his questioner that Amin "was constantly giving me assurance, through cables, that Americans would not be hurt."

Other callers had questions about how to handle their own personal problems. A North Carolina woman begged the President to help get the drug Laetrile legalized so it could be used to treat her father's cancer; Carter promised to have someone more expert on the problem from the Department of Health, Education, and Welfare call her back about the matter. One woman wanted assistance in straightening out her mother's G.I. Bill benefits; another

1

wanted help with problems with a civil service job; still another requested information about an Indian land claim. In each case the President said that he would check with appropriate officials and see what could be done about the situation. Also contributing to the President's seeming concern with citizens' problems was his practice of referring to callers by their first names.

Not all the calls, however, were friendly ones. A Marylander asked why the President's son Chip, together with his family, was living in the White House at the taxpayer's expense; Carter explained that he and members of his family paid all their personal expenses themselves, that "we're not mooching off the American taxpayer." A Vietnam veteran from Carter's home state complained of the President's pardoning draft resisters, to which the Chief Executive replied that he had no apology to make for that decision; however, he assured the caller that he had no intention of issuing a blanket pardon to deserters from the armed forces and quipped, "I thought I might get a friendlier question from Georgia."

All parties concerned were pleased with the results of "Ask President Carter." Toward the end of the program Carter said to Cronkite, "Walter, I liked it . . . my inclination would be to do this again." White House aides praised the President's performance as did many persons in the TV and radio industries. Even some of the persons who asked the President critical questions were satisfied with his answers. One New Yorker said that Carter's reply that the enforcement of drug laws was not a waste of taxpayers' money was "quite good and fair"; another who queried the President about spending for foreign aid exclaimed, "It seemed like talking to somebody next door. He is so down to earth." And a Pennsylvania woman reacted in a way designed to warm the cockles of a Democratic officeholder's heart: "As a registered Republican, I am behind you 100 percent."

Two weeks later, Carter tried out another format in his "Power-to-the-People" campaign. He paid a visit to Clinton, Massachusetts, arriving precisely in the middle of the two-day St. Patrick's Day celebration being held by the strongly Irish community. Appearing at a mock town meeting in the city hall (Massachusetts Senator Ted Kennedy sat in the balcony), the President fielded

Clinton, Massachusetts's most famous town-meeting participant.

questions for ninety minutes from town residents preselected by lot. As with the call-in show, most of the queries concerned personal problems, to which the President also responded with a personal touch. Replying to a plea for help for small-business men, Carter recalled his own modest business beginnings: he had lived in a housing project and didn't make enough his first year to pay the rent. When another Clintonian complained about inflation, the President responded that his own grocery bill for his first ten days in office was $600. Following the meeting, Carter spent the night at the family home of Edward Thompson, a local beer distributor who had been a campaign worker in Carter's presidential campaign. The next morning the President rose early, made his own bed, and wrote out notes for the Thompson children to take to school: "Please excuse (Jane) for being late. She had a house guest."

The "call-in" and "town meeting" programs initiated by Jimmy Carter were designed to convince ordinary citizens that their President was not an aloof figure, but a person who cared about common people and their problems. Carter and his advisers also claimed that the programs would alert the President to the kinds of concerns that were on the minds of his fellow Americans. Thus the communication was to be a two-way process, a kind of dialogue between the new President and his constituents.

Yet for the overwhelming number of Americans, the communication described above between the President and the citizens was a vicarious experience, something they heard or watched but did not personally participate in. Over nine million persons tried to place a telephone call to the President on that March afternoon; only forty-two were successful in talking with him. Even in the small town of Clinton, the proportion of persons who actually got to ask the President a question was small: of the community's 13,383 residents, only 18 were able to query the Chief Executive.

The call-in and town-meeting incidents thus point up the practical difficulties involved in trying to establish meaningful communication between political officeholders and the people in a large, diverse country like the United States. Yet the essence of a democratic form of government lies in the fact that those in positions of political authority are responsible to the citizenry at large for their actions. In this first chapter, we will examine two models of government designed to keep political leaders responsible to the people: direct democracy as epitomized by Athens, a Greek city-state; and representative democracy, the type of government used in countries like Great Britain, Switzerland, and the United States. This examination will focus on the political techniques and institutions of direct and representative democracy as well as on the values and assumptions about human nature upon which these two forms of government are based.

The initial sections of this chapter are concerned with the "theory" of democracy, how it *ought to operate* if it is to meet the expectations those who developed the concept of democratic government. They thus focus on the "promise" of democracy, a standard by which our government can be judged.

Evaluating the way American democracy *actually works in practice*—that is, its "performance"—is a matter we will be concerned with throughout the book. Towards the end of this chapter, we consider some of the major challenges and problems our government faces today—the sheer size of our country, its geographical and social diversity, major changes occurring among its people and

The North Carolina legislature in the 1970s: representative government in operation.

the complexities with which they must deal, our private economy, and the world community in which we live. Following that discussion, we summarize two overviews of our political system—one that suggests that it has for the most part met these and other challenges and lived up to the "promise" of democracy; another that argues that we have not dealt effectively with our problems and that the "performance" of American government falls far short of democratic ideals.

The purpose of the first chapter is thus to provide you with some general standards by which to judge our institutions; an appreciation of the kinds of challenges American democracy faces today; and some understanding of the general assessments other persons have made of the supposed strengths and weaknesses of our political system. However, as an individual you should ultimately make your own judgments on American democracy. Others can provide ideas of what to look for and facts and interpretations to consider, but they cannot and should not decide such matters for you.

THE GENERAL NATURE OF DEMOCRACY

The word democracy is derived from two Greek roots—*demos*, which means "people," and *kratia*, which connotes "rule." Thus democracy literally means "rule by the people." For a society to be democratic, then, a large number of its people must enjoy the right to have some say over important decisions that seriously affect their lives. To express it another way, democratic government is based on the consent of the governed. Viewed thus, democracy is concerned with *how* political decisions are made, the *procedure* by which ordinary people participate in the making of such decisions.

While democracy is most often defined in terms of *how* governmental decisions are made, it is also associated with the *content* of those decisions. In other words, democracy involves not only the process of making public policies but also the *results* of the process. Democratic governments by definition produce policies that foster certain basic democratic *values* such as liberty, equality, and justice.

The underlying idea, of course, is that if a large number of people participate in the making of governmental decisions, those decisions will produce liberty, equality, and justice for the great bulk of citizens. Therefore, democracy is also based on certain *assumptions about human nature,* namely, that the ordinary person is rational enough to use his political influence for the purpose of fostering those values.

While there is agreement on these general features and beliefs of democracy, there are differences of opinion on their specifics. For example, what constitutes participation or some "say" over government decisions by ordinary citizens? Is it sufficient that they be able to choose public officials who make decisions, or must the citizens themselves have more direct influence over the content of policies? If so, how much influence, and in what manner is it to be exercised? What is meant by the term *equality?* Are we talking about political equality, legal equality, economic equality, or what? How far does the rationality of the average person go? Must he himself be able to determine what kind of policy is needed to bring more liberty or equality in a society? Or is it sufficient that he judge between policies suggested by others?

There are no definite answers to any of these questions, and reasonable people equally committed to democracy differ over them. In this respect, there is one general "theory of democracy," but there are many "theories" about the specific procedures, ideals, and assumptions associated with a democratic society. Nonetheless, it is possible to discern certain general types of democracy that have prevailed in various countries in different historical eras.

ATHENIAN DIRECT DEMOCRACY

Athens, a city-state in ancient Greece with some 300,000 inhabitants, is known as the cradle of democracy. There in the fifth century B.C. a society developed with institutions and beliefs that were clearly democratic. Today we would refer to the Athenian system as "direct" democracy because all adult male citizens (women, slaves, foreigners, and free men under twenty years of age were excluded) were permitted to play an important part in the governance of the community. And in fact a significant number of eligible citizens actually did play a role.

Political Techniques and Institutions

All adult, male citizens in Athens belonged to the Assembly, a town-meeting type of gathering that met ten times a year to conduct public business. This body, however, was too large and met too infrequently to handle all the political problems of the city-state; much of the real governance was in the hands of a 500-man Council that, in turn, divided itself into ten committees to expedite the consideration of problems. In addition, there were large juries composed of citizens who heard and decided legal controversies.

The system was not the pure, direct democracy in which the average citizen participates in each and every political decision; nonetheless, he played a significant part in many of them. Although the Council and its committees initially handled many problems, major issues came back to the Assembly for final disposition. That body, for example, gave its approval to declarations of war and negotiations of peace, the forming of alliances, the levying of direct taxes, and the like.

Officeholding by ordinary citizens was widespread. The 500-member Council was drawn by lot from persons elected by small geographical units, *demes,* the equivalent of our wards, townships, or parishes. Service on the Council and in most other political posts was typically for one year, so positions rotated from one person to another quickly. The large juries, ranging in size from 200 to 500 persons, were also drawn by lot from a panel of 6000 citizens selected each year. Because different juries were assigned to sit in particular courts, many juries were operating simultaneously. Such a system clearly called for broad participation by citizens: about one in six held some political office in any given year.

The operating principles of Athenian democracy were also distinctly democratic. The give-and-take of spirited debate and extensive discussions was the prevailing means of exploring and clarifying public problems. The final decisions in both the Assembly and the juries were reached by majority vote.

Values and Assumptions

Underlying the political institutions and operating principles of Athenian society were certain values that expressed what its citizens felt were the important things in life. Foremost of these was the belief that a citizen could achieve happiness and personal development only through *participation in the life of the community.* He was expected to attend to family and business affairs, but these were not to interfere with his duties to the broader community. His loyalty to the city-state was expected to supersede his private concerns and his attachments to less inclusive groups.

Political equality was another ideal of Athenian democracy. All citizens, regardless of their social station or financial situation, were given equal opportunity to participate in the political life of the community. To ensure that the poor could afford to take part in political affairs, most offices were paid; in some instances, individuals were even compensated for attending sessions of the Assembly.

Along with political equality went a *respect for the law.* The Athenian had great faith in the procedures by which the Assembly, Council, and popular juries reached their decisions, and he was inclined to follow those decisions once they were made. For the Athenian the rule of law was distinctly Greek as contrasted to the edicts of arbitrary rulers under which barbarians were forced to live.

The whole political system was predicated on a great faith in the essential *rationality* of the ordinary citizen. Athenians attributed no special political competence to persons of higher social or economic standing in the community. Nor did they have particular regard for the expert; they rather extolled the virtues of the "happy versatility" of the average citizen—what we would term today the ability of the "amateur." Although Athenians did not expect everyone to originate public policies, they considered each man a sound judge of policies. The belief in man's rationality was also reflected in the discussions and debates that characterized the Athenian political process. The faith that a wise law or good institution could bear the scrutiny of many minds was a basic assumption under which their democracy operated.

Athenian government was thus direct democracy in which a large sample of citizens participated in decisions of the Assembly while also exercising control over actions of the Council through the Assembly. At the same time a great number of citizens served on the Council and even more sat as members of the large juries.

Such political institutions have had little application throughout history. In the long period following the decline of Athens (which fell largely as a result of military encounters with its neighbors), people were governed by kings, merchant-princes, generals, religious leaders, aristocrats, or nobles. When democracy was revived in the form of direct citizen involvement in decision making, it was confined to small units like Swiss cantons and New England town meetings.

The governance of large countries such as Great Britain and the United States required a different form of democracy. The general type of government that developed in these nations in recent centuries serves as the major example of democracy in the modern world. It is known by many names: Western democracy for the geographical location of the countries in which it originated; constitutional democracy for its emphasis on limiting government through legal means; and liberal democracy for its concern with the liberty of the individual. I will refer to it simply as Western representative democracy for its source and for the basic technique it utilizes to implement the ideal of government by the people.

WESTERN REPRESENTATIVE DEMOCRACY

Representative democracy is a system of government in which ordinary citizens do not make governmental decisions themselves but, instead, choose public officials to make decisions for them. In modern nations encompassing millions of people, only a relatively few persons hold public positions, especially in the national government. Thus each member of the United States House of Representatives represents almost a half-million persons.

Democratic representative government as we know it today first developed in three Western nations: Great Britain, Switzerland, and the United States. In these countries in the late eighteenth and early nineteenth centuries a large number of people first began to select their political leaders. From this narrow base, democracy spread to other Western European nations and to the British Commonwealth. Representative democracy, then, is a form of government that is restricted to a relatively small group of nations in recent centuries.

In fact, if full democracy requires that the majority of the population have the right to affect governmental decisions by choosing its leaders, then this type of government is an even more recent phenomenon. Great Britain and the United States did not provide for universal manhood suffrage until the latter part of the nineteenth century, and women were not permitted to vote in na-

The British House of Commons at the turn of the twentieth century.

tional elections until the 1920s. Switzerland did not fully extend the suffrage to women until nearly fifty years later.

Political Techniques and Institutions

As we have already observed, in a representative democracy ordinary citizens do not govern; rather they choose those who do. Aristotle referred to such a system as the "rule of the few watched by the many." The crucial part of the phrase is not "rule by the few," since under all political systems a small minority of the populace holds major political offices. The key idea is the *many watching those few.*

Representative democracy, however, requires more than mere watching; the many must also be able to implement their observations through political action. The system has to give the people control over their leaders, so that the latter can be held responsible for their actions. If the general populace is unable to exercise such control, then the government does not differ from an oligarchy in which political authority is vested in a few persons who are not accountable to the people.

The particular mechanism that representative democracies have developed to keep their political leaders responsible to the general populace is *elections.* Indeed, democratic societies deliberately create insecurity of tenure for major officeholders, who are periodically required to go before the people to have their terms of office renewed. As Walter Lippmann, a perceptive writer and

Victory Dinner-Dance

Colonie Hill   Thursday,
Hauppauge, N. Y.   March 10, 1977

columnist, once put it, those "outside" the government pass judgment on those "inside."

If the citizens in a democracy are displeased with what those in public office are doing about major problems facing the society, the remedy is to replace them. Thus a democratic system of government must provide the electorate with competing groups of political leaders. The power of the people is effective only if they have the opportunity *to choose* one group over another.

All democratic societies, then, must develop some means of providing political leaders for the consideration of the populace. The institution that typically fills this need is the political party which puts forward candidates for public office. In order to provide the element of choice for the voters, there must be at least two competing parties that propose candidates. A voter can then choose a candidate from Party A over one from Party B because he feels that the former will do the more satisfactory job in making political decisions that affect his interests. Since at least two parties must be present, it is entirely consistent with the theory of democracy that three or four (or more) parties should offer potential leaders to the voters.

Because no political party in a democracy can be permitted to be the sole provider of candidates for public office, each party must recognize the right of others to compete. The parties must accept one another's existence as a necessity; beyond that, they must be willing to coexist peacefully. Accordingly, the party (or parties) presently in control of a government must allow the opposition party (or parties) to criticize what the leaders are doing and to propose alternative courses of action for the voters' consideration. Moreover, the incumbents must hold elections in which they can be replaced by members of the opposition. Thus, today's majority must be prepared for the possibility of becoming tomorrow's minority.

It is precisely this spirit of tolerance and willingness to allow themselves to be voted out of office that presents the most difficulty for leaders of nations that are first experimenting with democracy. There is a natural tendency for those in political power to consider persons who question their policies—indeed their very right to remain in control of the government—as subversive. We are familiar today with this attitude among leaders of emerging nations like South Korea and Nigeria, but as we shall see later, a similar attitude existed among the early party leaders of our own country. The idea of a "loyal opposition" presupposes a considerable amount of maturity and sophistication in the ways of democracy. It is perhaps best exemplified today in the British system of government, which not only tolerates opposition but actually fosters it by including a post known as her "majesty's loyal opposition." That position, which is occupied by the leader of the party out of power, carries the right to use funds provided by the government to criticize the party in power.

The minority party (or parties) has more than the responsibility of criticizing the policies of the majority and of suggesting alternatives; it also has the obligation to accept the verdict at the polls and to permit the majority party to remain in office until the next election. One of the most eloquent statements of the proper attitude of a losing candidate in a democracy was made by Adlai Stevenson on the occasion of his defeat by Dwight Eisenhower in 1956. (Stevenson had also lost the presidency to Eisenhower in 1952, and the margin of loss was wider in the second election than in the first.)

To you who are disappointed tonight, let me confess that I am too! But we must not be downhearted. . . . For here in America, the people have made their choice in a vigorous partisan contest that has affirmed again the vitality of the democratic process. And I say God bless partisanship, for this is democracy's life blood.

But beyond the seas, in much of the world, in Russia, in China, in Hungary, in all the trembling satellites, partisan controversy is forbidden and dissent suppressed.

So I say to you, my dear and loyal friends, take heart—there are things more precious than political victory; there is the right to political contest.

Adlai Stevenson conceding defeat.

Democracy provides the electoral machinery whereby competing groups of leaders contest for political office by vying for the votes of the public. The winners take responsibility for developing policies to deal with the major problems of society; the losers have the obligation to criticize those policies and the right to use their criticism as a means of attracting enough supporters at the next election to assume political office themselves. The majority (the general populace) has the responsibility of deciding which of the competing minorities will be permitted to govern until the next election.

Democracy not only requires competition between minorities who seek to govern with the consent of the people; individuals, too, must be permitted to become candidates for public office themselves and, if elected, to serve. The system must thus be open to everyone regardless of his social or economic status.

Beyond elections, which occur periodically, a democratic society must provide means of continuous communication between the leaders and the general populace so that personal views on public issues can be transmitted to those who make major political decisions. There is no obligation binding on those in political power to carry the suggestions into effect, but citizens must be entitled to have their viewpoints heard.

Although individuals can express their attitudes on various matters, to be effective they must join with other like-minded persons to form groups that can communicate their demands to decision makers. The institution that democracies have developed to transmit demands to those in political power is called an interest group. Even these groups are likely to contain only a small proportion of the total population, but they enable a public officeholder to gain some understanding of how a number of people in a common situation—say, businessmen, laborers, or farmers—feel about such matters as taxes, wages, or farm prices. Moreover, because communication is a two-way process, interest groups not only press demands on decision makers but also transmit proposals of political leaders to their memberships, which serve as potential sources of support for the proposals.

Marlboro senior power— Marlboro, Vt.

Just as parties compete in a democratic society to place their men in public office, so interest groups vie with one another to influence public policy. If the system is operating properly, they check and balance one another's efforts so that no one group or small number of groups dominates the political process. All kinds of groups representing persons with different social and economic backgrounds and concerns should be able to make themselves heard effectively by officials who make crucial governmental decisions.

The public officials who make the decisions in representative democracies are more diverse and specialized in training than were those who held office in Athenian democracy. Although members of the general public still serve on juries in courtroom controversies, they decide on the facts of the case only, while judges with extensive legal training rule on questions of law. Specialists also serve in the executive arm of the government. Only the legislature remains as the branch of the political "amateur," and, as in the Greek Assembly, decisions are typically made by majority vote.

While representative democracy supports majority rule, at the same time it protects the rights of minorities. Representatives of minority viewpoints are permitted to be heard and to criticize the opinions of the majority. Moreover, the system provides the opportunity for present minorities to become future majorities.

Minorities in a democracy, however, enjoy other rights besides that of eventually turning themselves into a majority. As we shall see below, certain fundamental rights are protected from infringement by public officials even when they are acting with the support of the majority. The protection comes through constitutions and courts that limit what the government can do. It also derives from attitudes and political customs that determine the proper way for the majority to act towards minorities.

Thus far we have discussed how representative democracies go about making political decisions. But democracy is more than a set of procedures; it also involves values that the procedures are designed to foster and protect.

Values

The single most significant idea in democratic thought is belief in the *basic integrity of the individual*. This overriding concern is best expressed in the command of philosopher Immanuel Kant to "treat all individuals, not merely as a means to an end, but as an end in and of themselves." In this view all persons are entitled to consideration simply because they are human beings. As such, they possess dignity and moral worth that everyone is obliged to respect.

One of the consequences of this concern is the belief that the government, or the state, exists for the individual, not the individual for the state. This idea is captured in the Declaration of Independence, which proclaims that men "are endowed by their Creator with certain unalienable rights," and that "to secure these rights, Governments are instituted among Men, deriving their just powers from the consent of the governed." Government does not create these rights; rather *it* is created by men to safeguard their natural rights.

This idea of the proper relationship between the individual and his government may seem too idealistic, yet it continues to be an important part of the democratic creed. David Lilienthal, the first director of the Tennessee Valley Authority, one of the nation's outstanding public servants with a wealth of experience in practical, everyday affairs, expressed the same basic thought in testimony before a Senate committee:

I believe, and I conceive the Constitution of the United States to rest, as does religion, upon the fundamental proposition of the integrity of the individual, and that all government, and all private institutions, must be designed to promote and protect and defend the integrity of the individual.

Another major value of democracy is *liberty*. Liberty involves a person's freedom to select his own purposes in life together with the means to accom-

plish those purposes. Obviously, neither of these liberties is absolute. Society, acting through the government, will impose reasonable restrictions; it will not permit a person, for example, to choose to become the world's most skillful thief. Or even if he selects a lofty aim for himself—say, the presidency of a great corporation—he will not be allowed to deal violently with rivals who stand in his path. There is a difference between liberty and *licence,* which is the *unrestricted* freedom to choose one's purposes and methods. Society will not let anyone "do his thing" if it interferes with the rights of others or even, in some cases, if it harms himself. Nonetheless, in the ideal democratic society such restrictions are minimal, and citizens retain the liberty to develop themselves to the fullest extent of their capacities.

Liberty carries with it the idea of *privacy,* the freedom to be left alone. Individuals have the right to their own thoughts and their own property, and the government cannot force them to share such personal attributes with their fellow citizens or with the government itself. Again, of course, privacy is not absolute; for example, an individual will be required to pay his share of taxes to provide government services—military and police protection, education, and the like. Nonetheless, democracy maintains as many private preserves for the individual as possible. Democracy thus involves freedom *from* as well as freedom *to.*

Another major value of democracy is *equality.* There are, however, many kinds of equality. The one that is most often accepted as part of the democratic creed is political equality. This involves the right of all adult citizens to vote for their political officials, with each vote counting as one and only one. Everyone is also equally entitled to seek and, if successful, to serve in public office. Political equality applies to other, nonelectoral, activities as well, such as the opportunity to form interest groups or to discuss and debate political issues.

Equality not only relates to participation in influencing or making governmental decisions; it also involves being subject to those decisions. Thus everyone is entitled to equality under the law. In other words, the law is to be applied impartially without regard to the identity or status of the individual involved. Few persons quarrel with this concept.

Somewhat more controversial than political and legal equality is the concept of social equality. It has as its basis the idea that people should be free of class or social barriers and discrimination. While many agree on the desirability of this ideal, they disagree on what, if anything, the government should do to require individuals to abide by it. The long battle over racial equality described in chapter 6 reflects differing attitudes on this basic question.

Economic equality is the most controversial of all democratic concepts, primarily because people attribute different meanings to it. Under a strict interpretation, each person would receive the same amount of worldly goods regardless of his contribution to society. This is what Karl Marx had in mind when he wrote, "From each according to his abilities [society should take from the individual what he is able to contribute]; to each according to his needs [he should receive from society what he must have to get along in life]." If everyone's needs are basically the same, then each person should receive the same amount of economic wealth.

Although Western democracies have generally favored a fairly wide distribution of wealth, they have not construed economic equality to mean that everyone must obtain the same amount of material possessions. Rather, all persons should have equality of opportunity, the chance to develop themselves to the fullest extent of their capacities. But even that concept has different interpretations. Does it mean merely formal opportunity in the sense that positions are open to everyone on the basis of capacity? Or does it require that material conditions be equalized by universally providing basic services (good health care, education, and the like) that are vital to individual self-development? This latter position suggests that, although a democratic society need not ensure equality at the end of the developmental process, it should see to it that people are made equal at the beginning of it.

One of the reasons Western democracies such as Great Britain and the United States favor the equal-opportunity concept is that it permits them to reconcile the two values of liberty and equality. If individuals differ in ability, then to give every person the liberty to develop himself to the fullest extent of his capacities will result in some acquiring more goods than others. In other words, Western democracy gives individuals the *equal opportunity to become unequal.*

Assumptions About Human Nature

Advocates of representative democracy urge the participation of the average person in government because they believe that people are, for the most part, rational and capable of deciding what is good for them personally. Even if their judgments are not always correct, they are more likely to be so than if an elite makes decisions for them. The democrat assumes that no elite group is wise enough or unselfish enough to rule in the interests of the remaining members of society. The only way to ensure that the interests of everyone will be taken into account is to give the bulk of the population the right to influence the basic decisions that affect their lives.

The greatest influence most people have on those decisions is exerted through their choice of candidates for public office. Representative democracy does not, therefore, require that the average person himself make decisions about public problems; it only asks him to determine whether political leaders who do make such decisions are doing so satisfactorily. The populace thus acts as a consumer of public-policy decisions produced by others. As one student of democratic theory, A. D. Lindsay, has suggested, "Only the ordinary man can tell whether the shoes pinch and where." In other words, only the individuals subject to rules and regulations know how they are personally affected by them. To determine this effect, the average man does not have to know how to make governmental decisions any more than he has to be a cobbler to know that certain shoes hurt his feet.

The democrat is skeptical about the possibility of knowing what is absolutely "good" or "true." He takes issue with belief in an objective truth that can be discovered by a special group of individuals set apart from the rest of the populace by intelligence and training. The democrat assumes either that no such absolutes exist or that, even if they do, they cannot be discovered by mortals, however intelligent or educated they may be. For all practical purposes, then, the truth is a relative matter. As Supreme Court Justice Oliver Wendell Holmes put it: ". . . the best test of truth is the power of the thought to get itself accepted in the competition of the market. . . ." By this he meant that in a democracy a variety of ideas and viewpoints can be expressed, and what emerges as the choice of the people is the closest thing to truth that can be achieved.

This lack of certainty about truth renders possible another assumption of democracy, namely, that individuals can *tolerate* viewpoints that differ from their own. Since no one has a private pipeline to eternal verities, a person ought to be able to face up to the possibility that he *may* be wrong about a given matter and that the other person may be right. The adherent of democracy assumes that a spirit of give-and-take and a willingness to *compromise* will develop among individuals, enabling them to resolve their differences in a peaceful manner.

The democrat also takes the position that decisions made by a large number of people are more likely to be good ones than those made by a few. E. B. White, an American writer, expresses this idea in his statement that "Democracy is the recurrent suspicion that more than half of the people are right more than half of the time." In other words, a majority is more likely than a minority to decide the correct thing to do. But White's statement underscores the tentative nature of democratic faith in the majority.

In fact, the proponent of democracy does not always trust the majority and consequently is not willing to allow it to decide all matters that affect peoples' lives. Minority rights are also to be respected. Democracy evolved in Western Europe and America in the eighteenth and nineteenth centuries from an earlier concept known as constitutionalism, which had as a major principle the idea that government should be limited. For example, in the United States and Great Britain it makes no difference that more than half the population are Protestant: they are not permitted to tell persons of the Catholic or Jewish faith how to worship. Likewise, in democratic nations the individual's right to private property is respected and his personal goods cannot be taken from him even for a public use (as, for example, when a university takes private land to expand its operations) without just compensation. It is precisely this limitation on the scope of government—based on a concern for privacy as well as on limited faith in majority rule—that distinguishes a democratic society from a totalitarian one.

Democracy presupposes neither a wholly optimistic nor a wholly pessimistic view of human nature. It does not rest on the faith that people are innately good, "beautiful," or cooperative, nor on the assumption made by some advocates of totalitarianism that the average person is depraved. The democrat's ambivalence toward human nature is aptly expressed in the comment of the late theologian Reinhold Niebuhr that "man's capacity for justice makes democracy possible; but man's inclination to injustice makes democracy necessary."

This combination of political techniques and institutions, values, and assumptions regarding human nature underlies the type of Western democracy we Americans normally associate with our own political system as well as with the systems of certain nations of Europe and the British Commonwealth. The question remains, however, whether this system of government is adequate to meet the challenges posed by American society today.

Hare Krishna.

CHALLENGES TO AMERICAN DEMOCRACY

The United States has changed greatly over the course of more than two centuries of existence. As a result, the conditions that political officials face today are radically different from those with which the Founding Fathers were familiar when they devised our basic system of government in the late 1780s. Moreover, the pace of change has accelerated in recent years: the United States is significantly different from the nation into which the children of the 1950s and 1960s were born. The alterations in American life are many and varied; here we focus attention on only a few of the major examples.

Size: Area and Population

The first census of the United States, taken in 1790, indicated that the territory included within the thirteen original colonies that came under the jurisdiction of the new nation covered less than 900,000 square miles. As Figure 1.1 indicates, the nation and the territories under its jurisdiction have been expanded on several occasions since 1803, when we bought the Louisiana Territory from France, until we purchased the Virgin Islands from Denmark in 1917. Today the 50 states, covering all of continental United States, Alaska, and Hawaii, include over 3,600,000 square miles. Thus the area included within our country (not counting its overseas territories) has quadrupled since the nation's founding.

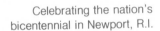

Celebrating the nation's bicentennial in Newport, R.I.

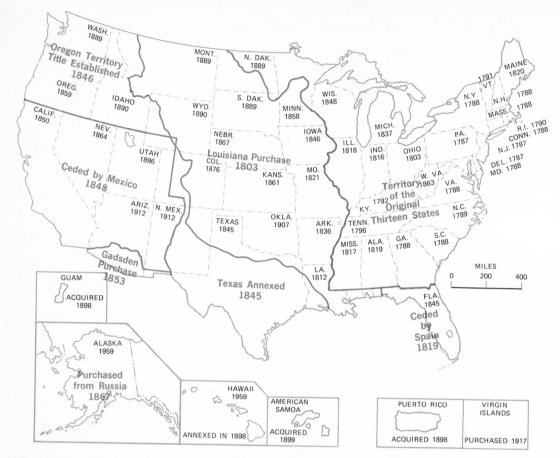

The increase in our population has been even more significant. The 1790 census showed that fewer than 4 million persons were included in our nation; at the outbreak of the War of 1812, that figure had doubled; by the turn of the twentieth century, it stood at 76 million. As Figure 1.2 indicates, the turn-of-

Figure 1.1
Territorial expansion of the United States and acquisitions of other principal areas.
Source: U.S. Bureau of the Census.

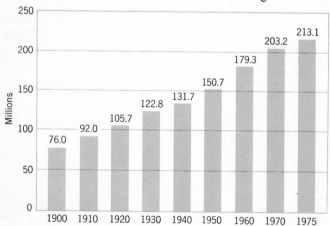

Figure 1.2
U.S. population growth, 1900–1975.
Source: U.S. Bureau of the Census.

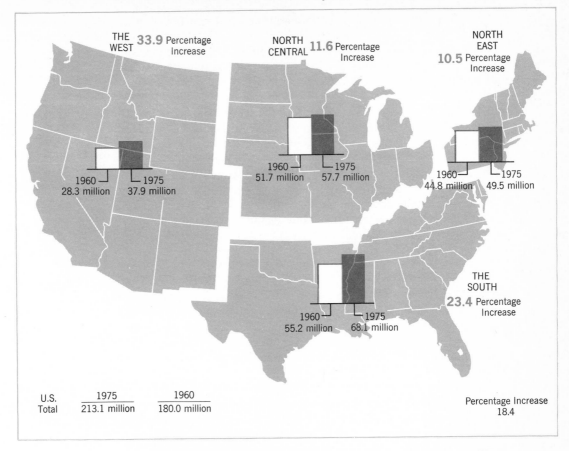

Figure 1.3
Population changes in the
United States, 1960–1975.
Source: U.S. Bureau of the
Census.

the-century population almost doubled by mid-century and virtually tripled by the three-quarter mark. The population growth over the total period of our nation's history thus increased more than fifty times, from 4 million in 1790 to 213 million in 1975.

Diversity: Geographical and Social

Our nation is not only large but also diverse. The states run the gamut from tiny Rhode Island with 1200 square miles to mammoth Alaska with 566,000. In population the latter state is the smallest, with an estimated 350,000 residents in 1975, whereas California, the nation's most populous state, had an estimated 21,000,000 people. Moreover, the various regions of the country are experiencing disparate rates of growth. As shown by Figure 1.3, the West and South had great population increases in the period from 1960 to 1975, while the numbers of people living in the North East and North Central regions remained fairly stable.

Another dominant population trend in American politics has been the movement of persons off the farms and into urban areas. The first wave of this migration into the cities was due to the job opportunities fostered by the Industrial Revolution that began in the middle part of the nineteenth century. By the third decade of the twentieth century, however, a new phase of the process began to assert itself as many persons began to move out of the cities and into surrounding suburbs. Automobiles, improved roads, and electrical interurban railroads served as vehicles and avenues of escape from the crowded cities. In increasing numbers persons gravitated towards the new promised land of lower rents and what was generally thought to be the better life of the suburbs, while continuing to maintain economic and social ties with the city.

The end result of these two population trends has been the development of metropolitan areas—urban communities composed of central cities surrounded by suburbs. In 1950 the Census Bureau designated such areas as standard metropolitan areas (the term was later changed to standard metropolitan statistical areas) which included any central city with a population of 50,000, together with the county in which that city was located and any other counties that were economically and socially integrated with the county of the central city. With some minor modifications, that same definition has been used to describe such areas since 1950.

In the third quarter of this century, there has been a great increase in the number of persons living in our metropolitan areas. In 1950, 56 percent of Americans resided in 168 SMSAs; in 1974, 73 percent lived in 264 SMSAs. The largest metropolitan area in 1974 was the New York-New Jersey area with a total population of 9.6 million, followed by Chicago and Los Angeles-Long Beach with almost 7 million residents each. Within such areas, the dominant trend has been the loss of population by many central cities (particularly older ones located in the North East and North Central regions) and a burgeoning of suburban communities.

As far as particular social groups are concerned, the most significant population trend in recent years has been the movement of blacks from the South to the North and from rural to urban areas. In 1940, 77 percent of blacks lived in the South and only 22 percent in the North East and North Central regions; by 1974 barely over half—53 percent—of all blacks still lived in the South and 38 percent in the two northern regions. (Meanwhile, the population of blacks residing in the West rose from 1 to 9 percent.) Within the urban communities,

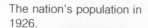

The nation's population in 1926.

The nation's population as 1976 approaches.

Los Angeles: West-Coast megalopolis.

Figure 1.4
Population changes in
metropolitan areas by race,
1950–1970. Source: U.S.
Bureau of the Census.

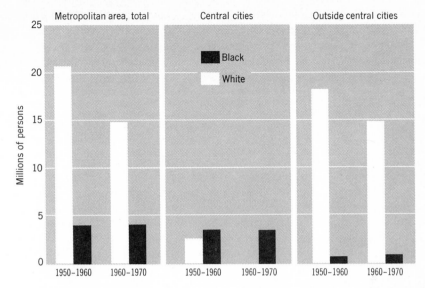

Figure 1.4
Population changes in
metropolitan areas by race,
1950–1970. Source: U.S.
Bureau of the Census.

blacks have settled primarily in the central cities. As indicated by Figure 1.4, growth in the population of central cities in the period between 1950 and 1970 came more from Negroes than whites, particularly in the decade between 1960 and 1970; in contrast, the burgeoning suburban population during both decades was overwhelmingly white. As a result, our central cities have become increasingly black while more and more whites have migrated to the suburbs.

Along with the migration of blacks from Southern rural areas to Northern central cities, there has been yet another major social development in recent years: the movement of women out of the home and into the job market. In 1950, 31 percent of women of working age were included in the work force; by 1975, that figure had climbed to 46 percent. Particularly affected by this development were married women. In 1950, they constituted 52 percent of the female work force; by 1975, married women were 62 percent of that force. Over the course of the 25-year period, attitudes also changed concerning working

Who says it's a man's world?

mothers of young children: in 1950, 12 percent of mothers with children under 6 years of age were in the female work force; by 1975, that figure had tripled to 36 percent. The kinds of jobs that women filled also changed: the percentage of women employed in professional and technical occupations doubled from 9 to 18 percent during the period from 1950 to 1975; during the same period, those employed as operatives (unskilled blue-collar jobs) dropped from 23 to 12 percent.

Complexities: The Economy and the World Community

Unlike many other countries in which the government owns manufacturing industries (like steel and oil), financial institutions (banks and insurance companies), and transportation facilities (railroads and airlines), in the United States these great economic ventures are privately owned and operated. Moreover, such ownership is widely spread. In 1973, there were 10.6 million proprietorships (businesses owned by one person) in the United States; over a million partnerships; and 1.9 million corporations. All together, these 13.6 million businesses had receipts of almost $3 trillion and net profits of $176 billion. Thus private business in the United States is diverse.

At the same time, there is a considerable concentration of that private wealth. Of the $176 billion in net profits earned by the three major kinds of businesses in 1973, $120 billion went to corporations. Moreover, great concentration occurs within the corporate category of businesses. For example, in 1973, of the total assets held by the 1.9 million corporations, 62 percent were in the hands of 1000 of them. There has also been a tendency towards greater concentration of corporate wealth in recent years: in 1955, the 1000 largest companies owned a somewhat smaller share of total corporate assets—43 percent.

Along with big business has come big labor in the United States. As indicated by Figure 1.5, over the period from 1966 through 1975, the total labor force climbed from 79 million to 95 million persons. Also presenting a problem for government was the fluctuating rate of unemployment over the ten-year period. After remaining under 5 percent for the first half of the decade, the unemployment rate rose, reaching an average of over 8 percent in 1975.

Figure 1.5
Trends in the labor force, 1916–1976. Source: U.S. Bureau of the Census; data from U.S. Bureau of Labor Statistics.

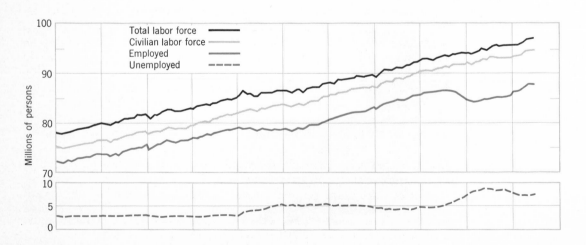

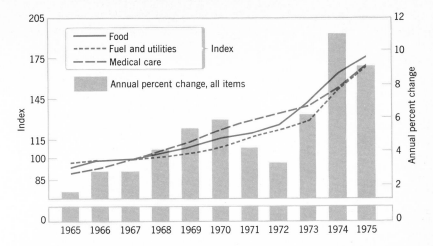

Figure 1.6
Consumer Price Indexes,
1965–1975 (1967 = 100).
Source: U.S. Bureau of the
Census; data from U.S.
Bureau of Labor Statistics.

Another major economic challenge for American democracy in recent years has been the rise in prices that consumers must pay for goods and services. Using the cost of items in 1967 as the index of 100, Figure 1.6 shows a constant rise in prices for food, fuel and utilities, and medical care over the nine-year period through 1975. To take an example, if we make the index of 100 equal to $1.00, in 1975 a consumer had to spend $1.75 for food items that he could have bought for $1.00 in 1967. Also rising dramatically after 1973 was the cost of medical care and fuel and utilities. (A separate breakdown of costs for fuel oil and coal alone shows they rose from a price index of 136 in 1973 to one of over 235 in 1975.)

A final major challenge to the American political system comes in the area of international affairs. We are members of a world community composed of over 150 nations with a total population of some 4 billion. The sovereign countries that belong to the United Nations range in area from tiny Maldives with 115 square miles to the Union of Soviet Socialist Republics with 8.6 million square miles, and in population from Sao Tome and Principe with 78,000 residents to the People's Republic of China with 814 million. Figure 1.7 indicates how the area and population of the United States compare with those of some of the other leading nations of the world.*

The United States also has increasingly close economic ties with other nations. As shown by Figure 1.8, sales of multinational companies (foreign affiliates with a U.S. ownership of at least 50 percent) have risen dramatically in recent years. While the majority of sales of these companies have been to developed countries (especially to countries in the British Commonwealth, Western Europe, and Japan), recently our sales to developing countries (particularly to those in the Middle East) have risen rapidly. At the same time—as indicated by Figure 1.9—we have become increasingly dependent on other nations (especially those in the Middle East) for our supply of petroleum.

In various chapters of this book we will analyze the ways in which American democracy has been affected by these and other challenges. For example, chapter 9 discusses how the apportionment of the House of Representatives and the number of votes in the electoral college for choosing the President have been

---

* Not shown in the figure is Canada, which ranks second among the nations in area with 3.9 million square miles; however, its 1974 population was only 22.5 million.

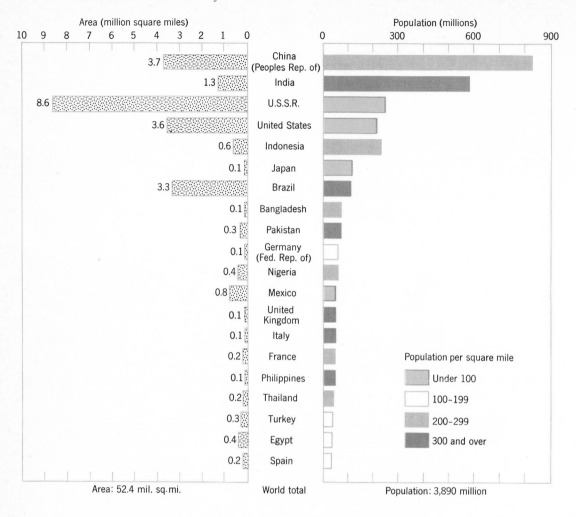

Area (million square miles)

| 10 | 9 | 8 | 7 | 6 | 5 | 4 | 3 | 2 | 1 | 0 |

Population (millions)

| 0 | 300 | 600 | 900 |

Area	Country	
3.7	China (Peoples Rep. of)	
1.3	India	
8.6	U.S.S.R.	
3.6	United States	
0.6	Indonesia	
0.1	Japan	
3.3	Brazil	
0.1	Bangladesh	
0.3	Pakistan	
0.1	Germany (Fed. Rep. of)	
0.4	Nigeria	
0.8	Mexico	
0.1	United Kingdom	
0.1	Italy	
0.2	France	
0.1	Philippines	
0.2	Thailand	
0.3	Turkey	
0.4	Egypt	
0.2	Spain	

Population per square mile

- Under 100
- 100–199
- 200–299
- 300 and over

Area: 52.4 mil. sq. mi.   World total   Population: 3,890 million

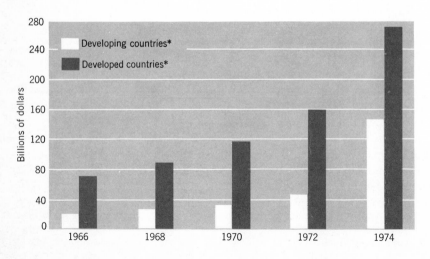

Developing countries*
Developed countries*

Billions of dollars

| 280 | 240 | 200 | 160 | 120 | 80 | 40 | 0 |

1966   1968   1970   1972   1974

Figure 1.7
Area and population: United States and leading countries, 1974. Source: U.S. Bureau of the Census; data from Statistical Office of the United Nations.

Figure 1.8
U.S. multinational companies: sales by majority-owned foreign affiliates, 1966–1974. Source: U.S. Bureau of the Census; data from U.S. Bureau of Economic Analysis.

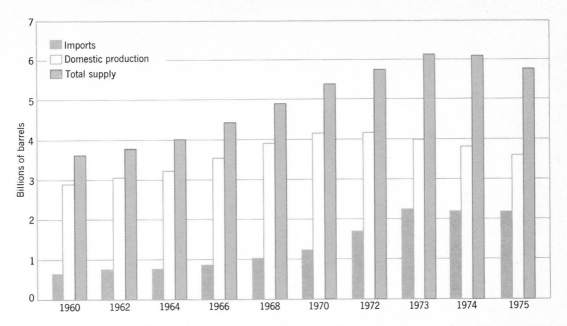

Figure 1.9
Supply of petroleum:
domestic production and
imports, 1960–1975. Source:
U.S. Bureau of the Census;
data from U.S. Bureau of
Mines.

adjusted to meet the expansion of our nation's area and population, while chapter 3 analyzes the ways in which our federal system has been influenced by regional patterns of growth. Chapter 6 describes how blacks and women have used the political process to further their interests; the role of the President and Congress in dealing with foreign affairs is analyzed in chapter 13. However, before turning to a detailed analysis of the establishment of American democracy and how it has changed over the years, we examine two conflicting interpretations of how successful our political system has been in meeting major challenges and still retaining its democratic character.

CONFLICTING VIEWS OF AMERICAN DEMOCRACY

Students of our political system differ fundamentally on the basic state of American democracy today. Some view it as a successful, if not the most successful, example of democracy in the modern world, one that has for the most part lived up to its ideals or promises. Others feel that its performance falls far short of its promises and that some of these promises themselves are badly in need of revision.

The Case for American Democracy

The case for American democracy rests on the assessment that our political techniques and institutions operate for the most part according to democratic principles. The leaders of the Republican and Democratic parties compete for the support of the voters by tailoring their proposals to appeal to the wishes of a wide variety of groups that make up the electorate. The winning party, representing a broad coalition of such groups, must continue to keep the preferences of many groups in mind after it assumes office, and if it fails to do so, it can and will be replaced by the opposition party. The fact that the Republican and

Democratic parties are so competitive (seldom does the losing party draw less than 40 percent of the vote in a presidential election) means that overturns in party control are frequent, and even when they do not actually occur, the possibility that they will keeps the majority party responsive to public preferences.

Between elections public policy is primarily influenced by the activities of concerned minorities who work through interest groups to make demands on decision makers. Again, the system is competitive because groups such as business and labor take different views on public concerns and frustrate each other's ambitions. Therefore, no one group or small number of groups dominates the American political process.

American governmental institutions also ensure that a wide variety of interests will be taken into account when political decisions are made. Public officials in separate parts of the governmental system are responsive to different groups: for example, the House of Representatives favors the concerns of people who live in rural areas and small towns, while the President is receptive to ethnic groups in the large industrial states. Groups whose interests are not met by the national government can turn to state officials for help. As political scientist Robert Dahl puts it, "The normal American political process is one in which there is a high probability that an active and legitimate group in the population can make itself heard effectively at some crucial stage in the process of decision."

The American political system is, in this view, a highly pluralistic one in which power is distributed widely among many individuals and groups: businessmen, laborers, farmers, blacks, white-collar workers among them. Although some groups have more political assets in the form of money, numbers, and campaigning and propaganda skills than others, all have some political resources—at the minimum, the vote.

The American political system is also open in the sense that people from various ethnic, racial, and social backgrounds can become politically active. Indeed, some groups, notably the Irish, have worked their way up the social and economic ladder by using the political process to further their interests. Eventually one of them may win the highest position in the American political system, the presidency—as John F. Kennedy did. This process continues as Italians, Jews, and, most recently, blacks are elected to more and more political offices.

Those with favorable views of American democracy generally recognize that the successful operation of our political system depends primarily on persons who are interested and concerned about political matters. Referred to by various names—political "elites," "activists," or "influentials"—they are the citizens who offer themselves or others as candidates and who campaign for election, who fill the major appointive positions in the government, who propose policies for dealing with major problems, and who work through the political process to get their proposals enacted into law. They include not only individuals who hold public office but also those who are outside the formal structure of government in leadership posts in political parties, interest groups, private corporations, and labor unions, as well as newspaper editors, college teachers, and others who are in a position to shape the political opinions of the man in the street.

It is the political moves and countermoves by this broad variety of political elites that make the American political system work as it does. While they compete vigorously with each other, at the same time they appreciate and abide by the democratic "rules of the game" regarding the right of freedom of speech and the press for those who oppose them. They are also personally committed to the major values of a democratic society—the liberty of the individual, the right of privacy, religious freedom, and justice under the law. It is these political activists who are the major carriers of the American democratic creed; they can be counted upon to defend it when other, less politically aware and educated individuals are willing to deny basic rights to unpopular minorities.

In the final analysis, supporters of American pluralistic democracy feel that it serves well the interests of a wide variety of individuals and groups in our society. Competing elites take the initiative in public affairs, but at the same time they must take account of the interests of ordinary citizens on whom they ultimately depend to support their policies as well as their tenure in public office. The entire process, which takes place within prescribed democratic procedures, has moderated differences among our diverse people and brought the nation social peace as well as social progress.

Major Criticisms of American Democracy

Although most students of American democracy over the years have tended to support our system, it has also had its share of critics. Particularly in recent years, with the emergence of major social problems—increased violence, racial tensions, poverty, the war in Vietnam—and the decline of the credibility of public officials, critics have increasingly called into question the operation, ideals, and assumptions of our political system.

One of the major criticisms directed at American democracy is that it simply does not operate as its supporters claim it does. Rather than shape their actions to accord with the wishes of the voters, candidates and officeholders manipulate the attitudes of the populace by clever public-relations techniques and the skillful use of the mass media. Republican and Democratic candidates, it is charged, stand for essentially the same policies, which means that voters have no significant choice between them. Moreover, significant minorities—blacks, Mexican-Americans, American Indians, the poor, and the young—are not represented or served by either of the two major parties.

The critics view the making of public policy between elections in essentially the same light. None of the above-mentioned minorities is nearly as effectively organized as are more dominant, affluent groups. As political scientist E. E. Schattschneider has suggested, "The flaw in the pluralist heaven is that the heavenly chorus sings with a strong upperclass accent. Probably about 90 percent of the people cannot get into the pressure system." Moreover, the minorities that are organized do not actually check and balance one another as is generally claimed. Rather, each concentrates on getting what it wants in benefits from government: businessmen are served by the Department of Commerce, organized working people by the Department of Labor, and farmers by the Department of Agriculture. Instead of regulating such groups in the public interest, public officials grant them favors at the expense of the general tax-payer or of each other.

Nor do the critics feel that the system is equally open or responsive to all kinds of individuals and groups. Few if any women, blacks, laborers, or members of the lower economic classes sit in Congress, in the executive departments, or on the Supreme Court. Middle- and upper-class persons dominate all three branches of our national government, and those at the state level as well. Moreover, the increasing costs of political campaigns may make it even more difficult for those of limited means to hold elective office in the future, especially in the national government.

For such critics the American system is not pluralistic but rather elitist in the sense that organized minorities—checked neither by each other nor by the general populace—dominate the political process. Their privileged status in the society at large, together with their uneven representation in the government itself, enables them to set the "public agenda"—that is, to determine which matters become legitimate issues of governmental concern and action, and which remain "nonissues," ignored by public officials. The end result is a biased political system favoring the status quo—that is, established groups over unorganized ones and stability over change in American life.

As proof of their contentions, critics point to the public policies of American government, which they feel do not really implement democratic ideals. We have done little to develop equality in American life, whether it be social equality for such groups as the blacks, Mexican-Americans, or Puerto Ricans; economic equality for those same groups and others of the poor as well; or equal justice under the law for all our disadvantaged citizens. Thus critics contend it is not sufficient to provide individuals with the mere opportunity to participate politically or to have the law applied impartially to them. We should also see to it that all Americans are provided with the education, training, and necessary resources to make their participation effective—and with access to an attorney to ensure that their legal rights are fully protected.

America's first citizens in action.

Inequality, American style.

Critics of American democracy also charge that we have been far too willing to accept the view that political elites should run the political system because common people are apathetic about public affairs and are not committed to the democratic rules of the game. According to this view, that position underestimates the possibility of educating the average citizen to appreciate his own political rights as well as the right of others to oppose his views. Moreover, an important reason the common man or "little guy" does not participate politically is that he considers it futile; make the system more responsive to his needs, and he will take a greater interest in its operation. Thus we should not accept political apathy as endemic to human nature but rather as a condition that can be changed.

In fact, some critics suggest that we introduce more democracy into American life by utilizing its values and methods in other institutions besides the government. According to this view, corporations should not trade with South Africa because of its racist policies, boards of directors should include representatives of consumers and workers, and students should participate in the making of decisions that vitally affect their lives. Such actions would make these private organizations more humane; moreover, habits and experiences that citizens acquire in their operation would carry over into the functioning of our governmental institutions as well.

Finally, critics charge that we have been far too ready to judge American democracy on the basis of the stability it has provided for our society and its success in reconciling conflicts among selfish interests. In the process we have lost track of the fundamental purpose for which democracy was originally established: the full development of the individual's personality through participation in the life of the community. Such a line of thought reflects a desire to return to the kinds of values and assumptions that underlay direct Athenian democracy. Thus, today's mottoes of "participatory democracy" and the "new politics" have much in common with the Greek precept that the individual should involve himself in public affairs, that he must think not just of his own private interests but also of those of the community at large.

APPROACH AND ORGANIZATION OF THIS BOOK

With these models of democracy and conflicting views about the current state of the American political system in mind, we turn to a detailed analysis of that system in the chapters that follow. In the first section of each, key concepts are treated (e.g. a constitution is defined and its purposes explained); concepts are also distinguished from related ones (e.g. a political party from an interest group). The aim is to enable us to see important relationships and grasp essentials rather than to get bogged down in factual material unrelated to major ideas.

Many chapters also provide basic information on how our political system has evolved over time. Particular attention is focused on the early years, when the nation was struggling to establish its political institutions, and on periods of rapid change in our society. A student needs to understand how evolving forces mold and change political institutions; moreover, history provides an excellent basis of comparison. In evaluating our political system today, it is important to compare it not only with other models of democracy, but also with its own past accomplishments and failures.

With concepts and some historical perspective in mind, one is better able to appreciate the way our political system functions and how successful it is in dealing with current developments and problems in American society. An effort has been made to provide the factual information needed to judge how closely the performance of American democracy lives up to its promise. At the end of most chapters, the author gives his personal view of how the particular institution under study should be assessed. You are not necessarily expected to agree with this evaluation, but perhaps it will stimulate thought and controversy.

The book is divided into three major parts. The first analyzes the constitutional framework of American government together with the values and assumptions underlying that framework. It explores the basic features of American democracy as well as the limitations placed on all levels of government in the interest of individual liberty. This part thus focuses on legal powers and limitations and the role they play in establishing the basic rules of the game within which our political process operates.

The second part concentrates initially on the attitudes of citizens toward the American political system and the ways in which their attitudes are acquired. Succeeding chapters in Part 2 focus on the kinds of institutions Americans have developed to keep those in political power responsible to the general public and on the extent to which such institutions actually enable the public to influence and control their public officials.

The third part focuses on the three branches of government—the Congress, the executive branch, and the courts—which together make the official decisions that are binding on the rest of society.

These three branches are examined in terms of the kinds of persons who serve in them; their general structure; the procedures that each utilizes to carry on its activities; and the relationships that exist among the officials of the three branches. Also included at the end of most chapters are case studies describing in some detail how particular public policies were enacted into law. Such descriptions provide insight into how the political process actually works in American society and the extent to which that process satisfies Dahl's criterion that every active and legitimate group be able to make itself heard effectively at some crucial stage in the process of decision. By examining the *content* of such decisions, students can also assess how well our public policies foster the major values of a democratic society.

SELECTED READINGS

A classic study of the rise of modern democracy is A. D. Lindsay, *The Modern Democratic State* (New York: Oxford University Press, 1962). An extended treatment of the historical evolution and general nature of democracy is Leslie Lipson, *The Democratic Civilization* (New York: Oxford University Press, 1964).

Two excellent recent treatments of democratic theory are Henry Mayo, *An Introduction to Democratic Theory* (New York: Oxford University Press, 1960), and Giovanni Sartori, *Democratic Theory* (New York: Praeger, 1965). For a critique of the excessive optimism concerning human nature underlying some recent theories of democracy, see Reinhold Niebuhr, *The Children of Light and The Children of Darkness* (New York: Scribner, 1944).

The case for pluralist American democracy is set forth by Robert Dahl in several of his recent studies. Included are *A Preface to Democratic Theory* (Chicago: Phoenix Books, 1963), *Who Governs?* (New Haven: Yale University Press, 1961), and *Pluralist Democracy in the United States* (Chicago: Rand McNally, 1967). Other books expressing this same general viewpoint include Seymour Lipset, *Political Man* (Garden City: Doubleday, 1960), and V. O. Key, *Public Opinion and American Democracy* (New York: Knopf, 1961).

An excellent criticism of Dahl's theory is Jack Walker, "A Critique of the Elitist Theory of Democracy," *The American Political Science Review* 60 (1966): 285-95. For a more extended analysis of the same subject see Peter Bachrach, *Theory of Democratic Elitism: A Critique* (Boston: Little, Brown, 1967). Three articles expressing the same general viewpoint are Darryl Baskin, "American Pluralism: Theory, Practice, and Ideology," *The Journal of Politics* 32 (1970): 71-96; Michael Parenti, "Power and Pluralism: A View from the Bottom," *The Journal of Politics* 32 (1970): 501-30; and Roger W. Cobb and Charles Elder, "The Politics of Agenda-Building: An Alternative for Modern Democratic Theory," *The Journal of Politics* 33 (1971): 892-916.

Political Novels   At the heart of all democratic values is the human spirit itself. The power of this spirit in the face of overwhelming authority under the most hopeless conditions is movingly shown by Alexander Solzhenitsyn in his novel about a Soviet labor camp, *One Day in the Life of Ivan Denisovich* (New York: Bantam, 1963).

The strain of social and political persecution on human dignity is powerfully illustrated in Bernard Malamud's novel about antisemitism in czarist Russia, *The Fixer* (New York: Dell, 1969).

The significance of democratic values can best be appreciated when compared to systems that reflect absolute political authority, collectivism, and the absence of personal privacy. Such systems have often been the subject of excellent fiction. The exchange of personal freedom for physical comfort creates a bleak existence for those who inhabit Aldous Huxley's *Brave New World* (New York: Harper & Row, 1969). George Orwell in his classic novel *1984* (New York: New American Library, 1961), envisioned life under the total control of the "Big Brother" of political authority. A world devoid of individualism is described by Ayn Rand in *Anthem* (New York: New American Library, 1961).

THE AMERICAN CONSTITUTIONAL FRAMEWORK

The constitution of a democratic nation provides the basic principles that determine the conduct of its political affairs. These principles relate to three fundamental aspects of the political system. One aspect has to do with the *functions* of the government, the kinds of activities within public, as contrasted to private, control. The second bears on *procedures,* the manner in which the government carries out the activities entrusted to it. Closely related is the third aspect, *structure,* the particular mechanisms used to execute public functions. Together, these elements constitute the rules of the game by which political authority is exercised in the society.

Historically, constitutions have been linked to the concept that those in political power should be responsible to the populace for their actions. Thus the constitution becomes the practical means whereby the ruled exercise some control over their rulers. In democratic societies like Great Britain and the United States, constitutions have also been associated with limitations on government, ensuring that those in political power— even when they are acting with the consent of the majority—do not interfere with certain fundamental rights. In such countries, the constitution determines not only what the government *can* do but also what it *cannot* do; thus the constitution both channels and restricts the exercise of political power.

In the first chapter we found that public officials make binding decisions in the form of legal regulations that determine what private individuals and groups may and may not do and how they should conduct themselves toward their fellow men. A constitution performs a similar function for public officials themselves by determining what they can and cannot do and what their relationships should be with other officeholders as well as with the general populace. Reciprocity thus characterizes a constitutional form of government: the people grant public officials the power to enact laws and decrees that vitally affect their lives, but at the same time they control the manner in which that power is exercised.

A constitution, then, establishes legal relationships between leaders and followers; even more basically, it is at the heart of a nation's political process. On the one hand, it shapes that process by determining the rules to be followed in competing for political power. On the other hand, the constitution is itself shaped by the political process, as groups struggle to write the rules of the game to favor their own particular interests.

Our study of the American system begins in chapter 2 with an analysis of the political context in which our Constitutuion was created—the circumstances that gave rise to the calling of the Convention in 1787, the kinds of individuals and groups that participated in its deliberations, and the specific purposes they had in mind in forging the basic document to guide the nation's future growth. The latter part of the chapter examines the political beliefs of the Founding Fathers and the constitutional principles they chose to implement those beliefs. Chapters 3 and 4 analyze the part that two major features of the American constitutional framework— federalism and civil liberties—have played in shaping the continuing struggle for political power in the United States.

Chapter 2

During the summer of 1787 fifty-five delegates met in convention in Philadelphia to frame a new constitution for a young nation. In the group were many of the leading public figures of the day: the revered wartime commander, George Washington, the "Vesuvius of a man" who, despite his famed temper, presided over the four-month deliberations with fairness and dignity; beloved Benjamin Franklin, the nation's elder statesman (age eighty-one), admired like Washington not only in his own country but also in the capitals of Europe; youthful Alexander Hamilton, brilliant prime-mover of events that led to the calling of the Convention; and the diminutive James Madison, "no bigger," someone remarked, "than half a cake of soap," ultimately judged by historians the Convention's "giant."

Political history knows no more revered heroes than this assemblage of distinguished men. Americans of many generations have endowed the Constitution and its framers with almost divine qualities. Thomas Jefferson called his contemporaries "an assembly of demigods"; one of the more recent authors to chronicle those exciting days, Catherine Drinker Bowen, entitles her book *The Miracle at Philadelphia*. Nor has the adulation been restricted to our own citizens: William Gladstone, four-time Prime Minister of Great Britain, once described the Constitution as "the most wonderful work ever struck off at a given time by the brain and purpose of man."

Not all Americans, however, have joined in such veneration of our fundamental document. One outspoken opposition delegate at the Massachusetts ratifying convention, Amos Singletry, had this to say about Jefferson's demigods:

THE
AMERICAN
CONSTITUTION

These lawyers and men of learning, and monied men that talk so finely, and gloss over matters so smoothly, to make us poor illiterate people swallow down the pill, expect to get in the Congress themselves . . . get all the power . . . and then they will swallow up us little fellows, . . . just as the whale swallowed up Jonah.

The radicals: Patrick Henry and Samuel Adams.

Less partisan men than "plain-folks" spokesman Singletry have also questioned the purity of the Founding Fathers' motives. Scholars Vernon Parrington and J. Allen Smith viewed the Convention as a reaction against the era of the common man that followed the Revolutionary War; they thus regarded it as a "counterrevolution," an overturn of political power (though this time a peaceful one) by which the conservative, propertied classes recaptured control of the country from radicals like Samuel Adams and Patrick Henry, who had dominated politics in the Revolutionary and immediate postwar eras. A similar stream of thought flows through historian Charles Beard's classic study, *An Economic Interpretation of the Constitution of the United States,* which suggests that the Founding Fathers wrote the Constitution primarily to protect their own property interests. Although written in 1913, Beard's work remains the most controversial analysis of the Constitution, as scholars continue to attack, defend, and qualify his thesis.

We shall assess these conflicting interpretations in the concluding portion of the chapter. First, however, we need to examine the circumstances that led to the calling of the Convention and the type of Constitution that the proceedings produced.

THE PRECONSTITUTION PERIOD

A constitution provides the basic rules of the game that citizens must follow in competing for things they want from the political process. Such rules—dealing with governmental functions, procedures, and structures—are never entirely neutral: *they inevitably favor some persons at the expense of others.* To understand the background of the United States Constitution, we need to appreciate two major factors: first, the preceding frames of government—the national Articles of Confederation and state constitutions; and second, the economic conditions that created dissatisfaction with the existing governmental arrangements, leading some groups to seek a rewriting of the nation's constitutional framework.

Frames of Government

The Articles of Confederation and the early state constitutions reflected American experiences during the colonial period. Because the colonists attributed their particular troubles to the heavy hand of the London government, they feared centralized political power; as a result, they declared themselves to be independent not only of the mother country but, in essence, of one another as well. The Articles of Confederation specifically provided that "Each state retains its sovereignty, freedom and independence, and every Power, Jurisdiction and right" not "expressly delegated to the United States, in Congress assembled."

The functions so delegated to the national Congress were restricted primarily to matters of war and peace (raising an army and navy, entering into treaties and alliances, sending and receiving diplomatic representatives) that wartime experience indicated had to be vested in the nation. Missing, for example, was Congress's power to regulate interstate and foreign commerce; the Confederation's framers had associated this power with the abuses of the Acts of Trade and Navigation passed by the centralized authority of Parliament. A similar fear of the tyranny of taxation as practiced by the British against the colonists resulted in denying the national government the power to tax. Although it had authority to requisition funds from the states for its expenses, the taxes to pay these requisitions had to be levied by the states themselves. National troops also had to be furnished by the states. Lacking the authority to require the states to meet their obligations (which many did not) or to tax or conscript individuals itself, the national government was denied the means to carry out the few functions entrusted to it. Moreover, the Articles provided little opportunity for changing these arrangements, since all thirteen states had to consent to any alteration of the document.

The British experience colored the attitude of the Confederation's framers not only toward the distribution of authority between the nation and the states but also toward the particular branch of government that should be entrusted with important political powers. Memories of George III and his emissaries, the colonial governors, led Americans of the Revolutionary period to identify tyranny with the executive; at the same time, they associated liberty with the legislature, the arm of colonial government that represented their interests in battles with the King's governor. They had little use for the judiciary, which had been populated by representatives of the Crown.

These attitudes toward the various branches of government are directly reflected in the structures of both national and state governments in the post-Revolutionary period. The Articles of Confederation provided for a legislative body with a single house in which each state had an equal vote. There was no provision at all for independent executive and judiciary branches. In the states, too, the legislature was the dominant branch, even to the point of choosing most of the governors: only four states had a chief executive elected by the people. The state judiciaries were also generally weak, frequently appointed by the legislature, and usually given limited powers.

Beyond their particular fears of the national government and the executive, Americans in the Revolutionary era also had a profound distrust of political power in general. The Articles of Confederation and state constitutions provided checks on even the favored legislative bodies of the day. Terms of legislators were short—one year only in the national Congress and most of the states; Rhode Islanders were even more wary of officeholders, allowing their representatives only six months between elections. And for the popular legislator, there was an additional limitation in the form of forced rotation—for example, under the Articles of Confederation no person was "capable of being a delegate for more than three years in any term of six years"; similar provisions plagued ambitious state legislators. As for the unpopular delegate, the voters need not endure him even during his short term, for the national Articles and many state constitutions gave the electorate the power of recall at any time. As a final check on arbitrary government, state constitutions established bills of rights ensuring fundamental liberties like freedom of speech and conscience, and trial by jury.

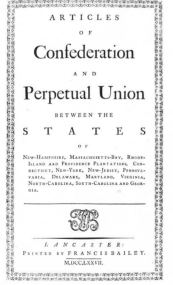

ARTICLES
OF
Confederation
AND
Perpetual Union
BETWEEN THE
S T A T E S
OF
New-Hampshire, Massachusetts-Bay, Rhode-Island and Providence Plantations, Connecticut, New-York, New-Jersey, Pennsylvania, Delaware, Maryland, Virginia, North-Carolina, South-Carolina and Georgia.

L A N C A S T E R:
Printed by F R A N C I S B A I L E Y.
M,DCC,LXXVII.

In time, a reaction set in against this legislative, semidirect democracy. The simple necessities of executive government required the national Congress to create departments of diplomacy, war, and finance, and to appoint eminent men like Robert Livingston, John Jay, and Robert Morris to head their activities. British occupation of New York required that state to develop a strong governorship free of legislative dominance in order to handle its military and civilian affairs. And in Massachusetts the voters adopted a constitution that departed radically from the strong legislative-democratic model. Conceived by John Adams, who favored a "mixed" government representing various social interests, it provided for a popularly elected house of representatives and an "aristocratic" senate apportioned on the basis not of population but of taxable wealth. Moreover, it included a popularly elected governor (eligible to succeed himself) with substantial powers, including that of vetoing legislative acts, and an independent judiciary. The New York and Massachusetts constitutions were important not only for their influence on other states but also because they constituted alternative models to which the Founding Fathers would ultimately turn in their deliberations at the Constitutional Convention.

While alterations were thus being made in the structures of both the national and state governments in the pre-Constitution period, attempts to change the allocation of powers between nation and state were continually frustrated. Before Maryland had even signed the Articles of Confederation, Congress submitted an amendment to the states to allow it to levy a duty of 5 percent on imported goods; the amendment failed of adoption because one state, Rhode Island, refused to ratify. Similar efforts to grant Congress authority to regulate foreign and interstate commerce and to require states to comply with requisitions of men or money owed to the national government ran afoul of the unanimous-consent requirement for amending the Articles. Financial affairs of the national government had reached such a sad state that its total income in 1786 was less than a third of the interest due on the national debt. Meanwhile, seven states exercised the power to issue money, with the result that the new nation lacked a common currency; nine states even retained their own navies. Thus the United States in the pre-Constitution period lacked authority over what are fundamental concerns of any viable, sovereign nation—finances, commerce, and external affairs. Yet as the following section indicates, it was precisely these matters that were of greatest concern to many Americans of that time.

Economic Conditions

Like many of the newly emerging nations in today's world, the United States in the 1780s faced a major period of adjustment following the successful revolt against Great Britain. Within a few years after the close of the Revolutionary War in 1781, Americans were experiencing an economic depression. Accounts differ about how serious conditions actually became: some historians suggest that the young nation was very near an economic disaster that threatened its very existence; others claim that the critical period was very short lived and that the United States was well on the way to recovery by the time the Convention met in Philadelphia in mid-1787. There is general agreement, however, that the economic downturn did not affect all groups in the same way. Small

Economic crisis in the pre-Constitution period: Shays' Rebellion and the currency of the day.

farmers and the few hired laborers of the day bore little of the impact, while persons in commerce and finance were hit the hardest.

One of the ironies of the success of the Revolution was that, while it brought relief from burdensome taxes imposed by the mother country, it also ended the favorable position of American businessmen in international commerce. After the war, in place of the preferential trade treatment and the assured markets they had enjoyed in the British empire, merchants faced an economic threat from British manufacturers who dumped their goods on the American market. Infant businesses naturally found it very difficult to compete with the products of well-developed British industries; moreover, under the Articles of Confederation the national government lacked authority to levy import duties on British merchants to protect the domestic market. Thus, having thrown off the political yoke of Great Britain, the United States was threatened with being shackled by the economic power of the mother country.

Nor was the commercial competition faced by American merchants restricted to foreign sources alone. Domestic rivalries also developed as states levied duties not only to raise needed revenue but also to protect local interests against out-of-state competitors. Particularly disadvantaged by such duties were those states with no seaports of their own. Madison suggested that "New Jersey between Philadelphia and New York was like a cask tapped at both ends, and North Carolina between Virginia and South Carolina was like a patient bleeding at both arms." Lacking the authority to levy duties on imports or to regulate interstate commerce, the national government was thus powerless either to erect a tariff barrier to protect American industries against the British or to break up the obstacles to free trade within the nation.

Another major group adversely affected in the postwar period was creditors who financed both private and public ventures in the young nation. Debtors could use the political process at the state level to lighten the burden of their debt in various ways. One technique involved enacting "stay" laws to postpone the due date of obligations past the time originally provided for in the promissory note. Another, similar type of legislation permitted a debtor to declare bankruptcy, pay off his obligation at less than the face value, and begin his financial life anew with a clean slate. Yet another advantage for debtors—and disadvantage for creditors—was the issuance of cheap paper money by state legislatures; this inflationary practice allowed obligations to be paid off with money that was worth far less in purchasing power than the currency originally borrowed.

Even more financially frustrated than private creditors were those who had lent the nation money to fight the Revolutionary War. No method existed for collecting on public securities issued by a government that lacked the financial ability to pay off its debts. Similarly affected were wartime veterans who lent not money but a more precious commodity, their services, for which they were to be later compensated by proceeds from government bonds.

Although the United States had theoretically achieved an independent status in the family of nations as a result of the war, in actuality numerous challenges to sovereignty persisted after the conclusion of hostilities. Unfriendly Indian tribes continued to inhabit lands in the West, so that veterans found their claims to such lands no more realizable than the worthless bonds they were issued for their wartime services. Beyond this, the Spanish closed the mouth of the Mississippi to all shipping, and the supposedly vanquished British troops refused to withdraw from certain northwestern forts until claims of British creditors were honored.

Group Rivalries and the Movement for a Convention

In the situation described above, the groups particularly aggrieved by the postwar situation were those involved in commerce and finance—manufacturers, merchants, shipowners, and public and private creditors. The professional classes—lawyers, doctors, newspaper editors—viewed matters from the perspective of their clientele, and that perspective was shared by former soldiers who felt cheated out of their rightful claims for services rendered in the cause of nationhood. All in all, these groups comprised a potent array of individuals longing for a change in the unfortunate circumstances in which they found themselves. Later, after the Constitution had been framed, these disparate elements were to be welded into an effective group working for its adoption under the name of "Federalists."

Although these groups were for the most part concentrated in the cities, some rural Americans also found their interests jeopardized by the postwar conditions. These were the commercial farmers who produced a surplus of crops that they wanted to dispose of in interstate and foreign markets. Typically large holders of fertile lands, with slave labor and locations on river arteries that linked them to the outside world, they found common cause with merchants whose futures were also linked to commerce.

Arrayed against the nascent Federalists in the economic and political rivalries of the day were those Americans who were not dependent on trade for their livelihood. The small subsistence farmers, scratching out a living on poor soil

Anti-Federalists: Luther Martin, George Mason, and Elbridge Gerry.

remote from river valleys, who produced crops entirely for their own families or who marketed their small surpluses in nearby localities, formed the core of the group that was basically satisfied with life in the postwar period. Also included in its ranks were small businessmen, artisans, mechanics (the small laboring class of that day), and debtors who welcomed governmental assistance in their eternal struggle to keep one step ahead of their creditors. It was their coalition of interests, labeled "anti-Federalist," that eventually led the fight to defeat the ratification of the Constitution.

The Federalists as a group were wealthier and better educated and held higher-status occupations than their antagonists, who tended to be lower-class, obscure men of modest means. Although the leadership of the anti-Federalists included such prominent Americans as George Mason, Richard Henry Lee, Patrick Henry, and George Clinton, they could not match either in numbers or in fame those who, like Washington, Hamilton, and Madison, lent their skill and prestige to the Federalists' cause. There were also major differences between the two groups of leaders: the anti-Federalists were "locals"—persons with interests and influence in their own states—while the Federalists were "cosmopolitans"—individuals with national reputations who were oriented to the world beyond their immediate communities. The latter enjoyed friendships across the breadth of the young nation, many bred by the camaraderie of common wartime experiences. A number of rich Federalists also acquired their wealth late compared to the established anti-Federalists like George Mason who, hailing from an old Virginia family, regarded George Washington as something of an upstart. Washington and Hamilton, by propelling themselves up the social and economic ladder through astute marriages, contributed to their nouveau-riche image among local anti-Federalist notables.

These, then, were the opposing leaders and interests that were to vie over the writing and ratification of the Constitution. The nascent anti-Federalists were essentially satisfied with existing governmental arrangements, while those who were later to become Federalists sought to overturn them in favor of a constitutional system that would provide relief from their mounting problems.

Two events converged in the fall of 1786 that enabled the Federalists to convert their desires into successful action. One was a meeting at Annapolis, Maryland convened to discuss problems of interstate trade and the possibility of adopting a uniform system of commercial regulations. When only five states showed up, Hamilton and Madison seized the opportunity to issue a report to the Continental Congress suggesting that a commission be assembled the following May to "render the constitution of the federal government adequate to the exigencies of the Union." The other event was the outbreak of an armed revolt in western Massachusetts; farmers there took to arms in response to an effort by the state to take their property for failure to pay taxes and debts in the "hard" money of the time. Although Shays' Rebellion (named for its leader, Daniel Shays) was put down, it badly frightened many Americans who regarded it as a threat not only to property rights but also to the very existence of government. Among such men was the most popular American of them all, George Washington. Appalled by the news that a former officer in his army had brought the state of Massachusetts to the brink of civil war, Washington lent his great prestige to the movement for the Convention. The following February the Congress called upon the states to send delegates "for the sole and express purpose of revising the Articles of Confederation." All except ever-recalcitrant Rhode Island, where debtor interests completely controlled the state, eventually responded, although the North Carolina delegation did not arrive until July, some two months after the deliberations first began.

THE CONSTITUTIONAL CONVENTION

Personnel: The Founding Fathers

In terms of the economic, social, and political divisions described above, the most important feature of the Constitutional Convention was that the over-whelming proportion of the delegates were would-be Federalists. Even though the anti-Federalists matched or even exceeded their opponents in numbers among the general populace, they sent only a few of their men to the delibera-tions. This failure is puzzling since the state legislatures of the day, which in many instances were under the control of the debtor forces, were also entrusted with selecting delegates to the Convention, and so they could have packed their delegations with anti-Federalists. The best indications are that they did not do so for two reasons. One is that some of the anti-Federalists did not want to dignify the constitutional assembly with their presence; a case in point was Patrick Henry, who stayed away because he "smelt a rat." The other is that they thought it was not important to attend, since the Convention was re-stricted to revising the Articles of Confederation; moreover, they could always ultimately block any undesirable changes in the Articles because such changes had to be approved by all the states. In any event, several persons who later opposed the Constitution refused their commissions to the Convention, a deci-sion lamented by one of them, Richard Henry Lee, who wrote, "The non-attendance of eight or nine men who were appointed members of the conven-tion, I shall ever consider as a very unfortunate event to the United States."

A sprinkling of future anti-Federalists did attend the Convention (including George Mason of Virginia, Elbridge Gerry of Massachusetts, Luther Martin of Maryland, and Robert Yates and John Lansing of New York), but they were badly outnumbered by their opponents, and even they belonged to the elite element of their group. The nation's subsistence farmers, who constituted the rank-and-file support of the anti-Federalist cause, were represented by only one delegate, a backwoods yeoman from Georgia. Since such farmers were the most numerous economic group in the nation at that time, the Convention's delegates were decidedly not a cross section of American life.

In fact, an analysis of the backgrounds of the members of the Convention indicates that they were definitely an elite group. Of the fifty-five delegates, thirty-four were lawyers; most of them held college degrees, nine of them from universities abroad. To their educational attainments they added a wealth of practical political experience. Over three-fourths of them had served in the Continental Congress; many had participated in the writing of the Declaration of Independence and were active in state politics of the period. Learned men, seasoned in political struggles in the past, they represented the cream of the young nation. Some foreign political leaders of the day, not normally given over to praising the newest member of the family of nations, conceded that the group matched in talents any that the most advanced European nations could muster.

The Father of the
Constitution: James Madison.

Key Convention
committeemen: James Wilson
and Gouverneur Morris.

Although almost all the fifty-five delegates took an active role in the proceedings, in a gathering of this size certain individuals naturally stood out as the major leaders of the Convention. Without a doubt, by far the most influential delegate was James Madison. Like a schoolboy preparing for an important examination, Madison spent the months preceding the Convention poring over treatises on government, including accounts of the constitutions of the republics of Greece and Rome, sent to him from Paris by Thomas Jefferson. The labors of the Convention's "egghead" were not to be in vain—his grasp of historical materials in addition to the practical experience he had enjoyed in state and national politics enabled him to play a creative role in the deliberations. As the author of the Virginia Plan, the first major proposal to be presented to the Convention, Madison became the leader of the movement to draft a constitutional scheme that would break radically with the principles of the Articles of Confederation. At the same time, Madison was a man of large enough character to compromise his ideas in the interest of solidarity. Madison's contributions to the Constitution transcended the Convention itself; he was a key figure in both the pre- and post-Convention maneuverings, and his diary constitutes the major historical source of information on the four-month-long proceedings. By any standard, Madison well deserves the epithet, Father of the Constitution.

Next in importance to the giant from Virginia were two delegates from Pennsylvania, James Wilson and Gouverneur Morris. Both in physical appearance and in personal style they were poles apart: Wilson, a solid Scotsman, aged forty-four, a shrewd lawyer with a penetrating, logical turn of mind, earned the title of the "unsung hero of the convention"; Morris, eleven years younger, a tall glamorous figure (considered by the ladies of the day "as very handsome, very bold, and very impudent"), possessor of a biting wit, became the convention's marathon talker, speaking on more occasions than did any other single delegate. Their views on human nature also diverged sharply: Wilson placed great faith in the common people, whereas Morris regarded them with an aristocrat's mistrust and disdain. But despite such differences, they had more vital matters in common: both were friends of a strong national government headed by a potent chief executive, and both were major figures on key committees of the Convention—Wilson, the one on Detail, and Morris, those on Style and Postponed Matters. Their convergence of views and their positions of power at the Convention permitted Wilson and Morris to shape both the contents and the phraseology of the document that ultimately emerged.

Two other figures, George Washington and Benjamin Franklin, contributed in an entirely different way to the eventual success of the Constitution. Neither had the slightest effect on its substance. Not until the final day did Washington address the Convention, but he did not miss a single session in his capacity as presiding officer; Catherine Drinker Bowen suggestively writes that "the spirit of compromise sat on his shoulder like a dove." The assumption that Washington would be the nation's first chief executive gave the delegates the confidence to create an office with great legal and political potentialities; his mere presence at the Convention made Americans in general feel easier about the entire affair. The aged Franklin had long since passed the peak of a political creativity that had formulated the Albany Plan of Union more than thirty years before the Convention. Moreover, few of his junior colleagues were inclined to adopt his

Convention proposals because they considered him to be something of a radical, too naive in his enthusiasm for the good sense of the common people. But his famed wit cooled tempers during the course of the heated debates, and he closed the proceedings on a benedictory note. Looking at the president's chair, Franklin observed that during many points in the long deliberations he had been unable to decide about the course of the sun that it bore as a decoration. "But now," he pronounced, "I have the happiness to know it is a rising and not a setting sun." In the ratification campaign that followed, no two Americans contributed more toward speeding the adoption of the Constitution than the young nation's greatest heroes, Washington and Franklin.

As with most human events, the Convention also had its failures. Most disappointing was Alexander Hamilton. Outnumbered in his own New York delegation by Yates and Lansing (sent to the Convention by anti-Federalist Governor George Clinton to keep an eye on Hamilton), he was also out of political step with the bulk of the delegates. His support for a life-tenured chief executive and senate smacked too much of the British model of King and House of Lords, with which the late colonists were all too familiar. Thus, ironically, the conservative ideas of the youthful Hamilton were as uncongenial to the Convention's thinking as the radical proposals of the aged Franklin. At one point Hamilton left the convention in frustration; for all he had accomplished, he might just as well never have showed up at all. Ultimately he was to atone for his failure by joining with Madison, his partner in the pre-Convention maneuverings, in successfully campaigning for the subsequent adoption of the Constitution.

The Convention conciliators: George Washington and Benjamin Franklin.

Agreement and Disagreement at the Convention

Accounts of the great debates of the Constitutional Convention frequently obscure the substantial agreement that existed among the delegates on a number of features of the new government. The authority of the national government to raise revenue by taxing imports and to regulate interstate and foreign commerce was accepted by the delegates, even by the anti-Federalists. The Convention proposal that most clearly reflected the attitudes of that group, the New Jersey Plan, vested such vital functions (along with those previously provided for in the Articles) in the national government. The same plan permitted Congress to act against states that failed to honor financial requisitions; it also granted the federal executive the authority to "call forth the powers of the confederated States" to enforce national laws and treaties against resistant states. Thus the very issues that had raised such difficulties between the nation and the states under the Articles of Confederation presented no serious conflicts at the Convention. Of course the absence of the most independent and antiunion state of the thirteen, Rhode Island, undoubtedly contributed to this harmonious state of affairs.

Nor were there serious differences at the Convention over the general structure of the national government. Most delegates concurred with Jefferson's assessment of the Virginia experience with legislative supremacy that "173 despots could be as oppressive as one" and that "concentrating all powers in the same hands was precisely the definition of despotic government." They were also mindful of the fact that under the Articles of Confederation the Congress had been forced to develop crude substitutes for the missing executive and judicial arms of the national government. The delegates were thus agreed upon the necessity for creating a government with three separate branches.

The greatest single cause of disagreement among the delegates was the general issue of nation-state relations. The conflicting proposals for dealing with this basic issue, and the way in which they were ultimately compromised, will be discussed in detail in chapter 3 (on federalism).

Closely connected to the issue of nation-state relations was the question how the states would be represented in Congress. The Virginia Plan provided for a two-branch legislature, the first branch to be elected by the people, the second to be chosen by the first from persons nominated by the state legislatures. The representation of a state in both branches was to be based on its financial contributions or population. Thus the plan would have been advantageous to the large, wealthy states from which it drew its major supporters. In contrast, the New Jersey Plan would have retained the Confederation's one-house legislative body with its equality of state representation. It was backed by delegates who wanted essentially to retain the confederation system as well as by those who favored a strong national government but did not want to see it dominated by the large states. Ultimately the Convention adopted a bicameral legislature—one house representing the States by population, the other the states on an equal basis—as the best solution to the representation dilemma. Labeled the "Connecticut Compromise" because the delegates from that medium-sized state worked so diligently for its acceptance, it became the most famous of the accommodations developed to bridge the differences among the various delegates. (As we shall see in the following chapter, the compromise also paved the way for the resolution of a number of issues bearing on the relationship between the national government and the states in the new constitutional system.)

The Convention eventually compromised a series of issues that divided its members. Just as crucial as representation for the new government was the composition and method of selection of the executive branch. As we shall see in detail in chapter 12, the presidential office that ultimately emerged from the deliberations differed greatly from the one contemplated in early Convention proposals.

Divergent views of the North and South on slavery were also compromised in Convention decisions to permit the continuation of the trade until 1808 and to count slaves as three-fifths of a free person for purposes of determining both the representation of a state in the lower house of the Congress and its share of direct taxes that were based on population. In addition, the desire of Southerners for free trade (as producers of raw materials like cotton they wanted to ship goods to Britain in return for finished products) led them to advocate requiring an extra majority (two-thirds) vote for navigation acts as a means of protecting themselves against tariffs favored by Northern manufacturers. While the Convention was unwilling to go this far in deferring to Southern interests, it did agree to a prohibition against export taxes.

This give-and-take process of the Convention has led one close student of the subject, Max Farrand, to label the Constitution a "bundle of compromises." A number of factors contributed to the willingness of the delegates to search for, and achieve, accommodations of their differences. Many genuinely believed that the new nation was on the brink of a dissolution that would divide the country into three separate parts, northern, middle, and southern; to fail in their purpose was thus to return the United States to chaos and eventual extinction. Moreover, since most of the delegates were Federalists, they agreed on the essential structure of the national government and on the necessity for making radical changes in nation-state relations. Their consensus on fundamental principles thus permitted the delegates to reach compromises on the particular application of those principles. Compromise was also fostered by the delegates' early decision to keep the proceedings secret: operating free of public scrutiny and pressures permitted them to change their minds and modify their stands in the process of groping for answers to the nation's difficult problems.

But the very conditions that promoted agreement at the Convention itself were precisely the same ones that threatened to make the subsequent ratification process so difficult. Far from seeing the nation as about to disintegrate, the anti-Federalists viewed difficulties under the Articles of Confederation as both manageable and temporary in nature. While the anti-Federalists were generally absent from the constitutional deliberations, they were well represented in the general population and the state legislatures. And the very secrecy that promoted cooperation among the delegates themselves created resentment and suspicion among those denied access to, and information about, the proceedings. Thus the delegates who worked so hard to create a new constitutional framework faced major obstacles in their final task—getting the rest of the nation to accept the product of their labors.

THE RATIFICATION CAMPAIGN

Before the delegates even left the Convention, they made decisions designed to facilitate the adoption of the proposed Constitution. They chose to ignore the unanimous-consent requirement for amending the Articles; instead, they provided that ratification by nine states would be sufficient for the Constitution's adoption. In this way they avoided the possibility that a state like Rhode Island—which had refused even to send delegates to the Convention—could block their efforts. The fear that state legislatures would refuse to accept a constitution that reduced their powers also prompted the delegates to substitute elected state conventions as the ratifying bodies. Such a procedure provided the Federalists with at least an opportunity for victory, since they could influence the selection of the delegates as well as the course of the state-convention deliberations. Cloaking their real purposes in the rhetoric of democracy, the framers claimed that such a ratification process would more directly involve the people than would the use of state legislatures. Surprisingly, the old Continental Congress, which had much to lose under the new constitutional system, forwarded the Convention's instructions to the states for action.

Having manipulated the rules of the ratification game to favor the Constitution's adoption, the Federalists set out to transform their opportunities into realities. They worked to get themselves and their sympathizers elected as state-convention delegates (twenty-five of the thirty-nine delegates who signed the document were so chosen), developed strategies for convention proceedings, and set out to sell the general public on the virtues of the new Constitution. In doing so, the Federalists were able to trade upon a number of political advantages they held over their opponents: prestigious leaders like Washington and

Franklin, whose endorsement alone was worth thousands of votes; continental figures, whose contacts across states and regions provided a communications link for the various state and local campaigns; and the bulk of the nation's phrase-makers—newspaper editors, lawyers, teachers, ministers—who could spread the Federalist propaganda by word of mouth and printed page. In addition, they had one vital asset that their opponents lacked completely: a positive program to sell. Placed in the difficult position of favoring some changes in the Articles of Confederation, but having no concrete plan to substitute for it, the anti-Federalists were forced to adopt a negative, defensive stance in the ratification battle. Meanwhile, the Federalists argued that rejecting the Constitution would mean a return to the chaotic situation under the Articles.

Having written the ratification rules and rallied their resources, the Federalists turned to the practical problem of winning support for the Constitution in the nine states necessary for ratification. Some, like Delaware and New Jersey, burdened with heavy tax and debt loads or plagued by interstate duties, could be counted on for ready support, as could vulnerable Georgia, described by Washington as having "Indians on its back and Spaniards on its flank." Others, notably Rhode Island, offered little hope for the Federalists. Four states were particularly important because of their size and political strength: Massachusetts, New York, Pennsylvania, and Virginia. Should any of these major states fail to ratify, even a legally constituted union of nine or more states would be a shaky one.

The activities of the Federalists in these four crucial states reveal the variety of tactics they used in order to win state-convention support for the Constitution. Threatened with loss of control of the Pennsylvania legislature in upcoming elections, they pressed for immediate action calling for delegate elections. When anti-Federalists tried to thwart this move by absenting themselves so as to deny a legislative quorum, they were unceremoniously dragged back to the chamber, thrust into their seats, and declared present for the crucial vote. The Federalists won two-thirds of the convention seats, and although they failed to convert a single anti-Federalist in the deliberations that followed, their margin held intact in the final convention vote. This early victory (only Delaware acted sooner than Pennsylvania) in the nation's second most populous state helped to start the campaign bandwagon rolling.

Five states had ratified the Constitution by the time the Massachusetts convention was held. When an early straw vote of the delegates indicated that the Federalists were in the minority, they set out to win over two of the state's

The Ninth PILLAR erected !
" The Ratification of the Conventions of nine States, fhall be fufficient for the eftablifhment of this Conftitution, between the States fo ratifying the fame." *Art.* vii.
INCIPIENT MAGNI PROCEDERE MENSES.

favorite sons to their cause—Samuel Adams and John Hancock. Ultimately it was necessary to make a political deal with Hancock; in return for his endorsement of the Constitution, the Federalists promised to support him for the vice-presidency under Washington or, in the event that Virginia failed to ratify, for the presidency itself. The Bay State Federalists also made an important concession on the content of the Constitution: a promise to have the first Congress initiate amendments to add a Bill of Rights to the document. Massachusetts's ratification of the Constitution with a specific recommendation to this effect established a precedent that other states would follow.

Madison's collaborators on the Federalist papers: Alexander Hamilton and John Jay.

The ratification battle in Virginia was crucial, even though the necessary nine states had approved the Constitution by the time the Dominion-State convention met. For the first time, the anti-Federalists had outstanding delegates capable of matching wits with the opposition: Madison, with the able assistance of young John Marshall (later to become Chief Justice of the Supreme Court), defended the Constitution against the criticisms of Patrick Henry, George Mason, and President-to-be James Monroe. The most influential Virginian of them all, George Washington, was not at the convention, but his known support of the Constitution (he even converted to the Federalist cause Governor Randolph, who had refused to sign the document at the national convention) swayed enough of the uncommitted delegates so that the result was a vote of eighty-nine to seventy-nine.

Like Virginia, New York had its share of able anti-Federalist leaders, including Constitutional Convention delegates Lansing and Yates, and Governor George Clinton. But the recent Virginia decision; the series of newspaper articles authored by Hamilton, Madison, and John Jay under the title *The Federalist Papers*, explaining and defending the Constitution; Hamilton's threat that New York City would secede from the state to join the Union if the state failed to ratify; and, perhaps most important of all, the prestige of Washington and Franklin—all these brought the Federalists a narrow convention victory (thirty to twenty-seven) and New York into the fold as the eleventh state to ratify. North Carolina and eventually even reluctant Rhode Island (which also feared the secession of its major city, Providence) were later to make ratification unanimous. The pangs of the formation and adoption struggle were over; a new nation was born.

The above analysis of the political and economic conditions of the pre-Constitution period, the groups favoring and opposing the Constitution, and the process by which it was formulated and adopted provides some important clues to the intentions and motives of the men who established our constitutional framework. Before we can fully assess them or the Constitution itself, however, we must examine the political beliefs of the Founding Fathers and the techniques and institutions they chose to implement those beliefs.

THE POLITICAL PHILOSOPHY OF THE FOUNDING FATHERS

The fifty-five individuals at the Convention spanned the political spectrum from elitists to worshippers of the common man. Yet the greater part of the group was committed to the same general scheme of values and made similar assumptions about the nature of man. The delegate who most clearly articulated the common views was James Madison. In the eighty-five *Federalist Pa-*

POGHKEEPSIE,
July 2d, 1788.

JUST ARRIVED

BY EXPRESS,

The Ratification of the New Constitution by the Convention of the State of Virginia, on Wednesday the 25th June, by a majority of 10 ; 88 agreeing, and 78 dissenting to its adoption.

pers in general and Number 10 in particular, he set forth in plain and succinct terms the fundamental theory of the Constitution. Even though the *Federalist* was written as a political document for the ratification campaign in New York State, it remains to this day the best single source for the Founders' philosophy.

In reading the *Federalist,* it becomes obvious that the democratic value that Madison cherished the most was liberty, an individual's being able to choose reasonable goals for himself and the means to reach those goals. He assumed that one such goal would be the acquisition of private property. However, because of what he termed "the diversity in the faculties of men"—that is, differences in their individual abilities—Madison reasoned that some persons would succeed in acquiring more worldly goods than would others. This being the case, government must protect property interests because they reflect innate differences in individual capacities. Madison thus embraced the view of English political philosopher John Locke that, because individual intelligence and effort are involved in gaining property, it represents an extension of the human personality.

For Madison, property was not only a value to be protected but also a factor to be appreciated if one were to understand the basis for natural divisions among mankind. In *Federalist Paper* 10 he suggested that society is divided into various factions, which he defined as "a number of citizens, whether amounting to a majority or a minority of the whole, who are united and actuated by some common impulse of passion, or of interest, adverse to the rights of other citizens, or to the permanent and aggregate interests of the community." While conceding that the causes of factions are numerous, including differences of opinion over religion and government, Madison stated that "the most common and durable source of factions is the unequal distribution of property. Those who hold and those who are without property have ever formed distinct interests in society. Those who are creditors and those who are debtors, fall under a like discrimination."

Thus Madison's idea that property ownership was the major source of divisions in society paralleled Karl Marx's analysis of more than a half-century later. Unlike Marx, however, Madison had no desire to remove divisions by converting private property to common ownership among individuals because such differences reflect "the diversity in the faculties of men." Moreover, the government was not to wither away as it does in Marxist theory; instead, for Madison, it was the major institution to referee the natural conflicts that develop among various factions in society. In fact, the government provides the legal framework within which factions may compete politically in such a way that no major interest can extinguish another.

Since removing the *causes* of factions would be both unwise (factions are desirable) and impossible (they are also rooted in human nature), Madison set out to construct a system of government that would control the harmful *effects* of factions. As he viewed the matter, minority factions presented no difficulty since the majority of society could always protect itself through voting down their "sinister views." The real problem arises when one faction constitutes a majority of the population. As Madison himself put the issue: "To secure the public good and private rights against the danger of such a faction, and at the same time to preserve the spirit and form of popular government, is then the great object to which our inquiries are directed."

CONSTITUTIONAL PRINCIPLES OF THE FOUNDING FATHERS

Given the human impulse to pursue selfish interests, Madison saw little hope in either morals or religion as effective checks on the appetites of men. Since "men are not angels," society itself must create a series of obstacles to blunt and divert the opinions and wishes of the majority that threaten private rights and the public good. This aim can best be accomplished through a republican form of government, in which the people elect representatives to make binding decisions, as contrasted to a pure democracy, in which they make such decisions themselves. This is so for two reasons. First, a representative government provides for a "refinement and enlargement of public views" by passing them through a chosen body of citizens whose knowledge of the public good is superior to that of the general populace. Second, because representative government permits effective rule to be exercised over a larger and more populous territory than town-meeting government, it brings under its control a greater variety of people and interests than pure democracy does. This system thus

makes it difficult to construct a majority from a large number of groups: because of communication problems, such interests are often unaware of their common motives, and even if they are aware, they find it difficult to work together politically to exercise their will over minorities or the general public.

But Madison was not willing to trust to general principles of republicanism alone to contain the majority. He wanted to build additional controls within the governmental framework itself to protect minority rights. Reflecting his view of human nature, he suggested that "ambition must be made to counteract ambition." In other words, selfish persons occupying different political positions must be deliberately pitted against one another in the struggle for power. In the course of frustrating one another's ambitions, they indirectly protect the liberties of minorities and the general public.

Separation of Powers

A major feature of Madison's scheme to make "ambition counteract ambition" was the doctrine of the separation of powers, which he borrowed from a Frenchman, Montesquieu. That political thinker concluded from his studies that the liberties the English people enjoyed were attributable to the fact that political power under their constitutional system was not centralized in the hands of one person or clique but was rather distributed among the legislative, executive, and, to a lesser degree, the judicial branches of the national government. Thus Montesquieu associated tyranny with the concentration of political power and liberty with its dispersal.

The separation of powers might more accurately be termed a *separation of processes.* That is, each of the three branches or arms of the government carries on a separate portion of the total political process: the legislature has the primary responsibility for making the laws, the executive for putting them into effect, and the judiciary for interpreting them. This distinction is similar to Aristotle's idea of the deliberative, administrative, and adjudicative processes used in making political decisions.

The doctrine, however, does not call for a *total* separation of processes. Although each of the three branches has the *major* responsibility for one of these processes—that is, making, executing, or interpreting laws—each participates to some degree in the principal activities of the others. For example, under our system of government, the Congress has the primary responsibility for enacting legislation, but the President is authorized both to recommend measures to the Congress and to veto laws actually passed by that body. Similarly, the Senate can affect the President's execution of the laws by failing to approve his nominees for major positions in the executive branch. Likewise, Congress can affect the courts' interpretations of the laws by determining the kinds of cases they can hear.

By participating in one another's processes, the three branches are in a position to check and balance each other's influence and political power. A branch can assert and protect its own rights by withholding its support for the essential activities of a coordinate arm of the government. Thus the President may threaten to veto a piece of legislation as a means of preventing Congress from interfering with the operations of the executive branch. But since the three branches are dependent on one another, the system of shared processes ultimately forces them to cooperate in their mutual activities.

The two principles—separation of processes, and checks and balances—complement each other to achieve the desired effect in the political system. The first provides that no branch can usurp an activity that is the *primary* responsibility of another; the second allows the three arms of the government to counteract one another's influence. The end result is a decentralization of political power. Figure 2.1 illustrates the relationships among the governmental branches that the Founding Fathers favored.

But more than a partial separation of process is necessary to make Montesquieu's principle operate effectively. He also called for a *complete* separation of

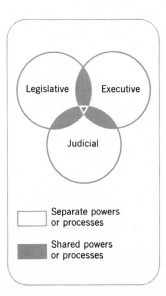

Figure 2.1
Governmental arrangements under the separation-of-powers doctrine.

governmental *personnel.* In other words, the same persons who occupy the legislative seats of government cannot also serve in the executive or judicial branches. (Our system does not permit congressmen to hold executive or judicial positions, and executives and judges are also similarly restricted.) To allow such a practice would concentrate all political powers in the same hands, the very definition of tyranny.

Another aspect of the doctrine reflected in the American system is the separation of constituency. That is, essentially different groups of people choose the personnel of the three branches. As originally conceived, the President, for instance, is selected by an independent group of electors, none of whom can be congressmen; senators are chosen by state electors; and representatives are elected by smaller local publics. Although members of the national courts are nominated by the President and confirmed by the Senate, no one branch chooses them; moreover, once appointed and confirmed, they enjoy life tenure. Thus the personnel of the three branches have largely separate and independent bases of political support and power.

Mixed Government

There is good reason to believe that the Founding Fathers provided separate constituencies not only because they wished the branches of the national government to be independent of one another but also because they wanted them to represent different kinds of social and economic interests.

The idea of "mixed" government—that is, one representing both property and number of people—was favored by John Adams, who succeeded in having the concept incorporated into the Massachusetts state constitution. Although he was in London at the time of the national Constitutional Convention, ideas expressed in the Federalist Papers, as well as the similarities between the structure of the national government and that of Massachusetts, indicate that as a political thinker, Adams influenced the Constitution.

Although the Constitution nowhere provides for property qualifications for either officeholders or voters, it is significant that originally the House of Representatives was the only political body directly elected by the people. (The direct election of senators was not authorized until the ratification of the Seventeenth Amendment in 1913.) The other major offices were somewhat insulated from the general populace. As Figure 2.2 indicates, according to the original document, members of the Senate were two, the President three, and the Supreme Court four steps removed from direct control of the people. (It should also be noted that the Founding Fathers gave the House of Representatives no role in choosing members of the Supreme Court.) In addition, the longer terms of senators (six years), the President (four years), and Supreme Court members (life) would make them less subject to public pressures than were members of the House of Representatives. And because fewer persons were to be chosen for the other three political bodies, their positions would be more prestigious than seats in the lower house of the national legislature. This, in turn, would have the effect of attracting more able persons to them, and since property ownership was considered reflective of natural ability (Adams and Madison agreed on this point), such men would be those of economic substance from the upper social classes.

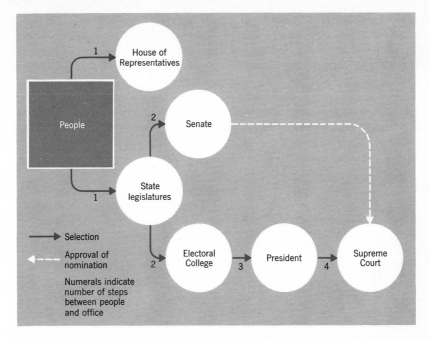

Figure 2.2
Relationship between the people and the selection of various officeholders of the nation under the original Constitution.

In all probability, the Founding Fathers expected the House of Representatives to represent the interests of the many in society, the common people who owned no private property of any consequence. It would be the democratic, popular branch of the government. On the other hand, the Senate, with a smaller, more prestigious membership, insulated somewhat from popular control both by its indirect method of selection and by its longer term of office, would represent the few in society with substantial possessions. It would constitute the oligarchic division of the legislative body.

It is somewhat more difficult to discern the exact intentions of the Founding Fathers concerning the kinds of interests the President and the Supreme Court were to represent in the governmental system. One interpretation calls for their standing above the many/few conflict as guardians of the general interest, promoting unity and justice in society. Another suggests that they were expected to join forces with the Senate to protect the interests of the propertied few against the excesses of the popular legislature. Given Madison's concern with safeguarding both the general interest and minority rights against the evils of a majority faction, it is probable that the President and the Supreme Court were expected to serve both purposes.

The Division of Powers

Madison conceived of one final check on the majority, which we will examine in detail in the next chapter—the division of powers between the national government and the states. His major concern is reflected in *Federalist Paper* 10: "The influence of factious leaders may kindle a flame within the particular states, but they will be unable to spread a conflagration through the other states."

Thus Madison's system for checking the evils of faction was to create a series of dikes to interfere with the free flow of majority will. First, majority interests are *filtered* by the actions of their elected representatives who have more refined views on the public good than do the voters themselves. Second, the wishes of the majority are *diluted* because republicanism allows the expansion of the sphere of government to take in a wide variety of interests. Moreover, the geographical distribution of powers under federalism *contains,* or *segregates,* the evil effects of a faction. Finally, the majority will is *diverted* into many channels by the joint effects of the division and separation of powers. As Madison himself put it in *Federalist Paper* 51:

In the compound republic of America, the power surrendered by the people is first divided between two distinct governments, and then the portion allotted to each subdivided among distinct and separate departments. Hence a double security arises to the rights of the people. The different governments will control each other, at the same time each will be controlled by itself.

This then was the type of political system the Founding Fathers had in mind for the new nation. As the following section shows, however, vast changes have since occurred in our constitutional framework.

CHANGING THE AMERICAN CONSTITUTION

A constitution necessarily reflects the interests and values of those groups responsible for its original formulation. In time, however, new groups arise that are dissatisfied with the status quo, the existing distribution of values, and quite often they seek to rewrite the rules of the democratic game to change that distribution. The press of events and the emergence of different attitudes on the part of leaders and the populace in general also require alterations in a nation's fundamental framework. Every democratic system of government must provide methods for bringing about such modifications peacefully or risk the danger that frustrated individuals and groups will turn to violence to accomplish their ends. Thus the question is not whether a democratic constitution will be changed, but rather what particular form such change will take.

Formal Amendments

One important method of changing the American Constitution has been the formal amendment process. Amendments can be enacted either by a two-thirds vote in both houses of Congress or by a national convention called by the legislatures of two-thirds of the states. (This latter method has never actually been used.) Amendments so initiated must then be ratified either by three-fourths of the state legislatures or by conventions in three-fourths of the states. (Only the Twenty-first Amendment has been adopted by the latter procedure.) By 1977, Americans had made twenty-six changes to the original document by means of the formal amendment process. (As discussed in chapter 6, a twenty-seventh, the Equal Rights Amendment, lacked ratification by only a few of the thirty-eight states required for its adoption.)

In analyzing the formal amendments, it is helpful to understand the particular types of alterations they made in constitutional principles—that is, whether they affected the functions, procedures, or structure of the government—and which level or levels, national or state, were involved. Even more important is an appreciation of the particular groups involved in the amendment process and of the kinds of values they sought to implement through a change in the rules of the game.

The anti-Federalists, who were primarily responsible for adding the first ten amendments to the Constitution, were concerned with civil liberties—protecting individuals against arbitrary governmental action affecting their rights of speech, press, and religion, or the taking of their lives, freedom, or property in criminal proceedings. The first nine amendments place limits on the procedures that the national government may use in such matters. The Tenth Amendment reflects the anti-Federalists' preoccupation with preserving the powers of the states against encroachment by the national government. The amendments thus reflect political beliefs that are much different from those of the Founding Fathers, who were most concerned with guarding property rights against the actions of state governments.

Many of the remaining amendments reflect still another major value of a democratic society: equality. The Thirteenth, Fourteenth, and Fifteenth relate to race, while the Nineteenth, Twenty-third, Twenty-fourth, and Twenty-sixth govern the voting rights of, respectively, women, residents of the District of Columbia, persons who live in jurisdictions that levy a poll tax as a condition for voting, and young people between ages eighteen and twenty-one. They are thus designed to allow formerly disadvantaged groups to participate in the political process and, through the Thirteenth and Fourteenth amendments, in the social and economic life of American society. It should be noted that this group of amendments primarily affects the states, not the national government.

Two other amendments, the Seventeenth and the Twenty-second, also relate to political participation. However, they affect the suffrage rights of all qualified voters, not particular groups. The former amendment, dealing with the direct election of senators, extends the rights of voters to choose members of the upper house of the national legislature; the latter, which affects the length of term of the President, prevents voters from choosing the same man more than twice. The two amendments are based on somewhat different assumptions about human capacities: the Seventeenth expresses faith in the electorate's ability to choose good senators; the Twenty-second evidences a fear that the voters may fall victim to the entreaties of a demagogue.

Four of the amendments—the Eleventh, Twelfth, Twentieth, and Twenty-fifth—bear no particular imprint of group influence or political philosophy. They rather relate to changes brought about by the press of particular historical events and affect primarily the structure and procedures of all three branches of the national government.

The one other amendment, the Sixteenth (the Eighteenth and Twenty-first, dealing with alcoholic beverages, cancel each other out), establishes the procedures that the national government may follow in levying an income tax; it provides that the government may do so without allocating the tax on the basis of population of the individual states. Although the amendment does not directly favor or disadvantage any group, the revenue measures developed by the Congress have some potential for economic leveling since the wealthy are taxed at a higher rate than the poor.

Some amendments to the Constitution were the result of a long, arduous struggle. The women's suffrage movement began in 1848; in the early 1900s these suffragists were still soliciting support; their efforts were not successful until the passage of the Nineteenth Amendment in 1920.

Other Methods of Constitutional Change

Although important changes have been made in the American Constitution by means of formal amendments, only twenty-six have made it past the extramajority* hurdles created by the amendment process, and ten of these came at once. Thus in a period of some 190 years (ignoring the Eighteenth and Twenty-first, which counterbalance each other), formal alterations in the Constitution have been made on only sixteen occasions.

But the formal amendment process does not begin to tell the full story of the vast changes that have occurred in the functions, procedures, and structure of the American political system over that period. The final document's brevity (it is much shorter than most of our state constitutions), as well as the vagueness of many of its provisions, has also led to changes through its *interpretation* by officials of the three branches of the national government. For example, the formal document says nothing at all about the removal of officials of the executive branch: can the President do so on his own, or must he receive the Senate's consent to such an action? As we shall see in chapters 12 and 14, that issue surfaced as a major factor in the impeachment action taken against President Andrew Johnson by the House of Representatives and Senate shortly after the Civil War, and eventually led to important Supreme Court decisions on the

* A majority is one over half. An extramajority is greater than that proportion, typically two-thirds or three-fourths.

matter after Presidents Woodrow Wilson and Franklin Roosevelt had also removed key executive officials. Moreover, as will be seen in chapters 6 and 9, within the last twenty-five years shifts in the Supreme Court's interpretations of the "equal protection of the laws" clause of the Fourteenth Amendment have revolutionized race relations in this nation and altered the composition of both the House of Representatives and the state legislatures. Thus changes in the direction of more political and social equality in American life have come through judicial interpretation of the Constitution as well as by formal amendment.

Moreover, *custom and usage* have also contributed to changes in the American constitutional system. Article II, Section 3 states that the President "shall from time to time give to the Congress information of the state of the Union and recommend to their consideration such measures as he shall judge necessary and expedient." As we shall see in chapter 13, the generality of the language has enabled various Presidents to utilize the power in different ways: some Chief Executives have delivered the message to Congress in writing while others have done so in person; some have been satisfied to deliver the one message, while others have followed it with a series of special messages on particular topics of concern and even suggested specific legislation to deal with them.

Thus the American constitution has contributed to both the stability and the flexibility of the American political system. The relative difficulty of the formal amendment process has helped ensure that fundamental aspects of our governmental functions, procedures, and structure will not be easily altered. At the same time, the conciseness and ambiguity of many parts of the document have enabled our constitutional system to change with the necessities of the times.

ASSESSMENT

As we piece together the various bits of evidence on the intentions of the Founding Fathers—the economic and social conditions of the day, the major provisions of the new Constitution, and the philosophy articulated in the *Federalist Papers*—it becomes clear that two concerns were paramount in their thinking. One was national unity, the necessity for drawing together, through an effective political union, the states that threatened to go their separate ways in the period immediately preceding the Constitutional Convention. In this respect the United States was faced with the same major problem that preoccupies the leaders of the emerging nations in the world today, namely, providing some sense of national identity for a people divided along lines of economic interests or regional loyalties. Such divisions, or "factions" as Madison called them, threatened the very existence of the American political system.

The other major concern of the Founding Fathers was the protection of private property against the incursion of majority rule. For property ownership was linked with their most cherished value, that of liberty, the right of each person to develop himself to the fullest extent of his capacities and to be free from arbitrary governmental action. It is significant that while the preamble of the Constitution refers to the "blessings of liberty," it nowhere mentions "equality." In fact, the *Federalist Papers* specifically refer to "the equal division of property" as a "malady" and express concern over the "leveling spirit" of men. (As political scientist Martin Diamond suggests, the only concept of equality of which the Founding Fathers would have approved, would have been the right to equal political liberty.)

Debates over which of these concerns—national unity or property rights—was most important to the Founding Fathers are meaningless, since the two issues were inexorably linked in their thinking. They felt that a young nation could not survive in a situation of interstate commercial rivalries, uncertainties involving the collection of debts, and a worthless currency. Similarly, attempts to determine whether their prime motivation in writing the Constitution was to protect their own personal property interests or to promote the public good miss the point that, for the Founding Fathers, there was no real difference between the two inducements. They believed that the ownership of property gave men a "stake" in society and hence made them better citizens; moreover, like most people, they tended to identify their own interests with that of society as a whole.

The constitutional movement therefore represented a reaction against some of the democratic values and assumptions of the Revolutionary period. Ironically, the same political philosopher, John Locke, provided some of the major ideas for both. But whereas the earlier era espoused Locke's concepts of majority rule and legislative supremacy, the Founding Fathers rather stressed his concern with property rights and his recognition of executive prerogatives. Thus different aspects of Locke's philosophy were borrowed for dealing with differing conditions in the two periods of national development.

The events of the pre-Constitution period tempered the essential optimism concerning human nature that characterized the earlier era. Even such a great admirer of the common man and the legislature as Thomas Jefferson referred to the "173 despots" in the Virginia legislature. It was thus experience, rather than a radical shift in leadership, that brought about a change in the dominant thinking of the two eras. For

essentially the same men were involved in both: Jefferson and Adams, the major architects of the Declaration of Independence, both heartily approved the new Constitution, while James Wilson, a major figure at the Convention, had signed the Declaration. Moreover, some of the Founding Fathers had endorsed the Articles of Confederation or served in its national legislature. Although some new leaders emerged in the constitutional period, no genuine "counterrevolution" occurred whereby one group of Americans completely replaced another. Rather, some of the key men changed their minds about the kinds of political institutions that were needed to channel human weaknesses (as well as virtues) to achieve the public good.

In place of the legislatively dominated governments of the Articles of Confederation period, closely tied to the public by short terms, forced rotation in office, and recall, the Founding Fathers sought to substitute the concept of a political system with three rival branches, removed in different stages from direct public control. They favored a "mixed" government that would reflect the interests of both the few with property and the many without. Although they did not embrace the principles of semidirect democracy, they turned their backs on both monarchy and oligarchical control of society by members of the upper class. They created the most democratic system of the day, as evidenced by the refusal of Catherine the Great of Russia to recognize the new government because of its radical nature.

An analysis of the American constitutional system thus indicates that the original rules of the game were written primarily by groups interested in protecting property rights and avoiding what they considered the harmful effects of direct democracy. Their most cherished value was that of liberty. The major changes that have been made in the original constitutional system over the years have come from groups particularly solicitous of civil liberties as compared to property rights, and from those persons who desire to open up the democratic process to additional groups in society. In place of the liberty that was so valued by our nation's founders, equality has become the dominant concern in our recent constitutional development.

SELECTED READINGS

The classic study of the Constitutional Convention is Max Farrand, *The Framing of the Constitution of the United States* (New Haven: Yale University Press, 1913). A recent interesting account of the event written in a journalistic style is Catherine Drinker Bowen, *Miracle at Philadelphia* (Boston: Little, Brown, 1966). Another excellent analysis, Clinton Rossiter, *1787: The Grand Convention* (New York: Macmillan, 1966), also contains valuable background information on the events leading up to the calling of the Convention that is not present in the above selections.

In addition to Rossiter, other good sources on the economic, social, and political conditions that surrounded the calling of the Convention are David Smith, *The Convention and the Constitution* (New York: St. Martin's Press, 1965), and Alpheus T. Mason's edited work with commentaries, *The States' Rights Debate* (Englewood Cliffs, N.J.: Prentice-Hall, 1964). The latter work, along with Jackson Turner Main, *The Antifederalists: Critics of the Constitution, 1781-1788* (Chicago: Quadrangle Books, 1961), contains valuable information on the opponents of the Constitution. Bowen, Rossiter, Mason, and Main also touch on the campaign for the ratification of the Constitution.

The most controversial interpretation of the motives of the Founding Fathers is Charles Beard's classic study, *An Economic Interpretation of the Constitution of the United States* (originally published 1913; reissued, New York: Free Press, 1965), which suggests that they wrote the Constitution primarily to protect their own property interests. Two recent criticisms of Beard's work are Robert Brown, *Charles Beard and the Constitution* (Princeton: Princeton University Press, 1956), and Forest McDonald, *We the People* (Chicago: University of Chicago Press, 1958). Main, in his work cited above, basically defends the Beard thesis.

There are a number of good sources on the political philosophy of the Founding Fathers. Included are Hamilton, Jay, and Madison, *The Federalist;* Smith's book cited above; and Paul Eidelberg, *The Philosophy of the Constitution* (New York: Free Press, 1968). Another work that touches on the subject as part of a larger historical study of values in American society is Seymour Lipset, *The First New Nation* (New York: Basic Books, 1963). An excellent recent analysis of the political philosophy of the framers of the constitution written at the time of the nation's bicentennial is Martin Diamond's contribution, "The Declaration and The Constitution: Liberty, Democracy, and The Founders," which appears in Nathan Glaser and Irving Kristol, eds., *The American Commonwealth* (New York: Basic Books 1976).

Political Novels   A perceptive treatment of the nature of political revolution is provided by Robert Heinlein in his science-fiction novel *The Moon Is a Harsh Mistress* (New York: Berkley Publishing, 1968), in which a computer masterminds the revolt.

The early days of the new American Republic are described with wit and irreverence by Gore Vidal in *Burr* (New York: Bantam, 1973). Two particularly colorful and well-written novels about the American Revolution are Howard Fast's *Citizen Tom Paine* (New York: Bantam, 1976) and Kenneth Roberts's *Rabble in Arms* (New York: Fawcett, 1969).

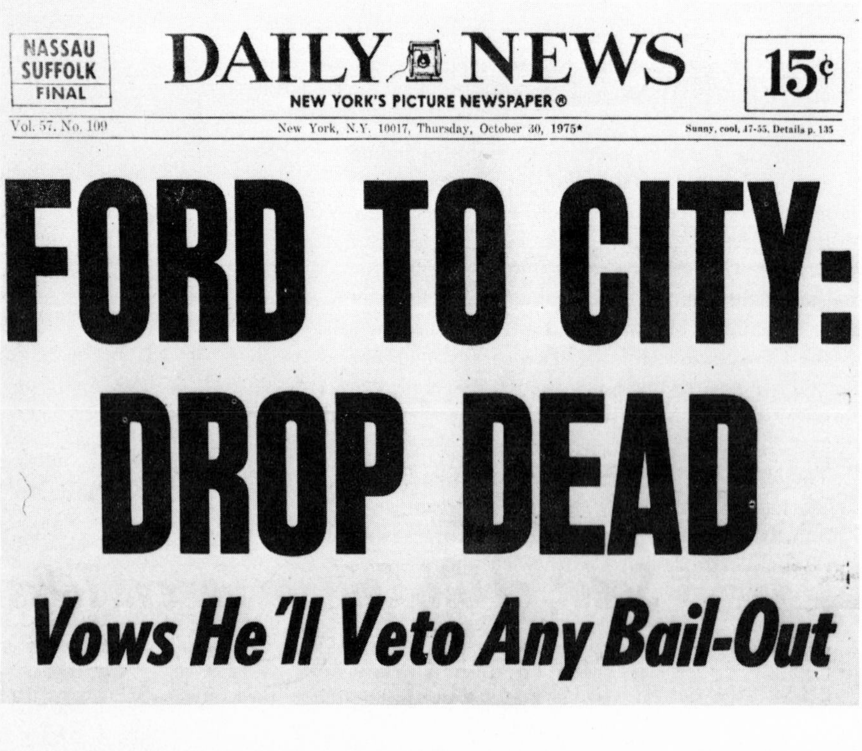

NASSAU SUFFOLK FINAL

DAILY NEWS
NEW YORK'S PICTURE NEWSPAPER®

15¢

Vol. 57. No. 109   New York, N.Y. 10017, Thursday, October 30, 1975*   Sunny, cool, 47-55. Details p. 135

FORD TO CITY: DROP DEAD
Vows He'll Veto Any Bail-Out

Chapter **3**

While many United States communities were experiencing financial difficulties in the mid-1970s, none was in as desperate straits as the nation's largest city, New York. On the one hand, governmental costs of the metropolis rose dramatically in recent years, a product of burgeoning social-welfare expenditures for its increasingly lower-class population, as well as its high wage and pension payments to municipal employees. On the other, the city's tax base dwindled as middle- and upper-class citizens, along with industry and commercial establishments, moved to the suburbs. Caught in this financial squeeze, the city borrowed heavily by issuing municipal bonds to raise money to meet its mounting deficits. In time, however, even this step failed to bring the necessary financial relief: the city found it difficult to pay off these obligations as they fell due, and the prospects of default on such bonds made it harder for New York to borrow any additional money from banks and other private investors.

In May of 1975, city and state officials approached the Ford administration for federal assistance to enable them to meet their financial obligations. However, their pleas fell on deaf ears. The President, Treasury Secretary William Simon, and Federal Reserve Board Chairman Arthur Burns all responded with the same message: do not count on federal help.

Faced with the refusal of the federal government to come to their aid, state and city officials took some direct actions on their own. In June, the state created a Municipal Assistance Corporation (dubbed "Big Mac") to sell long-term bonds guaranteed by the state, the proceeds to be used to pay off the city's short-term obligations. The city, in turn, froze wages for municipal employees, curtailed certain services, increased bus and subway fares, postponed spending for capital projects, and requested citizens to pay their property taxes in advance.

However, even these measures failed to meet New York City's mounting financial problems. Fears of such problems prevented investors from buying the "Big Mac" bonds, and in September the state approved a rescue plan providing financing of the city through November and placed a state-controlled board of overseers in charge of managing the city's fiscal affairs. In mid-Octo-

FEDERALISM

ber, when the city was about to default on its obligations, the United Federation of Teachers used $150 million from its pension fund to buy New York City bonds. Even that relief was temporary, however; the city was expected to run out of cash in early December and be forced to default on hundreds of millions of dollars' worth of debts due at that time.

As the city and state struggled to meet the situation, pressures began to build for federal aid. The president of the United States Conference of Mayors, Mayor Moon Landrieu of New Orleans, announced that his group would tell President Ford that federal assistance was needed for New York and other financially pressed cities. House of Representatives Speaker Carl Albert of Oklahoma told the New York delegation that they could count on his support for legislation, and the House and Senate banking committees developed legislation that would permit the federal government to guarantee bonds issued to enable the city to meet its obligations. Eventually even Federal Reserve Board chairman Arthur Burns became concerned about the effect that New York City's default might have on the financial money markets and the economic recovery of the nation.

Despite these pressures, Treasury Secretary Simon and President Ford stood firm against federal assistance during most of the fall months. In late September, Simon told the Joint Economic Committee of the Congress that he did not think New York would default and that even if it did, the effect on the capital money markets would be temporary and tolerable. The President also remained adamant on the issue: on October 29, he told the National Press Club that federal aid would only postpone the day when New York City would have to learn to live within its resources and that he would veto any legislation providing for a "federal bail-out" of the city.

Eventually, however, the federal government came to the city's assistance. In late November, President Ford ended his opposition to such assistance, arguing that the state's agreement at that time to raise New York taxes and reduce future expenses met his insistence that state and local officials bail themselves out of their financial difficulties. Moreover, the President's proposal for federal aid differed from that contemplated by the congressional banking committees: rather than have the federal government guarantee the payment of bonds, the Chief Executive favored direct federal loans to the city to help it meet expenses until the city collected the bulk of its tax revenues in the spring of the year. Thus the assistance was designed to help the city with temporary, seasonal deficits, not permanent ones.

Fearful that New York City would actually default in December and that a presidential veto of the proposed congressional legislation could not be overridden by the necessary two-thirds vote in each house, congressional leaders abandoned their own program and helped push the President's proposal quickly through both chambers. The bill that was signed into law by the President on December 9 was a tough-minded one: under its provisions, the city had to repay loans made in any fiscal year by the last day of that year (June 30) and was required to pay an interest rate 1 percent higher than the prevailing Treasury borrowing rate. The legislation, which provided up to $2.3 billion a year in federal loans until June 30, 1978, also barred the Secretary of the Treasury from making loans unless all previous loans had been paid on time, and also authorized him to withhold other federal funds due the city to offset the amount of any unrepaid loans.

Despite these stringent provisions, the legislation was passed over the objections of a number of House and Senate members. House delegations from Kansas, Nebraska, North and South Dakota, and a number of southern states voted solidly against it, as did 100 Republicans in the lower chamber. In the Senate, among others, 11 southern Democrats opposed it, along with 16 Republicans. These legislators expressed a common sentiment: their citizens should not be required to come to the rescue of New York City for living beyond its means; moreover, providing federal aid of this kind would establish a dangerous precedent that would encourage other communities to turn to the national government to solve their local problems.

For citizens of most other countries, the battle over federal aid to New York City was a curious and baffling one. Why should a country that has provided hundreds of billions of dollars in military and economic assistance to nations around the world, think twice about coming to the aid of the residents of its own largest city? Could anyone imagine the British or French parliaments seriously debating whether their national government should provide aid to Londoners or Parisians if their cities were in financial difficulties?

To make some sense out of the New York situation, we need to determine why political officials in the United States are so committed to the delicate and difficult task of dividing political power and responsibility among the various levels of our governmental system. To understand the sources of this attitude, we must examine the origins of the American concept of division of powers, the particular circumstances that resulted in an act of genuine political creativity: the establishment of the world's first federal system of government.

EARLY EFFORTS TO DIVIDE POLITICAL POWER

Working out proper relationships between central and local authorities has been a persistent problem in American statecraft. In fact, the issue predates the establishment of the nation. When the delegates assembled in Philadelphia in 1787, it was not the first but actually the *third* time that Americans had endeavored to solve the thorny problem of dividing political functions and authority between different governments.

The British Empire

The first American experience with the issue occurred while the colonies were still a part of the British Empire. Although the authorities in London never conceded that the colonies enjoyed any rights or powers except those that were granted to them by the mother country, over the years a division of authority had been worked out that gave the British control over foreign affairs, war and peace, and overseas trade, leaving to the colonists the exclusive right to tax themselves, to raise troops, and to run their own schools, churches, and land systems. This accommodation ended, however, with the termination of the French and Indian War in 1763. Abandoning the colonial policy that British statesman Edmund Burke referred to as one of "salutary neglect," the government of George III embarked on a new program designed to exercise far more extensive control over American affairs. Dissatisfied with the inability of some of the colonies to provide adequate military forces during the encounter with the French, the British decided to use their own troops to provide order in the colonies and to make the residents bear their share of the financial burden of these military forces, along with the debt the London government had incurred in the course of fighting the war. Further, the colonists would be required to provide funds from which royal governors and judges would be paid. (Earlier colonial legislatures had developed a practice of withholding moneys for the salaries of the King's representatives as a means of forcing concessions from them.)

The new British policy shattered the traditional division of authority between the mother country and the colonies. Having grown accustomed to their own military forces, Americans resented the presence of British soldiers in their midst. Equally if not more galling were the series of revenue measures that the British enacted to enable the colonies to assume their new financial responsibilities. Such activities invaded another touchy area formerly reserved for local authorities; moreover, the particular objects of the new taxes—wine, molasses, and tea, as well as newspapers, deeds, liquor permits, diplomas, and other legal papers which, under the terms of the infamous Stamp Act, required revenue stamps—struck at what colonists regarded as the necessities of life. Rallying around the basic constitutional principle of "no taxation without representation," Americans began to resist these British encroachments on their military and financial affairs in a series of actions that were to culminate in the Revolutionary War. Thus the British failed to solve the delicate problem of balancing central control and local self-government within their Empire; it remained for Americans to tackle the issue themselves.

The Articles of Confederation

As we saw in chapter 2, the high hopes of Americans for establishing a viable government of their own foundered within a few years after the close of the Revolutionary War in 1781. As with the British experience, the major flaw in the governmental system created by the Articles of Confederation was its failure to provide a satisfactory division of political functions and power between different governments. Reacting to the centralized control of London over trade, taxes, and troops, the authors of the Articles denied the new national government effective control over these vital matters; it was granted no power to regulate foreign and interstate commerce, and it was forced to depend on the states for the financial requisitions and troops so vital to the central government's existence. Thus as overcentralization proved to be the undoing of the British Empire in the colonies, so excessive decentralization led to the failure of the first American effort to deal with national-state relationships. The calling of the Constitutional Convention, however, provided the young nation's political leaders with one more opportunity of devising a workable method of balancing the interests of both the central government and the parts.

The Constitution

Although the Empire and Articles experiences ended in failure, they provided the Convention delegates with some object lessons. Alexander Hamilton stood virtually alone at the Convention in favoring the adoption of the British system of extreme centralization. His proposals to grant central authorities the power to pass "all laws whatsoever" and to allow them to appoint state executives who, in turn, could veto state laws died a quick death on the floor, despite his

Facsimile of the *Pennsylvania Journal* on the Stamp Act.

Draft of the Articles of Confederation.

eloquent pleas and arguments on their behalf. Also missing from the Convention was any appreciable sentiment for preserving absolutely intact the extreme decentralization under the Articles; persons with this general attitude (including some who were actually elected as delegates) were generally not present at the proceedings.

Although the delegates avoided the extremes that led to past failures to deal with central-local relations, they nonetheless differed on several basic issues relating to the division of political power in the new nation. Their views diverged sharply on the scope of the functions to be entrusted to the national government. They also disagreed on the kinds of controls that the two levels of government should be able to exercise over each other's activities. And perhaps most fundamentally, they differed on the very basis of authority over the central government: should it represent the people of the whole nation or should the states remain as sovereign units possessing ultimate legal authority?

Two plans introduced at the Convention reflected opposing attitudes on such issues. The first, the Virginia Plan, so named because it was introduced by Governor Randolph of that state (Madison was its actual author), represented the "Nationalist" approach. Although it did not go as far as Hamilton's proposal to give the central government the right to pass "all laws," the plan authorized it to legislate when the states were "incompetent" to do so or when their individual legislation would interfere with the "harmony of the United States." Further, the national legislature would be given the power to negate any state law that it deemed contrary to the national constitution. According to this plan the new government rested on popular sovereignty: representation in both legislative branches would be based on population or financial quotas rather than state equality, and the plan was to be ratified by the people in state conventions.

The opposing views of delegates committed to protecting state sovereignty were reflected in the New Jersey Plan, advocated by William Paterson of that state. Known originally as the "Federalist" proposal (as we shall see, a more appropriate name would have been "Confederationalist"), it proposed that limited changes be made in the Articles of Confederation. Although the plan granted the national government authority over commerce and taxes along with the power to act against states that failed to meet their requisitions or to obey national laws, no national powers could be exercised without the consent of an indefinite number of states. Moreover, the plan retained equal representation of states in the national legislature and required that amendments to the Articles obtain the approval of all the state legislatures.

Neither the Nationalists nor the Federalists had sufficient support to prevail at the Convention, and it remained for a third group, the "Unionists," to play the key role in breaking the deadlock. Committed above all to preserving the union of states, they labored to compromise the differences between the two plans. Attacking the most basic issue that separated the contending factions, namely, the method of representation in the national legislature, the Connecticut Compromise offered a half-loaf to each: the House of Representatives would be based on population, while states would be represented equally in the Senate. This decision served the practical purpose of mediating large-state/small-state conflicts; it also met the sovereignty issue by proposing that the national government represent both the people and the state governments.

The Connecticut Compromise paved the way for subsequent actions that resolved Nationalist-Federalist differences on a number of issues. Although the latter group succeeded in defeating the Virginia Plan proposal granting the national legislature a veto over state legislation, the delegates took a series of subsequent actions that favored the national government. A clause establishing the supremacy of the national Constitution, laws, and treaties over conflicting state constitutions and statutes was adopted. Moreover, by providing for appeal from state to federal courts on those matters (Jefferson made this suggestion in a letter to Madison from Paris), the delegates placed ultimate authority over such federal-state conflicts in an agency of the central government. The Convention also adopted a clause granting Congress power "to make all laws necessary and proper for carrying into execution" the enumerated functions assigned to it. As we shall see later in this chapter, such language paved the way for the indefinite expansion of the specific powers of the national government. Finally, the Convention undercut the basis of state sovereignty by providing that the Constitution would take effect when approved by nine states and that ratification could be accomplished by elected delegates in state conventions rather than by state legislatures.

Thus the give-and-take process of the Convention culminated in a division of powers in the new nation that differed both from the centralized systems of the Empire and the Virginia Plan and from the decentralized arrangements of the Articles of Confederation and the New Jersey Plan. The delegates had somehow fashioned a middle ground that avoided what Hamilton had claimed could not be avoided, that is, having the general government "swallow up" the states, or "be swallowed up by them." Madison explained in the *Federalist* that the new government depended "partly upon the states and partly on the people." Although the Founding Fathers did not realize it at that time, they developed an entirely new means for dividing power between levels of government, a system that came to be known as *federalism*.

MODELS OF DIVIDING POLITICAL POWER

Although societies employ a variety of methods to divide political power among governmental levels, it is possible to group the arrangements into three general categories—confederative, unitary, and federal systems. In understanding what federalism is, it is helpful first to analyze what it is *not*—that is, to see how it differs from the other two models of divided political authority.

Confederation   look up definition

The confederative system was employed by name under the Articles of Confederation. Assuming the people to be the ultimate source of political authority, one can illustrate the allocation of powers under a confederation as in Figure 3.1. The figure indicates that in a confederation the people grant political power over certain concerns to the governments of the component parts of the political system. These governments as a group in turn delegate power over certain of these concerns to the central government. In a confederation the scope of powers granted to the governments of the component parts is generally broad and covers all those activities that people feel should come under the control of public, as against private, authorities. In contrast, the scope of powers of the central government is narrow and is restricted to only those matters that the component parts feel must be handled by the large and geographically more inclusive unit of government. For example, under the Articles of Confederation the functions of the national government were restricted to concerns of war and peace, while the state governments exercised broad authority over the remaining activities entrusted to political authorities.

Under a confederation the people grant no political power directly to the central government; and thus that government cannot exercise direct legal control over the people. As suggested by Figure 3.1, the central government must depend on the governments of the component parts to enforce its authority over even the few concerns entrusted to it. Thus under the Articles of Confederation the national government had the power to raise an army and to levy certain taxes. Yet it could not exercise direct control over people to enforce that authority; rather, it was dependent on the state governments to provide money and troops. The national government also had to depend primarily on state courts to enforce its laws.

Two other features are usually associated with a confederation. One is the right of a component government to withdraw voluntarily from the larger union when it feels that its interests are not being served by the more inclusive unit of government. The other is the requirement that all the component parts of the union consent to any change in the division of powers between the two levels of government. Thus under the Articles of Confederation the national government could not be granted the power to levy import taxes because a single state (Rhode Island) refused to consent to an amendment granting this additional power to the central government.

A modern-day example of a confederation is the United Nations. In this body, of course, the nation-states (United States, Soviet Union, and so on) are the component governments, while the United Nations itself is the central political unit. The organization possesses the basic features of a confederation: the UN exercises only those powers granted to it by its members; its governmental authority is narrow compared to that retained by the nation-states; it depends on voluntary contributions of money and military forces of individual countries for its operations; it cannot enforce its provisions on individual mem-

Figure 3.1
Confederation.

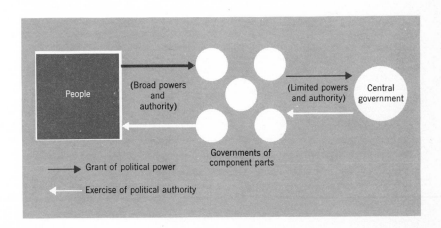

bers; and nations are free to withdraw from it at any time (as Indonesia did temporarily some years ago). Although the consent of two-thirds of the member nations is sufficient to ratify proposed changes in the charter of the organization, that two-thirds must include all the permanent members of the Security Council (United States, Soviet Union, United Kingdom, France, and China).

Unitary Governments

Diametrically opposed to a confederation as a means of dividing political power between levels of government is a *unitary* system. As Figure 3.2 indicates, the people grant power over their activities to the central government, which, in turn, delegates authority over some of these activities to the component parts. The powers retained by the central unit are usually more extensive or more important than those it grants to the lower political units. Moreover, the governments of the component parts may enforce their decrees on individuals only if they are authorized to do so by the central government.

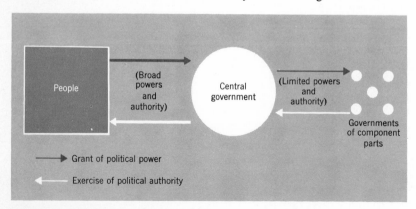

Figure 3.2
Unitary system.

A historical example of a unitary system of government is the British Empire in the period preceding the Revolutionary War. The colonial governments controlled only those activities granted to them by the mother country; they were likewise dependent on London for authority to enforce their laws. The British did not think it necessary to obtain the consent of the colonies before intervening in military and financial affairs formerly entrusted to the colonists, nor did the mother country recognize the right of the colonies to declare themselves independent of the British Empire. On the contrary, the Revolutionary War was fought for the purpose of forcing Americans to remain under that authority.

Most of the countries in the world today have unitary governments. So do the individual states of our own nation. And the arrangements between state governments and their lesser units are essentially unitary. The states determine what functions will be granted to local governments (counties, cities, villages) and decide whether these political entities can create their own agencies or must rely on those of the states to control individuals. Nor can the lower units generally block changes in state-local relationships or legally withdraw from the jurisdiction of the state government.

Federalism

At the time of the Constitutional Convention, the term *federalism* did not carry the definite meaning that we ascribe to it today. In the early stages of the proceedings, "federal" was used to describe a system in which political power was concentrated in the states. As we have seen, those who backed the New Jersey Plan were known as "Federalists," while the supporters of the Virginia Plan called themselves "Nationalists." This is the sense in which Oliver Ellsworth of Connecticut (a major figure in the development of the Connecticut Compromise) used the term *federalism* when he said that the new government was "partly national, partly federal." During the ratification campaign, however, the title *Federalists* was taken over by proponents of the Constitution like Madison and Hamilton, who favored a strong national government, while those who opposed its adoption because they felt that it violated states' rights became known as *anti-Federalists.* Thus a failure fully to grasp the possible variations in nation-state relationships (including the unique nature of the government that they themselves had created), in addition to the desire to capitalize politically on the favorable image of the word *federal* in the minds of the people, contributed to the loose and often contradictory meaning that the Founding Fathers ascribed to the concept of federalism.

When a political scientist uses the term *federalism* today, he refers to a system in which political power is divided between the central government of a country and the governments of its component parts so that each level is legally independent of the other within its own sphere of activity. In the American system neither the national government nor the government of an individual state depends on the other for its source of political power. The same is true of other federations in the world. Although the names of the component parts of given nations differ, the principle is the same: provinces of Canada, cantons of Switzerland, and länder in West Germany all have bases of power independent of their national governments. Figure 3.3 indicates the relationships that exist under a federal political system.

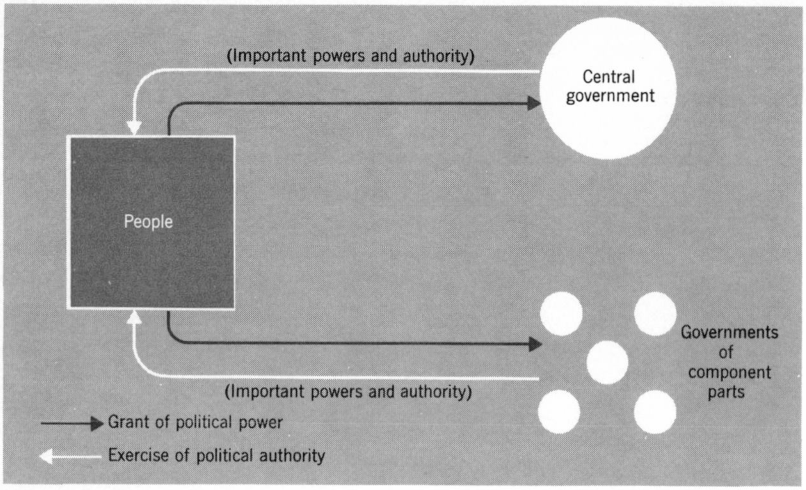

Figure 3.3
Federation.

Thus under a federal system each level of government is legally independent of the other. Each receives its grant of powers directly from the people. Each, in turn, has the concomitant right to exercise political authority over the people within its own sphere of activities without depending on the consent of the other level of government.

A federal system also has two other essential characteristics. First, both levels of government must participate in decisions to change the division of powers between them. Thus in the American system both the Congress and the states are involved in amending the federal Constitution. Second, the component parts are not free to leave the union voluntarily as may parts of a confederation. The major legal issue that precipitated the American Civil War was precisely this: the Southern states took the position that they had the right to secede from the Union; Lincoln and the Northern states disagreed. The issue was settled militarily on the battlefield, and subsequently the Supreme Court gave its legal blessing to the result by stating that "the Constitution, in all its provisions, looks to an indestructible Union composed of indestructible States." In the late 1960s a similar state of affairs developed in Nigeria: Biafra sought to pull out of the federation, and the central authorities used force to prevent it from doing so.

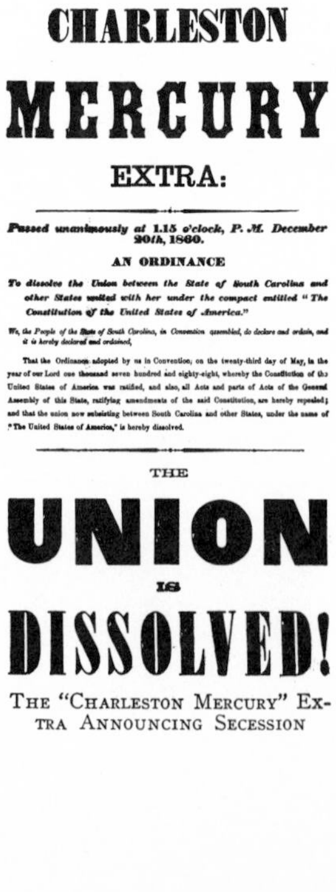
CHARLESTON

MERCURY

EXTRA:

Passed unanimously at 1.15 o'clock, P. M. December 20th, 1860.

AN ORDINANCE

To dissolve the Union between the State of South Carolina and other States united with her under the compact entitled "The Constitution of the United States of America."

We, the People of the State of South Carolina, in Convention assembled, do declare and ordain, and it is hereby declared and ordained,

That the Ordinance adopted by us in Convention, on the twenty-third day of May, in the year of our Lord one thousand seven hundred and eighty-eight, whereby the Constitution of the United States of America was ratified, and also, all Acts and parts of Acts of the General Assembly of this State, ratifying amendments of the said Constitution, are hereby repealed; and that the union now subsisting between South Carolina and other States, under the name of "The United States of America," is hereby dissolved.

THE

UNION

IS

DISSOLVED!

THE "CHARLESTON MERCURY" EXTRA ANNOUNCING SECESSION

It should be emphasized that differences between confederative, unitary, and federal forms of government are legal in nature. A division of political power occurs in all three. Moreover, considerable variations in the allocation of powers exist within each of the major systems. As weak as the national government was under the Articles of Confederation, it was granted more political power than the United Nations has today. Both France and Great Britain have unitary governments, but counties and towns exercise more important powers in the latter because of the British tradition of local self-government, as against the historic patterns of centralism in France. Nevertheless, the powers that central authorities in London grant local governments in Britain today can be legally withdrawn tomorrow. Such a possibility is not present in a federation. In fact, federations utilize a series of institutions to safeguard the independence of both levels of the governmental system.

INSTITUTIONAL SAFEGUARDS OF FEDERALISM

Although the Founding Fathers did not realize that they had created a new form of government (the word *federal* does not appear in the Constitution), the give-and-take process at the Convention led to the establishment of a number of devices and institutions that have come to be associated with a federal system of government because they are designed to protect both political levels in the system. Many such practices have been consciously borrowed (with some modifications, of course) by other nations, such as Canada and Australia, that have created federations similar to the one first developed by the United States.

The basic device the Founding Fathers used to distribute powers in the American system was a *formal written constitution.* Because they feared political power, they sought to curb its possible excesses by distributing it among different branches and levels of government, each of which was assigned definite responsibilities in the constitutional system. By spelling out in some detail the respective spheres of authority of the national government and the states, they hoped to protect the domain of each from invasion by the other. Other nations seeking to benefit from the American federal experience have likewise used written constitutions to distribute political powers among the central government and the component parts.

Federations can and do differ, however, on the particular means they use to divide political power. The American approach is to assign certain specific powers to the national government and to reserve all remaining powers to the states. (The details of this division of powers will be discussed later in this chapter.) Canada uses precisely the opposite technique of delegating particular powers to its provinces and permitting the Dominion (national government) to enjoy the remaining authority. Still other federations—for instance, West Germany—assign certain specific powers to one level of government and other specific powers to the other level. Whatever approach is used, the emphasis in all federations is on dividing political power so that important responsibilities are granted to both levels of government.

Since the two levels receive their respective powers from the written constitution, another practice logically follows in a federal system: *both* levels must participate in the formal process for altering that constitution. Otherwise, one of the governmental levels could change the original division of powers in its favor. Under the American Constitution the Congress initiates amendments, either by its own action or in response to a call from the state legislatures for a convention to consider proposed amendments. (This latter procedure has never been used.) The states, in turn, must ratify amendments through their legislatures or by conventions before they become effective. Similarly, in Australia and Switzerland the component parts (states and cantons, respectively) must approve amendments to their formal constitutions.

Another institution generally associated with a federal system is an *umpire* to settle disputes that inevitably arise between the two levels of government. No matter how carefully the language of a constitution is drawn, situations arise in which it is not clear from the division of powers which level of government is entitled to undertake a particular activity. In many instances, of course, the difficulty is unavoidable: constitution-framers cannot be expected to foresee all future developments—such as the rise of the modern corporation or the invention of television—and provide for them accordingly. Thus some agency must be provided for allocating new governmental responsibilities between the central unit and the component parts. In a typical federal system the ultimate authority for settling such nation-state disputes rests with the highest court in the land, such as the United States Supreme Court. (Switzerland, however, refers such issues to the people.)

Most federations also provide some protection for the states in the political process, generally a special house of the national legislature in which the component parts are represented as units. The purest form of this practice is absolute equality of representation as in the American and Australian senates. Other federations such as Canada give larger provinces more representation in their senates than smaller ones, but the disparity is not as great as it would be if population alone were the sole criterion.

Typically, federations create two separate sets of political institutions to carry on the constitutional responsibilities of the central government and those of its component parts. Each has its own legislative, executive, and judicial branches of government operating directly on individual citizens, and these two sets of institutions generally function independently of one another. In rejecting both Hamilton's proposal for having the national government appoint state governors and the New Jersey Plan's provision whereby state executives could remove their national counterpart, the Founders established the autonomy of the personnel of both levels of governments. They also refused to adopt the Virginia Plan proposal that the Congress be empowered to negate state laws and guaranteed the territorial integrity of the individual states by providing that boundaries could not be changed without the permission of the states' own legislatures.

By creating general governmental institutions like those described above, federal nations seek to maintain a balance between the central government and the parts. Whether such a balance is actually preserved depends on how such institutions work out in practice.

LEGAL SAFEGUARDS OF AMERICAN FEDERALISM

The operation of legal safeguards in the American federal system has been affected by two major factors: first, the method by which powers are divided in the Constitution between the national government and the states; second, how the Supreme Court has interpreted this division of powers in major cases.

The Division of Powers Under the National Constitution

Article I, Section 8 of the Constitution delegates certain specific, enumerated powers to the Congress. Included in its jurisdiction are such varied functions as regulating interstate and foreign commerce, raising an army and navy, controlling the currency, and establishing post offices and roads. Congress is also granted the power to levy taxes to pay national debts and provide for the defense and general welfare of the nation, as well as the authority to borrow money on the credit of the United States. At the very end of Article I, Section 8 there appears an important clause granting Congress the power "to make all laws which shall be necessary and proper for carrying into execution the foregoing powers. . . ." With this statement the Founders sought to expand the authority of the national government beyond those matters specifically listed in that section. In other words, they wanted the national government to have implied, as well as expressed, powers.

The national Constitution makes no specific grant of powers to the states. In fact, in its original form, the document made no mention at all of state prerogatives. By implication, the framers intended that all powers not granted to the national government would remain in the states. However, uneasiness among anti-Federalists over leaving states' rights to implication alone led to the adoption of the Tenth Amendment, which expressly provided that "The powers not delegated to the United States by the Constitution, nor prohibited by it to the States, are reserved to the States respectively, or to the people."

The general sources of political powers of the American states are their own constitutions. Although their powers (and limitations) vary somewhat, the states in general possess "police power" enabling them to pass laws for the "health, safety, and morals" of their people. This broad grant of political authority means that unlike the national government, a state government need not depend on a specific grant of power authorizing a particular function; unless an activity is specifically forbidden by the national or its own state constitution, or is considered by state courts to be an "unreasonable" use of the police power (such as permitting men, but not women, to drive motor vehicles), a state is free to legislate on it.

The resulting division of powers—whereby the national government can exercise specific enumerated powers, as well as powers implied from them, while the states are free to take advantage of the general police power—results in a broad area of concurrent powers. For example, both the national and the state governments are entitled to raise taxes to finance their activities. At the same time, the Constitution provides for settling possible conflicts that may arise between their operations. Article VI, paragraph 2 declares that if state laws or constitutional provisions are at variance with the national Constitution, laws, or treaties, the latter prevail because they are considered "supreme."

This, then, is the basic method of distributing governmental powers in the American federal system. Since the constitutional language is broad and general, however, and since new situations have arisen that the framers could not possibly have foreseen, the Supreme Court has had to act as umpire in legal disputes involving specific nation-state relationships. In deciding such disputes, the Court has had to interpret the meaning of certain key clauses of the Constitution.

The Supreme Court as Interpreter of the Division of Powers

The Court has had occasion to define a number of powers granted to the national government by the Constitution, three of which have been particularly crucial in shaping its jurisdiction: the "necessary and proper" clause; the power over interstate commerce; and the authority to tax and spend for the general welfare. In addition, the Court's interpretation of the Tenth Amendment has affected nation-state relationships.

The "Necessary and Proper" Clause. The national government was organized for only a year when Secretary of the Treasury Alexander Hamilton submitted

The first National bank.

a broad economic program to the Congress proposing the establishment of a national bank. Because he had some doubts about its constitutionality, President Washington turned for legal advice to two perennial antagonists in his cabinet, Alexander Hamilton himself and Thomas Jefferson. The former maintained that although the national government was granted no specific authority to establish a bank, "the necessary and proper" clause of Article I, Section 8 gave it the implied power to do so. Pointing out that Congress was authorized to raise money by taxation or by borrowing, Hamilton reasoned that the creation of a bank was a "convenient" means for keeping such moneys. He thus interpreted "necessary" to mean "convenient" or "appropriate." Jefferson took the opposite position that the word "necessary" should be strictly construed to mean "indispensable." Since the establishment of a national bank was not indispensable to the safeguarding of federal funds (they could be deposited in state banks, for instance), then it lay beyond the authority of the national government.

Ultimately, Washington accepted Hamilton's arguments over those of Jefferson and signed the national bank bill into law. About a quarter-century later, the bank again became a constitutional issue. The state of Maryland taxed a branch of the national bank within its borders; on the instructions of the bank's officials, its cashier, James McCulloch, refused to pay the tax on the grounds that this constituted state interference with a legitimate activity of the national government. When the Maryland Supreme Court decided in favor of the state, the ruling was appealed to the United States Supreme Court. The case, *McCulloch* v. *Maryland,* raised the basic issue of federalism first argued in the Washington administration: does the national government have the right to create a bank?

A battery of famous lawyers of the day argued the case before the Court. The major figure representing the United States was Daniel Webster; his courtroom opponent was the well-regarded Luther Martin of Maryland. The legal arguments were essentially the same as those made previously by Hamilton and Jefferson. Chief Justice John Marshall, a staunch Federalist and friend of a vigorous national government, not surprisingly wrote the Court's opinion in favor of that government. In doing so, he adopted Hamilton's interpretation of the necessary and proper clause. Necessary meant "appropriate," not "indispensable," or "absolutely necessary," as Jefferson and Luther Martin maintained. The national government had the authority to create a bank because it was an appropriate means for exercising its power to raise moneys.

This early judicial test of the powers of the national government resulted in a liberal interpretation of its authority and opened the door to the expansion of its activities through the use of implied, as compared to expressed, powers. Yet two specific powers expressly granted to Congress—authority over interstate commerce and the right to tax and spend for the general welfare—have proved to be even more important bases for national power.

Interstate-Commerce Power. The constitutional issue concerning the interstate-commerce power is essentially the same as that of the "necessary and proper" clause: how liberal or strict an interpretation to give the phrase. The same John Marshall who interpreted the latter clause liberally in the historic *McCulloch* v. *Maryland* of 1819 used essentially the same approach for the commerce clause five years later in the landmark case of *Gibbons* v. *Ogden.* In that instance he ruled that the national government had the authority to license the operation of boats on the waters of New York State because these passenger vessels were involved in interstate commerce, which he construed broadly to cover all "intercourse" between the states. In so doing, Marshall rejected the argument that interstate commerce should be limited to "traffic" involving only the buying and selling of goods.

Over the course of American constitutional history, justices of the Supreme Court have differed over which activities should be considered interstate commerce. When Congress began to use the powers increasingly to regulate (rather than to promote) the operations of American business, members of the Court who were opposed to governmental intervention in economic affairs narrowed the scope of such regulations by holding that only those activities directly involved in interstate commerce—such as transportation and communication— were subject to the jurisdiction of the Congress. This strict construction of the interstate-commerce power meant that that body could not regulate the manufacturing and mining of products or their local sale or distribution. This interpretation of the commerce clause was dominant in the waning years of the last century and into the third decade of the present one. In the 1940s, however, the Court changed the test from whether an activity is *involved* in interstate commerce to whether it economically *affects* such commerce. Using this approach, the Court in *Wickard* v. *Filburn* (1942) justified the national government's even regulating what a farmer fed to his own chickens on the reasoning that this activity economically affected the interstate market for wheat. This decision and others that followed have led students of constitutional law to conclude that, given the interdependent nature of American society today, there is almost no activity that the Court will consider beyond the scope of the commerce power.*

---

* A recent exception to the rule was the Court's decision in *National League of Cities, National Governors' Conference et al.* v. *Usury* (1976) that the 1974 Fair Labor Standards Act amendments extending federal minimum-wage protection to state and local employees were unconstitutional because they violated the concept of state sovereignty guaranteed in the Tenth Amendment.

"ARE THEY TOUGH? I'VE BEEN IN THIS COUNTRY ONLY THREE WEEKS, I'M UNEMPLOYED, AND THEY GOT $8,500 OUT OF ME."

The Power to Tax and Spend for the General Welfare. Like the "necessary and proper" clause, the power of the national government to tax and spend for the general welfare provoked an early debate between two of the nation's prominent leaders, this time Hamilton and Madison. Both, of course, were supporters of a strong national government at the Convention, and together they wrote the bulk of the *Federalist Papers*. Yet Madison subsequently parted company with his co-author on the proper interpretation of the taxing and spending power. Madison considered that function to be subsidiary to the enumerated powers of the Congress; in this view, the national government can tax and spend only for those activities over which it was given specific authority. Hamilton argued that the power was in addition to, and hence independent of, the enumerated ones; in other words, Congress can tax and spend moneys for functions that it could not otherwise control. The issue was ultimately resolved by the Supreme Court in favor of Hamilton's view.

A series of other constitutional questions relating to the taxing and spending power have also been decided to favor the national government. The Supreme Court will no longer inquire into the motive behind the enactment of a tax; thus Congress can use it as an indirect method of regulating an activity (such as a tax on gambling) as well as for the purpose of raising revenue. Moreover, the Court will not make a judgment about whether Congress's use of the taxing and spending power in particular instances is in "the general welfare" or not; nor will it interfere with the right of Congress to establish conditions under which the moneys it appropriates can be spent. The result is that the taxing and spending power of the Congress has been converted into a kind of national police power (power to enact laws for the "health, safety, and morals" of the people), since most government activity involves the expenditure of money.

Thus the two powers that the Founding Fathers thought most crucial to the operation of a national government—interstate commerce and taxation—have been the major bases for the constitutional expansion of national activities. At the same time, another key constitutional question of that early era—the relationship between national and state powers spelled out in the Tenth Amendment—has also played a major part in the continuous struggle over the division of political authority in the American system.

The Tenth Amendment. Constitutional questions raised by the Tenth Amendment concern its effect on the scope of national powers. Those friendly to an energetic central government have maintained that the Tenth Amendment is redundant—it merely expresses what was implied in the original document: that the states enjoy constitutional authority over any matter neither delegated to the national government nor forbidden to the states. The amendment in no way diminishes or restricts the activities of the national government that are based on its expressed or implied powers. Those opposed to strong centralism contend that the amendment limits the scope of national power by preventing the central government from exercising its otherwise legitimate powers if they impinge on matters of state and local concern. Some Supreme Court justices have also been inclined to read the word *expressly* into the amendment (". . . not *expressly* delegated. . .") with respect to delegated powers (no such word appears in the Constitution although it does in the Articles of Confederation) so as to negate any idea of implied powers of the national government. Since the 1930s, however, this position has lost favor among the justices, so that the Tenth Amendment is now considered the redundancy that the early friends of a strong government maintained it was.

The effect of these judicial interpretations has been legal support for almost any activity in which the national government chooses to become involved. This support, coupled with judicial checks over state actions that affect matters of national concern (states may not, for example, "burden" commerce through regulations that curtail interstate business activities, nor may they tax the operations of the national government), is evidence that the Supreme Court has had a *nationalizing* influence on American federalism. The legal checks provided by federalism have thus *not* operated (at least in recent years) to maintain a balance in our political system; they have rather favored the interests of the national government over those of the states.

Some advocates of states' rights have ascribed this favoritism to the non-neutrality of the Supreme Court in federal-state disputes. Rather than an umpire in such conflict, it is a member of the national team. To counteract this advantage, the Council of State Governments (an organization of state officials) some years ago proposed a constitutional amendment creating a Court of the Union to be composed of the chief justices of the highest courts of the fifty states, with authority to overrule the decisions of the United States Supreme Court on nation-state issues. Nothing serious came of the proposal, nor of a companion measure permitting state legislatures to amend the national Constitution without the concurrence of national officials. Fortunately for the states and their supporters, other safeguards have operated to protect their interests in the American federal system.

POLITICAL SAFEGUARDS OF AMERICAN FEDERALISM

Although the actions of the United States Supreme Court (particularly since the 1930s) have expanded the legal powers of the national government, the interests of the states have nonetheless been protected by our political processes. One reason for this development is the fact that, as lesser geographical units, the states are represented in the national government. Beyond equal state representation in the Senate, the Constitution requires that members of the House of Representatives be residents of the states they serve. (By political custom, they are also residents of the congressional district they represent.) These provisions, plus the legal control that states exercise over the nomination and election of their senators and congressmen (we will explore how this control operates in chapters 8 and 9), mean that the states possess considerable potential influence over the national legislature.

This potential is converted into actual influence by the realities of the American political-party system. One of the cardinal facts about our parties (the general subject will be treated in chapter 7) is that they are highly decentralized; power resides at the state and local, rather than the national, level. The choice of candidates for the House and Senate is determined not by the national committees of the parties but primarily by state and local party organizations. Moreover, the money for political campaigns comes not from the treasury of national headquarters but from the contributions of local groups and individuals.

Since representatives and senators are familiar with these basic facts of political life, their concern lies with the interests of the districts and states that they represent. This is reflected in their wish to see national legislation either positively benefit their areas or at least not harm them. Thus congressmen from urban districts and states typically seek aid for the cities, while those from areas whose businesses are threatened by foreign trade (such as states with textile mills) push for tariffs or quotas on the importation of competitive goods from abroad. This solicitude of individual legislators for state and local interests is further buttressed by important organizational features of the Congress: informal arrangements and understandings provide for committee seats to be assigned to representatives of the areas most vitally concerned with the work of the committee. Thus congressmen from working-class districts populate the committees concerned with labor legislation, while those from farming areas sit on the agricultural committees of the House and Senate.

Nor is the concern of congressmen for states and localities restricted to the legislative process. As overseers and financial providers of the activities of the executive branch (treated fully in chapter 14), congressmen are in an excellent position to ensure that the interests of their districts and states are taken into account. Thus key congressional leaders and committee chairmen can exercise considerable control over where a military base is located. It is no accident that so many defense and space installations were located in Texas and Georgia during the years that Texans Lyndon Johnson and Sam Rayburn (as Senate Majority Leader and Speaker of the House respectively) and Georgians Walter George and Carl Vinson (chairmen of the Senate and House Armed Services committees) were influential, benefiting their state and local economies. (Recently some congressmen have exerted the opposite kind of pressure, working to prevent the location of antiballistic missile sites in their districts out of fear that such complex weapons might malfunction or make their areas prime targets for enemy nuclear attacks.) All congressmen also spend a considerable portion of their time acting as liaison agents between individual constituents and executive agencies to see to it that "their" people are treated fairly.

Thus the two legislative houses of the national government, reflecting state and local interests, counterbalance the nationalizing influence of the Supreme Court in the American federal system. At times the legal and political processes come into direct conflict, as they did in the 1950s over the issue of tidelands oil. Both the national government and the states involved claimed title to valuable oil deposits located in submerged lands off the shores of Texas, Louisiana, California, and other coastal areas. After a lengthy period of litigation the Supreme Court ruled that the national government owned the disputed lands. The Congress, however, ultimately resolved the issue in favor of the states by passing legislation that deeded the valuable lands to them. On another earlier occasion in the 1940s the Supreme Court ruled that the national government had authority over insurance companies because of the interstate nature of their business transactions; Congress subsequently passed legislation permitting the states to continue to regulate insurance companies.

The legal aspects of American federalism thus permit the Congress to undertake almost any activity it wishes, but political forces tend to make it receptive to the interests of states and local areas. Together these factors have shaped the nature of the political system that has evolved in the United States.

THE GROWTH OF LOCAL, STATE, AND NATIONAL GOVERNMENT

An analysis of governmental developments points to one overriding pattern: the growth of activities at all levels of our political system. Local, state, and national governments are doing more today in providing services and regulating the actions of their citizens than they have ever done in the past; their total expenditures rose from under $2 billion in 1902 to some $480 billion in 1974, the last year for which actual figures are available. Therefore, any assessment of American federalism must be based on the *relative* activity of the various levels—that is, how much the national government is doing in public affairs at a given time compared to state and local political units. A good measure of the relative activity is the proportion of total expenditures made by the three political levels. Table 3.1 shows such figures for various years of this century.

The most striking overall trend shown by Table 3.1 is the comparative increase in the activities of the national government during the first half of this century. This development is most noticeable in three historical periods: 1913 to 1922, World War I and its aftermath; 1932 to 1938 (the period of the New Deal response to the Great Depression); and finally, the most dramatic change of all, the period from 1938—the beginning of the military build-up for World War II—to 1948, the first full postwar year for which expenditures are available. All told, the federal proportion of all governmental expenditures doubled in the period from 1902 to 1954.

These increases in the activities of the federal government are related to certain key factors during the first half of this century, particularly war and depression. Military matters have, of course, always been the paramount concern of the national government, so it is not surprising that wars should augment federal activities. The Great Depression, however, resulted in a change in traditional public attitudes against having the national government assume an active role in economic crises. As conditions worsened, neither private enterprise nor local and state governments proved capable of dealing with the unemployment problem; therefore people turned to the national government to get the country back on its feet. Armed with power over the currency, the banking system, and the regulation of interstate economic activities; supported by a good tax base (the Sixteenth Amendment, ratified in 1913, enabled the Congress to tap an excellent source of revenue—incomes of individuals)*; and guided by the powerful political leadership of President Franklin Roosevelt, the national government in the 1930s embarked on a series of new programs designed to lead the country to recovery. Thus the felt needs revealed by the military and economic crises in the first half of this century plus the fiscal and political capacity of the national government to meet these needs altered the division of governmental activities among the three levels of our federal system.

Table 3.1 also indicates that the comparative increase in government spending at the national level has been accompanied by a sharp decline in local expenditures. The latter stood at almost three-fifths of total governmental outlays in 1902; in 1954, they constituted slightly more than only one-fifth of the composite figure. The level of government least affected by overall trends has been the states: although their share of total expenditures increased somewhat during this century, state governments have continued to run a distant third to both the national and local governments in the spending of public funds.

Levels of Government	Year											
	1902	1913	1922	1927	1932	1938	1948	1954	1962	1967	1972	1974
Federal	34	30	40	31	33	44	62	67	58	59	53	53
State	8	9	11	12	16	16	13	11	14	15	18	18
Local	58	61	49	57	51	40	25	22	28	26	29	29

Table 3.1 Proportions of Total Governmental Expenditures Spent by Federal, State, and Local Governments, 1902–1972 (Figures in Percentages)

Source: Frederick C. Moser and Orville F. Poland, *The Costs of American Governments* (New York. Dodd, Mead, 1964). Table 3.2. The 1967 figures are derived from the 1967 Census of Governments and the 1972 and 1974 figures, from *The Statistical Abstract of the United States,* 1976, No. 418.

* Prior to the amendment, the tax had to be apportioned among the states on the basis of population, and since income is not related to population, the tax could not be administered.

Table 3.1 demonstrates another basic fact of American federalism: the comparative activities of the three governmental levels have stabilized considerably since the end of World War II. The military demands of the Korean conflict resulted in an increase in federal spending between 1948 and 1954, but this increase was not nearly so marked as were those associated with the two world wars. In the period when the country became increasingly involved in the hostilities in Vietnam (1962-67), no substantial change occurred in the basic pattern of American federalism. The latest figures for the most recent period show a slight decline in the federal proportion of total governmental expenditures from 1967 to 1972 and a stabilization in relative spending by the three governmental levels after the latter year.

The overall balance in American federalism since World War II has resulted from increased spending of the national government, particularly for national defense, offset by burgeoning state and local expenditures for major domestic programs such as education, highways, welfare, and health. From 1948 to 1974 federal spending for defense-related matters rose from $28 billion to over $105 billion. In the same two decades, however, state and local governments increased their expenditures drastically to meet pressing domestic needs—from $20 billion in 1948 to over $226 billion in 1974.

This information on governmental expenditures reveals the basic dimensions of American federalism in the twentieth century: an overall growth in federal activities, especially relating to military and economic crises, accompanied by the continuing vitality of state and local units undertaking increased responsibilities for the nation's domestic needs. But we cannot justifiably conclude from these gross figures that the division of functions in our political system has been simple, with the national government concerned almost entirely with military and foreign policy, while the states and local units go their own ways, raising public money and spending it on matters of exclusive concern to themselves. Instead, as the following section indicates, the governmental process of American federalism has been far more complex, involving close relationships among the various levels.

COOPERATIVE FEDERALISM

Students of American federalism frequently refer to recent developments in the system as a "new" federalism or, sometimes, a "cooperative" federalism. By

Cooperative Federalism:
Federal and State highways
bind together the metropolis.

this they mean that we no longer have three separate levels of government that undertake distinct functions and operate independently of one another; instead, they all share in carrying out various public functions.* Another dimension of the new federalism is that the various political levels no longer view each other as "rivals" for public support and the exercise of political power; rather, they regard themselves as "partners" in the great enterprise of government.

Cooperative federalism may have become more prominent in the United States in recent years, but it is not entirely "new." Even before the Constitutional Convention, the Congress in 1785 passed a statute, supplemented by the Northwest Ordinance of 1787, that granted designated sections of public lands to the states for educational purposes. Thus the national government financially assisted the states in establishing primary and secondary schools, long considered in the United States to be one of the most basic local functions. Subsequently Congress provided funds to both state and local governments to

* The late political scientist Morton Grodzins likened our system not to a layer cake but to a "marble" one characterized by an intermingling of colors in vertical and diagonal strands representing the mixing of functions at all levels.

develop internal improvements such as roads, canals, rivers, and railroads. During the Civil War a national law was enacted that has had a major impact on higher education in the United States: the Morrill Act donated lands to the states, the proceeds of which were to be used to establish colleges devoted to instruction in agriculture and mechanics. The "A and M" colleges, prominent in the Middle and Far West, thus owe their existence to the willingness of the national government to concern itself with traditional state matters.

These early grants involved a resource that the national government had in abundance: land. Toward the end of the nineteenth century a shift from land to cash occurred in the substance of grants. Moreover, the nature of the grants changed from once-only affairs to continuing appropriations made on an annual basis. This new form of subsidy is the grant-in-aid, familiar to the student of modern federalism in the United States.

Traditional Federal Grants-In-Aid

Development. Although a few federal grants-in-aid were established before 1900 (for example, in 1887 Congress provided the first continuing cash grant to assist states in establishing agricultural experiment stations), they are primarily a twentieth-century phenomenon. The grants are closely linked with a major fiscal development: the enactment of the income tax amendment in 1913. With the major new source of revenue available to the national government, and a President (Woodrow Wilson) and Congress willing and able to involve the national government more extensively in the economy than their predecessors had been, federal grant-in-aid expenditures increased from some $5 million in 1912 to almost $34 million in 1920. Not only were familiar objects of nineteenth-century subsidies favored (the Smith-Lever Act of 1914 established the agricultural extension program; vocational education and highways also drew major financial support), but the Congress provided the beginnings of modern assistance programs with provisions for maternal and child health.

The Republican administrations of the 1920s and early 1930s continued and improved the existing federal grant-in-aid program. However, no significant new starts were made during the twelve years between the Wilson and Roosevelt terms. In contrast, the New Deal ushered in a different era in grant-in-aid programs. Ignoring the advice of many of his advisers to let the national government itself administer burgeoning new programs in welfare, health, employment security, and public housing, President Roosevelt chose instead to funnel such expenditures through lesser political units. As a result, during the period from 1932 to 1939, grant-in-aid expenditures swelled from some $200 million to almost $3 billion. Two significant departures from the Wilson years were also apparent: a shift in emphasis in the programs from rural to urban needs and the channeling of some of the assistance directly from the national government to local units, bypassing the states in the process. For example, cities became the direct recipients of federal aid in public housing.

The outbreak of World War II brought a temporary decline in federal grant-in-aid programs as the national government harbored its resources for military necessities. Beginning in 1948, grant expenditures began to rise again, but it was not until 1954 that they reached their prewar level of some $3 billion. During the remainder of the Eisenhower administration, grant moneys increased as the Republicans sought to counter the centralization of domestic programs in Washington. Also, consistent with that party's philosophy, the administration was concerned not to bypass the states in favor of direct grants to cities.

The 1960s and early 1970s witnessed a major surge in federal aid programs similar to that of the 1930s. A major increase occurred in the Johnson administration (some two dozen new "Great Society" programs were inaugurated in 1964–65 alone) and continued during the Nixon administration, in which the number of federal grants doubled in the period from 1969 to 1973. Programs tended to concentrate on the problems of the large metropolitan areas of the nation (central cities and suburbs) and ranged broadly in welfare, economic development, education, and race relations. They brought still another feature to the evolution of federal grants-in-aid: some, such as the Community Action Program in the antipoverty field, bypassed not only the states but even local governments in favor of private groups that received funds and, in some cases, helped administer the programs.

The development of the federal grant-in-aid program in the United States has thus had a major impact on government expenditures and revenues during this century. Federal outlays during the period mushroomed from $3 million in

The "Great Society" and the little one.

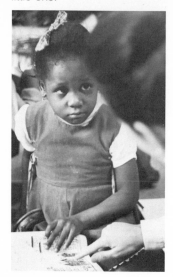

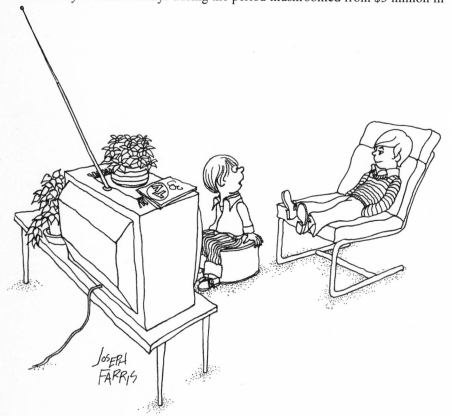

"The Great Society—did it come and go, is it yet to come, was it just talk, or what?"

Drawing by Joseph Farris; ©1976 The New Yorker Magazine, Inc.

1902 to an estimated $60 billion in 1976. By the latter year, one of every six dollars the national government spent was allocated to some federal grant-in-aid program; and such grants constituted almost one-fifth of all state and local revenues.

Characteristics. As we have already seen, one of the distinguishing features of federal grants-in-aid is that they generally involve cash payments (one exception is the surplus agricultural commodities used in the school-lunch and social-welfare programs) authorized by Congress on a continuing basis or for a specific period of years. The distinction between continuous- and specific-term grants has tended to be a legal one, however; Congress normally extends the short-term grants when their original authorization period has expired, so in actual fact they too are continuous. In other words, once enacted, few grant-in-aid programs have been terminated. Groups favored by such grants have used their political influence to prevent that termination. Thus the number of grant programs has swelled as new ones have been added to old ones.

The new programs have seldom been integrated with those already in existence. Instead they have developed as separate programs. The outcome of this process is a proliferation of programs, each of which is designed for fairly narrow purposes. For example, until recently there were various categories of public-assistance programs: those for the aged, the blind, and the disabled, each of which operated independently of the others. A recent estimate of federal aid programs indicated that there was a total of 530 of them administered by departments and bureaus of the national government.

Categorical grants vary considerably in method of distribution to state and local governments. A few, like some to vocational education, are "flat" grants, allocated in equal or minimum amounts to political units without any financial contributions by the units themselves. Most grant-in-aid, however, require states or localities to "match" federal funds by furnishing some of their own money for the program. But even in matching grants, there are various formulas for determining the specific allocation of funds between levels of government and the amount of money to which each political unit is entitled. Some are based purely on population, while others, including some in primary and secondary education, take into account the financial needs and capabilities of the recipient governments. In the latter instance, the federal share of the grant is higher for political units with a large number of citizens requiring assistance, as well as for those with limited tax resources, than it is for those without such handicaps. A few programs are "open-ended" in that the federal government provides a certain percentage of the state contribution. This arrangement has a built-in incentive: the more a state spends on a program, the more federal moneys it receives.

Federal grant-in-aid programs also impose other conditions for states or localities besides a financial contribution, such as the establishment of a single state agency to administer a given program or the use of a merit system for the employees of all agencies receiving federal money. Furthermore, the federal government agency administering a grant program is entitled to review and supervise the work of the recipient agency and to audit its expenditures.

One additional feature of some grant-in-aid programs is that they are of the "project" type—that is, they require the specific approval of the federal govern-

New Deal Firmament.

ment. For example, while any community might be entitled to apply for a grant
to build a waste-treatment plant, the total funds available may not be sufficient
to cover all the requests, which means that federal officials must choose among
them. One student of the subject, Michael Reagan, estimates that in the early
1970s about four of every five grant-in-aid programs were of the project type.

Administrative Problems and Changes. As the grant-in-aid programs have
multiplied in recent years, they have produced major problems of coordination
and control for all parties involved in their administration. Some of these problems center on a single level of government; the administration of the wide

variety of aid programs located in the myriad departments and bureaus of the national executive branch is a case in point. The compartmentalization of grants into these many agencies sometimes means that the federal left hand does not know what the federal right hand is doing: the Bureau of Public Roads develops highways in urban areas that displace low-income groups who are a major concern to federal officials in the Department of Housing and Urban Development. A similar confusion arises in agencies at the state and local level, since each agency has its closest relationships not with other state and local agencies, but the corresponding *federal* bureau in the same program area—health, education, welfare, and so on. The end result is that officials entrusted with viewing overall public needs—legislators (senators and representatives, their state counterparts, and city councilmen) and executives (the President, governors, mayors, and city managers)—have difficulty controlling the activities of specialized agencies and establishing priorities among them.

The other major type of administrative problem involves relationships among the three levels of government in the American political system. State officials complain that they are not properly informed and consulted by their federal counterparts in the formulation of administrative rules and practices relating to grant-in-aid programs, and that the red tape and delay in the forwarding of federal funds hampers their operations and prevents them from executing their programs as efficiently as they might. State governors, legislators, and administrators also oppose the recent trend in some grant-in-aid programs to bypass the states in favor of direct relationship with local governments. And political officials at all levels are concerned about an even more recent development, noted above: dispensing federal grants to private persons and groups who also play a major role in their administration.

A growing recognition of such problems by supporters as well as critics of federal grants-in-aid has led to concerted efforts in recent years to confront these problems. Lyndon Johnson's emphasis on what he termed "creative" federalism—that is, working out better relationships among officials at all levels of the federal system—resulted in some changes in the administration of federal grants-in-aid. The Congress sought to improve the coordination of federal urban programs by providing, in the Demonstration Cities and Metropolitan Development Act of 1966, that a metropolitan-wide planning agency screen all applications of federal grants relating to urban development projects in its metropolitan area. Richard Nixon's New Federalism also involved some administrative improvements, including the creation of Federal Regional Councils, through which a number of federal departments coordinate their activities with the cooperation of state and local officials.

Recent developments also reflect a particular concern for problems of state governments. The Intergovernmental Cooperation Act of 1968 directs federal agencies to speed up the dispersal of funds to state agencies; it also requires federal officials, upon request, to furnish the governor or legislature of a state with information on the amount and purpose of each grant to that state or its localities. A recent amendment to the Economic Opportunity Act of 1964, which originally created the Antipoverty Program, permits each governor to veto projects within his state. The Intergovernmental Personnel Act of 1970 provides grants to state (as well as local) governments for improving their personnel administration and training programs and permits their employees to work at another level of government for two years without losing any benefits (retirement, sick leave, and the like).

Block Grants

The most basic administrative reform sought in the federal grant-in-aid programs in recent years is the "block" grant. This approach has two major purposes: to channel federal grants-in-aid through state governments, rather than directly to local governments or private groups, and to permit state officials to allocate funds for some broad purpose—such as health, education, or welfare—rather than have the federal government delineate specific limited purposes for grants. The block-grant approach has been utilized by Congress in such fields as health care, juvenile delinquency, and law enforcement. Typically, under such legislation, applications for federal grants must be approved by a state agency that develops a comprehensive plan for spending moneys under the broad purposes of the governing act.

The block grant has become a controversial topic among persons interested in federal grant-in-aid programs. It has drawn particular support from state governors and legislators as well as Republican officials at the national level. Big-city mayors and administrators of the present categorical grant system, along with Democrats who have supported that system over the years, generally oppose the approach on the grounds that state officials siphon away funds that should go to urban areas and spend the grants for the wrong purposes. The battle between these contending groups has been particularly evident in the administration of the 1968 Omnibus Crime Control and Safe Streets Act, with critics charging state officials with distributing too much money to suburban police departments instead of to high-crime areas of the cities and with failing to allocate sufficient moneys for courts and correctional institutions. When the Act was renewed in 1970, it provided that no state plan be approved for funding by federal officials unless it allocates an adequate share for areas of high-crime incidence; moreover, it earmarked 20 percent of the funds for corrections.

This struggle involving categorical versus block grants became even more heated in the 1970s. In his 1971 State of the Union Message President Nixon recommended that some 100 grant-in-aid programs be consolidated into six broad-purpose ones dealing with education, law enforcement, job training, urban development, rural development, and transportation, but the predominantly Democratic Congress took no action on his proposals. Emboldened by his smashing election victory in 1972, the President began to eliminate some existing programs by impounding funds—that is, refusing to spend moneys appropriated by Congress for them; in his 1973 State of the Union Message he also suggested phasing out a number of other categorical programs in education, health, housing and community development, and manpower training, and consolidating them into broad block grants in those four fields. Liberal Democratic congressmen in particular adamantly opposed Nixon's actions, and only in the manpower and urban development areas were the contending parties able to resolve their differences by enacting laws in 1973 and 1974 that merged a number of federal programs (thus pleasing the President) and, in the 1973 law, also promoted public-service jobs in areas with a high unemployment rate (a provision favored by the Democrats).

Thus what at first blush appeared to be merely an administrative matter—consolidating existing grant-in-aid programs into broader and more flexible ones—took on a highly political character involving major differences in public policy. The President's approach to grants meant eliminating or reducing some categorical programs of which he disapproved, such as providing public housing for the poor, in favor of a broad block grant for community development. Many congressmen consider such a trade-off as most unfortunate: it results in reduced federal spending on social programs that the federal government has enacted over the years in order to attack national problems, without any assurance that states and localities that receive block grants will attempt to solve such problems themselves. It is essentially this same problem that has now begun to cause concern over the newest feature of cooperative federalism: revenue sharing.

Revenue Sharing

Development. Some students of American federalism concluded a number of years ago that there were fundamental defects in the grant-in-aid program that could not be remedied by the administrative changes outlined above, even those as drastic as the block-grant approach. Instead of using the various aid programs to channel federal moneys to states and localities to help them solve their domestic problems, they proposed distributing the superior tax resources of the national government directly to such units and letting them decide how to spend such moneys themselves. One device developed to accomplish this purpose became known as revenue sharing.

Supporters of revenue sharing pointed to two major advantages that it provided over the previous system. First, states and localities would not have to depend on congressional action to receive funds: the return of funds would be automatic. Second, under the principle of general revenue sharing, such units would have complete discretion in spending the funds and would not be limited by even the broad purposes spelled out in block-grant legislation.*

Over the years, the idea of revenue sharing won wide support in both parties. Proposed originally in 1958 by a Republican representative from Wisconsin, Melvin Laird, it was advocated in the early 1960s by Walter Heller, chairman of John Kennedy's Council of Economic Advisers. It was subsequently espoused by the conservative Republican senator from Arizona, Barry Goldwater, as well as by Hubert Humphrey, the liberal Democratic senator from Minnesota. In 1967 Gerald Ford, then Minority Leader of the House Republicans, declared that "tax-sharing would restore the needed vitality and diversity to our federal system." Moreover, the concept received an important political boost from President Nixon, who went before Congress in August 1969 with a dramatic message: "After a third of a century of power flowing from the people and the states to Washington, it is time for a New Federalism in which power, funds, and responsibility will flow from Washington to the states and to the people." To enable the states to assume greater responsibility for solving (not avoiding) problems, the President recommended that a set portion of the rev-

---

* The term special revenue sharing is used synonymously with block grants (such as those proposed in recent years by President Nixon).

enues from federal income taxes be remitted to the states. He also suggested that few restrictions be placed on how the dollars be used and that a proportion of them be channeled for the use of local governments. Terming such revenue sharing a "gesture of faith in American states and localities and the principle of democratic self-government," Nixon said it would also help to create an effective, responsive government with not only one center of power, but with many.

While the President's proposed measure was favored by leading figures in both political parties, the astronomical costs of the Vietnam war delayed congressional action as did disagreements on exactly how the money should be divided among the states and localities of the nation. Ultimately, the State and Local Fiscal Assistance Act of 1972 was passed, authorizing the return of $30.2 billion to state and local governments over a five-year period, two-thirds of the funds to be allocated to local governments and one-third to the states. As the President requested, relatively few strings were placed on use of the moneys: states could use them virtually as they pleased, while local governments could spend their funds for a wide variety of functions including public safety, environmental protection, public transportation, health, recreation, libraries, social services for the poor and aged, and for financial administration.

Soon after its passage in late 1972, the machinery of the act went into operation. The Office of Revenue Sharing of the Treasury Department allocated funds to more than 38,000 units of state and local government, and each unit began to make decisions on how it would spend its new-found moneys. Public hearings were held (particularly at the local level), in which individuals and groups argued for their pet projects.

Effects of Revenue Sharing. Official reports filed with the Office of Revenue Sharing show some definite patterns of expenditures of federal revenue-sharing funds. During fiscal 1974, states claimed to have spent 52 percent of their shared revenue for *education,* with such other functions as public transportation, health, governmental administration, and social services trailing far behind the educational expenditures. Local governments (which were forbidden by the 1972 Act from using such funds for education) reported spending 36 percent of their shared revenues for *police* and *fire protection,* followed by public transportation, government administration, environmental protection, health, and recreation.

Some close students of the subject, however, have discounted such claims on the grounds that states and localities have frequently mixed the shared revenue with other funds and thus lost track of how their federal moneys were really being spent. Some academic studies of spending patterns of states and localities have concluded that many of these governments are using the federal funds primarily to reduce taxes or to prevent such taxes from going up. Thus, rather than using federal revenues to expand governmental services, states and localities have been utilizing them as a means of reducing pressures on their own financial resources.

While most state and local officials have welcomed the new source of revenue as "manna from heaven" or "having Santa Claus come four times a year," there have been complaints about the operation of the new program. Some critics have charged that Presidents Nixon and Ford reduced or eliminated many categorical aid programs, so that states and localities have not more, but actually less, money with which to attack their problems. Moreover, there have been indications that health and social-service programs benefiting low-income and socially disadvantaged groups have not been receiving a significant proportion of general revenue-sharing funds. Finally, charges have been made that some state and local governments have used federal funds in programs that discriminate against blacks and other minorities.

Extension of Revenue Sharing. Despite the objections outlined above, revenue sharing was extended in the fall of 1976 shortly before the original legislation was scheduled to expire. This time Congress placed the program on a fiscal-year basis, providing for a total of $25.5 billion dollars to be distributed over a 45-month period from January 1, 1977 through September 30, 1980. Many of the basic features of the 1972 Act were retained, including the allocations of one-third of the funds to states and two-thirds to local units of government.

Some changes in the original program were made, however, to meet the criticism expressed above. Civil rights groups were accommodated by new stipulations making the antidiscrimination provisions applicable to any activity of state or local governments unless these jurisdictions could show by clear and convincing evidence that such activities had not been funded directly or indirectly through revenue sharing. Moreover, the antidiscrimination provisions that originally covered race, color, national origin, or sex were expanded to include age, handicapped status, and religion.

The new legislation also reflected the wishes of other groups. State and local officials won their battle to remove all restrictions on the kinds of programs that could be funded with shared revenues, and also to allow such funds to be used to match federal grants received under other programs. Groups demanding that there be more citizen participation in decisions on how shared revenues should be spent were appeased by requirements for full and specific information on how state and local governments intended to spend the funds, as well as for well-publicized public hearings before final decisions on such matters were made.

Thus various groups that look at federal revenue sharing from different vantage points were able to submerge their differences in the interests of the extension of the general program. It remains to be seen, however, whether such differences can remain reconciled after the program's administrators begin to deal with the practical problems involved in implementing the new legislation. For as the next section suggests, conflict in the political process continues to characterize American federalism in the last quarter of the twentieth century.

Conflict and Competition in Cooperative Federalism

While recent developments in American federalism have tended to stress the federal-state-local partnership, it should be recognized that conflict and competition continue to exist in our political system. One of the major rivalries in what has been referred to as picket-fence federalism has developed between the specialists in the various public-policy areas outlined in Figure 3.4 on the one hand, and policy-generalists such as governors and congressmen, state gover-

"Unaccustomed as I am to signing bills"—President Ford okays the extension of Revenue-sharing.

nors and legislators, and mayors, managers, and representatives of counties and cities on the other.* The former are professionals committed to enlarging programs in their specialized areas of expertise; the latter are politicians who must coordinate and establish priorities among the claims of these specialists for scarce public resources. Each group has its own type of organization to represent its interests: the specialists work through national associations of highway commissioners, social workers, teachers, and the like; while, as Figure 3.4 reveals, the generalists are organized into seven other kinds of associations—for example, the National Governors Conference and the Council of State Governments—collectively known as the "Big Seven." Moreover, the two groups prefer different mechanisms for distributing federal aid; the specialists favor the traditional categorical grant, while the generalists are partial to block grants and general revenue sharing.

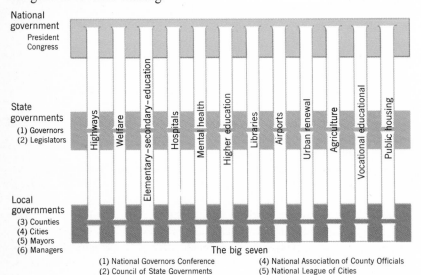

Figure 3.4
Picket-fence federalism: a schematic representation.
Source: © 1974 Deil S. Wright.

Of course, "picket-fence federalism" also creates competition and conflict among the specialists themselves. Each of the professional groups working in a particular functional area naturally thinks its own programs are move valuable than those carried on by other professionals: teachers believe that educating children and adults should have the highest priority among public needs, while social workers believe that caring for the disadvantaged persons in society is the most important activity for government to undertake. Thus specialists must compete with each other in attempting to obtain adequate public funding for their programs.

Other developments point up still another type of conflict and competition within the American federal system: that which exists between *regions* of the

---

* As shown by Figure 3.4, the pickets represent the vertical relationships among officials at all three levels who work in the same functional area (highways, welfare), while the cross rails depict the horizontal relationship between executive and legislative officials within the same level of government.

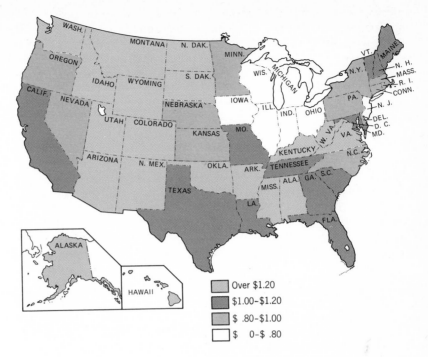

Figure 3.5
Winners and losers in the
contest for federal spending.
In some states the
government spends more
than $1 for every $1 of
federal tax revenue it collects;
in other states it spends less
than it collects.
Source: *National Journal* (26
June 1976), p. 879.

Over $1.20
$1.00–$1.20
$ .80–$1.00
$ 0–$ .80

United States. Recent trends indicate that the Western and Southern states are winning the contest for federal spending over states from the Northeastern and Midwestern areas. This disparity among regions is primarily attributable to the greater defense spending in the first two areas, but also results from major highway and sewer construction in the Mountain states and the payment of high social security retirement benefits to people in Florida. On the other hand, the Northeast and Midwest have contributed more proportionately in federal taxes than have other areas of the country. As indicated by Figure 3.5, the combined effect of different levels of federal spending and tax burden favors the South and West over the Northeast and Midwest.

Recently public officials in the Northeastern region have organized to try to do something about the above developments. The six New England states have formed a Congressional Caucus, a Coalition of Northeastern Governors, and a research arm (The New England Research Office) to press demands for a greater share of federal moneys. In particular, they are attempting to obtain more defense and public-works spending for their area and also to get Congress to change the formulas of major federal grant-in-aid programs to take into greater account such factors as population, unemployment rates, incidence of poverty, and cost of living, with a view to benefiting the Northeastern states.

Finally, while cooperative federalism has resulted in a stronger federal-state-local partnership, it has not resolved all the conflicts between officials of the three levels of government. National officials still believe that they have a broader and more enlightened perspective of the nation's problems than do their more parochial state and local counterparts; the latter complain that people in Washington do not appreciate the special circumstances and conditions of their particular areas. Moreover, political officials at all levels continue to struggle over the specific arrangements of the partnership: what policies will be established with respect to governmental programs? how will they be financed? and who will have the major control over their operation? Thus the give-and-take of the political process that led to the initial establishment of the American federal system continues to shape its character two centuries later.

ASSESSMENT

If majority rule is the most important feature of democracy, there is no doubt that our federal system is essentially undemocratic. It permits interests that are nationally in a minority on some issue, but in the majority in some individual states, to have their way on the matter, at least for a period of time. As William Riker has pointed out, the classic instance is the way in which Southerners utilized the rationale of states' rights to pursue their own policies on race relations over the years.

Yet the federal system has not operated to give the states a permanent veto on any issue. The South has been unable in recent years to prevent all three branches of the national government from pursuing policies favoring blacks and from having these policies applied in the states. The legal powers of the national government, in addition to its revenue sources, are such that almost no issue is beyond its scope, provided national officials have the political will to deal with it.

Over the years, economic elites have also espoused the virtues of federalism and states' rights because they have calculated that state governments are generally more protective of their interests than the national government is. Business concerns and wealthy individuals have frequently been able to dominate state governments so as to prevent regulation and the payment of taxes at a level necessary to meet public needs for education, welfare, health, and highways. Yet the post-World-War-II record of some states is impressive. New York and California in particular have pioneered in higher education and mental health. Indeed, both of them have budgets that exceed that of the national government in the years immediately preceding World War II. Although the other

states cannot match the record of these two giants, by the late 1960s more than half of the fifty states had combined state-local expenditures exceeding a billion dollars annually. States are also increasingly funneling financial assistance to localities; presently such total grants exceed those that state governments themselves receive from the national government. And as evidence of increased activity at the lower levels of the federal system, taxes and indebtedness have risen faster on the state and local levels in recent years than on the national level.

Beyond this, public services have been improved in all states, including the poorer and less advanced ones, by the operation of federal grant-in-aid programs that stimulate state efforts and ensure that some minimum level of services will be provided to citizens wherever they may live in the United States. In addition, the federal government has recently acted to force states into adequate regulation of matters that some have slighted too long; for instance, congressional legislation in air pollution, meat inspection, and disclosure of full credit information to consumers requires states to bring their controls up to national standards by a certain date or face the consequences of a federal takeover of those problems.

Of course, federalism can serve the ulterior purposes of persons who seek to prevent action on a given problem. For example, in recent years some individuals and groups unfavorable to low-cost housing developments have opposed certain national programs on the grounds that the responsibility for the projects should be local, knowing full well that the community itself would not or could not make the financial sacrifice necessary to resolve the issue. Thus a basic principle of federalism—in this case, that problems at the grass-roots level should be handled at that grass-roots level—can be used to masquerade the real motives of those who invoke the rhetoric of federalism: preventing *any* level of government from taking a course of action they oppose.

Although federalism can lead to negativism, recent experiences in the United States also indicate that it can have precisely the opposite effect. Groups unable to get one level of government to handle a problem can shift their efforts to another. This tactic has been successfully pursued since the 1930s by those who have persuaded the Congress to undertake urban problems that state governments refuse to act on. At times, groups have used both political levels to advantage. A case in point is public-welfare legislation: having persuaded Congress to establish welfare programs, interested persons subsequently persuaded states to supplement and expand federal services in this field.

The charge that federalism is inherently negative is refuted by the rapid expansion of public activities at all levels of the American system. Moreover, developments in cooperative federalism indicate that a system of divided powers can operate in a positive fashion to meet public needs. Problems in American federalism today no longer turn so much on the issue of which government will undertake a particular activity as on the question of how the various political levels will be utilized to accomplish our nation's purposes. Increasingly, our federation has evolved into a system wherein the national government appropriates moneys and establishes broad guidelines for programs that the states and localities administer on a day-to-day basis. A similar pattern is becoming prevalent within the states as they provide increased financing for programs (as in education) that local authorities administer.

It is difficult to assess the impact of the newest development in cooperative federalism, revenue sharing, because we have had such a limited experience with it to date. Insofar as it permits states and localities to set their own priorities and to involve citizens in the process, it is a healthy development for the democratic process. However, distributing funds (which the federal government raises through borrowing) to wealthy jurisdictions (some of which have surpluses) is financially questionable. Moreover, it remains to be seen whether disadvantaged groups whose interests have been increasingly protected by the national government in recent years will be as successful in persuading state and local governments to enact social programs favorable to them. It is also not yet clear whether the funds available from revenue sharing will compensate for cutbacks in categorical programs that have helped to meet major needs in American society.

SELECTED READINGS

For a general discussion of the issues involved in dividing political power in a society, see Arthur Maass, *Area and Power: A Theory of Local Government* (New York: Free Press, 1950). This book is particularly valuable in providing an analytical and theoretical treatment of the subject.

The classic study of the general principles of a federal system of government, together with the institutions and social, economic, and political conditions associated with such a form of government, is K. C. Wheare, *Federal Government* (London: Oxford University Press, 1953). Two other edited works that treat of many facets of federalism in various nations of the world are Arthur MacMahon, *Federalism, Mature and Emergent* (Garden City, N.Y.: Doubleday, 1955), and Valerie Earle, *Federalism: Infinite Variety in Theory and Practice* (Itasca, Ill.: Peacock, 1968). A particularly valuable essay in the latter book is the one by William S. Livingston, "Canada, Australia, and the United States: Variations on a Theme." For a provocative, critical analysis of federalism, see

William Riker, *Federalism: Origin, Operation, Significance* (Boston: Little, Brown, 1964).

Two books are particularly helpful in giving an understanding of the establishment of American federalism. One is Arthur Holcombe, *Our More Perfect Union* (Cambridge: Harvard University Press, 1950), chapter 2. The other is an edited work by Alpheus T. Mason, *The States Rights Debate: Antifederalism and the Constitution* (Englewood Cliffs, N.J.: Prentice-Hall, 1964).

Two excellent sources of information on the political philosophy underlying American federalism are Hamilton, Jay, and Madison, *The Federalist,* and, in the Maass book cited above, chapter 7, "The Founding Fathers and the Division of Powers," by Samuel Huntington.

For analyses of the role of the Supreme Court in settling legal disputes of federalism see, in Earle, cited above, "The Role of the Court," by Alpheus Mason, and Samuel Krislov, *The Supreme Court in the Political Process* (New York: Macmillan, 1965), pp. 80-95.

Two general treatments of federalism written primarily for the lay reader are William Anderson, *The Nation and the States, Rivals or Partners?* (Minneapolis: University of Minnesota Press, 1955), and Leonard White, *The States and the Nation* (Baton Rouge: Louisiana State University Press, 1953). The former is pronational, while the latter is more favorable to the states.

A broad treatment of federalism in the United States is Morton Grodzins, *The American System: A New View of Governments in the United States* (Chicago: Rand McNally, 1966). This book was edited by one of his former students, Daniel Elazar, after Grodzin's death. Subsequently, Elazar wrote his own general treatment of American federalism entitled *American Federalism: A View from the States* (New York: Thomas Y. Crowell, 2nd ed., 1972). Both books treat of a wide variety of topics and are particularly strong on the historical dimensions and political aspects of American federalism. Two excellent analyses of the operation of federalism at the local level are Roscoe Martin, *The Cities and The Federal System* (New York: Atherton, 1965), and James Sundquist, *Making Federalism Work* (Washington: The Brookings Institution, 1969).

A number of publications have been written in recent years on the subject of federal grants-in-aid. An excellent treatment of the subject is Deil S. Wright, *Federal Grants-in-Aid: Perspectives and Alternatives* (Washington: American Enterprise Institute, 1968).

Two good accounts of the passage of revenue sharing are Samuel Beer, "The Adoption of General Revenue Sharing: A Case Study in Public Sector Politics," *Public Policy* (Spring 1976): 127-195, and Paul Dommel, *The Politics of Revenue Sharing* (Bloomington: Indiana University Press, 1975). An excellent analysis of spending of shared revenues is David Caputo and Richard Cole, "General Revenue Sharing Expenditure Decisions in Cities over 50,000," *Public Administration Review* (March/April 1975): 136-142. Deil Wright's "Revenue Sharing and Structural Features of American Federalism," *The Annals of the American Academy of Political and Social Science* (May 1975): 100-119, focuses on the political and governmental impact of revenue sharing.

A very good, broad analysis of the New Federalism is Michael Reagan's book by that title (New York: Oxford University Press, 1972). Insights into its practical problems are contained in Leigh Groseneck, ed., *The Administration of the New Federalism: Objectives and Issues* (Washington: American Society for Public Administration, 1973). Two excellent articles dealing with recent fiscal developments in American federalism are Neal Peirce, "Fiscal Crises Show Interdependence," *National Journal,* 22 February 1975, pp. 280-292, and a Special Report, "Federal Spending: The North's Loss is the Sunbelt's Gain," *National Journal,* 6 June 1976, pp. 878-891. For an overall assessment of recent developments in American federalism see Deil Wright, "Intergovernmental Relations:

An Analytical Overview," *The Annals of the American Academy of Political and Social Science* (November 1974): 1-16.

Finally, there are many good studies dealing with specific problems of federalism made by public agencies. One series of reports was issued in the 1950s by the Commission on Intergovernmental Relations appointed by President Eisenhower. Another series of very helpful reports has been published in recent years by the Advisory Commission on Intergovernmental Relations, an agency established in 1959 to make continuous analyses of the problems of American federalism.

Political Novels   The fragile balance inherent in maintaining a political system in the face of many external and internal threats is chronicled by Isaac Asimov in *The Foundation Trilogy* (New York: Avon Books, 1974). Set in the distant future, this novel describes the creation, dissolution, and re-creation of a vast federal system.

Now hear this.

Chapter 4

June 21, 1973 was a banner day for persons concerned with obscenity and pornography in the United States: on that date the United States Supreme Court handed down decisions in seven separate cases involving that general issue. The major case decided that day involved the activities of Marvin Miller, who had mailed unsolicited brochures advertising four books—*Intercourse, Man-Woman, Sex Orgies Illustrated,* and *An Illustrated History of Pornography*—and a film titled *Marital Intercourse* to a restaurant in Newport Beach, California. The brochures (which consisted primarily of pictures and drawings depicting men and women in groups of two or more engaging in a variety of sexual activities, with genitals often prominently displayed) were opened by the manager of the restaurant and his mother, both of whom complained to the police. Miller was ultimately convicted of violating California's criminal statute forbidding the distribution of obscene matter; he appealed the conviction to the United States Supreme Court on the grounds that the statute in question infringed on the right of free speech guaranteed by the Constitution of the United States. In a split 5-4 decision, the Court upheld the law and actions of the California authorities as not constituting an infringement on freedom of speech.

Chief Justice Warren Burger wrote the opinion for the majority of the Court. Citing former Supreme Court decisions that obscene material is not the kind of speech that is entitled to constitutional protection, the Chief Justice explained: "In our view, to equate the free and robust exchange of ideas and political debate with commercial exploitation of obscene materials demeans the general conception of the First Amendment and its high purposes in the historic struggle for freedom. . . ." In his opinion, the Chief Justice also enunciated a new position for the Court: in determining whether a particular matter is obscene, the standards of morality and taste to be applied are not those of the entire

"THAT'S TO TAKE CARE OF OBSCENITY CASES"

Copyright 1977 by Herblock in The
Washington Post.

nation but rather "community" standards. In justifying this position, the Chief
Justice stated: "It is neither realistic nor constitutionally sound to read the First
Amendment as requiring that the people of Maine or Mississippi accept public
depiction of conduct found in Las Vegas or New York City. . . . People in
different states vary in their tastes and attitudes, and this diversity is not to be
strangled by the absolutism of imposed uniformity."

Justice William Douglas (who served longer on the Court than any man in
our history) countered the Chief Justice's views in a sharply worded dissenting
opinion: "The idea that the First Amendment permits punishment for ideas
that are 'offensive' to the particular judge or jury sitting in judgment is astound-
ing. No greater leveler of speech or literature has ever been designed. . . . The
First Amendment was not fashioned as a vehicle for dispensing tranquilizers to

Albany Film Conviction Is Overturned

Tough Smut Curbs Set by High Court

Local Standards Can Be Used to Ban Books, Films

BY LINDA MATHEWS
Times Staff Writer

WASHINGTON — Reversing a long trend toward permissiveness, the Supreme Court Thursday handed down tough obscenity standards that could lead to a nationwide crackdown on pornographic books and movies.

The new guidelines, announced in a series of 5-4 decisions, grant greater discretion to law enforcement agencies, judges and jurors to decide whether, under local community standards, material should be condemned as obscene.

the people. Its prime function was to keep debate open to 'offensive' as well as to 'staid' people." Justice Douglas also differed sharply with the Chief Justice's decision to use contemporary community standards to determine what is obscene: "That test would make it possible to ban any paper or any journal or magazine in some benighted place."

Whatever the merits of the majority and dissenting opinions in *Miller* v. *California* may be, the Court's adoption of contemporary community standards to determine obscenity had an immediate impact in states and localities across the nation. Copies of *Playboy* were seized from newstands in a variety of small towns across the United States. In Chicago the operator of a movie theater was fined $1000 a day for showing *Deep Throat*, while theaters in Detroit were urging citizens to see the film perhaps for the "last time ever." *Carnal Knowledge*, starring Ann-Margret, was banned in Georgia at the same time that it was being shown without protest in hundreds of theaters outside that state.

In fact, the latter film became the subject of a case, *Jenkins* v. *Georgia*, which reached the Supreme Court in June of 1974, just a year after the *Miller* decision. In a unanimous opinion written by Associate Justice William Rehnquist, the Court overruled the conviction of a Georgia theater owner who had shown *Carnal Knowledge;* in so ruling, the Court held that the *Miller* decision did not give juries "unbridled discretion in determining what is patently offensive." Justice Rehnquist went on to explain that despite the fact that there are suggestive scenes of sexual acts in the film, "there is no exhibition of the actors' genitals, lewd or otherwise"; he also stated that "nudity alone is not enough to make material legally obscene." The Court took a similar position in a 1975 case, *Erznoznik* v. *City of Jacksonville*, in overturning a city ordinance banning drive-ins from showing movies containing nudity.

Thus the law of obscenity in the United States is in a highly uncertain state. The Court rules on the one hand that community standards of morality and taste are to be applied in determining what is obscene; on the other, it reserves for itself the right to overrule judgments of local juries on just such matters. Publishers, film-makers, actors and distributors are thus faced with the problem of deciding what will be acceptable to communities throughout the United States. The peril of making such judgments was illustrated in rapid succession in 1976 and early 1977: Al Goldstein, the publisher of *Screw* magazine, was convicted in Wichita of sending obscene material through the mail; Harry Reems, who played the male lead in *Deep Throat*, was found guilty by a Memphis jury of obscenity for his performance in that film; and Larry Flynt, editor and publisher of *Hustler* magazine, was convicted in Cincinnati not only of obscenity but also of involvement in "organized crime" (defined under Ohio law as "the participation of five or more people in an illegal activity for profit,"), and sentenced by the judge to 7-25 years in jail and $11,000 in fines.

These cases cited above were merely part of a national trend as city councils, prosecutors, and police, responding to pressure from citizens, cracked down on pornography. Detroit passed zoning laws limiting the number of adult entertainment businesses that could be located in a particular area; Boston tried the opposite approach of requiring such businesses to be concentrated in a two-block area known as the "Combat Zone." In San Francisco the district attorney ordered the police to seize *Young Lolitas or Youthful Lust*, a film showing children having oral sex with adults of both sexes. From New York to Califor-

Larry Flynt, publisher of *Hustler* Magazine, being hustled to jail.

nia, city councils passed laws shutting down massage parlors; in Fremont, a city in the San Francisco Bay area, citizens took matters into their own hands, picketing such parlors and recording on signs the license numbers of patrons' cars, a strategy that brought immediate results as alerted wives burst into parlors looking for their husbands.

Thus the battle against obscenity was being fought on many fronts with diverse tactics. We will examine this issue in more detail later in this chapter. First, however, we need to explore the broad issue of civil liberties in the United States.

LIBERTY AND AUTHORITY IN AMERICA

The clash between the rights of the individual on the one hand and the general interests of society on the other reflected in *Miller* v. *California* is just one instance of the inevitable conflict between liberty and authority in a free society. Both concepts have exerted powerful and divergent influences on our nation's development. Many of the early settlers came to America for religious liberty, the right to worship God as they saw fit rather than as prescribed by the dictates of an established church. At the time of the Revolutionary War, Patrick Henry proclaimed his choice, "Give me liberty or give me death," and a century later the country fought a bloody civil war over the liberty of the black man. Yet the place of authority in the American political tradition is reflected in the colonists' initial reluctance to use violence to overthrow British rule and in our people's continuing attachment to law and order and the attendant legal system inherited from the mother country.

Indeed, the classic problem of all democratic societies is how to reconcile liberty and authority. Madison grasped the essential nature of the issue for constitution builders when he stated in *Federalist* 51, "In framing a government which is to be administered by men over men, the great difficulty lies in this: you must first enable the government to control the governed; and in the next place, to control itself." Lincoln pointed up the same problem for those seeking to preserve constitutional order. Calling on Congress in July 1861 to support a series of measures he deemed necessary to the nation's survival, he posed the rhetorical question, "Must the government, of necessity, be too strong for the liberties of its own people, or too weak to maintain its own existence?"

Democratic governments must somehow preserve political authority at the same time that they promote the liberties of their people. The issue becomes not a matter of liberty *or* authority but of liberty *and* authority. For without the minimum conditions of order, individual liberties are meaningless; concomitantly, *perfect* order is present only in the deadening security of a prison. The crux of the issue is, how much liberty and how much authority? How can a free and secure society achieve a balance between these two values?

Even if a democracy manages to strike a delicate balance between individual liberty on the one hand and governmental authority on the other, another knotty problem remains: how can it also resolve conflicts that arise because the exercise of certain liberties by some persons impinges on different rights claimed by others? A classic case is the newspaper editor who, in the course of enjoying freedom of the press, publishes information relating to a crime that jeopardizes the right of the accused to a fair trial. To assess this issue properly, we must spell out what we mean by civil liberties and examine the kinds of specific freedoms that Americans enjoy.

THE NATURE OF OUR CIVIL LIBERTIES

Use of the Term

Unfortunately, there is no agreed-upon definition of civil liberties. Some persons use the term to refer only to those freedoms that are protected against infringement by the government, not by private individuals. This is correct historical usage since civil liberties did develop, initially in Great Britain and later in the United States, in the context of the relationship of the individual to the state. In recent times, however, civil liberties problems in the United States have involved the issue of safeguarding such freedoms against violation by private individuals. In fact, the government is now frequently interposed to protect individual freedoms against private infractions.

A closely related issue is the source of civil liberties. Again, the traditional view is that they originate in constitutional provisions alone. Yet a number of fundamental rights now enjoyed by Americans stem not from our basic document but from statutes passed by Congress. For example, the historic Civil Rights Act of 1964 protects minority groups from discrimination in a number of areas—schools, jobs, and public accommodations among them. Moreover, the act forbids discrimination by both governmental agencies and private individuals.

There is also confusion over the terms *civil liberties* and civil rights. Some persons use them interchangeably (we will do so in this book); others restrict the latter to issues involving discrimination against any minority group; still others simply equate civil rights with Negro rights. This last, highly limited, usage has been prevalent in the United States in recent years, but it is worth keeping in mind that the first ten amendments of the Constitution are referred to as the Bill of Rights, and none of them deals with problems of race.

Whatever way the term civil liberties is defined, it covers a broad spectrum of freedoms in America today. Included are such diverse matters as the First Amendment freedoms of religion, speech, press, assembly, and petition; the rights of the accused in criminal cases; the protection of private property; the right to vote; and freedom from discrimination not only in political matters but also in certain economic and social activities. The growth and expansion of such rights constitute one of the major developments of the modern age.

Rights "in" Government and Rights "From" Government

It is helpful to distinguish between two major types of liberties protected by the American Constitution, those "in" government and those "from" government. The former relate to *participation in the political process.* The most obvious such right is voting; however, Americans can affect what the government does in other ways as well. For example, the First Amendment freedoms of speech, press, assembly, and petition permit individuals to communicate their ideas on public issues to government officials as well as to their fellow citizens.

Rights "in" government may properly be viewed from the standpoint not only of the individual who enjoys them but also of the government, which is their ultimate beneficiary. As we noted previously, democratic societies assume that there is no single discoverable political truth and that the closest we can come to this ideal is to adopt what emerges as the political choice from the marketplace of ideas. Thus the exercise of the franchise, together with the ancillary rights of speech, press, assembly, and petition, are essential to the operation of a democratic form of government because they become the means for achieving one of the major aims of constitutionalism: holding the rulers *responsible* to the ruled.

The other major aim of constitutionalism is *limiting* the scope of government, walling off areas of human activity from governmental interference. Rights "from" government, then, relate to *the private preserves that individuals enjoy against the state.* A primary example is freedom of religion, which is safe-guarded by the First Amendment. Another is the sanctity of an individual's house (a reflection of the traditional British concept that a man's home is his castle), as well as his person, papers, and effects, against unreasonable searches and seizures. The Second through the Eighth amendments of the Constitution all serve to protect an individual's property, his freedom of movement, and his life by providing that he may not be deprived of those by the government except under carefully prescribed conditions. For example, his property may be taken by the government for public use only if he receives just compensation. A person may be fined, imprisoned, or even put to death for committing a crime, but only after the government has followed definite procedures designed to safeguard his interests.

Rights "from" government are thus related to a basic democratic value, that of *privacy,* which was discussed in chapter 1. This concern with the right of

VIRGINIA BILL *of* RIGHTS

DRAWN ORIGINALLY BY GEORGE MASON AND
ADOPTED BY THE CONVENTION OF DELEGATES

June 12, 1776.

A Declaration of Rights made by the Representatives of the good People of Virginia, assembled in full and free Convention; which Rights do pertain to them, and their Posterity, as the Basis and Foundation of Government.

privacy has been reflected in some major Supreme Court cases in recent years dealing with such controversial issues as the dissemination of information on birth control and the right of a woman to have an abortion, subjects that we shall discuss in the concluding portion of this chapter.

The American Constitution thus provides a variety of rights designed to keep the government both responsible to the people and limited in its intrusion into their personal affairs. Moreover, our federal system provides safeguards against improper actions by either the national government or the states. As we shall see, however, the sources of such protections are different.

CONSTITUTIONAL RESTRICTIONS ON THE NATIONAL GOVERNMENT: THE BILL OF RIGHTS

Those who took the initiative in calling the Constitutional Convention were primarily concerned with protecting property rights from threats of state governments. In contrast, they gave almost no consideration to safeguarding civil liberties from actions of national authorities. When George Mason (a major author of the Virginia Declaration of Rights) proposed toward the end of the Convention that a committee be appointed to prepare a Bill of Rights for the document, Roger Sherman replied briefly that the various states already had bills of rights and, therefore, one for the national government was unnecessary. The delegates quickly sided with Sherman on the issue, and Mason's motion failed to draw support from a single state. With the exception of the idealistic (and nonbinding) language of the Preamble referring to "Justice" and "the Blessings of Liberty" and the few restrictions on Congress in Article I, Section 9, the original Constitution emerged from the Convention with few safeguards for civil liberties.

In the ratification campaign the absence of a Bill of Rights became one of the major targets for those opposed to the Constitution. Even Adams and Jefferson, who favored its adoption, were unhappy that the framers had not included a statement of rights. Hamilton said that none was necessary since the national government possessed certain enumerated powers only and thus had no authority to invade individual liberties; Wilson argued that enumerating rights would be dangerous because any not expressly listed would be presumed to have been purposely omitted. And Randolph held that listing rights was futile—"You may cover whole skins of parchment with limitations, but power alone can limit power."

The proponents of a Bill of Rights eventually had their way, however: several of the states ratified the Constitution with the express understanding that the first order of business for the first Congress would be the drawing up of a Bill of Rights to be submitted as amendments to the Constitution. Acting under a moral rather than legal obligation, Washington in his first inaugural address asked Congress to give careful attention to the demands for such amendments, and Madison took the leadership in coordinating the suggestions of state ratifying conventions and introducing them into the House. Congress pared down the list of proposals, and ten were eventually ratified. Both anti-Federalists and Federalists gained from the process: the former saw their initial support for a Bill of Rights vindicated while the latter gained additional popular support for the Constitution they authored.

Thus the struggle over protection of civil liberties against the national government took place within political arenas: the Constitutional Convention, the Congress, and the ratifying state legislatures. But we shall see that a similar battle against encroachments of state officials came primarily through the medium of the courts.

CONSTITUTIONAL RESTRICTIONS ON STATE VIOLATIONS OF CIVIL LIBERTIES

Early in our constitutional history the states rather than the national government showed the greater concern for civil liberties. Jefferson and Mason drafted Virginia's Declaration of Rights shortly before the Declaration of Independence was signed. In it they set forth the same general tenets that were later echoed in the more famous document: men are entitled to certain inherent rights of life, liberty, property, and the pursuit of happiness. Moreover, the Virginia Declaration spelled out in much greater detail than the national one the basic freedoms of the press and religion, and the right to a jury trial, that were safeguarded against action by Virginia officials. Other jurisdictions followed suit, with the result that all the early state constitutions either contained a separate bill of rights or incorporated similar provisions as part of the basic document.

When the first Congress turned to the development of a Bill of Rights, its primary attention was focused on the national authorities for obvious reasons: this was the level of government that persons concerned with civil liberties feared, and in any event state officials were restricted by their own constitutions. At one point the House proposed an amendment prohibiting states from infringing on the right to trial by jury in criminal cases or on rights of conscience, speech, and the press, but the measure was defeated by the Senate. Although the first ten amendments nowhere stated specifically that they were to apply to the national government and not the states (the First Amendment does read, however, "Congress shall make no law," and presumably this phrase is to be read into the amendments that follow), this was undoubtedly the intention of the persons who drafted them in the early 1790s, and four decades later the Supreme Court so ruled in *Barron* v. *Baltimore* (1833).

What the Senate and the Court initially refused to do—that is, to utilize the first ten amendments to restrict state as well as national authorities—has largely come to pass today as a result of a number of decisions of the Supreme Court. In 1925 the Court held in *Gitlow* v. *New York* that freedom of speech and the press are such fundamental rights that they should be construed as "liberties" protected by the Fourteenth Amendment from impairment by states. Subsequently, by similar judicial reasoning, all the other First Amendment freedoms and some others as well (such as the right to privacy) have been added to the liberties so protected. To date the Court has been unwilling to say that the Bill of Rights applies *in toto* to the states, but, as we will see in chapter 15, almost all the procedural safeguards set forth in Amendments Four through Eight, which federal authorities must respect in criminal cases, have now been held to bind state officials as well in proceedings against persons accused of violating state laws. So the afterthought of the national Constitution—the first ten amendments—has become a major source of rights "in" and rights "from" government at the state level, while state constitutions—which served as inspirations for the Bill of Rights—have proved to be less effective in protecting civil liberties.

Thus the Bill of Rights, in addition to those rights construed by the Supreme Court as basic "liberties" under the Fourteenth Amendment, provide the federal constitutional framework for the protection of civil liberties in the United States. The remainder of this chapter focuses on how these constitutional safeguards have affected our most fundamental freedoms—those set forth in the First Amendment plus freedoms recently recognized by the Supreme Court as part of the right of privacy. Elsewhere in the book we shall examine other basic rights relating to voting (ch. 10), procedural safeguards in criminal trials (ch. 15), and equal opportunity for the American black (ch. 6).

FREEDOM OF RELIGION

Americans, who enjoy freedom from governmental interference in religious matters, frequently assume that this right has been traditional ever since the Puritans fled England in the early 1620s and came to Massachusetts to escape the dictates of the official Anglican church. The facts of the matter, however, are that the Puritans proceeded to establish a church of their own—the Congregational—and forced all inhabitants to follow its religious precepts. Other colonies followed a similar practice, and as late as the Revolutionary War most of them had established churches.

The established churches that prevailed before the Revolution did not survive long in the postwar period. The Virginia Declaration of Rights of 1776 contained an article on religious freedom drafted by Patrick Henry, and three years later the Anglican church there was disestablished. A proposal favored by Patrick Henry and George Washington to make all Christian churches state religions of equal standing and to support them by taxation was rejected in favor of the preference of Madison, Jefferson, and Mason for the separation of religious and civil affairs. As this policy was enunciated in the famous Virginia Statute of Religious Liberty of 1786, "no man shall be compelled to frequent or

Religion, Populist style.

support any religious worship, place, or ministry whatsoever." This general attitude towards church-state relations also became dominant in other states as the proliferation of religious sects made it the only practical course of action to pursue.

Religious freedom also became a national policy. It was written into the Northwest Ordinance of 1787 providing for the governance of those territories and that same year was implemented in the constitutional clause prohibiting the use of a religious test as a requirement for public office (Article VI). Finally, religious freedom was guaranteed in the First Amendment's provision that "Congress shall make no law respecting an establishment of religion, or prohibiting the free exercise thereof."

Historically the Bill of Rights served as a check on the national government only, and therefore actions of state and local officials on religious matters were not affected by the provisions of the national Constitution. In 1940, however, in the case of *Cantwell* v. *Connecticut*, the Supreme Court extended the principle of its previously mentioned 1925 decision on free speech (i.e. it is so fundamental that it should be construed as a "liberty" safeguarded by the Fourteenth Amendment) so as to make it also applicable to the states. With this decision, the First Amendment protection of free choice in religion, which had been of little constitutional importance up to that time (few activities of national authorities touched on religious matters), became a matter of great concern as state and local actions affecting religious freedom began to be challenged in the federal courts.

It should be noted that the relevant First Amendment provisions contain two separate concepts: (1) the government cannot by law establish religion, nor (2) can it prohibit the free exercise of religion. Thus public authorities cannot take either positive or negative action with respect to religious matters. Although these two concepts are somewhat related, for the most part they convey distinct ideas and have been so treated by the courts. For these reasons, we will examine them separately.

Prohibition Against the Establishment of Religion

The first major case in which the Supreme Court directly articulated the concept of separation of church and state was *Everson* v. *Board of Education*, decided in 1947. The case arose in New Jersey, where, pursuant to state law, a local school board reimbursed parents for costs they incurred in transporting their children to parochial schools. Since the Court by this time had ruled that religious liberty was protected against state action by the Fourteenth Amendment, the issue in the case was whether such expenditure of funds constituted the establishment of religion.

The majority opinion written by Justice Hugo L. Black interpreted the principle of the separation of church and state to mean that neither the federal nor a state government can pass laws that "aid one religion, aid all religions, or prefer one religion over another." Nor can either levy a tax to support any religious activity. He went on to adopt Jefferson's thesis that there must be a "wall of separation" between church and state, even though no such language appears in the First Amendment itself. (Jefferson used the famous phrase in 1802 in a letter to a religious group explaining his interpretation of the First Amendment.)

But having enunciated what appeared to be a strict interpretation of church-state relations, Justice Black and the majority of the Court nevertheless held that the reimbursement of parents did not violate the wall-of-separation principle and hence was constitutional. They took the position that the use of public funds for transportation did not aid religion or the church, but rather benefited the children by contributing to their safety. Four justices dissented from the majority opinion. Justice Jackson said that the majority view reminded him of Byron's heroine, Julia, who "whispering 'I will ne'er consent'—consented." Another contended that the child-benefit theory employed by the majority could be employed with equal justification for other expenditures for parochial schools, including teachers' salaries, buildings, equipment, school lunches, textbooks, and so forth, since all ultimately benefit the child who attends the school.

Over the years the Supreme Court has had to draw fine lines on this difficult issue. It has tended to strike down financial support for parochial primary and secondary schools on the grounds that aid for such items as teachers' salaries, auxilliary services (testing and counseling), instructional materials, or reimbursement of tuition or tuition tax credits for parents who send their children to nonpublic schools—all advance the religious activities of such schools or "foster excessive governmental entanglement" with religion. On the other hand, the Court has generally approved expenditures of both federal and state grant moneys to church-related colleges and universities. In doing so, the justices have emphasized not the specific form of the aid, but rather the character of such institutions of higher learning, finding them not to be so "pervasively sectarian" that aid would have the primary effect of advancing religion. The distinction the Court seems to be drawing is one between aid to parochial schools that have a self-professed purpose of instilling religious values in children and which are subject to church control, and aid to church-related colleges and universities in which religion plays a minor role in the school curriculum and where the institutions themselves are largely independent of church authorities.

Behind the dispute over the application of the child-benefit theory to expenditures for parochial schools lies a more fundamental difference in attitude concerning the role that such schools can and should play in a democratic society. Those who support expenditures for parochial schools take the position that they are important for the education of a large number of students in our society, and that without them the public schools would be forced to absorb more students, with a consequent rise in educational costs. They also point out that, as the Supreme Court held in a 1925 case, *Pierce* v. *Society of Sisters*, parents have a legal right to send their children to parochial schools, and if this right is to become meaningful, then some assistance for those schools is needed to relieve the double financial burden of parents who now must pay taxes for public schools that their children do not attend. Finally, the parochial schools are not viewed as raising serious religious problems in American society because they devote most of their activities to educating students in secular rather than sectarian subjects.

Those who oppose public expenditures for parochial schools take the general position that public schools have had an important democratizing influence by bringing together children of various religious backgrounds in their formative years. They regard the separation of children in the schools on the basis of religion as undesirable, particularly since religious differences are often related to ethnic, social, and economic distinctions among individuals. They therefore do not want to see the government take any action that may foster parochial schools at the expense of public ones. They feel that if parents want to send their children to church-supported rather than to public schools, they should bear the financial burden of that choice themselves and not expect the rest of society to assist them in it. Finally, they believe that it is not possible in the educational process to draw clear distinctions between sectarian and secular matters and that religious points of view have an effect on how nonreligious subjects are taught.

The Supreme Court has been faced in recent years with another issue relating to the establishment of religion: whether public schools themselves may foster religious exercises in any way. In a 1948 case, *McCollum* v. *Board of Education,* the Court held that school officials in Illinois violated the establishment clause by permitting religious leaders to come to the school during the regular hours to conduct religious classes for students whose parents desired that they receive such instruction. (Other students were given a study period during that time.) Subsequently, however, in *Zorach* v. *Clauson* (1952) the Court held that a similar practice in New York was constitutional because the instruction took place off school property. Dissenting justices argued that where the instruction took place was unimportant and that the use of New York's compulsory school-attendance law to promote religious instruction during regular school hours constituted an establishment of religion.

Recent cases indicate that, while the Court will tolerate religious instruction held off school property during the school day, it will not permit school authorities to conduct religious exercises. In *Engel* v. *Vitale* (1962) the justices declared unconstitutional a practice in New York State of reciting during the regular school period a prayer composed by state officials. That the prayer was religiously neutral, favoring no sect or creed ("Almighty God, we acknowledge our dependence upon thee and we beg thy blessings upon us, our parents, our teachers, and our country"), and that the prayer was voluntary, so students who objected to it did not have to participate in the ceremony, made no difference to the justices. The following year, the Court, in *Abington Township School District* v. *Schempp,* outlawed the reading of the Bible or the recitation of the Lord's Prayer in the public schools. In both cases there was only one dissenter, Justice Potter Stewart, who declared that none of these practices constituted the establishment of religion.

As with the issue of financial aid to the parochial schools, important policy differences exist between those who favor and those who oppose religious exercises in public schools. The former argue that majorities as well as minorities have rights, and it is no great burden on the students who do not want to participate to remain quiet during the ceremonies. The opposition takes the position that the failure to participate in such exercises tends to brand the individuals involved as "oddballs" in the eyes of their fellow students, and that, in any event, religious instruction should be left to other institutions in society—the family and the church—that are better able to offer it than the public schools, which are designed to provide secular education.

Beyond differences about whether a particular practice is wise or unwise for good church-state relationships in a free society, there is also fundamental disagreement over exactly what the Founding Fathers meant to prohibit concerning the establishment of religion. One general line of thinking is that they merely wanted to prevent government officials from preferring one religion to another. Under this interpretation the national government (and now state or local ones) can financially support religious activities or foster them in other ways so long as they do not discriminate among various sects and churches in the process. A stricter interpretation of the establishment clause is that those who wrote it into the First Amendment desired to prohibit public officials from undertaking activities that would promote any or all religious groups. Under this reasoning the clause is designed to prevent discrimination not only among religious groups but also between religious and nonreligious ones. Thus atheists, who do not believe in a Supreme Being, and agnostics, who have doubts about the existence of one, are also meant to be protected by the establishment clause.

Whatever the historical merits of these two interpretations may be, we do not have a complete separation of church and state in the United States. Financial support for religion exists in the form of salaries paid to chaplains that serve the spiritual needs of members of Congress, the service academies, and military forces. Indirect financial assistance is also provided to churches in the form of exemption from the payment of taxes on property used for religious purposes, a practice that has recently been declared constitutional by the Court. Nor have we removed all vestiges of religion from our public life. Even though the Supreme Court has banned prayers from the public schools, they are still used to open sessions of Congress and the Supreme Court, and each year since 1952, under congressional authority, the President has declared a National Day of Prayer. Finally, the phrase "in God we trust" appears on both our coins and paper money, and during the Eisenhower administration the words "under God" were added to the Pledge of Allegiance to the Flag.

It remains to be seen how many (if any) of the above practices will eventually be successfully attacked as unconstitutional. With the exception of the holding of religious exercises in the public schools, to date public authorities (including Supreme Court justices) have not been inclined to adopt a strict interpretation of Jefferson's concept of a wall of separation between church and state.

The Free Exercise of Religion

Cases involving the free exercise of religion reached the Supreme Court prior to those relating to the establishment of religion. The first major case, *Reynolds* v. *United States,* arose in the late 1870s over the Mormon practice of plural marriages. Congress passed a law against polygamy in the territories, and the issue posed by its action was whether this law violated the First Amendment clause prohibiting the national government from interfering with the free exercise of religion. In its decision the Court made a clear distinction between religious beliefs and actions stemming from those beliefs. Thus, the justices reasoned, Mormons could hold the belief that God permits men to have as many wives as possible, but they had no right to implement their belief, because it violates social duty and order.

In other instances, however, the Court has permitted religious groups to act on their beliefs even though in so doing they affect the rights of others. A classic series of cases arose in the 1930s and 1940s as a result of activities of members of the Jehovah's Witnesses sect. Acting on the belief that each member of the group is a minister and has the duty to spread the gospel, Witnesses distributed and sold religious literature in the public streets without complying with state and local laws relating to permits, fees, or taxes. The Court upheld their activities and also sustained the right to pass out religious tracts door to door in residential areas. In sustaining such actions the Court balanced the religious liberty of Jehovah's Witnesses to propagate their faith against the right of individuals to privacy—that is, the freedom of individuals not to be bothered by persons seeking to convert them to religious beliefs—and found the former to be more important.

Another line of cases relating to the free exercise of religion turns on the issue of whether public authorities can force persons to take actions that run counter to their religious beliefs. Two landmark cases in the early 1940's put to constitutional test the practice in some states of requiring students as a part of daily exercises to salute the flag under penalty of being expelled from school. In the first one, *Minersville School District* v. *Gobitis* (1940), the Supreme Court upheld the statute on the grounds that if the legislature felt that the ritual instilled patriotism in children and thus promoted national unity, the Court ought not to interfere with that judgment. Just three years later, however, in *West Virginia State Board of Education* v. *Barnette,* the Court overruled the earlier decision under the reasoning that public officials could not compel students to utter words which they did not believe. In so ruling, Justice Roberts held that under our Constitution, no official can prescribe what is orthodox in politics, nationalism, or religion and force others to confess to such beliefs. In a recent case, *Wisconsin* v. *Yoder* (1972), the Court upheld the right of Amish parents to refuse to send their children to public schools beyond the eighth grade. Speaking for the majority, Chief Justice Burger held that the worldly values such schools teach are in marked contrast with those inculcated by the Amish way of life, which he characterized as resting on a religious, and not merely a philosophical, basis.

Still another related issue is the observance of days of rest. In a 1961 case, *McGowan* v. *Maryland,* the Supreme Court upheld the constitutionality of Sunday closing laws against attacks that they denied freedom of religion to individuals who closed their stores on Saturday in keeping with their beliefs. In so doing, the Court held that, although Sunday was originally celebrated as a day of rest for religious reasons, it is now a secular holiday, set aside for recreation and family activities. Thus closing laws are no longer related to religious beliefs. The Court also pointed out that persons who celebrate Saturday as a religious holiday are free to close their stores on that day. While recognizing the potential economic burden (their stores would then be closed on both Saturday and Sunday), the justices held that this is merely the indirect effect, and not the purpose, of a law regulating secular activity.

Thus the Supreme Court has tried to balance the religious rights of individuals against the interests of other individuals and of society generally. As the following section indicates, the justices have struggled to achieve a similar equilibrium with respect to other vital First Amendment freedoms.

Amish school boy.

FREEDOM OF EXPRESSION

In addition to freedom of religion, the First Amendment spells out a number of other rights with which Congress may not interfere: freedom of speech and the press, the right of peaceful assembly, and the right to petition the government for a redress of grievances. Together they constitute means by which individuals or groups express their views and communicate them to one another, as well as to their public officials. Insofar as such expressions relate to public issues, they are rights "in" government, enabling citizens to try to influence public decisions. When they pertain to nonpublic affairs and concerns, however, they are rights "from" government, for they protect the freedom to communicate views on private matters.

The Supreme Court has recently recognized another related freedom, that of association, even though no such right appears in the language of the First Amendment itself. In protecting a Southern chapter of the National Association for the Advancement of Colored People from a state law requiring it publicly to divulge its membership, the Court ruled, in *NAACP* v. *Alabama* (1958), that "freedom to engage in association for the advancement of beliefs and ideas is an inseparable aspect of the 'liberty' assured by . . . the Fourteenth Amendment which embraces freedom of speech." The Court did not restrict this freedom of association for public issues only; it rather said that "it is immaterial whether the beliefs sought to be advanced by associations pertain to political, economic, religious, or cultural affairs." Thus freedom of association is to be added to other First Amendment rights. (Because the case involved not only the right to associate but also the right to keep group membership lists confidential, the decision also indicates the Supreme Court's concern with the issue of privacy.)

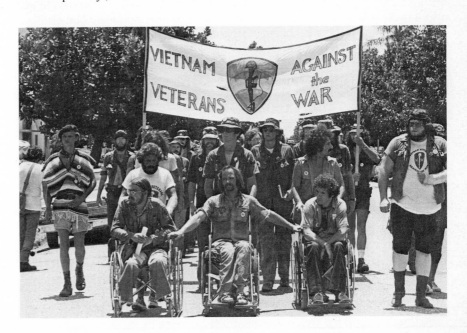

Like religious freedom, those First Amendment liberties relating to expression did not become a matter of major concern for the Supreme Court until relatively recent times. It was not until 1919 that the highest tribunal first directly faced an issue of free speech, in *Schenck* v. *United States,* a case (to be discussed below) concerned with antiwar activities during World War I. As we shall see, this general problem of reconciling freedom of expression with national security has continued to be a major concern of the Court in the post-World-War-II era as well. In the 1960s civil rights and Vietnam protests presented the Court with still other vital issues involving First Amendment liberties.

Before discussing decisions in these areas, it will be helpful to analyze the general approaches the Court has adopted in seeking to reconcile the right of personal expression with society's concern for order and authority. With these approaches in mind, we will then examine how the Court has applied them to specific situations.

General Approaches to the Issue

Of the various approaches to the issue of freedom of expression, the one advocated by the late Supreme Court Justice Hugo Black is the most *absolute.* Black argued that the Founding Fathers wanted the words of the First Amendment to be taken literally; the phrase that Congress shall make "no law" abridging the freedom of speech or of the press means just that—national authorities (and presumably state ones as well) cannot take any action that interferes with the free expression of views. Justice Black even went so far as to suggest that the First Amendment means that libel and slander actions (suits brought by private individuals against others who have defamed their character or reputation through written or oral statements) cannot be brought in federal courts. He was also unwilling to have restrictions placed on newspaper comments on criminal cases even though these comments jeopardize the right of the accused persons to a fair trial.

While Justice Black held absolutist views regarding the constitutional sanctity of the oral and printed word, he did not extend this attitude to conduct or action. For example, he did not recognize picketing as an absolute right, even though the Supreme Court ruled in *Thornhill* v. *Alabama* (1940) that it is a form of symbolic speech and is thus entitled to the protection of the First Amendment. Moreover, Justice Black took a rather conservative position on the methods by which speech can be implemented. He stated that freedom of speech does not mean that a person can express himself whenever, wherever, and however he pleases. In line with this reasoning, he contended that one person cannot use another person's private property to exercise freedom of expression, and that there are even limits on the utilization of public property for such a purpose. Thus Justice Black believed the First Amendment protects absolutely the *content* of speech but not the *manner* by which it is expressed.

A similar general view on freedom of expression was advocated by the late philosopher Alexander Meiklejohn. His attitudes, however, derived not from the historical meaning of the First Amendment itself but from the logic of *self-government.* He argued that freedom of expression is important not only for the individual but also for society; it is not just his right to speak that is involved but also society's obligation to hear what he has to say. The only way to assure that a free society will arrive at good decisions is to see to it that all viewpoints are considered, no matter how wrong or dangerous we may consider some of them to be. Meiklejohn suggested that it is not a question of balancing intellectual freedom against public safety; rather, that freedom is the bulwark of public safety.

The major difference between Black's and Meiklejohn's views is that Black would apply his absolutist approach to expressions relating to both public and private concerns, while Meiklejohn would restrict his to public affairs. Thus the philosopher, unlike the justice, would not bar private libel and slander suits and would tolerate other reasonable restraints on utterances not relating to "community thinking" or "self-government." Like Black, Meiklejohn would allow restrictions to be placed on the manner in which speech is expressed. For example, the government may suspend utterances until order is established, so that all views may be heard. As he himself expressed it, "When the roof falls in, the moderator may, without violating the First Amendment, declare the meeting adjourned."

Two other general approaches to freedom of expression concern the posture the Supreme Court should take in passing on speech and allied rights. We will examine the general role of the Court with respect to judicial review in chapter 16; it is sufficient for our purposes here to say that judges differ on the extent to which they feel they should interfere with the actions of legislators and executives on the grounds that they are unconstitutional. Some argue for an "activist" role for the Court, requiring judges to scrutinize carefully the activities of other public officials and to invalidate those that violate what they conceive to be constitutional principles; others feel that Supreme Court justices should assume a "nonactivist" role by presuming the actions of legislators and executives to be constitutional and seldom substituting their constitutional judgments for judgments of those officials.

Those who adopt a preferred-position approach to the expression issue (the position is generally associated with former Supreme Court Justices Harlan Stone and Wiley Rutledge, but other judges have also followed it) believe that when speech and allied rights become involved in litigation, the Court should take an activist role in reviewing the actions of legislators and executives. The reason is that the First Amendment freedoms are so basic to maintaining the openness of our political system and society that they deserve special or preferred treatment by the courts over other issues. Thus the Court should carefully scrutinize actions of public officials relating to freedom of expression at the same time that it presumes that their activities regulating economic affairs are constitutional. The basis for this special solicitude for rights of free expression is that such rights are particularly important for unpopular minority groups that frequently cannot protect their interests in the political processes of the legislative and executive branches. The special phrasing of the First Amendment (the Congress "shall make no law" respecting religion and expression) further justifies the Court's looking carefully at governmental regulation of such matters rather than presuming them to be constitutional.

The difference between the preferred-position approach and the views advocated by Black and Meiklejohn is thus one of degree. The latter two argue that political authorities cannot place any restrictions on the content of political expressions, while those who adopt the preferred-position approach are willing to permit some restrictions, but only under very special circumstances. All three approaches evidence a special solicitude for First Amendment freedoms and require that they be granted a special place in our constitutional order of values.

Felix Frankfurter.

The man most critical of all the above approaches was former Supreme Court Justice Felix Frankfurter. He was a "nonactivist" who felt that judges should be very reluctant to substitute their constitutional judgments for those of legislative and executive officials on all kinds of issues, including those pertaining to expression. He attacked the preferred-position approach to the problem as a "mischievous phrase" that "attempts to express a complex process of adjudication by a deceptive formula"; he also rejected the absolutist positions of Black and Meiklejohn as doctrinaire. In place of such approaches Frankfurter called for a pragmatic "balancing"—that is, a case-by-case weighing of competing values, and the exercise of judgment in deciding when restrictions on freedom of expression are warranted in order to protect society's interest in order and authority, or the rights of other individuals or groups. Thus Frankfurter rejected the idea that freedom of expression is either an absolute value or one that is to be necessarily preferred over other legitimate interests.

Although these general approaches to freedom of expression reflect important basic attitudes towards this vital issue, they have not proved to be very helpful in dealing with the wide variety of pertinent cases that have come to the Supreme Court in the last half-century. Although Justice Douglas moved closer to Black's position in his last years on the bench, no other justices have been willing to adopt an absolutist approach. The preferred-position and balancing approaches have been expressed in opinions from time to time, but both reflect a general mood rather than a usable guideline. Thus the former merely suggests that restrictions on freedom of expression are constitutional only under unusual circumstances without indicating what those circumstances are; the latter calls for a balancing of interests without determining the specific interests to be balanced and the weights to be assigned to each.

In attempting to develop more usable guidelines, the Supreme Court has turned to another type of attack on the problem. Rather than look at the issue from the standpoint of the historical meaning of the First Amendment, the logic of self-government, or a general philosophy concerning the role of the Supreme Court vis-à-vis legislators and executives in the protection of free speech, some judges have placed the issue on an *empirical* basis. In doing so, they have utilized certain basic tests relating to the actual *consequences* of given expressions.

Tests of The Consequences Of Expression

The judge most prominently identified with analyzing freedom of expression on the basis of consequences was Justice Oliver Wendell Holmes, Jr. In the *Schenck* case of 1919 referred to earlier, which involved the indictment of a Socialist for violating the World War I Espionage Act by circulating antiwar leaflets to members of the armed forces, the celebrated jurist spelled out the test to be applied in free-speech cases. Rejecting an absolutist approach by suggesting that no man had the constitutional right to falsely shout fire in a theater, Holmes stated:

Oliver Wendell Holmes, Jr.

The question in every case is whether the words are used in such circumstances and are of such a nature as to create a clear and present danger that they will bring about the substantive evils that Congress has a right to prevent. It is a question of proximity and degree.

In this particular case Justice Holmes upheld the conviction on the basis that the antiwar actions did create a clear and present danger to the prosecution of the war, an evil that Congress had the right to prevent. Later that same year, however, in a dissenting opinion in *Abrams* v. *United States,* Holmes held that restrictions on the publication of pamphlets that attacked the sending of an American expeditionary force to Russia were unconstitutional because the circumstances failed to fulfill the requirements of the test.

The key to the test proposed by Holmes is the meaning of the words *clear* and *present* as they are used in conjunction with danger. Some construe the former to mean "obvious"; Holmes himself never defined "clear" with any exactitude, but he seems to have had in mind the *probable effect* of the speech. Equally crucial to the application of the test is the interpretation of the word *present.* Holmes stated his meaning with considerable precision in the *Abrams* case, in which he said it was a danger that "imminently threatens immediate interference with the lawful and pressing purposes of the law." In any event, the test is considered favorable to freedom of expression, since it places the burden on those that seek to limit expression to demonstrate that restrictions are necessary to prevent the imminent occurrence of an evil that will probably result from the utterance involved.

In contrast with the "clear and present danger" test is the bad tendency rule, first utilized by the Supreme Court in *Pierce* v. *United States,* decided just one year after the *Schenck* opinion. Again, Socialists were convicted for distributing antiwar pamphlets, but in this instance there was no indication that any of this literature reached members of the armed forces or had an immediate effect on the war. Even so, the Court upheld the conviction on the ground that the action might eventually have a tendency to cause insubordination and disloyalty among the troops. In so ruling, the Court lifted from those doing the restricting the burden of proving that the speech in question would probably result in an immediate evil and substituted the less onerous requirement of demonstrating that the utterances *might tend* to bring about an evil sometime in the future.

Finally, in 1950 the Supreme Court developed a third empirical standard for evaluating the constitutionality of restrictions on freedom of expression; this standard has come to be known as the gravity of the evil or sliding scale test. In the 1950 *Dennis* case (we will examine this case in detail below) Chief Justice Fred M. Vinson ruled that "the Court must ask whether the gravity of the evil, discounted by its improbability, justifies such invasion of free speech as is necessary to avoid the evil." Thus the decision added a new dimension to the issue: the nature of the evil to be avoided. If the evil is grave enough—such as the violent overthrow of the government by force—then one need not demonstrate that the expression to be regulated will probably result in the immediate occurrence of the evil. However, if the evil to be presented is not so grave— such as a local disturbance—then those seeking to regulate expression must show that it will probably and imminently bring about the disturbance. Although the Court did not say so, it seemed to be suggesting that if the evil is serious enough, the "bad tendency" test is to be employed; if the evil is not so serious, the "clear and present danger" standard is applicable.

Although the empirical tests provide more definite guidelines for analyzing freedom-of-expression issues than do the preferred-position and balancing approaches, they leave unanswered a number of major questions. For example, in the "clear and present danger" test, *to whom* is the occurrence of the evil to be "clear"—the Congress, the President, or the jury that tries the case? What is meant by "present"—tomorrow, next month, next year? In the "gravity of the evil" test, how grave is "grave," and what criteria does one take into account in deciding that question?

The plain fact of the matter is that verbal formulas cannot capture all the complexities of social situations, and judges must ultimately exercise considerable discretion in deciding freedom-of-expression issues. They look at the total circumstances of the particular case before them. Thus it may make a difference *who* made the statement in question—a college freshman or a major official of the Communist party? *When* the statement is made may well be the crucial factor in the Court's thinking—in the midst of a war or threat of war, or during a period of relative calm in international affairs? *Where* the words were said may well be determinative—in a university graduate seminar or at a mass meeting containing militant groups opposed to the speaker's point of view?

Therefore, we need to look at the broad environment and the events associated with particular freedom-of-expression issues if we are to understand the nature of such issues and the considerations that are taken into account in dealing with them. In the remaining portions of this chapter we will focus on some of the major areas in which the important problems of free speech have arisen in recent years.

The Communist "Threat"

One of the more perplexing problems for American society in the post-World-War-II era has been the perceived communist threat to national security. In chapter 13 we will examine the foreign-policy aspects of this issue; we focus here on the domestic side of the problem as it relates to internal subversion.

One approach is that of the classic civil libertarian who argues that in a free society all viewpoints must be expressed and that democracy has little to fear from such a policy. As the poet John Milton put it, "Let truth and falsehood grapple. Whoever knew truth put to the worse in a free and open encounter?" In the same vein is the philosophy of Thomas Jefferson that a free society should be able to withstand the severest criticisms of its political institutions. Such an approach leads to the conclusion that our society need not concern itself with the activities of communist groups unless they resort to actual acts of violence. Regulating them may even have the unfortunate consequence of driving the groups underground, making it more difficult to counter their philosophy with our own and to scrutinize their activities that may lead to violence.

Those who favor the regulation of communist activities in this country argue that this particular group does not fit the classic case of the political opponent or dissenter. For one thing, they claim, communists do not believe in or follow one of the most fundamental tenets of democracy: the use of peaceful means to reach political decisions. Since they fail to abide by the rules of the game in a free society, democracy need not extend them rights traditionally accorded to members of the loyal opposition. Beyond this, communists do not seek the relative truth that is the goal of a free exchange of ideas; they have already decided what absolute truth is and distort matters that do not fit their preconceived ideas. Rather than come out in the open to state their unpopular views and to identify themselves, as heretics traditionally do, they conspire behind the scenes, using "front" organizations and legitimate groups to masquerade their real purposes and identity. They are not native dissident groups but rather serve foreign powers such as the Soviet Union; although they may not yet have resorted to violence, they are preparing for the day when the time is ripe to do so. All such assumptions logically lead to the necessity for regulating communists in this country.

At the end of World War II, this latter position won the day. The national government, as well as many states, embarked on a program of regulating communists. Inevitably, some of the major issues ended up in the Supreme Court as that tribunal struggled with the problem of reconciling freedom of expression with the interests of national security.

The Smith Act. The Smith Act, technically known as the Alien Registration Act, was passed by Congress in 1940. In addition to its provisions on aliens, it forbade the advocacy of, or teaching, the overthrow of any government in the United States by force or violence, the organization of groups having such purposes, and conspiracy to commit such acts. In addition, it contained a clause that prohibited "knowing" membership in any group advocating forcible overthrow of government.

The Smith Act was not originally aimed at the Communist party but rather at the greater enemy in 1940, fascism. Yet the language of the act dealing with violent overthrow of government fitted the nation's major postwar rival, international communism. In 1948 the government secured convictions against eleven major officers of the American Communist party for conspiring to teach the overthrow of the government by force as well as conspiring to form groups advocating such an overthrow. The accused appealed and the Supreme Court ruled on the matter in the famous *Dennis* case in 1951.

The Court upheld their convictions and the constitutionality of the Smith Act itself on the basis of the "gravity of the evil" test. In so ruling, the Court found that the defendants intended to overthrow the government "as speedily as the circumstances would permit" and that the government did not have to wait until "the putsch is about to be executed" before acting to preserve itself. Following the *Dennis* case, similar indictments were obtained under the Smith Act for nearly 150 other, lesser, communist officials.

The first major judicial check on prosecutions under the Smith Act occurred in the *Yates* case, decided by the Supreme Court in 1957. The opinion drew a distinction between the advocacy of the abstract doctrine of revolution (as contained in the writings of Marx, Engels, and other communist theoreticians) and the advocacy of action now or in the future. The Court construed the Smith Act to refer to advocacy of action rather than mere belief. The Court also held that the portion of the Smith Act outlawing the organization of groups advocating or teaching revolution applied only to the act of establishing the Communist party in the United States in its modern form in 1945; prosecutions for that crime were no longer possible after 1948 because of a three-year limitation on suits of this nature. The *Yates* case not only freed the communist

Alien registration card

officials involved but also made it difficult for the government to prosecute other persons for violations of the Smith Act, for the reasons that participation in the formation of the American Communist party in 1945 was no longer subject to legal action and that convictions for individual advocacy of revolution had to be based on evidence of incitement to violent action against the government.

One other potential basis for Smith Act prosecution of communists remained: the membership clause making it a crime to belong to an organization knowing that it has a revolutionary purpose. In the *Scales* case, decided in 1961, however, the Supreme Court construed "knowing" membership to mean not passive or paper affiliation but personal activity in a group's efforts directed toward the violent overthrow of the government. Although the Court ruled that the government had met the test in the present case, this strict construction of the Smith Act made it difficult to prosecute other individuals concerning whom the necessary evidence was lacking.

The end result of the major Smith Act cases was that the Supreme Court upheld the act's constitutionality but at the same time, through a process of judicial interpretation, made it difficult for the government to meet the standards of proof necessary for successful prosecutions under its provisions.

Communist investigator and political opportunist, Senator Joseph McCarthy at hearings.

The McCarran Act. In the midst of government prosecutions under the Smith Act in 1950 Congress passed an anticommunist statute known as the Internal Security Act ("McCarran Act"). Its major approach to the problem of internal subversion posed by the communists was to expose their organization and members and to remove communists from vital positions in American life. Under the provisions of the act, "communist action" organizations (defined as those "substantially dominated, directed, or controlled by . . . the world communist movement"), as well as "communist front" organizations (those similarly influenced by "communist action" groups), were required to register with a Subversive Activities Control Board composed of five members appointed by the President with senatorial approval. If any group believed by the Attorney General to fit either category failed to register, he was empowered to petition for a hearing before the board; if it found that the group was a "communist action" or "communist front" organization, the board had the power to compel registration. The act required affected organizations to indicate on mailed publications and on radio or television programs they sponsored that the information was being disseminated by a communist group. Members of these organizations were to be notified of the action taken against their groups and given the opportunity to prove before the board that they had no association with them. Individuals considered to be members of such organizations were barred from government employment, work in a defense facility, and the use of a passport.

The government's attempt to utilize the McCarran Act proved to be even more frustrating than its efforts under the earlier Smith Act. At first, after a series of inconclusive legal skirmishes, the Supreme Court, in the 1961 case *Communist Party* v. *Subversive Activities Control Board,* upheld the board's finding that the Communist party was a "communist action" organization and should be required to register and divulge the names of its officers and members. One will recall the 1958 Supreme Court ruling that the NAACP did not have to provide similar information to Alabama officials; however, in the Communist-party litigation Justice Frankfurter used the "balancing" approach to arrive at the conclusion that society's interest in national security outweighed the private right of association. (Presumably the cases could also be distinguished on the basis that the purposes of the NAACP were legal whereas those of the Communist party were not.)

The government's initial victory turned out to be a temporary one, however. Efforts to force the party to register failed because officers of the organization would have to register for the group, an act in violation of the clause of the Fifth Amendment that forbids compelling a person to incriminate himself. An attempt to force certain individuals to register as members of the Communist party was declared unconstitutional in the 1965 case of *Albertson* v. *Subversive Activities Control Board*. The Supreme Court further limited the usefulness of the McCarran Act by declaring invalid those portions denying members of a communist organization the right to travel with a passport *(Aptheker* v. *Secretary of State,* 1964) and the right to work in a defense industry (*United States* v. *Robel,* 1967).

In 1967 Congress amended the Internal Security Act to meet some of these difficulties. It removed the requirement that communist organizations or individuals be forced to register and provided that the Subversive Activities Control Board hear such cases on petition from the Attorney General. However, there have been few actions filed under the amended act. As with the Smith Act prosecutions, the government has found it difficult to use the McCarran Act effectively.*

In 1972 Congress cut the SACB's budget by 50 percent, and in 1973 President Nixon's budget message omitted all funds for it. These developments, coupled with improved Soviet-American relations in the 1960s and 70s, makes the internal subversion issue less salient today than it was in the recent past. There has been a shift to other kinds of problems relating to the First Amendment freedoms, problems we will now discuss.

Political Protests

The dominant domestic political problem in the United States in the 1960s was the civil-rights revolution, a topic that we examine in chapter 6. During the last half of the decade the war in Vietnam emerged as the major issue in foreign policy. Political protest was an important part of both developments. In the civil-rights movement, protests were leveled against the entire structure of segregation and discrimination in the United States; the antiwar protest had as its main targets the military, along with Congress and the executive branch, as epitomized by the many demonstrations that took place in Washington, D.C.

The protests over civil rights and the war in Vietnam involved different purposes and methods. In some instances protesters sought to stay within the law, as did most of those involved in the various demonstrations in the nation's capital; however others, such as those who tried to occupy the Pentagon in

---

* The Supreme Court also frustrated state actions in the field of internal subversion by ruling in *Pennsylvania* v. *Nelson* (1952) that states cannot prosecute persons for sedition against the United States because the national government has "pre-empted" this problem itself.

1967, deliberately chose to violate regulations, knowing full well that they would be arrested for doing so.

This latter type of protest, known generally as civil disobedience, has been most prominently identified in the United States with Martin Luther King and the antisegregation movement. Borrowed from Mahatma Gandhi, who used civil disobedience successfully against the British in India (Gandhi himself had borrowed the technique from an earlier American protester, Henry Thoreau, who refused to pay taxes used to prosecute the Mexican War), it is based on the philosophy that individuals need not obey laws that they consider unconstitutional or immoral. Rather, as a matter of conscience and in order to communicate their disapproval of such laws, they are obliged to disobey them. At the same time, if persons follow the doctrine of civil disobedience as taught by leaders like King and Ghandi, they are expected to use passive resistance, not violence, as a tactic and to be willing to accept the legal consequences of punishment for violating laws if their validity is upheld by the courts.

Civil disobedience in the United States in recent years has taken two major forms. In some instances, protesters have deliberately broken a specific law to which they object; thus blacks sat in at southern lunch counters in violation of segregation statutes in order to show their disapproval of those laws. On other occasions dissenters have violated laws to which they did not specifically object in the course of registering their displeasure with other concerns: an example of this method is the attempt of some protesters to interfere with the flow of traffic into Washington, D.C. in the spring of 1971 in order to publicize their views on the war in Vietnam.

The Supreme Court has never condoned civil disobedience as a means of registering dissent, yet its use by political protesters has raised fundamental constitutional issues for the Court. For example, the infraction of segregation statutes brought into question the constitutionality of such laws, a matter we will examine in chapter 6. In addition, deliberate violations by protesters of regulations regarding the use of public property, along with innocent infractions by others not committed to the idea of civil disobedience, have forced the Supreme Court to determine how far political officials can go in restricting the actions of demonstrators without interfering with their constitutional right of free expression. We examine this latter issue next.

Civil-Rights Demonstrations. The most fundamental freedom-of-expression issue raised by recent civil-rights demonstration cases concerns the kinds of limits that may constitutionally be imposed on the place and manner in which political protests are conducted. A 1963 case, *Edwards* v. *South Carolina*, involved a demonstration held on the grounds of the state capitol by Negroes protesting discriminatory practices. Police ordered the crowd of 200 protesters to disperse and, when they failed to do so, arrested them for breach of the peace. The Supreme Court reversed their convictions, emphasizing that the demonstrators were peaceful, that their protest had not interfered with pedestrian or vehicular traffic into the capitol area, and that it had not resulted in a threat of violence either from the demonstrators themselves or from the crowd of onlookers. The Court further held that a state may not make criminal the peaceful expression of unpopular views, even though such views may anger some persons who hear them.

Other recent cases have sustained the use of public property for demonstrations, provided they are peaceful and do not interfere with the operation of the facility. In a 1966 case, *Brown* v. *Louisiana,* the Supreme Court upheld a sit-in at a public library by five black adults protesting segregation of this public service. The majority opinion, written by Justice Abe Fortas, stressed that the defendants had the right to protest the segregation of public facilities by "silent and reproachful" presence in a place "where the protestant has every right to be." Four judges dissented in an opinion written by Justic Black, arguing that the Negroes were expressing their protest in an inappropriate and unauthorized place, since they had no right to be there after they had completed their business.

Although Justice Black's views did not prevail in that instance, they did in the 1966 case of *Adderly* v. *Florida,* which concerned a demonstration of 200 college students outside a county jail. Their convictions for violating a trespass law were upheld by Justice Black and four of his colleagues on the grounds that the students had no right to be on a part of the jail grounds that was set apart for security purposes and not open to the public. In so ruling, Black held that the state, like a private individual, has "the power to preserve the property under its control for the use to which it is properly dedicated." The opinion also contained the statement, typical of Justice Black, that people who engage in protest do not have the right to do so "whenever, however, and wherever they please." Three other judges joined Justice Douglas in dissent, arguing that a county jail housing political prisoners is an obvious center for protest and that the students had not upset the jailhouse routine.

Antiwar Protests. Cases concerning the Vietnam war that reached the Supreme Court did not involve demonstrations by large numbers of people but, rather, protests by individuals. Typically, they arose from acts of disobedience and defiance directed against the war and the military, such as the burning of draft cards and the wearing of black armbands in schools. The major legal issue raised by these cases is what constitutes permissible symbolic speech, since political views are expressed through conduct rather than words.

In the first major case of this nature, *United States* v. *O'Brien* (1968), four young men were convicted for burning their draft cards in violation of a federal statute making such destruction or multilation a crime. Chief Justice Warren, speaking for the majority of the Court, sustained their convictions on the grounds that not all conduct can be labeled speech simply because the person engaging in it intends to express an idea, and that the use of draft cards contributed to the administration of the Selective Service System. He held that acts of dissent can be punished if the government has "a substantial and constitutional interest in forbidding them, the incidental restriction of expression is no greater than necessary, and the government's real interest is not to squelch dissent."

The Supreme Court held, however, in a 1969 case—*Tinker* v. *Des Moines Independent Community School District*—that local school officials could not punish students for violating regulations against wearing black armbands to protest the war in Vietnam. Justice Fortas held this conduct to be "closely akin to pure speech" and pointed out that it had not resulted in any substantial disruption of, or material interference with, school activities. Justice Black in dissent expressed his usual sentiment that a person does not have the constitutional right to express himself whenever, wherever, and however he pleases and also objected to transferring the power to regulate pupils from school officials to the Supreme Court.

The Court has thus exhibited a high tolerance for protests against established authority. Other types of actions upheld by the justices have included denouncing the United States flag (*Smith* v. *Goguen,* 1971), wearing a military uniform in a play that was unfavorable to the United States (*Schacht* v. *United States,* 1970), and sporting a jacket in public that had the words "f--- the draft," emblazoned on it (*Cohen* v. *California,* 1971). At the same time, the Court has not extended such rights to all individuals under all circumstances: in *Parker* v. *Levy* (1974), it upheld the court martial of an army doctor who, in the course of his hospital rounds, made statements that American involvement in the Vietnamese war was wrong and that black soldiers should refuse to serve there. In doing so, the justices took account of the special need of the military to accomplish its major task of defending the nation, a need that justifies regulating a broader range of conduct than is permitted in civilian life.

This same concern for the circumstances under which free speech is exercised has also led the Court to examine another aspect of freedom of expression: the kinds of limitations that may be placed on campaign speeches and advertisements by political candidates.

Campaign Speeches and Advertisements

One might assume that campaign speeches and advertisements would enjoy a high priority in a democratic society. They are central to the process by which voters acquire information about candidates competing for political office and make decisions about which ones to vote for. Moreover, such speeches and advertisements are less threatening to political authority than are political protests. Despite these considerations, the Court in recent years has tolerated a number of restrictions on the circumstances surrounding such campaign speeches and advertisements. In so doing, the justices seem to be following

Justice Black's distinction between protecting the content of expression on the one hand, and on the other hand, establishing limitations on when, where, and how such expression may take place.

For example, two recent cases have recognized restrictions on *where* political speeches and advertisements may be delivered and displayed. In *Greer* v. *Spock* (1976), the Supreme Court upheld a ban imposed by the base commander of Fort Dix, New Jersey against the holding of political rallies and the distribution of campaign literature by minor-party candidates, including Dr. Benjamin Spock, on the grounds that the historical and traditional function of military bases has been to train soldiers, not to serve as a place for freedom of expression and assembly. In *Lehman* v. *City of Shaker Heights* (1974), the justices ruled that a municipal transit system had the right to refuse to sell placard space for a political advertisement to a candidate for the Ohio General Assembly even though the system allowed such space to be used for paid commercial advertisements. In so doing the Court reasoned that the acceptance of political advertisements could create problems for the city in allocating space among competing candidates so as to avoid the appearance of favoritism among them and could also subject the "captive audience" of commuters to the "blare of political propaganda."

The Supreme Court has also recognized the First Amendment right of the mass media to refuse to publish or broadcast comments by political candidates and party officials. In *Miami Herald Publishing Co.* v. *Tornillo* (1974), the justices declared invalid a Florida statute that granted political candidates the right to reply to adverse editorials, thus preventing a person running for the Florida House of Representatives from responding to a *Miami Herald* editorial criticizing him and endorsing his opponent. In so doing, the justices reasoned that such legislation would curtail rather than stimulate public debates by imposing an economic cost on a newspaper's decision to publish election editorials, and that it was unconstitutional for government to compel newspapers to publish that which "reason tells them should not be published." In a similar ruling, *Columbia Broadcasting System, Inc.* v. *Democratic National Committee* (1973), involving an attempt by the Committee to purchase time to comment on political issues and to solicit funds, the Court ruled that neither the First Amendment nor the Communications Act of 1934 requires radio and television to sell broadcasting time for editorial advertising.

Commercial Advertising

Interestingly enough, while the Court recently has been recognizing limitations on when, where, and how political speeches and advertising may be delivered and displayed, at the same time it has accorded commercial advertisements the same First Amendment status that had previously been granted to literary and political expression. In *Bigelow* v. *Virginia* (1975), involving the publication of an advertisement in a Virginia newspaper for abortions to be performed in New York, the Court ruled that the public interest in, and content of, an advertisement is important in determining the scope of its protection under the First Amendment. In striking down the Virginia statute prohibiting all advertising or other dissemination of information having the effect of encouraging an abortion, the Court emphasized the fact that the abortion was legal in New

York where it was to take place, and that the advertisement concerned the constitutional right to abortion (a matter we will analyze in the last section of this chapter), which gave it a stronger claim to constitutional protection.

In the following year in *Virginia State Board of Pharmacy* v. *Virginia Citizens Consumer Council, Inc.* (1976), the Court extended the principle of the Bigelow case in voiding another Virginia statute prohibiting the advertisement of prescription drug prices. Ruling that consumers and society as a whole have an interest in commercial advertising, the justices emphasized that such information is more than a convenience for the poor and aged who must shop carefully to conserve their incomes. The Court went on to say that the State of Virginia has no legitimate interest in keeping consumers in ignorance, and that if aggressive price competition (resulting from the advertising) threatens to bring a decline in the quality of drugs, such a result can be prevented by existing laws regulating such standards.

Obscenity

No civil-liberties issue in recent years has given the Supreme Court more difficulty than that described in the *Miller* case at the beginning of the chapter. Most of its members have agreed on the fundamental constitutional question (with the exception of Justices Black and Douglas, all have followed the rulings in two key 1957 cases, *Roth* v. *United States* and *Alberts* v. *California*, that obscenity is *not* protected under the freedom-of-speech principle); however, the justices have frequently disagreed over what materials are in fact obscene and the kinds of regulations that can be placed on the distribution and use of such materials.

One major issue has been the development of a satisfactory standard by which to judge obscenity. The test developed in the *Roth* and *Alberts* cases was "whether to the average person, applying contemporary community standards, the dominant theme of the material taken as a whole appeals to prurient interest." In other words, it is not sufficient that the material appeal to the lewd interest of a person especially sensitive to such matters or fail to appeal to a particularly insensitive person; rather, the attitudes and tastes of the *average* person are to be taken into account. Another important requirement of the *Roth-Alberts* standard is that one cannot focus on isolated passages of a film or piece of literary work to judge its obscenity; instead, it is necessary to look at the dominant theme of the entire work.

Another major issue in the area of obscenity concerns the value of the material in question. In a 1966 ruling, *Memoirs* v. *Massachusetts*, a plurality of the Court added a requirement to the *Roth-Alberts* standard: the work must be "utterly without redeeming social value" in order to be declared obscene. This naturally had a liberalizing effect on the obscenity problem since it is very difficult to prove that material has no social value whatever. Speaking for the Court in the *Miller* case, Chief Justice Burger specifically rejected that standard, substituting in its stead whether a work has "no serious literary, artistic, political, or scientific value." While this latter test takes a variety of types of consideration into account, it is easier to demonstrate that material has no serious value than it is to establish that it is entirely without value.

As we saw at the beginning of the chapter, another change in the law of obscenity enunciated in the *Miller* decision involves an interpretation of the

"The redeeming social value is there, all right—
it's the pornography that's weak."

word *community* in the phrase "contemporary community standards." For a number of years *community* was construed to mean the nation as a whole, but Chief Justice Burger changed that interpretation to mean a smaller geographical area; however the opinion is not clear whether the area is to be a state or a locality. In *Jenkins* v. *Georgia,* the Court seems to leave the area up to the trial court: the judge can instruct the jury to apply a statewide standard, but such an instruction is not mandatory, and hence *community* can be construed to mean the community from which the jurors come.

Some of the key cases indicate that the Court is willing to go beyond the above tests and look at the total situation in determining whether certain materials are obscene. In *Ginzburg* v. *United States* (1966) the Court not only examined the three works in question (*Eros* magazine, the newsletter "Liaison," and a book, *The Housewife's Handbook on Selective Promiscuity*), but also determined that the "leer of the sensualist" permeated the advertising for them, a practice the Court termed "pandering—the business of purveying textual or graphic matter openly advertised to appeal to the erotic interest of their customers." Two years later in *Ginsburg* v. *New York* (1968), the Court also indicated that the *audience* makes a difference in the obscenity issue: authorities can regulate the sale of materials to minors that would not be constitutionally permissible in dealing with adults.

One of the more puzzling aspects of recent obscenity cases has to do with the possession and distribution of obscene materials. In *Stanley* v. *Georgia* (1969), the Court held that authorities cannot prohibit a person from viewing obscene materials (in this case it was films) shown in the privacy of his own home. As the Court put it: "If the First Amendment means anything, it means that a State has no business telling a man sitting alone in his own home, what books he may read or what films he may watch." Yet in two 1971 cases decided the same day, *United States* v. *Reidel* and *United States* v. *Thirty-seven Photographs,* the Court ruled that Congress may constitutionally prevent the mails from being used for distributing obscene materials, and that it may also prohibit an individual from importing such materials from abroad even for his own private use. Thus the Court recognizes the right of a person to read or view obscene works in his own house but denies him the major means of obtaining them.

A basic controversy also exists over the reasons for attempting to establish controls over obscene materials. A 1970 Report of the Commission on Obscenity and Pornography (a group of private citizens appointed by President Lyndon Johnson to look into the matter) concluded that there was no empirical evidence that exposure to explicit sexual materials plays a significant role in the causation of social or individual harms such as crime, delinquency, sexual or nonsexual deviancy, or severe emotional disturbances. For these (and other reasons) the commission held that "there is no warrant for continued governmental interference with the full freedom of adults to read, obtain or view whatever such material they wish." However, President Nixon (who was in office when the commission's report was issued) repudiated the report and its recommendations as "morally bankrupt" and called on states to enact anti-obscenity laws. Moreover, in a 1973 case, *Paris Adult Theater* v. *Slaton,* Chief Justice Burger also expressly rejected the commission's reasoning in holding that "a sensitive key relationship of human existence, central to family life, community welfare, and the development of human personality can be debased and distorted by the crass commercial exploitation of sex"; he went on to suggest that "nothing in the Constitution prohibits a State from reaching such a conclusion and acting on it legislatively simply because there is no conclusive evidence or empirical data." Nor did the Chief Justice think it important that the theater had prevented juveniles from seeing the films involved and given adequate notice to adults concerning the nature of the films.

There is little question that the obscenity area constitutes a judicial thicket. Justice Burger himself has conceded that it is "an area where there are no eternal verities." Others have gone further: the late Justice Black once complained that "I can imagine no task for which this Court of lifetime judges is less equipped to deal," and in his dissent in the *Miller* case Justice Douglas opined: "There are no guidelines for deciding what is and what is not 'obscene.' The Court is at large because we deal with tastes and standards of literature." It remains to be seen how successful the Court will be in dealing with what former Justice Harlan referred to as "the intractable obscenity problem."

Rights of Newsmen

In recent years two major issues have emerged that bear on the rights and responsibilities of newsmen. One pertains to comments they make on public officials and public events; the other relates to their keeping certain information confidential from governmental officials. While both matters are of imme-

HIGH COURT CURBS
PUBLIC OFFICIALS
IN LIBEL ACTIONS

———

It Rules for New York Times
and 4 Negro Ministers in
Alabama Suit on Ad

———

DECISION IS UNANIMOUS

———

Says Malice Must Be Shown
—Opinion Likely to Aid
Press Freedom in South

diate concern to persons involved in the business of gathering and disseminating news, they also have a major impact on the free flow of information and the public's right to be informed.

The landmark case regarding the right of comment is *New York Times Company* v. *Sullivan* (1964). In that decision the Court overruled a libel judgment against the newspaper for printing a full-page advertisement by Negro clergymen, charging local officials in Montgomery, Alabama with conducting a "wave of terror" against civil-rights demonstrators. Although some of the material contained in the advertisement proved to be false, the Court held that the public officials could not recover damages because the printed statement was not made with "actual malice"—that is, with knowledge that it was false or with "reckless" disregard of whether it was false or not. In adopting this position, the Court reasoned that "debate on public issues should be uninhibited, robust, and wide-open, and that it may well include vehement, caustic, and sometimes unpleasantly sharp attacks on government and public officials." The Court went on to state that "the constitutional protection of freedom of speech and press does not turn on the truth, popularity, or social utility of the ideas and beliefs which are offered."

Subsequently the principle enumerated in *New York Times* v. *Sullivan* has been expanded to cover comments about a candidate for a public position (as well as someone serving in office). In *Rosenbloom* v. *Metromedia* (1971) the Court went a step further in holding that a radio station broadcasting news reports on the arrest of a person alleged to be involved in distributing obscene magazines could be sued for libel only if it were guilty of actual malice. The important point was not whether the person involved was a public or private figure, but whether he was involved in "an event of public or general interest." These decisions may well be construed as an adaptation of Professor Meiklejohn's approach on freedom of expression relating to public affairs.

Recently, however, the Court appears to be moving away from the latter focus on the nature of the reported event to an emphasis on the identity of the persons involved. It has held than an attorney (representing the family of a youth slain by the Chicago police) who was falsely called a Communist by a right-wing organization, need only prove negligence, not malice or recklessness, to recover damages. The Court applied the same rule to a socialite whose divorce was the subject of a *Time Magazine* story that she claimed contained some false statements. In both cases, the Court stressed that the individuals involved were not public figures who had chosen to run the risk of close public scrutiny, but private persons who had made no such choice.

While the news media have succeeded in expanding their right to comment on public affairs, they have not been granted the right to withhold confidential information, including the identity of their sources for such information, from grand juries looking into the commission of crimes. In three related cases involving newsmen who refused to divulge their sources of information involving the use of drugs and to activities of the Black Panthers (*Branzburg* v. *Davis, in re Pappas,* and *United States* v. *Caldwell*) five members of the Supreme Court in 1972, speaking through Justice White, stated: "We perceive no basis for holding that the public interest in law enforcement . . . is insufficient to overrride the consequential, but uncertain burden on news-gathering which is said to result from insisting that reporters, like other citizens, respond to relevant questions

put to them in the course of a valid grand jury investigation or criminal trial."
Representing the view of the minority was Justice Stewart who held: "The
Court's crabbed view of the First Amendment reflects a disturbing insensitivity
to the independent press in our society . . . the right to gather news implies . . .
a right to a confidential relationship between a reporter and his source . . . the
presence of confidentiality may be a necessary prerequisite to a productive
relationship between a newsman and his informants."

The conflict represented by the various Court opinions has been carried over
into the legislative arena. Some twenty states have granted newsmen the privilege under certain conditions to withhold information and their sources from
law-enforcement agencies. In recent sessions the Congress has also had under
consideration a number of bills designed to afford some sort of federal protection for newsmen. These measures have varied considerably; some would grant
an absolute privilege, while others would extend a qualified privilege applying,
for example, only to representatives of established newspapers or news-produc-
ing media (as contrasted to "underground" ones), or permitting reporters to
withhold only information received under an express promise of confidentiality.
Opinions also differ over the proper scope of the newsmen's privilege: should it
apply only against national law-enforcement agencies or should Congress pass
a law that would be available against state officials as well? Thus freedom of
expression remains one of the most vital civil-liberties issues in the United
States today. Another matter that has become increasingly important in recent
years is the right of privacy.

THE RIGHT TO PRIVACY

Of course, there is nothing new about the right of privacy. The late Justice
Frankfurter once referred to it as "the right to be left alone—the most comprehensive of rights and the right most valued by civilized man." Alan Westin, a
close student of the subject, associates it with a number of elements in American political philosophy—individualism, limited government, and the linkage
between private property and liberty that Madison borrowed from John Locke.
Morevoer, as we have already suggested, the right of privacy underlies some of
the basic Bill of Rights amendments protecting an individual's thoughts and
religious beliefs, his home, other property, and his person itself from arbitrary
imprisonment or even death at the hands of law-enforcement officials.

Rather, what is new is the Supreme Court's expanding the right of privacy
beyond its linkage with such traditional protections and granting it an independent status of its own. The leading case in which the Supreme Court indicated
its willingness to take this approach to the right of privacy is *Griswold* v. *Connecticut* (1965). In ruling that the State of Connecticut could not prohibit the
use of contraceptives by married couples, the majority of the Court enumerated
a right of marital privacy even though it conceded that none was specifically
provided in the Constitution. Justice Douglas spoke of "zones of privacy" created by various guarantees of the First, Third, Fourth, Fifth, and Ninth
amendments that help give such guarantees "life and substance": included is
that of marital privacy, which he claimed was older than the Bill of Rights.
Justice Goldberg preferred to locate this right in the due process clause of the
Fourteenth Amendment as one "so rooted in the traditions and conscience of

our people as to be ranked as fundamental"; he also noted that the Ninth Amendment provides that "the enumeration in the Constitution, of certain rights, shall not be construed to deny or disparage others retained by the people." Speaking in dissent, the late Justice Black voiced his usual sentiment for a literal interpretation of the Constitution: "I like my privacy as well as the next one, but I am nevertheless compelled to admit that government has a right to invade it unless prohibited by some specific constitutional provision."

The Court has since indicated its willingness to extend the reasoning of *Griswold* to the decision whether or not to have children. In *Eisenstadt* v. *Baird* (1972), the Court held that it was also unconstitutional to try to forbid the dissemination of birth control information and devices to unmarried persons. Speaking for the majority, Justice Brennan stated: "If the right of privacy means anything, it is the right of the individual, married or single, to be free from unwarranted governmental intrusion into matters so fundamentally affecting a person as the decision whether to bear or beget a child." A further extension of this same principle came in two 1973 decisions, *Roe* v. *Wade* and *Doe* v. *Bolton,* invalidating statutes of Texas and Georgia regulating abortions. In these decisions the Court reaffirmed the personal right of privacy enumerated in *Griswold* and *Eisenstadt* in ruling that during the first trimester of pregnancy the abortion decision is up to the woman and her attending physician. (The Court did say, however, that during the second trimester of the pregnancy, a state can regulate abortion to protect the mother's health, and in the stage after viability—when the fetus is potentially able to live outside the mother's womb—it can prohibit abortion because of the potentiality of human life.)

As might be expected, the abortion decision triggered opposition from clergymen, doctors, mothers, and others concerned with the moral, psychological, and physical aspects of the problem. The issue was also interjected in the 1976 presidential contest: Ellen McCormack, a Massachusetts housewife, entered several Democratic primaries as an avowed anti-abortion candidate; in the general election campaign, Jimmy Carter opposed a constitutional amendment on the issue, while Gerald Ford favored leaving the matter to regulation by the individual states. A number of states have also enacted new anti-abortion statutes tailored to take account of the Supreme Court decisions.* Thus the subject of abortion remained one of the most controversial issues in American society. *John C. Danforth, Attorney General* (1976).

However, while the Court was extending the right of privacy to cover some highly personal areas of an individual's life, it was ruling that others lay outside the scope of that right. For example, it has struck down a Georgia law allowing newsmen to be sued for publishing or broadcasting the name of a rape victim, ruling that states may not impose sanctions for the publication of truthful information contained in official court records open to public inspection (*Cox Broadcasting* v. *Cohn,* 1975). It has also refused to exempt from disclosure under the Freedom of Information Act summaries of honor-code cases of the Air Force Academy from which the names of cadets have been deleted (*Department of the Air Force* v. *Rose* 1976). In such cases, the right of privacy has given way to that of freedom of expression and information. The right of privacy and confidentiality of individual bank accounts was also recently denied by a Supreme Court decision (*U.S.* v. *Miller,* 1976), ruling that the government has the right to obtain records of checks and other transactions relating to

Ellen McCormack, anti-abortion candidate for President.

* However, major portions of one such statute passed by Missouri that provided for the consent of the father to the abortion as well as parental consent for abortions of women under 18 years of age were declared unconstitutional by the Supreme Court in *Planned Parenthood of Central Missouri v. John C. Danforth, Attorney General* (1976).

ASSESSMENT

For the most part, basic constitutional guarantees are in a healthy state in the United States today. While the Court has tolerated some breaches in the wall of separation between church and state, it has become increasingly strict about such matters as expending public funds for salaries of instructors in parochial schools and granting tuition reimbursements or tax credits to parents who send their children to such schools. Moreover, it has taken a definite stand against religious exercises in the public schools. The Court has also adopted a very liberal position on the rights of religious minorities to proselytize for their beliefs and to refuse to take actions contrary to

their beliefs, such as saluting the flag or sending their children to public schools beyond the eighth grade.

The area of freedom of expression has also been characterized by a considerable degree of forebearance on the part of the Court. It has interpreted congressional statues regulating communist activities so as to protect freedom of expression and has shown considerable toleration of political protests, including those directed against the Vietnam war. Its position that persons are liable only for such comments about public figures and events as are characterized by actual malice has encouraged a vigorous discussion of public affairs, as envisaged by Professor Meiklejohn.

There are some areas of freedom of expression, however, where the record of the Court is less impressive. Several of the rulings pertaining to campaign speeches and advertisements seem unduly restrictive of such activities. The Court did not indicate specifically how the holding of a political rally on a military base was incompatible with the normal activity of a specific part of that base at a particular time; also, its reasoning that it would be difficult to allocate political advertising space in a bus so as to avoid the appearance of favoritism seems strained (how does one then avoid similar charges of preferential treatment for certain commercial advertisements?), as does the argument that such ads would subject commuters to the "blare of political propaganda." Also, given the virtual monopoly that radio and television stations and many newspapers have over the dissemination of political information and opinions, it seems only fair that they be required to allow candidates and political parties to use their facilities to defend themselves and to present their own political views.

The Court also appears to have embarked upon a questionable course of action as far as obscenity is concerned. While one can certainly make a good argument that obscene materials should not be accorded as important a place as political expression in a free society, it seems futile as a practical matter for judges to try to determine what is or is not obscene; moreover, interpreting community standards to mean those of states or localities presents enormous problems in a society in which books and films are produced for and distributed to a national audience. Rather than trying to outlaw allegedly obscene material altogether, it would be better for the Court to allow communities to regulate them through such measures as restricting the materials to certain geographical areas where consenting adults would have to go to view them and where impressionable juveniles would not be exposed to them.

The ruling on the newsmen's privileges also seems unduly restrictive: physicians and lawyers, for example, are entitled to withhold from law-enforcement officials any confidential information that they gain from clients; also, the importance of protecting newsmen's sources is illustrated by the fact that a number of them have gone to jail in order to do so. At the least, the government should be compelled to show that the crime involved is a very serious one (such as murder) and that it cannot obtain the necessary information from any other source besides newsmen.

The student should keep in mind, however, that Supreme Court cases do not automatically bring about the actual practice of civil liberties. Legal rights must be implemented and become accepted by public officials and private citizens alike if they are to become effective. Moreover, as the following section indicates, the opportunity of participating in the political process does not necessarily mean that people will take advantage of the opportunity. It is to this general subject that we now turn.

SELECTED READINGS

One of the better histories of constitutional developments in the United States, including civil-liberties issues, is Alfred H. Kelly and Winifred A. Harbison, *The American Constitution: Its Origins and Development* (New York: Norton, 1976). The classic legal study of freedom of speech during the period from 1920 to 1940 is Zechariah Chafee, *Free Speech in the United States* (Cambridge: Harvard University Press, 1942). A broad social and political analysis of human rights in American from World War I until the early 1960s is found in John Roche, *The Quest for the Dream* (New York: Macmillan, 1963).

The historical evolution of church-state relations in the United States is treated in Alan Grimes, *Equality in America* (New York: Oxford University Press, 1964). Philip Kurland, *Religion and The Law* (Chicago: Aldine, 1962), analyzes Supreme Court cases pertaining to religion.

Two recent analyses of the role of the Supreme Court in free-speech cases and the approaches used to resolve such issues are Martin Shapiro, *Freedom of Speech: The Supreme Court and Judicial Review* (Englewood Cliffs, N.J.: Prentice-Hall, 1966), and Samuel Krislov, *The Supreme Court and Political Freedom* (New York: Free Press, 1968). Justice Black's views on free speech are contained in a compilation of his statements edited by Irving Dilliard under the title, *One Man's Stand for Freedom: Mr. Justice Black and the Bill of Rights* (New York: Knopf, 1963). Alexander Meiklejohn sets forth his opinion of freedom of expression in *Political Freedom: The Constitutional Powers of the People* (New York: Oxford University Press, 1965). A recent treatment of the subject is Thomas Emerson, *The System of Freedom of Expression* (New York: Random House, 1970).

The issues involved in the attempt to control alleged communist subversion in the United States in the late 1940s and early 1950s are treated in Harold Chase, *Security and Liberty: The Problem of Native Communists 1947-1955* (Garden City, N.Y.: Doubleday, 1955). Philosopher Sidney Hook sets forth his views on the difference between legitimate and illegitimate opposition in a free society in *Heresy, Yes, Conspiracy, No* (New York: John Day, 1953).

Paul Kauper discusses recent judicial trends in such areas as church and state, obscenity and censorship, and freedom of association in *Civil Liberties and the Constitution* (Ann Arbor: University of Michigan Press, 1962). Milton Konvitz treats these same First Amendment issues in his study, *Expanding Liberties: Freedom's Gains in Postwar America* (New York: Viking, 1966). A brief analysis of the problems posed by protests and demonstrations is contained in a book by former Supreme Court Justice Abe Fortas, *Concerning Dissent and Civil Disobedience* (New York: New American Library, 1968). For an excellent analysis of the obscenity issue, see Elliot Slotnick, "The Courts and Obscenity," which appears in Randall Ripley and Grace Franklin, eds., *National Government and Policy* (Itasca, Ill.: F. F. Peacock, 1977).

An excellent general analysis of the right of privacy is Alan Westin, *Privacy and Freedom* (New York: Atherton, 1967).

Supreme Court decisions are published in official volumes of the *United States Reports*. Until 1973, a brief yearly analysis of major decisions appeared in the December issue of *The Western Political Quarterly*. A more extended treatment of such cases is published each year in the November issue of *The Harvard Law Review*.

Political Novels Political freedom may best be appreciated when we observe the workings of a society in which it is absent. Such a system and its effect upon human beings is shown by Alexander Solzhenitsyn in a novel about life in a Soviet political prison, *The First Circle* (New York: Bantam, 1969).

A society so afraid of free thought as to require the burning of all books is described by Ray Bradbury in his science fiction novel *Fahrenheit 451* (New York: Ballentine, 1976).

The fragile balance between individual rights and the need for a society to protect itself, as well as the problems of implementing Supreme Court decisions, are shown by Joseph Waumbaugh in his realistic novels about police work, *The New Centurians* (New York: Dell, 1972), and *The Blue Knight* (New York: Dell, 1972).

In his story about an important obscenity trial Irving Wallace explores the relationship between free expression and censorship—*The Seven Minutes* (New York: Simon and Schuster, 1969). The importance of free speech and freedom of religion is shown very clearly by Jerome Lawrence and Robert E. Lee in their play *Inherit the Wind* (New York: Bantam, 1960).

POPULAR CONTROL

As we have seen in chapter 1, the most distinctive feature of democratic government is that citizens have a major voice in determining the public decisions that vitally affect their lives. In pure, direct democracy people arrive at those decisions themselves; however, in modern political units encompassing millions of individuals, responsibility for lawmaking must be vested in a small minority of the population, the political officeholders. The fundamental issue in a representative democracy thus concerns the amount and kind of influence that the general populace exercises over the policymaking of public officials.

One possible solution would be to maximize the influence of the mass over political decisions. In effect, the duty of those in public office would be to find out what the majority of the people want to do about a public issue—such as whether or not to place a special tax on large cars ("gas guzzlers")—and then enact their wishes into law. Representatives thus would act as the agents of the people by converting their sentiments into public policy. Such a process would require the average person to take an interest in, and be informed about, political matters and also to be rational enough to know what course of action should be taken to deal with the problems of his society. Given that condition, his wishes would be respected—and indeed courted—by those in public office.

At the opposite extreme, the public could play a minimal role in the enactment of governmental policy. Essentially, the people in a democracy would have only one task: to elect public officials and let them make major political decisions without being hamstrung by the opinions of the general populace. This view would be predicated on the belief that the mass of people has neither the interest nor the capacity to deal with political problems in any meaningful way. Therefore, those that have the interest and capacity—the ones who hold political office—should have no obligation to heed their desires.

Neither view fits the realities of the situation in the United States. Communication between the people and those who hold office is in fact a two-way process: the public presses certain demands on political decision makers and provides support for them and their actions; in turn, those in office respond to the demands of the people in some respects while also seeking their support to take initiatives of their own on public policy matters.

The following six chapters explore the nature of public attitudes on political issues and how such attitudes are channeled to political decision makers. Chapter 5 analyzes the general substance of the political views of citizens, how they are acquired, and the various outlets that exist for expressing attitudes through the political process. Chapter 6 focuses on the major means for expressing views between elections: the interest group. Chapters 7, 8, 9, and 10 examine the role that political parties and the electoral process play in conveying public preferences to political officials.

America's the greatest land of all.

Chapter 5

In the midst of the Watergate crisis in August 1973, the Senate Subcommittee on Intergovernmental Relations of the Committee on Government Operations contracted with a private public-opinion firm to undertake a study of public attitudes towards government. Over a ten-day period in mid-September, Louis Harris and Associates conducted personal interviews with a cross section of some 1600 Americans,* inquiring into their views on the responsiveness of government at the federal, state, and local level as well as soliciting their suggestions for increasing the responsiveness and efficiency of government at all levels. Simultaneously the staff of the subcommittee surveyed the attitudes of 68 state and 206 local officials in various parts of the country on the same topics. In December the findings of these surveys were reported in a 342-page document entitled *Confidence and Concern: Citizens View American Government,* the most comprehensive study of public attitudes towards government in the nation's history.

The most dramatic findings of the survey were the lack of satisfaction the American people expressed with general conditions in the country and their feeling that political leaders were unresponsive to their concerns. Fifty-three percent of the public agreed with the sentiment that "there is something deeply wrong in America today" compared with 39 percent who felt that way in 1968; by a 45-35 percent margin, Americans also expressed the view that "the quality of life" in the country had grown worse rather than improved in the last decade. The percentage of persons who agreed with the statement "what you think doesn't count much anymore" rose from 37 to 61 from 1966 to 1973, while those believing "people running the country don't really care what happens to you" increased from 36 to 55 percent. Particularly significant was the fact that these sentiments came from all segments of the American public—the old as well as the young, Southerners along with Easterners, upper-middle-class citi-

* The technique known as random sampling permits information to be obtained from a smaller number of persons (the sample) which is representative of the views of a larger group (the population). The important statistical principle involved is that each person in the population must have an equal chance of being chosen in the sample.

zens together with laborers, and city dwellers as well as those who lived on the nation's farms.

The survey also uncovered the particular concerns that were bothering Americans. Asked to name the two or three biggest problems facing the country they would like to see something done about, 72 percent mentioned the economy and inflation, 43 percent integrity in government, and 17 percent identified crime as a major issue of concern to them. When queried on the matter they would like to talk to the President about if they had a chance, three-fourths said "integrity of government and lack of confidence," one-half mentioned economic matters, while one in five expressed a concern with some foreign-policy matter.

The Harris study also revealed the public's disenchantment with the people running the nation's key public and private institutions. Since 1966 the number of persons expressing "a great deal of confidence" in leaders of the three branches of government, the military, colleges and universities, business concerns and organized labor declined precipitously. Of some twenty-two institutions and functions surveyed, only medicine and local trash collection received an affirmative vote from a majority of the American people!

Another major finding that emerged from the study was the tendency of the American public on the one hand, and state and local officials on the other, to view matters in an entirely different light. Only 35 percent of the former thought that the quality of life in America was improving, but 61 percent of the officeholders believed that it was. While 70 percent of the public felt that corrupt politicians are a real problem for most citizens, less than half of the officials did. Moreover, three in five Americans believed that the "inability of government to solve problems" is a high-priority matter, but only about a third of the government leaders shared that view. As we noted previously, this disparity in views between the political leaders on the one hand, and the mass of citizens on the other, raises fundamental questions of governance in a democratic society, questions with which we are concerned throughout this book.

Despite the general pessimism revealed by the survey, there were some bright spots in what Americans thought about the government and themselves. Most encouraging was the fact that more than 80 percent of the public thought that the "best people" could be brought into government, that a "concern for the general welfare" could dominate "special interests," and that public officials could be found dedicated both to "helping the country" and to "caring about the people." Moreover, not all institutions received the same degree of criticism: the number of persons expressing a great deal of confidence in people in charge of television news rose from 25 to 41 percent in the period from 1966 to 1973.

Subsequent developments, and the reactions of Americans to them, also indicated that the generally pessimistic attitudes expressed in the Harris study were not permanent. As the nation's economy improved and the memories of Vietnam and Watergate faded, our citizens became more optimistic. In a Gallup poll published in January 1977, 65 percent of Americans expressed satisfaction with the future facing themselves and their families, compared to 53 percent who expressed that sentiment in 1973. The same poll also showed that the percentage of persons predicting rising unemployment fell from 87 at the beginning of 1974 to 57 at the start of 1975, and further down to 37 as 1977 dawned.

Moreover, Americans became more confident about the nation's influence in international affairs: in early 1974, only 29 percent expected the United States to increase its power in the world during that year; in 1976, that figure rose to 42 percent; in 1977, it stood at 58 percent. Another study, done by Potomac Associates, also showed a rise between 1974 and 1976 in the proportion of Americans who expressed trust and confidence in the Office of the presidency. (The details of that study will be examined later in this chapter.)

Thus public attitudes on the state of the nation and its political institutions reflected the events and experiences through which the American people passed in the early and mid-1970s. Before examining that matter further, however, we need to explore the general nature of political attitudes, how people acquire them, and how such attitudes relate to political participation.

THE NATURE OF POLITICAL ATTITUDES

Viewed in the broadest sense, attitudes exist on a variety of matters that affect the operation of a political system. Most fundamental of all are the feelings that citizens have toward their country and their sense of identity with it. For example, a problem frequently encountered by new nations is the difficulty its members may find in giving up their primary loyalty to a tribe, region, or religious group with which they have been closely associated. Until a substantial portion of persons in a society feel a sense of community with their fellow citizens and believe that they should be part of the same overall political system, the delicate act of governing them will be difficult if not impossible.

Closely allied to this sentiment of national identity are basic attitudes persons have toward their political system—that is, whether they consider it the legitimate vehicle for making the decisions that will affect their lives. This, in turn, depends on their attitudes towards the constitutional order—the functions, procedures, and structures of their government—or what we have been calling the rules of the game. Important here are not only formal rules set forth in legal documents but informal agreements and understandings concerning what is proper and improper in the realm of politics.

The feelings people have toward government officials themselves also determine whether the public will accept their decrees as legitimate and binding. Again, public support, active or passive, of such decrees must exist if the political process is to be effective in a society. In a democracy like the United States, the selection of major public officials through free elections in which the mass of people participate, and the ease of removing and replacing the officials at reasonable intervals, provide a basis for general acceptance of their rule.

These basic attitudes that people hold towards their political system have been termed by political scientist Gabriel Almond a nation's "political culture," which he defines as "a particular pattern of orientation to political actions." More specifically, political culture refers to such fundamental beliefs as: (1) the ends or purposes of political activity, (2) the general nature of the political process, and (3) the part that individual citizens play in the process. The term is frequently used to include citizens' attitudes on how these basic elements of a political system *should* operate as well as their perception of how they work *in fact*. Viewed in this way, political culture is concerned with the "promise" and the "performance" of a political system as viewed by the people that live under that system.*

Below the level of political cutlure—that is, basic beliefs concerning the nation, the rules of the political game, and governmental leaders—there also exist public views toward matters that affect the day-to-day operation of the political system. In particular, people have ideas concerning the most important issues facing the nation and what policies the government should follow in dealing with these issues. They react to the personalities of candidates for office. They may also identify psychologically with particular groups, such as political parties or social, economic, or geographical divisions in the population and shape their attitudes on issues and candidates accordingly. These views, which are generally assumed to be less stable and enduring than political culture beliefs, are often referred to by political scientists as matters of "public opinion."

Whether one is speaking of political culture or public opinion, the important point is that these are attitudes of the general populace, not those of political leaders who, as previously indicated, often have strongly differing political views. (Such attitudes are referred to as elite political culture or elite opinion). But, of course, the number of persons having a view depends on the particular matter involved: most have basic attitudes concerning their nation and its political system, but fewer have definite opinions on what, if anything, the United States should do about the Arab-Israeli conflict. It would thus be more accu-

The candidate and the crowd.

* It should be understood that "political culture" refers to the *overall views of the general public;* there are often distinctive political attitudes held by blacks, chicanos, Southerners, Easterners, and the like, which are often referred to as political "subcultures."

rate to speak of not one "public," but rather a series of "publics," separate groups of people with views on different political matters.

But if the public does not include all citizens, it must involve enough persons to have an impact on the political process. Yet a public is not composed of any precise minimum number of opinion-holding individuals, because the effectiveness of opinions depends on how intensely they are held and the political resources and skills of those who hold them. V.O. Key's definition that public opinions are "those opinions held by private persons which governments find it prudent to heed" comes as close as possible to expressing the basic elements of the concept because it focuses on the influence of public attitudes on official decision making.

Ultimately, of course, the importance of "publics" in the political process depends not only on their size and resources, but also on the ways in which they channel their views to those in positions of political authority. Before turning to that topic, however, we need to examine the substance of individual political attitudes and the methods by which they are acquired.

THE FORMATION OF POLITICAL ATTITUDES

Teaching citizens proper attitudes and information about their government has long been a concern of political philosophers, as evidenced by Plato's views on the importance of civic education in the Greek city-state. Only very recently, however, have scholars begun to conduct empirical examinations into the ways in which individuals actually come to acquire their political attitudes. The learning process is called political socialization.

Like political culture, political socialization is given different meanings. Some persons equate it with the study of how children acquire their political attitudes. Others restrict political socialization to the acquisition of the prevailing values and beliefs of the society, not deviations from them. In other words, they focus on how leaders instill a respect for the status quo in citizens. Here, however, we will interpret political socialization more broadly to mean the process by which individuals acquire all kinds of political attitudes (unfavorable as well as favorable to the existing political system) over a period of time that includes adulthood as well as childhood. Moreover, we will look at not only the individual who acquires political attitudes but also the agencies that shape those attitudes.

The Development of Political Attitudes

Guided by theories of psychologists, psychiatrists, and sociologists that emphasize the crucial importance of the formative years in molding a person's attitudes and beliefs, students of political socialization have focused most of their attention on the development of political opinions in children. They find that people begin to develop some awareness of the political world when they are quite young.* This earliest political orientation generally takes the form of strong patriotic feelings toward their country, as children react favorably

* Most studies deal with school-age children, but some have discovered the beginnings of political attitude in preschoolers.

toward symbols like the flag. The political system itself is personified for them primarily by the major officials. They first become aware of government executives at the top and bottom levels of the system—at the national level, the President; at the local, the mayor or the policeman. The identity with the government, as with the nation itself, is generally positive; that is, children by and large look upon the President, mayor, or police chief as a "good" person who "helps" people and "gets things done." They also feel that they should respect and obey such persons. Thus a child's early orientation to the political system is essentially one of allegiance and support.

A young child is also inclined to find his own particular place in the political world that he has become aware of. In particular, he seeks to identify with a group, to associate himself with some persons in society—and to distinguish himself from others. He may form an early psychological attachment to a political party. Indeed, children as young as seven already regard themselves as Republicans or Democrats; they also come to think of themselves as white or black, rich or poor, Protestant or Catholic. These identifications with social and economic groupings, like those with political parties and the nation and its political system, have deep emotional underpinnings, and therefore they tend to persist throughout subsequent stages of a person's political life.

Later, as the average person approaches or enters his teens, his conception of the political world begins to change. He becomes more critical in his thinking and is less likely to think that the President, mayor, or police chief is all-benevolent and all-powerful. These figures no longer personify his view of the political system as they did; for example, the older child is able to disapprove of a particular individual serving as President without necessarily losing respect for the office itself. He is also aware that Presidents and mayors share the running of the government with other groups, such as the Congress, the Supreme Court, and the local city council. He also adds the state level of government to his view of the political system. Furthermore, he begins to develop some notion of what concepts like "democracy" and "communism" mean, though typically his views on such matters are superficial or, in many instances, erroneous.

Towards the end of childhood, an individual becomes even more politically sophisticated. He begins to associate differences with being a Republican and a Democrat, particularly in terms of the social and economic groups (business, labor, rich, poor, black, white) that each party favors. He also develops reactions to political personalities. Moreover, public policy issues, particularly those of a general nature, like race relations and international conflicts, become matters of concern to the older child. In addition, he may have ideas how such problems should be handled by those in public office. He may also develop a better understanding of democracy and its procedures—majority rule, minority rights, and the like.

Information on the political socialization of adults is sparse. We have no studies of particular individuals over a long period of time that enable us to spell out in any detail how political attitudes of persons change after they reach maturity. What evidence is available indicates that political learning continues as the individual is exposed to new experiences in life, such as getting a job, raising a family, moving to other areas of the country, or associating with people and groups that differ from those he previously knew.

Thus political socialization is a developmental process. In the early years, a person's political orientation is general, positive, and based on strong emotional attachments toward nation, government, and officials. Later on, as a person becomes more knowledgeable and discriminating, he may develop expectations of what public officials should do about particular social issues. In short, his attitude toward political leaders changes from offering unqualified support to making demands.

This is not to suggest, however, that all persons follow this pattern. For example, studies have found that black and chicano children, as well as white children from Appalachia, a region characterized by poverty and physical isolation, are less favorably disposed toward the nation's political leaders than are middle-class white children from affluent suburban areas. Moreover, people do not acquire political attitudes at the same pace: children from wealthier and better-educated families are more knowledgeable and discriminating about political matters than are those of a similar age from poorer circumstances. As a rule, boys develop political interests and sophistication faster than girls do; young people of both sexes with high IQs politically outdistance their less intelligent classmates. Nor are people's eventual level of development the same. Some never proceed past the early stage of generalized emotional attitudes towards the political system, while others develop a keen interest in trying to analyze political issues and events objectively.

It is difficult to determine precise reasons for differences in the development of political opinions of various individuals. One obvious factor, however, is the variation in associations with the key social groups that shape political orientations.

Agencies Affecting Political Opinions

A vast number of influences affect a person's political opinions. Some of them, like the family, are felt early in life, while others, such as work groups, affect political orientation as an adult. Some of the agencies of political socialization are primary groups in which a person has close face-to-face relationships with the same individuals over a considerable length of time—again, the family is the prime example. Others are secondary groups like labor unions or employers' associations, in which contacts among members are more limited and frequently involve not a continuing common core of individuals but rather a range of different persons over time.

Family. By far the most potent group in shaping individual political attitudes is the family. It exercises its major effect on a person during his most impressionable years, he has his closest emotional ties with it, and it influences his political attitudes during the time when other agencies have not yet begun to affect them. In fact, the family enjoys a near-monopoly over a person's political attention during his early years in life.

The family shapes the most basic aspects of a person's political opinions. A child who respects his parents is inclined to transfer this feeling to other authorities outside the family, such as the President. He will also imitate his parents' political opinions and behavior: if they think and speak well of the President, the child too will tend to favor him. Parents who do not hold the

Chief Executive in high regard may keep their adverse feelings to themselves to avoid undercutting the child's respect for authority. If so, their child also will develop a favorable image of the President.

Parents also affect another basic feature of the child's early political attitudes: his identification with a political party, as well as with social and economic groups. Young children are likely to identify with the same political party as their parents, particularly if the parents share strong partisan attachments. If there is a difference of opinion between the two parents about political parties, then their children may avoid the delicate problem of choosing between the mother's and father's views by declaring themselves political independents. Children also acquire from their parents a sense of identity with religious, racial, or social groups and so learn to think of themselves as Jews, blacks, or laboring-class people.

While parents have a major influence on the political attitudes of their children, a major study of high school seniors by political scientists M. Kent Jennings and Richard Niemi points up the limitations of that influence. Many parents do not consciously try to shape the views of their offspring and are often unaware what such views actually are. The degree of transfer of political attitudes from one generation to another depends upon the particular object of such attitudes: concrete matters like partisan affiliation, which are also meaningful for most persons on a constant, long-term basis, are more likely to be successfully transmitted than are more abstract ideas such as the characteristics of a good citizen or a transient political issue like prayer in the public schools. Moreover, even the transfer of partisan affiliation suffers when the two parents have different party preferences. Finally, as the child grows older, other influences begin to shape his views on political matters.

Public Schools. Another major organization that shapes political attitudes is the public school, which like the family has its major impact during the early years of a person's life. One of the major reasons why societies establish schools is to transmit values to the young; therefore teachers instill in students favorable attitudes toward their country and government. Thus symbolic exercises like saluting the flag, singing patriotic songs, and honoring the nation's heroes engender positive feelings toward the nation and its system of government. Teachers, like parents, try to develop a respect for authority, and children are inclined to transfer their respect of classroom supervisors to political leaders.

There are, however, some major differences in the shaping of political attitudes between the home and school. In the interest of maintaining good relationships with all kinds of parents, teachers are generally careful not to appear to favor one political party over another. If the schools are to fulfill the function of promoting harmony among children from various kinds of economic and social backgrounds (as many people feel they should), then teachers must also strive to avoid partiality toward any such groups. Thus unlike the family, schools do not generally shape a child's orientation toward his particular niche in the political world.

In the secondary and high schools the curriculum typically contains instruction in civics or the problems of democracy. Yet such courses often have relatively little impact on the political opinions of most students, partly because by the time a student takes such courses his basic political attitudes are already formed, and most of the material presented in such courses is redundant for them. Even so, children who have not been exposed to political matters in the home (most likely those from minority groups and the poor and uneducated in general) may be influenced about their duty to vote and to respect the rules of the democratic game regarding the toleration of opposing viewpoints, and about how to make their wishes known to those in positions of authority.

Other factors besides the curriculum shape students' political attitudes. Teaching techniques employed by particular instructors may have an impact: students acquire an understanding of the democratic process from the instructor who encourages debate and questioning in the classroom, in contrast to the authoritarian taskmaster who runs his classes with an iron hand. Extracurricular activities also influence political attitudes of students as they learn to govern themselves in voluntary clubs and organizations. The way in which principals and other school authorities treat children, and the kinds of rules and regulations developed by school boards regarding attire and personal appearance, affect students' attitudes toward authority in general and political authority in particular. The nature of the student body is also important: students from lower-class backgrounds are sometimes affected by the attitudes of their middle-class classmates on such matters as the importance of personal liberty and the duty to vote, as well as on the necessity for using other means besides voting to affect the political process. Thus the total social setting of the public school shapes political attitudes.

College. Many young people who go on to college (9.7 million were enrolled in American institutions of higher learning in the fall of 1975) experience a marked change in political attitudes. Colleges generally encourage a critical approach to problems, and courses are much less likely to defend the status quo than are those taught in the public schools. College faculties, particularly those in the social sciences, tend to be liberal in their political orientation (that is, they favor greater public concern with social problems in general and the plight of disadvantaged groups—blacks and the poor—in particular), and some students who come from politically conservative families are influenced by their values.

Other factors may be even more important in changing the political attitudes of college students. Going away from home is a major social dislocation for many students, for it involves breaking with families and the values learned from them and becoming exposed to ideas of other persons with backgrounds quite different from their own. Particularly important at this point is the influence of their peers—that is, their contemporaries. While peers, of course, shape students' political attitudes earlier than during the college years, classmates are particularly influential at this time because students live together and are in constant association with one another. This common situation of breaking with the past and of close physical proximity, in addition to easy communication among college students, is conducive to their forming distinct attitudes and values, including ways of looking at the political world.

Other Peer Groups. As he becomes an adult, a person's political attitudes may be influenced by other peer groups, such as churches, clubs and ethnic groups. The extent of that influence depends on a number of factors: how important political concerns are to the group; how closely its members agree on such matters; whether the individual himself thinks it is proper for the organization to be involved in political issues (some persons, for example, feel that churches should not take political stands); and how closely the individual identifies with the group. Thus a person who belongs to a politically active labor union composed of like-minded members, who approves of the activities, and who thinks of himself as a "union" man is likely to be strongly affected by the political beliefs of his fellow union members.

It is also possible for individuals to have their political attitudes shaped by groups to which they do *not* belong. Thus a white liberal who is sympathetic with the plight of the underdog in society may identify with the National Association for the Advancement of Colored People or with black groups in general, so that he favors government programs that benefit Negroes even though he personally does not benefit from them. Such groups are called reference groups, or sometimes reference symbols, because they provide guideposts from which individuals take their social and psychological bearings. Of course, reference groups or reference symbols can be negative as well as positive: the self-made businessman may be against a proposal that he believes will benefit labor unions or social welfare organizations because he has unfavorable images of such groups.

The Mass Media. Another agency in our society with a potential for shaping political opinions is found in the mass media, comprising television, radio, newspapers, and magazines. In fact, many political observers in the United States in recent years have expressed increasing concern that those who control the media may be able to manipulate political attitudes of the population at will, that Madison Avenue techniques projected over the tube result in a nation of political puppets. Undoubtedly, the mass media do have an appreciable effect on political attitudes—particularly in creating an interest in public affairs and in stimulating reactions to the personalities of candidates—but there are a number of built-in limits on the long-term influence of the media.

The CBS team.

One such factor is the nature of the messages carried by the media. Most television programs, for example, are nonpolitical. Advertisers who pay the high costs of television time want the maximum audience for their dollar; since most people are far more interested in being entertained than they are in being informed on public affairs, few programs with political content are sponsored by private companies or groups. Under regulations of the Federal Communications Commission, networks and individual stations themselves, of course, carry a certain amount of "public affairs" programs, but most of these are not controversial (such as the astronauts' trips to the moon), because the owners of the stations do not want to antagonize viewers and because they have an obligation to provide free "equal time" to those with opposing viewpoints. For these reaons, few stations have taken advantage of the opportunity provided by regulations of the Federal Communications Commission to carry editorial comments, instead confining their news broadcasts to fairly objective accounts of the facts of political developments.

In newspapers, as on television, much of the content is nonpolitical, for editors seek to avoid antagonizing their readers and advertisers. Although editorial pages print controversial viewpoints, relatively few readers examine these columns. (The comics, sports, social, and financial sections are likely to capture more interest.) Some news magazines, notably *Time, Newsweek,* and *U.S. News and World Report,* carry a great deal of political information, but the readership of such publications is fairly limited.

Even the minimal political content of the mass media has less effect on people than may be supposed. Communication depends, after all, not only on the messages sent but also on the messages received. Some persons screen out political information entirely because they have no interest in it; a television viewer, for instance, may turn off the set or turn his attention to other matters when political comments are carried on the air. Others select only the messages they want to hear: thus the liberal may read the *New Republic,* the conservative, the *Chicago Tribune.* Still others actually misperceive what they hear or read; they interpret an editorial or other political comment to mean what they want it to mean, not what the conveyer of the message is trying to say.

Students of the mass media have discovered something else that bears on their impact on political attitudes; there is often a "two-step" or "multi-step flow" in the communication process. That is, many messages do not reach the average citizen directly because he is not interested enough to expose himself to them; instead, they are transmitted to him indirectly via "opinion leaders" (party and interest-group officers or local "influentials" such as lawyers, doctors, bankers, and teachers) who are especially attentive to the media and who discuss their content with less-informed persons. In the process, of course, these transmitters alter the messages in keeping with their views and biases.

The end result of all the above factors is to minimize the independent influence of the mass media on individual political opinions, especially those that persist over a period of time. Those persons who pay the most attention to the media are the very ones who already have well-established political views; those with vague and insubstantial opinions that offer the greatest potential for change are least likely to expose themselves to whatever political content the media do carry.

As we have seen, however, there are some ways in which the media do influence political attitudes. The kind of image a political candidate or officeholder projects on television can affect voters' perceptions of his personality and character. Moreover, there are some dramatic events such as military combat scenes, civil rights demonstrations, or Congressional hearings that lend themselves especially well to visual presentation. Such presentations of events, particularly if they are recurrent ones, can shape the perceptions that individuals have of the world around them.

Political Events and Experience. We are by now aware that the developmental approach to political socialization focuses on the effects of various phases of the life cycle of an individual. In other words, one's political attitudes evolve as one progresses from an initial association—primarily with the family—to associations involving teachers and fellow students in public schools and colleges, and ultimately to adult contacts with fellow workers and other peers. However, this conception of the political socialization process leaves out another major influence in the formation of political views: political events and experiences.

There are indications that even the fundamental political beliefs of children are affected by what is happening in the general political world in which they live. A study by political scientist F. Christopher Arterton of three groups of children in the third through sixth grades of elementary school—the first group in school in 1962, the second in 1973, and the third in 1975—showed a great variation in their attitudes towards the American President. The first group, who were in the primary grades when John Kennedy was in the White House, expressed the traditional attitude that the Chief Executive is a benevolent figure who would help them if they needed it and that he would also protect them. The second group, who were in school in 1973 during the midst of Nixon's troubles, were much less inclined to think that the Chief Executive would take such helpful actions. The third group, who were students after Gerald Ford had succeeded to the presidential office, held an intermediate position on the issue: they were not as sure of the President's benevolence as were the 1962 students, but not as skeptical about it as the 1973 primary graders had been.

Another study by Roberta Siegel and Marilyn Brooks analyzed the political attitudes of students when they were in the fourth, sixth, and eighth grades in 1966, and then again in 1968, when they had advanced to the sixth, eighth, and tenth grades respectively. Interviews with the students indicated that during that two-year interval, several dramatic events, including the war in Vietnam, the assassination of Martin Luther King Jr., and the riots in Detroit (the area in which the study was conducted), were matters of great concern to them. The study found that individual students in 1968 were less inclined to think that the government, and particularly the President, were responsive and helpful to people than they had been two years earlier, a result that could be attributed to their additional maturity and/or the events described above. Moreover, a comparison of different groups of students who were in the same grades (fourth and sixth) in 1966 and 1968 respectively, showed the same results, which more clearly demonstrated the impact of the above-mentioned events, since the student groups in each of the two years were the same ages (The fourth-graders were nine years old, and the sixth-graders were eleven.) Interestingly enough, however, while students were more critical of government and of the President in 1968 than they were in 1966, they were also more politically involved, that is, they talked politics with friends and their family more in the latter year than in the former one. Thus political concern can affect political participation, a matter that we will explore in the last section of this chapter.

In addition to doing so in the early childhood years, political events have a marked effect on individuals during pre- and early adulthood (usually considered age 17–25). Political scientists and sociologists refer to age "cohorts" (groupings) that share prominent and significant political experiences during those impressionable years as constituting a political generation. Thus persons who were between 17 and 25 years of age during the period of economic distress from 1929 to 1935 are frequently referred to as the "Depression" generation. Similar generations are identified with other dramatic events, such as the Vietnam war and the Watergate scandals. Such experiences are thought to have lasting effects on persons living through them. Thus persons who grew up in the 1930s are especially sensitive to economic problems and tend to vote Democratic because they associate the Depression with Herbert Hoover and the Republican party, crediting Democrat Franklin Roosevelt with leading the United States out of those difficulties. It remains to be seen whether the Vietnam and Watergate experiences will have similar long-term effects on the attitudes of the political generations associated with them.

Finally, even though the political attitudes of adults are considered to be generally more established and stable than those of young children and young adults, persons over age 25 are also affected by political events and experiences. As we saw at the beginning of this chapter, the Americans whose views were elicited in the 1973 Harris poll (most of whom were adults) expressed much more pessimistic views about general conditions in the United States and the responsiveness of our political leaders than had been voiced in similar polls seven years earlier. Thus political attitudes of adult citizens concerning even such basic matters as the state of the nation and its major political officials are subject to change as a result of dramatic and significant political events.

Political events vary in the extent to which they affect the political attitudes of persons of different ages. A major study by Jennings and Niemi of the political views of high school seniors on the one hand, and of their parents on the other, over the period from 1965 to 1973 revealed that some events affected the two generations similarly, while others had a different impact. For example, both groups reacted similarly to the issue of the role of the federal government in school desegregation: they were less likely in 1973 than they had been in 1965 to think the federal government should help to integrate the schools, an attitude that the authors attribute mainly to the busing controversy. On the other hand, the views of the two generations differed on whether prayers should be allowed in the public schools: the seniors were more inclined than their parents to say no in 1965, and the differences between the two generations on that issue were even more pronounced eight years later. Jennings and Niemi attribute this difference to the fact that the high school seniors were socialized in a more secular era than that in which their parents came of political age.

Thus political attitudes of individuals are shaped by three major factors. One is life cycle, the various stages of life—early family relations, school, college, work—through which one passes. Another is political generation influences, the outstanding political events experienced during the pre- and young adult

*"That's the worst set of opinions I've heard
in my entire life."*

Drawing by Weber; © 1975 The New
Yorker Magazine, Inc.

years. The third is period effects, events that have a similar impact on persons
of all ages. Together these factors mold the political attitudes of all of us.

POLITICAL ATTITUDES OF AMERICAN CITIZENS

Although we have not determined with any precision how political views
change over the course of a lifetime, we can analyze the general nature of the
views held by Americans. As previously suggested, attitudes exist on a variety
of political subjects, including basic orientations toward the nation and to the
government and public officials that are vital to the very existence of a political
system. Public reactions to the vital issues of the day also shape the public
policies political leaders develop to meet them. The remainder of this chapter
and all of chapter 6 treat those aspects of public opinion that affect the everyday operation of our government. Attitudes toward political parties, social and
economic groups, and political personalities that relate closely to the periodic
electoral process are discussed in later chapters.

Attitudes Toward the Nation

The strong sense of loyalty to the nation that children in the United States develop very early in their lives persists in adulthood. A nine-nation survey taken by Gallup-affiliated organizations in 1971 indicated that fewer Americans (12 percent) than citizens of the other nations who were questioned said they would like to settle in another country.* (The countries Americans would most like to go to were Australia, Canada, Great Britain, and Switzerland; the group most desirous of emigrating were persons with college training between the ages of 18 and 29.) Moreover, a Gallup poll taken in early July of 1973 after the Watergate revelations found that 74 percent of the American people gave the United States a "highly favorable" rating. Three years later, in November 1976, that figure had risen to 85 percent.

Attitudes Toward the American Political System

Surveys of public attitudes taken in the United States, Great Britain, West Germany, Italy, and Mexico during 1959 and 1960 by Gabriel Almond and Sidney Verba also reflect the favorable opinion Americans have of their government. When asked what things about their country they were most proud of, 85 percent of those questioned in the United States cited some feature of their political system, such as the Constitution, political freedom, or democracy. By way of comparison, only 46 percent of the Britons, 7 percent of the Germans, 3 percent of the Italians, and 30 percent of the Mexicans prized aspects of their government or political tradition. As indicated by Table 5.1, citizens of these nations were more inclined than Americans to emphasize other aspects of their national life.

A Gallup Poll taken in mid-1973 confirmed the above attitudes. When asked what they would tell foreign visitors was the "best thing about the United States," Americans responded by citing features related to "democracy" and "freedom" as their main preferences. A middle-aged electronics engineer said: "The freedom of opportunity in this country impresses me most—no matter what state or station in life you're born into, there's an opportunity to move out of it." That same sentiment was expressed three years later in a 1976 Gallup poll by a 65-year-old retired farmer who said: "I do not know of another country that has as much to offer its people as the United States. I think the opportunity to better ourselves is here if we wish to put forth the effort to do so. All it takes to be successful in this country is to be willing to work."

The general attitudes evinced toward our political system raise a related concern: to what extent does the American public subscribe to the basic tenets of democracy discussed in Chapter 1? Are there any differences among our citizens in such matters?

Attitudes Toward Democratic Principles and Values

It will be recalled that democracy is based on certain operating principles. In particular, as it has developed in Western nations like the United States, de-

* The percentages in the other countries were: Great Britain, 41; Uruguay, 32; West Germany, 27; Greece, 22; Finland, 19; Sweden, 18; Brazil, 17; the Netherlands, 16.

			Nation		
Characteristic	U.S.	U.K.	Germany	Italy	Mexico
Governmental, political institutions	85	46	7	3	30
Social legislation	13	18	6	1	2
Position in international affairs	5	11	5	2	3
Economic system	23	10	33	3	24
Characteristics of people	7	18	36	11	15
Spiritual virtues and religion	3	1	3	6	8
Contributions to the arts	1	6	11	16	9
Contributions to science	3	7	12	3	1
Physical attributes of country	5	10	17	25	22
Nothing or don't know	4	10	15	27	16
Other	9	11	3	21	14
Total percentage of responses*	158	148	148	118	144
Total percentage of respondents	100	100	100	100	100
Total number of cases	970	963	955	995	1,007

Table 5.1
Sources of National Pride (Responses by Nation in Percentages)

* Percentages exceed 100 because of multiple responses.

Source: Gabriel Almond and Sidney Verba, *The Civic Culture* (Princeton: Princeton University Press, 1963), p. 102.

mocracy employs certain techniques and procedures of governance. Included among them are the concepts of majority rule and minority rights. Thus the question arises whether American citizens really believe in these two basic principles.

We have limited information on the subject, but one study of citizen attitudes in two cities—Ann Arbor, Michigan and Tallahassee, Florida—made a number of years ago by two political scientists, James Prothro and Charles Grigg, indicated overwhelming public support for both principles. A sample of registered voters in each of these communities was asked whether every citizen should have an equal chance to influence public policy; they were also questioned about whether they agreed with the statements that the minority should be free to try to win majority support for these opinions. The rate of agreement on these statements ranged from 94.7 to 98 percent.

Agreeing on abstract principles is one thing; applying the principles to particular situations is another. When the citizens of the two cities were asked their opinion toward a number of concrete questions that required them to make such an application, the responses shown in Table 5.2 resulted. The table shows that on none of the ten statements does agreement on the democratic responses reach the 90 percent figure that was associated with the four more abstract principles pertaining to majority rule and minority rights. On only three statements (3, 7, and 9) do three-fourths or more of the respondents agree on the democratic response.

At the same time, the table indicates that the responses of the voters to the questions vary with education and income as well as with the community in which they live. Persons with more education and income in both cities tended

Table 5.2
Percentage of
"Democratic"
Responses to Basic
Principles of
Democracy among
Selected Population
Groups

Statements	Total N = 244	Education† High N = 137	Education† Low N = 106	Ann Arbor N = 144	Talla- hassee N = 100	Income ‡ High N = 136	Income ‡ Low N = 99
Majority Rule							
1. Only informed vote*	49.0	61.7	34.7	56.3	38.4	56.6	40.8
2. Only taxpayers vote*	21.0	22.7	18.6	20.8	21.2	20.7	21.0
3. Bar Negro from office*	80.6	89.7	68.6	88.5	66.7	83.2	77.8
4. Bar Communist from office*	46.3	56.1	34.0	46.9	45.5	48.9	43.0
5. AMA right to bloc voting**	45.0	49.6	39.2	44.8	45.5	45.5	44.4
Minority Rights							
6. Allow antireligious speech**	63.0	77.4	46.5	67.4	56.6	72.8	52.1
7. Allow socialist speech**	79.4	90.2	65.7	81.3	76.8	83.8	73.7
8. Allow Communist speech**	44.0	62.9	23.5	51.4	33.3	52.2	36.7
9. Bar Negro from candidacy*	75.5	86.5	60.2	85.6	58.0	78.6	71.1
10. Bar Communist from candidacy*	41.7	48.1	30.3	44.1	38.2	44.8	34.4

* For these statements disagreement is recorded as the "democratic" response.

** For these statements agreement is recorded as the "democratic" response.

† "High education" means more than 12 years of schooling; "low education," 12 years or less.

‡ "High income" means an annual family income of $6000 or more; "low income," less than $6000.

Source: James Prothro and Charles Grigg, "Fundamental Principles of Democracy: Bases of Agreement and Disagreement," *Journal of Politics* 22 (1960): 285.

to give more democratic responses than did less educated and less affluent persons, as did residents of the northern city as a whole in comparison with those in the southern community. Of the three factors, education was the most important in differentiating between respondents. Yet even the more highly educated voters achieved the 90 percent figure on only one statement (7), and on three propositions (2, 5, and 10), less than half gave the democratic response.

Another survey of democratic attitudes of a nationwide sample of American adults conducted by Herbert McClosky generally confirmed the findings of Prothro and Grigg. In none of the twelve specific statements submitted to them relating to democratic rules of the game (principles of fair play, respect for legal procedures, and the rights of others) did the national sample achieve a 75 percent level of agreement. However, when McClosky put the same questions to a sample of 3000 political influentials drawn from the delegates and alternates who attended the Democratic and Republican presidential nominating conventions in 1956, he found that they achieved a 75 percent agreement on eight of the twelve specific statements.

McClosky also tested the attitudes of the general public and the political influentials toward a major value of democratic society—equality. As with his analysis of beliefs in the democratic rules of the game, he developed a list of concrete statements that required the respondents to apply the principles of political, social, and economic equality to specific situations. Table 5.3, which gives the responses of the two groups, indicates that neither members of the general public nor the political influentials achieved much agreement on these statements relating to political, social, and economic equality. Compared to the public, the influentials tended to take more equalitarian stands on political and social matters but were less likely to support the idea that the government should mitigate economic inequalities by providing the basic necessities of life for all individuals.

Items	Percentage Agreeing	
	Political Influentials (N = 3020)	General Electorate (N = 1484)
Political Equality		
The main trouble with democracy is that most people don't really know what's best for them.	40.8	58.0
Few people really know what is in their own best interest in the long run.	42.6	61.1
"Issues" and "arguments" are beyond the understanding of most voters.	37.5	62.3
Most people don't have enough sense to pick their own leaders wisely.	28.0	47.8
It will always be necessary to have a few strong, able people actually running everything.	42.5	56.2
Social and Ethnic Equality		
We have to teach children that all men are created equal but almost everyone knows that some are better than others.	54.7	58.3
Just as is true of fine race horses, some breeds of people are just naturally better than others.	46.0	46.3
Regardless of what some people say, there are certain races in the world that just won't mix with Americans.	37.2	50.4
When it comes to the things that count most, all races are certainly not equal.	45.3	49.0

Table 5.3
Political Influentials versus the Electorate: Responses to Items Expressing Belief in Equality

Table 5.3 *(continued)*

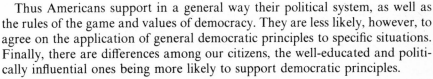

The trouble with letting certain minority groups into a nice neighborhood is that they gradually give it their own atmosphere.	49.8	57.7
Economic Equality		
Labor does not get its fair share of what it produces.	20.8	44.8
Every person should have a good house, even if the government has to build it for him.	14.9	28.2
I think the government should give a person work if he can't find another job.	23.5	47.3
The government ought to make sure that everyone has a good standard of living.	34.4	55.9
There will always be poverty, so people might as well get used to the idea.	40.4	59.4

Source: Herbert McClosky. "Consensus and Ideology in American Politics," *The American Political Science Review* 58 (June 1964): 369.

Thus Americans support in a general way their political system, as well as the rules of the game and values of democracy. They are less likely, however, to agree on the application of general democratic principles to specific situations. Finally, there are differences among our citizens, the well-educated and politically influential ones being more likely to support democratic principles.

Attitudes Toward Political Leaders

Traditionally, Americans have tended to maintain the faith in public officials that they originally acquired in childhood. For example, 83 percent of the Americans questioned in the five-nation survey mentioned above expected to be treated as well as anyone else if they had to take a tax-regulation or housing problem to the government office concerned. The same question drew the following percentages of similarly favorable responses from the citizens of the other four countries: Great Britain, 83; Germany, 65; Italy, 53; and Mexico, 42. Thus only the British expressed as much confidence in their public officials.

However, public opinion polls taken in recent years have shown a steady erosion in the confidence and trust that Americans have in their political leaders. Surveys conducted over a seven-year period by Louis Harris and Associates show a dramatic increase in a sense of alienation and powerlessness felt by the American people. As we can see in Table 5.4, almost twice as many people experienced these general feelings (as evidenced by their replies to four key questions) in 1973 as did in 1966.

A similar poll taken in 1976 by Harris showed a continuation of the above trend. This time 77 percent agreed with the statement, "The rich get richer and the poor get poorer," and 64 percent with, "What you think doesn't count much any more." Moreover, 63 percent concurred with the assertion, "Most

Agree with Statement	1973	1972	1971	1968	1966	Change 1966– 1973
The rich get richer and the poor get poorer	76	68	62	54	45	+31
What you think doesn't count much anymore	61	53	44	42	37	+24
People running the country don't really care what happens to you	55	50	41	36	26	+29
Feel left out of things going on around you	29	25	20	12	9	+20
Average feeling alientated and powerless	55	49	42	36	29	+26

Table 5.4
Trend in Alienation and Powerlessness Felt by the American People (Expressed in Percentages)

Source: U.S. Congress, Senate, Subcommittee on Intergovernmental Relations of the Committee on Governmental Operations, *Confidence and Concern: Citizens View American Government: A Survey of Public Attitudes,* 93d Cong., 1st sess., 3 December 1973, pt. 1:30.

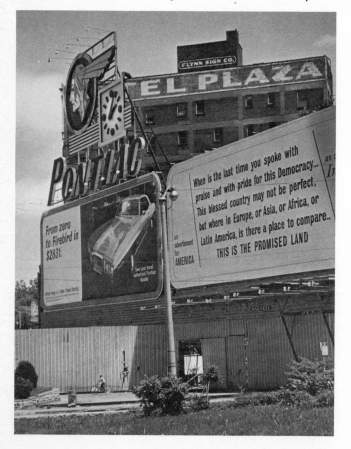

people with power try to take advantage of people like yourself," and 74 percent with "The tax laws are written to help the rich, not the average man."

Other evidence on public attitudes towards the leaders of some of the nation's major political and private institutions is provided by recent polls taken by Potomac Associates. In such surveys, Americans were asked to indicate how much trust and confidence they had in the leaders of a variety of our basic institutions; scores were then computed on a scale from 0 to 100, with "none at all" assigned a 0 score; "not very much," 33 points; "a fair amount," 67 points; and "a great deal," 100 points. Table 5.5 shows the composite scores for each of the matters about which our citizens were questioned in 1972, 1974, and 1976.

The information contained in Table 5.5 does add some support to the pessimistic findings of the Harris polls. Public trust and confidence declined significantly from 1972 to 1976 in the federal executive and legislature as well as in the federal government's handling of international and domestic affairs. Meanwhile, only two institutions—the mass media and state government—showed an actual increase in public trust and confidence between 1972 and 1976, and those increases were not statistically significant.

Table 5.5
Public Trust and
Confidence
(Composite Scores)

	1972	1974	1976
1. American people	*	71	70
2. Military leadership	*	*	68
3. Young people	67	69	67
4. American system	*	68	66
5. Mass media	60	60	62
6. State government	60	64	61
7. FBI	*	*	60
8. Federal judiciary	60	62	59
9. Local government	57	61	57
Politicians	58	58	57
11. Federal legislature	62	59	55
Federal executive	67	45	55
13. Business and industry	55	54	54
14. Government officials generally	*	50	53
Federal government (International)	66	67	53
16. Federal government (Domestic)	61	52	50
17. CIA	*	*	48
18. Labor unions	47	51	45

* not asked

Source: Francis Rourke, Lloyd Free, and William Watts, *Trust and Confidence in the American System* (Washington, D.C.: Potomac Associates, 1976), p. 11.

However, as the authors of the Potomac Associates' study point out, their findings are not as negative as those of Harris. Only two of the eighteen institutions about which Americans were questioned received less than a 50 percent score—the CIA in 1976 and labor unions in 1972 and 1976, with only the latter being significantly below the 50 percent mark. Moreover, unlike the Harris poll findings that showed a continuous increase in the alienation of Americans and their feeling of powerlessness, those of Potomac Associates reveal fairly stable attitudes on most of the eighteen objects of inquiry from 1972 to 1976, and a significant increase in the public's rating of the federal executive between 1974, the last year of the Nixon presidency, and 1976, the second year of Gerald Ford's term in office. Finally, the American system, our young people, the leadership of the armed forces,* and the American people themselves all received relatively high ratings in the Potomac Associate surveys.

Attitudes On Policy Issues and Personalities

Among political attitudes, those on policy issues and personalities change the most rapidly. For example, a survey taken in 1964 by the Institute for International Social Research showed that the five matters of greatest concern to Americans were: (1) keeping the country out of war; (2) combating world communism; (3) keeping our military defense strong; (4) controlling the use of nuclear weapons; and (5) maintaining respect for the United States in other countries. It should be noted that all of these matters concerned foreign and military policy; none involved a domestic problem.

Over the years since 1964, public perceptions of issues facing the American people changed considerably. By 1968, surveys of the same institute showed that concern with domestic issues had increased, so that two major problems—maintenance of law and order, and inflation and the cost of living—were among the five issues that bothered Americans the most. In mid-1972 a study by Potomac Associates indicated that the four matters of greatest concern to Americans—rising prices and the cost of living, violence, drugs, and crime—were all domestic ones. (Vietnam rated in fifth place in the survey.) An identical survey taken by the same organization in the spring of 1974 indicated that sixteen domestic problems (including "collecting and disposing of garbage, trash, and other solid wastes") concerned Americans more than the most salient foreign-policy issue—"keeping our military and defense forces strong." A similar 1976 Gallup poll that asked Americans what the biggest problem facing our nation was found that nine domestic matters (headed by the high cost of living and unemployment) bothered Americans more than did defense spending, the foreign-policy issue that evoked the greatest concern.

Dramatic events can change public perceptions even more rapidly. Surveys conducted by Louis Harris and Associates in 1972 and again a year later showed that the percentage of Americans naming "integrity in government" as one of the two or three biggest problems facing the country jumped from 5 to 43 percent; meanwhile, "taxes" as an issue fell from 40 to 11 percent, and "the

* One of the problems of many surveys is that the particular phraseology of a question may affect public responses to it. Thus a survey undertaken by Proctor and Gamble showed that some two-thirds of Americans had a "great deal of confidence" in the Army, Navy, and Air Force, 48 percent had high confidence in the military, and 21 percent were positive towards "military leaders."

war in Indo-China" from 29 to 4 percent. Even more dramatic was the alteration in public concern with the energy problem: it rose from none to 10 percent between the first and second Harris surveys, and in a Gallup Poll taken in early 1974 it was named by almost half of all Americans as the most important problem facing the country.

Also variable was the public response to President Ford's performance in office. As indicated by Figure 5.1, the percentage of Americans approving his handling of the job fell from 71 percent who regarded his performance favorably one week after taking office in August 1974 to 37 percent who felt the same way about him in January 1975, shortly before he delivered his first State of the Union Message. As the figure shows, after Ford pardoned former President Nixon, the new President's ratings fell 16 points. Economic conditions also contributed to the decline in President Ford's popularity in the early months of his presidency. On the other hand, his ratings rose 11 percentage points in May 1974, after he sent marines to rescue the *Mayaguez* and its crew when it was seized by the Communist government of Cambodia. Another possible factor affecting the upswing in the President's popularity was the fact that he was in the midst of a European trip at the time.

These, then, represent the kinds of public attitudes that exist in the United States on a broad range of political matters. However, having an attitude on such a matter is one thing; doing something about it politicallly is another. As the following section indicates, some people undertake a variety of political activities, while others take little or no part in public affairs.

POLITICAL PARTICIPATION

In a sense, everyone participates in the political process since each is subject to laws and commands of political officials that may require such things as payment of taxes, performance of jury duty, or, service in the armed forces. However, political participation is generally used by political scientists to include, as Herbert McClosky suggests, "those voluntary activities by which members of a society share in the selection of rulers and directly or indirectly, in the formation of public policy."

Forms of Political Participation

Political involvement may take many forms. Two recent students of the subject, Sidney Verba and Norman Nie, divide citizen participation into four major types of acts, or what they term "modes": (1) *voting,* which is the most widespread and regularized activity; (2) other kinds of *campaign activities,* such as working for, or contributing money to, a party or candidate; (3) *citizen-initiated contacts* with government officials, in which a person acts on a matter of concern to him; and (4) *cooperative activities,* which involve group or organizational activity by citizens to deal with social and political problems.

Verba and Nie also point out that these four basic modes of political activity possess different characteristics. For example, voting involves political conflict in the sense of a choice between competing candidates, seeks some collective outcome such as broad social policies for dealing with problems of concern to many persons, and requires little initiative on the part of the citizen. In contrast, citizen-initiated contacts typically do not involve conflict with other citi-

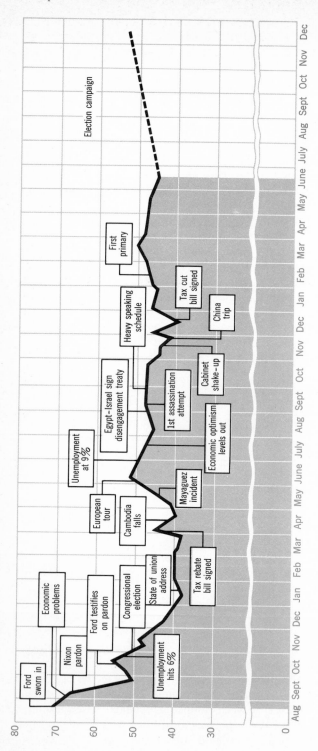

Figure 5.1
Percentage of Americans
approving Ford's performance
as President (1974–76).
Source: *The Gallup Opinion
Index,* Jan. 1977, pp. 14, 15.

zens, may seek a particularized outcome such as the repair of a sidewalk, and generally require a lot of initiative on the part of the citizen.

Using these four basic modes of involvement to analyze political activities of American citizens as reported in a 1967 national survey (a joint venture of the Survey Research Center of the University of California—Berkeley and the National Opinion Research Center at the University of Chicago), Verba and Nie develop six basic categories of participators. The "inactives," some 22 percent of our citizenry, do not take part in political life in any form. Another 21 percent, termed the "voting specialists," vote in presidential elections and always, or almost always, in local elections; but this is the extent of their political involvement. A very small group—some 4 percent of Americans, called the "parochial participants"—are average voters, do not engage in campaign or communal activities, but do initiate particularized contacts with governmental officials on matters that affect their personal lives. Another 20 percent of the population, the "communalists," are active in cooperative ventures in community affairs but avoid the conflict of political campaigns; while still another group, the "campaigners," (some 15 percent of the populace) concentrate their efforts in this mode of participation and have little to do with communal activities. Finally, some 11 percent of Americans are "complete activists," who engage in all types of political activities with great frequency. Thus Americans vary greatly in their political involvement: some avoid all forms of activity; others tend to concentrate their efforts in different kinds of participation, whereas a few have the time and energy to engage in a broad range of political acts.

Other recent surveys on political participation provide information on specific political activities undertaken by our citizens. Table 5.6, based on data gathered by the Center for Political Studies at the University of Michigan, indicates the percentages of Americans who have participated in activities associated with six recent presidential elections. As the table shows, different proportions of persons participate in the various campaign activities analyzed; however, the percentage of Americans who involve themselves in each of these actions has remained fairly constant over the twenty-year period.

Table 5.6
Percentage of
Americans Professing
to Have Participated
in Various Political
Activities, 1952–1972

Activity	1952	1956	1960	1964	1968	1972
Work for political party	3	3	6	5	5	5
Attend political rally or meeting	7	10	8	9	9	9
Contribute money to campaign	4	10	12	11	9	9
Use political sticker or button	*	16	21	16	15	14
Give political opinions	27	28	33	31	30	31

* not asked

Source: John P. Robinson, Jerrold G. Rusk, and Kendra B. Head, *Measures of Political Attitudes* (Ann Arbor: Center for Political Studies, 1968), p. 591; data for 1968 and 1972 from the Center election studies made available through the Interuniversity Consortium on Political Research.

Data from the 1973 Harris survey included in Table 5.7 provide some basic information on certain nonelectoral activities of the American public. It also shows a hierarchy of activities ranging from participation in a violent demonstration to the signing of a political petition.

Thus there are important distinctions among the various forms of political participation. There are also important differences among the kinds of persons who involve themselves extensively in public affairs as compared to those who participate little or not at all in such matters.

Factors Affecting Political Participation

There are no easy answers to the question of what disposes some people to participate in politics and others to avoid such activities. Nonetheless, students of the subject have been able to identify certain basic factors that are associated with both participation and nonparticipation. These include: (1) the social background and position a person occupies in society; (2) his psychological attributes and attitudes; and (3) the general political setting in which participation takes place.

The factor that correlates most closely with political participation is social-class status. Well-educated persons are likely to be highly conscious of political matters and to possess the self-confidence to deal with them; the affluent see a financial stake in politics; and lawyers and teachers have important intellectual and social skills that are transferable to the political arena. Besides such individual attributes, the general social situation of persons of high status gives them advantages: they are likely to receive political information and stimulation from persons with whom they associate—that is, they are most likely to be in the political center rather than on the periphery of the world of politics. Moreover, persons from the middle and upper classes are more likely than members of the lower classes to feel that they have the civic duty to participate in political affairs even if they are not personally interested in such matters.

Other social circumstances also affect participation. Verba and Nie report that participation in voluntary associations as well as political parties tends to

Took part in a demonstration where violence occurred	2
Picketed or took part in a street demonstration	11
Visited or talked in person with their senator	11
Visited state legislator in the state capital	14
Written a letter to a local government official	19
Visited or talked in person with their congressman	22
Written a letter to their senator	25
Participated in a school board discussion	27
Written a letter to their congressman	33
Actively defended the action of a public official in private discussion	56
Signed a petition	69

Table 5.7
Involvement of Public in Various Kinds of Political Activities (Expressed in Percentages)

Source: U.S. Congress, Senate, Subcommittee on Intergovernmental Relations of the Committee on Governmental Operations, *Confidence and Concern: Citizens View American Government: A Survey of Public Attitudes,* 93d Cong., 1st sess., 3 December 1973, pt. 1:83–84.

increase the political activities of citizens. Moreover, the heightened group consciousness of blacks in recent years has led to their greater involvement in political concerns and to a narrowing of the traditional gap between their participation and that of white citizens.

Some of the *psychological* attributes associated with participation have already been suggested as reasons why persons in positions of high social status become politically involved: they have a sense of confidence in their abilities and may also think that they have a duty to participate. Participants tend to feel politically efficacious,—that is, they believe that government officials will respect their views and do something about them. Psychological motives associated with political involvement are of two general types: (1) instrumental, in which persons seek a specific goal such as a victory for a particular candidate or the passage of a bill, or (2) expressive, in which persons seek personal satisfaction at having done the "right" thing, even though they may see no real chance that their candidate will be elected or a favored bill enacted.

There are also different psychological reasons why people do *not* participate in political matters. One is sheer *indifference*—that is, some persons simply find politics dull and so prefer to devote their time and efforts to matters that they find more rewarding such as sports, entertainment, business activities, and the like. Others are not disinterested in politics, but they feel a sense of *powerlessness* in their personal ability to affect the political process or a general *cynicism* or *mistrust* of politicians, who they think are unfair and/or dishonest.

There is no general consensus among political scientists concerning the relative importance of these various reasons for nonparticipation in politics. Certainly the evidence on the point is not clear. For example, in the Harris study cited at the beginning of the chapter, 60 percent of the American people admitted that they were not up-to-date on events in the federal government. One possible reason for that lack of knowledge was the general feeling of alienation and powerlessness indicated by Table 5.4. Yet when asked in the same survey what they could do to "change things they didn't like about government," 94 percent said that they would vote against a public official, 84 percent would write their congressman, and 79 percent would work through a group to which they belonged, all responses that would seem to indicate a belief that the political process is responsive to American citizens and that their lack of interest in politics is due to indifference rather than disillusionment.

Finally, the political setting affects participation, a topic that we will explore in depth in chapter 10 relative to voting in presidential and congressional elections. For now, it is sufficient to note that different kinds of political races draw more interest than others; for example, more people vote for the President than for congressmen. Moreover, people who live in areas where politics has traditionally been an important activity or where political contests are close tend to be drawn into the campaign process more actively than people who reside in areas of low political interest and competition. Verba and Nie also report that the type of community in which persons live also affects participation: as communities grow in size and lose the characteristics of "boundedness" that distinguish the independent city from the suburb, participation declines.

ASSESSMENT

Traditionally most Americans have supported our nation, its form of government, and major public officials. However, recent surveys indicate a significant erosion of the trust that Americans have in their political officials. At this point it is difficult to assess how significant the erosion is. As we have already seen, there are some signs that such attitudes may have hit their low point in 1974 and are now beginning to improve again as Americans put Vietnam, Watergate, and related incidents behind them. Moreover, even the polls taken during these crises showed public dissatisfaction with the particular individuals occupying our major political offices rather than a disillusionment with our basic institutions themselves.

Studies of the political attitudes and participation of the average American indicate that he hardly meets the model of the Athenian citizen, highly interested and actively involved in political affairs. Rather, he tends to be an apathetic or passive spectator of what is going on in the political process. Thus few persons become active in political campaigns or are interested or knowledgeable about major political issues.

There is, however, a minority of political activists in the United States who are concerned about public issues and who take the time and effort to participate in the campaign process. The factor that is most closely related to both political interest and political participation is social-class background, particularly the amount of formal education a person has. The well-educated not only participate more, but they also have a greater appreciation for the rules of the game and the values of democracy.

There are certain advantages in the fact that persons who know little about issues and do not understand the democratic rules of the game do not participate more in the political process. Otherwise, uninformed opinions would be transmitted to political officials. There is also a danger that the rights of minorities and democratic values in general would not be protected. Viewed in this light, democracy is best protected by the present system, whereby the political activists bring their knowledge and understanding of procedures to bear on the problems of governing our nation.

Yet there is also danger in the present situation. There is no assurance that the politically apathetic will always remain so: they may, for example, become exercised over a controversial issue such as communism or race relations and suddenly enter the political arena in support of leaders and policies that may be highly undemocratic. Also, there is no guarantee that upper-class activists will always take into account the interests of lower-class apathetics.

An ideal solution to the problem would be to politically educate everyone to protect his own interests and to understand the democratic rules of the game. Political-socialization studies provide some evidence that disadvantaged persons can be given a greater appreciation of democratic procedures and values in high school civics courses. Yet it would be naive to assume that such courses alone could accomplish miracles. It is much more realistic to think that political socialization must take place through many social institutions and at various stages of a person's life. Moreover, we must face the fact that some persons will never become politically interested and involved, however much we may want them to do so.

There are some signs, however, that changes in our society may result in increased political interest and participation (especially in other ways besides voting) on the part of more Americans. It is significant to note that the conditions that are most closely associated with political understanding and involvement are also those that are becoming more prevalent in the United States. Thus more citizens today are attending college, going into the professions, and becoming part of the middle class. Also, with all their limitations, the mass media, particularly television, are providing political information to persons who have never before been exposed to it. It is also encouraging to find that blacks have begun to close the participation gap that has traditionally existed between them and white Americans.

Another factor also bears on political participation: the extent to which our political institutions effectively channel the concerns of citizens to public officials. It is to this general subject that we now turn.

SELECTED READINGS

The findings of the Harris survey are reported in *Confidence and Concern: Citizens View American Government: A Survey of Public Attitudes,* Subcommittee on Intergovernmental Relations of the Committee on Governmental Operations, U.S. Senate, 3 December 1973, pt. 1. Other recent studies of political attitudes of Americans are William Watts and Lloyd Free, eds, *The State of the Nation, 1972* (New York: Universe Books, 1972), and a subsequent volume by the same authors, *The State of the Nation, 1974* (Washington, D.C.: Potomac Associates, 1974). They also joined with Francis Rourke in a series of short monographs published by Potomac Associates in 1976 on public attitudes on a variety of matters, including *Trust and Confidence in the American System.* Louis Harris Associates and the Gallup organization of Princeton, New Jersey periodically publish the results of polls and attitudes of Americans on a broad variety of subjects. For an analysis of some of the problems involved in such polls, see Seymour Lipset, "The Wavering Polls," *The Public Interest* (Fall 1976): 70-89.

The concept of political culture is utilized in Gabriel Almond and Sidney Verba, *The Civic Culture* (Boston: Little, Brown, 1963). A recent study that emphasizes a high degree of political consensus in the United States is Donald Devine, *The Political Culture of the United States* (Boston: Little, Brown, 1972).

The best modern treatment of the role that public opinion plays in the American political system is V.O. Key, Jr., *Public Opinion and American Democracy* (New York: Knopf, 1961.) Using survey data on political attitudes of the American public, the author traces the linkages between such attitudes and decision making by public officials. A good short analysis of public opinion, with particular emphasis on how such opinions are formed, is Robert E. Lane and David A. Sears, *Public Opinion* (Englewood Cliffs, N.J.: Prentice-Hall, 1964). A book relating public opinion to democratic theory is Bernard Hennessy, *Public Opinion* (Belmont, Ca.: Wadsworth, 1965). Two good recent studies of public opinion are Robert Erikson and Norman Luttbeg, *American Public Opinion: Its Origins, Content, and Input* (New York: Wiley, 1973), and James Best, *Public Opinion: Micro and Macro* (Homewood, Ill.: Dorsey, 1973).

An analysis of the political socialization of elementary-school children that pointed the way for other studies is Fred Greenstein, *Children and Politics* (New Haven: Yale University Press, 1965). Other major works in the field are Robert Hess and Judy Torney, *The Development of Political Attitudes in Children* (Chicago: Aldine, 1967), which focuses on the psychological aspects of political development, and David Easton and Jack Dennis, *Children in the Political System* (New York: McGraw-Hill, 1969), which emphasizes the way political attitudes learned early in life contribute to the stability of the American political system. A book incorporating data on political socialization in Jamaica as well as the United States is Kenneth Langton, *Political Socialization* (New York: Oxford University Press, 1969). An excellent general treatment of the subject, which synthesizes the findings of a number of studies and places them within a meaningful analytical framework, is Richard Dawson and Kenneth Prewitt, *Political*

Socialization (Boston: Little, Brown, 1969). More recent general analyses of political socialization include Robert Weissberg, *Political Learning, Political Change and Democratic Leadership* (Englewood Cliffs, N.J.: Prentice-Hall, 1974), and a book edited by Richard Niemi and Associates, *The Politics of Future Citizens* (San Francisco: Jossey-Bass Publishers, 1974). Kent Jennings and Niemi collaborated on a major work on the political attitudes of high-school students entitled *The Political Character of Adolescence: The Influence of Families and Schools* (Princeton: Princeton University Press, 1974) and on an excellent article, "Continuity and Change in Political Orientations: A Longitudinal Study of Two Generations," *The American Political Science Review* 69 (1975): 1316-1335. For an interesting analysis of the effect of the Watergate scandals on the political attitudes of children, see F. Christopher Arterton, "Watergate and Children's Attitudes Towards Political Authority Revisited," *Political Science Quarterly* 90 (Fall 1975): 477-496.

A pioneering study of political attitudes of citizens in the United States, Great Britain, West Germany, Italy, and Mexico, is the Almond and Verba study cited above. Based on survey data, the analysis focuses on basic orientations of individuals in these five countries towards their government and the role that they expect to play in its operation. Two analyses of citizen attitudes on democratic principles and values are James Prothro and Charles Grigg, "Fundamental Principles of Democracy: Bases of Agreement and Disagreement," *Journal of Politics* 22 (1960):276-94, and Herbert McClosky, "Consensus and Ideology in American Politics," *The American Political Science Review* 58 (1964):361-82. For an analysis of the results of a variety of recent polls dealing with trust and confidence in our political leaders, see Everett Ladd, Jr., "The Polls: The Question of Confidence," *Public Opinion Quarterly* (Winter 1976-77): 544-552.

Excellent works that draw together a large number of studies treating various facets of political participation are Robert Lane, *Political Life: Why People Get Involved in Politics* (New York: Free Press, 1959), Lester Milbrath, *Political Participation: How and Why Do People Get Involved in Politics?* (Chicago: Rand McNally, 1965) and Herbert McClosky's treatment of the subject in the *International Encyclopedia of the Social Sciences*, 2nd ed., s. v. "Political Participation." The best individual empirical study of political participation is Sidney Verba and Norman Nie, *Participation in America: Political Democracy and Social Equality* (New York: Harper & Row, 1972).

Political Novels   Sometimes even those who most deeply believe in a political system become its victims. The moving story of a man destroyed by the system his ideas helped to create is told by Arthur Koestler in *The Darkness at Noon* (New York: Bantam, 1966). The consequences of surrendering personal moral beliefs to political authority are illustrated in *Judgment at Nuremburg* (New York: New American Library, 1961) by Abby Mann.

The development of authority relationships, socialization, and behavior modification are aptly shown by William Golding in his story about a group of boys stranded on an island, *The Lord of the Flies* (New York: Capricorn, 1955).

How certain political figures can manipulate popular attitudes so as to acquire awesome personal power is the subject of Robert Penn Warren's acclaimed novel *All the King's Men* (New York: Bantam, 1968). The potential for the manipulation of irrationality in the American public provided Sinclair Lewis with the material for his novel about an emerging fascist state in this country, *It Can't Happen Here* (New York: New American Library, 1970).

Chapter 6

In the mid-1970s Congress faced a continuing problem of vital concern to environmentalists and American industry alike: the protection of the nation's air against pollution. The 1970 Clean Air Act, one of the first of a series of federal laws designed to clean up the environment, established standards designed to eliminate existing pollution by the end of the decade, but it was silent on the issue of air that was presently cleaner than that required by the 1970 law. Should it be maintained at its present relatively clean state, or should it be permitted to deteriorate to the level permitted by the federal legislation? The matter had subsequently been fought out in the courts and before the Environmental Protective Agency (a unit of the executive branch established to carry out the provisions of the 1970 Clean Air Act), but because of some uncertainties, the parties concerned were asking the Congress itself to decide the highly controversial issue.

Leading the effort to maintain the quality of air in regions of the United States with relatively clean air were a variety of organizations. Included were environmental groups like the *Sierra Club* and *Environmental Policy Center;* a health organization, the *American Lung Association;* and two prominent public-interest groups, the *League of Women Voters* and *Common Cause.* Joining efforts under an umbrella organization, the *National Clean Air Coalition,* the groups kept their members informed of the progress of legislation on the issue and urged them to write their congressmen to support a law that would prevent further deterioration of the nation's clean air. Following a week of air pollution alerts in the national capital, on April 22, 1976 the *Washington Coalition for Clean Air* held a press conference calling for a strengthening of the 1970 law. Similar events were held that same day in other large cities in the nation.

Opposing the above groups was another broad coalition of organizations called the *Washington Environmental Coordinating Committee.* Included among its participants were a variety of business groups, including the *U.S. Chamber of Commerce,* the *National Association of Manufacturers,* the *American Petroleum Institute,* the *Business Roundtable,* industry trade groups, and individual firms. Arguing that provisions to maintain clean air at its present state would prevent industrial development in up to 50 percent of areas in some states, the

Chamber sent its members a map of the affected areas and urged them to write, wire, or telephone their congressmen about the issue. The Committee also encouraged local businessmen to present their views to members of Congress during the spring recess of that body. Also joining in the battle was the *Electric Utilities Clean Air Coordinating Committee,* which claimed that utilities could not afford the pollution control equipment required on new plants built in clean-air regions without raising their rates.

Another pollution issue faced by the national lawmakers was that of controlling exhaust emissions from automobiles. The 1970 Clean Air Act set standards for the emission of three pollutants—hydrocarbons, carbon monoxide, and oxides of nitrogen; standards for the first two were to be met by the automobile industry by 1975 and the latter by 1976. The imposition of such standards, although subsequently delayed by the Congress three times, was nevertheless to take effect in 1978 if Congress did not act on the matter prior to that time.

A constellation of groups similar to that which battled over the nondeterioration issue formed on the emission controversy. The automobile industry, as represented by General Motors, Ford, and Chrysler, claimed that the technology to meet the emission standards had not been developed, and that such standards would reduce fuel efficiency. The environmentalists, led by the *National Clean Air Coalition,* countered that a new catalytic converter could be developed to control excessive emissions and that such controls need not reduce gas mileage. Also drawn into the fray was the *United Automobile Workers* (UAW), a liberal union with a genuine interest in the pollution problem that was nonetheless concerned that too hastily implemented standards could hurt the automobile industry and cost it members jobs.

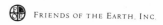

FRIENDS OF THE EARTH, INC.

During the 1976 session of Congress, the contending forces struggled to influence action in both the House and Senate on the issues of antideterioration and automobile emissions. The two chambers developed separate bills but in the last week of the session compromised their differences with a measure that placed restrictions on additional pollution in clean-air regions and extended the imposition of stricter standards for hydrocarbon and carbon monoxide pollutants to 1979 models, and for oxides of nitrogen to 1981 cars. However, a last-minute filibuster in the Senate prevented action on the bill, and it died at the end of the legislative session.

These developments illustrate the variety of organizations that can become involved in public issues in American society and the kinds of motives—economic, moral, and political—that prompt their actions. They also depict the diverse techniques that groups in the United States use to influence decisions made by public officials. Before examining such matters further, however, it will be helpful to consider a fundamental question: *what do all interest groups have in common?*

NATURE OF INTEREST GROUPS

An *interest group* is *any collection of persons with a shared attitude on some matter who make certain claims or demands on others in society with respect to that matter.* It should be noted that not every groups fits this definition. People who have red hair, or who earn $10,000 or more a year, or who are members of the Jewish faith share something, have certain characteristics in common. (So-

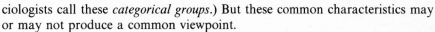

ciologists call these *categorical groups*.) But these common characteristics may or may not produce a common viewpoint.

Shared attitudes develop among people who have a common interest in a particular subject; typically, they interact with one another over it. Thus people who like symphonic music may meet as a group to listen to records or to attend concerts. Or they may work together to sponsor a visit of a touring orchestra. Such a group does not qualify as an interest group, however, unless it meets the second requirement of the definition: that it make some claim on other people. If they demand that a local radio station stop playing nothing but rock music and devote certain hours to classical concerts, they are acting as an interest group.

In many instances the claims that interest groups make on others do not involve the political process. If the symphony-lovers merely try to influence radio station owners to play their preferred music, they do not qualify as a political interest group. But if the group demands that the Federal Communications Commission (an agency of the national government that grants licenses to radio stations) force every station to devote a certain percentage of air time to symphonic music under pain of losing its license, it is acting as a political interest group. This is the kind of interest group that is of primary concern to the student of government.

Typically, symphony-lovers in the United States do not turn to the political process to further their intersts, but there would be obvious advantages if they did. A radio station owner that refused to cooperate voluntarily in playing symphonic music might do so under threat of losing his license. Moreover, symphony-lovers might persuade their city council to subsidize a local orchestra by using public funds to make up any deficit the group might incur. In doing so, they would be taking advantage of the government's ability to take money from people who do not necessarily like orchestral music and use it for the enjoyment of those who do. Thus public officials are particularly helpful to groups because they can do what private individuals cannot: issue commands that people will have to consider legitimate and utilize the taxing and spending power to benefit some persons at the expense of others.

Political interest groups have available two basic approaches for attempting to influence public officials. They may seek *positive benefits,* such as requiring radio stations to play symphonic music or convincing city councils to subsidize a local symphony orchestra. Or they may try to *prevent* the government from taking an action; for instance, those who do not appreciate symphonic music may try to stop public officials from pursuing either of the above policies. Groups that are generally satisfied with the present distribution of values attempt to preserve the status quo by taking defensive actions in the political arena. The two approaches are not mutually exclusive, however, and groups frequently pursue both simultaneously: at the same time that music-lovers are attempting to influence the city council to subsidize a local symphony, they may try to prevent the use of public money to support a baseball team.

Interest groups also attempt to accomplish their purposes through private channels. Although labor unions exert extensive influence in government, they also make demands on employers and the general public through strikes and picketing. Other groups also seek to satisfy their demands by dealing directly

with private individuals and organizations; students have sought to bring about major changes in universities through negotiation, as well as confrontation, with school officials.

Thus interest groups attempt to achieve some of their objectives by private means and others through political channels. This is one of the characteristics that distinguish an interest group from a *political party,* which focuses its activities almost entirely on political processes. In addition, the primary methods by which interest groups and political parties attempt to accomplish their purposes differ. Political parties seek to staff governmental positions by running candidates for office; interest groups typically attempt to influence the actions of whatever officials are in office.

This distinction is a matter of emphasis only; the division of political labor between the two kinds of organizations is not complete. As we shall see in chapter 7, some persons who participate in political party activities are concerned with issues and support a party or its candidates primarily because of their stands on such issues. Conversely, some interest groups try to influence the selection of political officeholders because they believe that certain persons will be more likely than others to pursue sympathetic courses of action. Yet the primary purposes of the two types of organization differ. Political parties *always* run candidates for office, and frequently issues are not a major factor in campaigns. Interest groups typically try to influence public officials on issues in which the group is concerned; quite often they make no attempt to determine who is chosen; and they *never* (at least in the United States) run a candidate for office under the label of their own organization.

A final note is in order on the name pressure group, an older term for interest group, often used in disapproval by persons who think of such groups as selfish, irresponsible organizations seeking privileges for their members. Yet some groups have members who devote themselves to causes that benefit others; many white persons, for instance, belong to the *National Association for the Advancement of Colored People* (NAACP) because they sympathize with the problems of blacks. The word *pressure* implies that such groups use improper means—force, bribery, threats—to achieve their purposes. But, as this chapter will show, the techniques by which interest groups attempt to wield political influence vary greatly and include methods like conveying factual information to political officials, which can hardly be said to constitute "pressure" in the sense in which that term is normally used. To avoid any emotional connotation or inaccurate characterization of what the groups under discussion actually are or do, the more neutral and descriptive term "interest group" is used here.

INCENTIVES FOR JOINING INTEREST GROUPS

People join interest groups for a variety of reasons. These reasons may be grouped in three general categories that political scientists Peter Clark and James Wilson suggest are incentives for membership in any organization. One is the material benefits that one receives from membership. Another is the solidary benefits that accrue to persons who belong to a group. The third is what Clark and Wilson refer to as purposive benefits from organizational membership.

Material benefits are tangible rewards that persons seek to gain through membership in an interest group. These may be monetary in nature, such as

higher wages that workers believe a labor union can achieve for them through negotiaing a new contract with their employers. Material benefits may also be nonmonetary ones, such as providing safety for coal miners through congressional laws requiring that mine owners use certain equipment and take particular precautions to prevent mine cave-ins or explosions.

Solidary incentives are basically intangible in nature. As Clark and Wilson suggest, they include such rewards as "socializing, congeniality, the sense of group membership and identification, the status resulting from membership, fun and conviviality," and the like. Thus a person may join a farm organization primarily because he and his family enjoy the opportunity to escape the isolation of their daily work and to socialize with other persons involved in agricultural work.

Purposive incentives are those that transcend an individual's own material or solidary interests; they are benefits directed at other persons besides oneself. As noted later in this chapter, whites who established the *National Association for the Advancement of Colored People* were motivated to improve not their own situation but that of blacks in the United States. Some persons have even broader goals in mind: seeking changes that will benefit society as a whole. Individuals who belong to public interest groups like *Common Cause* (to be discussed later in this chapter) are primarily concerned with purposive incentives.

It should be understood that material, solidary, and purposive incentives are not mutually exclusive; the same organization may provide all three kinds of benefits. Thus the *United Automobile Workers* furnishes material benefits to its members in the form of wages that it obtains through contracts with management. At the same time, the UAW sponsors recreational and other activities that are of social appeal to the workers. Moreover, the organization in recent years has sought broad social and economic reforms to benefit disadvantaged groups as well as society in general. Thus the UAW provides divergent kinds of incentives that appeal to different individuals or in some cases to one and the same individual.

One of the problems of many interest groups is that frequently the benefits that they help to achieve cannot be restricted to their members alone. Thus a union may negotiate a contract for increased wages that covers *all* the workers in a plant whether or not they belong to the organization; or a veteran may receive government benefits even though he is not a member of the *American Legion* or *Veterans of Foreign Wars* that helped get the legislation through the Congress.

As economist Mancur Olson suggests, under these circumstances it is not rational for an individual to belong to an interest group, since he enjoys the benefits of its efforts without having to invest his time or money in its activities. However, groups have several ways of overcoming this problem. One is to get legislation passed requiring *compulsory* membership in an organization. Thus some states *require* a worker to join a union within a specified period of time if a majority of his fellow workers have voted to have the union represent them;* also membership in the state bar association is required of all attorneys in some states. Moreover, as Olson suggests, groups can utilize "selective benefits" as incentives to induce persons to join their organization. These benefits, which are restricted to members alone, include low-cost life insurance and health plans for workers, malpractice insurance for doctors, the distribution of profits of cooperatives to farmers, technical information to businessmen, and the like. Finally, members can use social pressure to persuade persons to do their part in achieving group goals by joining and contributing to the organization; and they can threaten to ostracize those that do not.

Thus individuals are induced to join an interest group for many reasons. As political scientist Robert Salisbury suggests, the formation of such groups is

* Such an arrangement, referred to as a *union shop,* is permitted by the Taft-Hartley Law if a state passes legislation providing for it. However, the federal law also permits states to have an *open shop,* which does not require a worker to join a union favored by his fellow employees. Organized labor has attempted unsuccessfully over the years to have the Taft-Hartley Law changed so as to require all states to have a union shop.

often dependent upon *entrepreneur* organizers* who provide the kinds of benefits discussed above to members in exchange for their dues as well as for the time and effort that some individuals invest in the activities of the organization. If the arrangement proves not to be worthwhile, members will probably leave the organization and perhaps join a similar one. Moreover, if the organizer fails in one venture, he may apply his entrepreneurial skills to the establishment of another organization, usually of the same general type (farm, business, good "cause") with which he has had previous experience. The end result of the process is the development of a wide variety of interest groups in the United States.

INTEREST GROUPS IN AMERICAN SOCIETY

Americans have long been known as joiners. Alexis de Tocqueville, a young French nobleman who came to America in the 1830s and wrote a perceptive analysis of American society, *Democracy in America*, had this to say on the subject:

The Americans of all ages, all conditions and all dispositions constantly form associations. They have not only commercial and manufacturing companies in which all take part, but associations of a thousand other kinds, religious, moral, serious, futile, restricted, enormous or diminutive. The Americans make associations to give entertainments, to found establishments for education to send missionaries to the antipodes. Wherever at the head of some new undertaking you see the government of France or a man of rank in England, in the United States you will be sure to find an association.

Tocqueville's impressions of the part that associations played in American society during the Jacksonian era are generally confirmed by recent studies of voluntary groups in the United States. The Five-Nation study referred to in the last chapter showed that Americans are more likely to join voluntary associations than are citizens of the other countries studied: 57 percent of our citizens were members of some such organization, compared to 47 percent of Britons, 44 percent of Germans, 30 percent of Italians, and 24 percent of Mexicans. Subsequent studies have shown the same general level of citizen involvement: the 1967 survey of Verba and Nie revealed that some 62 percent of Americans belong to at least one voluntary association, and the Harris study in 1973 reported a figure of 53 percent.

At the same time Tocqueville's statement is undoubtedly too sweeping. Not *all* Americans today (and, in all probability, not in his time either) belong to voluntary associations; in fact, almost half do not belong to even one. Moreover, there are marked differences in membership among people of different "conditions." The Verba-Nie study showed that fewer than one-half of those who were not high school graduates belonged to a voluntary organization compared to almost four-fifths of those who had done some college work. Education also affected the degree of involvement of persons with groups: only about one-quarter of the non-high-school graduates were active in at least one organization to which they belonged, but about three in five persons who had attended college were.

---

* Entrepreneur is a term usually applied to a person who starts his own business and hires persons to work for him.

The student of government, of course, is particularly interested in political associations, those that turn to the political process to accomplish at least some of their purposes. There are no precise statistics on how many of the more than 13,000 voluntary groups reported in the 1976 edition of the *Encyclopedia of Associations* are political in nature, but the Verba-Nie study provides information on the extent to which organizations mentioned by respondents become involved in community affairs and/or participate in political discussions.

Table 6.1 indicates that there is a fairly high level of involvement in community affairs among all groups with the exception of those devoted to literary pursuits, hobbies, and sports. There are more organizations that tend to avoid political discussions, including youth and church-related groups, as well as fraternal associations, trade unions, school fraternities and sororities, and hobby and sports clubs. Perhaps the most surprising finding is the relative infrequency of political discussions in trade unions compared to service clubs and professional associations: this disparity probably relates to the higher social-class composition of members of the latter two groups.

Type of Organization	Percentage of the *Population* Who Report Membership	Percentage of *Members* Who Report the Organizations Involved in Community Affairs	Percentage of *Members* Who Report that Political Discussions Take Place in the Organization
Political groups such as Democratic or Republican clubs, and political action groups such as voters' leagues	8	85	97
School service groups such as PTA or school alumni groups	17	82	54
Service clubs, such as Lions, Rotary, Zonta, Jr. Chamber of Commerce	6	81	64
Youth groups such as Boy Scouts, Girl Scouts	7	77	36
Veterans' groups such as American Legion	7	77	56
Farm organizations such as Farmer's Union, Farm Bureau, Grange	4	74	61

Table 6.1
The Types of Organizations to Which Individuals Belong

Table 6.1 *(continued)*

Nationality groups such as Sons of Norway, Hibernian Society	2	73	57
Church-related groups such as Bible Study Group or Holy Name Society	6	73	40
Fraternal groups such as Elks, Eagles, Masons, and their women's auxiliaries	15	69	33
Professional or academic societies such as American Dental Association, Phi Beta Kappa	7	60	57
Trade unions	17	59	44
School fraternities and sororities such as Sigma Chi, Delta Gamma	3	53	37
Literary, art, discusssion, or study clubs such as book-review clubs, theater groups	4	40	56
Hobby or garden clubs such as stamp or coin clubs, flower clubs, pet clubs	5	40	35
Sports clubs, bowling leagues, etc.	12	28	30

Source: Sidney Verba and Norman Nie, *Participation in America: Political Democracy and Social Equality* (New York: Harper & Row, 1972), pp. 178–79.

Of course, discussing poltics is one thing; doing something about a political problem is another. Groups that use political means differ in the extent to which they do so. Thus some become politically involved only on rare occasions, while others do so almost constantly. Groups also vary with respect to the scope of their political activities. Some turn to government to accomplish a broad range of purposes; others restrict their political involvement to one major issue.

Historically, economic groups have been most frequently involved politically in a broad range of issues. At the very outset, commercial cliques (manufacturers, merchants, ship owners, and large farmers) and noncommercial ones (small businessmen and farmers, artisans, and mechanics) contended over the writing of the Constitution, and Madison himself considered the major differences among men to be based on the distribution of property. Over the years these same kinds of groups, operating under the broad constellations of interests known as business, agriculture, and labor, have been most prominently involved in the American political process. The discussion that follows focuses on the activities of these three major economic groupings.

Recently, however, groups that have not traditionally been politically active have emerged as important forces in American politics. Later in this same section we examine two such groups: those representing public employees and those dedicated to pursuing the "public interest." The final portion of the chapter analyzes the ways in which blacks and women have used the political process to further their interests.

Business Interest Groups

The first national organization representing a variety of businesses was established in 1895 in response to an economic depression. Taking the name *The National Association of Manufacturers,* the group initially had a positive goal of promoting trade and commerce but soon shifted to the negative aim of counteracting the growing strength of organized labor. During the 1930s the NAM came under the control of large firms; it remains the major spokesman for big business today. Its 14,000 members consist of firms engaged in manufacturing; it also has "cooperating" members (financial institutions and transportation companies with close relationships to manufacturers) that contribute financially to the organization. Its major policy goals are counteracting the power of organized labor (although the organization now accepts the general principle of labor unions), lowering individual and corporate taxes, preventing extensive government regulation of business activities, and promoting free enterprise not only in the United States but also in other nations of the world.

The NAM never claimed to represent state and local chambers of commerce or a large number of trade associations operating at the regional and national level. In 1912 the Taft administration sponsored a meeting of such groups from various parts of the nation to establish an organization that would legitimately

speak for the general business community. At that meeting the *Chamber of Commerce of the United States* was born. Today it consists of 4000 chambers of commerce and trade associations plus 34,000 business firms and individuals with an underlying membership of more than 4,500,000 firms and individuals. Since its membership is broader than that of the NAM, its officials can speak more legitimately for the entire business community; however, because the Chamber represents such a wide range of businesses, frequently it cannot take stands on certain important issues. For example, the Chamber has avoided enunciating a definite position on reciprocal trade (exchanging goods between countries with little or no duty) because some members fear competition from companies abroad whereas others want to export goods free of foreign duties. The general political goals of the Chamber parallel those of the NAM: counteracting the power of organized labor, reducing taxes and government regulation, and promoting the virtues of a free economy.

A third business interest group, composed of businessmen and professional economists with somewhat different policy goals from those of the NAM and the national Chamber, is the *Committee for Economic Development.* Founded in 1942 by persons who felt that business groups had been too negative toward the New Deal without developing positive economic programs of their own, the organization played a major role in the enactment of the Full Employment Act of 1946, under which the national government assumed the responsiblity of promoting high employment, high production, and economic growth in the American economy. In keeping with this greater appreciation for the role of government in the affairs of the nation, several of the major leaders of the CED have occupied top positions in Washington. Most notably one of the founders of the organization, Paul Hoffman, served as the first director of the Economic Cooperation Association, which dispensed financial aid through the Marshall Plan to European nations after World War II. Favoring greater economic cooperation with other nations, the CED also played a major part in the establishment of the International Monetary Fund and the World Bank. In recent years the organization has also turned its attention toward the management of the federal government as well as to economic and political problems of states and urban areas.

For much of American history, business groups dominated the political system. The depression of 1929, however, shook public confidence in the business community, which failed to prevent the passage of major New Deal legislation. The general prosperity after World War II restored some of that confidence so that business organizations once again became more politically effective. In recent years, however, they have become concerned with a lack of unity within the business community. In 1974 the NAM moved its headquarters from New York to Washington and began a concerted effort to work more closely with the *U.S. Chamber of Commerce,* the *National Industrial Council* (an NAM-supported umbrella organization of some 300 national, state and local manufacturing and commercial associations), as well as *Business Roundtable,* a group of Washington representatives of major corporations. Among the current issues of common interest to such organizations are threats of government controls over wages and prices, land use, energy conservation, and the quality of the environment, epitomized by the "clean air controversy" described at the beginning of the chapter.

Agricultural Interest Groups

Today American farmers are represented by a variety of organizations. The largest, with a membership of over 2 million, is the *American Farm Bureau Federation*. Established in 1919, the organization has traditionally had close ties with Extension Agents of the Department of Agriculture, who demonstrate new agricultural techniques to farmers, as well as with state land-grant colleges that carry on programs in agricultural research. During the 1920s and early 1930s, the Federation worked with other farm groups to get the national government to guarantee the farmer a "fair" price* for his products. Since the end of the 1930s, however, the organization has opposed a price-support program for basic crops and now favors a reduced role for government in agriculture and a free market for determining the level of food prices. The Federation's change in attitude is due to its having increasingly come under the control of wealthy, large farmers in the Midwest corn and hog belt, as well as of cotton planters in the South. Such farmers, who benefit from the economics of large-scale farming, can now compete effectively in a free market; moreover, withdrawing price supports from small farmers forces many of them out of agriculture, thus removing economic rivals of the large-farmer clientele of the *Farm Bureau*.

The primary voice of the less advantaged farmer today is the *National Farmers' Union*, founded in 1902 and with a current membership of 250,000. This group, which draws its support from wheat farmers of the Plains states who are particularly vulnerable to vagaries of the weather (particularly droughts), favors a high level of government support for farm products and the provision of cheap credit. In recent years the NFU has also fought for legislation to protect migratory farm workers. The organization proclaims itself the champion of the dirt farmer, the man who devotes his life to farming as a way of life, rather than what the NFU calls the corporation farmer (represented by the *Farm Bureau*), who looks at farming strictly as a business.

Located somewhere between the *Farm Bureau* and the NFU in terms of clientele and general goals is the *National Grange,* the oldest of the farm organizations (founded in 1867). Today, with a membership of 600,000, the organization has its major base of support among dairy farmers in the New England, Middle Atlantic, and Pacific states. Traditionally concerned with providing social activities for farmers, and less militant than the other two farm organizations, the *Grange* has moved closer politically in recent years to the NFU, primarily because it opposes the *Farm Bureau*'s ultimate goal of abandoning governmental farm support programs.

Like labor, agriculture is experiencing a decline in its organizational potential because of technological developments. Mechanization and improved fertilizers mean that fewer farmers are needed to raise the nation's food supply. As a result, more and more people have left the farm in recent years to seek employment in the cities. (In 1960 our farm population was between fifteen and sixteen million; by 1969, it had fallen to between ten and eleven million; by 1975 it stood at 8.9 million.) Furthermore, farmers are not much inclined to

* The price is generally referred to as parity, meaning the dollar figure needed to maintain a balance between what a farmer has to pay for things he buys and what he can sell his crops for. Thus if the cost of items a farmer purchases goes up, so should the price he is paid for his products.

The Founding Father: Samuel Gompers of the AFL and his working-class friends?

join interest groups. Today only about one in four farmers belongs to any of the major farm organizations.*

Labor Interest Groups

The first successful national organization, the *American Federation of Labor,* was established in 1886. Representing primarily skilled craftsmen—carpenters, bricklayers and the like—the economic goals of the AFL were essentially conservative: using the governmental process in a negative way, primarily to seek protection against court orders forbidding strikes, rather than for positive benefits in the form of minimum wages, public housing, or social security for its members. (In 1932, three years after the beginning of the Great Depression, the AFL still opposed unemployment insurance for workers on the grounds that such payments constituted governmental interference in concerns that should be left to management and labor.) The group's political tactics were similarly cautious: following the advice of the organization's founder, Samuel Gompers, to "defeat labor's enemies and reward its friends," the union avoided blanket endorsement of candidates of either major political party, including those running in presidential elections.

The growth of mass industries (coal, steel, and automobiles) in the 1920s and 1930s created unskilled jobs rather than openings in the skilled crafts; the appropriate organizational units for the new giant concerns were industry-wide unions joining all steelworkers, all autoworkers, and the like. The AFL leadership, however, was not eager to bring a flood of unskilled workers into the organization to threaten the dominance of skilled craftsmen, and so refused to permit workers in the mass industries to be organized permanently along industrial lines. This decision led John L. Lewis, head of the *United Mine Workers,* to leave the organization and form a new national union known as the *Congress of Industrial Organizations.* Unlike its parent group, the CIO sought positive political goals such as public housing for low-income groups, social security, minimum wages, and the like. The new organization also departed from the cautious political techniques of the AFL by establishing a Political Action Committee in 1944 to work for the reelection of Franklin Roosevelt.

This division in labor's ranks contributed to the movement's inability to prevent the passage in 1947 of the Taft-Hartley Act, a law placing restrictions on union activities. Eventually this outside threat from labor's traditional enemy—big business—forced the craft and industrial unions together so that the two organizations merged in 1955 as the *AFL-CIO.* However, tensions developed between the organization's new president, George Meany (former head of the AFL), and Walter Reuther, president of the Industrial Union Department of the new organization, who previously headed the *United Auto Workers* of the CIO. Besides the personal power struggle between the two men, there was also a difference in policy: Reuther charged that the organization was not involving itself in broad social causes he favored, such as ending racial segregation in all areas of American life (including the construction industry, which AFL unions

* A fourth general agricultural interest group, established in 1955, is the *National Farmers' Organization.* Concentrated primarily in Missouri and Iowa, it has tried unsuccessfully to withold products from the market until a satisfactory price is received from food processors and purchasers. The group does not publish its membership size.

George Meany of the
AFL–CIO: a man for all
Presidents.

dominate). Differences in style between Meany, a cautious man with limited verbal abilities, and Reuther, called by many the "Billy Graham of Labor," also created personality clashes between them.

Ultimately the break came in 1968 as Reuther's union, the *United Auto Workers*, left the AFL-CIO and shortly thereafter joined forces with another major ex-CIO union, the *Teamsters* (this union, led by Jimmy Hoffa, had been expelled in 1957 for alleged ties with gangsters and a misuse of union funds by its officers), to form a new group called the *Alliance for Labor Action.* Soon a third body, the *International Chemical Workers Union,* joined the organization. Boasting a membership of some four million, the new group dedicated itself to a Reuther-inspired program calling for broad social and economic reforms and to an effort to forge links with the youth of America and the intellectual community. However, the organization lasted only a few years: the *Chemical Workers* returned to the AFL-CIO, while the UAW and *Teamsters* reverted to the status of independent unions.

The result of these developments is a weakened labor movement. Two of the nation's largest individual unions—the *Teamsters* with more than 1,800,000 members and the UAW with 1,500,000—lie outside the AFL-CIO as do other important elements of the organization such as the railroad workers. Thus labor speaks with a divided voice. Moreover, all labor organizations together today represent less than one-fourth of the civilian work force.

Crosscurrents are operating in the labor movement today. Automation has eliminated many blue-collar jobs of industrial employees who have traditionally joined unions. On the other hand, unions are now zeroing in on persons who have generally remained outside their ranks, such as migrant farm work-

Labor leader Cesar Chavez.

ers, service employees (hospital workers and the like), and employees of the burgeoning new industries of the South. Moreover, they have experienced great success in recent years in organizing an increasingly important group in the nation's work force: public employees.

Public-Employee Interest Groups

Historically public officials have opposed the unionization of public employees on the grounds that allowing them to share in decisions regarding compensation and working conditions would compromise the concept of governmental sovereignty: public officials should decide such matters themselves. In addition, unions have been associated with strikes, a weapon considered dangerous when it involves interrupting vital public services such as education and transportation. However, a change of attitude began to occur at both the state and national level in the early 1960s. Between 1962 and 1973 the number of states in which public employees had the right to enter into a formal relationship with their employers rose from two to twenty-seven. In 1962 President Kennedy issued an executive order that granted official recognition to unions of federal employees and provided machinery for voting on exclusive bargaining agents for such employees. Subsequently President Nixon issued additional executive orders permitting employees to have union dues deducted from their pay checks and providing for binding arbitration of employee grievances in the event that such grievances could not be settled amicably with government officials.

This new legal climate for the organization of public employees soon resulted in a dramatic growth in the union memebership of such employees. In 1968 (the first year for which full figures on membership are available from the Bureau of Labor Statistics), 2.5 million persons belonged to state and local organizations; by 1974 this figure had increased to 3.9 million, a rise of almost 60 percent. Meanwhile, union membership of federal employees went from 1.4 million in 1968 to 1.7 million in 1972, a gain of over 20 percent. In contrast, during the same six-year period, membership in unions in the private sector of the economy rose only 3.7 percent. By 1974 more than one-fifth of all union members in the United States were public employees.

Today a number of organizations represent persons employed in the public sector. Two of the major ones—the *American Federation of State, County and Municipal Employees* (AFSCME) and the *American Federation of Teachers* (AFT)—are members of the AFL-CIO's Public Employee Department. However, the largest single public-employee organization (with a 1976 membership of 1.7 million) is an independent one, the *National Education Association* (NEA). In addition the *Teamsters Union** represents some 200,000 public employees, primarily in the field of law enforcement.

These public-employee unions have not only grown dramatically in size but have also experienced a great change in their essential character. Starting as primarily social and professional organizations, they have become more militant in their dealings with employers. Led by aggressive leaders like Jerry Wurf of the AFSCME and Albert Shanker of the AFT, public unions have pressed

---

* Officially known as the *International Brotherhood of Teamsters, Chauffeurs, Warehousemen and Helpers of America.*

hard for wage increases for their members and resorted increasingly to strikes (some of which have been illegal) to achieve their purposes. Moreover, the NEA has become increasingly active on the political front, spending large sums of money in federal, state, and local election campaigns in recent years.

Thus organizations providing primarily material benefits for their members have been among the most important interest groups in American society. However, as we shall see, those with essentially "purposive" goals have become more prominent in the United States in the last decade.

Public Interest Groups

While citizens' associations and taxpayers' groups have been involved in American politics for a number of years, their effective organization at the national level can be traced primarily to the late 1960s and early 1970s. Consumer advocate Ralph Nader, made famous by his book *Unsafe at Any Speed* (an exposé of the lack of adequate safety devices on automobiles), lauched a series of investigations into foods and drugs, air and water pollution, nursing homes, banking, pesticides, and many other aspects of American life. Staffed initially by idealistic law students and some practicing lawyers (called "Nader's Raiders"), he eventually established an organization called *Public Citizen, Inc.* to solicit funds in nominal amounts (usually $15) to finance major activities in which he and his associates were interested: investigating, exposing, recommending, and, when necessary, litigating, in order to bring about needed changes to protect the interests of the consumer. (Though not a membership organization, *Public Citizen* is supported by an estimated 175,000 contributors annually.) Nader was also instrumental in helping to establish Public Interest Research groups on college and university campuses through which students petition to have a portion of the fees paid to their school allocated to the support of full-time representatives to engage in citizen action.

Another organization that moved to the forefront of the public-interest-group movement was *Common Cause.* Established in 1970 by former Secretary of Health, Education, and Welfare John Gardner, this association soon gathered substantial contributions from foundations and corporations and a dues-paying membership ($15 a year) to finance its activities. Within six months the organization has reached its initial goal of 100,000 members; spurred by the public's reaction to the Watergate scandal, by early 1974 more than 300,000 Americans had joined the organization, whose budget exceeded $6 million. After that crisis subsided, the membership of *Common Cause* declined somewhat and the organization is currently trying to maintain it at a minimum of 250,000 persons.

Common Cause has placed its major emphasis on opening up the political process and making public officials more accountable to the general public. To that end, it has supported public disclosures of the sources of campaign financing, the lobbying activities of interest groups, and the personal finances of officeholders. It has also called for "open" meetings of public leaders and the end of closed sessions of legislative committees and secret voting on the floor of Congress. Although primarily a national organization, *Common Cause* has also helped to organize offices in state capitals to pursue the same kinds of reforms in state and local government.

The people's advocate.

John Gardner of Common Cause.

The major focus of activities of *Public Citizen* differs from that of *Common Cause*. Nader's groups have been more inclined than Gardner's to get involved in substantive issues, particularly economic ones such as energy and tax reform. While *Common Cause* has concentrated most of its activities on Congress and state legislatures, *Public Citizen* has been very active in supporting the claims of citizen groups in the courts and before executive agencies.

Despite differences in the basic emphasis of the two organizations, the division of labor between them is not complete. *Common Cause* has supported substantive issues, such as ending the war in Indochina and opposing the supersonic transport plane (SST) and, more recently, the B-1 bomber; it also occasionally becomes involved in litigation, joining with others, for example, in the suit challenging the Campaign Finance Law of 1974 (discussed in ch. 9). On the other hand, Nader and his associates undertook *Congress Project,* which profiled every member of that body running for reelection in 1972, and one of his current groups, *Congress Watch,* focuses on energy and consumer issues before the national legislature. In fact, the two organizations occasionally join forces as they have done recently on tax reform and in preventing the Clean Air Act from being weakened.

Thus a variety of interest groups in American society pursue different goals through different means. We will examine the nature of these means later in this chapter. First, however, we need to look at another important matter that affects the operation of interest groups: the relationship existing between the leaders and regular members of such organizations.

INTERNAL OPERATION OF INTEREST GROUPS

In theory, at least, interest groups are internally democratic in the sense that the rank-and-file members have a say over policy decisions as well as the selection of officers. A small voluntary group operating at the local level takes the form of direct democracy, with its periodic meetings as the equivalent of the Greek Assembly or the New England town meeting. Officers serve the group by presiding over such meetings and carrying on the group's activities between them. Interest groups that are important in national politics, however, encompass thousands or even millions of members who are organized on a nationwide basis. Given their size, these organizations use institutions and procedures of representative democracy that permit a relatively few persons to act on behalf of the entire membership.

Most national interest groups have similar means for governing themselves. A national convention attended by delegates chosen at the state and local level usually meets once a year to pass on major policy matters and to select the persons who will be responsible for carrying on the activities of the organization between conventions. The latter group generally consists of an executive body composed of elected officials that meets periodically to discuss group affairs. (This body, in turn, often selects a permanent staff headed by an executive secretary, who carries on the day-to-day activities of the organization.) Thus the operating principles of interest groups are democratic in form, and the few who handle the organization's affairs are held responsible to the many through representative institutions and procedures.

As a matter of fact, however, internal governance in most interest groups works in precisely the opposite way: an active minority runs the organization,

Politics, United Mine Workers' style.

and the rank-and-file members exercise relatively little control over their activities. Conventions held once a year attended by persons who have limited knowledge of the details of the group's operations can hardly be expected to serve as a meaningful check on the actions of the group's leadership. Typically the convention adopts the leaders' policy proposals with relatively little debate. Elections at the conventions also generally result in acceptance of the leadership's nominees for office. In fact, it is not uncommon for the same persons to be elected year after year without significant opposition. The *United Mine Workers,* for instance, had no seriously contested election for its presidency for almost half a century—from 1926 until 1969, when the incumbent president, Tony Boyle, beat off a challenge to his leadership by another official of the organization, Joseph Yablonski.*

A number of factors contribute to this internal situation. For one thing, the active minority has certain advantages in dealing with the rank-and-file membership. Besides a great knowledge of the group's affairs, the experience the leaders gain in office helps them develop managerial and political skills that few regular members can match. They are also in a position to dominate the group's affairs in various ways: by appointing the "right" persons to key committees, by determining what views will be carried in the organization's news-

---

* Boyle ultimately lost his presidency in 1973, but only after he was implicated in the murder of Yablonski that occurred three weeks after the 1969 election; moreoever, the federal government stepped in and conducted the 1973 election, which resulted in a victory for Arnold Miller a candidate of the rank-and-file members of the union.

paper (referred to generally as the *house organ*) which is distributed to all members, and by seeing to it that group's finances are used for the proper purposes. Thus power over personnel, the pen, and the purse enable the officers and staff of most interest groups to control their organization's activities.

Also contributing to the active minority's dominance is the fact that checks and balances are not built into the internal governance of most interest groups. Generally, no organized opposition (like a political party) exists to field a slate of candidates against the incumbent leadership and criticize what it is doing. (Some groups have regulations forbidding members from conducting campaigns or holding behind-the-scenes meetings to line up support for elected officials; others have an informal understanding that such activities will not occur.) Nor is there a contending group of permanent officeholders present (such as a legislative body) to counter the ambitions of the ruling clique. Thus the concept of competing elites that operates in public democratic bodies is generally absent in private interest groups.

The situation described above characterizes *most* interest groups in the United States, but of course the active minority cannot always control all organizations: the *International Typographical Union,* for instance has had two separate groups (or "parties") vying for leadership within the organization for years. Moreover, splits sometimes occur within a group's leadership: David McDonald, for many years the president of the *Steel Workers of America,* ultimately lost his post to another officer of the organization, Walter Abel. Also, an official who threatens the autonomy of local units may also lose his top-level post: James Carey, longtime president of the *International Union of Electrical Radio, and Machine Workers,* is reported to have been defeated on that issue in the 1965 election.* Nor does, the leadership of an interest group succeed entirely in imposing its policies on the rank-and-file membership: not all doctors subscribe to the AMA's fears concerning socialized medicine, and some state and local chapters of the AFL-CIO have failed to implement the desegregation edicts of the union's national headquarters.

Most interest groups, however, are able to reach substantial agreement on the organization's political goals and policies. The following section discusses the techniques they utilize to try to influence public officials to adopt those policies.

INFLUENCING PUBLIC POLICY

In order to accomplish its primary purpose of influencing public policy, a poltical interest group seeks "access" to official decision makers—that is, the opportunity to present its point of view to them. For an interest group, however, access means more than mere contact with decision makers; it also connotes a willingness to consider the group's views, whether or not the official ultimately decides to adopt them.

The process by which interest groups seek access to public officials is called lobbying. The term originated in the practice common to interest group repre-

---

* Carey sought to have union dues deducted from employees' pay checks sent directly to the central organization rather than to the local. Such a procedure would have denied locals the weapon of withholding dues from the central orgaization if they disagreed with its policies or procedures.

sentatives of frequenting the lobbies of government buildings in order to contact officials. Those who did so were referred to as "lobbyists" and the activity itself became known as '"lobbying."

Lester Milbrath, a close student of the subject, defines lobbying as a process by which someone (the lobbyist) communicates with a governmental decision maker* to try to influence what he does (or does *not* do) about a particular matter. Milbrath confines lobbying to communications made on behalf of someone else: a citizen who acts solely for himself concerning some public policy is not usually considered a lobbyist.

Lobbyists

As Milbrath suggests, interest groups make various arrangements to have their views presented to national officials. Large trade associations that have major offices in Washington typically use executive officials of the association as lobbyists, as do national labor unions, which are headquartered there. Groups with offices elsewhere must depend on a "Washington representative" to handle their lobbying; these persons normally handle the political affairs of a number of organizations. Some law firms located in Washinton not only carry on a standard legal practice before the courts but also represent clients on essentially political matters before legislative and executive officials. In addition, individual "lobbyist-entrepreneurs," who specialize in particular matters not requiring legal expertise, farm out their services to groups on a fee basis.

Whatever the arrangement, interest groups look for persons who possess information and skills that make them effective loyybists. Ex-senators and former members of the House of Representatives (along with former members of their staffs) are knowledgeable about particular legislation and also understand the complexities of the legislative process and enjoy contacts with former colleagues. As former legislators, they have the right to go on the floor of the legislative chambers, a priviliege that supposedly gives them an advantage in influencing legislation, particularly at the crucial time of a vote.† Despite these advantages, however, more lobbyists come from the executive than the legislative branch in Washington. The executive has a far larger number of former employees than the latter to draw from, and as we shall see in chapter 14, more and more crucial decisions are made by administrative officials. Therefore, persons knowledgeable about a given government agency are invaluable to organizations with business before it.

The skills of two professions—law and journalism—are particularly helpful to lobbyists. Lawyers are able to analyze the provisions of legislation as well as of executive regulations. Persons trained in writing and public-relations work can utilize those skills effectively in communicating with decision makers, members of their own organizations, and the general public—all targets of lobbying activities as discussed below.

---

* Although interest groups seek access to all three branches of government, the means by which they try to influence judges are very different from those they use on legislators and executive officials. We will examine the techniques they utilize before the courts in chapters 15 and 16.

† Former House members, however, are forbidden to go on the floor if they are in the employ of an organization that is interested in the particular legislation under consideration.

Lobbying is not a profession for which people specifically prepare themselves. Most go into the work by happenstance. Serving a stint as a lobbyist for a business organization is often part of the broad training of executives. Labor lobbyists are typically people who have previously demonstrated their political and verbal skills in the activities of a union. Former employees of the legislative and executive branches are often sought as lobbyists by interest groups who have observed them in their previous capacities.

Even though lobbyists do not specifically prepare themselves for that career, most of them enjoy the work and continue in it. Particularly rewarding is the sense of accomplishing something for their organization, the opportunity to interact with other people, and the challenge involved in preparing and defending an argument supporting their group's point of view. Pay and working conditions are also good, particularly for those lobbyists who represent business and professional groups.

Types of Lobbying

Lobbyists utilize a variety of approaches in communicating viewpoints to decision makers. Some involve direct contacts with public officials; others utilize intermediaries to try to influence such officials. The former method is called *direct* lobbying, the latter, *indirect* lobbying.

Direct lobbying. The lobbyist who is trying to influence Congress has a variety of options open to him. Since, as we shall see in chapter 11, the fate of legislative proposals largely depends on congressional committees that initially consider them, lobbyists appear before those committees to express their group's viewpoint on pending legislation. This approach permits the lobbyist to reach a number of influential legislators at one time. It also allows his group to get its views on record, since a transcript of committee hearings is made and distributed to concerned parties (including members of the interest group, who are thus furnished with proof that their lobbyist is working on their behalf).

Lobbyists, however, rate direct personal communications with individual representatives or senators as a more effective technique of persuasion than appearances before committees. Congressmen are frequently absent from committee meetings, or they have their minds on other matters while testimony is being taken. A personal visit to a congressman ensures attention and is more likely to convey the impression that the lobbyist thinks the individual legislator is important enough to warrant special consultation.

The above techniques are applicable to direct communications with officials of the executive branch, before whom more and more lobbying takes place. Government agencies also hold official hearings to take testimony of private groups, and lobbyists frequently call on executive officials to discuss problems of their clients.

Indirect Lobbying. Lobbyists work through intermediaries to try to influence decision makers. Congressmen and top executive officials with busy schedules depend heavily on their assistants to keep them briefed on legislative and executive matters. Therefore lobbyists who are able to persuade staff members of the merits of a client's point of view may be able to reach a major public official through his trusted employees.

Lobbyists often find it advantageous to work through other persons who enjoy special relationships with a decision maker whom they hope to influence. Personal friends of officials, of course, may provide an entrée, but even more helpful in reaching senators and representatives are their constituents, particularly those who are in a position to affect their political careers. If a lobbyist is able to get a heavy contributor to a congressman's campaign or a newspaper editor who supported that congressman for election to adopt his interest group's point of view and convey it to the elected official, he is virtually assured that it will be well received.

Lobbyists frequently use intermediaries to contact congressmen and executive officials who are not generally sympathetic to their organization's political goals. By working through neutral persons, not only do they avoid rebuffs, but they also hope to counteract any prejudice that might prevent their group's case from being examined by public officials on its merits. Lobbyists also use intermediaries as a means of increasing the number of people concerned with a particular issue. By widening their public, they seek to increase the political support for (or opposition against) a program of concern to their group.

One natural source of political support for a lobbyist is the membership of the organization he represents. Individual members are often unaware of the stands that their lobbyist takes in Washington, but they can be made aware of them through letters from the leadership or through the organization's newspaper. Thus the *American Medical Association* ran stories in its weekly journal for years against "socialized medicine."

Lobbyists frequently enlist the aid of members of groups that they represent to try to influence public officials. One technique is to get a person to write to his congressman or to the executive officials involved, expressing his views. A flood of mail can serve to alert a decision maker to the importance an issue has for some segments of the American public. At the same time, experienced public officials are able to detect a contrived letter-writing campaign stimulated by a lobbyist, by such clues as letters with identical wording, those sent on the same day, as well as those coming in disproportionate numbers from a particular area of the country. The wise lobbyist advises members of his organization to express their views in their own words and seeks to solicit letters written at different times from various parts of the nation.

Besides letter writing, other possibilities for using group members include getting them to talk to representatives and senators when they are back home campaigning or visiting, having individual members call on their congressmen when they are in Washington, and perhaps most effective of all, calling a conference in the nation's capital to let the lawmakers know firsthand how concerned individuals and groups feel on a particular issue.

A further broadening of the public involves getting diverse interest groups to join forces in the effort to influence congressmen and executive officials on a particular matter. This approach indicates to politicians that an issue is of concern to more than an isolated segment of the public. Groups that join political forces in this way are frequently drawn together as natural economic allies: General Motors, Ford, and Chrysler officials worked together with leaders of the *United Auto Workers* to delay the imposition of emission standards because, despite their differences over labor-management problems, all of them feared that they would be harmed economically by having to meet the timetable favored by the environmentalists. Business interest groups also take on the political battles of their customers: prior to the fuel shortage certain railroads opposed the importation of oil from abroad because so much of their freight business comes from coal companies that were hurt by the rival fuel.

Beyond immediate interests that lead groups to join forces on a particular issue, there is an increasing tendency for certain organizations with divergent interests to adopt each other's political causes. Thus the *Chamber of Commerce of the United States* typically sides with the *American Farm Bureau Federation* on agricultural policy questions, while the latter takes the Chamber's side on business issues before the Congress. Similarly, the AFL–CIO and the *National Farmers' Union* tend to end up on the same side of most political issues. This form of logrolling,* or exchange of support, has obvious political advantages for all parties concerned, but the practice also develops because members of various interest groups share certain fundamental values and political attitudes. Thus "liberal" organizations like the *United Auto Workers,* the *National Farmers' Union,* the *Americans for Democratic Action*, and the *Federal Council of Churches* generally advocate that the national government develop programs to help the disadvantaged. "Conservative" groups such as the *National Association of Manufacturers,* the *American Farm Bureau Federation*, the *American Legion,* and the *Young Americans for Freedom* prefer that the poor and deprived help themselves, or, if outside assistance is necessary, that it come from private groups or state and local governments. Such opposing ideologies frequently result in two general constellations of interests—those that support and those that oppose governmental programs to change the status quo in favor of underdog groups in American society.

Besides rallying the support of members of their own organizations and forming alliances with like-minded groups, lobbyists in recent years have turned their attention to an even more inviting target for indirect lobbying: the general public. If an interest group can make enough people sympathetic to its desires and persuade them to convey their sentiments to those in public office, then it has achieved a major strategic objective: getting other people to lobby for it.

The effort to shape public attitudes on issues takes different forms and involves various strategies and groups. Frequently, lobbyists use members of their own organizations to influence the general public. In the fight against "socialized medicine" some years ago, the leadership of the *American Medical Association* got doctors to distribute literature and to talk to their patients about the matter. The organization capitalized on the layman's tendency to respect his own physician and to regard him as an expert on health issues. As another technique the testimony of independent authorities can be presented to persuade the public of the merits of a particular view. Some years ago, when the development of an Antiballistic Missile (ABM) system to be placed around the nation's cities was under consideration, both the pro-and anti-ABM forces used this technique; the *American Security Council* published a booklet signed by a Nobel-prize-winning chemist supporting the weapon, while the other side countered with a publication by a former science advisor to President Kennedy setting forth his objections to it.

---

* This term is usually used to describe the practice whereby legislators back each other's bills to their mutual advantage.

Yet another tactic is to operate through an organization whose name conceals the true identity of its supporters. Some years ago a group called the *Small Business Economic Foundation* was formed purportedly to speak for the views of the modest entrepreneur. On investigation, it was determined that among the small businesses behind the organization were United States Steel, Goodyear Tire and Rubber, the Texas Company, and a number of other firms of comparable size. This same attempt to capitalize on symbols to which the public responds favorably* is reflected in the title of an organization called the *Committee for Constitutional Government,* which is backed primarily by a number of conservative business groups in the United States. It has a counterpart, the *Public Affairs Institute,* through which liberal groups, particularly certain labor unions, convey their views to the public.

Interest groups also use the mass media to transmit ideas in ways that camouflage their true source: letters-to-the-editor columns of newspapers frequently carry statements signed by individuals that in actuality are drafted by lobbyists. A similar practice is the preparation of "canned" editorials. The harried editor of a weekly newspaper who must handle all aspects of the paper's operation may welcome prepared statements on public issues that save him the effort of writing original editorials—especially when the material expresses his own viewpoint and is better organized and written than anything his busy schedule would permit him to develop. (Both parties benefit from such an arrangement: the editor is made to look like a perceptive and critical analyst of public issues, and the interest group gets its views purveyed without the public's knowing their real source.)

Television is another natural outlet for interest groups that seek to shape public attitudes on controversial issues. When President Kennedy outlined his program on medical care for the aged on national networks, a representative from the *American Medical Association* responded shortly thereafter with the physicians' case against the program. Standing alone in a bare studio, the AMA spokesman sought to convey the image of the solitary citizen battling to preserve his liberties against the organized forces of the national government and the awesome power of the presidency.

Thus lobbying has become increasingly complex and sophisticated over the years as interest-group representatives have directed their efforts at a broader array of targets and utilized a greater variety of techniques in their quest to influence public policy. Whereas communications were once directed essentially to legislators, lobbyists have now broadened their efforts, directing them to the executive branch of government, where more and more key decisions affecting private groups are now being made. At the same time, they have expanded their activities to take in various intermediaries—including the general public itself—that can assist them in their lobbying efforts. Their techniques have also undergone change as interest groups employ modern methods in influencing public attitudes through the mass media.

Along with such changes has come a supplementary activity: keeping communication channels open to decision makers so that when future lobbying takes place, it will be effective. In other words, lobbyists seek to create good

---

* An additional advantage in using such titles is the possibility that the organization will be considered an "educational" group by the government, thus qualifying it for certain tax advantages or exempting it from registering under federal legislation regulating lobbying.

relationships with legislative and executive officials to ensure that their messages to them will be well received. They also strive to develop a generally favorable impression with the American people so that they may benefit from that impression when they later try to exert influence on behalf of their group.

Opening Communication Channels

In a democratic society the relationship between public officials and interest groups is a two-way process: private groups not only press demands on officials; they also serve as potential bases of support for them. Thus lobbyists can keep communication channels open to congressmen and members of the executive branch by undertaking activities of value to them.

The most basic support an interest group can provide any public official is to help him get into office in the first place. If he seeks an appointive office, the group's representatives can use whatever political influence they have to see to it that persons responsible for the appointment are made aware of the man's qualifications and the high esteem in which he is held by that organization. As we shall see in chapters 14 and 16, many interest groups become involved in appointments to major executive posts and to seats on the federal bench; in the process, they try to persuade the President, who makes the nominations, and the Senate, which must confirm his nominees, to choose men who will be receptive to their organizations' political views.

Interest groups are also in a position to provide important political support for a man who is running for an elected office. This support can take many forms: making financial contributions to his campaign; providing information or writers for his political speeches, along with audiences for them; running favorable publicity for the candidates in the house organ, besides endorsing him publicly; or helping to get voters registered and to the polls to vote for him. In addition, an interest group can help him in the nomination process (discussed in ch. 8) and in the general election (analyzed in ch. 9). The earlier the group provides a person political support and the more extensive that support is, the more likely he is to grant access to the representatives of that organization.

Yet there are also political dangers involved for the interest group that commits itself to a would-be official. If he fails to be appointed or elected, it is not likely that the group will have access to his opponent. Moreover, it is by no means certain that an organization can deliver its members' votes in an electoral contest: despite organized labor's endorsement of the Democratic presidential candidate, Adlai Stevenson, in 1952 and 1956, many rank-and-file workers voted on both occasions for his opponent, Dwight Eisenhower. Or even if a group can persuade its members to support a particular candidate, they may be so widely scattered geographically that they have little impact on the election. The group must also consider the possibility that if it throws its active political support one way, its political enemies may be stimulated to enter the contest on the other side. Thus an organization's representatives must weigh the advantages and disadvantages of active political involvement in support of a particular political party or candidate.*

* One technique employed by some groups is to contribute financially to more than one candidate or to have various leaders or members support different would-be officials. Then, presumably, no matter who wins, the organization has access.

Whether or not an interest group decides to try to play a role in the selection of public officials, it typically performs important services for those who are already in office. Included are the furnishing of factual information and, if the official desires it, the writing of speeches to be given before his constituents. Lobbyists can also provide officials with ready-made audiences through their own membership and can rally their support for measures favored by the officials. Such services are designed to make a public official grateful and incline him to be receptive to future lobbying.

Another technique for keeping channels open to public officials is entertainment, or the "social lobby." Frequently the general public is treated to newspaper exposés that play up such socializing as though it were the only form of lobbying. Undoubtedly this tactic is successful with some national officials, yet most of them are so busy that they reserve the few moments they can spare from the pressures of their job for their family and close personal friends. The social lobby may be more successful in state capitals, where legislators are away from their families during the week and hence have more time for (and less family scrutiny of) social activities.

Lobbyists are frequently pictured as stealthy figures with little black satchels stuffed with money that they disperse as bribes to win favorable decisions from congressmen and officials of the executive branch. There is little question that bribery does occur at times. In 1956 lobbyists for an oil company were accused of offering Republican Senator Francis Case of South Dakota a $2500 campaign contribution (which he rejected) to influence his vote on a natural-gas bill. Moreover, allegations were made that dairy interests contributed to the 1972 Nixon campaign in return for an administration decision to increase milk prices, and that the International Telephone and Telegraph Corporation (ITT) made a pledge of financial support for the proposed Republican National Convention in 1972 in San Diego (later changed to Miami) in exchange for a favorable settlement of a government antitrust suit against the multinational conglomerate. More recently, Korean businessmen have been accused of providing gifts and financial contributions to members of Congress in order to influence governmental decisions regarding their economic interests. However, such instances are the exception rather than the rule: lobbyists who engage in activities of this nature run the risk that exposure will ruin their professional reputation and damage the interests of their client as well.

Lobbyists also try to keep communication channels open to the American public in order to shape basic attitudes that are favorable to their respective groups. One approach is to work through the schools to promote particular textbooks; business prefers those that support the free-enterprise system, while labor looks with favor on books that emphasize the dignity of work and the contributions that unions have made to American life. Groups from both camps frequently send materials to teachers for use in the classrooms. Some have gone so far as to subsidize the writing of textbooks favorable to their general point of view on public issues. Another technique is institutional advertising, which seeks to sell a political point of view as well as a commercial product. A recent example of this approach is the advertisement, printed on the next page, recently run in the media by Mobil Oil Company.

A more subtle way of keeping channels open to the American people is through publicizing activities that reflect credit on a group. A number of years

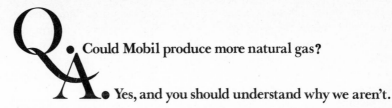

Q. Could Mobil produce more natural gas?

A. Yes, and you should understand why we aren't.

Q. Well, why not?
A. For several reasons—some economic, some technical, some involving conservation, and in some cases, because of regulatory delays. When we make a new gas discovery, we must ask: is there enough gas and is the price we'll get for the gas high enough to make commercial development of the field feasible? Will the expected revenue support the cost of drilling and equipping development wells? Is a pipeline company willing to link up to the field? And we hope there will be enough profit to help pay the cost of finding the *next* new field.

Q. You mean more natural gas would be produced if the price were higher?
A. No doubt about it. Producers would have the incentive to develop smaller fields, or those in remote areas, which aren't commercially feasible at today's prices.

Q. You mentioned other reasons besides price. How does conservation figure in?
A. Sometimes, for conservation reasons, we do not produce a field as fast as possible. We produce as much as we can consistent with sound field-conservation practice. Producing too fast may harm certain fields and reduce the amount of gas we can ultimately get from them. Such conservation will make this fuel available for future winters.

Q. Today's prices have gone up. Why must they go up still more?
A. Today's prices for natural gas have been totally distorted by 23 years of federally imposed, artificially low prices at the wellhead. Recent price increases granted by the Federal Power Commission may help, if the courts approve them. But the price of natural gas is still below its real worth. Remember, it's a premium fuel: piped right to the customer and cleaner than coal or oil. Yet, the average price of interstate natural gas at the well equates in terms of energy content to a crude oil price of about $3.50 per barrel. Currently, the average price of domestic crude is about $8.60 a barrel.

Q. Is Mobil holding off on producing gas until prices reach the "real worth" level?
A. No. We are bringing into production those new fields which are commercially viable at today's prices. Production of marginal discoveries must hinge on higher price levels.

Q. What incentive do you have to produce as much as possible?
A. Over a billion dollars of investments since 1970 for federal lease bonuses in the Gulf of Mexico. After paying the additional costs of drilling exploratory wells and of developing the fields we found (which were mostly gas), we naturally want to start recouping our investment as fast as possible. We have brought five new offshore blocks into production since last September, and expect to be producing from nine more by July. Our total U.S. gas production, after declining for several years due to natural depletion, may rise over the next three years because of new discoveries coming into production.

Q. How about the stories in the press about shut-in wells?
A. Most shut-in wells are out of production for technical reasons—for routine maintenance, or to wait until a pipeline is built to connect to a new field. Besides, any shut-in gas will be available for future years. Sometimes, wells are shut in until government red tape is unsnarled.

Q. How can government red tape shut in a well?
A. Here's one example. A couple of years ago, the FPC tried to change a contract already agreed to between Mobil and one of our customers, by attempting to extend its jurisdiction and making unprecedented demands. The terms we were proposing were the same as those in effect elsewhere, and were in accordance with industry and FPC practice. After a full year's delay, the FPC finally issued the necessary permits to hook up the pipeline. So for about nine months, gas was not permitted to be sold to the market.

Q. Let's go back to what interests consumers most—prices. If price regulation were ended, how high would prices go?
A. What should concern consumers most is an assured supply of natural gas. As to price, Mobil is urging that only new natural gas be decontrolled. There would therefore be no sudden major price jolt, because new gas volume will be relatively small initially. And old gas under existing contracts would continue to be sold at a much lower price. Hopefully, when these contracts expire, a program for gradual decontrol of any remaining old gas would apply. Such decontrol would encourage the search for new supplies, cause producers to bring previously marginal discoveries into production, and persuade some customers to shift to oil or coal.

Q. What would that mean, specifically, for the homeowner?
A. It's hard to cite any figures. The wellhead price of interstate natural gas represents only a portion of the average homeowner's gas bill. Indeed, in cold-weather areas, transportation and distribution are the major cost factors. Besides, if new gas were decontrolled today, contracts already in force would remain in force. Consumers' bills would go up gradually as old contracts run out and new gas fields come into operation, replacing old gas.

Q. Is there anything the nation should have learned from this winter's natural gas crisis?
A. For parts of the country, this winter has been one of the coldest on record. It's easy to accuse the producers of holding back gas. But a basic cause of the crisis was a 23-year-old mistake, which can't be corrected overnight. At least, we should start correcting such a long-term error by deregulating new natural gas.

ago certain chain stores in California faced the possibility that a tax on their operations passed by the legislature would be approved in a referendum set for a year later.* A public-relations firm determined that their unfavorable public image could dispose the voters to support the tax. With the assistance of the firm, the stores launched a campaign publicizing a plan to improve their employees' wages and working conditions. They also cooperated with peach growers in helping to absorb an unforeseen surplus of their crop. In addition, the chains offered to close their businesses on Sundays if independent stores would do likewise. A poll taken immediately before the referendum indicated a change in public attitude toward the chain stores, and the electorate subsequently voted down the proposed tax decisively.

Many interest groups today do not wait for an issue to develop before attempting to shape public attitudes; they rather work constantly to create a reservoir of good will toward their organization from which they can draw when the occasion arises. Public-relations men see to it that favorable publicity about a group's members is released: when business executives and labor leaders head Red Cross drives and United Fund campaigns or offer their services voluntarily in building a Boy Scout camp or fixing up a church, news of their philanthropic activities is not hidden under a bushel but instead is displayed widely to the American people. Thus groups seek to keep the channels open to the general public as a means of ensuring that when they want to lobby on issues that concern them, their communications will fall on receptive ears.

Legal Regulation of Lobbying

Lobbying is regarded in the United States as a legitimate method for influencing public policy. It has been granted constitutional sanction as coming within the basic rights of free speech and petition guaranteed by the First and Fourteenth Amendments to the Constitution. Congress has, however, placed two types of restriction on lobbying: (1) certain limits on the kinds of activities interest groups may engage in; (2) requirements that lobbyists and organizations disclose their identity as well as certain basic facts about their operations.

One type of lobbying that is clearly considered beyond the rules of the game is bribery. Federal laws make it a crime for persons to offer a congressman "anything of value" for the purpose of buying his vote or otherwise trying to influence his official actions. Congressmen who accept such offers are also subject to criminal charges. The difficulty with enforcing the law is that it is almost impossible to prove that a favor was tendered for the purpose forbidden by the act. (For example, it does not constitute bribery for a lobbyist to promise a congressman future political support in order to influence his vote on legislation.) Most students of the subject consider this legislation ineffective in preventing questionable dealings between interest-group representatives and congressmen.

The role of lobbies in making financial contributions to political campaigns is limited by law. We will explore the subject of campaign finance in chapter 9,

---

* Laws passed by legislatures in most states can be referred to the voters for approval or rejection in referendum elections.

including the abuses that occurred in the 1972 presidential campaign. It is sufficient for the present to note that certain organizations (foreign governments, for instance) are prohibited from making any campaign contributions in federal elections, and other groups face limitations on the amount of contributions they may make.

With these exceptions, interest groups are free to lobby at will. But Congress has taken the position that its members, as well as the American people, have the right to know who is supporting and opposing legislation, and that financial arrangements of lobbyists and interest groups with business before the national legislature ought to be a matter of public record. Thus lobbying activities are not to be prohibited but, rather, illuminated.

Although lobbyists for certain groups were singled out by Congress in the 1930s and made to disclose information about themselves and their clients (included were lobbyists for public-utility holding companies and shipping firms as well as those representing foreign governments), it was not until 1946 that a law was passed requiring similar information of lobbyists and interest groups in general. Enacted as part of a broad statute dealing with the reorganization of Congress, the Federal Regulation of Lobbying Act requires any person (or group) hired by someone else for the "principal purpose" of influencing congressional legislation to register with the Secretary of the Senate and Clerk of the House and file quarterly reports on his receipts and expenditures for lobbying with the House Clerk. Organizations that collect money to engage in such activities but do not hire themselves out as lobbyists for someone else are required to file similar financial information with the Clerk of the House.

It is generally agreed that the law contains so many loopholes that it has not been effective. Groups ostensibly affected by the act avoid its application by arguing either that they spend their own funds for lobbying rather than soliciting them from outside sources or that the outside funds they collect are not raised for the "principal purpose" of influencing Congress. Lobbying directed to executive agencies or the general public is not covered by the law, nor is testifying before legislative committees.

The law also leaves it up to groups themselves to determine the portion of their total lobbying expenditures that needs to be reported; as a result, organizations with large financial outlays claim to spend very little, arguing that most of it goes for research and public information (which are not covered by the statute) rather than direct personal contact with congressmen. Finally, even the information that is reported is almost worthless, since no agency is empowered either to investigate its truthfulness or to ensure that violations of the law are enforced. Until such time as these deficiencies are rectified (to date, Congress has been unwilling to do so),* the act will fail to accomplish its major objective—disclosure of activities of major lobbyists and interest groups in the United States.

Despite the lack of effective legal regulation of lobbying, however, Washington observers agree that most persons tend to respect certain informal rules of

---

* Both houses of Congress passed bills in 1976 to revise the 1946 law, but the session adjourned before they could agree on the specifics of the proposed legislation. Only *Common Cause,* Nader's *Congress Watch,* and the AFL-CIO among the major interest groups supported the revision. However, it was given a good chance of passage in a later Congress.

the game in attempting to influence public policy. Aside from matters of individual conscience, lobbyists naturally desire to protect their reputations with their colleagues and, even more importantly, with public officials. If a lobbyist provides false information to an official and is found out, he will certainly lose the very thing he works so hard to achieve: access to that individual. In all probability, the official will also tell others of his unfortunate experience, so that the lobbyist will find himself cut off from a number of important persons who make vital decisions affecting his group. Thus the denial of access is a powerful deterrent to lobbyists who may be tempted to engage in improper activities in seeking to influence public decisions.

A wide variety of interest groups in American society seek access to the political system to further their purposes. In so doing, they employ a number of techniques to influence decision makers in all three branches of the national government—legislative, executive and judicial—to enact and carry out policies that will provide benefits to their members. The following sections focus on the activities of two increasingly important groups in American politics, blacks and women, and the ways in which our political system has responded to their demands.

PRESSURING THE SYSTEM: THE CASE OF BLACKS

Of course, blacks belong to a wide variety of voluntary organizations. Many of these groups do not relate to racial matters and have a predominently white membership; there are black members of the *United Automobile Workers,* the *United States Chamber of Commerce,* the *National Farmers Union, Common Cause,* and the like. Moreover, many major all-black organizations such as churches and fraternal organizations, that have traditionally been so important to Negroes, have not attempted to place demands on government. Here, however, we are concerned only with interest groups that speak to the needs of black Americans in particular and attempt to use the political process to meet those needs. As the following discussion indicates, there have been a number of such interest groups with different goals, types of leaders, and techniques for accomplishing their purposes.

Interest Group Activities

While black interest groups existed prior to this century (for example, a *Colored Farmers Alliance* was organized in Texas in 1886 and grew rapidly for a time in the South), the beginnings of today's important groups can be timed to the first decade of the twentieth century. A serious race riot occurred in Springfield, Illinois in 1908, and the following year a group of white and black intellectuals assembled in New York City to found the *National Association for the Advancement of Colored People* (NAACP). Concerned with violence directed against blacks and the general worsening of race relations in the United States, the organization had as its major goals eradicating prejudice and promoting equality in education, employment, suffrage, and before the courts and the law. The single most important leader of the organization, W. E. B. DuBois, a Harvard-educated Negro social-scientist who taught at Atlanta University, served as the organization's first publicity director and editor of its organ, *The Crisis.* However, the organization was also given great prominence and

W.E.B. DuBois of the NAACP.

visibility through the efforts of well-known white leaders, including the philosopher and educator John Dewey; the founder of Hull House, Jane Adams; and the eminent lawyer Clarence Darrow.

A year after the establishment of the NAACP, three organizations working in New York City to mitigate the problems of blacks who had migrated there from the South merged to form the *National League on Urban Conditions among Negroes,* which came to be known as the *National Urban League.* Composed of conservative Negroes, white philanthropists, and social workers, it concentrated its efforts on finding employment opportunities for blacks and helping them to adjust to urban life. In so doing, it adopted a conciliatory approach in persuading employers that Negroes were good workers. Like the NAACP, the organization was distinctly middle-class in its orientation.

While the two organizations have naturally changed somewhat over the years (for example, blacks have largely replaced whites in leadership positions), these two interest groups have retained their essential character. They still are interracial and attract financial contributions and support from the white liberal community. Moreover, the same kinds of persons who founded the two organizations—professionals and other highly educated individuals—remain as the major activists in the two groups.

The techniques used by the NAACP and the *National Urban League* have also remained substantially the same over the years. The former has sought social change through the law, primarily by bringing suits in the courts to challenge all forms of racial discrimination in education, employment, recreation, housing, and in participation in the political process; the organization has also lobbied both the Congress and the executive branch to obtain equal opportunities for blacks. The *National Urban League* retains its emphasis on providing direct social services to blacks living in urban areas, expanding such services in recent years from traditional concerns such as education, employment, housing, and welfare, to newer areas of interest like family planning, consumer and youth affairs, and the development of minority businesses. The organization has also become more politically active in recent years, joining with the efforts of the NAACP to eliminate discrimination and segregation from American society.

The actions of the NAACP and the *National Urban League* have done much to provide a legal basis for the removal of the black's inferior status in American society and to help those living in metropolitan areas adjust to the harsh realities of urban life. Their emphasis on working within the present social and political system has helped to avoid interracial hostility and to win the sympathy of many elements of the white majority to their cause. But many blacks consider the approaches of the two organizations to social change to be too slow and cumbersome, resulting in legal victories that exist on paper only and that do not actually result in significant changes in the lives of blacks, particularly those belonging to the lower class. Moreover, there is a feeling that the traditional techniques used by the NAACP and the *National Urban League* have done little to raise the political consciousness of poor blacks and to stimulate them to initiate their own action to improve their situation in life.

The Rise of Nonviolent Protest Groups. As the race riots in Springfield in 1908 helped precipitate the formation of the NAACP, so an incident in Montgomery, Alabama in late 1955 set into motion forces that led to the rise of a new type of black interest group, using nonviolent protest as a major means of registering its demands. A black woman, Rosa Parks, refused to give up her seat in the front of a city bus to a white man and was arrested for violating a city ordinance. The black community quickly organized a bus boycott to protest the incident and chose a young Baptist minister, Dr. Martin Luther King Jr., to direct the effort. An association composed of Montgomery blacks called for the end of segregated seating in the city's buses; after some violence and the jailing of King and other protest leaders, the association ultimately prevailed when the United States Supreme Court ruled against segregated seating on municipal buses.

The importance of the bus incident, however, lay not in the successful legal conclusion of that particular matter, but rather in its bringing to national prominence the Reverend Dr. King, who worked to achieve full integration of Negroes in all aspects of American life. His approach was that of nonviolence, or passive resistance, a technique that he borrowed from Mahatma Gandhi, who has used it successfully against the British in India. In 1957 King founded the *Southern Christian Leadership Conference* (SCLC), a loose organization of Southern clergymen who joined together to fight against segregation and for Negroes' voting rights, particularly in the South. King's dominant role in the civil rights struggle, however, stemmed not from his position with that organization but from the symbolic leadership that he provided for blacks generally, many of whom were affiliated with other organizations.

One such group that came to prominence in the early 1960s was the *Student Nonviolent Coordinating Committee* (SNCC). Composed of Negro college students who initially protested against segregation at Southern lunchcounters early in 1960, it was officially founded in April of that year at a meeting attended by King and other civil rights leaders. SCLC provided SNCC with financial and other assistance, as did other Negro organizations such as the NAACP. In time Northern college students also helped with the group's primary activities: sponsoring sit-ins and freedom rides to protest segregation in

"I have a dream"—Martin
Luther King, Jr.

public accommodations and transportation, and registering Southern Negroes to vote. Under the leadership of John Lewis, SNCC, as its name stated, was also committed to the principle of nonviolence.

A third group, which also assisted SNCC and joined the civil rights effort in the South, was the *Congress of Racial Equality* (CORE). Established in Chicago in 1942, the organization carried out a successful sit-in the following year to protest segregation in restaurants in that city. The interracial group, composed of students of the Federated Theological Seminary of the University of Chicago and college graduates engaged in white-collar occupations, attracted little attention during the remainder of that decade or in the one that followed; but in the spring of 1961, shortly after James Farmer became its national director, the organization launched freedom rides through the South to test whether nondiscrimination policies were actually being observed in interstate transportation.

These three organizations formed the nucleus of the movement to achieve integration and secure Negro political rights through direct-action techniques designed to bring quick results. Sympathetic whites from the North contributed financially to the movement, and many of them, particularly college students, went to the South to assist with the integration of public facilities and the registering of Negroes to vote. The coalition of blacks and white liberals reached a high point in August 1963 when some 200,000 persons responded to the call of A. Philip Randolph and the pacifist socialist Bayard Rustin (who had first experimented with personal sit-ins in the 1940s) to join a march on Washington as a means of persuading Congress to enact civil rights legislation. It was at this gathering (remarkable for its orderliness, given the number of people that participated) that Dr. King delivered his famous "I have a dream" speech ("I have a dream that my four little children will one day live in a nation where they will not be judged by the color of their skin but by the content of their character. ...").

Just as the civil rights movement seemed to reach new heights, however, it began to develop frustrations. Direct-action techniques failed to bring results in desegregating facilities in Mississippi and Alabama; the Negro Mississippi political party, the Freedom Democratic party, which came to the Democratic presidential convention in the summer of 1964 to challenge the seating of the regular Democratic delegation on the grounds of Negro disenfranchisement, was granted only token representation: two at-large seats. In the North direct action proved ineffective both against de facto segregation of the schools occasioned by residential segregation of the races and against job discrimination by employers and labor unions alike. Violence broke out in some of the nation's major cities: Harlem experienced difficulties in the summer of 1964, and the nation was shocked the following summer when the Watts section of Los Angeles exploded in the worst riot in the nation's history.

In the period from 1964 to 1966 more and more blacks became dissatisfied with nonviolent, direct action as a means of achieving their goals. Contrariwise, many white liberals became alarmed at the incidents of violence and began to withdraw their support (particularly financial) from the civil rights movement. Martin Luther King experienced increased difficulty in bridging the gaps between Negro factions and between the two races. The stage was thus set for a new phase in the Civil Rights battle.

The Shift to Black Power. As the Montgomery boycott ushered in the initial stages of the Race Revolution in the mid 1950s, an incident that occurred a decade later in Mississippi triggered a new phase of the racial struggle in the United States. James Meredith (whose enrollment at the University of Mississippi in 1962 had touched off a riot that led to the intervention of federal troops) began a Freedom March through that state in the summer of 1966 to interest blacks in registering to vote. The march had barely begun when Meredith was shot and wounded. King rushed to the scene to resume the march, cautioning the participants to remain nonviolent. In contrast, however, a young Howard University graduate—Stokely Carmichael, chairman of the *Student Nonviolent Coordinating Committee,* who had recently replaced John Lewis—urged Mississippi blacks to follow a new approach in the civil rights battle: "Black Power."

Carmichael never defined what he meant by the term Black Power. It has remained vague, partly because it represents a general mood or call for action rather than a specific program with concrete goals, and partly because it means different things to different people. Nonetheless, it is possible to spell out certain ideas that have come to be identified with Black Power.*

Black Power for some of its advocates has meant primarily *economic power* in the form of more black businesses (black capitalism) as well as getting white firms to do business with such companies and to hire more black workers. Others have emphasized *political power,* electing blacks to public office, particularly in the rural South and urban areas of the North where the black population in the United States tends to be concentrated. Still other interpret black power to mean the idea of *black consciousness,* a feeling of pride in race that is reflected in the establishment of Black Studies programs in colleges and universities to acquaint members of the race with their cultural heritage, and in moves to have blacks gain control of primary and secondary schools in areas where they live, substituting black teachers for whites and tailoring the curriculum to fit the special needs of their children.

Carried to its extreme, black power means separation of the races rather than the integration of them. Such a goal has been strongly opposed by the NAACP

---

* One recent survey of interpretations given the term by black citizens in Detroit indicated that many of them associated it with a traditional goal of the civil rights movement: "a fair share"— that is, equal rights for Negroes. However, most Negro leaders appear to regard Black Power as involving new approaches to race relations, as discussed below.

The young militant—Eldridge Cleaver.

and the *National Urban League* and has drawn little sympathy from the SCLC. However, the leadership of both CORE and SNCC moved in the direction of separation in the mid-1960s when Stokely Carmichael and Floyd McKissick respectively replaced moderate James Farmer and John Lewis, who formerly headed those organizations. Moreover, two other interest groups explicity embraced an extreme policy of segregation by advocating that separate geographical areas be set aside for blacks.

The *Black Muslims*, founded in 1930, want to establish an exclusive black state in the United States where no whites are to be allowed. Believing that blacks originally lived in a high state of civilization in Mecca but were conquered by whites and made to worship the white Jesus, the *Black Muslims* believe in the superiority of the black race and hence the desirability of separation. One of the former leaders of the organization, Malcolm X (who was slain in 1965 by another Black Muslim), likened blacks in the United States to a colonized people such as those in Africa who must win freedom from their white oppressors.

The second separatist group with beliefs similar to those of Malcolm X is the *Black Panthers*, who want the central cities to be controlled by blacks. Marxist in orientation, Black Panther leaders like Eldridge Cleaver sought ties with the ex-colonial Third World as well as with white revolutionaries in the United States, in order to overthrow the capitalist system, which they feel enslaves both blacks and whites.* Founded in Oakland, California in 1966 to protect blacks there against alleged police brutality, the *Black Panthers* have been involved in periodic shoot-outs with police (however, some of these have not been entirely of the *Panthers'* making), whom they consider agents of the white society that holds them in colonial bondage.

It has never been very clear whether the use of violence is considered to be part of Black Power and, if so, under what circumstances such use is permissible. Carmichael himself vacillated on the issue, and the leaders of CORE sanction it only in self defense. Only the *Black Panthers* overtly advocated it as a weapon of guerrilla warfare to be used against white oppressors such as the police. Moreover, much of the violence associated with urban riots in Los Angeles, Detroit, Washington, and other major cities in the mid-to-late 1960s appears to have resulted from spontaneous reactions by masses of blacks to specific events (such as alleged police brutality and the assassination of black leaders like Martin Luther King Jr.) rather than demonstrations planned and executed by organized interest groups and their leaders.

Recent Interest Group Activities. Like the 1950s and 1960s, the 1970s have been characterized by changes in interest group activity on behalf of blacks. Some organizations like SNCC have disappeared from the scene altogether in recent years, while others like the *Black Panthers* in Oakland seem to have abandoned the rhetoric of revolution in favor of such community-action programs as providing free meals to hungry ghetto children and escort service to

* Cleaver, at one time Minister of Information for the Black Panthers, abandoned his anti-U.S. stand and commitment to violence and voluntarily returned to the United States in 1975, after seven years abroad, to face charges of attempted murder and assault stemming from a 1968 shoot-out with the Oakland police.

protect the elderly against muggings. At the leadership level of the *National Urban League*, Vernon Jordan has replaced the deceased Whitney Young, and Benjamin Hooks has become Executive Director of the NAACP, succeeding the long-time holder of that post, Roy Wilkins.

The leaders of the national interest groups referred to above no longer dominate the civil rights struggle as they did in the past. No individual comparable to Martin Luther King exists today in whom the overwhelming proportion of blacks have faith. Black leadership tends to be fragmented, with new aspirants acquiring (and often soon losing) influence with certain kinds of blacks. The civil rights movement also has tended to focus more at the local level in recent years. As Julian Bond, a black member of the Georgia legislature, expressed the situation: "Black people aren't so much interested now in marching from Selma to Montgomery as they are in doing something right there in Selma."

Another recent development is the redirection of black demands into traditional political channels. The protests of the early 60s in Selma and Birmingham in the South and the urban riots in Watts, Detroit, and other northern centers in the latter part of the decade have been replaced by blacks seeking and obtaining political office. Organizations of black officeholders have also emerged as exemplified by the *Congressional Black Caucus* as well as the *National Poltical Convention of Elected Officials and Political Activists,* both of which propose programs of interest to blacks and lobby white officeholders to enact them into law. Thus blacks have begun to pressure the political system from within as well as from without.

Interest group activity on behalf of blacks has undergone substantial change in this century. As a close student of the movement, political scientist Charles Hamilton, describes it, the fight for racial justice has moved "from court to street to politics." The following section analyzes the kinds of responses such actions have brought from the national government.

The Government Response

Interest group activities on behalf of blacks over the years have been aimed at different governmental targets: some have been directed at the courts while other actions have sought to engage the powers of executives and legislators in improving race relations in the United States. As the following discussion indicates, the responses of the three branches of the national government to such activities have also differed over the course of the civil rights struggle.

The Judiciary. The early stages of the struggle for racial equality in the United States were fought out almost exclusively in the courts. The newly established NAACP won its initial judicial victory in *Guinn* v. *United States* in 1915 when the Supreme Court invalidated the "grandfather" clause of the Oklahoma Constitution exempting persons from a literacy test if their ancestors were entitled to vote in 1866; the Court viewed this as a deliberate (and not too subtle) attempt to avoid the Fifteenth Amendment's prohibition against denying citizens the right to vote on account of "race, color or previous condition of servitude." The Association subsequently waged a number of legal battles against the white primary (a device excluding blacks from participating in

Hizonor, Maynard Jackson

choosing nominees of the Democratic Party in southern states), culminating in *Smith* v. *Allright* (1944), in which the Court held such an election to be a *public* function (rather than the business of *private* organization, the Democratic party) and hence forbidden by that same Amendment. A 1966 decision, *Harper* v. *Virginia,* eliminated the poll tax as a requirement for voting in state elections by ruling that it violated the "equal protection of the laws" clause of the Fourteenth Amendment. Thus the NAACP went to the courts to vindicate the political rights of blacks, thereby opening up the governmental process to them.

The NAACP has also used the judicial arena to eliminate segregation and discrimination in various areas of American life. Municipal ordinances providing for residential segregation in housing were outlawed in 1917, and ultimately in a 1948 decision—*Shelley* v. *Kraemer*—the Court held that restrictive covenants in deeds (clauses preventing property from being sold to nonwhites) could not be enforced in court because they violated the "equal protection of the laws" clause of the Fourteenth Amendment. The Supreme Court has since struck down segregation in public transportation and recreational facilities; it has also forbidden discrimination in private organizations that use public facilities and ruled that a community swim club could not deny membership to a black man leasing a home in the community served by the club.*

Most significant, however, of all the legal battles for blacks has been that to achieve equal treatment in the public schools of the nation. Considered by many leaders to be basic to the concept of equality of opportunity, it has also proven to be the most controversial area, and the one in which it has been most difficult to achieve significant results. In chapter 16 we shall examine in detail the nature of that long struggle, including the complex issue of busing of children to achieve racial balance in the public schools.

The courts have thus been very important in the civil rights struggle in the United States. Benefiting from the prestige accorded the federal judiciary and the freedom from political pressures provided by life tenure, federal judges have reacted earlier and more positively than executives and legislators to the aspirations of black Americans. However, as indicated by the following section, in recent years the other two branches have become more responsive to the demands for racial equality.

The Executive Branch. Presidents possess a number of powers that can be used positively to affect the interests of blacks. One is to ask Congress to pass helpful legislation and then to use presidential influence with the legislators to see that proposals receive favorable action by them; another is to issue executive orders, without the concurrence of Congress, that have the binding effect of law. Presidents can also appoint blacks themselves or persons sympathetic to their needs to high executive or judicial positions and also see to it that executive agencies use their powers to benefit black citizens.

---

* In recent years, however, there have been some exceptions to this general pattern of Supreme Court cases: *Palmer* v. *Thompson* (1971) upheld the decision of a city to close all public-owned swimming pools that could not be operated safely and economically on an integrated basis; *Moose Lodge, 107* v. *Irvis* (1972) ruled that a private club's possession of a state liquor license did not constitute "state action" so as to make the club's discriminatory policies a violation of the equal protection clause of the Fourteenth Amendment.

Despite this range of powers, Presidents in this century were slow to utilize them on behalf of blacks. While some might expect that to have been true of "conservative" Presidents like Harding, Coolidge, and Hoover, it was also true of "liberal" Chief Executives as well. Theodore Roosevelt arbitrarily discharged three black companies of soldiers on unproven charges of rioting in Brownsville, Texas. Woodrow Wilson would not permit Negroes in the Marines in World War I. And Franklin Roosevelt introduced no major civil rights legislation, limiting himself to an executive order establishing a Committee on Fair Employment Practices in 1941—after A. Philip Randolph, President of the *Brotherhood of Sleeping Car Porters,* threatened to lead a march on Washington to secure job opportunities for Negroes.

Ironically it was a border-state politician, Missourian Harry Truman, who took the first significant executive actions in behalf of blacks. He issued executive orders banning segregation in the armed services and in civilian jobs of the national government, ordered firms doing business with the federal government not to discriminate in hiring, proposed a broad civil rights program to Congress, and appointed a committee to study race relations in the United States. Truman's successor, Republican Dwight Eisenhower, had more of a mixed record on race relations. He did continue the desegregation of the armed forces that Truman had begun and took the leadership in ending segregation in the District of Columbia as well. However, "Ike" refused to speak out personally in favor of school desegregation and only belatedly sent federal troops to enforce a court order ordering integration of schools in Little Rock, Arkansas. Moreover, only reluctantly and under pressure from liberal Republicans did he propose any civil rights legislation to Congress.

John Kennedy was more sympathetic to black demands than was Eisenhower. The young President spoke out against the moral evil of discrimination, appointed Negroes to high public office, dispatched troops to Mississippi and Alabama to protect blacks entering state universities, and signed an order forbidding discrimination in federally assisted housing. But such bold executive actions were not matched by Kennedy's record as legislative leader. Not until the spring of 1963, after Americans had viewed police brutality against Martin Luther King Jr. and his followers in Birmingham on nationwide television, and the country's churches rallied to the cause of blacks, did Kennedy finally send a broad civil rights bill to Congress for action. When JFK was assassinated in November 1963, his successor, Lyndon Johnson, used his great political skills to get Congress to pass the Kennedy proposals in 1964 and, as we shall see below, continued to push for further legislation that was ultimately enacted into law in 1965 and 1968. Moreover, the Southerner from Texas also used executive powers extensively on behalf of blacks, appointing Thurgood Marshall to the Supreme Court and Robert Weaver to his cabinet (the first Negroes to serve in these bodies) and establishing a President's Commission on Equal Opportunity under the chairmanship of Vice-President Hubert Humphrey to coordinate activites of various executive agencies on behalf of blacks.

Blacks found a much less sympathetic Chief Executive in Richard Nixon. Honoring a campaign pledge to Southerners to take their interests into account in his presidency, the new Republican Chief Executive slowed administrative efforts to achieve school desegregation by threatening to withhold federal funds from recalcitrant school boards, came out strongly in opposition to the busing

Justice Thurgood Marshall.

of children to provide greater racial balance in the schools, and, as discussed in chapter 16, unsuccessfully tried to place Clement Haynsworth of South Carolina and G. Harrold Carswell of Florida on the United States Supreme Court. On the other hand, the Nixon administration provided financial assistance to black business entrepreneurs, stepped up "affirmative action" programs to increase minority hiring by organizations having contracts with the federal government, and initiated the Philadelphia Plan (named after the city in which the plan was begun) whereby contractors on construction projects financed by federal funds set "goals" or "quotas" for the employment of additional blacks. Nixon's successor, Gerald Ford, generally continued these same Republican policies, emphasizing the economic rather than the social aspects of the civil rights struggle; thus the Ford administration backed "affirmative action" programs, but strongly opposed busing.*

The Congress. Of the three branches of the national government, the Congress was the slowest to respond to black demands. In the 1920s the NAACP began a long campaign to make lynching of blacks a federal crime, but Southern senators' use of the filibuster prevented its passage into law. Efforts in the 1940s to secure legislation ending job discrimination against blacks by contractors for the federal government also failed as did President Truman's broad civil rights program presented to Congress in 1948. Interest group activity on behalf of civil rights failed to bring a favorable response from a Congress dominated by Southern committee chairmen and possessed of the power to block legislation through the use of the filibuster.

In time, however, the situation began to change. In 1955 NAACP lobbyist Clarence Mitchell initiated a meeting with congressmen from both political parties sympathetic to civil rights, and it was decided that they should push for the enactment of legislation protecting the Negro's right to vote. Meanwhile, Herbert Brownell, Attorney General under President Eisenhower, convinced the reluctant Chief Executive to submit a bill giving the Attorney General the right to seek judicial relief against persons violating any kind of civil rights of blacks, including that of voting. The bill passed the House, and a major battle loomed in the Senate between the legislation's supporters and Southerners who were ready to use their favorite weapon, the filibuster, to block its passage. Ultimately, however, the Senate majority leader, Lyndon Johnson, used his influence in favor of a compromise: the Southerners agreed to forego a filibuster if the bill were restricted to the protection of the right to vote only, not of other civil rights as well. Following the outbreak of racial violence and difficulties in enforcing school desegregation and the right to vote in some Southern states, Congress in 1960 passed additional legislation strengthening somewhat the enforcement of voting rights and providing limited criminal penalities for bombings and the obstruction of federal court orders on school desegregation. Thus the initial congressional response to black demands was essentially a moderate one.

The next stage in the legislative battle over civil rights was of a far different character. The *Conference on Civil Rights*, representing some fifty organiza-

---

* President Ford did, however, show somewhat more political sensitivity to blacks than did Nixon. Early in his administration Ford met with leaders of the *Black Congressional Caucus;* he also appointed a black, William T. Coleman, as Secretary of the Department of Transportation.

tions, pushed in 1963 for comprehensive legislation: equality of access to public accommodations, fair employment, stipulations for cutting off federal funds to state and local programs practising discrimination, and the provision of the original 1957 bill empowering the Attorney General to seek judicial relief for the violation of *any* civil right, not just that of voting. President Kennedy moved in that direction prior to his assassination; ultimately—with the help of the new Chief Executive, Lyndon Johnson (who urged that the legislation be enacted in the slain President's memory), with outside pressure from churches, organized labor and other liberal groups, joined by a bipartisan coalition in Congress—the most comprehensive civil rights bill was enacted into law in the summer of 1964. The next year, President Johnson supported new legislation to eliminate barriers to voting. Following violence growing out of voting-rights demonstrations led by Martin Luther King in Selma and a nationwide television speech by Lyndon Johnson in which he linked Selma with Lexington, Concord, and Appomattox as places that shaped a "turning point in man's unending search for freedom," Congress responded with the Civil Rights Act of 1965. It suspended literacy tests and authorized the appointment of federal examiners to supervise electoral procedures in areas using such tests where less than one-half the voting population was registered or voted in November 1964.

One major area remained outside the legislative accomplishments of the 1950s and 1960s: housing. (President Kennedy's executive order of 1962 excluded existing homes, and its restriction to housing insured or guaranteed by federal agencies left about 80 percent of new housing unaffected.) In early 1966 President Johnson asked the Congress to enact broad housing legislation, but the political situation differed greatly from that of the early 1960s: the legislation aimed not only at discrimination in the South but also at all-white suburbs in the North; churches that had been so active on behalf of previous legislation

Equality of home ownership.

did not come to its support; and in place of peaceful demonstrations, there were riots in Chicago and Cleveland, and cries of "Black Power!" As a result, the housing bill failed to come to a vote in either house of Congress in 1966 and 1967. The next year, however, prodded by President Johnson and the *Leadership Conference* (that now included 100 organizations), and shocked by the assassination of Martin Luther King Jr., the Congress finally enacted into law a housing bill that also included protection for civil rights participants. Thus the last major piece of civil rights legislation came into effect during the final year of the administration of Lyndon Johnson, the Southerner who ironically had done the most for racial equality in the United States.*

The battle for civil rights in the United States has thus been waged by various groups utilizing different techniques and zeroing in on all three branches of the national government. As we shall see in the following section, the same has been true of the struggle for the rights of American women.

REFORMING THE SYSTEM FOR AMERICAN WOMEN

The Historical Background

One of the interesting features of the struggle for the rights of women in the United States is the fact that it has often been clearly tied to the cause of blacks. Women were a part of the anti-slavery movement in the United States from its beginnings. The reasons for their taking up the battle for the rights of blacks varied. Many women came from families that opposed slavery, while others undoubtedly identified with the slave. As one close student of the subject, Catherine Stimpson, put it, "Recognizing the severe oppression of the black, they saw, perhaps for the first time, an image of themselves." But whatever the reason, women joined with male abolitionists in attempting to ban slavery in the United States.

Ironically, however, women soon found that many of the men who were battling for the cause of slaves did not welcome them as equal participants in the struggle. When women showed up at a convention held in Philadelphia in 1833 to form the *American Anti-Slavery Society,* the convention refused to seat them as delegates. Five days later, the women (both black and white) met to found a separate *Female Anti-Slavery Society.* Nor was prejudice against women in the antislavery movement restricted to the United States. The expanding abolitionist movement resulted in the holding of a World Anti-Slavery Convention in London in 1840; the women delegates were relegated to the galleries and not permitted to participate in any of the proceedings. Among those women delegates were a group of Americans, including Lucretia Mott and Elizabeth Cady Stanton. The two women decided to hold a women's rights convention when they returned to America. Eight years later in 1848 some three hundred persons assembled in Seneca Falls, New York and approved a Declaration of Sentiments, modeled after the Declaration of Independence— "We hold these truths to be self-evident: that all men *and women* are created equal. ..." From 1848 until the beginning of the Civil War similar conventions were held nearly every year in different cities in the East and Midwest. Thus

Early battlers for women's rights: Susan B. Anthony and Elizabeth Cady Stanton.

REPORT

OF THE

WOMAN'S RIGHTS

CONVENTION,

Held at SENECA FALLS, N. Y., July 19th and 20th, 1848.

Janet Cowung

ROCHESTER:
PRINTED BY JOHN DICK,
AT THE NORTH STAR OFFICE.

* The Voting Rights Act of 1965 was subsequently extended in 1970 and again in 1975.

women's rights activities in the United States can be traced directly to the previous participation of many women in the cause of blacks.

When the Civil War began in 1861, women's rights advocates were urged to forego their cause and throw their full support behind the war effort. While some like Stanton and Susan B. Anthony continued to argue that the struggle for the rights of blacks and women were inseparable, the movement for women's rights essentially stopped during the war. However after the hostilities were over, a battle developed over the suffrage issue. The more militant feminists wanted to add "sex" to the "race, color, or previous condition of servitude" language of the Fifteenth Amendment as a reason for which the right to vote could not be denied. However, black leaders like Frederick Douglass opposed linking women and black suffrage on the grounds that it would make it easier to defeat the Amendment. Some women's rights advocates agreed with Douglass and reasoned that if black men were enfranchised first, it would ultimately make their gaining the vote for women easier. Ultimately the view of Douglass and his allies prevailed, and the women's rights movement separated itself from the cause of racial equality.

The feminists were agreed on the need for female suffrage but the movement split into two factions based on differences over goals and tactics. In 1869 Anthony and Stanton organized the *National Suffrage Association;* six months later, Lucy Stone and others formed the *American Women Suffrage Association.* The former organization advocated the broad cause of women's rights and regarded the vote as a means to achieve the general improvement of women's situation in the United States; the latter concentrated on the suffrage issue

alone and, for the sake of appearing "respectable," deliberately avoided taking stands on controversial issues involving marriage and the church. The *National* group also pushed for an amendment to the federal constitution, while the *American* association sought change on a state-by-state basis. In time more and more women threw their lot in with the more conservative *American* association, and the Anthony-Stanton group ultimately shifted its focus more toward the suffrage issue alone. In 1890 the two organizations merged as the *National American Women Suffrage Association,* which subsequently became increasingly conservative and a single-issue organization.

In time, however, a new generation of women suffragists came to the forefront. Particularly important was Alice Paul, a young, militant woman who in 1913 formed a small radical group known as the *Congressional Union* (later to be reorganized as the *National Women's Party*). The purpose of the organization was to work exclusively for an amendment to the federal constitution (some previous gains in women's suffrage had been made at the state level, but these were limited primarily to western jurisdictions) and to use unorthodox means if necessary to win the right to vote, including organized parades, mass demonstrations, and hunger strikes; moreover, some of the members of the *National Women's Party* were willing to allow themselves to be arrested and put in jail in order to dramatize the issue. Eventually in 1920, seventy-two years after the Seneca Falls Convention, and a half-century after blacks had won the right to vote, women were finally enfranchised by the Nineteenth Amendment.

Having won its major battle for the right to vote, the women's movement virtually collapsed. Only a few groups continued to work for their cause. In 1923 the *National Women's Party* drafted an Equal Rights Amendment and had it introduced into Congress every year, lobbying vigorously for its passage, but without success. The *National Federation of Business and Professional Women's Clubs* (BPW), founded in 1919, urged that Civil Service examinations of the federal government be opened to women as well as men, lobbied for an equal pay bill, and in 1937 went on record in favor of the Equal Rights Amendment. However, the two organizations generally labored in vain, victims of the absence of political allies, a dramatic issue, or public support. It was not until the 1960s, forty years after the passage of the Nineteenth Amendment, that the women's rights movement began once again to come into its own.

The Reemergence of Women's Rights—Reform from within the Government

The struggle for women's rights reemerged in American life in the 1960s, not because of pressure from interest groups operating outside the political system, but rather as a result of initiatives taken by individuals within the federal government itself. When President Kennedy took office in 1961, he appointed as head of the Women's Bureau in the Department of Labor Esther Peterson, a long-time labor lobbyist who had been a member of Kennedy's staff during the 1960 campaign. She suggested that the new President establish a commission to investigate the status of women in the United States and to recommend measures to improve that status. Following that suggestion, Kennedy issued an executive order in December 1961 creating a President's Commission on the Status of Women, a body composed of thirteen women and eleven men from public and private life, headed by Eleanor Roosevelt, widow of the late President.

In October 1962, the Commission issued a report, *American Women*, composed primarily of factual information on the status of women in employment and education, together with some recommendations for governmental action. The recommendations were generally moderate in tone; for example, the Commission opposed the passage of the Equal Rights Amendment, favoring instead the judicial interpretation of the Fifth and Fourteenth Amendments as a means of equalizing opportunities of women with those of men; it also did not favor adding "sex" to an existing executive order barring racial discrimination by federal contractors on the grounds that sexual and racial discrimination involved different considerations. However, two of its moderate recommendations did bring about concrete results: in 1962 President Kennedy at the urging of his brother Robert, issued a directive revising the interpretation of an 1870 law that barred women from high-level federal employment; the following year the Congress passed the Equal Pay Act, amending the Fair Labor Standards Act of 1938 to require that men and women receive equal pay for equal work performed under equal conditions.

One other major piece of legislation affecting women's rights was also passed by Congress in 1964: Title VII of the Civil Rights Act. This legislation included "sex" as well as "race, color, religion, and national origin" as reasons for which private companies could not discriminate in hiring. However, the act contained some important exceptions. It did not cover either employees of federal, state, and local governments or teachers and administrators of educational institutions. Moreover, the Equal Employment Opportunity Commission (EEOC), the executive agency entrusted with the enforcement of the act, had to depend primarily upon employers' voluntarily complying with its findings since it was given no authority to sue them for discriminatory practices.

Thus this early phase in the reemergence of the women's rights movement was essentially a moderate one. Some feminists had serious doubts about the purposes behind some of these developments. For example, they regarded the appointment of the Commission on the Status of Women as an easy way for President Kennedy to pay off his political obligations to women who were active in his 1960 campaign and also as a way of currying their support for the 1964 election; some also charged that it was a means of heading off a move for the Equal Rights Amendment. (It will be recalled that the Commission opposed the passage of such an Amendment in its final report.) They also questioned motivations behind the passage of the 1963 Equal Pay Act and Title VII of the 1964 Civil Rights Act. The former was explained as a way to increase the job security of men by preventing their replacement with lower-paid women; the latter as the unforeseen result of an attempt to kill the Civil Rights Bill of 1964 by burdening it with prohibition of sex as well as racial discrimination.*

For all this, the fact remains that these actions in the early 1960s were important initial steps in the reemergence of the women's rights movement after forty years of dormancy; further, they led to the events that followed. The 1961 Commission on the Status of Women left some important legacies: similar commissions were established in state after state across the nation, and when the federal commission went out of existence, it was succeeded by a Citizen's Advisory Council on the Status of Women. Moreover, as we shall see, the increased publicity given the issue of women's rights, and the desire to expand the gains made in the early 1960s, stimulated the emergence of a variety of new feminist interest groups.

New Feminist Interest Groups

The Friedan mystique.

In the mid-1960s a series of events converged to stimulate the formation of a new type of interest group to press for women's rights. Betty Friedan, whose book *The Feminine Mystique* (1963), had stimulated many women to question their general situation in society, began commuting to Washington to gather material for a second book. While there she discussed her ideas with a number of women working in Congress, the executive branch, and the Citizens' Advisory Council. Many of these women were concerned with getting the Equal Employment Opportunity Commission (EEOC) to take sex discimination in private employment as seriously as it did racial discrimination. When the two largest politically oriented organizations—the *National Federation of Business and Professional Women's Clubs* (BPW) and the *League of Women Voters*—refused to launch an anti-sex-discrimination campaign for fear of being labeled as "feminist" or "militant," some of the women working inside the government suggested privately that what was needed was the formation of group that

---

* The fact that Representative Howard K. Smith of Virginia, an avowed opponent of the Civil Rights Act, offered the amendment to add "sex" to its language naturally aroused the suspicion of many persons. However, most feminists, including those in Congress, supported the amendment.

would speak on behalf of women and pressure the government for action in the same way that civil rights groups had done for blacks.

Within that general atmosphere, a specific issue and a particular event combined to set off the movement for a feminist interest group. The issue was the failure of the EEOC to prevent newspapers from running want-ads with separate listings of jobs for men and women. The event was the third annual conference of State Commissions on the Status of Women that met in Washington in late June 1966. The women agreed that the conference should pass a strongly worded resolution condemning sex discrimination in employment but were told that the conference was not allowed to pass resolutions or take action. This convinced the women that a new organization had to be set up at once. A group, including Friedan, met and, acting on her spur-of-the-moment suggestion, decided to call the group NOW *(National Organization for Women).* They also sent telegrams to the EEOC urging that it issue guidelines prohibiting "Help Wanted—Male" and "Help Wanted—Female" columns in newspapers.

From these beginnings NOW soon moved into the forefront of the women's rights movement. In late October 1966 its incorporation was announced at a press conference in Washington, Betty Friedan was elected the first president, and the group adopted a resolution calling for action "to bring women into full participation in the mainstream of American society *now,* exercising all the privileges and responsibilities thereof in truly equal partnership with men." It later became involved in almost every area of feminist activity, pressuring the EEOC for favorable rulings, opposing the nomination of G. Harrold Carswell to the U.S. Supreme Court for his antifeminist positions, filing suits against the nation's 1300 largest corporations for sex discrimination, lobbying for federal and local funds for child-care centers, and picketing "all-male" bars.

In time, however, the women's movement became too broad to be accommodated within one interest group. Major differences developed regarding the goals of women as well as the best means of securing these goals. A variety of organizations were formed in the late 1960s, which students of the women's movement generally divide into two major groupings: the first is referred to as the "women's rights" branch, the second as the "women's liberation" branch.

Persons active in the "women's rights" wing of the movement are typically middle-class in background, professionally oriented, and employed by private industry, the government, or the academic world. Their major purpose is to achieve equality for women and to do it through traditional political and legal channels. Such a group is the *Women's Equity Action League* (WEAL). Formed in 1968 by persons who felt NOW's controversial call for the repeal of anti-abortion laws would damage the organization's image, it has focused its efforts on removing discrimination against women in employment, education, and tax policies. Two other similarly oriented organizations also established in 1968 are the *Federally Employed Women* (FEW), a group that seeks to remove sex discrimination within the national government, and *Human Rights for Women, Inc.* (HRW), which provides free legal assistance for women seeking legal redress to remedy sex inequities practiced against them. While such groups have different emphases and memberships, they have the common approach of seeking to improve the situation of women by working within the existing political system and utilizing traditional means to change its practices.

It's never too late to learn.

In sharp contrast to the "women's rights" branch of the movement was the "women's liberation" one that also developed in the late 1960s. Participants in this segment were also middle-class in background but typically had participated in three areas of protest activities in the early and middle 1960s: civil rights, the peace movement, and the "New Left"—a vague collection of persons who sought to bring about radical change in American society through "participatory democracy" and confrontation with the existing "establishment."* While differing on their political goals, all three of these protest movements had one thing in common: a refusal to take the aspirations of women seriously. (When a woman tried to present a paper entitled "The Position of Women in SNCC," Stokely Carmichael countered, "The only position for women in SNCC is prone"; those who tried to get a plank on women's liberation adopted at an SDS convention were hit with tomatoes and thrown out of the meeting.) Enraged at such treatment, women withdrew from these organizations and established groups in major metropolitan areas to fight for women's liberation. In keeping with their origins, such groups excluded men, unlike women's rights organizations that welcomed sympathetic males to their ranks.

Both the goals and operating methods of the women's liberation organizations differed radically from those of the women's rights branch of the movement. Instead of seeking to equalize the economic and educational opportunities of men and women as the latter did, the liberationists attacked more fundamental aspects of the male-female relationship in society, including traditional roles of women in raising children, doing housework, and cooking. Instead of "purposive" undertakings such as lobbying for executive, judicial, and legislative actions to change sex discrimination, the women's liberation groups were interested in "solidary" activities, the holding of "rap sessions" and practicing "consciousness-raising" techniques designed to educate themselves to the fact that what many of them had previously conceived as *individual* problems in their lives were actually experiences *common to all women.* Moreover, the participants in women's liberation activities condemned the large national organizations and tightly structured associations of the women's rights branch and deliberately created small, local groups without formal offices that operated under the principle of participatory democracy.

Unlike the women's rights groups that were well structured and permanent, the women's liberation groups were amorphous and temporary. The fact that the latter's goals were remote (radically changing basic male-female relationships in society) and their operating principles vague and structureless (consciousness-raising through group sessions with no formal leaders) made them less purposive and well-organized than the women's rights organizations. There was also a serious cleavage within the liberation movement between the "politicos," who blamed woman's plight on capitalism and sought a socialist society as a means of remedying such ills, and the "feminists," who attributed women's problems to men in general rather than to a particular economic system. More-

---

* The best-known "New Left" organization was the *Students For a Democratic Society* (SDS), established in 1962 by a group of college students. Operating primarily on college campuses, its particular targets were racism, militarism, and "impersonal" institutions—corporations, universities, churches, and the like. The organization split into warring factions in 1969 and soon disappeared from the American political scene.

over, extremists from both groups tried to take over the movement, the former through the *Socialist Workers Party* (SWP) and/or its youth affiliate, the *Young Socialist Alliance* (YSA), which sought to co-opt liberation members for their own Marxist purposes, and the latter by means of a lesbian clique, which argued that the best way to fight a male-dominated world was to have no sexual association with men. This combination of remote goals, structureless-ness, and bitter infighting within the liberation branch of the movement, to-gether with the intense, emotional demands placed upon women to prove their commitment to the cause, resulted in a high turnover in its membership.

Feminist Gloria Steinem.

The struggle for sexual equality has undergone significant changes in the United States in recent years. While the women's rights–women's liberation elements of the movement are still present, the schism between them is less significant today than it was in the late 1960s. (In recent years the term *women's liberation* has come to refer to the women's movement in general rather than to only one branch of its activities.) The consciousness-raising techniques of the movement are no longer lodged in radical organizations; instead they have become a part of the activities of women's centers located on college campuses and in local communities throughout the nation. Moreover, national organiza-tions such as the *Women's Action Alliance* (WAA), conceived by Gloria Stei-nem at about the same time as *MS* magazine, act as clearinghouses for infor-mation for consciousness-raising groups across the country.

NOW has also expanded its activities to include concerns of the liberation branch. While it once considered lesbians a threat to the survival of the organi-zation, it has recently established a *Task Force on Sexuality and Lesbianism.* Meanwhile WEAL, FEW, HRW, and other similar groups continue to seek legal changes in the status of women in American society. There is an increased realization among women that a variety of organizations are required to meet their needs (the 1976 edition of the *Encyclopedia of Associations* lists some fifty separate feminist organizations) and that they must join forces if they are to accomplish their purposes. They have also come to appreciate the importance of politics as a means of accomplishing their goals, as evidenced by the estab-lishment of the *National Women's Political Caucus* (NWPC) to encourage the election and appointment of women to political office and to raise women's issues during and between elections. We shall see below that such activities have begun to generate a response from the national government.

Recent Governmental Response to the Women's Movement

Like the demands of blacks, those by women have received different responses from the various branches of the national government. As indicated below, the executive has been most receptive to feminist interests, but Congress and the courts have also become important arenas in the struggle for women's rights.

The Executive Branch. In the latter part of the 1960s the national government began to respond more affirmatively to the increased demands for women's rights. Much of the initial activity came from the executive branch. The Equal Employment Opportunity Commission, entrusted by Title VII of the Civil Rights Act of 1964 with preventing sex discrimination in private employment, issued new guidelines in 1968 prohibiting newspapers from publishing separate want-ad columns for men's and women's jobs. The following year the same

Commission ruled that state "protective" legislation (laws passed in the early part of the twentieth century restricting the employment of women to certain occupations, and establishing maximum hours, minimum wages, maximum weights to be lifted and the like) were no longer relevant to the expanding role of the female worker in the American economy and had been superseded by Title VII of the 1964 Civil Rights Act prohibiting discrimination in employment on the basis of sex. In 1965 President Johnson issued an executive order preventing those with federal contracts from discriminating in their employment on the basis of "race, color, religion, and national origin"; two years later, following extensive lobbying by women's groups, the word *sex* was added to the executive order as a reason for which federal contractors could not discriminate. That same order, as amended, also prohibited discrimination in employment by the federal government itself. Thus women began to achieve what had earlier been denied them: getting executive agencies to pay as much attention to discrimination against them as they did to that directed against blacks.

Congress. Women also began to turn to the Congress for help in their battle against sex discrimination. Both the Comprehensive Health Manpower Training Act and the Nurses' Training Act enacted in 1971 contained anti-sex discrimination provisions; that same year Congress also passed a Child Development Act providing free day-care for children of families of limited income, but this was successfully vetoed by President Nixon.* Important congressional victories for women in the 1970s included the Equal Opportunity Act of 1972, which extends the coverage of the anti-discrimination provisions of the 1964 civil rights law to educational institutions and state and local governments, the Education Amendments Act of that same year, which prohibits sex discrimination in all federally aided education programs, and a 1974 law that extends the jurisdiction of the U.S. Commission on Civil Rights (an independent bipartisan group originally set up to study problems of minorities) to include sex discrimination.

But for the advocates of women's rights by far the most dramatic congressional victory for their cause was the passage of the Equal Rights Amendment. Originally introduced in Congress in 1923, and first endorsed by both Republican and Democratic parties in their 1944 platforms, the Amendment passed the Senate in 1950 and 1953 but failed to clear the House of Representatives either year. In the early 1970s the pressures for its enactment became overwhelming. Backed by the Citizens Advisory Council on the Status of Women, the Woman's Bureau, and President Nixon himself, Democratic congresswoman Martha Griffith of Michigan took over the task of helping to steer ERA through the national legislature, while a National Ad Hoc Committee for the ERA, composed of almost every women's interest group and such allies as *Common Cause* and the liberal *Americans for Democratic Action,* kept up pressure for its passage. Finally in March, 1972, almost a half-century after it was first introduced in Congress by the *National Women's Party,* the Equal Rights Amendment received the needed two-thirds vote of both the House and the Senate and was ready for ratification by three-fourths of the state legislatures.

* The Revenue Act of 1971 did, however, permit families with combined incomes of $18,000 a year or less to take income tax deductions for child care.

Initially ERA had easy sailing at the state level as twenty-eight legislatures ratified it during the first year. However, in January 1973 a national "Stop ERA" campaign surfaced led by Phyllis Schlafly, an articulate woman from Illinois who was noted for her leadership in conservative causes. Rightist organizations, including the *John Birch Society,* the *Christian Crusade,* and *Young Americans for Freedom* joined the opposition effort, claiming that ERA would result in the drafting of women and deny wives the support of their husbands and mothers the custody of their children. State legislatures soon felt the same kind of outside pressure to oppose ERA that congressmen had earlier experienced for its passage. As a result, the momentum went out of the pro-ERA movement as only four more states ratified the Amendment in 1974. Moreover, some state legislatures that had voted to ratify the Amendment rescinded their previous action.* By mid-1977 thirty-five states—three short of the necessary thirty-eight needed for passage—had ratified ERA.†

The Courts. The women's movement also pressed its cause before the *courts.* Initially it won some important victories such as the abortion decisions (described in ch. 4) and rulings supporting equal pay for equal work, equal opportunities in education and sports, and equal treatment in hiring and the receipt of credit. But later in 1976, and in one week's time, the Supreme Court dealt three separate setbacks to women's rights forces, ruling that employers with employee disability programs are not required to provide women with pregnancy benefits, that divorced women are not entitled to all the Social Security benefits that go to married women, and that a state can require a married woman to adopt her husband's last name before receiving a driver's license.

It is difficult to determine whether the opposition to the ratification of the ERA and the judicial decisions cited above are only temporary exceptions to the success of the women's movement or whether they represent a significant slowing in the battle for sex equality in the United States. As Jo Freeman, an astute participant-observer in the movement has observed, early political successes of women were to a great degree due to their ability to ride on the coattails of the civil rights movement. However, issues like child care and abortion, as well as the abolition of sex-role stereotypes, have no civil rights precedents. Freeman goes on to warn: "Here the movement will have to learn to fight its own battles, and will not find the going so easy."

* There is a serious legal question whether a state can rescind its previous ratification of a constitutional amendment.

† Under the terms of the amendment, it must be ratified by 1979 if it is to become legally effective.

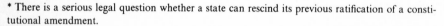

ASSESSMENT

Interest groups clearly make a valuable contribution to the American political system. By channeling demands of citizens to those in positions of public authority, they inform leaders on what people in various segments of our society think about important public issues. They also educate officials by providing them with factual information and arguments relating to vital issues. Although each interest group naturally presents its own side, legislative and executive officials are able to examine a wide range of views and can balance the merits of one against another in making decisions.

One major weakness in American interest groups is that not everyone benefits equally from them. Well-educated persons from the upper social classes are more inclined to join organizations than are the less educated and the poor. Beyond the matter of representation, business and professional organizations have more financial resources to spend on lobbying than do other interest groups. They also benefit from their prestige and the deference accorded their members by officeholders and the general public as well. The result is that upper- and middle-class Americans are more likely to have their demands satisfied than are less advantaged persons.

Yet groups that have traditionally been disadvantaged are better organized today than they have been in the past. The two examined in detail in this chapter—blacks and women—indicate what can be accomplished by persons who are determined to make the political process better operate to their advantage. By organizing and pressing their claims through a variety of methods and channels, both groups have been able to persuade significant elements of the American public, as well as those in positions of political authority (overwhelmingly white and male), to respond favorably to their demands. The outcome has been an increased public awareness of the inferior status of blacks and women in American society and the enactment of legislation, together with executive and judicial decrees, designed to change that status.

Another encouraging development is the rise of public interest groups as represented by *Public Citizen, Inc.* and *Common Cause.* These groups have succeeded in involving many citizens who have not been politically active in the past. They have also been well received by the public: 49 percent of the respondents in the Harris poll expressed the view that "groups of citizens and organizations are having more effect in getting government to get things done, compared with five years ago." It remains to be

seen how much staying power public interest groups demonstrate, but despite a high turnover in the memberships of both *Public Citizen, Inc.* and *Common Cause,* both organizations have generally been able through effective recruiting campaigns to replace departing members with new persons willing to support their activities. By targeting their efforts on a limited number of issues, both groups have been able to develop more political muscle than many veteran observers of the Washington scene thought possible for citizens' lobbies.

Another major aspect of interest groups that deserves comment is their internal operation. The form of their governance is democratic but the practice is oligarchical. Members typically have little control over their leaders, and competing internal elites do not frustrate one another's ambitions.

There are, of course, certain political advantages in that situation. Longterm leaders who are knowledgeable and experienced about group affairs are able to effectively represent the interests of the members in the political arena. Being cohesive and disciplined also assists an organization in combating its political rivals and in speaking with a united voice.

The danger in the internal situation, however, is that group leaders will pursue their own interests rather than those of the general membership. This has happened, for example, in certain labor unions where officers have misused moneys (especially in the administration of pension funds) and have also made arrangements with employers that benefited them but not the rank-and-file members. In some instances, moreover, group leaders promote political goals that have little appeal for the general membership.

Describing the problem of the internal governance of interest groups is much easier than figuring out ways to improve it. It seems unrealistic to expect such organizations to develop opposition candidates, together with other institutions and techniques that operate in public bodies; almost none has done so to date. Government regulation of certain aspects of internal governance—such as requiring disclosure of financial affairs and ensuring that elections of officers are honest—has been utilized, especially with respect to labor unions. Even so, there are limits to how much public authorities should intervene in the affairs of private organizations in a democracy.

There are, however, some mitigating circumstances. Rival organizations do exist in some instances, so that a person who is not satisfied that the leadership of one organization is adequately representing his interests can join another. Furthermore, as the following chapters indicate, demands and preferences can be channeled to decision makers through agencies and means besides interest groups, such as political parties and elections.

SELECTED READINGS

The most comprehensive treatment of interest groups is David B. Truman, *The Governmental Process: Political Interests and Public Opinion* (New York: Knopf, 1951). Emphasizing the theoretical aspects of group behavior, it stimulated a number of studies in the 1950s on the role of interest groups in our society and today is still considered the classic work on the subject. Other good recent studies supplementing Truman's work are Harmon Ziegler and G. Wayne Peak, *Interest Groups in American Society* (Englewood Cliffs, N.J.: Prentice-Hall, 2nd ed., 1970), and Abraham Holtzman, *Interest Groups and Lobbying* (New York: Macmillan, 1966). The latter book also analyzes the activities of interest groups in Great Britain and Italy and compares them with those in the United States.

Peter Clark and James Wilson discuss the basic inducements for joining organizations in "Incentive Systems: A Theory of Organizations," *Administrative Science Quarterly* 6 (1961): 129-166. Mancur Olson analyzes reasons for joining or nonjoining interest groups from the standpoint of rational choice in *The Logic of Collective Action* (Cambridge: Harvard University Press, 1965). Robert Salisbury attributes the formation of many interest groups to the entrepreneurial activities of their founders in "An Exchange Theory of Interest Groups," *Midwest Journal of Political Science* 13 (1969): 1-32.

Tocqueville's perceptive analysis of voluntary associations in the United States is contained in his classic study, *Democracy in America,* edited by Phillips Bradley (New York: Knopf, 12th ed., 1954).

Analyses of the organizations and purposes of major interest groupings in the United States are included in the Truman and Ziegler books cited above. Other excellent treatments of the subject are V. O. Key, Jr., *Politics, Parties and Pressure Groups* (New York: Thomas Y. Crowell, 5th ed., 1964); J. W. Peltason and James M. Burns, *Functions and Policies of American Government* (Englewood Cliffs, N.J.: Prentice-Hall, 2nd ed., 1962); and R. Joseph Monsen, Jr., and Mark W. Cannon, *The Makers of Public Policy: American Power Groups and Their Ideologies.* (New York: McGraw-Hill, 1965).

A recent compilation of articles published on various interest groups by the *National Journal* (including articles dealing with the National Association of Manufacturers, public employee unions, and public interest groups) is *National Journal Reprints,* "Interest Groups," 1975-76 edition (Washington, D.C.: National Journal, 1975).

For an analysis of the internal operation of interest groups in terms of democratic theory, see Grant McConnell, "The Spirit of Private Government," *The American Political Science Review* 52 (1958): 754-70. For general treatments of the subject of the internal governance of interest groups, see chapter 2 of Holtzman and chapters 5, 6, and 7 of Truman. Two excellent studies of the internal operation of specific interest groups are Oliver Garceau, *The Political Life of the American Medical Association* (Cambridge: Harvard University Press, 1941), and Seymour Martin Lipset, Martin Trow, and James S. Coleman, *Union Democracy: The Internal Politics of the International Typographical Union* (New York: Free Press, 1956). The former discusses the methods by which the leadership of the American Medical Association dominates its affairs; the latter examines the unusual "two-party" system of the ITU that results in alternative groups of leaders being offered the rank-and-file membership.

A recent analysis of the internal operation of unions in Britain and the United States is J. David Edelstein and Malcolm Warner, *Comparative Union Democracy: Organization and Opposition in British and American Unions* (New York: Wiley, 1976).

The general treatments of interest groups cited above include analyses of the techniques by which interest groups attempt to influence the making of public policy. The best empirical study of the characteristics of lobbyists who operate in the nation's capital and the means they use to communicate their desires to congressmen is Lester W. Milbrath, *The Washington Lobbyists* (Chicago: Rand McNally, 1963). A good analysis of group activities in the nation's capital that includes some interesting case studies of lobbying on recent issues is *The Washington Lobby* (Washington, D.C.: Congressional Quarterly, Inc., (2nd ed., 1974). Another inside look at the practical aspects of lobbying in Washington is Lewis Dexter's *How Organizations are Represented in Washington* (Indianapolis: Bobbs-Merrill, 1969).

Included among studies of Negro interest groups are Howard Zinn, *SNCC: The New Abolitionists* (Boston: Beacon, 1964); Inge Bell, *CORE and the Strategy of Non-Violence* (New York: Random House, 1968); and C. Eric Lincoln, *The Black Muslim in America* (Boston: Beacon, 1961). Martin Luther King Jr. gives his views in *Why We Can't Wait* (New York: Harper & Row, 1964), as do James Farmer in *Freedom—When?* (New York: Random House, 1965), and Whitney Young Jr. in *To Be Equal* (New York: McGraw-Hill, 1964). The concept of Black Power is analyzed in Stokely Carmichael and Charles V. Hamilton, *Black Power* (New York: Random House, 1967). Two recent excellent studies of the political activities of blacks are Lucius Barker and Jesse McCorry Jr., *Black Americans and the Political System* (Cambridge: Winthrop, 1976), and Milton Morris, *The Politics of Black America* (New York: Harper & Row, 1975).

A provocative historical analysis of the relationships between the struggles of blacks and women in the United States is Catherine Stimpson's, "Thy Neighbor's Wife, Thy Neighbor's Servants: Women's Liberation and Black Civil Rights," which appears in Vivian Gornick and Barbara K. Moran, *Women in Sexist Society* (New York: New American Library, 1971). Two excellent general treatments of the women's movement are Jo Freeman, *The Politics of Women's Liberation* (New York: David McKay, 1975), and Judith Hole and Ellen Levine, *Rebirth of Feminism* (New York: New York Times Book Co., 1971).

Two books that stress the contributions of interest groups to American democracy are those by Truman and Milbrath cited above. Critical of the narrow perspectives of such groups are E. E. Schattschneider, *The Semisovereign People: A Realist's View of Democracy in America* (New York: Holt, Rinehart and Winston, 1960); Grant McConnell, *Private Power and American Democracy* (New York: Knopf, 1966); and Theodore Lowi, *The End of Liberalism: Ideology, Policy, and the Crisis of Public Authority* (New York: Norton, 1969).

Political Novels How strong interest groups are created by dedicated leadership and the consequences of the acquisition of political power is the theme of Howard Fast's novel *Power* (New York: Doubleday, 1962). Fast's book describes the creation of a major labor union and the awesome political influence assumed by its leadership.

An account of group manipulation by a power-hungry, ruthless politician is provided by Eugene Burdick in *The Ninth Wave* (New York: Dell, 1956). Burdick makes the important point that interest groups can be manipulated by the very political figures they seek to control. A classic story of the corrupting influence of unchecked interests in politics is told by Upton Sinclair in *Oil* (New York: Washington Square Press, 1966).

Candidates wear many hats.

Chapter 7

In September 1796, six months before the end of his second term as President, George Washington announced to the American people his decision to eliminate himself as a candidate in the upcoming election. His famous Farewell Address set forth his hopes and fears for the young republic. What troubled Washington most was the possibility that it would be destroyed by the "baneful effects of the spirit of party." For he saw parties, particularly those based on geographical divisions, as threatening not only to national unity but also to popular government itself.

Almost two centuries later, at the end of the turbulent decade of the 1960s, a Gallup poll of American college students revealed the same mistrust of political parties. As Table 7.1 indicates, they ranked lowest of nine major American institutions in the estimation of the students. Statistically, not even one student in five rated political parties excellent or good, compared to two out of three who were favorably disposed towards universities. For a college generation not known for its satisfaction with institutions of higher learning, the poll pointed up how critical students are of political parties.

Nor did unfavorable student attitudes towards political parties disappear when American politics became calmer in the mid-1970s. In a Gallup poll published in September 1975, only 15 percent of college students were "highly favorable" to the Democratic party. Their attitude towards the Republican party was even more negative. Only 7 percent of the students were "highly favorable" to the GOP as compared to 10 percent that were "highly unfavorable" to it; moreover, of the eleven basic American institutions and groups about which they were questioned, only one, the Students for a Democratic Society, was rated below the Republican party. Even the Pentagon was regarded more favorably by the students than the GOP! The negative attitudes of the college students towards both parties was reflected in the fact that over half of them—52 percent—declared themselves to be Independents.

That today's vocal and critical young people would find themselves in agreement on a key political matter with the nation's chief father figure—a charter member of the American Establishment—is perhaps ironical. What is even more ironical is that despite Washington's attitude, the first democratic political parties in the world developed right here in the United States. In fact, they were already in existence at the time of the Farewell Address. Moreover, they have persisted: the Democratic party, indeed, is the world's oldest political party. Further, as indicated in chapter 10, most Americans today identify with either the Republican or the Democratic party.

Such conflicting attitudes indicate that the national experience with parties has been ambivalent. Americans created a major political institution that exists in all democratic societies in the world, yet many of them have great misgivings

POLITICAL PARTIES

Table 7.1
How Students Rate
American Institutions

Institutions	Responses (in Percentages)		
	Excellent	Good	Total Favorable
Universities	12	56	68
Family	23	35	58
Business	12	44	56
Congress	7	49	56
Courts	6	40	46
Police	6	34	40
High schools	4	33	37
Organized religion	7	26	33
Political parties	2	16	18

Source: The Newsweek Poll—The Gallup Organization, *Newsweek* (December 29, 1969), p. 43.

about the value of what they created. Why this is so is not clear, but exploring a number of questions may help to explain the situation: what is a political party and what part should it play in the governance of a free society? what are the major characteristics of political parties in the United States? and what have they actually contributed to the political system and to American society in general?

THE NATURE OF POLITICAL PARTIES

Students of government have experienced as much difficulty in defining a "political party" as they have had in explaining what is meant by "political culture." Particularly confusing has been the failure of political scientists to identify the specific features of a political party that distinguish it from other political agencies linking the general public to political officials.

Political Parties, Interest Groups, and Factions

The writings of some of the Founding Fathers illustrate the same problems of definition. In *Federalist Paper* No. 10, Madison uses three separate terms to describe divisions in society. One is *faction,* a concept we explored in some detail in chapter 2. Another is *interest,* which he calls the most durable source of factions, using as illustrations a manufacturing interest, a mercantile interest, and the like. Elsewhere in the same selection, the Father of the Constitution refers to conflicts of rival *parties.* Washington's Farewell Address is similarly vague: his condemnation of the "spirit of party" seems to reflect an unhappiness with the general state of divisiveness and bickering among citizens rather than an attempt to single out a particular kind of political agency—the party—for criticism.

A student of government today has different things in mind when he uses these three terms. A political party is a group of persons who run candidates for public office under a label. It is this activity that distinguishes a party from an "interest," or what we would today call an *interest group.* Members of the latter care about who holds office and may try to influence voters' decisions: business

groups tend to support Republican candidates who they feel are generally sympathetic to their policies, while labor unions favor Democratic ones for the same reason. But neither group offers its name to persons seeking office: no one runs under the banner of the United States Chamber of Commerce or the AFL-CIO.

Frequently, if inaccurately, political parties are distinguished from interest groups on other grounds, such as the number of persons associated with each. Typically, political parties attract more supporters than interest groups: far more people identify with either the Republican or the Democratic party in the United States than belong to the *Chamber of Commerce* or the AFL-CIO. But the same is not true of minor political parties. Only about 9500 persons voted for the Socialist-Labor candidates for President and Vice-President in 1976, as compared with the more than fourteen million Americans who belonged to the nation's largest labor organization that year.

Nor can political parties necessarily be distinguished from interest groups on the basis of their *purposes*. Not all political parties have as their primary goal the capture of public office. Witness the succession of minor parties that have appeared from time to time in American politics. Although some members of these parties undoubtedly thought that their candidates had a chance to win, most members have worked through these organizations as a means of registering their political demands. They have reasoned that even if their party could not win, because of the publicity given its goals during the course of the campaign or the electoral threat posed to the two major parties, their demands might receive more attention than if they worked only through interest groups. As we shall see later, many policy proposals of minor parties have eventually been adopted by officeholders and the major parties, evidence that such political calculations of minor-party backers have been vindicated.

On the other hand, not everyone who supports a political party does so because of its policies. Many people develop a psychological attachment to a particular party at an early age and, as discussed in chapter 10, back its candidates without regard to their stand on issues. Some persons participate in party activities because they expect to be rewarded with some concrete benefit, such as a job or other political favor. Others enjoy the excitement of party activities or the social contacts with other participants.

In brief, the crucial factor that distinguishes a political party from an interest group is neither size nor purpose; it is, rather, the *method* each chooses to make its influence felt in the political arena: a political party is the only organization that runs candidates for office under its label.

It is also necessary to distinguish a political party from a *faction*. Historically, factions preceded political parties; they were groups of persons who joined together on an ad hoc basis to win some political advantage for themselves. Thus certain people in England worked as a group to influence the King or to control Parliament. After the advent of elections to choose public officials, factions formed around particular persons or families (such as the Clintons in New York State) to vie for political posts. In the days of a restricted electorate and relatively few elective offices, these factions were able to control elections fairly effectively. However, as a greater number of people gained the right to vote, and more and more offices became elective, and the political arena was broadened to include a greater diversity of social groups, it became necessary to organize electoral efforts more extensively and to place them on a more permanent basis. Particularly important was the task of identifying candidates so that voters could tell who represented which group. It was then that factions took the crucial step that turned them into political parties: running candidates for office under a common label.

The term faction is still used today, primarily to designate groups that are part of a larger political entity. Sometimes it is employed to describe portions of an interest group, such as the two groups vying for control of the International Typographical Union described in the last chapter. More often the term is used to designate some grouping within a political party based on a particular personality, philosophy, or geographical region. Thus we speak of the Daley faction of the Illinois Democratic party (after the late powerful mayor of Chicago), the conservative faction of the Republican party, or the Southern faction of the national Democratic party. In this sense, faction is synonymous with *division* or *wing*.

A faction typically centers on some political personality, local political elite, or occasionally a particular political issue. Factions generally lack the features of a major political party—a permanent, well-organized structure and a symbolic relationship with their followers—that enable parties to transcend particular personalities or issues. For this reason, factions are less likely to persist over a series of elections than are parties.* They also frequently operate behind the scenes rather than out in the open because they lack the legitimacy of political parties in that people are not willing to grant them the right to run candidates for office. In any event, they do not do what we have suggested is the hallmark of a political party: run candidates for public office under a given label.

Membership in American Political Parties

Another difficulty in dealing with political parties is the problem of identifying its members. Most Americans do not go through the formality of joining a political party and paying dues to it as is common in interest groups and in many European political parties. Thus the Socialist party of France or the *American Farm Bureau Federation* of the United States can state that it has so many members, but the Republican and Democratic parties cannot. When we speak of those who belong to our two major parties, whom are we talking about?

One way to decide who should be considered members of a party is to determine the ways in which various individuals are involved in the kinds of party activities discussed in chapter 5. We could start with the following general categories:

1. *Party leaders:* the persons who hold major positions in the party, such as the chairman and members of the national, state, or local committee.

---

* Exceptions do exist, particularly in certain Southern states. For instance, former Senators Harry Byrd of Virginia and Huey Long of Louisiana dominated the politics of their states for years; even after they died, their respective followers continued to be associated as members of the Byrd and Long factions.

2. *Activists:* persons who work extensively in party affairs, raising money, re-cruiting candidates, making speeches for candidates, attending rallies, and canvassing voters.
3. *Supporters:* those who support the organization by donating money to the party or its candidates and by displaying labels, buttons, and bumper stick-ers.
4. *Voters and identifiers:* those who regularly vote for the party's candidates in elections or who, when asked, say that they consider themselves Republicans or Democrats.

Although this approach does make some important distinctions, it also has some major limitations. First, the somewhat arbitrary categories may not re-flect the actual influence various persons have in party affairs. Many activists, for example, swing more actual weight in party matters than those in formal party positions. Second, the realities of political life are such that no one re-mains in a category on a permanent basis: a person may become an activist in one election because of his interest in a particular candidate or issue, whereas in the next contest he may be merely a supporter or even an ordinary voter. In which group should he then be placed? Finally, the categories do not include everyone who is associated with a party. The prime example is a senator, representative or state legislator, or executive official. Although a person in one of those positions does not hold an official party post, he is elected under the party label or is appointed to his position primarily because of his relationship to a particular party. Moreover, in the course of his official activities he is expected to reflect the views of his party. He may thus be considered a party representative.

Aware of such difficulties, V. O. Key and Frank Sorauf identify three major divisions of political parties associated with different activities and different persons who participate in them. The three are:

1. The party organization: those who are active in party affairs, whether they hold an official party post or not. These are the individuals who carry on the major campaign activities of the party, contributing their time, money, skills, and effort.
2. The party in the government: those who hold official positions in the legisla-tive and executive branches and, as indicated above, are considered to be party representatives.
3. The party in the electorate: those who have a more casual relationship with the party—the supporters, voters, and identifiers.

These categories point up a major characteristic of political parties: they are broad-based and undertake a variety of activities. As the next section indicates, they also appeal to individuals for a variety of reasons.

INCENTIVES FOR JOINING POLITICAL PARTIES

The general incentives for belonging to political parties are similar to those previously described for interest groups. Included are *material benefits, solidary benefits,* and *purposive benefits.* Political scientist James Q. Wilson has divided those participating in political party activities into two major categories: those

Politicking professional style: The late Mayor Richard Daley congratulating the winner of a primary.

Amateur politicians at work.

whose incentives are primarily material and social in nature are known as professionals, while persons who primarily pursue purposive goals are called amateurs. As indicated below, these two types of party activist also differ on other matters, such as the role of compromise in political disputes, whether or not political patronage should be used to reward persons who help the party, and how political parties should be governed internally.

Party *professionals* are primarily in politics because they want something tangible for themselves such as a patronage job or a government contract, or because they like to exercise control over other persons' lives or enjoy the deference paid to them by others owing to the position they hold or the power they wield. They also tend to enjoy the "game" of politics for its own sake—the quest of victory, the maneuvering for advantage, and the camaraderie of working and socializing with other people in the political party.

The major goal of professionals is to win elections rather than to see to it that political programs or policies, such as better health care, environmental protection, and racial integration, are enacted into law. They may personally favor a particular program, but they evaluate it primarily in terms of its attracting political support needed to allow their candidate to win; if such a program threatens to cost the party an electoral victory, professionals will not hesitate to change the program to meet objections or abandon it altogether. Professionals understand the importance of compromise in political affairs and are tolerant toward those who differ with them on political matters. As far as the internal affairs of the political party are concerned, professionals expect it to be oligarchical in nature, with the people in top positions in the organization deciding how it should be run.

The prototype of a party organization run by professionals was the old-time political "machine" dominated by a "boss," such as James Curley of Boston,

The kingfish: Huey Long

Ed Crump of Memphis, Frank Hague of Jersey City, Tom Pendergast of Kansas City, Huey Long of Louisiana, and Gene Talmadge of Georgia. The arrangement between the boss and the people who supported him was of a reciprocal nature. The boss used his influence to see to it that his supporters or members of their families or friends were given public jobs or lucrative government contracts, that they received loans or gifts when they were in financial difficulties, a turkey at Thanksgiving or Christmas, or help when they got into trouble with the police. The political organization also sponsored picnics, beer parties, and other events for their supporters, many of whom were immigrants looking for new friends and outlets for their social interests. In return, the boss received votes from the recipients of his largesse, political contributions from those on the public payroll (usually a certain percentage of their salary, known as a lug, and "kickbacks" from those with government contracts.

In contrast, as Wilson suggests, political *amateurs* are persons who find politics intrinsically interesting because it expresses a concept of the public interest. They are thus concerned not with using political parties to further their own personal interests, but rather to help other individuals or groups, or society in general. They believe in certain principles and values (such as racial equality or "free enterprise") and are dedicated to seeing to it that those principles and values are implemented by means of public programs and policies.

This devotion to principle means that winning elections is not the primary goal of political amateurs. While they would, of course, prefer to be on the winning side, they will only back candidates who stand for the "right" things; it is better to support a loser who espouses their principles than a winner who does not. Unlike professionals, amateurs will not compromise their principles or even their favorite programs; rather, as political scientists Nelson Polsby and Aaron Wildavsky suggest, they are "purists" who believe that purism outside office is better than power inside government.

Amateurs also differ from professionals in other respects. Their purism makes them intolerant of persons who differ with them on political matters. Even if parties or candidates agree with political amateurs on most issues, that is not sufficient; they must prove themselves on *every* issue in order to be worthy of support. Moreover, political amateurs are very much opposed to patronage: they believe that people should participate in party activities out of a concern for the public interest, not for the sake of personal benefits. Finally, amateurs believe in internal party democracy; they are suspicious of strong party leaders and want rank-and-file members to have a major voice in the operations of political parties.

Wilson traces the development of organizations of amateurs to political clubs formed in New York City, Chicago, and Los Angeles in the 1950s. While these clubs operated at the city level, many of the persons helping to establish them had been drawn into politics originally by the presidential candidacy of Adlai Stevenson in 1952; moreover, many of the issues in which these amateurs were interested were national rather than local in nature. Since that time political amateurs have been closely associated with presidential candidates in both parties, including liberals who worked for Democrats Eugene McCarthy in 1968 and George McGovern in 1972, and conservatives who backed Republicans Barry Goldwater in 1964 and Ronald Reagan in 1976. Thus political amateurs represent both ends of the political spectrum.

It should be realized, however, that the political professional and the political amateur are "pure" or "ideal" types, and it is doubtful whether any individual or organization fits either category completely.* Few so-called professionals are totally disinterested in political programs, and few persons who are classified as amateurs will refuse to compromise on any occasion. Also, a person's motivations for participating in political parties can change over time: studies indicate that some who first become politically active as amateurs eventually adopt the goals and techniques of political professionals. Nonetheless, it is possible to distinguish the major political orientation of many persons or organizations as being essentially professional or amateur in nature. Moreover, as indicated at the end of this chapter, assessments of American political parties often turn on whether they are judged by the standards of a political professional or of an amateur.

FUNCTIONS OF POLITICAL PARTIES

What do parties do? Some of their functions are specific and observable, such as recruiting candidates. Other functions are general and intangible, such as contributing to the peaceful settlement of disputes in society. A party's action may have a very specific intention, as when it runs a candidate with a particular ethnic background for office in order to attract the votes of members of that ethnic group. Yet a given action may also have a significant byproduct—in this example, giving members of the minority group a feeling of importance, a sense of belonging to the society and an allegiance to its government. In talking about party functions we must also distinguish between things that parties *should* do, if they operate according to democratic theory (as discussed in ch. 1), and the things that they *actually succeed in accomplishing*. We must also delineate those functions that are characteristic of all parties compared to those that are peculiar to only some.

One function that all parties perform is running candidates for public office under their label. Sometimes party leaders themselves actually go out and induce persons to become candidates. Political candidates are also recruited in other ways, however. A person may be approached by an interest group, another officeholder, or by acquaintances to seek public office. Or he may be a self-starter, himself deciding to become a candidate. Ultimately, however, he must run under some party label if he hopes for any success, at least in national and most state elections.†

---

* It should be noted that the traditional political machine, epitomizing the "professional" organization, has largely disappeared in the United States in recent years, the exception being the Daley organization in Chicago. It remains to be seen whether Daley's successors can retain control over the politics of that community.

† Many local elections are nonpartisan in the sense that no label appears on the ballot. Judges in some states and state legislators in Minnesota and Nebraska are also elected in this way. The rationale behind nonpartisan elections is that by removing party labels from the ballot, "politics" is removed from the selection process. Studies indicate, however, that the political affiliations of the candidates are known by many voters anyway; moreover, removing party labels from the ballot does not eliminate politics—it merely *changes* the politics so that interest groups and newspapers (rather than the traditional parties) become influential in recruiting and backing candidates.

In addition to providing political leaders, parties take the initiative in policy matters. The dominant party in particular helps to identify the major problems—social, economic, and political—that require the attention of the citizens of a society. As President Kennedy stated, it is the responsibility of these party leaders to lay the unfinished business of America before its people for discussion and action. Besides setting an agenda, party leaders have the obligation of recommending specific programs to help mitigate the problems that they have identified.

Leaders of the party in the government also have the responsibility of using their influence to see that policies are implemented. The majority party organizes the legislative and executive branches of government so that the programs it favors can be enacted into law. The minority party has the function of criticizing the programs of the majority and of proposing alternative solutions to social problems.

Thus the major functions of political parties relate to three aspects of the political process: providing leadership through participation in elections; identifying problems and proposing programs to deal with them; and organizing and managing the government. There is little question that, of the three, the first is paramount. It is also the function on which American political parties have concentrated. Our two major political parties have been somewhat less concerned than European political parties, for example, with developing concrete social programs; they have also been less successful in organizing the legislative and executive branches of government so as to enact party programs into law.

Minor American political parties have also been deficient in regard to these latter two aspects of the political process. Although a variety of them have developed specific proposals for dealing with particular problems (witness their plans for removing the evil influence of alcoholic beverages, for dealing with currency problems, for giving relief to the farmer, and for controlling the trusts), they have not dealt with the broad range of issues demanding public attention. Nor have third parties performed the governing function. They have lacked the power to organize the political branches, and in most cases their representation has been so limited that they have not even been able effectively to criticize the proposals of the major parties.

These activities of political parties produce certain side effects that benefit individuals, groups, and the entire society of a democratic nation. The party helps to structure the voting choice of many citizens. As we shall see in chapter 10, many persons are unwilling to put in the time and effort to study the issues and the candidates' stands on them. Nor are they generally familiar with the background and abilities of the aspirants for public office. Lacking such information, some voters find it difficult to cast their ballots. For them the party serves as a point of reference, a guide to which is the best-qualified candidate and the one who is most likely to approach problems from their own general point of view. As imprecise as such guidelines are, they nonetheless provide clues for distinguishing the "good guys" from the "bad guys" in a large number of American electoral races.

For some, the party serves as more than a point of reference in voting; it also helps to meet their economic, political, and social needs. The classic case is the previously mentioned American political machine of the latter part of the last

century and early years of the present century; whatever else can be said of it, the machine helped assimilate immigrants into American society by furnishing them with the necessities of life, finding them jobs, educating and socializing them in the ways of our political system, and sponsoring social activities for them. Few persons today in the United States are so dependent on party organizations or receive so many benefits from them; nonetheless, many continue to derive substantial satisfactions—psychological, social, and economic—from participating in party affairs.

Like interest groups, political parties also channel the views and demands of individuals and groups to public officials. But rather than *articulate* particular desires as interest groups do, major political parties *aggregate* multiple demands—that is, combine them and accommodate their differences. Parties do so because if they hope to win power at the polls (some minor parties may not), they must develop broad-based programs that appeal to a wide variety of groups. Working out accommodations among diverse—and at times conflicting—demands of various groups enables the party to satisfy enough persons to win control of key governmental positions.

Finally, the activities of political parties contribute to the stability of the political system and of the larger society. A personal identification with, and commitment to, a political party helps create a sense of allegiance to the government. The process whereby parties reconcile and accommodate a broad spectrum of views and demands assists in the settlement of conflicts in society and in the development of significant areas of agreement among citizens of various backgrounds and perspectives. The creation of such a consensus, in turn, permits political parties to provide, and citizens to accept, the most basic feature of a democratic society: the pursuit and maintenance of political power by peaceful means and, when the populace desires it, the transfer of that power into other hands.

These, then, are the functions of political parties. Not all parties discharge them equally well; in fact, some parties do not perform a number of these functions at all. Nor are political parties the only organizations that carry on such activities: interest groups, factions, and ad hoc groups also participate in recruiting candidates, organizing campaigns, and proposing public policies. It is even conceivable that a democratic society might not need political parties at all, that other institutions might be developed in their stead. The fact remains, however, that no democratic nation has ever done so: all have depended on political parties to perform these vital functions. The remainder of this chapter focuses on the oldest party system in the world: our own.

THE DEVELOPMENT OF AMERICAN POLITICAL PARTIES

If there was any one matter on which the political leaders discussed in chapter 2 were agreed, it was that the nation should not divide itself into warring political camps. Madison and Washington were particularly concerned lest divisions imperil the national unity at a time when the young republic was fighting for its very existence against disruptive forces of geographic and economic rivalries. Hamilton, who had little faith in the common man (at one time he told Jefferson that the "people" were a "great beast"), quite naturally had no use for political organizations that would enable the public at large to influence decisions that he felt were better left to persons of superior intellect and training. Even Jefferson, who did place great trust in the masses and their ability to be educated politically, did not regard parties favorably: he declared in 1789 that "If I could not go to heaven but with a party, I would not go there at all." Instead, he assumed that political officials would respond to currents of public opinion without the necessity of channeling public attitudes through political parties. Yet within less than a decade after the creation of the national government under the Constitution that they all favored, all four became key figures in the establishment of rival political parties.

What precipitated the formation of the two parties was the economic program that Hamilton, as the first Secretary of the Treasury in the Washington administration, proposed to the Congress in 1790. Designed to promote manufacturing and commerce and to place the new government on a sound financial basis, the plan called for a number of controversial measures, including the assumption by the national government of debts owed by the states as well as the creation of a national bank. Madison, who was serving in the Congress, opposed the assumption of debts on the grounds that many Southern states had already paid theirs off and should not be taxed to help satisfy the obligations of Northern states. Jefferson, who was serving in the Washington administration as Secretary of State, worked out a political compromise whereby the debts would be assumed by the national government in return for the location of the capital in the South, specifically what was to become Washington, D.C. But Jefferson was unwilling to consent to the creation of a national bank (he regarded it as a dangerous monopoly that would benefit only mercantile interests, not the farmers for whom he had such admiration) and joined forces with Madison in trying to defeat the proposal in the Congress. Hamilton's supporters prevailed, however, and the bank was authorized in 1791.

A number of other domestic issues contributed to the growing split between the former political allies. Hamilton's economic program called for financial measures that clearly favored the industrial sections of the nation: a tax on foreign goods (a tariff) was levied not only to raise revenue for the national government but also to protect American manufacturers and merchants from

This Federalist cartoon of 1793 shows the Republicans as a band of lawless cutthroats keeping company with the devil. Jefferson is shown standing on a bench and ranting wildly.

foreign competition. Farmers who purchased manufactured goods bore the brunt of the tax since prices on foreign commodities were raised to cover the amount of the tariff. Even more vexing to them was the excise tax on liquor. While Eastern distillers could pass on the tax to their consumers, it was a direct levy on farmers who made liquor for their own use. Some frontiersmen in western Pennsylvania refused to pay the tax, intimidated government collectors, and dealt drastically with those who assisted revenue officers. Ultimately an insurrection known as the Whiskey Rebellion broke out there in 1794, and Washington sent a military force over the Alleghenies to put down this threat to the legitimacy of the new government.

While domestic economic concerns thus contributed to a growing split between the contending forces, ideology and foreign policy widened the cleavage. The eruption of the French Revolution in 1789, coupled with the outbreak of hostilities between the new revolutionary regime and Great Britain some four years later, polarized Americans. The followers of Jefferson viewed the French Revolution as a logical extension of our own, with the common people of both nations removing the political yoke of the upper classes. Hamiltonians agreed with the British statesman Edmund Burke that the stability of society was threatened by the excesses of the French mob. Hamilton's belief that the affairs of state should be entrusted to the national aristocracy was completely at odds with Jefferson's faith in the basic equality of man and his disdain for the nobility.

Injected into this general ideological climate was the highly controversial agreement negotiated with the British in 1794 by the Washington administration. Although the Jay treaty (so named because John Jay was the American negotiator) settled some major controversies with the British (they agreed, for example, to withdraw troops from forts in the Northwest), it failed to satisfy

SIM GREENE

A NARRATIVE OF THE WHISKY
INSURRECTION

Being a Setting Forth of the Memoirs of the Late
David Froman, Esq.

BY

RICHARD T. WILEY

———

THE JOHN C. WINSTON COMPANY
PHILADELPHIA 1906

two basic American grievances: compensation for slaves that the British had carried away during the Revolution and the impressment into British service of American sailors who were serving on ships that the British seized for trading with the French. Overnight the treaty became the target of bitter attacks by the anti-Hamiltonians (their favorite curse was "Damn John Jay! Damn everyone who won't damn John Jay! Damn everyone who won't put out lights in his windows and sit up all night damning John Jay!"), and it was necessary to throw the great prestige of Washington into the political battle to win its approval in 1795.

Out of this series of controversies over domestic issues, ideology, and foreign policy, the Federalist and Republican parties were born. The former, with Hamilton as the initiator of policies and Washington as the popular leader around whom men could be rallied, had formed by the early 1790s and soon had candidates running for Congress under its label and voting in the legislature in favor of the Hamiltonian programs. Jefferson's resignation from the Washington administration at the end of 1793 over the national bank issue paved the way for the establishment of the opposition, who came to be known as the Republicans. Although Jefferson returned to his home in Monticello, Madison remained in the Congress and organized the party so well that by the middle of the decade an anti-administration block in the Congress was voting together consistently; soon congressional candidates were being identified with the party as well. With the retirement of Washington at the end of his second term, the party rivalry spread to presidential politics when Adams, the Federalist candidate, narrowly defeated Jefferson, the Republican, in 1796.

During the next four years the partisan battle became even more intense. Direct taxes were levied on three major property sources of farmers, who supported the Republican party—land, houses, and slaves. The passage of the Alien and Sedition laws and their partisan application against Republicans (particularly newspaper editors) by Federalist judges served to deepen the partisan schism in the young nation. The stage was thus set for the crucial presidential election of 1800, in which the Republican ticket of Jefferson and Burr decisively defeated the Federalist team of Adams and Charles Pinckney at the polls, and the Republicans gained control of both the Senate and the House of Representatives.

Thus within a decade the United States had gone through crucial stages of political development. Many had viewed Washington as a "patriot king" who would rule in the interests of all the people, but it soon became apparent that there were major differences among groups that could not be settled by a neutral political figure, no matter how fair-minded or popular he might be. It also soon became apparent that traditional electoral organizations—factions based on local or state political personalities—would not be sufficient to capture control of the Congress and the presidency: to sponsor and help identify candidates for the growing electorate, permanent, visible, and broadly based organizations would have to be created. And so the world's first democratic political parties were established in the United States. When the Federalists, however grudgingly, relinquished control of the national government to the Republicans in 1800, another political first was achieved: the peaceful transfer of power from one party to another. Orderly, nonviolent competition has continued to characterize the American party system ever since.

GENERAL NATURE OF PARTY COMPETITION

Political scientists distinguish three types of electoral situations: one-party, two-party, and multiparty. In the first, representatives of one political party hold all or almost all the major offices in the government. This condition may prevail where only one party is legally permitted to run candidates—as in Nazi Germany and Fascist Italy between the two world wars and in the People's Republic of China and the Soviet Union today—or where opposition parties are legally recognized but, for one reason or another, only one party is successful in election contests—as in Mexico, where the Institutional Revolutionary Party has won election after election for over forty years despite the fact that other groups like the National Action Party run opposition candidates. In the United States the Democratic party held a similar monopoly in most Southern states from the end of the Reconstruction period following the Civil War until recently. In a one-party system, if electoral competition exists, it involves only factions within the dominant party.

Under a two-party system, two, and only two, political parties have a reasonable chance to control major political offices. Both parties seek total political power, but neither is able to eliminate its rival at the ballot box. Each party is capable of capturing enough public positions to govern, but the opposition party continues to draw a sufficiently large vote to threaten the party in power. The result is that those in control of the various governments must take public wishes and sentiments into account lest they lose out to the opposition party at the next election. Moreover, the system works best if the opposition threat is realized from time to time, so that the two parties alternate in governing at reasonable intervals of time. According to Leon Epstein, a student of comparative political parties, only six nations have two-party systems: Australia, Austria, Canada, Great Britain, New Zealand, and the United States.

Under a multiparty system, three or more parties compete effectively for political offices, and none of them expects to win control of the government on its own. Rather, representatives of a combination of parties share the major positions of public authority. Generally, multiparty systems operate in countries with a parliamentary form of government, wherein the legislative body chooses the major leaders of the executive branch. Typically a coalition is formed of parties that together control a majority of the seats in the legislature; these parties in turn divide up the cabinet seats among persons from their respective organizations. Examples of nations with a multiparty system are France and Italy.

Only the one- and two-party systems have operated to any significant extent in the United States. Minor or "third" parties* have appeared from time to time, but they have had relatively little success in winning political office, particularly at the national level. Yet, as the discussion later in this chapter indicates, they have nonetheless had some important political effects in the United States.

The Whig campaign of 1840.

---

* This is the term typically used for minor American parties, but it would be more precise to designate them as "third," "fourth," or "fifth" parties, depending on their relative electoral strength.

AMERICAN PARTY COMPETITION AT THE NATIONAL LEVEL

The Historical Record

The Republican candidate of 1872.

The Republican campaign of 1888.

As we have seen, the United States within a few years of its establishment had an operating two-party system. Although the Federalist Adams edged out the Republican Jefferson for the presidency in 1796, and his party also managed to win control of the House of Representatives (at that time senators were chosen by state legislatures), the Republicans swept them from power in both branches in 1800. After that crucial election, the Federalist party continued to operate nationally for the next decade and a half, but it never again gained control of either the presidency or the House. The demise of the party has been ascribed to a number of causes: the split in the party organization created by differences between Adams and Hamilton; an elitist political philosophy that prevented Federalist leaders from expanding membership to less-advantaged persons and from organizing at the grass-roots level; and the pro-British attitude of many Federalists (particularly in New England) during the War of 1812, which served to associate the party with disloyalty to the nation. The party disappeared completely from the national scene around 1816.

There then followed a period of one-party government. This so-called "era of good feeling" culminated in James Monroe's almost unanimous election as President in 1820. After that, however, competition broke out within the Republican party as "factions" formed around John Quincy Adams and Andrew Jackson. Gradually these factions developed into genuine parties: the followers of Adams became known as the National Republicans, those of Jackson as the Democratic Republicans. In the late 1830s the National Republican party was replaced by the Whigs; when in 1840 the Whig candidate, William Henry Harrison, defeated the incumbent President Martin Van Buren (who now ran under the label of the Democratic, rather than Democratic Republican, party), true two-party competition returned. It continued into the middle 1850s when the Whig party disappeared, only to be succeeded by another group, the Republican party, which ran its first presidential candidate, General John Frémont, in 1856. Since that date, the Democratic and Republican parties have dominated American politics in the oldest continuous two-party competition in the world.

The Republican and Democratic rivalry over the years clearly meets the requirements of a two-party system. In the period from 1856 through 1976, the Republicans were successful in eighteen presidential elections, the Democrats in thirteen. The competition every two years for control of the House of Representatives has been even closer: the Democrats won thirty-five such elections and the Republicans twenty-six. In this century alone, the results are also fairly close: through 1976, the Republicans captured the White House on ten occasions and the Democrats on ten; in the same period the Democrats enjoyed a 26-13 edge in contests for the control of the lower branch of Congress. Thus both Republicans and Democrats have been able to win political power in both the executive and legislative branches of the government.

Besides winning control of the national government, both parties have managed in defeat to win a substantial portion of the popular vote. "Landslide" presidential elections—those in which the winning candidate gets more than 60 percent of the vote—have occurred only four times in this century: Warren Harding's victory in 1920, Franklin Roosevelt's in 1936, Lyndon Johnson's in 1964, and Richard Nixon's in 1972. Contests for the House of Representatives since 1900 have been even closer. Only twice has the losing party received less than 40 percent of the vote—the Democrats in 1920 and the Republicans in 1936.

As for the alternation of parties in power, the record has been mixed. In their century-long rivalry, the Republicans and Democrats have generally been able to oust each other from office at fairly frequent intervals, although there have been some notable eras of one-party dominance. The newly formed Republican party controlled the presidency from Lincoln's election in 1860 until Cleveland won the office for the Democrats in 1884. The latter party, in turn, held the office over a twenty-year span from 1933 until 1953, with Franklin Roosevelt's four consecutive victories followed by Truman's upset victory in 1948.

There have also been extended periods of one-party control of the House of Representatives. The Republicans maintained majorities for sixteen-year periods on three separate occasions, 1859-1875; 1895-1911; and 1917-1933. In turn, the Democrats have dominated the chamber in recent years, from 1933-1947 and again since 1955; in fact, they have been in control of the House for forty-two of the forty-six years from 1933 through 1979, being out of power only from 1947 to 1949 and again from 1953 to 1955. Thus if one were to focus only on the recent situation in the House of Representatives from the standpoint of alternation of party control of that chamber (the same condition has prevailed in the Senate during this period), it would be proper to refer to the congressional electoral system as a one-party Democratic one.

However, on balance, the American system at the national level must be considered a two-party affair. The near-equality of Republican and Democratic victories over many years' time, the fairly close division of the popular vote, and the considerable degree of alternation in power—particularly for the presidency—place the system in the two-party category.

Reasons for the National Two-Party System

Political scientists have long puzzled over the question of why a given country has a one-, two-, or multiparty system. There is no ready answer because it is difficult, if not impossible, to demonstrate that certain social, economic, or political conditions actually "cause" the formation and operation of a given party arrangement. Yet it is possible to investigate the kinds of conditions that are associated with particular party systems and to deduce logical reasons for these associations.

Historical Factors. One reason for the original formation of that system was the early division into two general groups over political issues facing the young nation. As we saw in chapter 2, two broad constellations of interests appeared in the battle over the Constitution: the Federalists representing the manufacturers, merchants, shipowners, and commercial farmers—all of whom were dependent on trade for their livelihood; and the anti-Federalists speaking for the subsistence farmers, artisans, and mechanics—who were not thus dependent. This same general split persisted over the Hamiltonian economic pro-

The Republican campaign of 1900.

The Democratic campaign of 1932.

Promotional display for Republican campaign of 1932.

gram, with the commercial classes rallying to its support and agricultural interests generally opposing it.* This basic breach widened further when the large landowners (who supported the Constitution and Hamilton's early program) subsequently became disenchanted with the Federalists because the Jay treaty provided them with no compensation for the slaves the British carried away during the Revolution. Thus the two parties, the Federalists and the Republicans, represented two disparate groups: the former, the business and commercial elements of the nation that tended to be concentrated in the North, particularly along the coasts; the latter, the agricultural interests that predominated in the South and in the interior, along the "frontier."

Two broad constellations of interests have continued to characterize our party division. In the period of Jacksonian democracy, the Western-frontier forces were allied against Eastern monied interests. As the slavery issue became more salient, the East-West schism was replaced by a new sectionalism arising from conflicts between the North and South. This cleavage, based on differences in the economies of the two regions (the industrial Northeast versus the more rural South), the memories of the Civil War, and the problems of race, persisted through the first third of this century. In fact, the period from the Civil War until the 1920s was characterized by *sectional* politics—the Republican party based in the Northeast and the Democrats in the South, with both vying for the support of the West and Midwest, which held the balance of political power.

Beginning in the late 1920s a new dimension was introduced into American politics by increasing urbanization. This development caused a breakup of sectional unity as industry increasingly located in the West and South. The result was the development of *class* politics, as the Republicans gathered the support of the upper and upper-middle economic groups, while the working class, together with ethnic groups (especially immigrants from central and southern Europe and their children) and Negroes (who had traditionally been wedded to the Republicans since the Civil War), increasingly moved into the Democratic camp. The pattern continues to prevail today, but it is further complicated by the reemergence of race as a major issue in American politics: more Southerners, together with some working-class whites and ethnics, have begun to cast their votes in presidential elections for Republican candidates (whom they perceive as being less pro-Negro than Northeastern and Western Democrats).

This historical sketch of party divisions is admittedly simplified (we will examine the nuances and complexities of elections and voting patterns in more depth in ch. 10), but it does indicate that the two parties have been able to develop broad coalitions of groups and that between them they have managed to absorb and aggregate the major interests in our society. Unlike many European nations, we have not developed a number of major parties, each representing a fairly narrow range of groups and concerns.

The Democratic campaign of 1952.

Consensus. Another factor that has contributed to the American two-party system is the considerable consensus that has existed on the fundamental goals

---

* Not all individuals, however, followed this pattern: Madison and Jefferson supported the Constitution, but founded the Republican party. Still, most pro-constitutionalist leaders supported the Federalist party, while the anti-constitutionalists typically became Republicans.

of our society and the major means for reaching these goals. Most Americans have shared the views of Locke and Madison on the importance of individual self-development, including the right to acquire private property. There has been little sentiment for vesting the ownership of the means of production in public ownership, a common goal elsewhere. This being so, the dispute between the parties has focused not on whether there should be private property or not, but rather on how it should be distributed. The Republicans have tended to represent the interests of the haves and the Democrats the have-nots who want to become haves. Certainly this division has not been absolute, but as historian Charles Beard expressed the idea some years ago, "The center of gravity of wealth is on the Republican side, while the center of poverty is on the Democratic side."

Agreement on fundamentals extends beyond economic matters to political and social concerns as well. Thus Americans have been committed not only to the private enterprise system but also to our basic political institutions. No sizable group has ever advocated another form of government, such as monarchy, which many Frenchmen have proposed over the years. Because a feudal system never existed in the United States, there has been no aristocratic social class to establish an oligarchy in order to protect its privileges, as has happened in other countries. Finally, religious divisions that have plagued many societies and spawned a variety of parties have played no meaningful role in American politics. As suggested in chapter 4, the early decision to separate matters of church and state has prevented that result here.

This agreement on fundamentals has meant that American society has not been rent by the variety of basic cleavages—economic, political, and social— around which multiple parties have clustered in other nations. Keeping religion out of the politics, for example, has meant the absence of Catholic and Protestant parties or of groups supporting and groups opposing the subsidizing of religious institutions, an issue that has divided parties in France and Italy. Nor have we had significant monarchist or socialist parties. Instead, American parties have generally split on only one significant issue—how economic goods and privileges should be allocated among the population—and two parties have been sufficient to represent most opposing views on that issue.

The economic nature of party differences has also made compromise possible in the American political system. Although individuals may not see eye to eye on the matter of who should have how much of the good things of life, conflicts in viewpoint are not irreconcilable. The issue is not an either-or proposition; everyone can receive something in terms of material comforts. Our great natural resources and expanding economy have made it possible to distribute economic benefits to ever more people without threatening the interests of those who already have considerable possessions. Few significant groups have found it necessary to go outside our two major parties to protect their economic interests.

Very recently, however, some of the basic consensus in American society has begun to erode as issues have expanded beyond economic matters to racial and cultural concerns as well. As we shall see in chapter 10, these developments have left our traditional two-party situation in a highly uncertain state at the present time.

The campaign of 1960.

The Republican campaign of 1964.

Campaign memorabilium: 1968.

The Democratic campaign, 1972.

Electoral Rules. The rules of the democratic game are seldom, if ever, neutral; they tend to favor some interests over others. One factor that has permitted the American two-party system to survive—and, indeed, to flourish—is that certain features of our electoral system give the major parties advantages over third parties. We will examine the electoral process in detail in chapter 9; for the moment it will be sufficient to note the two points most relevant to our party system.

The way we elect our President favors a two-party system. In nations with a parliamentary form of government under which the Chief Executive (the prime minister or premier) is chosen by the national legislative body, a minority party can become a part of a coalition that controls a majority of the legislative seats and may have one of its leaders chosen for that post. As will be explained in detail in chapter 9, however, to win the American presidency a candidate must win a majority of the electoral votes, which means that he must have a large proportion of the popular vote. Third parties do not achieve that success, and as a consequence they have not survived: a party that cannot capture control of the highest office—the presidency—cannot be a major force in the nation's politics.

Our method of electing representatives also favors the two major parties. Although most states elect several representatives to the House of Representatives (only Alaska, Delaware, Nevada, Vermont, and Wyoming send one) they are not chosen under a system of multimember constituencies and proportional representation as in many European countries. Under that electoral system, voters select a number of representatives, and the seats are allocated to the parties on the basis of their share of the popular vote. If, for example, Missouri, which is entitled to ten members of the House of Representatives, used such a system, a minor party that won 20 percent of the popular vote would have two of its candidates sitting in Washington as representatives of that state. Under the single-member district method used by Missouri and other states, it is divided into ten separate House districts, and voters cast their ballots only for the candidates for the one representative of their particular area. The winner is the contestant who gains a plurality of the votes (that is, more than any other candidate) for that district. Under this arrangement a minor party whose candidate draws 20 percent of the popular vote in any or all the ten districts does not gain any representation in Washington, since under our two-party system that proportion would not constitute a plurality of votes. As with the presidential contest, our single-member-district-plurality method for choosing congressmen operates under a winner-take-all principle; thus losing minor parties receive no electoral rewards for their efforts.

Natural Perpetuation of the Two-Party System. One final factor that supports the two-party system in the United States is that certain built-in mechanisms tend to make it self-perpetuating. As we saw in chapter 5, children develop an attachment to a political party at an early age. This psychological identification, which they acquire primarily from their parents, tends to deepen during the course of their adult lives. In a society where the two major political parties have been dominant for over a century, the citizens, in overwhelming proportion, naturally learn to think of themselves as Republican and Democratic. In other words, traditional party patterns, plus the political-socialization process by which attitudes are passed on from one generation to another, combine to perpetuate the two-party system in the United States.

Our two-party system also serves to concentrate the political leadership of the nation in the Republican and Democratic parties. Persons aspiring to political positions know that unless they can use one of these labels, they have little chance of succeeding in their quest for public office. Thus political talent is attracted towards the two major parties and away from minor parties, which typically back losing candidates.

The two-party system also perpetuates itself by channeling political conflict into two major outlets, the organization in power and the one out of power. Support for, and opposition to, the government and what it is doing tends to polarize around two distinct (party) groups. Under this arrangement citizens who are unhappy about the current state of affairs not only vote against the present office holders but also give their support to candidates of the other major party, which serves as the only real political alternative to the party in power.

COMPETITION AT THE LOWER LEVELS OF GOVERNMENT

Students of American politics who speak of a two-party system are referring primarily to electoral competition at the national level. What about the lower levels of government? Table 7.2 (as well as Fig. 7.1), developed by Austin Ranney, which classifies the state party systems on the basis of competition for

Figure 7.1
State party systems. Source: "Parties in State Politics," in Herbert Jacob and Kenneth Vines, *Politics in the American States* (Boston: Little, Brown, 3rd ed., 1976), p. 62.

One–party Democratic
Modified one–party Democratic
Two–party
Modified one–party Republican

the governorship and both branches of the state legislature in the period 1962–73, indicates that only twenty-three of the fifty states had a two-party system during that time. Of the remaining twenty-seven states, twenty leaned toward political control by one of the two major parties, and the other seven were clearly dominated by the Democrats. Thus less than one-half of the states during the period under analysis had party systems resembling that of the nation as a whole.

Further down the levels of the American political system, electoral contests become even less two-party in nature. The overwhelming proportion of the approximately 3000 counties in the United States are dominated politically by one of the two major parties, as are municipalities that use partisan ballots to elect their officials; typically, the large central cities are controlled by the

Table 7.2
The Fifty States
Classified According
to Degree of
Interparty
Competition,
1962–1973*

One-party Democratic	Modified one-party Democratic	Two-party		Modified one-party Republican
Louisiana (.9930)	North Carolina (.7750)	Nevada (.6057)	Delaware (.4947)	North Dakota (.3463)
Alabama (.9520)	Maryland (.7647)	California (.6020)	Michigan (.4903)	Idaho (.3445)
Mississippi (.9145)	Virginia (.7543)	Alaska (.5760)	Pennsylvania (.4705)	Colorado (.3390)
South Carolina (.8935)	Tennessee (.7443)	Connecticut (.5670)	Utah (.4647)	Kansas (.3380)
Texas (.8780)	Florida (.7410)	Montana (.5553)	Arizona (.4377)	South Dakota (.3373)
Georgia (.8710)	Hawaii (.7313)	New Jersey (.5437)	Illinois (.4245)	Vermont (.3307)
Arkansas (.8645)	Oklahoma (.7297)	Washington (.5420)	Wisconsin (.4245)	Wyoming (.3205)
	New Mexico (.7107)	Nebraska (.5127)	Indiana (.4160)	
	Missouri (.7085)	Oregon (.5075)	Iowa (.4113)	
	Kentucky (.7037)	Minnesota (.5037)	New York (.4053)	
	West Virginia (.6945)		Maine (.4045)	
	Rhode Island (.6860)		Ohio (.3693)	
	Massachusetts (.6730)		New Hampshire (.3600)	

Source: Austin Ranney, "Parties in State Politics," in Herbert Jacob and Kenneth Vines, *Politics in the American States* (Boston: Little Brown, 3rd ed., 1976), p. 61.

* *Scale.* 1.000—completely Democratic; .0000—completely Republican.

Democratic party, while suburban communities, particularly those populated by the well-to-do, favor the Republicans.

Factors Affecting Competition Below The National Level

Interestingly enough, some of the very same factors that are associated with the national two-party system have had precisely the opposite effect at lower levels of the American political system. As Table 7.2 makes clear, the trauma of the Civil War, which split the nation into the Republican North and the Democratic South, created one-party politics within both of these regions. All seven of the one-party Democratic states fought on the side of the Confederacy, while of the thirteen modified one-party Democratic states, eight were Confederate or border states, and two others—New Mexico and Oklahoma—were settled originally by Southerners. And of the seven modified one-party Republican states, two—Kansas and Vermont—supported the Union, while the others contained many persons whose ancestors came from states that fought on the Union side. Thus, more than any other single historical event or issue, the Civil War shaped state partisan politics in the post-World-War-II era.

The race issue has been particularly instrumental in shaping the one-party Democratic politics of the Southern states, for it has suppressed natural economic divisions in the electorate there that might have led to a competitive party system. For a short period in the early 1890s it appeared that the Populist party (to be discussed later in this chapter) might be the vehicle for an alliance between blacks and poor whites against the Bourbons, the upper-class planter group that had traditionally controlled Southern politics. When that possibility occurred, the latter protected their interests by using the race issue as a means of splitting the poor whites from their natural economic allies, the blacks. This ploy, coupled with the demise of the Populists after the presidential election of 1896, restored Southern politics to its traditional one-party mold with the Bourbons in political command. The Democrats continued to use the race issue to brand the Republican party as the political enemy, the party of treason, with which no true Southerner would have any association. Moreover, differences with the rest of the nation, particularly the North, over racial matters (as well as economic issues, such as a low vs. a high tariff) tended to drive Southerners together, with the Democratic party serving as an instrument for regional unity.

Other factors have also operated to preserve the one-party politics of states and localities. Just as traditions and political socialization have perpetuated loyalties so that, overall, nationally a two-party system persists, so have they continued the one-party inclinations of staunch Northerners and Southerners. Political leadership has also been channeled into regionally dominant parties, as ambitious candidates have taken the only practical route open to political office. As we will see in chapter 9, the rules of the electoral game have also been manipulated to favor the prevalent party at the state level. State legislatures have drawn single-member districts in contests for their own seats (as for the national House of Representatives) to favor candidates of the dominant party. In addition, these legislators have passed laws giving all the state's electoral votes in presidential elections to the candidate that wins a mere plurality of the popular vote. In this fashion, the traditional majority party in one-party states has been able to deny a struggling minority vital political offices or influence that is so desperately needed if it is successfully to challenge the traditional one-party control of the state.

Although these factors help to explain the lack of party competition at the state and local levels in the United States, they fail to account for the twenty-three states listed in Table 7.2 that have two-party systems. A number of these, particularly in the Northeast, are highly urbanized states with a diversified economy and a population composed of many ethnic, religious, and social-class groups. Thus the changes in these highly industrialized states in the direction of class politics—upper-class suburbanites and residents of the small towns and rural areas aligned against working-class and ethnic groups in the central cities—have supplanted the one-party politics promoted by the Civil War.

There are in the two-party group, however, a number of Western states that are not urbanized, such as Alaska, Montana, Nebraska, Utah, and Arizona. Their two-party systems appear to be associated with two other factors. As newer states, they have not been so greatly affected by the memories of the Civil War. Also, they have been populated by persons from other parts of the country, both North and South, which has meant that political traditions (including partisan ones) have not been very important in shaping their politics. Indeed, the variety of settlers has provided a partisan mix and a competitive two-party system.

Patterns of State Competition

Even though states with one-party systems have no meaningful electoral contests between the candidates of the major parties, they are not totally without political competition. The nature of the competition is simply different, occurring within the framework of the dominant party: the focus of electoral combat shifts from the general election to the nominating process. In one-party states, particularly those of the once-solid Democratic South, more voters participated in the primary contest of the majority party than cast their ballots for the candidates of both parties combined in the general election. When the primary was over, people knew who would hold office for the next term, since the dominant party's candidate had little to fear from his rival in the general election. Thus one-party politics substitutes intraparty struggle for interparty competition.

States with one-party systems, however, differ significantly among themselves. V. O. Key, Jr., in his classic study of politics in the American South in the 1940s, *Southern Politics in State and Nation*, distinguished two separate patterns of intraparty competition. One is bifactionalism, wherein contests within the majority party between two identifiable groups persist over a series of elections. Good examples of bifactionalism are the previously noted Byrd/anti-Byrd and Long/anti-Long splits in the Virginia and Louisiana Democratic parties that continued after the death of both leaders, as the contending groups took on an identity that transcended the particular personalities involved. A student of politics in the New England states in the 1950s, Duane Lockard, found a similar situation in Republican Vermont between the supporters and opponents of the long-powerful Proctor family there.

The second of Key's basic patterns of intraparty competition is multifactionalism. He applies this term to Florida and Arkansas (Lockard to Maine), where several factions typically vie for the top state offices. In such a situation factional alliances among political leaders are loose and often change from one election to another. Moreover, almost everyone fends for himself as each candidate builds his own personal organization.

Key and others have concluded that, of the two kinds of intraparty competition, the bifactional type provides the voter with the more meaningful choice. Typically in a multifactional race, each candidate does well in his own geographical area, gaining what Key calls "friends and neighbors" support. In these situations elections turn on the appeal of the hometown boy rather than on differences between candidates over social, economic, and political issues. Bifactional competition is more likely to reflect such differences—as it has, for instance, in Louisiana, where the Long faction has generally championed the interests of the dirt farmer and other economically disadvantaged groups (including blacks) against the business community and wealthy planters that have constituted the major support of the anti-Long faction. Even where such clear liberal-conservative differences do not exist (they have been less apparent, for example, in Virginia between the Byrd and anti-Byrd factions), bifactionalism creates the potential for such a division. In any event, deciding between two major candidates for each office is less confusing to the voter than trying to distinguish among a large number who cannot be characterized on the basis of their association with different economic or social groups.

This is not to say, however, that bifactionalism offers the voter the same choice as a two-party system does. Quite often factions do not run a complete slate of candidates as do the major parties. Even when they do, not all voters know which particular candidates are associated with each of the two factions, since no designations appear on the ballot. As we have previously stressed, parties offer voters what factions cannot: a label on the ballot that helps to identify which candidate belongs to which electoral group.

One final pattern of state party politics combines elements of both one- and two-party competition. John Fenton, a student of the Border states (Kentucky, Maryland, Missouri, and West Virigina), in the 1950s, suggests that they have three identifiable political groups that are increasingly vying for political power. Two operate as factions within the Democratic party: a liberal wing, with its principal political support among labor, blacks, and ethnic groups from the urban areas; and a conservative counterpart, with its major base in the Bourbon class. In addition, an opposition has grown in recent years among traditional Republicans from the mountain areas of these states,* new arrivals from the North, and residents of the burgeoning suburbs. Fenton sees this three-way competition not only as the prevailing pattern in these states but also as the wave of the future in the South as states in that region take on more of the characteristics (growing industrialization and a more potent political alliance between Negroes and organized labor) of the Border states.

Recent Trends in State Party Competition

There have been a number of changes in Southern politics in recent years. Perhaps most important has been the increased role played by blacks in South-

---

* During the Civil War, persons from mountain areas who owned no slaves sided with the North. Many of these areas have remained as pockets of Republican strength over the years.

ern politics, a development stimulated by the Voting Rights Act of 1965, which made it easier for them to register and vote. Blacks have overwhelmingly thrown their electoral support to Democratic candidates, especially progressive governors like Dale Bumpers of Arkansas, Reubin Askew of Florida, John West of South Carolina, and Jimmy Carter of Georgia. Organized labor has also supported the same kind of candidates, but it has not become as potent a force in Southern politics as Fenton has predicted. The passage of right-to-work laws in many Southern states has prevented unions from organizing as many workers as they have in Northern and border states. Also handicapping organized labor in the South is the fact that many of the new companies locating there in recent years are not heavy industries but rather light ones with white-collar workers that labor has traditionally found difficult to organize.

A group of scholars under the leadership of political scientist William Havard, who analyzed Southern politics in the late 1960s, found other changes had occurred there in the two decades since V. O. Key's classic study. Particularly important were three changes in the internal operation of the region's dominant Democratic party. Unlike the 1940s with the Byrd organization in Virginia and the Long equivalent in Louisiana, there were no comparable state-wide permanent factions in any Southern state in the 1960s. Moreover, the bifactional rivalries that according to Key characterized the politics of those two states—along with North Carolina, Tennessee, and Texas—operated only in Louisiana when Havard and his colleagues studied Southern politics twenty years later. Finally, the "friends and neighbors" phenomenon of the 1940s also became less important, probably as a result of the increased influence of television in allowing candidates to communicate more easily with voters in all parts of their state.

The Republican party has become a more significant force in the South in recent elections, but primarily in national elections, especially the presidency and to a lesser extent for senatorial and congressional seats as well. Individual Republican candidates have been able from time to time to win gubernatorial posts, such as Winthrop Rockefeller in Arkansas and Claude Kirk in Florida, but the party has been unable to retain such offices; moreover, Republicans have not been able to make significant inroads into Democratically controlled state legislatures. If we compare the competitive situation of states shown in Table 7.2 for major state executive and legislative offices with a similar list compiled by Austin Ranney for a prior period, we find that only one state, Florida, moved from the one-party Democratic category in the earlier period (1946-63) to the modified one-party Democratic category in the later period (1962-73).

In fact, a similar comparison of other states shows that in recent years there have been greater changes in party competition in other regions of the country than in the South. The Democratic party has improved its situation in two areas in particular—New England and the Midwest. Rhode Island, Massachusetts, and Missouri have gone from being two-party states to modified one-party Democratic states; and Maine, New Hampshire, Iowa, and Wisconsin have changed from modified one-party Republican states to two-party states. On the other hand, three Western states—Colorado, Idaho, and Wyoming—are now modified one-party Republican states, rather than the two-party states that they were in the period from 1946 to 1963.

Thus party competition in the United States has been of either the one- or the two-party type. The former has prevailed in cities, counties, and about half the American states. The latter has been prominent in the remaining states and in contests for national political offices. We have not had meaningful multiparty competition at any level of the American political system. Minor parties have continued to exist in the United States, however, and although they have never captured a significant number of national offices and have seldom been successful in states and localities either, they have nonetheless had considerable impact on American politics—enough so that it is worth considering their record in some detail.

MINOR AMERICAN PARTIES

There has been a wide variety of minor, or third, parties in American history. Some, like the Anti-Masonic party of the 1830s, contested a single presidential election and disappeared almost immediately from the political landscape. Others, like the Socialist party, have fielded candidates in a hopeless electoral cause over a number of years. The Prohibition party has zeroed in on what members regard as the tragic flaw in the national well-being, while the Communist party has sought to overhaul the entire economic and political structure of a basically "decadent" society. The Progressives of the early part of this century genuinely expected to capture key offices and succeeded to some extent in doing so; the leaders of the Vegetarian party have accepted political realities and run presidential candidates for publicity. But despite these differences, minor parties have one thing in common: a feeling that certain values and interests that they consider important are not being properly represented by the two major parties.

Goals and Types of Minor Parties

Some of the minor parties have promoted ideologies that are entirely foreign to the nation's traditional beliefs—notably the parties that were introduced into the United States from Europe but failed to adapt to our essentially free-enterprise economic environment. Included in this general category are the Socialist party, which advocates public ownership of basic industries but is satisfied with moving toward its goal gradually through the workings of parliamentary democracy; the Socialist Labor party, which also seeks to eliminate the capitalist system through essentially peaceful, but not too clearly defined, means; and the American Communist party, with traditionally close ties to the Soviet Union, which has not generally ruled out violence as a method to bring about a classless society.

Of the three, the Socialist Labor party has been the most long-lived, running presidential and vice-presidential candidates in every election since 1896. On the other hand, the Socialist party has been by far the greatest vote-getter, polling close to a million votes in 1912, the first election in which it competed, and combining with the Progressive party in 1924 to give their joint candidate, Robert La Follette, almost five million votes. After 1932, however, it never again commanded a significant electoral following and ceased running presidential candidates regularly after 1956. Meanwhile, the forays of the Commu-

Campaign poster of the Greenback Party of 1876.

Teddy Roosevelt's 1912 Progressive campaign.

The ballot: 1920.

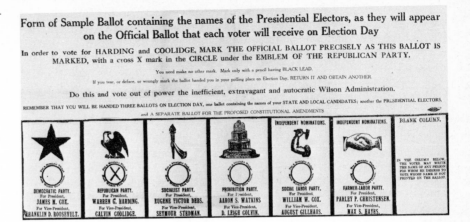

nist party into American electoral politics have been both sporadic and uniformly hopeless.*

The most successful minor parties in the United States have, like the Marxist ones, protested economic injustices. Rather than tracing their origins and ideologies to foreign sources, however, they have been indigenous and have proposed programs that remain within the American consensus of a free-enterprise system. Included in this category are two groups of the past century: the Greenback party, which ran candidates in the 1870s, and the Populists, who came into prominence in the 1890s. The former called for assistance to debtor farmers by way of issuing more cheap paper money; the latter proposed an expansion of the money supply in the form of free and unlimited coinage of silver, along with gold, at a ratio of sixteen to one, as well as a graduated income tax, the public ownership of railroads, and other measures designed to break the financial hold of the industrial East over the producers of raw materials in the West and South.

Twentieth-century minor parties have continued this tradition of sounding the call for reform while staying within basic institutions to achieve them. In 1912 former Republican President Theodore Roosevelt headed the Progressive party, which attacked abuses of both economic and political power in the United States. To correct the former, the party proposed governmental control over monopolies; for the latter, it urged adoption of such "direct democracy" devices as the initiative (allowing citizens to propose legislation), the referendum (referring laws to the voters for an ultimate decision), and the recall (permitting citizens to oust unsatisfactory officeholders between elections). Later on, as we have seen, another minor party adopted the label of the Progressives and joined the Socialists in backing Robert La Follette for President in 1924. This group's concern for the problems of the farmer paralleled that of the Populist party a quarter-century earlier, but in addition it spoke for the labor-

* The party ran presidential candidates from 1924 through 1940 and again since 1968. Its highest vote total was 100,000 in 1932 (compared to Franklin Roosevelt's 23,000,000); in 1976 its supporters numbered some 59,000.

ing man who wanted the right to organize. Thus the two Progressive parties of the first quarter of this century* expanded economic protest beyond the rural areas of the West and South to the urban areas of the Northeast.

The race issue has also recently spawned some new developments in party competition. In 1948 a group of dissident Southern Democrats walked out of their party's presidential nominating convention over the issue of civil rights, formed a States' Rights Democratic party (Dixiecrat party) and nominated J. Strom Thurmond of South Carolina and Fielding Wright of Mississippi as President and Vice-President. Rather than use that label on the ballot for the selection of presidential electors (this matter will be explained in detail in ch. 9), they chose instead to offer them as the "official" Democratic nominees in Alabama, Louisiana, Mississippi, and South Carolina, a tactic that paid off with victories in those four states. Twenty years later, a third party with similar views on the race issue headed by George Wallace ran candidates under the label of the American Independent party. Although its candidates, Wallace and vice-presidential nominee Curtis LeMay, appeared on the ballot in all fifty states, they prevailed in only five—Alabama, Arkansas, Georgia, Louisiana, and Mississippi.

Third parties have also operated in state and local elections. The Socialists have elected mayors in Milwaukee and Hartford. Even before the Farmer-Labor party of Minnesota merged with the Democratic party in the 1940s, it had won the governorship of that state on its own. In New York the American Labor party, and more recently the Liberal party, operating under provisions of that state's electoral laws that permit a candidate to be the nominee of more than one party, have contributed to the election of candidates in the Empire State. The former combined with the Republicans to elect Fiorello La Guardia as mayor in 1937, and thirty years later the latter joined electoral forces with the same major party to put John Lindsay in that post. In other instances, the Liberals have come to the assistance of the Democrats, as they did when Herbert Lehman narrowly defeated John Foster Dulles for the Senate in 1949, and in 1960 when John F. Kennedy won a close victory over Richard Nixon in New York. Yet another New York minor party—the Conservatives—elected their own candidate, James Buckley, to the United States Senate in 1970. (However, he ran under the Republican label in 1976 and was defeated by Democratic candidate Patrick Moynihan.)

For the most part, however, third parties in states and localities have met the same fate as those operating on the national scene; little success in winning public office and frequently a short political life. The absence of strong minor parties at the top level of the American political system has made it difficult for such groups to operate effectively at lower echelons as well. For the two national political parties have determined which parties can also compete in state and local political arenas.

Socialist party campaign poster of 1904.

Gregory for President: 1968

---

* Still another party using this name ran Henry Wallace for President in 1948. Its major emphasis, however, was on foreign affairs—in particular, a more conciliatory policy toward the Soviet Union.

Effects of Minor Parties

At first blush one might conclude that third parties have been of little significance in American politics. Judged by the major criterion for evaluating parties—namely, their electoral victories—the record of such parties could hardly be less impressive. None has won the major prize in the American political system, the presidency, and few have even managed to capture much in the way of other political offices (the most successful, the Populists, won a few seats in the House, three governorships, and hundreds of local posts). Generally speaking, they fail to win any electoral votes at all in the presidential election (the most earned was Roosevelt's eighty-eight in the 1912 election). Since the Civil War only four have gained more than 10 percent of the popular vote for President: the Populists in 1892, the Progressives in 1912, the Progressives in 1924, and the American Independent party in 1968.

The significance of minor parties, however, is greater if they are viewed from another perspective: the effect they have had on the two major parties in the United States. In some instances, such as the presidential election of 1912, their presence on the ballot has contributed to taking victory from one party and giving it to another. Even though this may not have been the only reason for Taft's defeat that year, it certainly was a major factor in bringing a Democratic candidate into the White House for the first time since the early 1890s. In other instances, minor parties have made a difference in individual states where the vote between the candidates of the two leading parties was close. Richard Nixon's popular-vote margin over Hubert Humphrey was less than the size of the vote for George Wallace in no fewer then seventeen states in 1968. In 1976, votes cast for third-party candidates (primarily Eugene McCarthy) were greater than the winning candidate's plurality in ten states. (Of the ten, Ford prevailed in eight and Carter in two.) Many observers also believe that if McCarthy had succeeded in getting on the ballot in New York State, he would have drained away enough votes from Carter to have given the state to Ford. Had that happened and the state's 41 electoral votes been cast for Ford instead of Carter, the incumbent President would have won the election.

Besides affecting the division of the vote at election time, minor parties frequently have an impact on the general policy orientation of the major parties. One of the two may clearly borrow the ideas of a third party—as in 1896 when the Democrats under William Jennings Bryan took over the position of the Populists on free and unlimited coinage of silver. In the process, the Democratic party was pushed to the left and its differences with the "sound-money," gold-standard policies of the Republican party became more apparent. A similar phenomenon occurred in the aftermath of the Progressives' show of strength in 1912 and 1924, for the Democratic party absorbed some of the basic ideas of Roosevelt and La Follette (such as the regulation of large corporations and the promotion of labor interests) for which the Republicans had little concern. It is precisely this kind of process that has led to the demise of many minor parties, as they find their programs and followers siphoned away by one of the two major parties. Many third-party supporters are not distressed by this result, however, since it means that the rationale for the party's formation no longer exists; the two major parties are now representing values and interests they formerly ignored.

Candidate Eugene McCarthy signs an autograph while campaigning in New Jersey.

Finally, third parties play a role in the composition of the two major parties. When the Wallace Progressives of 1948 fielded candidates who advocated a more conciliatory policy with the Soviet Union, they drained away from the Democratic party some of its supporters who agreed with that position. At the same time, they pushed back into the party fold some traditional Democrats, particularly Catholics, who had been alienated by the nation's close relationship with Russia during the Democratic administrations in World-War-II years. Thus differences among the various factions of the principal parties—in particular the majority party, which wins elections because it represents such a wide variety of interests—may result in the defection of a group that feels it is losing out in basic conflicts over key issues within the national party. This analysis would help explain the formation of the Progressive party from the ranks of the Republicans in 1912, and the Dixiecrats and the American Independent party from the Democrats in 1948 and 1968 respectively. Moreover, the process may eventually lead to the migration of such groups to the other major party, with the minor organization serving as a half-way house en route to the new party home. Recent cases in point are former Dixiecrats, including political leaders like Strom Thurmond, who have now affiliated themselves with the Republican party.

ASSESSMENT

Generally speaking, the historical record of American political parties has been a good one. Established in the very early years of the republic, they became the world's first permanent electoral organizations, models that other democratic countries have emulated. Another measure of their success is the persistence of our party system for almost two centuries.

The success of American political parties has been due in large part to the favorable environment in which they have been located. A general American consensus on basic social, economic, and political values and institutions has spared our parties the problem of trying to represent and reconcile deep cleavages on such matters, cleavages that have plagued party leaders in other societies. Our expanding economy has also made it possible for a wide variety of groups to satisfy their demands through the rival parties without having the rivalry become an all-out, do-or-die struggle.

American political parties, in turn, have contributed to the successful operation of our democratic institutions. Both have recruited and backed many able men for public office. In addition, the close competition that has existed between the two major parties over the years, together with their representation of different economic and social interests, has provided voters with significant choices of personnel and policies.

On the other hand, American political parties have also had some notable failures. Their inability to deal with the race issue resulted in a bloody civil war. That issue and the memory of that war have continued to confuse party divisions over the years and spawned one-party politics in many areas, thereby denying the voters a meaningful choice between rival candidates and policies. As we shall see in chapter 10, the race issue also confuses the American electoral scene at the national level today.

In recent years, a number of political scientists have criticized our existing parties. One group associates itself with a 1950 report of the Committee on Political Parties of the American Political Science Association, entitled "Towards a More Responsible Two-Party System." This report advocates that our parties present alternative policy programs in their platforms and then use discipline exercised by a strong national party organization over its members in Congress to get such programs enacted into law. Besides this ''responsible party government'' group, Austin Ranney also identifies another that favors ''representative party structures''—that is, parties that represent more accurately the views and interests of rank-and-file members of the party. It should be noted that these are the same ''programmatic'' and ''internal democracy'' goals that were previously described as being associated with political ''amateurs.''

Not all political scientists, however, agree with the advocates of responsible party government. In fact, defenders of the existing party system attack the reformers on three separate grounds. One is that their goals are undesirable: if the two parties did present highly different programs to Americans and the winning party then proceeded immediately to carry out these programs, the result would be a heightening of political conflict as losers would resist implementation of public policies that threatened their basic values and interests. Also, more intraparty democracy would mean that decisions on the selection of candidates and the adoption of policies would be made by rank-and-file party members who are not as knowledgable and skilled with respect to such matters as are more experienced party leaders. Secondly, even if the goals of the reformers are desirable, they cannot be attained: it is unrealistic to expect programmatic national parties to develop in the United States with its federal system of government and tradition of pragmatism and of protecting minorities' rights; also, rank-and-file members of parties will not take the time and effort to participate actively in party affairs. Thirdly, the charges the reformers level against the American party system are untrue: as a matter of fact, our parties do present alternative programs in their platforms, and the party members in Congress actually see to it that such programs are enacted into law; moreover, rank-and-file members of parties do play a major role in helping to select candidates and adopt policies.

It would be premature at this point to assess which of the above groups and their various arguments is correct, but the student should keep them in mind as we examine the part that American political parties play in various aspects of American politics. In chapters 8, 9, and 10, we focus on their role in the electoral process. In subsequent chapters we analyze the part that the party in the government plays in the making of public policy.

SELECTED READINGS

Particularly helpful for discussions of the nature of a political party and of how it differs from other groups linking the general populace to political leaders are chapter 1 of Leon Epstein, *Political Parties in Western Democracies* (New York: Praeger, 1967), and Austin Ranney's selection, "The Concept of 'Party,'" that appears in a book edited by Oliver Garceau entitled *Political Research and Political Theory* (Cambridge: Harvard University Press, 1968).

Classic studies of political machines include Harold Gosnell, *Machine Politics, Chicago Style* (Chicago: University of Chicago Press, 1937) and Dayton McKean, *Boss: The Hague Machine in Action* (Boston: Houghton-Mifflin, 1940). For an excellent journalistic account of the lives of six bosses—Hague, Curley, Crump, Long, Talmadge, and Pendergast—see Alfred Steinberg, *The Bosses* (New York: New American Library, 1972). Two recent highly readable accounts of Daley's political organization are Mike Royko, *The Boss* (New York: Dutton, 1971) and Len O'Connor *Clout* (Chicago: Henry Regnery, 1975).

James Q. Wilson draws the distinction between amateurs and professionals in *The Amateur Democrat* (Chicago: University of Chicago Press, 1962); Nelson Polsby and Aaron Wildavsky made the same distinction between professionals and "purists" in their *Presidental Elections* (New York: Charles Scribner's Sons, 4th ed., 1976). Two studies applying this distinction to national convention delegates are John Soule and James Clark, "Amateurs and Professionals: A Study of Delegates to the 1968 Democratic National Committee," *The American Political Science Review* (Sept. 1970): 888-898, and Thomas Roback, "Amateurs and Professionals: Delegates to the 1972 Republican Convention," *Journal of Politics* (May 1975): 435-467.

The roles that political parties play in various kinds of societies are analyzed in Sigmund Neumann, *Modern Political Parties* (Chicago: University of Chicago Press, 1956). Their role in underdeveloped countries is treated in Gabriel Almond and James Coleman, *The Politics of Developing Nations* (Princeton, N.J.: Princeton University Press, 1960), and in Almond's subsequent study with G. Bingham Powell, *Comparative Politics: A Developmental Approach* (Boston: Little, Brown, 1966). The best analyses of the part that they play in American politics are V. O. Key, Jr., *Politics, Parties and Pressure Groups* (New York: Thomas Y. Crowell, 5th ed., 1964), and Frank Sorauf, *Party Politics in America* (Boston: Little, Brown, 3rd ed., 1976). The latter book has a thoughtful discussion of what is meant by a "function" of a political party.

The best treatment of the original establishment of political parties in the .United States is William Chambers, *Political Parties in a New Nation: The American Experience* (New York: Oxford University Press, 1963). It is especially valuable in distinguishing parties from factions and in indicating how the transition from the latter to the former took place. Two good studies of American parties in the Jeffersonian era are Noble Cummingham, *The Jeffersonian Republicans in Power: Party Operations, 1801-1809* (Chapel Hill, N.C.: University of North Carolina Press, 1967), and James Young, *The Washington Community, 1808-1828* (New York: Columbia University Press, 1966). The latter extends beyond the Jeffersonian years and focuses broadly on politics in the nation's capital. A good series of selections dealing with various stages in the growth of American parties is contained in a book edited by William Chambers and Walter Burnham, *The American Party System: Stages of Political Development* (New York: Oxford University Press, 2nd ed., 1975).

Epstein's book cited above has an excellent discussion of various types of party competition, as does an article by Hugh McDowell Clokie, "The Modern Party State," *The Canadian Journal of Economics and Political Science* (May 1949): 139-57. Good discussions of two-party competition at the national level in the United States, including the reasons associated with that particular type of party competition, are included in the Key and Sorauf books cited above.

V. O. Key's classic work, *Southern Politics in State and Nation* (New York: Knopf, 1949), is an excellent study of the patterns of politics in the one-party South. He subsequently published another analysis of the politics of other parts of the nation in *American State Politics: An Introduction* (New York: Knopf, 1956). Two of Key's students have analyzed party competition in other regions of the United States: John Fenton in *Politics in the Border States* (New Orleans: The Hauser Press, 1957), and *Midwest Politics* (New York: Holt, Rinehart and Winston, 1966); and Duane Lockard in *New England State Politics* (Princeton, N.J.: Princeton University Press, 1959). Austin Ranney has a chapter on party politics in Herbert Jacob and Kenneth Vines, *Politics in the American States: A Comparative Approach* (Boston: Little, Brown, 3rd ed., 1976). William Havard and a group of other scholars analyze the South on a state-by-state basis in a book edited by him entitled *The Changing Politics of the South* (Baton Rouge: Louisiana State University Press, 1972).

Chapter 10 of Key, *Politics, Parties and Pressure Groups,* cited above, has an excellent analysis of minor parties in the United States.

E. E. Schattschneider's book *Party Government* (New York: Holt, Rinehart & Winston, 1942) makes the case for responsible party government, as does a Report of the Committee on Political Parties of the American Political Science Association chaired by Schattschneider, entitled "Towards a More Responsible Two-Party System," published as a Supplement to the September 1950 issue of *The American Political Science Review.* More recent books supporting this general position are James MacGregor Burns, *The Deadlock of Democracy* (Englewood Cliffs, N.J.: Prentice-Hall, 1963) and David Broder, *The Party's Over* (New York: Harper & Row, 1972). A classic defense of the American party system is Pendleton Herring, *The Politics of Democracy* (New York: W. W. Norton, 1965—reprint of the 1940 edition); a recent example of a book with the same point of view is Polsby and Wildavsky, cited above. Austin Ranney has two books analyzing the general subject of party reform, *The Doctrine of Responsible Party Government* (Urbana: University of Illinois Press, 1954) and *Curing the Mischiefs of Faction* (Berkeley: University of California Press, 1975).

Political Novels   In his prize-winning novel about party politics, *The Last Hurrah* (New York: Bantam, 1957), Edwin O'Connor shows how the old city machines worked and why they eventually died. In a later novel O'Connor describes the evolution of the "new" politics in his story about a politically ambitious, wealthy, Irish-Catholic family in New England, *All in the Family* (Boston: Little, Brown, 1964).

Party politics and its dangerous influence on representative government was exposed by Henry Adams in a novel about life in Washington in the late nineteenth century, *Democracy* (New York: Airmont Publications, 1968).

Stephen and Ethel Longstreet in *The Politician* (New York: Funk and Wagnalls, 1959) provide a sympathetic view of party politics and describe the rise of an aristrocratic politician to the presidency.

Chapter 8

As Democrats viewed their party's presidential candidates in January of 1976, two names headed the list of the Gallup poll: Minnesota Senator Hubert Humphrey, the party's unsuccessful presidential candidate in 1968, was favored by 29 percent, while 20 percent chose Alabama Governor George Wallace, the 1968 candidate of the American Independent party.* Next in line came the party's defeated presidential candidate in 1972, Senator George McGovern of South Dakota, with 10 percent of the voters' preference, followed closely by Washington Senator Henry Jackson, who had unsuccessfully sought the party's nomination in 1972. Trailing these four front-runners (as well as Senator Edmund Muskie of Maine, Indiana Senator Birch Bayh, and the party's 1972 vice-presidential candidate, Sargent Shriver) was former Georgia governor Jimmy Carter, who was preferred by a mere 4 percent of the Democrats polled. Also doing poorly in the poll was Morris Udall, a member of the House of Representatives from Arizona and the first candidate to publicly announce for the presidency, having done so in the fall of 1974.

Fast-moving events, however, soon resulted in an entirely different presidential picture. Humphrey announced that while he was willing to accept the nomination if the party turned to him, he would not actively seek it by entering presidential primaries or contests in states using caucuses and conventions to choose their delegates. Carter led all other candidates in delegate contests held in Iowa precinct caucuses in mid-January and also won the nation's first presidential primary in New Hampshire on February 24. When the former Georgia governor also scored primary victories in March in Vermont, Florida, Illinois, and North Carolina, he clearly established himself as the leading candidate for the Democratic nomination.

This first phase of the campaign not only advanced Carter's candidacy, but also resulted in the elimination of a number of contenders, including Bayh and Shriver as well as Governors Milton Shapp of Pennsylvania and Terry Sanford of North Carolina. Wallace's candidacy was also severely damaged by his

**THE
NOMINATION
PROCESS**

* Senator Edward Kennedy had announced in August 1975 that he would not be a presidential candidate in 1976. At the time of his announcement he was leading both Humphrey and Wallace in the Gallup poll by a wide margin.

Major Democratic contenders: Jimmy Carter, Henry Jackson, "Mo" Udall, Jerry Brown. And then there was one. . . .

southern losses to Carter in Florida and North Carolina, as was Udall's by his failure to win *any* primary, despite strong-second-place showings in New Hampshire and Massachusetts. Henry Jackson, the winner in the latter state, was the only candidate in this early period to score a primary victory against the front-running Carter.

While Carter thus dominated the initial phase of the presidential contest, most of his victories were in small, northern states and in the South, where he was expected to do well. His fourth-place finish in Massachusetts and again in New York on April 6 (Jackson won there as in Massachusetts) led Jackson to conclude that Carter could not prevail in industrial states in the North with large Catholic and Jewish populations. Udall also expected to do better after the withdrawal of Bayh and Shriver, with whom he was presumably sharing the liberal vote.

However, both hopes proved to be illusory: Carter edged Udall in Wisconsin, the state in which the Arizonan was expected to do best, and also defeated Jackson in late April in Pennsylvania despite overwhelming support of the senator by local party professionals and union leaders. Following that latter defeat, these two groups urged Humphrey to come into the presidential contest, but after an agonizing period of soul-searching, the Minnesota senator reluctantly decided not to enter his fourth presidential race. (Humphrey had been an unsuccessful candidate for the Democratic nomination in 1960 and 1972, and he had narrowly lost the presidency to Richard Nixon in 1968). Thus the second phase of the presidential race, like the first, ended in victory for Jimmy Carter.

The third stage of the 1976 Democratic contest, however, was of a different character. Two new candidates—Senator Frank Church of Idaho and Governor Edmund Brown, Jr. of California—entered the race and soon began to administer defeats to the front-runner. The Idaho senator won not only his own state's primary but also primaries in Nebraska, Oregon, and Montana. The governor surprisingly defeated Carter in Maryland and again later in Nevada and in his own state, California. However, Carter scored some important victories to offset his defeats: the same day he lost in Idaho, Nevada, and Oregon, he won in Arkansas, Kentucky, and Tennessee. Moreover, on the last day of the primary season, June 8, he took the sting out of his California loss to Governor Brown by winning a crucial primary contest in Ohio. Following that victory, opposition to his presidential candidacy collapsed, and party leaders and rival candidates rallied around the former Georgia governor as the Democratic standard-bearer in the 1976 presidential contest.

Unlike the previous two Democratic conventions, the 1976 gathering was harmonious. There were no significant disputes over the seating of delegates, the passage of rules for the convention, or the adoption of the party platform. The only suspense created at the four-day proceedings came over Carter's choice of a vice-presidential running-mate. After screening a broad range of candidates and narrowing the final list to Senators Muskie of Maine, Church of Idaho, Glenn of Ohio, Stevenson of Illinois, and Mondale of Minnesota, he chose Mondale, a protégé of Humphrey who was expected to serve as a bridge for Carter to the liberal northern wing of the Democratic party and thereby enhance his chances of election in November.

The Republican presidential contest in 1976 pitted the incumbent, Gerald Ford, against a single challenger—former governor of California and a long-

Senator Frank Church.

Picking the "Veep."

time favorite of many Republican conservatives, Ronald Reagan. Narrowly defeating Reagan in two crucial primaries—New Hampshire and Florida (in the former state, the percentage was 51-49; in the latter, 53-47)—the President also won early victories in Massachusetts, Vermont, and Illinois, thus sweeping all of the first five primaries. Leaders of the President's campaign organization declared Ford the winner of the presidential contest and called upon Reagan to withdraw his candidacy in the interests of party unity. However, the challenger refused, vowing to stay in the race until it was ultimately decided the following August in Kansas City at the Republican National Convention.

While many observers considered Reagan's statement merely campaign rhetoric, he did take his candidacy all the way to the convention floor. After scoring his first victory in the North Carolina primary on March 23, the challenger went on to battle the President on even terms in successive primaries, scoring victories particularly in southern and western states, including California, where the former governor won all 167 delegates to the national convention. All told, in the seventeen primaries in which voters expressed their preferences for a Republican nominee, Ford finished ahead in ten states and Reagan in seven; however, Reagan won 51 percent of the total popular vote in those states compared to 49 percent for the President. The nonprimary states were also the scene of spirited contests, with party leaders and Republican governors leading the battle for the President against the "amateur" Republicans who formed the nucleus of the governor's enthusiastic supporters.

Unlike the Democratic contest, which had ended for all practical purposes on June 8 when Carter won the Ohio primary, the Republican delegate-hunting contest continued during the summer months as both candidates wooed uncommitted delegates. Both sides claimed commitments from many of these, waging psychological warfare to convince wavering delegates that they should jump on the winning bandwagon. In the final stages of the contest, some uncommitted delegates received personal communications from both the President and the former California governor.

On July 26, Reagan made a dramatic move, announcing that if nominated, he would choose liberal Pennsylvania Senator Richard Schweiker as his vice-presidential running-mate. Designed to win additional support from uncommitted delegates in large states like Pennsylvania and New York, the choice of Schweiker also demonstrated that Reagan was not a doctrinaire conservative, but a candidate who sought to broaden the party's appeal in the November general election. However, the move alienated many conservatives, including the chairman of the uncommitted Mississippi delegation, who was thought to be leaning to Reagan until the Schweiker announcement, after which he came out publicly for the President.

The choice of Schweiker continued to be a key factor during the convention proceedings. The Reagan forces moved to amend the convention rules by requiring presidential candidates to announce their vice-presidential choice twelve hours prior to the balloting on the presidential candidates. This move was made to force Ford to name a running-mate in advance and thus risk the loss of supporters disappointed with his decision. However, the President's supporters (aided by the Mississippi delegation, which invoked the unit rule to cast all its 30 delegate votes against it) defeated the amendment by an 1180-1068 margin. The result, which ended Reagan's hopes for the nomination, paralleled the subsequent tally on the first ballot of the Republican nomination, which ended in a 1187–1070 victory for the President.

Having defeated the Reagan forces on the crucial decision of the presidential nomination, the President and his supporters then took action at the convention designed to placate the California governor and to reunite the party for the fall campaign. Included was a decision not to contest an amendment to the party platform praising the Soviet writer, Alexander Solzhenitsyn (whom the President had refused to greet for fear that the author's visit would antagonize Soviet leaders) and implicitly criticizing Ford and Secretary of State Henry Kissinger for making secret international agreements and discouraging the hope of freedom for victims of the Communist system. Another overture to the Reagan camp was the President's choice as his running-mate of conservative Senator Robert Dole of Kansas, who received the blessing of the California governor.

While candidates for other public offices do not experience the special rigors of a presidential contest, they must all pass through the crucible of the electoral process in which a free people test their political leaders. To top it off, the procedure involves two separate tests of political strength. First, as we shall see in this chapter, a candidate must win his party's nomination; then he must emerge victorious in the general election, a subject to be examined in chapter 9.

PURPOSE AND IMPORTANCE OF THE NOMINATION PROCESS

As we saw in chapter 7, one of the major functions of political parties is to present alternative groups of candidates for the electorate's consideration, thereby structuring the voter's choice and making his task more manageable. To do so, however, each party must itself have some method of deciding which person is to wear its label for each office. That method is the nomination process.*

Although the selection of a candidate by political parties is important in all democratic political systems, it is particularly so in the United States. For one thing, we elect to public office far more officials than any other nation in the world (a recent estimate set the number at about a half-million), not only because our population is large but also because Americans have been little disposed toward appointive political positions. The "Jacksonian Revolution" (associated with President Andrew Jackson), which swept the nation in the 1830s and 1840s and left lasting marks on politics, was based on faith in the common man and in his ability to choose his political leaders wisely. As a result we traditionally *elect* many officials, particularly at the state and local levels, who are *appointed* in other democracies.

Andrew Jackson.

* Even in nonpartisan elections, some method is generally used to narrow down the number of candidates. Typically, if no person receives the majority (one over half) of the votes in the initial election, a second election is held involving the two top runners. Recent examples occurred in Los Angeles mayoralty contests. In 1969 a Negro councilman, Thomas Bradley, who led all fourteen candidates on the first ballot, did not receive a majority vote and was beaten in the run-off by the incumbent mayor, Sam Yorty. Four years later, the same two candidates faced each other in the run-off election, but this time Bradley won. (In 1977 he received a majority vote on the first ballot.)

Another basic feature of our politics that contributes to the importance of the nominating procedure is the large number of one-party areas in the United States. As we previously noted, in such constituencies the significant competition involves opposing candidates and factions within the dominant party; the locus of the struggle is thus not the general election but the process by which the party chooses its candidates.

Finally, the nomination process is important even where genuine two-party competition exists, because our parties provide the voter with such a limited choice: he must pick between Republicans and Democrats—unless he is willing to back a third-party candidate, who, he knows, will rarely be successful in American politics. By way of contrast, in a multiparty system a range of candidates is available for consideration in the general election. Thus American citizens have a special incentive for taking an interest in the nomination process so as to avoid being presented with an undesirable choice in the general election.

As the following section shows, this problem has been a matter of concern over the course of the nation's political history as citizens have continued to seek improvements in the operation of the nomination process.

EVOLUTION OF THE NOMINATION PROCESS

Political parties appeared early in the history of the United States and so did the need to develop some means of choosing candidates to run under their labels. Races for local offices as well as for state legislatures and the House of Representatives presented no real difficulty, since they involved a limited number of voters. Therefore parties simply held caucuses—that is, meetings of their most active supporters to nominate candidates.

Selecting candidates for statewide offices presented more problems, however. Given the transportation of the day, it was difficult to assemble politicians from all over a state to choose a party's candidate for governor. Moreover, even if such a group could be convened, it would be too large and unwieldy to function efficiently. Of course, nominating the President and Vice-President, with their national constituency, presented the same problems in greater compass.

The Legislative Caucus

The parties soon moved to a more appropriate method of choosing nominees for state and nationwide offices: the legislative caucus. Under this method a party's members in state legislatures and the House of Representatives assembled to choose, respectively, candidates for statewide office and for President and Vice-President. By the end of the eighteenth century this procedure, popularly known as *King Caucus,* was in general use at both the state and the national level.

The legislative caucus made a lot of sense in the early stages of party development. State legislators and congressmen were already convened in one location, and since they were few in number, the nominating task was manageable. Moreover, legislators were likely to be highly knowledgeable about potential candidates from all parts of the political unit in question. Thus members of the party in the government were logical agents to choose candidates representing large constituencies.

There were, however, obvious defects in King Caucus. For one thing, it violated the separation-of-powers principle of the Constitution to have members of the legislative body play a key role in determining the occupants of major executive positions. The provisions of the Virginia and New Jersey plans to allow Congress to choose the President had been rejected by the Constitutional Convention. Yet now the legislative caucus threatened to bring the parliamentary system in the back door via the nomination process. This possibility eventually became near-actuality when the Republican legislative caucus in effect chose Madison and Monroe as Presidents of the United States during the era of one-party politics.

The legislative caucus also proved to be deficient in representing various party elements. For example, when a party lost an election in a legislative district, state or congressional, that area was not represented in the decisions of the party's legislative caucus. Although this defect was eventually remedied by permitting local party leaders from such areas to sit in the caucus, a more fundamental flaw remained: interested and knowledgeable citizens who participated in party activities at the grass-roots level (especially in campaigns) had no direct say in nominations. The legislative caucus thus became too limited and centralized a group to make key decisions for parties that were increasingly local in organization and increasingly dependent for political victories on active members who did not hold legislative posts.

The fate of the legislative caucus is exemplified by what happened to the Republican congressional caucus in 1824. No fewer than five candidates emerged that year with support from various elements of the party. Only one-fourth of the Republican legislators attended the caucus, and in the general election that followed, no candidate received a majority of the electoral votes. As a result, the election was thrown into the House of Representatives; to make matters worse, that body chose not Andrew Jackson—the candidate with the greatest number of popular and electoral votes—but John Quincy Adams. Adams benefited from a political deal with Henry Clay, one of the five nominees, who threw his support in the House to Adams in return for being named Secretary of State. This unfortunate combination of events discredited King Caucus as a means of nominating a presidential candidate.

After 1824, presidential nominations swung briefly to the state level: the Tennessee legislature chose Jackson for the 1828 campaign, and other "favorite son" candidacies followed as John Quincy Adams and John Calhoun were put into nomination by Massachusetts and South Carolina. But if the legislative caucus had proved to be too centralized for the political necessities of the day, selection by individual states was too decentralized for selecting a nationwide official. What was needed was some process that would represent party elements in various parts of the country and at the same time facilitate the nomination of a common candidate by these diverse groups.

The Convention

The nomination method that emerged to meet these needs was a national party convention composed of delegates from various states. It was not a major party but a minor one, the anti-Masonic party, that pioneered the way in 1831. The National Republicans (who, like the anti-Masons, had no appreciable representation in Congress, and thus could not have used the legislative caucus effectively even if they had wanted to) called a similar convention the following year. So did the Democratic Republicans under President Jackson, who saw a convention as an ideal means for getting his handpicked candidate, Martin Van Buren, chosen by the delegates as Vice-President.

Although the anti-Masons disappeared from the political scene almost immediately, they left the national convention as a legacy that the major parties have used continuously since 1840 to nominate their presidential candidates. Moreover, as we will examine in more detail below, their model contained two basic features that have persisted to this day: the selection of delegates by each state through whatever means it deems appropriate, and the allotment of delegates to states on the basis of the size of their congressional delegations (senators and members of the House of Representatives).

For a number of years the convention became the dominant means of nominating candidates at both the state and the national level. Delegates to state conventions were chosen either directly by party members in their localities (towns, cities, or counties) or, more often, by county conventions whose delegates themselves had been selected by party members in smaller local units. The state convention in turn selected candidates for statewide office and also chose the state's delegates to the national presidential convention. The system thus allowed rank-and-file members of the party to participate in the choosing of delegates but left the nomination process itself in the hands of the delegates. Viewed in the way we analyzed political parties in the last chapter, actual candidate selection lay with the party organization—that is, those who were most active in party affairs.

In time, however, disillusionment with the convention set in. Critics charged that instead of representing various elements of the party, the convention was the instrument by which a small clique controlled the nomination process for private purposes. These critics pointed out that the convention system lent itself to manipulation at various stages of the process: ad hoc meetings to choose delegates were frequently called without proper notice to all interested parties, and such meetings could be packed by ineligible participants; contests between rival delegations from a particular area were common, and the convention that ultimately ruled on the disputes frequently did so unfairly or without full knowledge of the facts; finally, the convention proceedings themselves placed in the hands of the presiding officers great powers over such key matters as the recognition of speakers, ruling on motions, and the taking of votes. Rather than eliminate the injustices of convention rules, however, foes of the convention chose instead to develop an entirely new means for nominating officials that would give the general public a greater role in the process. The method they chose was the *direct primary*.

The Direct Primary

The direct primary permits voters themselves to decide who will be nominated for public office. In contrast to the convention system, whereby the voters indirectly decide who will be nominated by choosing delegates who actually make the nomination decision, in the primary the voters select the nominees themselves.

The direct primary in the United States is chiefly the product of this century. Although it was actually used before the Civil War in some localities and was

"I'm thinking of entering the Democratic primaries."

adopted voluntarily by the Democratic party in several Southern states in the post-Reconstruction period when it became apparent that the nomination process there was in effect the election, the movement to make the primary mandatory developed in the early 1900s. It became a part of the general Progressive movement that called for taking government out of the control of the political bosses of the day and placing it where it belonged—in the hands of the people.* Under the leadership of Robert LaFollette, Wisconsin in 1903 passed the first law for a statewide, direct primary. Other states soon followed suit, and by 1917 all except a few used it for most party selections. Today the direct primary is utilized by all fifty states for some, if not all, nominations.

* In addition to the popular primary, other "direct democracy" devices proposed by the Progressives included the initiative, referendum, and recall procedures referred to in the last chapter.

Nominations in the United States have thus become progressively democratized as the selection of candidates has passed legally from the party in the government to the party organization and, ultimately, to the party in the electorate. Even so, as the rest of this chapter will indicate, the process differs from one office to another. Presidential candidates, for instance, continue to be nominated by national conventions rather than by a popular primary. In addition, primary laws themselves vary, so that candidates chosen by this general method do not all face the same rules of the game. And finally, aside from the legalities of the nomination process, political forces shape the particulars of various electoral contests.

NOMINATING THE PRESIDENT

No other political candidate faces the range of obstacles that confront a man with presidential ambitions. The rules that govern the nomination process for him are infinitely more complex than those for congressional aspirants or state and local politicians. But even more important, presidential-nomination campaigns place demands of time, energy, resources, and planning on candidates and their staffs that dwarf the efforts required of any other office-seeker.

The Allocation of National Convention Delegates

A presidential candidate starts out with a well-defined goal in mind: he must win a majority of the votes at his party's national convention in order to be nominated for the presidency. In 1976, 1130 votes out of 2259 were required at the Republican Convention; for the Democrats, the figures were 1505 out of 3008.

Although the numbers of their convention votes differ, both parties use the same general principles in deciding how many votes each state is entitled to. They generally take into account the size of a state's congressional delegation and its population as well as its record in supporting the party's candidates in recent years. The Republicans are concerned with voting not only for the presidential nominee but also for governors, senators, and candidates for the House of Representatives; however, they generally do not take into account the *size* of the popular vote for these officials. In contrast, the Democrats primarily focus on voting in recent presidential elections, but are concerned with the total number of popular votes cast for their candidates. The end result of the two formulas is that smaller states tend to be benefited somewhat in Republican conventions, while large states do comparatively better in Democratic ones.

The Selection of Delegates

State delegates to the national conventions of both parties are chosen by three major methods. One is selection by *party leaders,* such as members of the state central committee, the party chairman, or the governor (if the party controls that office). The second is choice by a state convention composed of persons themselves elected at caucuses and conventions held at lower geographical levels, such as precincts, wards, counties, and congressional districts. The third is direct election by the voters themselves in presidential primaries. In some instances, states combine one or more of the methods; for example, in 1976

'THAT MUST BE PRESIDENT FORD AGAIN .... MERLE'S AN UNCOMMITTED DELEGATE, Y'KNOW...'

Chicago Tribune—New York News
Syndicate

both parties in Pennsylvania used a primary to elect district delegates but allowed their respective state committees to choose the at-large delegates.

Traditionally, the selection of delegates has been dominated by professionals in both parties. This was only natural under the first method, which uses party officials to formally appoint the delegates; but domination also prevailed under the second system because professionals manipulated the caucuses and conventions to get themselves and their loyal supporters chosen as delegates. Moreover, the same kind of persons ran successfully as delegates in presidential primaries, and since many states did not legally require them to vote at the national convention for the candidate favored by those participating in the primary, they were free to vote their own preferences rather than those of rank-and-file voters.

In recent years, however, there has been a definite trend away from allowing party professionals to control the selection process. The trend has rather been towards increased participation by the party in the electorate. In 1968 only sixteen states chose delegates by a presidential primary; four years later that figure rose to 23; by 1976 it was thirty. Meanwhile, the proportion of total national convention delegates chosen in such primaries climbed from 42 to 63 to 75 percent. In the process, the primary replaced the convention system as the dominant method for choosing delegates to the national convention.

Many of the new primary laws passed between 1968 and 1976 also contain provisions designed to increase the influence of rank-and-file voters over their party's ultimate choice for President. States encourage delegates chosen in such primaries to indicate which candidate they personally support for President so that voters will know how such delegates may be expected to vote at the national convention. Some states also permit voters themselves to indicate their own personal preferences for President and legally bind delegates to support the preferred candidates for one or more ballots at the convention. Moreover, under many of the new state laws, a person's name is placed on the ballot if his

candidacy is generally advocated or recognized by the national news media, and if he wants to remove himself from the race, he must file an affidavit swearing that he is not a candidate in any state that presidential year. Such a system prevents candidates from picking and choosing on their own which particular state primaries they personally want to enter, thus allowing voters to pass judgment on a broader range of potential nominees than would otherwise be available to them.

Along with the passage of new primary laws by state legislatures have come actions by the national political parties themselves designed to reform the selection of delegates to the national conventions.

Democrats. Following the chaotic Democratic convention in 1968, that party's National Committee established a Commission on Party Structure and Delegate Selection under the Chairmanship of Senator George McGovern to assist state parties in granting "all Democratic voters a full, meaningful, and timely opportunity to participate" in the selection of delegates. The commission developed a list of specific guidelines designed to accomplish that purpose, and it subsequently worked with state parties to see that such guidelines were implemented in time to affect the selection of delegates to the 1972 Democratic convention.

The McGovern Commission's guidelines brought about major changes in delegate selection that presidential year. The traditional influence of party leaders was reduced by regulations forbidding them to serve automatically as ex-officio delegates to the national convention. Their control over caucuses and conventions was also diminished by requirements of written party rules, adequate public notice of all party meetings, and the elimination of proxy voting. At the same time, wider participation of rank-and-file voters was stimulated by guidelines urging states to remove restrictive voter-registration laws in order to make it easier for non-Democrats and unaffiliated voters to become party members and to assure widespread involvement of such members in making up candidate slates.

Two McGovern Commission guidelines in particular had a major effect on the 1972 convention and also stirred up bitter battles within the Democratic party. The first required that minority groups, women, and young people (those between 18 and 30) be represented in state delegations "in reasonable relationship to the groups' presence in the population of the state." While the Commission itself noted that this goal was "not to be accomplished by the mandatory imposition of quotas," many state parties actually adopted a quota system. A major convention fight over the issue resulted in a decision not to seat the Illinois delegation headed by Mayor Daley on the ground (among others) that it did not contain an adequate representation of youth, women, and minorities.

The other commission recommendation that ultimately became a major bone of contention at the 1972 convention related to "the fair representation of minority views on presidential candidates." Aimed at the injustices of the California type of "winner-take-all" primary that awarded all delegates to the candidate receiving a mere plurality of the popular vote, the guideline was merely "urged" on state parties by the commission rather than "required" of them (as some of the other guidelines stipulated). Californians refused to repeal their primary law, so that the "winner-take-all" provision was still in effect in June 1972 when Senator McGovern edged out Senator Hubert Humphrey by a 45–39 percent popular-vote margin. Evoking the "spirit" of the guidelines, the convention's Credentials Committee voted to divide the California delegation vote proportionately to the percentage of the primary vote received by each candidate. However, the entire convention decided to follow the "letter of the law" (the actual provisions of the California statute at the time of the primary) and awarded all 271 delegates to Senator McGovern. The votes of these delegates ultimately proved to be decisive in his first-ballot victory at the convention.

While the McGovern forces thus prevailed in the presidential nomination contest, the battle over the commission guidelines led to deep resentment among many elements of the Democratic party. Minority groups such as Italian- and Polish-Americans who had traditionally supported the party questioned why *they* were not included in the special quotas established by the guidelines. Also embittered were experienced national officeholders (senators and congressmen) and professional party leaders, like Mayors Daley of Chicago and Yorty of Los Angles, who found their places taken at the convention by women, blacks, young people, and other political "amateurs" who rallied to the McGovern cause. (Some 80 to 90 percent of the 1972 delegates were attending their first national convention.) The disaffection of the professionals in the 1972 general election contributed to the overwhelming defeat Senator McGovern suffered at the hands of Richard Nixon.

Determined to reunite the party, the Democratic National Committee appointed a new Delegate Selection Commission in 1973 to work out more satisfactory rules of the game for the 1976 presidential contest. Working under the chairmanship of Baltimore Councilwoman Barbara Mikulski and assisted greatly by the efforts of National Chairman Robert Strauss, the Commission

Chairperson Barbara Mikulski.

managed to work out rules that satisfied both the "amateurs" and the "professionals" among the party's activists.

Particularly important was the specific elimination of a quota system and the substitution of "affirmative action plans" whereby each state party specially undertook to encourage "minorities, Native Americans, women, and other traditionally underrepresented groups to participate and be represented in the delegate selection process and all Party affairs." The new rules also encouraged the selection of "public officials, party officials, and members of traditionally underrepresented Democratic constituencies" as at-large delegates and required states to employ proportional representation in allocating delegate votes.* These new rules clearly accomplished the desired effect—unlike the situation in 1972, in 1976 there were no significant battles over the credentials of state delegations, and party unity prevailed at the Democratic National Convention that year.

Republicans. While not under the pressure for reform that Democratic leaders have faced, the Republican party has also made some changes in delegate selection in recent years. A Delegate and Organization Committee (known as the DO Committee) chaired by Missouri National Committeewoman Rosemary Ginn recommended some proposals that were implemented in the choosing of delegates to the 1976 convention. Included were provisions similar to those of the McGovern Commission reducing the traditional influence of party leaders by eliminating them as *ex-officio* delegates, regularizing the nomination process by informing citizens how to participate in it, and maximizing participation by opening primary and convention systems to all qualified citizens.

At the same time, the Republican party has not attempted to regulate selection of national convention delegates nearly as extensively as has the Democratic party. The 1972 Republican National Convention turned down recommendations of the DO Committee to include in future conventions persons under twenty-five years of age in "numerical equity to their voting strength in a state" and to have one man, one woman, one person under twenty-five, and one member of a minority group on each of the convention's major committees. In 1975 the Republican National Committee refused to adopt the recommendation of a new committee chaired by Representative Steiger of Wisconsin that all states be required to have their "affirmative action plans" approved by the National Committee. Nor have the Republicans moved to abolish California-type winner-take-all primaries. Thus the national Republican party has been much less willing than its Democratic counterpart to intervene in state decisions involving the selection of delegates to the national convention.

The Nomination Campaign: The Pool of Candidates

Although many persons entertain presidential ambitions (the bug is considered to be almost incurable once it strikes), comparatively few are seriously considered as potential nominees by the two major parties. Those that are considered possess what is generally called political availability—that is, they have the

---

* The "winner-take all" principle, however, was permitted under state laws in contests at the congressional-district level that came to be known as "loop-hole" primaries. However, the 1976 Democratic convention eliminated the use of such primaries in the future.

characteristics and experiences that supposedly make them attractive candidates both to party activists and to the general voting public. There is, however, no definite check-list of job qualifications for the presidency. About the closest that one can come to determining what particular characteristics and experiences put a person in line for a presidential nomination is to look at past candidates. But even this approach poses some difficulties, since the attitudes of political leaders and the American public change over time.

The dominant background characteristics of presidential nominees in both major parties has been service in an elective political office.* The major position for presidential nominees in the past century has been a *state governorship.* Beginning in the 1960s, however, new political posts emerged as training grounds for presidential hopefuls. One is the *United States Senate.* All four of the Democratic nominees during the period from 1960 through 1972—Kennedy, Johnson, Humphrey, and McGovern—served in that chamber as did the two Republican standard-bearers, Nixon (nominated in 1960, 1968, and 1972) and Goldwater (1964). Moreover, all the serious contenders for the Democratic nomination during that time (Stuart Symington in 1960, Eugene McCarthy and Robert Kennedy in 1968, and Edmund Muskie and Hubert Humphrey in 1972) were former senators. Governors were more prominent as candidates in the Republican party, but they were limited both in number and in the seriousness of their candidacies. Nelson Rockefeller of New York made noises as a contender in the first three presidential years, but without much success, and frequently with little concerted effort. William Scranton of Pennsylvania and Ronald Reagan of California made belated attempts to stop Goldwater and Nixon in 1964 and 1968 respectively, while Governor George Romney of Michigan withdrew from the race in the latter year before the first presidential primary was held in New Hampshire.

The other office that has become a major launching pad for presidential candidates in recent years is the *vice-presidency.* Three of the eight candidates in the last five presidential elections (Nixon was nominated three times by the Republicans during that period) formerly served in that capacity. In fact, a close linkage has developed between a Senate seat and the vice-presidency as successive stepping-stones on the way to a presidential nomination: Truman, Johnson, Humphrey, and Nixon were all nominated as vice-presidential candidates while they were serving in the upper chamber, and three went on to the presidency from that position.

There are several possible reasons why senators have suddenly become prime presidential prospects. One is that they receive a great amount of coverage in the mass media, particularly network television, which focuses more closely on national news and events in Washington than on happenings in the states. Beyond this, the nation's increasing involvement in foreign affairs naturally places the Senate in the public's eye because of the influential role the upper chamber plays in the conduct of relationships with other countries. Also, the

---

* There are, of course, exceptions to the rule, particularly in the Republican party. For example, Wendell Wilkie and Dwight Eisenhower were private citizens prior to winning nomination in 1940 and 1952; Charles Evans Hughes and Herbert Hoover served in appointive positions (justice of the Supreme Court and Secretary of Commerce) prior to their being chosen in 1916 and 1928 respectively.

six-year term of senators means that they can frequently try for the presidency without giving up their legislative seat: of the senators running for the presidency in this century, only Barry Goldwater lost his place in the upper chamber as a result of his candidacy.

Recent vice-presidential experiences also help explain why that post has become more important for higher office.* As national figures, Vice-Presidents have benefited in recent years because Presidents began to give them duties that not only were meaningful but also resulted in increased exposure to both party leaders and the general public. Eisenhower, for instance, virtually turned over the job of political campaigning and forging ties with Republican party professionals around the nation to Nixon, who in turn assigned similar duties to Spiro Agnew. Johnson also permitted Humphrey to continue to cultivate the friendships he had so long enjoyed with Democratic chieftains. All three men also traveled widely abroad as representatives of the country and received the publicity that naturally attends such globe-trotting on the nation's behalf.

There are a number of reasons why a governorship is no longer so important a training ground for presidential candidates as it once was. Only chief executives of states with cities of the size and complexity of New York, Los Angeles, and Chicago, which serve as communication centers for the nation, get anything like the publicity that surrounds activities of the national officials in Washington, D.C. Beyond this, governors have no responsibilities of consequence in foreign affairs and frequently do not appear as well versed in such matters as they should be. They are also more tied physically to their home states (particularly when the state legislature is in session) than are senators and Vice-Presidents, who are expected to move freely about the country. Finally, many governors serve short stints in office (in some cases, due to legal limitations on their tenure; in others, because they fail to meet public expectations that major domestic problems be solved without an increase in taxes), and therefore find it difficult to become well-enough known to be visible presidential candidates.

In 1976, however, persons with gubernatorial experience once again emerged as presidential candidates in both political parties. As indicated at the beginning of the chapter, Ronald Reagan was a major threat to President Ford's renomination, while Jimmy Carter emerged victorious from a large group of candidates vying for the Democratic nomination. Also included were Governor Milton Shapp of Pennsylvania and two former governors: George Wallace of Alabama and Terry Sanford of North Carolina.

At this point it is still too early to determine whether the 1976 situation was unique or whether long-term forces are at work. There is little doubt that the perceived anti-Washington mood of the electorate that year encouraged persons to run for the presidency who had not served in national political office; whether future presidential candidates can continue to run on an "anti-establishment" theme remains to be seen. However, continuing citizen concern with increasing costs of government and the problems involved in controlling the federal bureaucracy (a subject that we will examine in depth in ch. 14), should

* Prior to Nixon's nomination in 1960, the last incumbent Vice-President who was nominated for the presidency was Martin Van Buren, who was chosen in 1836 while he was the second man to President Andrew Jackson.

"Candidates are the friendliest people."

continue to make governors attractive presidential candidates: they can claim valuable executive experience in managing large-scale public enterprises and thousands of state-government employees as contrasted to a senator's essentially legislative duties and small personal staff. Finally, it is possible that the American public's declining interest in foreign affairs will counteract the advantages senators held over governors as presidential candidates in the years prior to our withdrawal from Vietnam.

Whatever the public-office backgrounds of today's presidential aspirants may be, they do not have to be concerned with a number of matters that traditionally plagued potential candidates. They no longer need to be from populous Northern states, as indicated by the recent candidacies of Goldwater (Arizona), Johnson (Texas), McGovern (South Dakota) and Carter (Georgia). Nor is a Catholic or a Jewish background any longer a bar to a presidential bid: John Kennedy's candidacy in 1960 violated the traditional preference for Protestants, and once he had succeeded, people seemed not to notice that two of the major Democratic contenders in 1968—Robert Kennedy and Eugene McCarthy—were of the Catholic faith. Nor did Republicans seem concerned in 1964 that Senator Goldwater, although an Episcopalian, came from a Jewish background on one side of his family.* The related traditional preference for English stock did little to deter the nomination of the Irish John Kennedy or Goldwater with his Russian genealogy.

Taking the place of geographical, religious, and ethnic considerations that used to affect presidential candidates is an increasing concern in recent years with their political philosophy and public-policy preferences. Barry Goldwater clearly represented the conservative viewpoint on public affairs whereas George McGovern spoke for persons on the opposite side of the political spectrum. Moreover, more centrist candidates have been associated with national political issues: Johnson with social welfare legislation and Nixon with a tough stand on law and order in American society. Jimmy Carter, the Democratic standard-bearer in 1976 was less clearly identified with specific substantive issues than other recent candidates; however, even he was associated with a more general type of issue: honest and competent government and with executive reorganization as a means of accomplishing that goal.

Another piece of evidence on the growing importance of national forces in presidential politics is the changing attitude of party leaders toward defeated candidates. American history has generally relegated the losers to political oblivion (exceptions were two Democrats: Grover Cleveland, who won in 1884, ran again but lost in 1888, and was renominated and reelected in 1892; and William Jennings Bryan, who was nominated in 1896, 1900, and 1908); yet in the twenty years after World War II, three defeated candidates were selected a second time by their parties: Dewey by the Republicans in 1948, Stevenson by the Democrats in 1956, and Nixon by the GOP in 1968. Recent political experience thus indicates that if a defeated candidate does not lose by too wide a margin (as did Goldwater and McGovern), he may well have another chance to head his party's ticket.

---

* An amusing story made the rounds in 1964 to the effect that when the senator was refused admittance to a golf course because of his religious background, he demanded the right to play nine holes on the rationale that he was only half Jewish.

If even a defeated candidate has a fair chance at renomination, a winner has a virtual monopoly of his party's nomination the second time around. In this century no incumbent President who sought another term of office has been denied renomination. Even Herbert Hoover, hardly the nation's most popular political figure during the depression years, was chosen to lead his party again in 1932 against the Democrats. Moreover, Vice-Presidents who have succeeded to the presidency on the death or resignation of their predecessors have all been renominated by their party in this century—Theodore Roosevelt, Calvin Coolidge, and Gerald Ford by the Republicans, Harry Truman and Lyndon Johnson by the Democrats. It is interesting to note, however, that none of the former Vice-Presidents who were eligible sought a *second successive full term.* Roosevelt retired in 1908 (he attempted a political comeback against President Taft in 1912 but failed); Coolidge "chose not to run" in 1928 (some students of the era claim, however, that he actually wanted to be renominated and was bitterly disappointed when his party took him at his word); while Truman and Johnson withdrew in 1952 and 1968 (their exact reasons are unknown, but both had been challenged and embarrassed politically in the New Hampshire primary by, respectively, Estes Kefauver and Eugene McCarthy).

Preconvention Strategies: Early Maneuverings

While the formal nomination process does not officially begin until the start of the election year, political maneuvering takes place long before that time. John Kennedy decided almost immediately after he lost the try for the vice-presidential nomination in 1956 to run for the presidency in 1960; George McGovern made a similar decision as soon as the 1968 presidential contest was concluded.

Carter's dynamic duo: Jody Powell and Hamilton Jordan.

The candidate and *New York Times'* columnists Tom Wicker and James Reston.

A few days after the 1972 presidential election, Jimmy Carter's staff provided him with a seventy-page memorandum laying out the plan he should follow for winning the 1976 Democratic nomination.

In the interim period prior to the new presidential year, an aspirant takes actions designed to further his candidacy. Especially important are the *media* that are in a position to provide the candidate with name recognition and favorable publicity needed to make him a viable contender. Carter's staff recommended in the above memorandum that he compile a list of important political columnists and editors (such as *New York Times* columnist Tom Wicker and *Washington Post* editor Katherine Graham) and cultivate them by making favorable comments on their articles and columns and, if possible, by scheduling personal visits with them. Some candidates may also appear in the printed media themselves, writing magazine articles or even books, such as Kennedy's *Profiles in Courage,* Nixon's *Six Crises,* and Carter's *Why Not the Best?* They also use television and radio, showing up with some regularity as guests on "Meet the Press," "Face the Nation," and "Issues and Answers." They may even employ a syndicated radio program or news column of their own as Ronald Reagan did to advance his political views and, indirectly, his candidacy.

Persons with presidential ambitions typically take other steps to further their prospects. Edmund Muskie, who was nominated for Vice-President by the Democrats in 1968, began accepting speaking engagements outside his home state of Maine soon after his and Hubert Humphrey's defeat that year. Jimmy Carter assumed the position of Coordinator of the 1974 Democratic Congressional Campaign, a job that took him to 30 states in which he had the opportunity to get acquainted with Democratic leaders. A trip abroad may also serve to keep the candidate in the news and, if he has not had much experience in foreign affairs, help to counteract the charge that he is not knowledgeable in this vital area that consumes so much time of the American President.

Not all candidates, however, face identical problems in cultivating party leaders and the American voter. Prominent senators and incumbent Vice-Presidents, whose duties place them in the public eye, do not have to work as hard at making themselves politically visible as do state governors, comparative newcomers to national public life, and those persons not presently holding a public office. Since the defeated presidential candidate (called the *titular leader*) is most likely to be in the latter category, it is especially important that he keep his political fences mended by maintaining contact with both national and local party leaders. A titular leader who hopes to be renominated also generally speaks out on public issues as a means of conveying the impression that he remains the leader of the party out of power.

Besides gaining broad exposure in the early period, the presidential aspirant must also begin acquiring two vital resources for the nomination campaign ahead: *workers* and *money.* In recent years, the former have been generally recruited especially for the candidates' own personal organization. Professional politicians and regular party workers have not only been generally reluctant to commit themselves in advance of the nomination contest for fear they might be backing a loser (one general exception is when a President is seeking renomination), but, even when committed, have seldom possessed the enthusiasm that characterized "amateurs" like those who worked so effectively for such candidates as Carter, Goldwater, McGovern, and Reagan.*

Traditionally, presidential candidates gathered their *campaign funds* from a relatively few large donors (often referred to as "fat cats") simply because it is much easier to collect a sizeable amount of money that way rather than to seek small donations from a large number of people. However, abuses of the Nixon presidential campaign in 1972 led to the passage of new legislation that has radically changed the "rules of the game" for campaign financing.† Not only are contributions in excess of $5000 forbidden, but the law also provides matching federal funds to a candidate who is successful in raising a total of $5000 in each of 20 states in amounts of $250 or less. The new law thus puts a premium on early efforts to raise funds from a wide variety of persons so that the federal funds will be available for the race ahead.‡

This early period, which political scientist Donald Matthews refers to as "the emergence of presidential possibilities," often helps to determine the eventual outcome of the nomination contest. As Table 8.1 indicates, in the period since 1936, the person leading in the Gallup poll at the beginning of the presidential year has almost always been ultimately chosen as the nominee in both parties. However, in the two most recent instances, the Democratic front-runner has been ultimately replaced as the party favorite by a dark horse—McGovern, who was preferred by only 3 percent of the Democrats in January of 1972, and Carter, the choice of only 4 percent in the same month of 1976. Thus front-runners cannot afford to rest on their early popularity: the final decision on the nominee eventually depends upon the presidential primaries as well as delegate-selection contests in non-primary states.

Campaigning in Presidential Primaries

For today's aspiring presidential candidate, the primaries are virtually a "must." Not only do three-fourths of the delegates to national conventions now come from the primary states, but the past records of both parties indicate that party leaders and the general public expect candidates to prove their vote-getting abilities in presidential primaries. Of the sixteen persons chosen by the two parties in the eight presidential elections held since the end of World War II (1948 through 1976), only two candidates—Adlai Stevenson in 1952 and Hubert Humphrey in 1968—secured the nomination without entering the

---

* Even though Reagan lost the nomination to President Ford, the narrowness of that loss to an incumbent was noteworthy; moreover, most observers of that contest felt that the Reagan staff and supporters were generally more effective than those in the Ford camp.

† Because of the relationships and comparisons that exist between the financing of the nomination and election of candidates, it is both confusing and redundant to try to discuss the two matters separately. The entire subject, including the financing of both presidential and congressional contests, is analyzed in detail in the following chapter, which treats the general election process.

‡ In 1976, thirteen Democratic candidates, along with President Ford and Ronald Reagan, received a total of $24 million in federal funds. Reagan received the most ($5.1 million), followed by Ford ($4.7 million), Carter ($3.5 million), and Wallace ($3.3 million).

Table 8.1
Continuity and
Change in
Presidential
Nominating Politics,
1936–1976

Year	Leading Candidate at Beginning of Election Year	Nominee
Party in Power		
1936 (D)	Roosevelt	Roosevelt
1940 (D)	Roosevelt	Roosevelt
1944 (D)	Roosevelt	Roosevelt
1948 (D)	Truman	Truman
1952 (D)	Truman	Stevenson
1956 (R)	Eisenhower	Eisenhower
1960 (R)	Nixon	Nixon
1964 (D)	Johnson	Johnson
1968 (D)	Johnson	Humphrey
1972 (R)	Nixon	Nixon
1976 (R)	Ford*	Ford
Party out of Power		
1936 (R)	Landon	Landon
1940 (R)	?	Willkie
1944 (R)	Dewey	Dewey
1948 (R)	Dewey-Taft	Dewey
1952 (R)	Eisenhower-Taft	Eisenhower
1956 (D)	Stevenson	Stevenson
1960 (D)	Kennedy	Kennedy
1964 (R)	?	Goldwater
1968 (R)	Nixon	Nixon
1972 (D)	Muskie	McGovern
1976 (D)	Humphrey*	Carter

Source: James Barber (ed.), *Choosing the President* (Englewood Cliffs, N.J.: Prentice-Hall, 1974), p. 54. The question mark shows that no single candidate led in the polls.

* The 1976 information is taken from the January Gallup poll.

primaries.* The typical pattern is for the nominee of the party out of power to emerge victorious from the primaries after a spirited battle; aspirants who opt to stay out of such contests, such as Humphrey in 1976 and Rockefeller in 1968, watch others walk off with the nomination. Candidates for the nomination of the party in power, including the incumbent President, are also expected to enter the primaries, but generally the latter has little difficulty in soundly defeating his challengers. Thus the Ford-Reagan primary battle in 1976 was highly unusual, most likely occasioned by the unique circumstances under which the former took office (he was the first Vice-President to become President without having been elected to the vice-presidency), and his lackluster performance on the campaign trail as compared to that of Reagan, the former movie star and television personality.

* Both were unusual circumstances: in all probability, Stevenson did not really want to be nominated in 1952 and have to run against the extremely popular Republican nominee, Dwight Eisenhower; Humphrey was prevented from entering many primaries in 1968 because President Johnson did not withdraw from the race until the last day of March.

For the serious presidential contender today, then, the crucial question is not *whether* he should go into the primaries; rather, it is *which particular ones* he should enter. However, even those options are not as great as they were at one time. As we know, the trend in recent state primary laws—to enter a person automatically in the race if his candidacy is generally advocated or recognized by the national media and making it difficult or impossible for him to withdraw—forces candidates to contest in such states. Moreover, candidates are increasingly expected to demonstrate their strength in various parts of the country. As a result, in 1976 Jimmy Carter's name appeared on the ballot of 26 of the 27 states with presidential preference primaries (the exception was West Virginia, whose favorite son, Senator Robert Byrd, won); following close behind were Wallace in 24 states, and Udall and Jackson in 22 each.

Of course, having a candidate's name appear on a state ballot does not mean that he will wage an all-out campaign there. Limitations of time, energy, and money force a presidential aspirant to establish priorities among the large number of primaries. On the one hand, he must avoid actively campaigning in so many states that his efforts are dissipated and ineffective. On the other, he must not concentrate on too few states and run the risk of not being victorious in them, or even if victorious, fail to demonstrate broad geographical support for his candidacy.

Candidates take a number of factors into account in deciding which primaries they should emphasize in their nomination campaign. One is the *time* the primary is held. The earliest contest, traditionally in New Hampshire, generally attracts most of the major contenders because it constitutes the first test of popular sentiment. Although the number of delegates involved is small, winning this initial contest focuses immediate attention on the winner as it did for Kennedy in 1960 and Carter in 1976. Moreover, even if a candidate loses in New Hampshire but draws a greater percentage of the vote than expected, the media may interpret the results as a "moral" victory for him, a determination that benefited Eugene McCarthy in 1968 and George McGovern in 1972.

On the other hand, other primaries provide a late indication of voter preferences. California has often served this purpose, since it traditionally holds its contest at or near the end of the primary season. Some candidates, such as Goldwater in 1964 and McGovern in 1972, owed their ultimate nomination to the fact that they scored victories in California and thus projected the image of a "winner" as delegates throughout   ntry looked ahead to the upcoming national convention.

The California primary possesses other general characteristics that are of interest to presidential contenders. It reflects attitudes of voters in the nation's largest state, a western one populated by persons living in urban centers as well as in small communities and rural areas. The state is also divided politically between the liberal north, represented by San Francisco and the Bay area, and the conservative south, epitomized by Los Angeles and Orange County. The fact that California has received so many migrants from other states also helps to make it a microcosm of the nation at large. Finally, the "rules of the game" for presidential nomination make the Golden State an attractive target: not only does it have more delegates at both party conventions than any other state, but for Republicans its "winner-take-all" provision provides a large bloc-vote for the winning candidate.

Thus the timing, location, representativeness, and delegate strength of the various presidential primaries are factors that candidates take into account in deciding where to concentrate their campaign efforts. They also naturally try to choose states that they think they have the maximum chance of winning. In 1976, Jimmy Carter campaigned heavily in Florida, not only because its primary was held early in the year, but also because it is next to his home-base of Georgia, which he could draw upon for campaign workers. That same year Henry Jackson chose Massachusetts and New York as special targets because both contained large numbers of Catholics, Jews, and labor-union members with whom the Washington senator felt he had close political ties; Morris Udall also zeroed in on Massachusetts and, in addition, Wisconsin because he expected to do well in the liberal academic communities concentrated in those states. The two Republican contenders in 1976, Gerald Ford and Ronald Reagan, worked hard in their home states of Michigan and California respectively to advance their candidacies.

In some instances, however, a presidential contender may deliberately choose to contest a primary that is *not* considered advantageous to his candidacy to demonstrate that he has a broader appeal than is generally recognized. John Kennedy went into the West Virginia primary in 1960 to prove that a Catholic could win in a state that was 95 per cent Protestant. Sixteen years later, Jimmy Carter campaigned in the Pennsylvania primary to demonstrate that a southern Baptist from a rural background could score a victory in a northern, urban state with a heavy Catholic population. Both risks proved to be good ones that dramatically advanced the two candidacies.

The candidate who makes judicious choices and campaigns effectively in primaries so that he wins most of them, or who scores significant victories in some key contests, goes a long way toward establishing his claim for the presidential nomination. The wise presidential aspirant, however, does not put all his efforts into the primaries; he works to garner as much support as he can from other sources as well.

Gathering Delegate Support in States without Primaries

As we have seen, party professionals traditionally dominated the selection of delegates in nonprimary states. Few rank-and-file citizens took the time and effort to attend the caucuses and conventions through which delegates were selected. Those who did, found themselves outnumbered and outmaneuvered by persons active in party affairs. As a result, party loyalists were chosen as delegates and took their cues on how to vote at the national convention from the delegation chairman or other influential leaders in the state party who helped to get them chosen. These leaders, in turn, were generally willing to bargain their delegation's votes at the national convention for benefits for themselves or their state; they were also willing to support a compromise candidate who had the best chance of winning in November.

In recent years, however, political amateurs have turned out in large numbers at such caucuses and conventions. They have sought to choose delegates committed to candidates on the basis of their stands on issues rather than upon the criteria favored by party professionals: acceptability to all elements of the party and ultimate electability. While the professionals have sometimes prevailed in such contests—as they did on behalf of Hubert Humphrey in 1968, for example—the amateurs have also scored some notable victories. Supporters of George McGovern in 1972 benefited from the 1972 Democratic guidelines opening up the selection process to broader participation by persons not traditionally active in that party. In 1976 conservative enthusiasts for Ronald Reagan won many contests in party caucuses and conventions, as did amateur supporters of Jimmy Carter.

While there are fewer delegates chosen today from nonprimary states than there were in the past, contests in such states can still be important in presidential nominations. If no clear-cut verdict on the preferred candidate emerges from the primaries (as in the 1976 Republican contest), the delegates chosen in party caucuses and conventions are in a position to help determine who the ultimate nominee will be. Moreover, how a contender does in such contests may affect his candidacy in primary states as well: Carter's initial victory over other candidates in the Iowa precinct caucuses was considered by many observers to have given him a psychological edge shortly thereafter in the New Hampshire primary.

Recent Trends in Preconvention Politics

The contest for the presidential nomination has undergone significant change in recent years. New groups have arisen to supplement, and in some cases to replace, the traditional influence that state party professionals exercised over the choice of the party nominee. One such group is the *amateurs,* who encourage issue-oriented candidates to become presidential candidates and wage concerted battles in both primary and nonprimary states in their behalf. Another is the *media,* which help determine in the early stages of the contest who are and who are not viable candidates; project and assess the image, presidential qualifications, and stands on issues of would-be contenders; predict in advance the outcome of the various primaries; and then interpret who the "real" winners and losers of such contests are. Also involved are the political *pollsters,* who provide periodic evidence of how the American people feel about the various candidates. Finally, there are the *rank-and-file voters* who participate in the increasing number of presidential primaries. (In 1976 some 43 percent of the eligible electorate in the thirty states with presidential primaries cast their ballots in the Democratic and Republican contests.)

The end result of these new developments has been the increasing *popularization* of the presidential nomination contest. Moreover, the various forces affect each other: a candidate who receives favorable treatment from the media tends to do well in the primaries which, in turn, raises his standings in the polls. Favorable polls also impress representatives of the media as well as political activists and many rank-and-file voters, resulting in more victories for the poll leader in nonprimary and primary contests. The presidential contender who benefits from this reinforcing process often gains the necessary support for the nomination before the convention meets. Still, he cannot be sure until then whether promises of votes to him will be kept. Moreover, as indicated in the following section, the convention serves other purposes for the man who has his eye on the White House.

The National Convention

The convention is important to the presidential candidate for two major reasons. First, whatever may have transpired beforehand, it is that body which

The pollsters: George Gallup and Louis Harris.

makes the actual nomination. Second, the convention provides opportunities for the candidate to strengthen his chances to win the general election the following November.

A number of decisions that precede the balloting on presidential nominations can have significant effects. In some instances, the location of the convention is important.* Illinois governor Adlai Stevenson's welcoming speech to the Democratic delegates assembled in Chicago in 1952 is credited with influencing their decision to nominate him that year. In 1968 the events growing out of the confrontation between protestors and Mayor Daley's police in that same city contributed to Hubert Humphrey's defeat in the general election.

Also important in some instances are contests between rival slates of delegates from states where there have been disputes in the selection process. There were no fewer than eighty-two separate challenges involving thirty states and over 40 percent of the delegates at the 1972 Democratic convention, most of which stemmed from alleged violations of the McGovern-Fraser guidelines. Ultimately all were settled by the Credentials Committee except the fight over the California delegation and another that led to a convention decision not to seat an Illinois delegation linked with Mayor Daley of Chicago on the grounds that it did not contain an adequate representation of youth, women, and minorities and was chosen through closed slate-making processes.

Fights over rules of the convention proceedings also sometimes take on great significance. As indicated at the beginning of this chapter, one such battle occurred at the 1976 Republican convention when the Reagan forces moved to amend the rules to require candidates to name their vice-presidential choice in advance of the balloting on presidential candidates. The defeat of that amendment helped pave the way for President Ford's victory on the first ballot of the convention that year.

Another major convention decision is the writing and adoption of the party platform. Although these documents have traditionally been ridiculed as meaningless promises the party does not intend to keep, or as vague phrases produced by the necessities of compromise, the fact of the matter is that many delegates have taken them seriously. In 1948 some Southern delegations walked out of the Democratic convention because they felt that the platform was too liberal on the issue of civil rights; twenty years later the delegates of the same party debated the Vietnam plank of the platform before a nationwide television audience in an amazing display of self-criticism by the party in power.

Republicans have also had their share of platform disputes. In 1960 Nelson Rockefeller threatened to lead a floor fight over the platform unless it committed the party to stronger programs for national defense and civil rights. To avoid that fight, Richard Nixon agreed to the Rockefeller demands and used his influence to get the changes included. As we have seen, the Ford forces pursued a similar course of action in 1976 by not contesting a platform amendment by Reagan supporters criticizing our policy of détente with the Soviet Union. However, at the 1964 convention the Goldwater forces adopted the opposite tactic: they refused to make any concessions to party liberals like

---

* This decision is made officially by the National Committee. For the out-party, the chairman of the National Committee has the greatest say in the matter; for the in-party, the President does.

Governors Rockefeller and Romney on such issues as civil rights and political extremism.

For potential presidential candidates, credentials contests, the adoption of rules of procedure, and the party platform all provide tests of strength as well as opportunities for forging the kinds of political alliances necessary to win the nomination. They have other effects as well. Ronald Reagan lost the Republican nomination in 1976 to President Ford but was successful in getting many of his conservative ideas incorporated in the GOP platform that year. The statement of party principles may also influence the general election campaign, since party leaders who oppose such matters may not be inclined to work too hard on the party's behalf. Republican Governors Rockefeller and Romney did little to help the Goldwater cause in 1964, and many Democrats opposed to the pro-administration plank on Vietnam in the party's 1968 platform did not bestir themselves in the general election campaign that year. Four years later many conservatives and centrists in the party, unhappy with some planks in the Democratic platform (amnesty for war-resisters and the endorsement of busing to achieve racial balance in the schools), refused to work for McGovern in the fall.

Although the candidate must concern himself with such matters during the early stages of the convention, he and his supporters must work at the same time towards the most crucial decision of the assemblage: the balloting that normally occurs on the third or fourth day of the proceedings. In the interim, plans are laid for that fateful roll-call vote. Presidential hopefuls appear before caucuses of state delegations to solicit support. Polls are taken of delegates so that candidates know how many votes they can count on and from whom they might pick up additional support. Individual delegates are also wooed. In 1960 Edward Kennedy retained contacts with the Wyoming delegates he had worked with the previous spring and was in their midst when the state's votes put his brother over the top on the first ballot. That same year Richard Nixon arranged to have his picture taken with each delegate at the Republican convention.

The kind of strategy a candidate employs in the balloting for the nomination depends on the amount of delegate support he has. If he is the front-runner, as President Ford claimed he was in 1976, he concentrates on holding the votes he has been promised and on picking up any additional ones he needs to win a majority on the initial ballot. To this end he and his workers use the band-wagon technique—that is, they argue that since he is going to win the nomination anyway, delegation chairmen or individual members who are smart politically will come out now for his candidacy and not wait until the matter has already been settled. The candidate, it is suggested, will take early support into account in the future when he is in a position to do political favors. Franklin Roosevelt did so quite specifically after he was elected in 1932 by determining whether a person seeking a political position was for him "before Chicago."

Candidates with weak delegate support attempt to counter the bandwagon technique with strategies of their own. They typically encourage delegates who do not support them to cast their ballots for favorite sons or other minor candidates. The important thing is to hold down the vote for the front-runner on the first roll-call. Candidates also attempt to forge alliances to stop the leader. They may agree, for example, that at some point in the balloting, the

The 1976 Democratic Convention.

The 1976 Republican
Convention.

one who falls behind in the voting will throw his support to the other. The difficulty with making such an arrangement, however, is that frequently minor candidates may have greater differences between themselves than either has with the leader. The only alliance that might conceivably have stopped Richard Nixon at the 1968 Republican convention would have been one between Nelson Rockefeller and Ronald Reagan. Yet given their divergent views on vital issues of the day, plus Rockefeller's failure to support Goldwater in 1964 (Reagan had made the best speech of that campaign in his behalf), the two governors were hardly a compatible political combination.

The front-runner, as well as minor candidates, holds forth various enticements in bargaining with possible political supporters. Some persons are interested in getting the party to take a particular stand in the platform. Others have more tangible concerns: a senator or governor may seek the candidate's support in his own campaign; another political leader may have his eye on a cabinet post. Although a presidential candidate himself may refuse to make such commitments so that he can go before his party and the electorate as a "free" man beholden to no one, his supporters do not hesitate to make promises on such matters. One delegate to the 1960 convention claimed to be the nineteenth person to whom the Kennedy forces had offered the vice-presidency!

A definite trend in recent conventions is an early victory for the candidate who arrives at the convention with the greatest number of pledged delegates. In the sixteen conventions that have been held in the two major parties in the post-World War II era, only two nominees—Thomas Dewey in 1948 and Adlai Stevenson in 1952—failed to win a majority of the convention votes on the very first ballot. Thus the convention has increasingly become a body that legitimizes the decision on the presidential nominee that has already been made by the time the delegates gather to officially choose a candidate.

The selection of the vice-presidential nominee is the final decision of the convention. Although in theory the delegates make the choice, as a matter of political custom they allow the presidential nominee to pick his own running-mate. On rare occasions the nominee may decide not to express a preference of his own and thus permit the convention to make an open choice, as Adlai Stevenson did in 1956. Typically, however, the presidential nominee confers with leaders whose judgment he trusts, and when he makes his decision on the matter, the word is passed to the delegates. Even though some may resist a particular vice-presidential candidate, the presidential nominee generally gets his way. Franklin Roosevelt threatened to refuse to accept the presidential nomination in 1940 unless Henry Wallace was chosen as his Vice-President. In 1960 John Kennedy insisted on Lyndon Johnson as his running-mate against the objections of some liberal elements of the party, including his own brother Robert. Thus, in effect, the Vice-President is the winning presidential candidate's first political appointment.

Various considerations underlie the choice of a vice-presidential candidate. Traditionally there has been an attempt to balance the ticket—that is, to select a person who differs in certain ways from the presidential nominee himself. For example, the two may come from separate parts of the country. The Democratic party often chose Southerners to run with presidential nominees from other, two-party areas; the Kennedy-Johnson ticket in 1960 was such a combination. In 1976 when a southerner (Jimmy Carter) won the Democratic presidential contest for the first time since before the Civil War, the process worked in reverse: he chose as his running-mate Senator Walter Mondale from the northern state of Minnesota. In 1972 Senator Thomas Eagleton was originally chosen by George McGovern as his running-mate (as indicated below, he was ultimately forced off the ticket) because he possessed certain characteristics that the South Dakotan lacked: affiliation with the Catholic church; ties to organized labor; and previous residence in a large city (St. Louis). Balancing the ticket in these ways is designed to broaden its appeal so as to strengthen the party's chances in the general election.*

There are indications, however, that some presidential candidates are at least giving consideration to how the vice-presidential candidate will perform in office. The trend towards assigning the second-in-command important responsibilities has led some candidates to choose as their running-mates persons with whom they feel they can work effectively. This factor apparently led Hubert Humphrey to select Edmund Muskie to share the ticket with him in 1968. The senator's views on a variety of public issues (including Vietnam) paralleled those of Humphrey; moreover, the presidential nominee also admired Muskie's effective work in the Senate, where Humphrey had also served with distinction. The possibility of succession to the highest office (we will discuss this matter in ch. 12) has also led Presidents to choose running-mates who they felt would be best able to step into their shoes should anything happen to them. There is evidence that John Kennedy regarded Lyndon Johnson as the most capable leader among his rivals for the presidential nomination in 1960.

Of course these factors are not mutually exclusive. It is possible to choose a man for the second place on the ticket because of more than one of these considerations. Thus Kennedy chose Lyndon Johnson not only because he regarded him as an effective political leader, but also because he calculated that Johnson's presence on the ticket and his campaign efforts in the South would help the Democratic party's chances in that region.

Whatever the considerations may be that prompt a presidential nominee to choose a running-mate, there is little question that the decision is typically made far too quickly and frequently without a full knowledge of the candidate's background. A classic case occurred in 1972 when McGovern and his staff gathered the morning after his nomination (many of them having had only two or three hours' sleep) and by five o'clock that afternoon finally settled on Senator Thomas Eagleton. The Missourian accepted the nomination after several other persons either had turned it down, could not be contacted, or were vetoed by key McGovern supporters. In the process, no one turned up the information on Eagleton's past experiences with mental illness that ultimately led McGovern to force him off the ticket.

With the choosing of the vice-presidential nominee, the last major decision of the national convention is completed. The final night of the proceedings is given over to acceptance speeches. This is a time for attempting to bring back together the various candidates and party elements that have battled each other during the long preconvention campaign and the hectic days of the convention

---

* Carried to the extreme, the balancing principle would lead to the selection of a candidate who differs in many respects from the presidential nominee. One wag suggested in 1960 that what Richard Nixon needed for a running-mate was a Negro nun from the South who was president of a labor union!

itself. Typically, major party figures are expected to come to the convention stage to pledge their support for the winner in the campaign that lies ahead. At times, however, personal feelings run too high and wounds fail to heal sufficiently for a show of party unity. Major figures of the liberal wing of the Republican party in 1964, and many McCarthyites among Democrats in 1968 (including their candidate himself), refused to endorse the chosen nominee, at least immediately. In 1972 some prominent Democratic leaders, including George Meaney of the AFL-CIO, did not support McGovern. Thus the convention does not always achieve one of its major objectives: rallying the party faithful for the coming general election battle.

For the presidential candidate, the nomination process is a long and arduous effort involving complicated legal arrangements for the selection of delegates and voting at the convention itself, as well as difficult strategic decisions of a highly political nature. For the congressional candidate, the path to the nomination is less complex from both legal and political standpoints. Nevertheless, he too must take into account a variety of factors as he maps his campaign to win his party's nomination for the Senate or House of Representatives.

THE NOMINATION OF CONGRESSMEN

Although senators and members of the House of Representatives are national officials in the sense that they enact laws that govern the entire nation, they are more commonly considered to be representatives of smaller geographical units. This being so, their method of selection is left, under the Constitution, to the individual states. How a congressman or senator gains his party's nomination, therefore, depends on state law.

Primary Laws

Most states nominate both senators and members of the House by means of a direct primary. There are, however, differences among primaries, which span the months from late winter to early fall. Most are "closed"—that is, restricted to voters who are affiliated with a party as evidenced by declaration of their affiliation when they register to vote or by pledging that they have supported the party's candidates in the past or that they will in the future. Some states, however, have "open" primaries that allow a voter to choose which party's primary he wants to vote in, and a few use a "wide-open" primary that permits a person to vote in one party's primary for some officials and in another's for different officials. In most states the *plurality* candidate—the one receiving the largest number of votes—wins the nomination. In the remaining states (primarily in the South) a *majority vote* is needed to win; if no candidate receives a majority on the first ballot, a run-off election is held between the top two vote-getters.

While most states let the party in the electorate choose congressional candidates, a few grant that right to party activists by using state conventions to nominate senators or members of the House of Representatives. Other states use a combination of the party organization and the party in the electorate to nominate candidates. In some of these states official endorsement of candidates by the state central committee or state party convention precedes the primary;

in others the process is reversed: the convention is used to choose a candidate in the event that the top vote-getter in the primary does not receive the requisite proportion of votes (usually 35 percent).

The congressional aspirant thus faces a variety of legal requirements in seeking his party's nomination. The political factors affecting his candidacy, however, are even more diverse and complex.

The Politics of Choosing Congressional Candidates

It is far more difficult to discuss the naming of congressional candidates than the nomination of the president. For one thing, students of politics have focused more of their attention on the presidency. Moreover, even if a researcher has data on the politics of some individual congressional nominations, he cannot properly conclude that these are necessarily typical of 535 races for the national legislature (100 Senate and 435 House). Nonetheless, the limited information we have on the subject reveals certain basic political patterns in congressional nominations.

Senatorial candidates have generally been drawn from two major pools: state governors and members of the House of Representatives. State legislators constitute a third, but less frequent, source of senatorial aspirants. The national executive branch has also become a good recruiting ground for senators: former Vice-President Hubert Humphrey returned to a Senate seat, and Abraham Ribicoff, one-time Secretary of Health, Education and Welfare, went to the Senate after serving in that post; John F. Kennedy's presidential assistants Pierre Salinger and Theodore Sorensen also ran for the upper chamber, although unsuccessfully. Of late, celebrities like movie star George Murphy and pioneer astronaut John Glenn have become senatorial candidates. The position of United States senator is so highly prestigious that it attracts persons from all areas of public life.

The same cannot be said of the House of Representatives. Few governors or officials of the national executive branch are likely to consider a position there as a move up the political ladder. Sitting senators naturally have no interest in the less prestigious House, and even those that are defeated for reelection are more likely to seek some other position—a governorship, a place in the national executive branch, or employment as a lobbyist—than to run for the more parochial lower chamber of Congress. So where do members of the House come from? Primarily from state legislatures and from county or city posts. Some House aspirants, indeed, have no previous political experience at all.

Congressional candidates are recruited in various ways. Some are self-starters who take the initiative on their own. At other times party leaders, other senators or representatives, interest-group representatives, or personal friends stimulate a candidacy. However the process is initiated, it usually involves those groups eventually. In other words, a candidate who first decides to seek congressional office on his own will try to determine how much support he can rally from these various sources. For without help from at least some of them, he is unlikely to have the resources necessary for the nomination and election contests that lie ahead.

The extent to which state and local party organizations become involved in congressional nominations varies. In states that use a party convention either to officially nominate or to screen congressional candidates, an aspirant must generally win the support of party leaders if he is to have a chance for the nomination, especially for the Senate. He must also do so in nonconvention states where strong party organizations make a practice of committing resources (mainly workers and money) in the primary. Thus most potential Democratic senatorial aspirants in Illinois simply did not run if they could not win the support of Chicago's Mayor Daley. Although few states in the nation have had such a potent party organization as his, the support of political activists is essential for a congressional nomination in some other urban areas as well.

In some instances, however, the support of party organizations is not crucial for congressional nominations. In states like California and Wisconsin, laws prevent official party organizations from endorsing candidates in the primary.* Even where no such legal restrictions exist, party organizations or individual party leaders may think it wise to remain neutral in intraparty contests in order to avoid antagonizing unendorsed candidates, some of whom may eventually win despite the lack of organizational support. Finally, party support in contests for the House of Representatives is hampered because in many states there are no official party organizations for congressional districts, only for counties and the state. All these circumstances force congressional candidates to build their own personal organizations of workers and financial contributors for primary campaigns.

If assistance in many congressional primaries is minimal from state and local party groups, it is almost nonexistent from national party officials and leaders. As a matter of political custom, congressional nominations are considered state and local concerns into which national leaders should not intrude. Even as popular a political leader as Franklin Roosevelt was unsuccessful in his attempt in 1938 to purge certain Southern congressmen in the Democratic primaries because they had voted against his liberal legislative proposals. Most Presidents consider it politically unwise to try to unseat congressional incumbents of their party. Not only do defeats in those primaries result in a loss of presidential prestige; they also make political enemies of the victors, on whom the Chief Executive may have to depend for support of his legislative program.

About the only congressional primaries in which national leaders are likely to intervene are in those areas where the other party controls the seat or where the incumbent in their own party is not running for reelection. In such circumstances the President or other national officials may encourage a person to enter the primary and even go so far as to offer him financial assistance to do so. For example, in 1970 national Republican leaders persuaded Attorney-General John Danforth of Missouri to seek their party's senatorial nomination against the Democratic incumbent, Stuart Symington. Even in these cases, national officials are wary of intraparty squabbles and generally support only candidates who are acceptable to most, if not all, important party leaders. Most instances of national party intervention involve contests for the Senate rather than for the House, because individual senators are more important politically to the president than are the more numerous members of the lower chamber.

---

* Sometimes extralegal groups are organized to get around this restriction. The California Republican Assembly and the California Democratic Council have endorsed candidates in primaries of their respective parties for years.

One final fact of political life is that most congressional primaries are not competitive, in part because most congressional elections, particularly for the House of Representatives, are not competitive. Candidates of the minority party in an area do not ordinarily battle vigorously for the honor of going down to defeat in the general election. On the other hand, candidates of the majority party might be expected to be more plentiful; however, if the incumbent himself is seeking reelection, challengers in his own party generally have little chance against him. Previous campaign experience, close relationships with voters, greater knowledge of issues, and superior financial resources* give the veteran congressman almost insurmountable advantages over his opponents. Recent estimates indicate that, on the average, only 1 percent of incumbent representatives are defeated for renomination.

Senatorial nominations are more competitive than are those for the House. The prestigious nature of the position draws multiple candidacies even in the state's minority party, and the majority party naturally has a good share of contested nominations. Incumbent senators, however, tend to be fairly successful in hanging on. In the twenty-five years after World War II, an average of only two senators per election year failed to be renominated.

Even though congressional nominations are generally noncompetitive, spirited battles do occur at times, particularly when the incumbent is not seeking reelection or when he is considered politically vulnerable for some reason. The reasons may include his age, his status as a one-term congressman with comparatively little seniority and campaign experience, or a change in the district he has been representing, so that a new constituency with a different electorate is created.

For the congressional or presidential candidate, the nomination process constitutes the first of the two hurdles he must clear if he is to hold public office. For a nominee in a competitive situation with the candidate of the opposition party, the general election campaign ahead may be even more trying than the one he has just completed. Before turning to that subject, however, we should assess the nomination process.

* As previously indicated, the financing of congressional campaigns is discussed in the next chapter.

ASSESSMENT

As we have seen, the process of choosing presidential nominees has become more and more democratic in recent years. The growth in the number of presidential primaries, plus the passage of rules in both parties opening up caucuses and conventions to broader participation by candidate enthusiasts and rank-and-file voters, has ended the domination of the selection process by party professionals. Moreover, the mass media and public-opinion polls are important factors in the process by which the presidential nominees are chosen.

While these developments are generally favorable for democratic government, they nevertheless raise both practical and theoretical problems. The undue favoring of amateurs over party professionals by the McGovern Commission contributed to the choice of a candidate and the writing of a platform in 1972 with views that were distinctly at odds with the sentiments not only of those professionals but also of many rank-and-file voters as well. The practical effect was the defection of many traditional Democratic supporters that year and an overwhelming defeat of the party's candidate in the general election. Also affected was the broader issue of democratic responsiveness: professional politicians who are in public life on a permanent basis are more likely to be sensitive to, and concerned about, public sentiment than are candidate enthusiasts who come into the political process merely to nominate a President and then return to their private concerns. This being the case, the decision of the Mikulski Commission to encourage the selection of public and party officials as at-large delegates to the national convention is to be commended.

The Mikulski Commission also brought about other improvements in the nomination process for Democrats. The use of quotas to represent certain groups in the nomination process (as was done in 1972) is neither wise nor consistent with democratic theory. Americans have never assumed that persons must be represented by legislators from their own social groups; once quotas are assigned to some groups, why not to others—the elderly, for example, who have special needs? Equality in the American context has always meant equality of *opportunity,* not of *results;* the right to participate equally in the political process, not a guarantee of success. Thus the decision of the Mikulski Commission expressly to eliminate quotas in favor of affirmative-action plans requiring states to take positive steps to encourage the participation of formerly underrepresented groups, is a healthy corrective in the nomination process.

The nomination process should be pluralistic enough to reflect a variety of views: those of party leaders and office-holders as well as political amateurs and rank-and-file voters. The present system, with the quotas now removed and the undue favoring of amateurs over party activists having been ratified, is a judicious blend of these elements. It draws upon the wisdom and experience of party professionals in helping to screen candidates, and at the same time it

ensures that the preference of rank-and-file voters will determine the final choice of the nominee.

Another advantage of the present nomination process is the fact that it is such an *open* one. Recent changes in the ''rules of the game,'' including the public financing of a portion of campaign costs, make it possible for political underdogs successfully to challenge more established candidates in both political parties. Certainly the results of the 1976 contests attest to this fact—an obscure, one-term governor of a southern state won the Democratic nomination, while another ex-governor battled an incumbent President down to the wire for the Republican party designation.

While the present presidential nomination system is generally a good one, it has some problems. One is the increased role that the media have come to play in the process. There is little evidence to indicate that their representatives are wiser and more informed about the merits of the various candidates than are party professionals who formerly dominated the recruitment and screening of candidates; moreover, the latter bear the responsibility of working with the candidate once he is in office, an obligation not assumed by members of the press or by television and radio commentators. The civic education of the American electorate would also be better served if the media spent less time and effort trying to predict and interpret the results of primary contests and worked harder at investigating the backgrounds and records of the contenders and their major advisers, some of whom are appointed to key government positions if their candidate wins the presidency. Media representatives should also do a better job of researching and analyzing the issue-stands of candidates rather than try to trap weary campaigners into ambiguous comments that can be quoted out of context.

Another problem is the recent proliferation of presidential primaries that not only exhaust the candidates but also confuse them with a hodgepodge of different legal provisions relating to the selection of delegates. Some analysts of presidential politics have concluded that since we have gone as far as we have in eliciting voter preferences, it might be best to go all the way and adopt a national primary to choose party nominees. Such a system (favored by almost three-fourths of Americans in a 1972 Gallup poll) would have the advantage of being direct and simple, readily understood by candidates and voters alike. It would come closest to the ideal of the "one-person–one-vote" principle and would eliminate the uncertainties of the present system in which early, key primaries decided by a small vote vitally affect the remainder of the process.

Despite these advantages, on balance a national primary would *not* be a good idea. It would eliminate the possibility of a lesser-known candidate's making a relatively limited investment of money and effort in key state primaries and, having won them, going on to wrest the nomination from the initial front-runner. Thus the system would be less open than the present one. A national primary in which a large number of persons were entered could also result in the winning candidate's receiving only 20 to 25 percent of the vote. While that possibility could be avoided by requiring a run-off election between the top two contenders, candidates would then be faced with making three nationwide campaigns (including the general election) within a relatively short period of time. Moreover, a nationwide contest would probably further increase the role of the media in the nomination process, with all the previously discussed disadvantages such a development would bring.

Another, less radical, proposal than the national primary is to go to a series of four or five regional primaries. Under this plan, states located in the same general geographical area would hold their primaries on the same day, and the regional contests would be scheduled about a month apart over the course of the nomination season. While such a system would undoubtedly ease the campaign scheduling of candidates, it would not solve some of the major problems of the present system, such as the increased role of the media. It would also increase the initial investment costs of the lesser-known candidate, who could no longer concentrate his initial efforts on a single state or two; at the same time, the winner of the first regional primary would have the same advantage in the presidential race as has the early state victor under the present process.* It is thus questionable whether the regional primary plan would be appreciably better than the current system.

There is, however, one feature of our present system that definitely needs to be changed: the selection of the Vice-President. Recent experiences with the choice of Spiro Agnew (who resigned from office under disgrace) and Thomas Eagleton (who was forced off the Democratic ticket because of past mental illness) clearly indicate the folly of the present custom of leaving the matter completely to the discretion of the presidential nominee (who often makes a quick decision on the matter less than twenty-four hours after he himself is chosen). One possibility for improvement is to extend the period in which the presidential nominee has to make the decision so that he can take sufficient time to get the information necessary for an informed choice. An even better idea would be to formally involve other groups in the process: for example, the presidential nominee might submit a list of three or four persons who are acceptable to him and let either the convention delegates or the National Committee make the final selection from among them.

---

* As William Keech has suggested, if the 1976 contest had begun with a western regional primary, the Republican nomination might have gone to Reagan rather than Ford; also there is some doubt whether Carter would have prevailed in the Democratic contest under those circumstances.

SELECTED READINGS

For an excellent treatment of candidate selection in democratic political systems see Leon Epstein, *Political Parties in Western Democracies* (New York: Praeger, 1967). Very helpful treatments of the nomination process in the United States are contained in V.O. Key, Jr., *Politics, Parties and Pressure Groups* (New York: Thomas Y. Crowell, 5th ed., 1964), and Frank Sorauf, *Party Politics in America* (Boston: Little, Brown, 1968).

A monumental study of the presidential-nomination contests in 1952, which contains detailed information on delegate selection in the various states, is Paul T. David, Malcom Moss, and Ralph M. Goldman, *Presidential Nominating Politics in 1952* (Baltimore: Johns Hopkins University Press, 1954). A one-volume condensation of the above study was published by Paul T. David, Ralph M. Goldman, and Richard Bain under the title of *The Politics of National Party Conventions* (Washington, D.C.: The Brookings Institution, 1960). This book was subsequently revised and condensed by Kathleen Sproul as a Vintage paperback (New York: Random House, 1964). Another excellent study of the subject is Gerald Pomper, *Nominating the President: The Politics of Convention Choice* (New York: Norton, 1966). A good analysis of presidential primaries and the role that they play in the nomination process is James W. Davis, *Presidential Primaries: Road to the White House* (New York: Thomas Y. Crowell, 1967). An excellent recent study of the presidential nomination process is William Keech and Donald R. Matthews, *The Party's Choice* (Washington, D.C.: The Brookings Institution, 1976). Keech updates this study in his paper, "The 1976 Presidential Nominations in the Context of the Previous Twenty," which was delivered at the annual meeting of the American Political Science Association held in Chicago September 2-5, 1976.

Treatments of presidential nominations are also included in broader studies that cover the general election process as well. One very good study is Nelson W. Polsby and Aaron B. Wildavsky, *Presidential Elections: Strategies of American Electoral Politics* (New York: Scribner, 1976). Theodore White's four classic studies of *The Making of the President (1960, 1964, 1968, and 1972)* (New York: Atheneum) are highly readable accounts of the nomination and election campaigns in these four election years. Another journalistic and exhaustive analysis of the 1968 race by three reporters of the *London Sunday Times,* Lewis Chester, Godfrey Hodgson, and Bruce Page, is *The American Melodrama: The Presidential Campaign in 1968* (New York: Viking, 1969). Donald Matthews's "Presidential Nominations: Process and Outcomes" and Austin Ranney's "Changing the Rules of the Nominating Game" are excellent political and legal analyses of the nomination process that appear in James David Barber (ed.) *Choosing the President* (Englewood Cliffs, N.J.: Prentice-Hall, 1974). Recent analyses of the role of the press in presidential campaigns include David Broder, "Political Reporters in Presidential Politics," in Charles Peters and Timothy J. Adams, eds., *Inside the System* (New York: Praeger, 1970) and Timothy Crouse, *The Boys on the Bus* (New York: Random House, 1970). A book edited by Ernest May and Janet Fraser, *Campaign '72: The Managers Speak* (Cambridge: Harvard University Press, 1972) examines the 1972 contest from the vantage-point of persons active in both the Republican and Democratic campaigns.

Studies of congressional nominations are very limited. Chapter 16 of Key's book cited above contains basic information on the subject. An excellent comparative study of ten congressional campaigns in 1962 in the Bay Area of California is David Leuthold, *Electioneering in a Democracy: Campaigns for Congress* (New York: Wiley, 1968).

A major criticism of primaries is in V.O. Key, Jr., *An Introduction to State Politics* (New York: Knopf, 1956). The David, Keech, Polsby, and Pomper books cited above all contain evaluations of the presidential nomination process.

Political Novels   A southern Senator's drive for nomination as President is imaginatively portrayed by Tom Wicker in *Facing the Lions* (New York: Avon, 1973). Wicker provides a realistic view of the effect of presidential ambitions upon the candidates and those around them as well as a penetrating picture of the politics of the "new" South.

Two other novels colorfully describe the events surrounding major party conventions: Allen Drury in *Capable of Honor* (New York: Doubleday, 1966) shows the desperate battle between extremism and moderation that often characterized nominating conventions in the 1960s; Fletcher Knebel and Charles Bailey II in *Convention* (New York: Bantam, 1965) provide a graphic account of the behind-the-scenes maneuvering during a major presidential nominating convention.

Squaring off before the American Public

Chapter 9

A few days before the Republican Convention in Kansas City in August 1976, President Ford assembled his top political advisers to plan the fall campaign. Political director Stuart Spencer found it necessary to deliver a painful message to the President: much as Ford loved to campaign, he was not adept at it and his efforts would probably cost him votes. Under the circumstances, it was best that he restrain his early campaign activities and play the role of incumbent, working hard at exercising the duties of the office. The advisers did believe, however, that the President could do well in political debates and suggested that he challenge Jimmy Carter to a series of them. They also recommended that Ford harbor his campaign funds for a media blitz in October, and that he ultimately hit the campaign trail hard in the ten days prior to the election. Although he found the assessment of his campaign activities a bitter pill to swallow, the President decided to accept the strategy outlined for him.

The "game plan" for Jimmy Carter was quite different from that of the President. Having captured the nomination as an outsider running against the Democratic Establishment, Carter's advisers suggested that he now enlist the support of such leading figures in the party as Senators Hubert Humphrey and Edward Kennedy, and Mayors Richard Daley of Chicago and Frank Rizzo of Philadelphia. It was also decided that Carter should continue the all-out campaign style that brought him his nomination victory, and that he target his efforts on the various groups comprising the New Deal Coalition first forged by Franklin Roosevelt—southerners, blacks, organized labor, Catholics and Jews, intellectuals, and big-city dwellers. The only feature of the Carter campaign strategy that paralleled Ford's was agreement on the debates: the Georgian accepted Ford's challenge immediately and claimed that he had originally intended to call for presidential debates himself.

The early stages of the presidential campaign reflected the basic strategies of the two candidates. Carter opened his campaign on Labor Day with a rousing speech in Warm Springs, Georgia, a resort that President Roosevelt had visited many times seeking comfort for his paralytic condition and where he died in 1945. The Democratic candidate then headed north to the industrial East and Midwest. Meanwhile President Ford waited until a week after Labor Day to open his campaign in Ann Arbor, Michigan, the scene of his college football triumphs, and then conducted most of his early campaign from the White House, where he received visitors, signed or vetoed bills, and called press conferences to make announcements and gather presidential publicity. The President also used the advantages of incumbency, recommending legislation to expand the national park system and to reduce the amount of down payments for mortgages guaranteed by the Federal Housing Administration.

During the first stage of the campaign, the Ford strategy appeared to be working. The eighteen-point spread in the public-opinion polls that Carter enjoyed in early September (it had been as high as 33 percent after the Democratic Convention in late July) soon began to narrow. While the President was playing it safe by sticking close to the Rose Garden, Carter was campaigning at a frenetic pace, a victim of over-scheduling and poor advance planning. The Georgian had a tendency to talk too freely to the press and to make mistakes when he was tired. In an ill-fated interview with a reporter for *Playboy* magazine, he confessed that he had "lusted after women in his heart," a remark that reportedly lost him some votes among religious fundamentalists in the Bible Belt, and said he would never lie to the American people as former Presidents Lyndon Johnson and Richard Nixon had done. (Carter subsequently apologized to Johnson's widow, but the statement was thought to have hurt him in Texas.) Carter also made some remarks to the press that were interpreted to mean that he favored increasing taxes on all persons with a medium income ($14,500 a year) or above. Also contributing to the decline in the Democratic candidate's fortunes was the fact that he was nervous and overly deferential to the President in their first debate in late September, a contest in which most observers felt that Ford had bested his challenger. As the time for the second debate in early October neared, the Gallup poll showed that the President had virtually closed the gap between himself and the challenger.

At about that time, however, Ford developed some troubles of his own. The Watergate Special Prosecutor began to look into contributions to his former congressional campaigns by two maritime unions and into an allegation that he had used campaign funds to pay his own personal expenses. It was also revealed that while he was Minority Leader of the House of Representatives, Ford had accepted paid golfing vacations from corporation executives. Moreover, a story by former White House counselor John Dean surfaced in *Rolling Stone* magazine, revealing that on the way back from the Republican Convention in Kansas City, Secretary of Agriculture Earl Butz had made a racial slur. Initially, the President merely reprimanded the secretary; but under increased pressure, Butz, a man popular with many Republican farmers, was forced to resign. Finally, the President not only lost the second debate to a much more confident and no longer deferential Carter, but also during the proceedings claimed that Eastern Europe (in particular, Yugoslavia, Romania, and Poland) was not under Soviet domination. To make matters worse, the President refused for several days to retract that statement and did so only under pressure from his staff.

This series of events ended the dramatic decline in public support for Carter (and the increased support for Ford) that had characterized the first month of the campaign. The second debate also stimulated the competitive instincts of the two candidates, and they began to attack each other much more vigorously.

Campaigning—Presidential style.

The peripatetic candidate.

Carter charged that other Presidents (like Richard Nixon who had been to Poland) "at least knew whose tanks"—the Russians'—were there. The President accused Carter of "slandering the good name of the United States" by asserting in the debate that we were no longer strong. Also contributing to the stridency of the campaign was the debate in mid-October between the two vice-presidential candidates, Republican Robert Dole and Democrat Walter Mondale. Dole charged that about 1.6 million Americans, "enough to fill the city of Detroit," had been killed in "Democrat wars" in this century; Mondale countered that Dole had "richly earned his reputation as a hatchet man by implying and stating that World War II and the Korean War were Democratic wars." However, advisers on both sides urged their candidates to cool the campaign rhetoric and negative attacks, and both Ford and Carter were on their good behavior for the third and final debate, which, unlike the first two encounters, was generally scored as even by most observers. Following the debate, both candidates launched their final ten-day efforts, concentrating on the industrial states in the East and Midwest, along with California; on the eve of the election, most pollsters estimated the contest to be a dead heat, too close to call.

On November 2, 1976, more than 81.5 million Americans went to the polls and favored Jimmy Carter by a 1.7 million plurality. However, the election was very close in many states; in eleven of them, the margin of victory was less than 2 percent. Moreover, a distinct regional pattern was evident in the voting: Carter carried eleven of the thirteen Southern states, rolling up a 1.8 million plurality in that region; he also won in seven of the twelve Eastern states (plus the District of Columbia), and swept that area by over a million votes. In contrast, Ford carried eight of the twelve Midwestern states, running up a 325,000-vote pluarlity there, and swept twelve of the thirteen Western states (only Hawaii went to Carter) for an 800,000-vote margin in that region.

These experiences of Gerald Ford and Jimmy Carter point up the calculations that candidates have to make in American presidential elections. In laying their campaign plans, they must make choices about how to concentrate their efforts to realize their major objective: winning the 270 electoral votes necessary for victory.

THE ELECTORAL COLLEGE

Earl Butz steps down.

One of the supreme ironies of the American political system is that the electoral college now governing the contest in which most Americans vote was not designed as a popular election system. In fact, it was a distrust of the ability of the common man to choose the nation's highest political official (Constitutional Convention delegate George Mason suggested that to allow the people such a choice made no more sense than "to refer a trial of colors to a blind man") that led the Founding Fathers to create the electoral college in the first place. They had already ruled out selection by Congress for two reasons: because that method violated the separation-of-powers doctrine, and because the delegates could not choose between state-unit voting, which favored the small states, and joint action of the two chambers, which benefited the large states with their greater voting power in the House of Representatives. To protect the interests of the national government, the delegates also rejected a proposal that the state legislatures choose the President.

Having decided against both popular election and selection by legislative bodies, the delegates proceeded to adopt an entirely new plan put forth by one of their own committees. The proposal provided that each state legislature choose, by whatever means it desired, a number of electors (none of whom could be congressmen or hold other national office) equal to its total of senators and representatives in Congress. The individual electors would assemble, at a fixed time, in their respective state capitals and cast two votes for President. These votes were then to be transmitted to the nation's capital, to be opened and counted in a joint session of Congress. The person receiving the largest number of electoral votes would be declared President, provided he received a majority; if no candidate received a majority, then the House of Representatives, voting by states (one state delegation, one vote), would choose the President from among the five candidates receiving the highest number of electoral votes. After the choice of the President was made, the person with the next highest number of electoral votes would be declared Vice-President. If two or more contenders received an equal number of electoral votes, then the Senate would choose the Vice-President from among them.

This complicated procedure reflected certain values and assumptions about human nature that are enunciated in *The Federalist Papers.** As mentioned above, the Founding Fathers felt that the average person did not have the ability to make sound judgments about the qualifications of the various presidential candidates; therefore, this crucial decision should be left to a small group of electors—a political elite who would have both the information and the wisdom necessary to choose the best men for the nation's two highest offices. Since the electors could not be national officeholders with connections to the President, they could approach their task without bias; because they assembled separately in their respective state capitals rather than as a single body, there would be less chance of their being corrupted by evil men or exposed to popular ferment; and because they were convened for a single purpose only, to be dissolved when their task was completed, the possibility was eliminated of tampering with them in advance or rewarding them with future favors.

Although philosophy largely shaped the presidential-selection process that the delegates adopted, so did a recognition of political factors. Some of the delegates evidently did not expect the electors to be entirely insulated from popular preferences on presidential candidates. They rather anticipated that each state's electors would cast one vote for a "native son," some locally popular political figure, and the other for a "continental character," an individual with a national reputation that they, as members of the political elite, would be aware of, even though he might not be well known to the average citizen of their state.† It was also expected that after George Washington's presidency, the electoral votes would be so widely distributed that few candidates would

"IT'S FORD — HE WANTS TO KNOW IF THERE'S ANYTHING WE FORGOT TO TELL HIM ABOUT EASTERN EUROPE"

Copyright 1976 by Herblock in The Washington Post.

---

* The particular selection is Number 68, which is generally attributed to Alexander Hamilton. It is difficult to determine whether the views expressed represent the attitudes of a majority of the Convention delegates or primarily those of Hamilton, who was more elitist than most of the others.

† Evidence for this assumption is provided by Article II, Section 1 of the Constitution, which states that at least one of the two persons for whom an elector votes must not be an inhabitant of his own state.

receive a majority, and therefore most elections would ultimately be decided by the House of Representatives. The electors would thus serve to "screen" (today we would say "nominate") the candidates, and the House would choose (elect) the President from among them. The same large-state/small-state conflict that was settled by the Connecticut Compromise on the composition of the Senate and House was also involved in the plan the delegates worked out for the selection of the Chief Executive. In the initial vote by the electors the large states had the advantage, since the number of each state's votes reflected the size of its House delegation. If no candidate got a majority, then in the secondary selection the small states were favored, since the contingent vote was by states, not by individuals, in the House of Representatives.

Subsequent events, however, soon nullified both the philosophical and political assumptions underlying the Founders' vision of the electoral college. The formation and organization of political parties in the 1790s proceeded at such a rapid pace that by the election of 1800 the electors no longer served as independent men exercising their own personal judgment on candidates' capabilities; they rather acted as agents of political parties and the general public. In fact, party discipline was so complete that all Republican electors in 1800 cast their two votes for Thomas Jefferson and Aaron Burr. Although it was generally understood that the former was the Republican candidate for President and the latter for Vice-President, the Constitution provided no means for the electors to make that distinction on their ballots. The result was a tie in electoral vote between Jefferson and Burr; neither won a majority (one over half), and the matter was thrown into the House of Representatives for a final decision. Ironically, the Federalists, despite their major defeat in the congressional elections of 1800, still controlled the lame-duck Congress (which did not expire until March 1801) and therefore were in a position to help decide which Republican would serve as President and which as Vice-President. At the urging of Alexander Hamilton, who disagreed with Jefferson on policy matters but distrusted Burr personally, some of the Federalist representatives eventually cast blank ballots, which permitted the Republican legislators to choose Jefferson as President.

One result of this bizarre chain of events was the ratification in 1804 of the Twelfth Amendment stipulating that electors cast separate ballots for President and Vice-President. The amendment also provides that, if no presidential candidate receives a majority of the electoral votes, the House of Representatives, balloting by states, will select the President by majority vote from among the three (rather than the five) candidates receiving the highest number of electoral votes; if no vice-presidential candidate receives a majority of electoral votes, similar procedures are to be used by the Senate in choosing between the two persons with the highest number of electoral ballots.

Other changes in the selection of the President soon followed, but these came not by way of constitutional amendments but rather as political developments that fit within the legal framework of the electoral college. Thus state legislators, who were granted the power to determine how electors should be chosen, began vesting this right in the general electorate. By 1804 a majority of the states had done so.

Another matter left to the discretion of the states—how their electoral votes would be counted—soon underwent change. Initially states were inclined to

The 1860 deadlock—Thomas Jefferson and Aaron Burr.

divide the vote by congressional districts: the candidate who won the plurality of the popular votes in each district received its electoral vote, and the remaining two electoral votes (representing the two Senate seats) were awarded to the statewide popular winner. However, legislatures soon began to adopt the "unit," or "general ticket," rule whereby all the state's electoral votes went to the candidate who received the plurality of the statewide popular vote. Two political considerations prompted this decision: it benefited the state's majority party, which did not have to award any electoral votes to a minority party that might be successful in individual congressional districts; it also maximized the influence of the state in the presidential election by permitting it to throw all its electoral votes to one candidate. Once some states adopted this procedure, others, wanting to maintain their political effect on the presidential contest, felt that they had to follow. As a result, by 1836 the district plan had been abandoned by most states and the unit system adopted in its stead.

One other major political development of the era changed the nature of the presidential election contest: the elimination on a state-by-state basis of property qualifications for voting. As we shall see in the next chapter, by the early 1840s *white manhood suffrage* was virtually complete in the United States. Thus the increasing democratization of American political life is reflected in the procedure for choosing the most important public official. Yet the formal provisions of the electoral college remain the same today as they were in 1804, when the Twelfth Amendment was adopted. The popular vote for the President has simply been grafted onto a system initially designed to place his selection in the hands of a select few.

This graft produces results that violate some of the major tenets of political equality. Not every person's vote really counts the same: the influence he has in the election of the President depends on the political situation in his particular state. For many Americans who support a losing candidate in their state, it is as though they had not voted at all, since under the general-ticket system all the electoral votes of a state go to the candidate who wins a plurality of its popular votes. Other citizens who live in populous, politically competitive states have a premium placed on their vote because they are in a position to affect how large blocks of electoral votes are cast. Nor does the electoral college ensure that the candidate who receives the most popular votes will win the presidency: John Quincy Adams in 1824, Rutherford B. Hayes in 1876, and Benjamin Harrison in 1888 went to the White House even though they trailed their political opponents, Andrew Jackson, Samuel Tilden, and Grover Cleveland. In 1976, Jimmy Carter almost suffered the same fate: if some 9,000 voters in Hawaii and Ohio had shifted their ballots to President Ford, the latter would have edged out Carter in the electoral college, 270–268.

The requirement that a candidate win a majority of the electoral votes or have the election decided by the House of Representatives also violates the idea of political equality. In 1948 Harry Truman defeated Thomas Dewey by over 2,000,000 popular votes, but if some 12,000 people in California and Ohio had voted for Dewey rather than the President, the election would have been thrown into the House of Representatives for a decision. The same thing could have happened in 1960 if some 9000 persons in Illinois and Missouri had voted for Nixon instead of Kennedy, and again in 1968 if about 42,000 persons in Missouri, New Jersey, and Alaska had cast their ballot for Hubert Humphrey

The Hayes-Tilden contest of 1876 provoked bitter electoral debate, and Congress spent three months counting the ballots. The pass at top is to the House gallery.

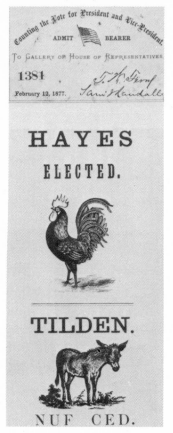

"WHEW! LET'S NOT TRY THAT ROUTE AGAIN"

Copyright 1976 by Herblock in The
Washington Post.

rather than President Nixon.* Permitting the House of Representatives, voting by states, to select the President of the United States is not consistent with the "one man—one vote" principle.

The 1968 election also illustrates another danger of the electoral college system: an elector need not cast his ballot for the candidate who wins the plurality of votes in his states. Had Nixon failed to win a majority of the electoral votes, third-party candidate George Wallace would have been in a position to bargain with him. Wallace could have asked his electors (forty-five)† to cast their ballots for Nixon, which would have given the latter enough electoral votes so that the election would not go into the House. While Wallace's forty-five electoral votes would not have been enough to give Humphrey a majority of the electoral votes (even if the Vice-President had carried both Missouri and New Jersey), the Alabama governor could have tried to bargain with the Vice-President by offering to use his influence with Southern representatives to get them to choose him over Nixon.

These problems have created a great deal of dissatisfaction with the electoral college over the years. The sentiment for changing it has increased recently, particularly in the wake of the above-noted elections of 1948, 1960, 1968, and 1976 in which a switch in votes of a relatively few persons in key states would have sent the selection of the President into the House or immediately changed the result. Yet while there is widespread agreement on the necessity for changing the electoral college, there is marked disagreement over what form that change should take. Four basic plans have been suggested as substitutes for the present system.

The first, known as the automatic plan, which would make the least change in the present system, would eliminate the possibility of "faithless electors" by abolishing the office and automatically casting a state's electoral votes for the popular-vote winner in that state. If no candidate received a majority of the electoral votes, a joint session of Congress would choose the winner with each representative and senator having one vote.

The second, known as the district plan, proposes that we return to the method the states used early in our history (and recently reinstated by Maine), under which the presidential candidate who received the plurality vote in each House district would receive its electoral vote, with the remaining two electoral votes going to the statewide popular winner. If no candidate received a majority of the electoral votes, senators and representatives, sitting jointly and voting as individuals, would choose the President from the three candidates having the highest number of electoral votes. This plan's major supporters have been congressmen and private groups from rural areas such as the *American Farm Bureau*. If the plan were adopted, the crucial areas would be the some seventy-five politically competitive congressional districts where the two major parties traditionally divide the vote 55 to 45 percent.

---

* In all these elections, persons other than the two major party candidates received electoral votes; therefore Dewey, Nixon, and Humphrey could have carried the above states and still not have had a majority of the electoral votes.

† Although Wallace actually earned forty-five electoral votes, he received forty-six because one elector in North Carolina (which went for Nixon) cast his vote for the Alabama governor. In 1960, 1972, and 1976, single electors in Oklahoma, Virginia, and Washington also did not cast their ballot for the candidate receiving the popular vote plurality in their state.

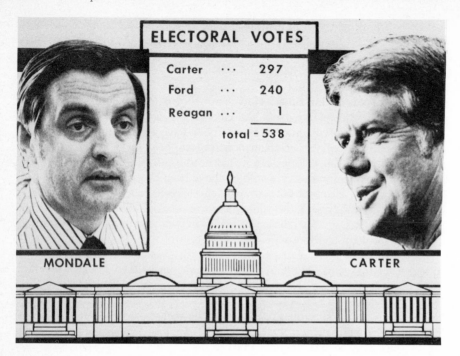

ELECTORAL VOTES

Carter	···	297
Ford	···	240
Reagan	···	1
	total -	538

MONDALE   CARTER

A third proposal, known as the proportional plan, would divide each state's electoral votes in proportion to the division of the popular votes: if a candidate received 60 percent of the popular votes in the state, he would receive 60 percent of its electoral votes. A plan of this nature introduced by Republican Senator Henry Cabot Lodge of Massachusetts and Democratic Representative Ed Gosset of Texas passed the Senate in 1950 but failed to be enacted by the House. The plan would eliminate the present advantage of the large states in being able to throw all their electoral votes to one candidate and has, therefore, been opposed by many of their legislators, including John Kennedy when he was a senator from Massachusetts. One possible consequence of a proportional division of the electoral votes would be a fairly even split between the two major candidates so that neither received a majority; hence there would be a greater likelihood of elections being thrown into Congress for decision.*

The fourth plan, direct popular election of the President, has picked up major support in recent years, especially since its recommendation in 1967 by a special commission of the *American Bar Association*. In addition, it has been endorsed by such politically disparate groups as the *Chamber of Commerce of the United States* and the AFL-CIO. In 1969 the House passed a constitutional amendment providing that the President (and Vice-President) be elected by a minimum of 40 percent of the popular vote and, if no candidate received so large a vote, that a runoff be held between the two front-runners. The Senate failed to pass the amendment, however, despite the efforts of its major sponsor,

---

* Most of the proportional plans have suggested lowering the winning electoral-vote requirement from a majority to 40 or even 35 percent to avoid the possibility of having the election go to the House. They have also proposed that, if no candidate receives the requisite proportion of electoral votes, the two houses, meeting jointly and voting as individuals, choose the President.

Birch Bayh, Democrat of Indiana. After Carter's narrow electoral college victory in 1976, Bayh indicated that he would reintroduce a similar amendment that would substitute congressional selection for a runoff election if the leading candidate received less than 40 percent of the popular vote.

We will assess the merits of these various plans, along with the present system, at the conclusion of this chapter. We next consider the rules for electing congressmen.

RULES FOR CONGRESSIONAL ELECTIONS

Unlike presidential aspirants, congressional candidates do not face complex rules about how special types of votes are determined and counted, an unusual proportion of the vote necessary for election, or contingency procedures if they do not achieve that proportion. All they need to do is win a plurality of the popular votes. Moreover, senatorial aspirants, as well as House candidates in the five states that have only one representative (Alaska, Delaware, Nevada, Vermont, and Wyoming), have an easily defined constituency—the whole state population. But those who seek a seat in the House from the other forty-five states face a very real problem: how are the geographical limits of their constituency to be determined? What rules of the game govern that decision?

The Constitution provides that members of the House of Representatives be apportioned among the states according to population. In order to keep the allocation of House seats current with changes in state populations, an enumeration of national population every ten years was prescribed, a practice that has been followed each decade since 1790.

The Constitution does not establish a permanent size for the House of Representatives, leaving the matter to Congress. Beginning with sixty-five members, the House gradually expanded over the years until it reached the size of 435 in 1912 after New Mexico and Arizona came into the Union. Congress has generally maintained the membership at that figure since then.*

Holding the size of the House of Representatives constant in the face of national population growth has resulted in an increase in the average number of persons represented by each congressman. In 1912 the figure was just over 200,000; in 1970 it was nearly 500,000. Apportioning the permanent House membership among the various states means that after each census, each state gains, loses, or stays even depending on how its population changed in relation to the national average in the preceding decade. In 1970 eleven seats were exchanged: five Southwestern and Western states gained seats in the House of Representatives, while nine others in the Midwest, East, and South lost.

Thus the provisions of the Constitution pertaining to apportionment and the laws of Congress establishing the size of the House of Representatives together provide the means for determining how many representatives each state is entitled to. For the congressional candidate, however, an even more salient issue remains: what method will be used to distribute congressional seats within a state?

---

* When Alaska and Hawaii were admitted into the Union in the 1950s, two representatives (one for each) were temporarily added to the House membership. After the 1960 census, the membership was again reduced to 435.

Legislative Apportionment of Congressional Seats Within States

For the first half-century of the nation's existence, each state was free to determine how congressional seats were to be apportioned internally. Many states elected their representatives at large, much as they allocated electoral votes for presidential candidates. Congress itself, however, reacted differently to the two situations: it permitted states to make their own decisions on electoral college matters but in 1842 intervened in legislative apportionment by requiring that members of the House of Representatives be chosen in separate, "single-member" districts.

Although single-member districts have the virtue of making individual legislators responsible to a limited number of constituents, they are also subject to the vice of having their boundaries drawn to favor certain groups over others, typically by distributing voters so as to maximize the political influence of a state's majority party. (A state legislature draws the boundaries of its own legislative districts as well as those of the state's congressional districts.) This feat is accomplished by concentrating voters who support the minority party in a few legislative districts, allowing their candidates to carry those constituencies by wide margins, or by spreading them fairly evenly and seeing to it that they are outnumbered by the majority party's supporters in the districts concerned. Both techniques have as their purpose minimizing the minority party's (and hence maximizing the majority party's) number of district victories.

The common result is legislative districts of strange shapes. Some are *noncontiguous;* others, while contiguous, are long, thin strips, *not compact* entities. In fact, one state legislative district in Massachusetts that resembled a salamander was responsible for the coining of a word, gerrymander (the Democratic governor at the time was Elbridge Gerry), that is used to describe the technique by which legislative district boundaries are manipulated politically.

Gerrymandering can benefit not only the majority party but also other kinds of political interests. Incumbent legislators manipulate boundaries of districts to protect themselves against electoral challengers from within their own party. Sitting state legislators as well as representatives avoid political battles against one another by maintaining the boundaries of their districts in the face of population shifts within the state that call for redistributing. This latter technique, known as the "silent" gerrymander, leads to the third abuse of legislative districts: *different-sized constituencies.* Areas that lose population are overrepresented in that their state legislators and congressmen represent relatively few people; regions that gain residents are underrepresented since their representatives have extra-large constituencies. Thus the silent gerrymander generally tends to benefit rural areas with dwindling numbers and to work to the disadvantage of urban localities with burgeoning populations.

For a number of years Congress gave an indication that it was aware of these abuses and that it might try to prevent them in congressional districts. An act passed in 1842, which first required states to choose members of the House of Representatives by single-member districts, provided that they consist of "contiguous territory"; in 1872 a requirement was added that House districts contain an "equal number of people"; in 1901 Congress went a step further, adding a stipulation that the districts be "compact." All three requirements—contiguity, compactness, and equality of population—were subsequently included in the Reapportionment Act of 1911.

There is little evidence, however, that Congress really intended to enforce the regulations. In 1901 and again in 1910 it rejected attempts to deny House seats to persons on the grounds that their districts did not meet federal standards. When a new reapportionment act was passed in 1929, none of the three requirements was included in its provisions. It was obviously asking too much to expect representatives, many of whom themselves came from malapportioned and gerrymandered districts, to commit political suicide by changing the system from which they benefited.

As the nation became urbanized, the silent gerrymander produced more and more unequal legislative districts. The disparities were particularly pronounced at the state level, where constitutional provisions granted local units (such as towns and counties) representation in the state legislature, frequently without regard to their size. In 1960 the most populous district of the California state Senate had 422 times as many people as the smallest one. At the national level, the differences were less marked; even so, the ratio between the largest and smallest congressional districts in Texas that same year was four to one. Yet neither state legislatures nor successive Congresses were disposed to change the situation. Representative Emanuel Celler of New York introduced a bill in 1951 seeking to reinstitute the former requirements of contiguity and compactness for congressional districts and to require that they not vary in size more than 15 percent from each state's average district population; he failed to rally the support of his colleagues. Faced with the unwillingness of legislative bodies themselves to remedy the situation, aggrieved parties turned to the courts for assistance.

The Supreme Court and Reapportionment

Attempts in the 1930s and 1940s to use the federal courts to rectify unfair congressional districts ended in failure. In a 1932 case, *Wood* v. *Brown,* involving redistricting in Mississippi, the Supreme Court ruled that although the 1929 Reapportionment Act had not specifically repealed the contiguity, compactness, and equal-population provisions of the 1911 act, its failure to mention these requirements specifically made them no longer applicable to congressional districts. In a 1946 suit, *Colegrove* v. *Green,* the Court considered a new approach to the problem: the plaintiff (a political science professor at Northwestern University) argued that the disparity in Illinois' congressional districts violated the Fourteenth Amendment provision forbidding states to deny persons the "equal protection of the laws." The Court, with Justice Frankfurter writing the majority opinion, refused to grant relief on the grounds that legislative apportionment is a "political" problem whose remedy lies not with the judiciary but with state legislatures and Congress.

By the 1960s, however, the composition of the Court had changed so that Frankfurter's nonactivist philosophy (that judges should be reluctant to substitute their constitutional judgment for that of legislative or executive officials) no longer prevailed. In a 1962 case, *Baker* v. *Carr,* the Court held that legislative reapportionment was not a "political" question, and, therefore, federal courts could hear such matters. Several landmark cases followed. In the 1964 decision in *Wesberry* v. *Sanders,* the Court invalidated unequal congressional districts in Georgia; citing the language in the Constitution providing that representatives be apportioned among the states according to population and that they be chosen by the people of the several states, the justices ruled that "as nearly as practicable, one man's vote in a congressional election is to be worth as much as another's." (The opinion was popularly condensed to "one man, one vote.") The same year, in *Reynolds* v. *Sims,* the Court held that the "equal protection of the laws" clause of the Fourteenth Amendment requires that state legislative districts also be substantially equal and that seats in both houses of a bicameral state legislature must be apportioned on the basis of population.

For a period thereafter it appeared that the Supreme Court would use the same approach to deal with the districting of both state legislatures and the House of Representatives. However, in the 1972 case of *White* v. *Weiser* the Court invalidated a Texas plan for congressional districts that provided for a maximum population disparity of only 4 percent between districts on the grounds that the plan did not meet the requirement of a good-faith effort to make the districts equal. By way of contrast, in *Mahan* v. *Howell,* decided that same year, the Court upheld a districting plan for the Virginia House of Delegates with a disparity of over 16 percent between districts under the reasoning that the state legislature was following a rational state policy, in this case of protecting political subdivisions (cities and counties) in order to provide representation for local governmental units. Thus the Court continues to seek precise mathematical equality among congressional districts at the same time that it remains satisfied with eliminating gross malapportionment for state legislative districts.

Political Repercussions and Effects of the Apportionment Decisions

Few decisions of the Supreme Court have had more immediate repercussions than those dealing with legislative apportionment. State legislatures throughout the country were forced to reapportion themselves, as well as draw new congressional districts. Hundreds of law suits have been filed challenging the validity of both old and new legislative districts. And Congress and the state legislatures have sought ways to avoid some of the effects of the reapportionment decisions. Most objectionable to state lawmakers has been the requirement that both houses of the state legislature be based on population. The late Senator Everett Dirksen of Illinois sought to initiate a constitutional amendment to allow one house to be based on some other criterion (such as geographical units), but it failed to pass the Senate. Subsequent attempts to initiate such an amendment through actions of the state legislatures have also been unsuccessful.

To date, the decisions have been generally successful in rectifying the disparities in population of both state-legislative and congressional districts. (As a result of redistricting following the 1970 census, 385 of the 435 congressional districts varied from their state's average district population by less than 1 percent.) But they have scarcely touched the other abuses of gerrymandering: drawing noncontiguous and noncompact districts with strange shapes to benefit particular groups. Thus it is possible for a state legislature to distribute residents equally among districts but still benefit the majority party or an incumbent legislator. A recent practice is to add suburban dwellers to an essentially rural constituency but to keep their number sufficiently small so that the rural residents still dominate the district. Candidates still have to contend with this situation in running for state legislatures and the House of Representatives.

Despite these efforts of legislators to preserve the status quo, the reapportionment decisions have nonetheless brought about changes in the character of both state-legislative and congressional districts. However, the fear of many persons that conservative Republican legislators from rural areas would be replaced by liberal Democratic legislators from large, central cities has generally been unfounded. What has rather happened is that fast-growing suburban areas, many of them populated by Republicans, have experienced the greatest increase in representation. Thus in many instances—particularly in the North, Midwest, and West—it is conservative, suburban Republicans (not liberal, big-city Democrats) that have replaced conservative rural Republicans both in state legislatures and in the House of Representatives.

The provisions of the electoral college and those that govern the election of representatives affect the kind of contests that are waged by candidates for the major offices in the American political system. The following sections analyze the dynamics of campaigns for those offices.

THE GENERAL NATURE OF POLITICAL CAMPAIGNS

A political campaign may be defined simply as the activities of a political candidate (and those working for him) that are designed to motivate other citizens to take the time and effort to vote, and to vote for *him*. Voters' minds are not, of course, blank pieces of paper on which campaigns activities are written. Rather, the political-socialization process described in chapter 5 has already left the average person with certain political opinions and ways of looking at the political world around him. The key to securing votes, then, is somehow to trigger a person's key political dispositions so that they result in decisions to vote for the candidate in question.

In chapter 5 we saw that people have political attitudes on a variety of matters. Some are quite general, determining whether a society will be governable at all—namely, the attitudes of persons toward their country, its constitutional system, and the right of public officials to make binding decisions that vitally affect their lives. Other opinions are more specific, relating to the particular persons who should be entrusted with carrying on the day-to-day activities of the government and the kinds of public policies that they should pursue. Included in this category are attitudes on political personalities, issues, and events. These, along with personal identifications with political parties and social, economic, or geographical divisions in the population, have most relevance for the key question facing the voter at election time: which of the alternative candidates should he choose?

During a campaign a candidate can try to affect the voter's perceptions of these matters. For example, he can project himself as having a *pleasing personality* with the kinds of traits that the average person admires in his leaders. In short, he can try to project an *image* to the public that is most attractive and believable.

If he is from the majority political party, a candidate will obviously emphasize his *party label*. If not, he may prefer to play down party affiliation and instead suggest that the voters should select the "best man." Or he may try to appeal to voters who are unhappy with their party's candidate by arguing that his opponent does not really represent that party anyway—that he, not his opponent, is the one who actually stands for the principles that their party has traditionally espoused over the years. Thus Richard Nixon could tell Southerners that he, not Hubert Humphrey, represented their views on states' rights.

Another possibility is for a candidate to associate himself with *major social, economic,* or *geographical groups.* Thus Jimmy Carter attempted to woo the support of farmers by emphasizing his work in the family peanut business. But even if a candidate is not a member of a particular group, he can indicate what he has done in his political career to further that group's interests. He can also solicit the endorsement of its leaders, as Carter did of the black community.

The candidate can also use his stand on *issues* as a means of attracting votes. He may decide to be quite specific about how to deal with an issue such as reducing the defense budget by a certain amount, or he may rather opt to make a general pronouncement on a subject like "law and order," hoping to trigger deep-seated fears of crime in the streets and to create the impression that he will somehow be able to handle the problem. Closely allied with this latter approach is the ploy of associating oneself and one's party with favorable *political events* and circumstances such as peace and prosperity, and the opposition with unfavorable ones, like war and depression.

By manipulating political objects and symbols and by playing on fears and hopes, a candidate seeks to tap basic political attitudes of the electorate in such a way that they will perceive him as the one who best represents them and their needs. But to do so the candidate must somehow *communicate* with the electorate and get his personality and views before it.

One way to communicate during a political campaign is to go before the people in a series of speeches and appearances *in person.* In state and local races a candidate can hope to reach a significant portion of the electorate in this fashion, but it is increasingly difficult to do so in contests for the House of Representatives and almost impossible in senatorial and presidential elections. Today's candidates must utilize the mass media—television, radio, and newspapers—to reach so large an audience.

Vital to all political campaigns are two final ingredients, *people* and *money*— people to communicate a candidate's message calling for votes, and money to pay for the campaign costs. Anyone who has too little of either is unlikely to do well in a modern political campaign, particularly for major national offices.

Thus a political campaign involves a complex combination of popular appeals, communicated by various means to voters through the utilization of people and money. As one student of political campaigns, David Leuthold, suggests, it is a process in which a candidate and those who assist him acquire a number of resources and use them so that they can be converted into votes. Because such resources are limited, difficult decisions must be made on the best means of gaining and utilizing them to achieve the maximum effect on voters.

Thus a candidate and his staff must wrestle with a series of key decisions. Should he emphasize his own qualifications and approach to public problems, or should he attack his opponent and his opponent's programs? Should he agree to a debate? Is it best to emphasize his party label, or will that antagonize independent voters? Should he discuss issues, and if so, which ones should he

Your typical peanut farmer.

single out for most attention? Which social and economic groups offer the best potential support for his candidacy, and how should he go about appealing to them? How much of the campaign budget should go to television, as compared to newspaper advertisements or radio broadcasts? Which are better—volunteers or paid political workers? Should campaign money be raised from a relatively few "fat cats" or from a large number of small donors?

Not only are such decisions difficult, but they must often be made when the candidate and his staff lack full information on which to base a judgment. At the time that Gerald Ford extended the challenge to Jimmy Carter to debate, the decision made a lot of sense. He was far behind in the polls and needed to do something to close that gap. Moreover, his training as a lawyer and long service as a member and later Minority Leader of the House of Representatives contributed to his debating skills; his experience as President also provided him with unique information and insights into national problems, particularly in the field of foreign and military affairs. On the other hand, Carter, trained as an engineer, was not known for his talents as speaker and debater, and his government experience was confined to one term as governor of a medium-sized state.

The first debate, in which Ford managed to best his hesitant and deferential opponent and—despite high unemployment and inflation—create the impression that he was a competent manager of the domestic economy, seemed to support the wisdom of his challenge to debate, particularly when Carter's lead in the polls thereafter continued to fall. However the second debate, dealing with foreign and military affairs (in which Ford was supposedly advantaged by his incumbency, as well by the peacemaking efforts and successful diplomatic ventures of Henry Kissinger in Asia, the Middle East, and Africa), resulted in a victory for the inexperienced Carter, and the President's embarrassment by his own unfortunate remark about Eastern Europe. Pollster George Gallup reported that the second debate stalled Ford's momentum and enabled his Democratic challenger to regain some of his earlier losses with the electorate. Carter himself said after the election that he felt that had it not been for the debates, he would have lost the election, since they had furnished the necessary reassurance that he had "some judgment about foreign affairs and defense."

Because it is difficult to foresee contingencies, and also because so much information must be gathered and so many activities coordinated, many political campaigns are not unlike some military battles where participants seem to go off aimlessly in all directions simultaneously. The overall management of campaigns demands leaders with superb administrative skills who can put together and utilize information on such diverse matters as voting patterns in past elections, public attitudes on issues, and the best format for a television presentation.

Traditionally, political campaigns in the United States have been devised by candidates, their personal advisers, and party leaders on the basis of intuitive judgments and experiences in successful contests of the past. Beginning in the 1930s in California, however, *public-relations firms* that had developed advertising programs for private businesses began to transfer their propaganda skills to persuading the public to vote for certain political candidates or propositions put to the voters in referendums. Both parties have used professional firms of this type since the 1952 presidential election, and subsequently more and more senators and representatives have sought their services. Some companies work for candidates of only one political party; others are "guns for hire," available on a first-come-first-serve basis.

These firms can provide a wide variety of services for a political candidate: they take public opinion polls, inquiring into voter attitudes on issues as well as their reactions to the candidate and his opponent; they research past voting patterns and political preferences of various social, economic, and geographical groups; they write speeches, plan press conferences, and oversee the use of mass media. Beyond that, firms will even plan and manage the overall campaign, budgeting funds and directing the use of personnel. Some have even entered into domains formerly reserved for the candidate and party leaders: raising funds and recruiting workers for the campaign.

Although all political campaigns face the basic problem of acquiring resources and converting them into votes, the particulars differ. Republicans, for example, typically have better access to money than do Democrats, who, on the other hand, have the edge in campaign workers, particularly from organized labor. Then, too, the type of appeal a candidate makes in his campaign, as well as his prospects for gathering resources, depends on whether he is an incumbent or a representative of the party out of power. Finally, the particular office sought significantly affects the entire process: a presidential campaign differs from a race for Congress.

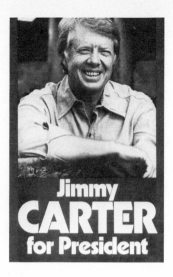

PRESIDENTIAL CAMPAIGNS

As the "world series" of politics, a presidential campaign entails far more time, effort, and money than any other political contest. To take one rough measure of its dominance, the Citizens Research Foundation (a private nonpartisan group that analyzes all aspects of campaign expenditures) estimated that in 1972, when the total cost of *all* political activities was $425 million, $138 million was spent on the presidential race alone—almost one-third of the total, to elect one man!

Manipulating Political Appeals

Candidate Image. **Because so much public attention is focused on the presidential contest, the personalities the aspirants project are especially important. Each party strives to create a composite image of the attractive attributes of its candidate. Yet the image must be believable. Thus the elderly Dwight Eisenhower was pictured as a benevolent "father," whereas the youthful John Kennedy was epitomized as a man of "vigor". (Robert Kennedy once remarked that the major contribution that his brother made to America was to make the people feel young again.)

Frequently presidential candidates take their opponent's image into account in shaping their own. In 1964 Lyndon Johnson pictured himself as the candidate of moderation, hoping thereby to point up the extremeness of some of Senator Goldwater's statements and views. Gerald Ford painted himself as a man of maturity and experience to counteract Carter's emphasis on being a "new face" and an "outsider" to the Washington scene. Besides shaping his own image to take account of his opponent's, a candidate can directly attack the opposition candidate to put him in a bad light with the voters. Accordingly,

I NEVER INTENTIONALLY TRY TO MISLEAD MY AUDIENCES. I KNOW I DON'T PREPARE MY ANSWERS IN ADVANCE. BUT AT THE SAME TIME, I DON'T SEE ANYTHING INHERENTLY WRONG IN TRYING TO SAY THINGS IN SUCH A WAY THAT I DON'T IRRITATE PEOPLE AS LONG AS I REMAIN CONSISTENT WITH MY BASIC POSITION. ER... WHAT WAS THE ORIGINAL QUESTION?

DO YOU WANT THICK OR THIN CRUST?

"Courtesy Copley News Service"

Gerald Ford described Jimmy Carter thus: "He wavers, he wanders, he wiggles, he waffles" and charged that his opponent had a strange way of changing his accent: "In California he tried to sound like Cesar Chavez; in Chicago, like Mayor Daley; in New York, like Ralph Nader; in Washington, like George Meany; then he comes to the farm belt and he becomes a little old peanut farmer." After Ford claimed in the second debate that Eastern Europe was not under Soviet domination, Carter countered that the President must have been "brainwashed" when he went to Poland, thus comparing Ford with George Romney, the former Michigan governor whose nomination campaign collapsed in 1968 after he said he had been "brainwashed" by the military in the course of a trip to Vietnam. The Georgian also said that during the second debate Ford had "showed very vividly the absence of good judgment, good sense, and knowledge" expected of a President.

Not all candidates, however, think it is politically wise to attack an opponent. Franklin Roosevelt, for example, thought that doing so only served to give him free publicity. Moreover, there is always the chance that voters will resent the tactics or that they may open the way to counterattacks by the opposition. A classic case occurred in the presidential campaign of 1884. Seeking to take advantage of the accusation that the Democratic candidate, Grover Cleveland, had fathered a child out of wedlock (an accusation Cleveland himself never denied), Republicans composed the campaign ditty, "Ma! Ma! Where's my Pa? Gone to the White House, Ha! Ha! Ha!" The Democrats responded with a slogan that sought to remind voters of the charges of political dishonesty directed against the Republican candidate, James G. Blaine: "James G. Blaine, the continental liar from the state of Maine." Thus the voters that year were presented with a dilemma: should they favor Cleveland, whose private life was morally questionable but whose honesty in public life had never been challenged, or should they vote for Blaine, whose family relationships were idyllic but whose conduct in public office made him seem risky? One of Cleveland's supporters offered a solution: "We should elect Mr. Cleveland to the public office which he is so admirably qualified to fill, and remand Mr. Blaine to the private life which he is so eminently fitted to adorn."

Generally speaking, however, candidates spend more time trying to project a favorable image of themselves than to cast an unfavorable light on their opponents. Thus in 1968 Nixon focused his attention on refurbishing his own former portrait as a humorless and overly aggressive political infighter. In touching up the picture he strove to present a "new Nixon" who could laugh at himself (referring to his 1960 loss to Kennedy and his performance in the presidential debates that year, he acknowledged being "an electoral college 'drop-out' who had flunked debating") and who had somehow matured and become more humane over the intervening eight years since he last ran for the presidency.

Party. Candidates deal with their party label in different ways. Given the Democrats' status as majority party since the days of Franklin Delano Roosevelt, it is not surprising that their candidates generally play up party affiliation and that their opponents do not. Thus John Kennedy stressed during the 1960 contest that he stood "where Woodrow Wilson stood, and Franklin Roosevelt stood, and Harry Truman stood." Nixon, in contrast, urged voters to ignore party labels and to vote for the "best man," the man with experience in foreign

Grover Cleveland.

affairs who had stood up to Khrushchev and bested him in the kitchen debate in Moscow.

In 1976, Jimmy Carter opened his campaign in Warm Springs, Georgia, to associate himself with Franklin Roosevelt; Gerald Ford invoked no past Republican Presidents and instead tied his candidacy to that of a former Democratic Chief Executive, Harry Truman, who as an underdog incumbent struggled successfully for the same goal as Ford's: election to the presidential office in his own right, not merely by succession.

Whether a candidate represents the majority or the minority party, prominent political figures in it must support his campaign. In 1964 Goldwater's candidacy suffered (although it is unlikely that he could have won the presidency in any event) from the fact that some leading Republicans dissociated themselves from their party's presidential nominee and conducted independent campaigns of their own. Senator Eugene McCarthy's lukewarm and belated endorsement of Hubert Humphrey in the last stages of the 1968 campaign did little to help the latter avert his narrow defeat that year. And in 1972 large numbers of Democratic candidates for Congress and state offices deliberately dissociated themselves from the McGovern-Shriver ticket.

Social Groups. Presidential candidates also attempt to rally members of important social groups to their cause. Typically a campaign organization itself has separate divisions designed to appeal to women, youth, older citizens, nationality groups, business, labor, and the like. Candidates and their staff must decide which groups to appeal to in particular, taking into account the size of the group as well as its geographical concentration, the likelihood that its members will be receptive to the candidate, and the extent to which appeals to certain groups will alienate others.

The classic case of the latter dilemma occurred in Nixon's 1960 campaign. Initially, he hoped to win a number of Negro votes (Ike had done well with blacks in 1952 and even better in 1956), for he capitulated to New York Governor Nelson Rockefeller's demands for more liberal platform provisions on race relations. Early in the general election campaign, however, he visited Atlanta, where he received what he termed "the most impressive demonstration he had seen in his fourteen years of campaigning." After that, Nixon vacillated between trying to woo the black vote and appealing to white Southerners. When Martin Luther King Jr. was jailed in Atlanta for refusing to leave a restaurant table, Nixon took no action; in contrast, Kennedy made a quick decision to take a campaign aide's advice to telephone Mrs. King and express his concern. King's father, who before the incident had been a Nixon supporter, switched to Kennedy, a move many observers credit with giving Kennedy enough black votes in close states like Illinois to win the election. Eight years later Nixon pursued a different tactic: he made a concerted effort to appeal to white Southerners and made no bow at all in the direction of the Negro community. In contrast, Hubert Humphrey appealed to blacks and made no overtures to white Southerners.

Issues and Political Events. Although presidential candidates talk a lot about discussing the issues, as a matter of fact they seldom do so in any detail. (In 1968 the *New York Post* remarked testily, "Mr. Nixon has published a collection of positions he has taken on 167 issues. It seems a pity he could not have made it a round 170 by adding Vietnam, the cities, and civil rights.") The candidates usually do focus on major problems in American society, but only in very general terms. Typically, a catchy slogan is used by the out-party to link the one in power with unfortunate political events; hence the "Korea, corruption, and communism" brand was stamped on the Democrats by Republicans in 1952. The party in power responds in kind, as when the Democrats defended their record with the plea to voters, "You never had it so good." In 1976 the situation was reversed: Democrats talked about Watergate, inflation and unemployment, and President Ford's pardon of Richard Nixon,* whereas President Ford claimed that his administration had cut inflation in half, brought peace ("Not a single American is fighting or dying") to the nation, and restored faith, confidence, and trust in the presidency.

It is this kind of general attack and defense that characterizes most presidential campaigns. The party out of power has the advantage of associating all the ills of American life with the administration; the latter is in the position of claiming that all the nation's blessings have resulted from its leadership. The candidate who is in the most difficult situation is the nonincumbent nominee of the party in power; recent examples are Nixon in 1960 and Humphrey in 1968. Both served as Vice-Presidents in administrations whose policies they did not fully endorse. Nixon, for instance, did not believe Eisenhower was doing enough in space exploration and national defense; Humphrey opposed the bombing of North Vietnam when it was first initiated in 1965. Yet each hesitated to criticize an administration in which he had served. Humphrey's inability to disassociate himself from the Johnson administration's approach to Vietnam is considered to be one of the major reasons for his defeat in 1968.

Not only are the issues framed in general terms in presidential campaigns, but also few concrete suggestions are made for handling them. Thus Kennedy urged in 1960 that he be given the chance to "get the nation moving again," but he was very vague about what, specifically, he would do to move the nation forward. Nixon was even more nebulous in 1968: he refused to spell out his plans for dealing with the major issue in American political life, Vietnam, on the excuse that if he did so, he might jeopardize the Paris peace talks that were being held to try to settle the problem.

A major exception to the above pattern was the McGovern campaign. Not only did it focus more on issues than did former ones, but the candidate also made more specific suggestions for dealing with such issues. Thus McGovern proposed that the defense budget be cut 30 percent, and early in his campaign advocated that all persons (regardless of need) be given a $1000 grant by the government.

In manipulating a variety of political appeals, candidates typically attempt to develop a *general theme* that will incorporate a wide variety of matters and leave the voters with some overall impression of the campaign. Sometimes the

---

* Carter himself refused to follow the recommendation of his staff to attack Ford openly on the pardon issue, but the Democratic vice-presidential candidate, Walter Mondale, took the offensive in his place.

theme focuses on the candidate himself, as did Humphrey's slogan, "He's a man you can trust." Or it may be essentially an appeal to a wide group, like Nixon's "Forgotten Americans" who did not break the law but did pay their taxes, go to work, school, and church, and love their country. At other times, the theme is directed at issues and political events ("Korea, corruption, and communism" or "peace and prosperity") or takes the form of Kennedy's general call for action, "We've got to get the nation moving again," McGovern's plea, "Come home, America," or Carter's promise to make the government as "truthful, capable and filled with love as the American people." Once the theme is established, a candidate tries by constant repetition to get the electorate to respond emotionally to it. His success in doing so, however, depends on another important aspect of presidential campaigns: the means by which political appeals are communicated to the American voter.

Communicating With The Public

No other aspect of political campaigns has undergone more change than the means of communicating political appeals to the voters. First radio in the 1920s and then, even more importantly, television in the 1950s have revolutionized campaign techniques and rewarded candidates who have been able to master their use. Franklin Roosevelt's radio skills did much to counteract the newspaper support given his Republican opponents; John Kennedy's adept use of television, particularly in the television debates, was a key factor in his 1960 victory over Richard Nixon. Nixon's triumph in 1968, in turn, is attributed at least in part to his ability to use the medium more effectively than he had eight years before.

In fact, some campaign observers consider Nixon's use of television in the 1968 campaign as the most successful exploitation of the medium to date. Calculating that long speeches on TV fail to sustain the interest of the voters, his advisers convinced him to utilize two other approaches: short, sixty-second spot announcements during popular programs like Rowan and Martin's "Laugh-in" and appearances before panels of citizens who asked questions to which Nixon could seem to reply in a spontaneous fashion. To guard against possible embarrassing questions, both the makeup of the panels and the questions themselves were carefully screened by his advisors. To make the show even more interesting, former football coach and television personality Bud Wilkinson intercepted the questions and lateraled them on to the candidate.

The use of television for political communication also underwent significant changes in 1972. While spot commercials continued to be used (one, for example, symbolized McGovern's proposed cuts in defense spending by a hand sweeping away toy soldiers and miniature ships and planes), there was a trend toward longer programs, as exemplified by a series of addresses by McGovern on Vietnam, the issue of corruption, and the like. Media consultants also determined that voters were more influenced by TV news than by political advertising; as a result, there was an increasing use of such semidocumentary formats as a candidate discussing issues with the "man in the street." Thus McGovern was filmed interacting with workers and small businessmen, and Nixon's trips to China and the Soviet Union were dramatized for television viewers.

The televising of the three presidential debates (the first since the 1960 confrontation between Kennedy and Nixon) plus the one between the vice-presidential candidates (the first ever held) was the major development in political communication in the 1976 campaign. In fact, the debates became by far the most important feature of the entire Ford-Carter contest. Barry Jagoda, Carter's television adviser, saw the debates as a "surrogate campaign," and Sander Vanocur, television columnist for the *Washington Post,* viewed the campaign as "intermissions between these moments when Ford and Carter perform their three acts." Sponsored and paid for by the League of Women Voters and merely covered as "news events" by the three networks (this ploy, permitted by the Federal Communications Commission, was used to get around the provisions of the Communications Act of 1934 that require networks to provide "equal time" to *all* candidates*), the debates succeeded not only in sharpening the contest between Ford and Carter, but also in cutting minor candidates like Eugene McCarthy out of the picture. McCarthy, who unsuccessfully carried his fight to be included in the debates to the Supreme Court, also complained that the television network newscasts ignored his rallies, speeches, and news conferences: "It's like walking through the snow. As soon as you pass, your tracks are covered over."

Both candidates also purchased their own time on television, with Ford using the medium somewhat more imaginatively than Carter. The President held an informal television interview with sportscaster and former baseball player Joe Garagiola, who tossed him some "gopher ball" questions: "How many foreign leaders have you met with, Mr. President?" to which Ford modestly replied, "One hundred and twenty-four, Joe." In the last stages of the campaign, the Ford forces also broadcast short television interviews with voters in Georgia, who described Carter as "wishy-washy." Carter's use of television concentrated on short commercials in which he looked directly into the camera and talked

---

* In 1960 the Congress temporarily suspended the provisions of the Act in order to allow the Nixon-Kennedy debates to be held. The legal fiction that the 1976 debates were really "news events" was exposed by the fact that the first one was interrupted for twenty-eight minutes until an audio failure could be repaired.

about various issues, aimed at counteracting Ford's version of him and picturing him as a strong, positive leader with specific programs.

Television possesses several advantages over the other mass media. First, it requires less effort to watch the screen than to read a newspaper. Second, it has now become the major source of political information for most Americans. And third, people are more inclined to believe what they see on television than what they read in the newspapers or hear on the radio. The illusion of being there on the spot (few are aware of the possibilities for staging a scene or event) helps create the feeling of political reality.

Radio and newspapers continue to be used, however. Nixon's 1968 campaign included five-minute excerpts on radio from his acceptance speech before the Republican convention. In 1972 Nixon made many more speeches on radio than he did on television, possibly because his staff felt that he came over better on the former medium. In 1976 Ford held a series of early-morning five-minute chats with the nation's commuters over hundreds of radio stations. Advertisements in newspapers offer the potential for visual effects: in 1960 the Democrats used pictures of their handsome candidate and his attractive wife in 60 percent of their ads; in 1976, the Republicans printed full-page ads comparing a cover of *Newsweek* magazine, featuring President Ford, with the cover of the issue of *Playboy* magazine touting its controversial interview with Carter.

Thus the mass media offer the candidate a wider audience than could be reached in the past. They also enable him to make direct contact with the public, and hence to bypass to some degree groups formerly relied on. Among such groups are political party workers who have traditionally carried the campaign to the voter. Yet as the following section indicates, it would be premature to write off those workers as a relic of the political past.

People: Campaign Workers

Interpersonal contacts remain an important instrument in shaping people's political decisions. As was previously explained, there is frequently a two-step or multistep flow in the transmittal of political information, so that the views expressed in the mass media are filtered through opinion leaders before they reach the average voter. Beyond that, personal contacts are particularly vital in getting many persons to make the most basic political decision: whether to vote at all. Sometimes the only thing that will overcome the apathy of a citizen is the dogged determination of someone who sees to it that he gets himself registered to vote and then takes him to the polls to do so.

That service has traditionally been provided by political party workers, particularly those who labor for party machines.* As we suggested in chapter 7, machines operated by a rule of quid pro quo: in return for his vote, a person was often given a job, furnished with the necessities of life, educated politically, and given social outlets for his energies. Particularly vulnerable were immigrants who desperately needed assistance in becoming assimilated into the American way of life. Indeed, they provided the major clientele for the oldstyle party worker.

---

* The word *machine* was used because of the efficiency with which party organizations "delivered" automatic votes.

The political machine, however, has been on the decline in the United States for the last thirty or forty years. A number of factors have contributed to its demise: the passage of restrictive laws cutting off the flow of immigrants; the provision of welfare and other regular governmental programs that have filled the needs formerly met through the informal largesse of the political boss; the enactment of legislation eliminating political appointments in many public-service jobs and placing them under the civil service; the general prosperity of the country, which has made low-paying public jobs less attractive than those available through the private sector of the economy; and the increased educational level of the populace, which has made more and more citizens self-reliant and independent in political matters.

The traditional political machine still exists in some cities of the nation (the late Richard Daley's Chicago is the prime example), but it is no longer the powerful force it once was in American politics. Moreover, even where it exists, it tends to have more effect in state and local races than in national elections. Even so, many observers attribute Hubert Humphrey's defeat in Illinois in 1968 to the failure or unwillingness of Mayor Daley to rally the party faithful to his cause.*

Aside from the classic political boss, party organizations in general are not nearly so potent as they are typically pictured to be. The standard organization chart shows a military-type chain of command proceeding from the precinct workers (the privates) up through ward leaders and county and state officers to, finally, the national chairman of the party (the general). All are presumably working round the clock on party affairs. The realities of the situation are that many party posts are not even filled (particularly in the minority party), and those who hold positions seldom stir themselves to do the hard and time-consuming chores that are crucial in getting out the vote: polling the precinct to see who is registered and who is not; discovering the party preferences of the people living there; and figuring out what can be done to get the "right" people to the polls on election day.

In the absence of potent party organizations, modern presidential candidates have turned to other means to get out the vote. In recent years organized labor has helped to carry out that vital function, chiefly to the benefit of the Democrats. In 1968 the AFL-CIO, working through its Committee on Political Education,† claimed to have registered 4.6 million voters, printed and distributed over 100 million pamphlets, operated telephone banks in 638 localities, sent out over 70,000 house-to-house canvassers, and provided almost 100,000 volunteers on election day to get people to the polls. Of course, this effort was extended on Hubert Humphrey's behalf and is credited with helping eventually to swing into line a number of workers who initially planned to vote for George Wallace.

---

* Before the Democratic convention, Humphrey wrote to Mayor Daley requesting that the protesters be given permits to demonstrate and halls in which to gather, but Daley did not even bother to reply.

† Like corporations, labor unions are forbidden by federal law to contribute money to either the nomination or the election of the President, Vice-President, or a member of Congress. The Committee on Political Education (COPE) was created as a separate organization to which union members can contribute voluntarily (union dues may not be used) for political activities.

By way of contrast, because of the antipathy of George Meany and other AFL-CIO leaders towards George McGovern, the organization remained neutral in the 1972 presidential race and concentrated its efforts on helping elect Democratic congressmen and state and local officials. In 1976 the AFL-CIO returned to its traditional policy of supporting Democratic presidential candidates and played a major role in getting its members and their families registered and to the polls on election day to vote for Jimmy Carter.

Another form of political organization that has become increasingly prominent in recent years is the *ad hoc committee* for a particular presidential ticket. Typically designated along the lines of "Citizens for Johnson-Humphrey" (sometimes the presidential candidate's name alone is used, or none at all, as with the Committee to Reelect the President, in 1972), they are designed to attract the support of persons who may not be willing to work with the traditional party organizations. They may appeal, for example, to people who consider political parties outdated or meaningless but who favor a particular candidate because of his personal magnetism or his stand on issues. They also can be valuable in winning the support of people who generally support the opposition party or are political independents. Also, in many instances, even fairly potent state and local organizations will not expend efforts for a presidential candidate either because they regard him as a loser who will hurt the party ticket (many Republicans took this attitude toward Goldwater in 1964, as did some Democratic leaders toward Humphrey in 1968 and toward McGovern in 1972) or because they feel that who it is that gains the presidency is not nearly so important for their interests as who it is that wins the county sheriff's race. (Sheriffs not only control some patronage positions—deputies and jail custodians—but also determine the extent to which laws against gambling, prostitution, and the like are enforced.)

The well-run presidential campaign should be able somehow to draw on all these sources of campaign workers. Some, however, tend to regard each other with mutual disdain. The "Citizens for" types often think of regular party workers as political hacks who are in politics only for their own materialistic interests and who will support any party candidate, no matter what his personality, character, or stand on issues may be. The party worker, in turn, often regards the citizens' group workers as "station wagon" types who come out of the political woodwork every four years to campaign for a particular candidate but who show no concern for the long-range prospects of the party and no loyalty to it as an institution. Squabbles among local, state and national party organizations are also common since each feels that election races at its particular level are most important.

Money: Campaign Finance

One of the major developments in American politics in recent years has been the rapid increase in the costs of conducting political campaigns. As Figure 9.1 reveals, moneys spent in presidential years tripled in the twenty-year period from 1952 to 1972. When Dwight Eisenhower was first elected, campaign costs for offices at all levels of the American political system totaled $140 million; when Richard Nixon was reelected to the presidency, comparable costs stood at $425 million. As Figure 9.1 also shows, costs rose faster than either the size of the vote cast or the general increase in the cost of living in the United States

Figure 9.1
Total political spending in
presidential election years
and indexes of total spending,
total votes cast for president,
and the Consumer Price
Index, 1952–1972.
Source: Herbert E. Alexander,
Financing the 1972 Election
(Lexington, Mass.: Lexington
Books, D.C. Heath, 1976), pp.
77–78; derived in part from
Alexander Heard, *The Costs
of Democracy* (Chapel Hill,
N.C.: The University of North
Carolina Press, 1960),
pp. 7–8, as cited in Herbert
Alexander, *Financing Politics*
(Washington, D.C.:
Congressional Quarterly
Press, 1976), p. 17.

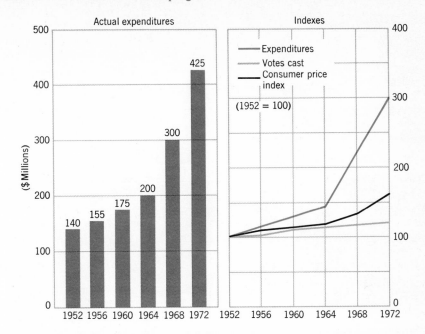

over the twenty-year period, with the increase in campaign costs being particularly pronounced after the 1964 elections.

A number of factors have contributed to this rapid increase in campaign costs. The major one has been the growth in the use of mass media, particularly television and radio. Figures of the Federal Communications Commission show that some $60 million was expended on these two media in 1972, one out of every seven dollars of the total ($425 million) spent on politics at all levels that year. The costs of television and radio have been more prominent in presidential campaigns: in 1968, the two major-party candidates together expended $19 million of the $37 million spent in the general election that year on the two media. Added to the above figure, which includes only network and station charges, are production and promotion costs, which sometimes ran as high as 50 percent of the media charges. Also contributing to the burgeoning of campaign moneys are the fees paid to political consultants for specialized services such as conducting polls, raising funds, preparing direct-mail appeals, and the like. Thus the increasing professionalization of American political campaigns has brought with it spiraling costs.

This great increase of campaign costs has raised the possibility of abuses in the financing of elections. One such issue is that of the *large contributor*: figures compiled by Herbert Alexander of the Citizens' Research Foundation indicate that in 1968, W. Clement Stone, chairman of the Combined Insurance Company of America, gave $2.8 million for the nomination and election of Richard Nixon; four years later Stewart R. Mott, heir to a General Motors' fortune, donated over $800,000 to liberal Democratic candidates, $400,000 to George McGovern alone. In 1972, 13 business and professional groups (including the *American Bar Association*, the *American Medical Association*, and the *American Petroleum Institute*) contributed $3.3 million to candidates, over 90 percent of it to Republicans; that same year organized labor made political donations of

Ronald Reagan at a Republican fund raising dinner in Long Island.

$6.2 million, primarily to Democratic candidates. Do such large contributors receive special consideration from office-holders for their generosity?

Another potential abuse of expensive political campaigns is the possibility that *they favor some candidates over others.* For example, over the years Republicans have generally been advantaged in financial resources over Democrats. Alexander's figures show that in 1964, 1968, and 1972, the advantage was about 2 to 1. For example, in 1972 Nixon spent $61 million compared to $30

President Carter greets a guest at a $1,000-a-plate dinner to help pay off the 1976 campaign debt.

million by McGovern in the general election. The presence of candidates with personal and family wealth like Nelson Rockefeller and the Kennedy brothers in presidential politics, and John Heinz III and Howard Metzenbaum in senatorial races, has also raised the possibility that such people buy their way into office at the expense of perhaps more able opponents. High campaign costs may also mean that some persons may be deterred from seeking public office at all.

Over the years, students of campaign finances have proposed a variety of means to deal with these potential abuses. One is *public disclosure*—providing the public with knowledge of who is giving how much to whom, so that people can be alerted to possible monetary influences on public officials. A second is *contribution restrictions*—that is, limiting the amount of money an individual or group can donate, or in some cases preventing certain persons or groups (such as residents of foreign countries) from making any contributions at all. A third is *expenditure limits,* to meet the problem created by a candidate's having far more funds to spend than his opponent. A fourth is *government subsidies*—that is, giving money to political candidates either to supplement what they receive from private sources or to replace private moneys altogether.

Despite these possibilities, effective federal regulation of campaign finance was virtually nonexistent until the 1970s. In 1907 the federal government did pass legislation forbidding corporations to contribute money to federal elections, but the law was easily circumvented by paying executives extra compensation and having them and members of their families make contributions of the bonuses in their own names. And when labor unions were also forbidden by the Taft-Hartley Act (1947) from making such contributions, they formed "political-action committees" to solicit voluntary donations from members and to spend the funds in the committee's name. The Federal Corrupt Practices Act of 1925, which required disclosure of contributions in federal elections, did not cover the selection of the President and Vice-President at all and applied only to congressional general elections, not to nomination campaigns. Finally, the Hatch Act of 1940, which limited individual contributions to a federal candidate or political committee to $5000, was not effective because numerous committees were formed for a single candidate, with each committee being entitled to accept a $5000 contribution.

Then, after decades of neglect, a wave of election reform swept the country in the 1970s. In rapid succession, Congress passed two pieces of legislation in 1971 and then amended that legislation in 1974, all affecting the financing of political campaigns. In addition, in January 1976, the United States Supreme Court handed down a decision invalidating major portions of the campaign finance legislation; later that year, Congress responded by enacting still further provisions regulating the use of moneys in federal elections. As we are about to see, these legislative and judicial activities have had a major effect on recent presidential and congressional elections. (Their effect on the latter will be treated separately in the next section of this chapter, which deals with congressional campaigns.)

The 1971 legislation utilized all the major means outlined above for dealing with campaign finance abuses. The Federal Election Campaign Act required candidates and committees to file reports with appropriate officials (the Clerk of the House for congressional races, the Secretary of the Senate for Senate contests, and the Comptroller General for presidential elections) *disclosing* detailed information on the money they raised and spent, including the names of all persons who contributed more than $100 and the nature of all expenditures of that same amount or more. The legislation also placed *restrictions* on the amount candidates and their families could contribute to their own campaigns ($50,000 for President or Vice-President, $35,000 for senator, and $25,000 for representative). It also set *limitations* on the amount candidates could spend on advertising in the media (10¢ per eligible voter or $50,000, whichever is greater—only 60 percent of which could go to television and radio time). The Revenue Act of 1971 encouraged small contributions by permitting individuals to take tax credits of up to $17.50 or deductions up to $50 for political contributions. It also provided for the establishment of future *government subsidies* of major presidential candidates (those receiving 25 percent or more of the previous election vote) in the amount of 15¢ for each U.S. resident over 18 years of age, the subsidy to be funded by taxpayers who on their federal tax form indicate their willingness to have $1 of their tax payment set aside for that purpose.

However, the 1971 legislation had a limited effect on the 1972 presidential campaign. The public subsidy provisions of the Revenue Act were not yet applicable, and the Campaign Act did not take effect until April 7, 1972, which resulted in a mad scramble to collect funds prior to that date. It is estimated that the Committee to Reelect the President (Nixon) raised as much as $20 million prior to that date. Both presidential candidates spent well under the $8.5 million limit in radio and television because more emphasis was placed in 1972 on direct mail, telephone, and door-to-door contact with voters. The one feature of the 1971 legislation that may have been effective was the tax credits and deductions that encouraged small donations from a broad variety of citizens: estimates indicate that 500,000 persons contributed more $13 million to the Nixon campaign, while 530,000 donated $15 million to McGovern.

One of the ironies of the 1972 presidential campaign—the first one conducted in the new era of election reform—was that it ranks as one of the most scandalous contests in American history. The Committee to Reelect the President raised large cash contributions from persons who did not want their identity known (many were traditional Democrats who did not like McGovern) and then sought to conceal their source in a variety of ways, including transmitting funds through banks in Mexico. Several executives of major corporations pleaded guilty to making illegal contributions to the presidential race, suggesting that the money was in effect extorted from them under pain of losing certain financial advantages that they enjoyed from the federal government if they refused to contribute. Allegations were also made that representatives of the dairy industry made large donations to the Nixon campaign in return for an increase in government support of milk prices. Finally, disclosures showed that moneys collected were used to finance "dirty tricks" against leading Democratic candidates, such as Senator Edmund Muskie in the nomination campaign, and to provide funds for persons involved in the Watergate burglary.

Reacting to the 1972 campaign abuses in October 1974 after President Nixon had resigned, the Congress passed, and President Ford reluctantly signed into law, legislation amending the 1971 Federal Election Campaign Act. The previous restrictions on contributions by candidates themselves and their families were retained and new ones added: a limit of $1000 for individuals and $5000 for committees for each primary or general election. In addition, a $1000 limit was placed on independent expenditures made on behalf of a candidate, while cash contributions of over $100 and those from foreign sources were barred altogether.* Previous limitations on media spending were repealed, replaced by overall expenditure limits of $10 million per candidate on presidential primary spending, $20 million on the general election. Particularly significant was the provision of partial public funding for presidential primaries (as we saw in chapter 8, matching funds up to $5.5 million were granted to any candidate successful in raising a total of $5000 in each of 20 states in individual amounts of $250 or less) along with full public funding of the costs of the general election. Finally, the 1974 legislation provided for full disclosure of campaign contributions and expenditures (including those by persons making independent expenditures on behalf of a candidate) and also created a full-time bipartisan Federal Election Commission composed of six members (two each appointed by the President, Speaker of the House, and President Pro Tempore of the Senate) to administer the federal election laws and public finance program.

The battle over campaign finance, however, soon shifted to the courts. On January 1, 1975, a number of disparate individuals and groups including, among others, conservative New York Senator James Buckley, former Minnesota Senator Eugene McCarthy (a liberal), the Conservative Party of the State of New York, and the New York Civil Liberties Union filed a case in the federal courts challenging the constitutionality of the campaign finance legislation. The case was eventually appealed to the Supreme Court, and on January 30, 1976, that tribunal handed down a historic decision in *Buckley* v. *Valeo*. Faced with balancing the two rights of (1) free speech involved in the use of money to communicate political appeals and (2) the rights of Congress to protect the integrity of federal elections, the Court declared certain provisions of the legislation unconstitutional while upholding others. The Court concluded that limitations on the amount of expenditures by candidates themselves and their families, and by individuals making independent expenditures on behalf of a candidate, together with overall limits on campaign expenditures, constituted direct and substantial restraints on political speech, and hence were unconstitutional. (However, the Court qualified its ruling on these matters by holding that while independent spending on behalf of candidates could not be limited, it was illegal to coordinate such spending with that of the candidate or his campaign organization, and that if a candidate accepted public financing—which the Court sustained—then he would have to accept the limitations on overall expenditures as a condition of the grant.)

On the other hand, the Court sustained the restrictions on the amount of contributions by individuals and political committees on the grounds that they constituted only a marginal restriction on the contributor's ability to engage in political communication. The justices also upheld the disclosure provisions of the campaign finance law as well as the concept of a bipartisan commission to administer it. However, the Court ruled that as long as the commission was within the executive branch of government, the separation of powers principle required that all its members be appointed by the President. The court granted the Congress thirty days to reconstitute the commission in that way.

---

* Comparable limitations were also placed on congressional campaigns; these are discussed in the next section.

This latter ruling forced the Congress to act again on campaign finance. The legislation, however, got bogged down in a new controversy—the role that corporations, labor unions, and membership organizations (such as trade associations) should be able to play in political campaigns—and failed to meet the thirty-day deadline imposed by the Supreme Court for reconstituting the Federal Election Commission. The Court extended the period for another twenty days, but the Congress missed that deadline also, and as a result, the Commission lost its authority to provide matching funds after March 22, 1976. It did not regain that authority until two months later in late May, when the legislation was eventually passed and President Ford chose the six new members of the Commission. In the meantime, however, Congress resolved the controversy by establishing a $5000 limitation on contributions by political action committees of corporations, labor unions, and membership organizations to a candidate in a single campaign, and also by providing that expenditures made by such groups in excess of $2000 per election which involve communications advocating the election or defeat of a clearly identified candidate must be reported to the Federal Election Commission. In addition, the 1976 legislation required individuals and political committees making an independent political expenditure of more than $100 for the defeat or election of a candidate to report the expenditure and to state that it was not made in collusion with a candidate.

Both campaign finance legislation and the *Buckley* v. *Valeo* decision had some effect on the 1976 presidential nomination race. As we saw in chapter 8, thirteen Democratic candidates plus President Ford and Ronald Reagan were able to qualify for federal matching funds, which probably enabled a number of them to remain in the race longer than would have been the case if they had had to depend upon private donations alone.* The two-month delay between March and May in the availability of federal matching funds did not seem to have been too harmful to the leading candidates in either party: President Ford's and Jimmy Carter's finances were in fairly good shape at the time of the cut-off in funds, and Ronald Reagan was able to borrow money until the federal funds to which he was entitled became available again.

The recent legislation and judicial actions on campaign finance had a much greater effect on the 1976 general election campaign for the presidency. Both Ford and Carter decided to accept the public funds ($21.8 million each) and were therefore restricted to that figure (plus another $3.2 million that each national committee could spend on behalf of its presidential candidate) for the entire campaign. This meant that the Republicans had to forego their traditional advantage in campaign funds; moreover, both sides had to conduct much more restricted campaigns than they did in 1972 when the Republicans spent $61 million and the Democrats $30 million. Both campaigns devoted about half their total moneys to television and other media advertising, which meant that they had a limited amount of funds available for organizing the campaign at the grass-roots level. Also largely missing were buttons, bumper stickers, and yard signs, which characterized former campaigns, as well as the fund-raising activities of former elections. Campaign organizations were even forced to turn

---

* One of the 1976 amendments, however, provides that in the future such funds will be cut off to a candidate who wins less than 10 percent of the vote in two consecutive presidential primaries in which he runs.

down "in-kind" (as contrasted to cash) donations such as hot-air balloons, sound trucks, and Coke machines for fear that they would violate legal restrictions against coordinating outside activities with those of the candidate's own organization. As a result, there was less spontaneity in the 1976 presidential campaign, a situation some observers felt affected voter turnout at the polls.

CONGRESSIONAL CAMPAIGNS

We have less reliable data on congressional than on presidential campaigns. Nonetheless, from the limited information available we can detect certain basic similarities and differences between the two types of contests.

The general campaign process itself shows similarity. The congressional candidate makes the same basic political appeals involving his personal image, his party label, pleas for group support, general positions on issues, and the development of a campaign theme. He also seeks the best means to communicate his appeals and the best use of money and manpower to do so. To that end, he acquires and allocates scarce political resources for conversion into votes.

There are, however, important differences. Perhaps most basic is the great advantage an incumbent enjoys over a challenger. First of all, he is likely to be running in a one-party district, whereas a candidate for the presidency has to compete for a more diverse nationwide constituency. (As we saw in chapter 7, the race for senators is competitive in only one-half of the states; in congressional seats, the figure is even less—about one-sixth). Second, even if the general party competition in a state or congressional district is close, advantages accrue to the incumbent simply because as a senator or House member he has contacts with many constituents and frequently does favors even for those who normally identify with the opposite party. Due to gratitude for such services, plus a belief that an incumbent may be unbeatable anyway, social and economic groups that generally support the other party often yield to his appeal.

As political scientist David Mayhew suggests, an incumbent senator or congressman can use his office to make various kinds of appeals to his constituents. One type of activity is *"advertising"*—getting his name before the electorate to create a favorable image of himself through making frequent visits to his constituency, addressing high-school commencements, and sending out infant-care booklets. A second activity is *"credit-claiming"*—creating the impression that he is responsible for the building of a new dam in his district or the awarding of a grant to a local government or university; he can also emphasize "casework" for individual constituents—seeing that older persons get their social security benefits, students the information needed to write term papers. The congressman can also engage in *"position-taking"*—making public statements or taking action such as cosponsoring legislation that will appeal to particular constituents. (In 1973 seventy-six senators supported a provision to block trade benefits to the Soviet Union until it allowed Jews to emigrate without paying high fees to leave the country.) As Mayhew suggests, the emphasis that congressmen give to their various activities varies: senators participate more in position-taking than do House members, who tend to favor credit-claiming.

As we shall see in Chapter 11, incumbent legislators enjoy a variety of privileges that enable them to carry on the above activities. Included are travel allowances for frequent trips home, the franking privilege that permits them to distribute a broad variety of literature to their constituents without mailing charges*, the opportunity to appear on local television and radio programs, and money to hire staff members to handle casework in their states or districts.

The incumbent also enjoys another advantage over his challenger: access to campaign workers. Unlike the presidential candidate, someone running for Congress has no pool of regular party workers to which he can automatically turn. Since many states do not have any party organization for congressional districts, individual candidates must build their own following. An incumbent can call on those who have helped him in past races, but a challenger who is seeking a congressional seat for the first time must start from scratch. In addition, incumbent congressmen can assign campaign duties to regular members of their staff situated in Washington or in their home state or district.

The campaign finance situation for congressmen also differs from that of presidential contenders. As we have seen, the latter now enjoy partial public financing for presidential primaries and full financing for the general election; but congressional candidates must raise all their funds from private sources. Moreover, there are spending limitations in presidential elections (a total of some $25 million), which are equalized between the candidates of the two major parties; in contrast, the limits set by the 1974 legislation on congressional spending in the general election ($150,000 each for senatorial candidates and $70,000 for House candidates) no longer apply since they were invalidated by *Buckley* v. *Valeo*. As a result, incumbents are advantaged: they find it easier to raise money than challengers (people are not moved to give money to probable losers) and usually outspend their rivals by a ratio of 2:1.† Even more difficult for challengers is the fact that the Supreme Court upheld the legislative limits on contributions ($1000 for individuals, $5000 for political committees), which means that money must come from a wide variety of sources (such as political-action committees of corporations, unions, or membership organizations) or depend on their personal or family fortune to support their campaign.‡

Thus both the rules of the game and the campaign strategies developed by the opposing candidates shape the outcome of presidential and congressional campaigns. Yet we know relatively little about the effect such activities actually have on the electorate. Winners tend to congratulate themselves on having conducted an effective campaign; losers are inclined to blame their defeat on circumstances they could not control, such as their minority-party status or the superior resources of their opponent, which even their best campaign efforts could not overcome. Some studies of presidential contests indicate, however, that one-third of the voters make up their minds even before the national

New York senatorial candidates, Republican James Buckley . . .

---

* In early 1977, both the House and the Senate adopted codes of ethics that provide, among other things, that mass mailings at public expense cannot be made less than 60 days before a primary or general election in which the incumbent is a candidate.

† In addition, Common Cause estimated in 1975 that the advantages of incumbency—such as trips home, franking privileges—were worth almost a half-million dollars.

‡ One candidate who definitely benefited from the Court ruling invalidating limits on such latter contributions was Republican John Heinz III, heir to the pickle fortune, who spent more than $4 million of his personal money in defeating Democrat William J. Green for a Senate seat from Pennsylvania. (Both were former House members seeking to fill the seat made vacant by the retirement of Senate Minority Leader Hugh Scott.)

and Democrat Patrick Moynihan.

conventions are held; another third do so during the conventions or immediately after; and the last third decide during the general election campaign.

The campaign, however, is only one of the factors that shape how persons decide to vote. Others include long-term political predisposition of individuals, which they acquire in the socialization process described in chapter 5, together with their reactions to short-term forces, such as particular candidates and issues involved in specific elections. Such matters are explored in depth in the next chapter dealing with voting behavior in both presidential and congressional contests. Following that discussion there will be an overall assessment of the rules of the game that govern American political contests, the nature of our political campaigns, and the voting patterns that prevail among our citizens.

SELECTED READINGS

An excellent treatment of the evolution and weaknesses of the electoral college is Lucius Wilmerding, *The Electoral College* (New Brunswick, N.J.: Rutgers University Press, 1958). More recent analyses of the subject are Neal Peirce, *The People's President: The Electoral College in American History and the Direct Vote Alternative* (New York: Simon & Schuster, 1968), and Lawrence Longley and Alan Braun, *The Politics of Electoral College Reform* (New Haven: Yale University Press, 1972). Good references on reapportionment are *Representation and Appointment* (1966) and *Congressional Districts in the 1970s* (1973), both published by Congressional Quarterly of Washington, D.C.

Several of the sources listed in the Selected Readings for the nomination process treated in chapter 8 are also helpful for general election campaigns. Included are Chester et al.; Leuthold, Polsby, and Wildavsky; White's four presidential-year analyses; and May and Fraser for the 1972 presidential campaign. Studies that focus on the role of the mass media and public relations firms include Joe McGinniss's journalistic best-seller, *The Selling of the President, 1968* (New York: Trident Press, 1968), Dan Nimmo's scholarly analysis, *The Political Persuaders: The Techniques of Modern Political Campaigns* (Englewood Cliffs, N.J.: Prentice-Hall, 1970), and Timothy Crouse, *The Boys in the Bus* (New York: Random House, 1970). Chapters by John Kessel and Murray Edelman that appear in James Barber (ed.), *Choosing the President* (Englewood Cliffs, N.J.: Prentice-Hall, 1974), contain insightful information on group coalitions and persuasive techniques used in recent campaigns. Jeff Fishel analyzes the role of challengers in congressional campaigns in his *Party and Opposition* (New York: David McKay, 1973), while David Mayhew emphasizes the advantages of incumbency in his *Congress: the Electoral Connection* (New Haven: Yale University Press, 1974).

Recent studies of campaign finance are Herbert Alexander, *Political Financing* (Minneapolis: Burgess Publishing Company, 1972), Delmar Dunn, *Financing Presidential Campaigns* (Washington, D.C.: The Brookings Institution, 1972), and Alexander's more recent and comprehensive *Financing Politics: Money, Elections, and Political Reform* (Washington, D.C.: Congressional Quarterly Press, 1976).

Political Novels Arthur T. Hadley's novel about the first computer to run for President, *The Joy Wagon* (New York: Viking Press, 1958), provides a satirical view of elections in the United States.

In *Dark Horse* (New York: Pocket Books, 1973) Fletcher Knebel describes the presidential campaign of an accidental candidate who, because he hasn't a chance, breaks all the political rules—and tells people the truth. The novel is a mixture of hope and despair as it explores the role of money, social position, and deception in elections.

An amusing science-fiction parable about elections is told by Isaac Asimov in "Franchise," in *Earth Is Room Enough* (New York; Fawcett, 1976).

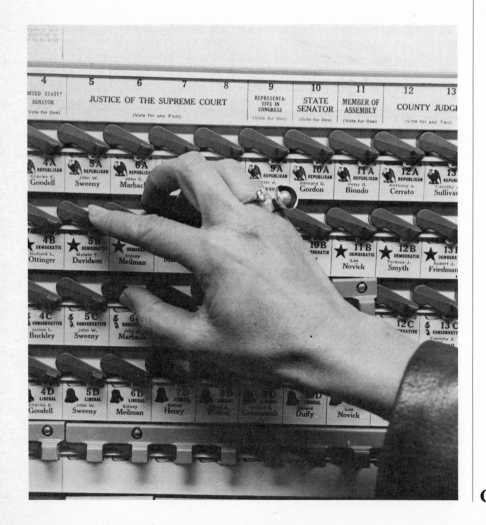

Chapter 10

As we saw in chapter 1, voting is the process by which those "outside" government pass judgment on those "inside." If citizens in a democracy are unhappy with what those in public office are doing about major problems facing the society, the remedy is to replace them. Thus democracies provide their people with competing leaders and enable them to choose between them.

Not all persons, however, actually participate in choosing their leaders. As we shall see, some do not possess the legal right to vote. Others possess that right but for one reason or another choose not to exercise it.

VOTING PARTICIPATION

One of the hallmarks of a democratic society is that instead of breaking heads, it counts them. According to democratic theory, each person is the best judge of his own interests. Accordingly, he must be able to vote for leaders who pursue policies that favor his interests and against those who do not. Everyone, then, should have the right to vote unless for some reason he is incapable of making judgments about his own self-interest.

The franchise in the United States has had a history of expansion, as a series of reasons for withholding the ballot from various groups have been eliminated over the years, either by the states or by the national government. Property qualifications (based on the assumption that the votes of the poor could be bought) disappeared at the state level by the end of the Civil War.* Almost immediately, the battle to enfranchise the Negro (who traditionally had been considered unable to think for himself) began. As described in chapter 6, this struggle persisted into the 1960s.

The twentieth century has seen the vindication of the voting rights of two other major groups, women and young people. As indicated in Chapter 6, the former ultimately defeated the legal notion that a woman's place was in the home (not in politics) when the Nineteenth Amendment, ratified in 1920, de-

VOTING BEHAVIOR

* The exception to this development is the requirement in some jurisdictions that voters be property owners in order to participate in referendums on bond issues.

335

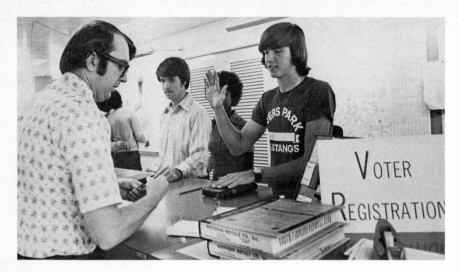

Eighteen-year-olds win the vote.

nied states the right to discriminate in voting rights on the basis of sex. Youth won its major victory in the early 1970s: Congress first passed a statute granting eighteen-year-olds the right to vote in national, state, and local elections, and when the Supreme Court ruled that a national law could only affect voting in national elections, the Twenty-sixth Amendment was enacted extending that right to state (and local) elections as well.

Two other voting restrictions were removed in the early 1960s with the passage of the Twenty-third and Twenty-fourth Amendments. The former granted the residents of the District of Columbia the right to vote in presidential elections, a privilege they had been denied since the nation's capital was located there at the beginning of the nineteenth century. The latter eliminated the payment of poll taxes (in use in five Southern states at the time) as a requisite for voting in primaries and general election contests for the President, Vice-President, senators, and members of the House of Representatives. (In a 1966 decision, *Harper* v. *Virginia,* the Supreme Court eliminated the poll tax as a requirement for voting in state elections by ruling that it violated the equal protection clause of the Fourteenth Amendment.)

Several other voting restrictions are still retained by most states. Some relate to special groups that are presumed not to have the intelligence or moral character necessary to cast a ballot. These include prisoners and the mentally incompetent, for example. Persons who are convicted of a crime are denied the right to vote in most states, a practice that was recently upheld as constitutional by the Supreme Court, even after the person has served his sentence.*

One voting qualification that has come under attack in recent years is the requirement of lengthy residence in state, county, or precinct. While residency requirements make sense in relation to state and local officials of whom a newcomer might have little knowledge, they are less justified in voting for the President and Vice-President. In the 1970 act that lowered the voting age to 18, Congress provided that persons can vote in an election for these officials if they have lived in the place concerned for at least thirty days.

Women get the vote: 1920.

* Another type of disability is alien status; all states today require voters to be citizens.

Table 10.1
Participation in
Presidential
Elections, 1932–1976

Year	Est. Population of Voting Age (Millions)	No. of Votes Cast (Millions)	Percentage of Vote Cast
1932	75.8	39.7	52.4
1936	80.1	45.6	56.9
1940	84.7	49.9	58.9
1944	85.7	48.0	56.0
1948	95.6	48.8	51.1
1952	99.9	61.6	61.6
1956	104.5	62.0	59.3
1960	109.7	68.8	62.8
1964	114.1	70.6	61.8
1968	120.3	73.2	60.9
1972*	140.1	77.7	55.4
1976*	149.2	81.5	54.4

* Elections in which persons 18-20 were eligible to vote in all states.

Source: Statistical Abstract of the United States, 1975, Table No. 727. The 1976 data are from *Congressional Quarterly Weekly Report* (Dec. 18, 1976), p. 3332 f.

Another major voting qualification that has been imposed by some states is *literacy.* The states differ, however, in the way they measure literacy. Some require minimal efforts such as writing one's name or filling out an application form to vote. Others, like New York, require voters to demonstrate their ability to comprehend certain reading passages. Some Southern states have administered their literacy tests to favor whites over blacks. To obviate the use of literacy tests for that latter purpose, Congress passed a law in 1965 suspending literacy tests in areas where less than 50 percent of the voting-age population was registered or voted in November 1964. The act was subsequently amended in 1970 to cover areas where a similar situation existed in November 1968. In 1975 the act was extended for seven more years and its provisions expanded to cover the voting rights of persons of Spanish heritage, American Indians, Asian-Americans, and Alaskan natives.

Thus the trend in the United States has been towards counting more and more heads. As the following sections will show, however, the right to vote and the actual exercise of that right are two separate matters.

General Trends in Voting Turnout

One of the ironies of American elections is that more and more of our citizens have acquired the right to vote in recent years, but there has been a trend towards a smaller and smaller proportion of them actually exercising that right. As Table 10.1 indicates, the estimated number of persons of voting age has almost doubled since Franklin Roosevelt was first elected to office in 1932, but after reaching a high point in 1960, the percentage of such persons who actually went to the polls has declined in the last four presidential elections. The most marked drop—over 5 percent—occurred between the 1968 and 1972 elections.

This decline in voting participation in recent years runs counter to some of the traditional themes that attempt to explain why people do not vote. Frequently, restrictive laws, particularly those relating to registration and voting, are said to prevent persons from going to the polls. Yet many states have eased such restrictions in recent years, so that it was generally easier for a person to register and vote for a President in 1976 than it was in 1960. Nonvoting is also often attributed to a person's lack of education; however, the level of education of American citizens was higher in 1976 than in 1960. The failure to vote is frequently linked to a lack of political information. Yet thanks to increased use of the mass media, and particularly to the televising of the Ford-Carter debates in 1976, more Americans than ever (an average of 87 million tuned in on the three debates) were exposed to the two candidates and their views on public issues. Finally, close political races are supposed to stimulate people to get out and vote because they think their ballot might conceivably make a difference in the outcome. All the pollsters correctly forecast that the 1964 and 1972 elections would be landslides and the 1968 and 1976 elections cliffhangers, but a smaller percentage of persons voted in 1968 than in 1964, and participation also declined between 1972 and 1976.

It is possible to attribute some of the decline in voter turnout in recent years to the extension of the right to vote to eighteen-year-olds, which first took effect in the 1972 presidential election. Analyses of participation in that election by age group show that 18–20-year-olds did not vote as much (proportionately to their number) as did persons 21 and over. Therefore, some of the overall 5 percent decline in voter turnout between 1968 and 1972 was attributable to the addition of persons to the potential electorate in the latter year who were less inclined to exercise their franchise. However, this factor does not help to explain the decline in participation between 1964 and 1968, and again between 1972 and 1976. Moreover, analyses of the 1972 election indicate that persons 21 and over did not participate as much proportionately as they did in 1968.

The precise reasons for the decline in voting in recent years are not known for certain, but it does seem that more and more people are making a deliberate decision not to cast their ballot. Some persons, particularly those with limited education and interest in politics, continue to fail to vote because of *indifference*, but they are being joined by other, better-educated individuals who *are* concerned with political matters but who do not vote because of *cynicism* and *mistrust of politicians.* A 1976 national study of a group of nonvoters (defined as those of voting age who had voted in two or fewer previous elections; who had not registered that year; or who said that their chances of voting in the 1976 presidential election were 50 percent or less) by Peter D. Hart Research Associates, Inc. of Washington, D.C. indicated that the major reasons why such persons said they did not vote were that "candidates say one thing and do another" and that "it doesn't make any difference who is elected, because things never seem to work out right." The same study also indicated that among the persons who did not intend to vote that year were a number of "political dropouts," individuals who had cast their ballots frequently in the past, particularly during and prior to the 1968 election. Reasons for nonvoting again pointed to lack of political leadership: 62 percent of the "drop-outs" said they would vote if the political system could produce a candidate worth voting for. (Asked to name a politician whom they admired most, 50 percent of the

'Now that's real alienation'.

total nonvoters chose John Kennedy and 20 percent Franklin Roosevelt; in contrast, 1 percent chose Gerald Ford and Jimmy Carter).

While there has been a general decline in voting turnout in recent years, the phenomenon is not universal. Some states have actually increased their participation in presidential elections. For example, every one of the twelve Southern states that Jimmy Carter carried had a greater percentage turnout in 1976 than it did in 1972, some evidence that regional pride was involved, along with the possibility that blacks in the South voted more (proportionately) than they had in the past. Thus political and social factors also affect the determination of voters to participate or not to participate in elections.

Political Factors In Voting Turnout

Among the factors that affect voting turnout in the United States are the general political circumstances of an election. As shown by Figure 10.1, there has been some variation in both presidential and congressional voting over the years: both generally rose between 1948 and 1960 (with the exception of the 1956 election); since 1960, however, participation in congressional contests, like that in presidential races, has declined markedly, particularly in 1974 after the Watergate revelations. Moreover, there is a difference in the turnout rate in the two types of elections. Typically in a presidential election year some 5 percent of those who cast their ballot for the Chief Executive fail to mark a ballot for a congressman; moreover, in the midterm congressional elections when there is no presidential contest to attract voters to the polls, voting in general is about 10 to 15 percent less than the presidential turnout figure.

A similar pattern prevails in elections for state and local officers. Governors draw more voters to the polls than do state legislators. The further one goes down the levels of government, the smaller the voting turnout becomes: fewer persons vote for a mayoralty candidate than a gubernatorial one. Thus a common argument in praise of grass-roots democracy—that the people have more interest in political officers of smaller geographical units—is simply not true, at least to judge by votes.

Figure 10.1
Voting turnout in elections for President and House of Representatives, 1944–1976. Source: *Statistical Abstract of the United States,* 1975, Table No. 727. Data for 1976 from *Congressional Quarterly Weekly Report* (18 Dec. 1976), p. 3333.

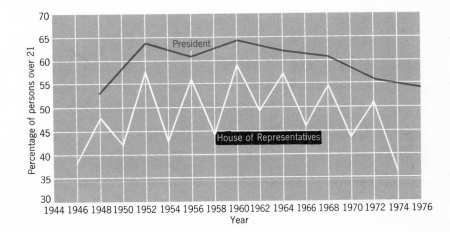

Why do voters take more interest in certain elections than in others? They may feel that a particular official can have more effect on their lives than others can. (Presidents can affect whether a son is sent off to war; the city council can improve the condition of the streets.) Moreover, contests for higher political positions attract wide public attention simply because candidates use the mass media (particularly television) so much. The networks themselves give more extensive coverage to what they view to be the more significant elections. It may even be that, generally speaking, more attractive candidates run for higher offices and thus stimulate voters' interests in their campaigns.

Voter turnout is also higher in close contests than in one-sided elections. As indicated in Table 10.2, the proportion of voters tends to increase with the degree of interparty competition in a state. One other pattern revealed by the table—the high turnout in Republican states—raises another issue related to electoral participation: the extent to which various groups take the time and effort to vote.

Group Differences in Voting Turnout

Besides differences in turnout based on the political circumstances, there are also variations among groups in participating in the same elections, as Table 10.3 shows. One significant pattern revealed by the table is that several low-participation groups—blacks, women, and young people—were formerly denied the franchise. One possible reason for this pattern of low participation is that some of the "newly" enfranchised may still be affected by public attitudes that originally denied them the right to vote. Thus, even after fifty years, some women (particularly older, less educated ones from the South) cling to the belief that their place is in the home and that politics is none of their business. Similarly, nonwhites, especially older people who grew up in the South, may feel that they are not able to make good choices between candidates. In time such attitudes may change (young, college-educated women and blacks now tend to outvote their male and white counterparts), but there is a lag between the legal elimination of an impediment to voting and the removal of the attitudes and reasoning that underlie it.

Some group differences in voter turnout are rooted in psychological feelings that, as we saw in chapter 5, affect all kinds of political participation, including

Degree of Party Competition†	Mean Percentage Turnout
One-Party Democratic	36.8
Modified One-Party Democratic	50.4
Two-Party	59.4
Modified One-Party Republican	63.4

Table 10.2
Mean Percent Turnout* in Presidential, Congressional, and Gubernatorial General Elections, 1962–1972.

* Based on number of persons of voting age.

† Based on competition for gubernatorial and state legislative contests 1962–1972.

Source: Turnout data: Herbert Jacob and Kenneth N. Vines, *Politics in the American States* (Boston, Little Brown, 3rd ed., 1976), Table 1, p. 54. The categorization of states: ibid., Table 4, p. 61.

Table 10.3
Voting Participation
of Various Groups
(by Percentage),*
1968, 1972, 1974

Group Characteristic	1968	Year 1972	1974
Male	69.8	64.1	46.2
Female	66.0	62.0	43.4
White	69.1	64.5	46.3
Negro	57.6	52.1	33.8
18–20 Years old	—	48.3	20.8
21–24 Years old	51.1	50.7	26.4
25–34 Years old	62.5	59.7	40.3
35–44 Years old	70.8	66.3	49.1
45–64 Years old	74.9	70.8	56.9
65 and over	65.8	63.5	51.4
Residence			
Metropolitan	68.0	64.3	44.7
Non-Metropolitan	67.3	59.4	44.7
North and West	71.0	66.4	48.8
South	60.1	55.4	36.0
School year completed			
Grade 8 or less	54.5	47.4	34.4
Grade 9 to 12	61.3	52.0	35.9
Grade 12	72.5	65.4	44.7
More than 12	81.2	78.8	54.9

* Based on estimated population of voting age.

Source: The Statistical Abstract of the United States, 1975, Table 728.

voting. The well-educated are more likely to be aware of political developments and the significance they have for their lives than are the poorly educated. In addition, they tend to feel politically efficacious, that is, to have a sense of confidence about the value of their opinions, to believe that people in public office will listen to them; therefore, they think that what they do has an important effect on the political process. Poorly educated persons, on the other hand, are likely to feel that political officials do not care about them or their opinions. General attitudes about other persons also affect voting behavior: those who trust people are more likely to cast their ballots than are those whose cynicism and hostility toward their fellow humans make them feel politically alienated.

The influence of a group itself is frequently important. Thus if a person belongs to a business orgainzation or labor union whose members talk much about political affairs, he is apt to develop an interest of his own in such matters. If so, his political interest will lead him to make the effort to vote.

Moreover, even if a person is not interested in politics, he may feel that it is nevertheless his duty as a citizen to vote. Such an attitude is much more likely to exist in the upper and middle classes than it is in the lower class.

If the reasons that prompt certain persons to vote and influence others to remain at home on election day are varied, the factors that shape preferences between competing groups of candidates are even more complex.

VOTING PREFERENCES

The reasons underlying voting decisions have long been of interest to students of democratic politics. Some political philosophers created the model of the rational citizen who carefully studies the major issues that his society faces, decides what public policies are needed to deal with them, and then chooses the candidate whose views on such matters are closest to his own. Viewed in this context, the results of elections turn on the "issues" and the candidates' stands on them. Historians, journalists, and other political observers writing on individual campaigns have similarly tended to focus on issues, along with dramatic events and personalities, as the key factors in election outcomes. They have also been inclined to attribute victory or defeat to campaign strategies.

Survey techniques developed in the United States in the 1930s have made it possible to interview a carefully selected sample of persons on some matter and, on the basis of their responses, to generalize how a much larger group feels about it. These techniques became highly useful for eliciting the reasons behind electoral decisions. Instead of relying on what other persons *thought* the reasons were, it was now possible to get them from the voters themselves. Moreover, rather than focusing on what the voters *should* consider in making voting decisions, the emphasis now turned to what they actually *did* take into account.

In-depth studies of voters' attitudes began in the 1940 presidential campaign of a single county (Erie) in Ohio; another followed of the 1948 campaign in a single city (Elmira, New York). These early studies, which were originally conducted to analyze the ways in which media coverage during the campaign changed voters' attitudes and behavior, rather demonstrated that voting behavior was more closely linked to long-term factors such as affiliation with social groups (churches, unions, political parties) and to social class differences in income, occupation and education. Thus the major approach of these studies was *sociological* in nature since they related voting behavior to group membership and social status.

In the immediate postwar period another group of specialists on consumer behavior at the Survey Research Center of the University of Michigan at Ann Arbor began to study voting in the 1948 election. Rather than concentrating on a single community, however, they interviewed a nationwide sample of Americans on how they voted in that election and why they voted as they did. Moreover, their general approach to voting was a *psychological* rather than a *sociological* one; instead of emphasizing the group affiliations and social status of persons, the Michigan group concentrated on the psychological motives that prompted individuals to vote as they did, including such major factors as their partisan identification or affiliation and their attitude towards the *candidates* and the *issues* of a particular election.

The 1948 venture was a pioneering, experimental one, but beginning with the 1952 election, the Michigan group provided a comprehensive and systematic

Table 10.4
Party Identification,
1952–1972

	1952	1956	1960	1964	1968	1972
Strong Democrat	22	21	21	26	20	15
Weak Democrat	25	23	25	25	25	25
Subtotal	47	44	46	51	45	40
Strong Republican	14	14	13	13	14	13
Weak Republican	13	15	14	11	10	10
Subtotal	27	29	27	24	24	23
Independent	22	24	25	23	30	35

Source: The University of Michigan Center for Political Studies.

analysis of each presidential election. In 1960, four of the scholars at the Survey Research Center published a classical study, *The American Voter,* based on data gathered for the 1952 and 1956 elections; for many years this study constituted the "bible" for students of voting behavior in the United States. Later the Michigan group established the Inter-University Consortium on Political Research, through which scholars from all over the United States and abroad share the election data gathered each four years. Ultimately this arrangement has borne fruit with the publication of a number of studies analyzing presidential voting for the entire period from 1952 through 1972. As we shall see, these latter studies indicate that there has been a substantial change in the voting behavior of Americans over the course of the two decades, particularly since the 1964 presidential election.

Voting In Presidential Elections

Party Affiliation. Analyses of presidential elections in the 1950s clearly indicate that the single most important determination of voting at that time was the *party affiliation* of the voter. This general psychological attachment, shaped by family and social groups, tended to intensify with age and to affect the way persons voted. For the average person in that era, looking for some guidance as to how to cast his vote amidst the complexities of personalities, issues, and events, the party label of the candidates was the most important reference point or cue. In this early period, partisanship was also fairly constant: when asked, an average of about 45 percent of Americans in the two presidential years said they thought of themselves as Democrats and about 28 percent as Republicans. When further asked to classify themselves as "strong" or "weak" partisans, identifiers in both parties tended to divide equally between those two categories. Independents in both 1952 and 1956 averaged about 23 percent of the electorate.

As Table 10.4 indicates, however, partisan affiliation began to change in the mid-to-late 1960s in the United States. In 1964, affiliation with the Democratic party rose about 5 percent and fell about a similar amount for the Republican party, with the Independents' share of the electorate remaining constant. However, beginning with the 1968 election, this latter group began to increase—

primarily at the expense of the Democrats—until it constituted one-third of the electorate in 1972. (Also noteworthy is the fact that even those persons who stayed with the Democrats were more inclined than formerly to say that they were "weak" rather than "strong" Democrats.) Moreover, after 1968, more persons considered themselves Independents than identified with the Republican party.

Another indication of the declining importance of political party identification in presidential elections is the increase in recent years in the number of "switchers," that is, persons who vote for one party's candidate for President one year and for another party's candidate in the following presidential election. V. O. Key's analyses of presidential voting from 1940 to 1960 showed that on the average one in six switched; recent information from the Center for Political Studies indicates that one in three Americans switched his vote in 1968 and again in 1972 from the party's candidate he preferred four years before. A similar phenomenon has occurred in split-ticket voting—that is, casting a ballot for candidates of more than one party for different offices at the same election. In 1956 some 30 percent of Americans voted a split ticket in state and local races; by 1972 that figure had risen to 58 percent. What is even more significant is the fact that even persons who claim to identify with the Republican and Democratic parties have increasingly displayed partisan disloyalty by switching and ticket splitting, particularly in 1968 and again in 1972.

Thus independence of political parties, whether measured by voters' subjective attitudes toward the parties themselves or reports of their actual behavior in the voting booth, has increased in recent years in the United States. However, this rise in Independents is not spread evenly across the voting population. It has occurred primarily among young people, particularly those that

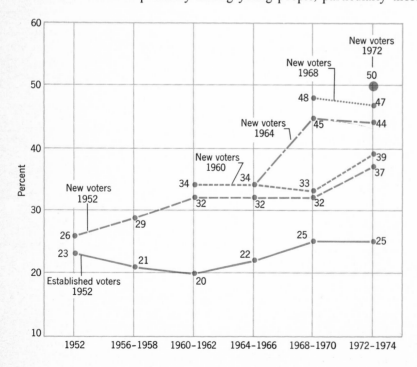

Figure 10.2
Proportion of Independents by age cohorts, 1952–1972.
Source: Norman Nie, Sidney Verba, and John Petrocik, *The Changing American Voter* (Cambridge, Mass.: Harvard University Press, 1976), p. 63.

entered the electorate in 1964 or later. As indicated by Figure 10.2, which traces *cohorts* of various aged voters over the twenty-year period, established voters (those who were twenty-five or older in 1952) have not become noticeably more Independent over the years: the percentage of increase is only 2 percent over the twenty-year period. The next two groups (new voters in 1952 and 1960) were somewhat more Independent when they entered the electorate than were the established 1952 voters, and they have also become more Independent over the years. Most affected, however, by the 1960s were the new voters in 1964, 1968, and 1972. The first group began with the same proportion of Independents as the 1960s cohort (34 percent) but then became considerably more Independent than the latter in 1968, while new 1968 and 1972 voters began with a high level of Independents.

The data in Figure 10.2 indicate that while some increase in Independents in this country in recent years has occurred because individuals have abandoned their party home, most of it has been due to the influx of new voters. The figure also shows that contrary to some assumptions, people do not necessarily become more partisan as they grow older: only the established 1952 cohort declined significantly in proportion of Independents and that by only a few percentage points for the period between 1952 and 1960. Thus partisan affiliation appears not to be related to *life cycle*—a particular chronological stage in an individual's life—but rather to *political generation,* the particular era when a person comes of political age.

Recent analyses of Independents in the United States indicate that not only have they grown dramatically in numbers but that they have also changed in character. Those in the 1950s tended to be less knowledgeable about political issues and candidates and to participate less in the political process than partisans. However, Independents in recent elections have been found to be just as knowledgeable about political matters as partisans. While not as likely to vote as the latter, Independents do participate as much as, or more than, partisans in other political activities, such as writing to political officials and voting on referendums. Thus nonpartisanship, rather than general political disinterest, characterizes many of the younger Independents, particularly those with a college education. What seems to have happened is that a new type of Independent has been added to the ranks of the older kind that was prevalent in the 1950s.

It is difficult to determine the precise reasons for the decline in partisanship among American voters. One factor has been a lessening in the transfer of partisanship from one generation to another. In the first three elections of 1952, 1956, and 1960, persons tended to identify with the same party as their parents; however since that time, younger voters have been less likely to retain family partisan affiliation. Nor do social groups shape partisan attitudes as much as they did formerly. As we shall see, to an increasing extent partisanship counts for less and issues count for more in the political world of the American voter.

Political Issues and Ideology. The Michigan scholars who analyzed the voting behavior of Americans in the 1950s suggested that as a matter of logic, issues are potentially important in determining how an individual casts his ballot only if three conditions are present. First, the person must be aware that an issue or a number of issues exist. Second, the issue or issues must be of some concern to him personally. Third, the voter must perceive that one party better represents his own position and thinking on the issue or issues than the other party does.

When the Michigan group applied these three conditions to the American voters in the 1952 and 1956 presidential elections, they found that relatively few voters met the three criteria. About one-third of the persons in their survey were not aware of *any* of the sixteen major issues about which they were questioned. Moreover, even the two-thirds who were aware of one or more issues frequently were not personally concerned about the matter. Finally, a number of those that were aware and concerned about issues were not able to perceive differences between the two parties on them. The end result of the analyses was the finding that at the most, only about one-third of the electorate *potentially* voted on the basis of issues. (The proportion who *actually* voted as they did because of issues could have been, and probably was, even lower than that.)

More recent studies of political attitudes in the 1960s and early 1970s show a rise in the potential for voting on the basis of issues. First of all, there has been an increase in the number and types of issues of which voters are aware. While the Eisenhower years were characterized by some voter concern for traditional domestic issues (welfare, labor-management relationships) and foreign policy concerns (the threat of communism, the atomic bomb), beginning with the 1964 election, the scope of such concerns broadened to include new issues like civil rights and Vietnam. The latter issue in particular continued to concern voters in the 1968 and 1972 contests, and was joined by such new matters as crime, disorder, and juvenile delinquency (sometimes referred to collectively along with race problems as "the social issue").

Analyses of political attitudes in the 1960s and early 1970s indicate that persons were not only aware of more issues and a greater variety of them, but that such issues had a greater personal impact on their own lives. Studies by Hadley Cantril show that in 1959 when Americans were asked about their hopes and fears for the future, they were most likely to refer to *personal* matters such as good or bad health or the aspirations or problems of their children. While such matters continued to concern Americans in 1964 and 1971, they were not as preoccupied with them and had begun to think more about *political* issues (those requiring the intervention of government) such as world peace, inflation, and—by the latter year—drugs, pollution, and crime.

Finally, the connection between voters' own attitudes on issues and their perceptions of where the parties stand on such matters has grown closer in recent years. As political scientist Gerald Pomper has demonstrated, beginning with the 1964 presidential election, voters' attitudes on issues became more related to their partisan identification. Democrats were more likely to express the "liberal" position on economic, civil rights and foreign policy issues than were Republicans. Also, voters in the 1960s perceived more clearly than voters in the 1950s that differences exist between the general approaches the two parties take on such issues. Moreover, there has been an increasing consensus among such voters that the Democratic party takes a "liberal" approach on such issues and Republicans a "conservative" one. These developments, coupled with the increase in voter awareness of political matters that are salient to them, means that the potential for voting on the basis of issues has increased in recent years. Correlations of voters' attitudes on issues with the way they voted in presidential elections in the 1960s as compared to the 1950s also show that this potential for issue voting has been converted into actuality.

Vietnam war, crime, drug abuse, pollution, inflation:
issues of recent concern to voters.

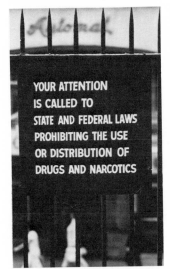

Recent analyses also indicate a change in the way that the American people think about politics. When voters in the 1950s were asked by the Michigan group to indicate what they liked or disliked about the candidates and the parties, only about one in ten responded in ideological terms by linking his attitudes on such matters to political issues or by utilizing such general concepts as "liberal" or "conservative" to describe differences between candidates and parties. Far more people made references to *group benefits*—such as Democrats helping the "working man," and Republicans "business,"—or to *the nature of the times,* linking Democrats to foreign wars and Republicans to economic downturns and depressions. Moreover, over one-fifth of the voters in the 1950s gave replies that had no issue content at all, such as "I just like Democrats better than Republicans," or "Ike's my man." More recent studies have shown, however, that the number of "ideologues" has increased considerably to as much as one-third of the electorate in an election year like 1964. What is particularly noticeable is a movement away from conceiving politics primarily from the vantage point of group benefits and towards viewing it in broader terms of issues and general political ideas.

Related to this broadening of the conceptualization of politics is the increased ability of the voters to be able to relate political issues to one another on the basis of a general liberal-conservative dimension. Studies of the electorate in the 1950s by Philip Converse of the Michigan Survey Research Center showed that voters displayed what he called "constraint"—that is, a low level of consistency—in attitudes on political issues. For example, persons who took the "liberal" position that government should take an active role in providing welfare for the needy did not necessarily think it should assume a similar role in encouraging racial integration in the schools; nor were voters' attitudes on either domestic matter related to their opinions on the foreign policy issue of what stand our government should take towards the threat of communism in the world. However, as Figure 10.3 indicates, beginning with the 1964 election

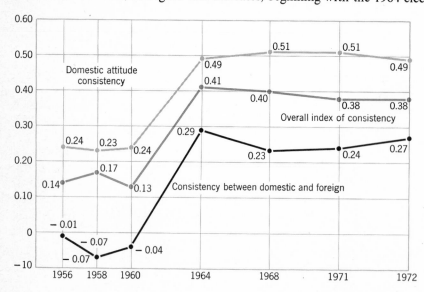

Figure 10.3
Changes in constraint on domestic and foreign issues, 1956–1972.
Source: Norman Nie and Kristi Andersen, "Mass Belief Systems Revisited: Political Change and Attitude Structure," *The Journal of Politics* 36 (August 1974), Fig. 4, p. 558, as cited in Herbert Asher, *Presidential Elections and American Politics: Voters, Candidates, and Campaigns Since 1952* (Homewood, Ill.: The Dorsey Press, 1976), p. 114.

there was an increase in the correlation of attitudes on the various issues; voters' positions on domestic issues were more likely to correlate with one another as well as with their attitudes on foreign policy issues than was the case in the 1950s.

Thus the interest of Americans in issues has increased in recent years, and voters are more likely than they were in the 1950s to be able to relate such issues to each other on the general basis of liberalism and conservatism. These changes could conceivably be due to the rise in the educational level of the electorate between 1952 and 1972. However, while analyses do show that better-educated persons are more knowledgeable and concerned about issues than the lesser-educated, still the greatest *increase* in knowledge and perceptions concerning issues over the twenty-year period occurred among persons who had not finished high school. What seems to be true is that the electorate's increasing sensitivity to political issues is not due primarily to alterations in the electorate itself, but rather to changes in the political environment in which elections have taken place in the period from 1952 to 1972. Political events such as the war in Vietnam and the developments in race relations in the United States were simply more dramatic and salient to voters than were the issues of the 1950s, such as the more abstract threat of international communism and the traditional economic conflict between labor and management. Moreover, presidential candidates like Barry Goldwater and George McGovern took more definite stands on controversial issues than candidates in the Eisenhower years did; they also tended to tie issues together more closely in liberal and conservative packages than had their predecessors. The end result of these developments was the sending of clearer signals to the electorate on where the respective parties and candidates stood on the vital issues of the 1960s and early 1970s.

Candidates. We have less systematic information on the influence that candidates exert on the outcome of elections than we do on the part that parties and issues play in voting in presidential elections. Voters' attitudes on candidates stem from several sources, including the associations they make between a candidate and his partisan affiliation, his stand on issues, perceptions on how he would manage the government, as well as his personal qualities. Moreover, even the latter category covers a wide variety of considerations, including the personal background and experience of the candidate, his personal or political "style," and his competence and trustworthiness. As political scientists Warren Miller and Teresa Levitin suggest, it is much easier to focus on the specific qualities of a particular candidate, such as Eisenhower's personal warmth, Kennedy's youth and Catholicism, and Johnson's expansive style, than it is to make systematic comparisons between and among candidates over a series of elections.

Recognizing these limitations, it is nonetheless possible to make some overall comparisons of how voters reacted to candidates over the period from 1952 to 1972. Each presidential year the Michigan group asked persons whether there was anything about each of the major candidates that would make them want to vote for or against that candidate. The total number of favorable and unfavorable comments can then be tabulated for each candidate and the difference between them computed; the more favorable (as compared to unfavorable) comments a candidate receives, the more positive his overall score is. The overall scores (positive and negative) of the two major party candidates can then be compared with one another to determine the relative appeal of the two candidates in any given election year. Figure 10.4 shows the relative appeal over the period from 1952 to 1972.

Two major finding are revealed by Figure 10.4. One is the great variability in the reactions that voters demonstrated toward the candidates over the course of the six presidential elections. The differences in candidate appeal were much less pronounced in 1952, 1960, and 1968 than they were in 1956, 1964, and 1972. The second major finding is that except for a single election—that of 1964—the Republican candidate was more favorably evaluated by voters than was the Democratic candidate. While it is not noteworthy that Dwight Eisenhower was more popular than Adlai Stevenson in 1956, and that Richard Nixon received a more favorable rating in 1972 from the voters than George McGovern did, it is somewhat surprising to find that Nixon was evaluated higher by the voters than John Kennedy was in 1960.

It is difficult to determine why Republican candidates have generally been more popular in recent years than their Democratic opponents, but political scientist Herbert Asher has suggested some possibilities. One is the fact that the Democratic party draws support from a broader variety of divergent groups than the Republican party does, and this makes it more difficult to please all elements of the Democratic party. Another possible explanation is that since Republicans are clearly the minority party, they have to be particularly con-

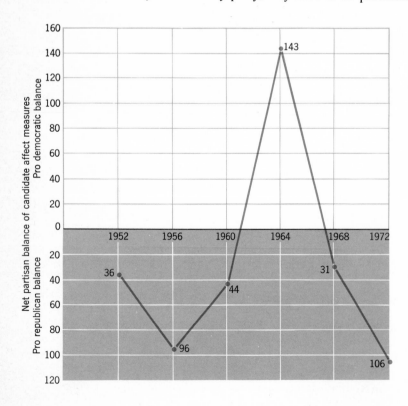

Figure 10.4
Difference in appeal evoked by Democratic and Republican candidates for President, 1952–1972.
Prepared by the Center for Political Studies, University of Michigan, for publication in Warren Miller and Arthur Miller, *Political Contours*, cited in Warren Miller and Teresa Levitin, *Leadership and Change: The New Politics and the American Electorate* (Cambridge, Mass.: Winthrop Publishers, 1976), p. 43.

cerned with nominating very attractive candidates. Finally, the general nature of the times has favored Republican candidates: in 1952 and 1968 the incumbent Democratic party was faced with defending the Korean and Vietnam wars, while such hostilities were over when the Republicans were the incumbent party in 1956 and 1972.

Social Groups and Social Class. The early voting studies of American politics in the 1940s showed an association between social group membership and social status on the one hand, and support for one of the two major parties on the other. For the most part, Democrats received their support from Southerners, blacks, Catholics, and persons with limited education and income and a working-class background. Republican candidates, in turn, drew their major support from Northerners, whites, Protestants, and persons with higher levels of education and income and a professional or business background.

Table 10.5 indicates how these various groups voted during the period from 1952 to 1972. One obvious fact revealed by the table is the great variability that occurred in group voting from one presidential election to another. Particularly noticeable is the effect of individual candidacies. In 1964 all the groups—including those typically supporting Republican candidates, such as college-educated and professional and business persons—voted for the Democratic candidate, Lyndon Johnson. In 1972, all the groups—including all the Democratically inclined ones with the exception of blacks—voted for the Republican candidate, Richard Nixon. Moreover, John Kennedy's religious background was particularly appealing to Catholic voters in the 1960 presidential election.

The table also shows a general decline in the support that some groups gave to their traditional party's candidates over the twenty-year period. Most noticeable is the sharp drop in the Southern vote for Democratic candidates in the last two elections. Also, the level of support of college-educated and professional and business persons for Republican candidates fell in the 1960s. The one clear exception to the rule is blacks. Their tendency to support Democratic candidates has become much more pronounced in recent years, particularly since the 1964 presidential election.

Recent analysis of voting by whites only in the four presidential elections of 1948, 1960, 1968, and 1972 by political scientist Everett Ladd, Jr., makes the changes in group and social-class voting even more apparent. (The 1948 election is a better indicator of traditional party voting than the 1952 and 1956 presidential contests, which reflect the particular appeal of Dwight Eisenhower; also, as we have noted above, the 1964 election results are distorted by the Goldwater candidacy.) As shown by Table 10.6, social-class support of the two parties has shifted drastically since 1948, when noncollege persons and those of a low socioeconomic status were most supportive of the Democratic presidential candidate, Harry Truman, with the middle and high SES (socioeconomic status) voters following in that order. By 1968, college-educated persons voted more proportionately for the Democratic candidate, Humbert Humphrey, than noncollege-educated ones did. Moreover, overall voting by the three social-class groups was virtually even, and among persons under 30 (and, to a lesser degree, women) the former pattern was actually reversed: high SES individuals were most supportive of the Democratic candidate, with the middle and low SES groups following in that order. The 1972 election continued the

Table 10.5
Vote by Groups in
Presidential Elections
Since 1952
(Based on Gallup
Poll Survey Data)

	1952 Stev. %	1952 Ike %	1956 Stev. %	1956 Ike %	1960 JFK %	1960 Nixon %	1964 LBJ %	1964 Gold. %	1968 HHH %	1968 Nixon %	1968 Wallace %	1972 McG. %	1972 Nixon %
NATIONAL	44.6	55.4	42.2	57.8	50.1	49.9	61.3	38.7	43.0	43.4	13.6	38	62
RACE													
White	43	57	41	59	49	51	59	41	38	47	15	32	68
Non-white	79	21	61	39	68	32	94	6	85	12	3	87	13
EDUCATION													
College	34	66	31	69	39	61	52	48	37	54	9	37	63
High school	45	55	42	58	52	48	62	38	42	43	15	34	66
Grade school	52	48	50	50	55	45	66	34	52	33	15	49	51
OCCUPATION													
Prof. & business	36	64	32	68	42	58	54	46	34	56	10	31	69
White collar	40	60	37	63	48	52	57	43	41	47	12	36	64
Manual	55	45	50	50	60	40	71	29	50	35	15	43	57
RELIGION													
Protestants	37	63	37	63	38	62	55	45	35	49	16	30	70
Catholics	56	44	51	49	78	22	76	24	59	33	8	48	52
REGION													
East	45	55	40	60	53	47	68	32	50	43	7	42	58
Midwest	42	58	41	59	48	52	61	39	44	47	9	40	60
South	51	49	49	51	51	49	52	48	31	36	33	29	71
West	42	58	43	57	49	51	60	40	44	49	7	41	59
Members of labor union families	61	39	57	43	65	35	73	27	56	29	15	46	54

Source: Excerpted from *The Gallup Opinion Index* (October 1976), p. 30.

	1948	1960	1968	1972
All				
High SES*	30%	38%	36%	32%
Middle SES**	43	53	39	26
Low SES***	57	61	38	32
Women				
High SES	29	35	42	34
Middle SES	42	52	40	25
Low SES	61	60	39	33
Under 30 years of age				
High SES	31	42	50	46
Middle SES	47	49	39	32
Low SES	64	52	32	36
College educated	36	45	47	45
Noncollege	56	49	33	30

* High SES includes persons having upper white collar and managerial occupations who have had college training.

** Middle SES includes persons having lower white collar or skilled manual occupations.

*** Low SES includes persons having semiskilled and unskilled occupations, service workers, and farm laborers.

Source: Data are from the following AIPO surveys: for *1948,* #430, 431, 432, 433; *1960,* #635, 636, 637, 638; *1968,* #769, 770, 771, 773; *1972,* #857, 858, 859, 860, as cited in Everett Ladd, "Liberalism Upside Down," *Political Science Quarterly,* vol. 91, no. 4 (Winter 1976-1977), p. 578.

same general pattern, except that this time it was the middle SES group, not the low one, that supported the Democrat George McGovern the least.

Ladd suggests some possible reasons for these shifts that reflect changes in both the composition of the different social classes and the nature of political issues that have developed over the period from 1948 to 1972. In recent years, more persons from the upper SES group are professionals and managers rather than business entrepreneurs, and the former are less committed to a conservative economic philosophy than are the latter; moreover, the high SES groups are "liberal" on some of the newer political issues, such as racial integration, Vietnam, and the handling of crime and urban disorders. Meanwhile, more and more persons from the traditional working class have moved up into the middle class, which now bears a greater proportional tax burden for expanded welfare programs than do the upper social strata. (As Ladd suggests, such persons have gone from being "beneficiaries" of social programs to "contributors" to them). Also noncollege-educated persons from the lower part of the middle class are more inclined to be conservative on the newer social issues than are those from the upper class. This means that liberal, upper-class persons are voting Democratic more than they formerly did, while conservative middle-class persons are increasingly casting their ballots for Republican presidential candidates.

Political Attitudes and the Presidential Vote. As we have seen, a variety of factors affect how a person decides to cast his vote in a presidential election. Included are his attitudes towards the political parties, the issues of the day, the opposing candidates, and the social groups he thinks the two parties favor or oppose. Because these factors are related to each other, and also because a person may vote for a candidate for more than one of these reasons, it is difficult to determine the particular considerations that shape an individual voter's decision. However, it is possible to look at the political attitudes expressed by the groups of respondents in the Michigan surveys over the years and make some estimate of the factors influencing their voting behavior in particular presidential elections.

Political scientist Gerald Pomper analyzed the comments made by respondents in a series of open-ended questions and placed them in nine subject-matter categories. Two had to do with the individual qualities of the Democratic and Republican candidates on such matters as experience, qualifications for office, and personal characteristics. The next four categories involved political issues, including those related to the "social issue" (race, poverty, public order, protest, as well as attitudes towards groups associated with such issues, such as blacks, persons on welfare, young people, and feminists); all other domestic issues; Vietnam; and all other foreign policy issues. The last three categories included attitudes towards the general philosophies of the parties and candidates; their performance as managers of political institutions (the nominating conventions, the party organization and the national government, spending and administrative policies, and record in office); and their association with social groups other than those included above in the "social issue."

Pomper then determined the percentage of the national vote that was gained or lost by each party and its candidate as a result of each category of attitudes. Figure 10.5 shows how attitudes on each of these nine categories effected the vote in presidential elections from 1960 to 1972.

The figure indicates the different patterns that exist for the various elections. The 1964 and 1972 contests were landslides for the Democratic and Republican parties respectively because virtually all the categories of attitudes in those years favored the winning party; even attitudes toward the losing party's candidates, Goldwater and McGovern, were negative and thus helped their opponents, Johnson and Nixon. In contrast, the 1960 and 1968 elections were close because both parties enjoyed advantages in some of the categories of political attitudes. In the former year, Democrats were favored by attitudes toward groups, towards candidate John Kennedy, and towards domestic issues; in turn, Republicans were advantaged even more by attitudes toward their candi-

Figure 10.5
Effects of political attitudes on the vote, 1960–1972. Bar length measures percentage of the national vote gained from each element. Elements aiding the Democratic party display bars left of the neutral point; those aiding the Republican party extend to the right. No bar is seen for an element that had no effect favorable to either party.
Source: Gerald Pomper, *Voters' Choice: Varieties of American Electoral Behavior* (New York: Dodd, Mead, 1975), p. 160.

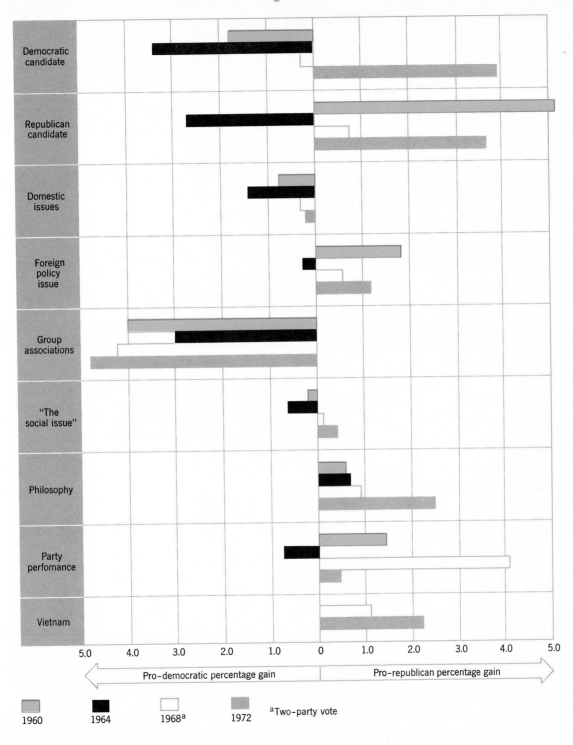

Pro-democratic percentage gain   Pro-republican percentage gain

| 1960 | 1964 | 1968[a] | 1972 | [a]Two-party vote |

date, Richard Nixon, as well as toward foreign policy issues and their party's philosophy and performance as manager of political institutions. In 1968 the major Democratic advantage stemmed from a favorable association with social groups and, to a lesser extent, from domestic issues and a positive evaluation of their candidate; while Republicans were favored by the party performance and philosophy, Vietnam as well as other foreign policy issues, the social issue, and a favorable assessment of their candidate.

Despite differences in the effect of political attitudes on individual elections, Figure 10.5 also reveals some general patterns that persist over time. The most likely sources of Democratic advantage are group associations and domestic issues. In contrast, Republicans are most often advantaged by their candidate, foreign policy issues, and voters' attitudes towards the party's philosophy and performance as a manager of political institutions. The only category that shows no significant party advantage is the "social issue"; despite the attention given to it by the press and political commentators, it was not a significant factor in any of the four elections, slightly favoring the Democrats in 1960 and 1964, and the Republicans in 1968 and 1972.

The 1976 Presidential Election. At the time of this writing, detailed systematic information on the 1976 presidential election is not available. After scholars have had time to analyze the data the Michigan group gathered from the nationwide sample of respondents that year, we will have a much clearer picture of the political attitudes of the electorate and the ways in which such attitudes affected the voting for candidates in that election. However, some preliminary information is available on the American public's attitudes and the general voting patterns that year; these form the basis of the tentative conclusions and assessments about the election that follow.

Carter, of course, enjoyed the usual *partisan* advantage that Democrats have had over Republicans since the 1930s. Gallup polls indicate that during the election year the percentage of Americans identifying with the Democratic party rose from 43 to 48 percent; the Republican figure stayed at about the 23 percent level; while those who said they were Independents declined from 34 to 29 percent. The same polls also showed that on election day some 82 percent of self-identified Democrats voted for Carter, as compared to 80 percent of such identifiers who normally vote for their party's presidential candidate. While Gerald Ford outdrew his challenger among Republicans by a 91 and 9 percent margin, and among Independents by a 58 to 38 percent advantage, it was not sufficient to overcome Carter's lead among the more numerous Democratic identifiers in the electorate.

As far as *political issues* were concerned, voters were preoccupied with domestic matters in 1976. When asked in Gallup polls which was the most important problem facing the nation, as well as which issue would determine how they would vote, the high cost of living and unemployment drew more responses than any other problem or issue. Moreover, other domestic issues—such as government spending, tax reform, energy, lack of trust in government, and welfare—were mentioned more often as affecting how people would vote than any foreign policy concern.

This preoccupation with domestic, economic issues redounded to Carter's favor. The Gallup poll in October showed that 47 percent of Americans thought that the Democratic party would be the best party for prosperity, compared to 23 percent for the Republicans. Moreover, when asked which candidate would do a better job of handling the specific domestic issues mentioned above, Carter outscored Ford in every one of them—inflation, unemployement, government spending, the tax system, energy, trust in government, and welfare. Ford did elicit more confidence than Carter on dealing with the Soviet Union, keeping the United States at peace, and handling relations with other countries; but the gap between public perceptions of the two candidates' ability to handle such matters closed after the second debate. Moreover, following that encounter, the Gallup poll showed that more people thought Carter would do a better job with national defense. In addition, an October Gallup poll showed that people slightly favored the Democrats over the Republicans (32 to 29 percent) as the party better able to bring peace in the world. Thus the issues favored Carter and the Democrats in 1976: not only were they advantaged by the electorate's primary concern with domestic affairs but also by the fact that the traditional Republican advantage in foreign affairs was not as pronounced as it has usually been.

There is also evidence that Carter's *personal appeal* was greater than Ford's in 1976. When asked to give their personal reactions to the two candidates as *individuals,* more persons rated the challenger highly than they did the President. Moreover, when they were also asked to name the personal characteristics and qualities they felt were most important for a President to have, the five most often mentioned were: putting the country's interest ahead of politics; intelligence; sound judgment in a crisis; competence; and concern for the average person and "little guy." Voters then went on to rate Carter higher than Ford on four of these qualities, with the two candidates receiving identical scores from the electorate on exercising judgment in a crisis.

The final Gallup poll taken before the election also showed that Carter succeeded in winning the support of many of the *social groups* that had been part

Jimmy Carter and friend.

of the Democratic coalition during the days of Franklin Roosevelt. Blacks continued their overwhelming support for Democratic presidential candidates, estimated to be 85 percent in 1976. Organized labor also came back to the Democratic camp, supporting Carter by a 63-percent vote, a figure surpassed only by Johnson and Kennedy among the Democratic candidates in the period since 1952. Moreover, 54 percent of Southerners supported Carter, the highest figure attained by a Democratic candidate during that same period. Carter also won back the Catholic vote the Democrats had lost in 1972, but the 57 percent support he obtained from that group was lower than the vote Democratic presidential candidates generally received from Catholics prior to 1972. There is also some indication from an NBC poll taken right after the election that Carter retained the Jewish vote, but, as with the Catholics, not by as great a margin as the Democratic party had been able to secure in the past.

There is also some indication that *social class* voting was more prevalent in 1976 than it was in either 1968 or 1972. The proportion of persons voting for Carter declined as one went up the educational attainment ladder: 58 percent of persons with a grade-school education voted for him, as compared to 54 percent of high-school graduates, and 42 percent of college-trained individuals. However, the differences in class voting were not as pronounced as they were in the 1936–1948 period, and the Gallup poll showed that among persons employed in managerial positions, Carter actually outdrew Ford. Moreover, there are some indications that the Georgia governor also drew from traditional Republican strength in some farm areas and suburban communities.

One general domain where Ford was probably advantaged lay in *political philosophy* or *ideology*. Gallup polls during the course of the election year showed that as the campaign progressed from the nomination to the general-election stage, more voters perceived Carter as being "liberal" and Ford as "conservative." In the process, voters increasingly saw the Democratic candidate as being out of step with their own political views, which were described in an October Gallup poll as 51 percent "conservative" compared to 37 percent "liberal." Thus at the time of the election, Ford was closer to the political philosophy of more voters than was Carter. It is also possible that a major reason for Carter's losing the substantial lead he once held over the President was the increasing realization by many voters during the course of the general-election campaign that Ford's overall political posture more closely resembled their own than did the basic views of the former Georgia governor.

There is no direct evidence at the time of this writing (mid-1977) on how the voters perceived the two parties and their presidential candidates as *managers of political institutions*. It is possible that Ford retained the traditional advantage that Republican candidates hold over their opponents on that issue, especially since the President stressed his long experience in political office and his record of promoting an efficient and financially sound administration. However, Carter talked much more than Democratic candidates normally do about the importance of government efficiency and his own abilities as a manager, which he claimed he demonstrated while serving as Governor of Georgia. There is also a distinct possibility that he succeeded in convincing many Americans on these matters: in a September Gallup poll, 41 percent of the voters thought Carter would do a good job of spending the taxpayer's money wisely compared to 33 percent who thought Ford would.

Thus the factors favoring the respective parties and their candidates were generally similar to those of past elections. Carter was advantaged by his party label, domestic issues, and group associations; Ford was favored by foreign policy issues, political philosophy, and perhaps by his party's traditional image as a successful manager of political institutions, although there is no clear evidence on that latter point. What seems to be different from most past elections is the superior personal appeal that the Democratic candidate demonstrated over his Republican opponent.

If one were to try to compare the 1976 election with other recent ones, it most probably would resemble the 1960 contest. The respective factors favoring the two candidates were generally the same in the two races, with the exception of candidate appeal, which favored Republican Nixon over Democrat Kennedy in 1960. In fact that single difference (which in 1976 favored Democrat Carter), together with Carter's greater appeal in the South, may account for the fact that he won the election over Ford by 1.7 million votes while Kennedy edged out Nixon by just over 100 thousand. As Figures 10.6 and 10.7 indicate, the regional voting in the two elections was quite similar.

Voting in Congressional Elections

As with nominations and campaigns, we have far less reliable information on voting in Congressional elections than we have in presidential elections. The limited information available indicates that while some of the same factors are at work that affect presidential voting, differences in the circumstances of the two kinds of races result in some variation in the way and the degree to which such influences are felt.

Figure 10.6
Electoral votes by states,
1960.
Source: *Presidential Elections Since 1789* (Washington, D.C.: Congressional Quarterly, Inc., 1975), p. 57.

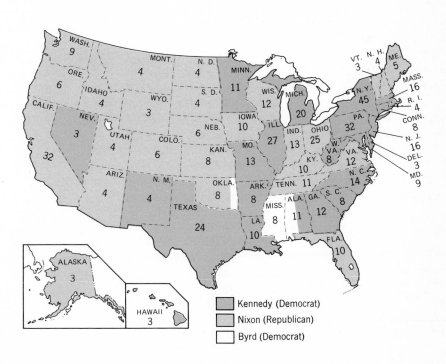

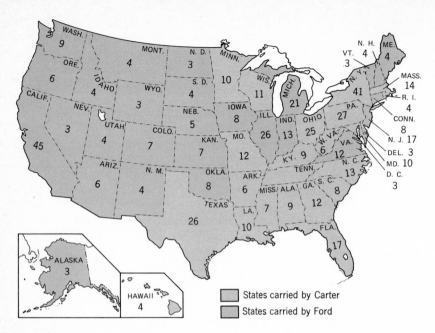

Electoral votes by states, 1976.
Source: *Congressional Quarterly Weekly Report* (6 Nov. 1976).

Party identification is more important in voting for congressmen than it is in presidential contests. While more persons who termed themselves Independents cast their ballots in congressional elections in the late 1960s and early 1970s than did so in the 1950s, Independents were still not as prevalent in congressional elections as they were in presidential races during the latter period. The same is true of the tendency of persons to depart from their traditional party and vote for the opposition congressional candidate; more individuals have done so in recent congressional elections, but the incidence is not as great as it has been in presidential contests.

Several reasons have been advanced for the prominence of party voting in congressional elections. One explanation that applies to midterm contests (as compared to those in presidential years) is that fewer persons turn out in such elections, and those that do, tend to be strong party identifiers who are more involved and interested in politics than Independents are. The person with less concern about politics, who may be motivated to vote in presidential elections because of the extensive coverage in the mass media, is not as likely to receive such stimulation from the less exciting off-year congressional campaign.

Another reason suggested for the prevalence of party voting in congressional elections is that other factors such as candidate appeal and issues mean less in such contests. The innate importance of the presidential race, plus the great amount of media coverage given to it, combine to make the presidential candidates much more familiar to the electorate than congressional candidates. In fact, some studies show that most voters cannot name either of the congressional candidates running in their district. The same tendency applies to the role of issues in congressional elections. Not only are voters unlikely to be familiar with issues before Congress but they also display little knowledge of how their congressman or his opponent stands on such matters. Moreover, many voters don't even know which party controls Congress. (This situation is more likely to obtain when there is divided control of the executive and legislative branches.) Thus the link in presidential elections between a voter's discontent with an issue or political event and his remedy of voting out the party in power is simply not available for some citizens who might like to hold Congress responsible for the nation's misfortunes, but don't know which party to blame.

Another factor that is becoming increasingly important in congressional elections is the effect of *incumbency*. This factor is particularly important in voting for the House of Representatives. Since House races seldom involve a contest between highly visible candidates or salient issues, the advantage is with the person in office: he may not be a household name to many voters but frequent visits back home and the provision of services to his constituents mean that he will generally be known to more voters than will his opponent. A classic example of the influence of incumbency is the phenomenal sucess enjoyed by the freshman Democratic House members who sought reelection in 1976. Despite the fact that many were elected in 1974 from traditional Republican districts—primarily because of voter disillusionment with Richard Nixon (who resigned in disgrace) and his successor, Gerald Ford (who subsequently pardoned him for crimes committed during his presidency)—only 2 of the 78 who ran for reelection in 1976 were defeated. Moreover, despite President Ford's strong showing, (he carried 27 states to Carter's 23), many of the freshman Democratic Congressmen won a much higher percentage of their district's vote in 1976 than they had in 1974, when Republican fortunes were at a low point. Observers of this phenomenon generally attribute the success of such individuals to their close attention to constituents' needs and their liberal use of the mailing privilege to get their names known to the voters of their districts.

The fact that congressional voting is determined largely by party loyalty and incumbency, whereas candidate appeal and isssues increasingly affect presidential balloting, means that the results of the two kinds of elections are increasingly different. In 1940 less than 15 percent of the House districts voted for one party's candidate for President and the other party's candidate for congressman; by 1964 that figure had risen to 33 percent; in 1972, 44 percent of the districts split their vote in that way. In that last year, of the 377 congressional districts carried by President Nixon, 188 elected Republican congressmen and 189 went Democratic.

Splitting the ticket.

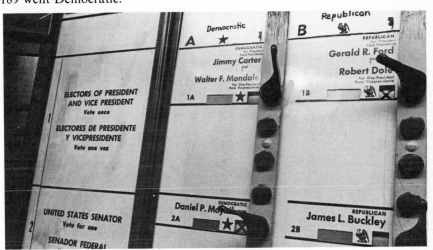

Party loyalty and incumbency are also important in Senate races, but not as much as they are in House contests. For example, in 1976 only 13 House members (8 Democrats and 5 Republicans) lost their seats, but 9 incumbent senators—more than one-third of those seeking reelection—were turned out of office. Sitting senators are more likely to be associated with policy issues than are House members, and this factor makes them more vulnerable to attacks by opponents. Moreover, since the mass media devote more attention to Senate than House races, challengers for seats in the upper chamber find it easier to become known to the voters than do candidates for the House.

The end result of the above developments is a tendency for presidential, senatorial, and House elections to involve different considerations and to bring about disparate results. Presidential contests increasingly turn on issues and the appeals of the individual candidates; Senate races are also frequently decided by such factors, but the candidate appeals and issues do not necessarily correspond to those involved in presidential voting; and the partisan and incumbency factors make more and more representatives virtually immune from the influence of presidential and senatorial contests. Thus the electoral process is an increasingly segmented one, with voters casting ballots for different reasons for candidates for President, the Senate, and the House of Representatives.

VOTING BEHAVIOR AND THE OPERATION OF THE AMERICAN POLITICAL SYSTEM

The collective decisions of individual voters determine not only the results of the elections but also the operation of the political system. Elections that turn on long-term forces such as traditional party loyalties build stability into the system because representatives of the majority party remain in power over a considerable period of time. Other short-term factors such as individual candidates or dramatic political events produce change as the party is turned out of office. Thus our political system contains elements that are conducive to both stability and change, desirable characteristics of any human institution.

In fact, students of American presidential elections have categorized them according to different clusters of electoral factors. An election in which the long-term partisan orientation of the electorate results in keeping the traditional majority party in power is a maintaining election. The majority-party candidate wins primarily because the voters choose him on the basis of their traditional party loyalties. Short-term forces, such as candidates and issues, are present, but rather than determining which party wins, they contribute to the size of the majority party's victory. When they favor that party, as they did in 1964 when the Goldwater candidacy benefited the Democrats, the vote margin separating the two major candidates is larger than usual. If short-term forces are in balance, as they were in 1948, the vote division approximates the proportion of voters who identify generally with the two parties.

While maintaining elections provide general continuity in governance, others result in change. A deviating election occurs when short-term forces sufficiently benefit the minority party that they override the long-term partisan preferences of the electorate. A particularly appealing candidate or some salient issue or event allows the minority party candidate to win with the support of some majority-party members, Independents, and a good share of new voters. The electorate does not, however, change its basic party preferences. Examples of deviating elections are those in 1952, 1956, 1968, and 1972: they were won by the Republican candidates, Eisenhower and Nixon, but the commitment of many persons to the major party—the Democrats—was unaltered.*

The election that brings about major political change is referred to as a critical, or realigning, election. Such elections involve a major realignment of electoral support among blocs of voters who switch their traditional party affiliation. An unusual number of new voters may also enter the electoral arena and cast their ballots disproportionately for one party's candidate. Unlike the deviating election, the effects of the realigning one tend to persist in the form of durable loyalties to the advantaged party. Political historians usually include five elections in the realigning category: 1800, 1828, 1860, 1869, and 1932.

It is somewhat misleading, however, to identify a single election as realigning. For one thing, it is not always possible to determine at the time of the election whether the new political alignment will persist. For another, the realignment process usually begins earlier and culminates in the election itself. Thus the realignment of 1932 had actually begun in 1928 when the Democratic candidate, Alfred E. Smith, gained significant support from ethnic groups in urban areas; moreover, it continued in 1930 when the Democrats made dramatic gains in the Senate and House of Representatives.

The realignment of partisan forces is associated with changes in social and economic conditions that have not been accommodated within existing arrangements. In the case just cited, the majority Republican party had not concerned itself sufficiently with the needs of immigrant and low-income groups from urban areas. The increased movement of these groups into the Democratic camp, plus the economic depression of 1929 that affected a wide variety of citizens, triggered a massive swing to the minority Democratic party by old and new voters alike and ushered in a long period of Democratic rule.

An indication that the parties are not meeting the needs of certain groups is the fact that a significant third-party movement often precedes the realignment. The rise of the Free Soil party and of the Republican party itself, which began as a third party, eventually culminated in the realignment of 1860; the Populist party played a role in the critical election of 1896; and La Follette's Progressives contributed to the reorganization of American politics that occurred in the late 1920s and early 1930s. The rise of the American Independent party in 1968 led some observers to predict that 1972 would be a realigning election that would usher in a new partisan era. As the following section indicates, however, such a realignment did not occur; a number of other predictions made in recent years about trends in American politics have also failed to come to pass.

TRENDS IN AMERICAN POLITICS

As we have already seen, American electoral politics in recent years has been in a considerable state of flux. In the seven presidential contests held since 1952, the minority party, the Republicans, have emerged victorious four times. During this same period we have also had three elections decided by very substan-

---

* Analysts of the Survey Research Center refer to an election following a deviating period as a reinstating one, because it reinstates the usual majority party in power. An example is the 1960 election when the Democrats returned to power after the two Eisenhower victories. Thus a reinstating election is like a maintaining one in that long-term partisan factors are controlling.

tial margins—1956, 1964, and 1972 (the latter two were of landslide proportions)—and three were close contests: 1960, 1968, and 1976 (the first two were genuine cliffhangers). Contributing to such occurences have been a decline in importance of the long-term factor of party affiliation and the increasing importance of short-term forces, such as individual candidates and issues. Such developments have made the American electoral and party systems volatile and difficult to assess. As a result, we have had a wide variety of assessments and predictions about the future course of American politics.

One scenario has called for a *reconstituted majority Democratic party*. After the 1964 debacle, Gerald Pomper suggested that that party might have succeeded in converting to its cause businessmen and other conservative groups that had traditionally been affiliated with the Republican party. During the summer of the 1972 presidential year, historian Arthur Schlesinger Jr. suggested that a "rejuvenated" Democratic party, composed of a coalition of the young, women, blacks, blue-collar workers, suburbanites, farmers, Mexican Americans, and intellectuals, had appeared on the American political scene. Some analysts have also recently proposed that a new "top-bottom" combination of highly educated professionals on the one hand, and economically disadvantaged persons on the other, has emerged as basic elements in a new Democratic coalition. However, such predictions have turned out to be short-lived: in the succeeding congressional elections of 1966 and 1968, Republicans quickly recaptured major groups that had temporarily been alienated by the Goldwater candidacy; the 1972 presidential debacle for the Democrats showed that Schlesinger's coalition was more of a hope than a reality; and the reemergence of class voting in the 1976 presidential election raised serious doubts about the viability of the "top-bottom" combination in an emerging Democratic coalition.

Other political analysts like Kevin Phillips predicted in the late 1960s that a *newly constituted Republican party* would soon replace the Democrats as the majority party in American politics. Noting the passage of about a third of a century since the last realignment in 1932 as well as the rise of Wallace's third party in 1968,* Phillips foresaw the emergence of a new Republican majority composed of traditional Republican groups, blue-collar and ethnic groups alienated by the pro-black policies of the Democratic party, and residents of the rapidly-growing "sun belt" of the South and Far West.† However, the 1972 presidential victory proved to be a personal one for President Nixon as Democrats continued to hold clear control of the Congress and recaptured most state governorships. Moreover, whatever hope existed for extending Republican presidential gains in 1968 and 1972 evaporated with the revelations of the Watergate scandals and the forced resignation of President Nixon.

Still another possibility of political trends has been the reemergence of the former *New-Deal Coalition* of Franklin Roosevelt. In 1972 Richard Scammon

---

* Previous realignments in 1800, 1828, 1860, 1896, and 1932 came at about that interval of time and may be attributed to the development of a new generation of voters since the previous realignment. The rise of third parties preceded several of the realignments; as previously indicated in chapter 7, such parties may serve as halfway houses for persons transferring their identification from one major party to the other.

† Phillips assumed that both retired persons living on fixed incomes and businessmen migrating to the Sun Belt would find the conservative political philosophy of the Republican party congenial to their interests.

and Ben Wattenburg advised the Democrats to take a hard line on the social issue—law and order, political protests, and the like—a tactic they felt would enable the majority party to neutralize this issue and allow traditional economic concerns that favor the Democratic party once again to dominate the political agenda. Shortly thereafter political scientist James Sundquist reported that the Democrats had actually managed to neutralize the social issue by using the "law and order" tactic; "cross-cutting" issues (those that run counter to the traditional economic issues that divide the parties) such as Vietnam, race, and law and order, had failed to divide voters along party lines. Sundquist went on to predict that other issues, such as social programs for the underprivileged, would be "coincident" with (that is, parallel to) traditional New Deal economic issues and tend, at least in the short run, to reinvigorate the old Coalition.

Finally, a number of analysts have suggested a *decomposition of the traditional American two-party system*. First given prominence by Walter Burnham, who suggested that our party system may already be "beyond realignment," this possibility has several variants. One is the emergence of a multiparty system in the United States to accommodate increased divisions that exist among voters on a variety of political issues. Another, suggested by Burnham himself, is the disappearance of political parties altogether as viable instruments for rallying majorities of individually powerless citizens, a consequence that he feels will allow the corporate business system to dominate American politics. Pomper has suggested still another result of the decline in importance of the two major political parties: the growing tendency of individual Presidents, operating free of party control, to increase their power in the American political system.

Of all the predictions outlined above, thus far Sundquist's has turned out to be the most accurate. As we have already observed, neither a reconstituted Democratic majority nor a new Republican one has emerged to date. A multi-party system, which looked possible in 1968, seems much less likely today, as does the decomposition of the party system that so concerned Burnham and Pomper. What seems to have happened in 1976 is that the cross-cutting issues of the 1960s and early 1970s have become less salient; meanwhile, coincident issues like unemployment and tax reform have once again emerged as the most important concerns dividing the voters and the parties. This development, as well as the concern of many Democrats with reuniting their party and Carter's wooing of the New Deal Coalition, enabled the party to win a "reinstating" presidential election with the support of many elements of that coalition.

It would be premature, however, to conclude that the 1976 presidential election has permanently restored the politics of the 1930s and 1940s. As political pollster Louis Harris has pointed out, the coalition of social groups that made up the New Deal Coalition constituted over 60 percent of the electorate during the era of Franklin Roosevelt, but today composes only 43 percent of the voters. Moreover, it is possible that only a Southerner like Jimmy Carter could have pulled together that traditional coalition in 1976. There is also no assurance that the divisive issues that emerged in the 1960s and early 1970s may not surface once again in the future. The electoral situation in the United States thus remains in a highly uncertain state.

ASSESSMENT

The rules of the game for choosing our nation's highest political figure are archaic and should be changed as soon as possible. As indicated earlier, the electoral college makes little or no sense in the present situation in which the President is expected to be chosen in a nationwide popular election: retaining it means playing a game of electoral roulette which the nation almost lost in four recent elections and can ill afford to lose at any time. A major argument for its retention that John Kennedy used in the 1950s—that its bias in favor of large urban states compentates for the rural bias in the House of Representatives—no longer applies with as much force since the congressional redistricting that has taken place to meet the one-man–one-vote principle.

The direct popular election of the President is superior to the district and proportional proposals. The first would incorporate into the selection of the president the gerrymandering abuses that still remain despite the reappointment decisions—manipulating House district boundaries (including noncompact, noncontiguous ones) to favor particular political interests. Although the proportional system is superior to the present general-ticket one, it still does not guarantee what should be guaranteed: that the President be the person who receives the most popular votes.

The major objections to the popular election of the President are that it violates the principles of federalism and discriminates against small states. Yet the principles of federalism, which we examined in chapter 3, do not include favoring state interests in the choice of the national executive; states are already given special protection in the composition of the Senate. No state should have special consideration in the selection of the President; he should represent all the American people, no matter where they live.*

There have been some encouraging developments in presidential elections in recent years. The ability of candidates like Goldwater, McCarthy, and McGovern to attract as volunteer workers political amateurs who had never before been active in the political process is evidence that campaigns are becoming more open to the general public rather than being the private preserve of the professional politician. It is also a healthy sign that both parties had increasing success in recent presidential campaigns in broadening the financial base of their support to include a large number of small contributors.

The new campaign finance law that first became effective in the 1976 election made a substantial change in the presidential campaign that year. The decision of both major parties to accept the complete government subsidy of their campaigns, along with the $25 million limit on such expenditures, served to equalize the resources available to the two candidates and spared both parties the problems and dangers associated with raising funds from private sources. It also meant, however, that citizens were deprived of the opportunity to donate funds and services to their favorite presidential candidate and also cut down on traditional party activities at the grass-roots level. Some thought should be given to the possiblity of using the same approach in general elections as is employed in the nomination phase of the

presidential contest: allow candidates to raise some of their financial support from private individuals and groups but place an overall limit on campaign expenditures and make the partial federal financing contingent upon the raising of moneys from small contributors. In any event, even if full federal financing of presidential general elections is retained, the amount of that funding should be raised to reflect the burgeoning costs of utilizing the mass media to communicate with voters.

Despite the above problems, the financing of presidential campaigns is more adequate and satisfactory than that of congressional contests. The advantages of incumbency, which have been overwhelming in recent years, should be mitigated by a partial government subsidy to provide challengers with sufficient funds to mount a serious campaign against sitting congressmen. Such financing could also have the advantage of making limits on campaign spending and the size of personal and family contributions once again effective: despite the fact that the Supreme Court has ruled that such restrictions are unconstitutional when applied to private funds, they would be binding on incumbents or challengers who accept the partial federal funding of their campaigns.

The 1976 presidential debates were a valuable addition to the campaign. While the candidates were often unresponsive to questions—and especially in the first encounter tended to overwhelm and confuse the audience with excessive facts and figures on the economy— the debates did acquaint the electorate with the candidates' views on a variety of political issues; they also enabled observers to make some judgments on the personal qualities of Ford and Carter, as well as their qualifications for office. Without the debates, voters would have known far less about the two candidates, especially since the $25 million campaign limitation restricted the amount of information that the

---

* It is interesting to note that under the direct popular election of the President, a small, one-party state might have more of an impact on the election result than a large, politically competitive state. In Nebraska, where some 540,000 votes were cast in 1968, Nixon's popular plurality over Humphrey was about 150,000; in New Jersey, where almost 2,900,000 voters went to the polls, the President's vote margin was about 60,000.

electorate received through traditional means. Such debates should be retained in the future, but the role of reporters in such debates should be reduced; other persons such as political scientists, economists, or public officials should be added to the questioners, and the candidates themselves should be permitted to ask each other some questions.

The role of the media was, if anything, less salutary in the general election than it was in the nomination stage of the presidential contest. Many media representatives delighted in badgering the two candidates, hoping that they would make a mistake or commit an indiscretion that could then be converted to dramatic news reportage. More notoriety was given to Carter's *Playboy* interview and Earl Butz's racial slur than to the positions of the two major candidates on the important problems facing the nation. The media should stop pandering to the worst instincts of our citizenry and begin to play their proper educational role in the campaign process.

There are indications that the voting decision itself has been more rational in recent elections. Beginning with the 1964 presidential contest, the American electorate has become more aware of issues and the candidates' stand on them; moreover, these factors are now playing a larger role in its presidential choice. This is an improvment over the past situation, in which most Americans voted as they did because of their emotional predisposition toward a political party rather than on the basis of what the respective candidates proposed to do about the nation's major problems.

There is also some indication that voters are learning to distinguish between relevant and irrelevant issues in presidential campaigns. It is a healthy sign that the voters concerned themselves primarily with the state of the American economy in 1976 and, despite the publicity given the *Playboy* and Butz incidents, Carter's religious views, and the abortion controversy, apparently largely ignored those matters when they made their voting decision.

There is, however, one discouraging aspect of recent elections: the decline in voter participation in both presidential and congressional elections since 1960. While it is possible that this decline might be attributable to a general public satisfaction with the current situation in the United States (if things are going well, why bother to vote?), the evidence presented in chapter 5 and earlier in this chapter is to the contrary: people are increasingly discouraged about the state of the nation and the unresponsiveness of political leaders to the needs of ordinary citizens. It seems much more likely, therefore, that many people are choosing not to vote because they perceive that their vote has little effect on how the nation's affairs are governed. Those who hold political office must do everything possible to regain the confidence of the American electorate; at the same time, however, voters themselves need to become more realistic about what government can be expected to accomplish in mitigating the many complex problems in our modern society.

SELECTED READINGS

The first in-depth analysis of voting (made of the presidential campaign in 1940 in Erie County, Ohio) was Paul Lazarsfeld, Bernard Berelson, and Hazel Gaudet, *The People's Choice* (New York: Columbia University Press, 1944). The first two authors published another community study (Elmira, New York) of presidential voting in 1948 with William McPhee, *Voting* (Chicago: University of Chicago Press, 1954). Two publications growing out of the national studies of the Survey Research Center at the University of Michigan are Angus Campbell, Gerald Guerin, and Warren Miller, *The Voter Decides* (New York: Harper & Row, 1954), and Campbell and Miller's classic study with Philip

Converse and Donald Stokes, *The American Voter* (New York: John Wiley, 1960). V. O. Key's analysis of presidential preferences expressed in Gallup polls over the years is *The Responsible Electorate: Rationality and Presidential Voting, 1936-1960* (Cambridge: Harvard University Press, 1966). There have been a number of excellent studies published recently that cover presidential elections over the period 1952-1972. Included are Herbert Asher, *Presidential Elections and American Politics: Voters, Candidates and Campaigns since 1952* (Homewood, Ill.: Dorsey Press, 1976); Warren Miller and Teresa Levitin, *Leadership and Change: The New Politics and The American Electorate* (Cambridge, Mass.: Winthrop Publishers, 1976); Norman Nie, Sidney Verba, and John Petrocik, *The Changing American Voter* (Cambridge, Mass.: Harvard University Press, 1976); and Gerald Pomper, *Voter's Choice: Varieties of American Electoral Behavior* (New York: Dodd, Mead, 1975).

A basic study of voting behavior in congressional elections is Milton Cummings, *Congressmen and the Electorate* (New York: Free Press, 1966). Chapter 11, "American Politics in the 1970s: Beyond Party," by Walter Burnham, which appears in a book edited by William Chambers and Burnham, *The American Party System: Stages of Political Development* (New York: Oxford University Press, 2nd ed., 1975), focuses on the increasing independence of congressional and presidential elections.

Two interesting studies with differing perspectives on recent partisan coalitions are Kevin Phillips, *The Emerging Republican Majority* (New Rochelle, N.Y.: Arlington House, 1969), and Richard M. Scammon and Ben J. Wattenberg, *The Real Majority* (New York: Coward-McCann, 1970). An excellent recent analysis of changes in party coalitions is Everett Ladd Jr., with Charles Hadley, *Transformation of the American Party System* (New York: Norton, 1975).

The first study analyzing types of presidential elections was V. O. Key, Jr., "A Theory of Critical Elections," *The Journal of Politics* 17 (1955): 3-18. Chapter 16 of *The American Voter* and chapter 5 of Gerald Pomper, *Elections in America* (New York: Dodd, Mead, 1968), contain methods of classifying presidential elections. An excellent extended analysis of realignment is Walter Burnham, *Critical Elections and the Mainsprings of American Politics* (New York: Norton, 1970), James Sundquist's *Dynamics of the Party System* (Washington: The Brookings Institution, 1973) is another excellent analysis of alignments and realignments of political parties in the United States.

The Burnham; Ladd/Hadley; Miller and Levitin; Nie, Verba, and Petrocik; and Pomper studies—cited above—all contain analyses of possible future developments in American electoral politics. The introduction to the Ladd/Hadley book contains an excellent summary of the major views expressed by various scholars on this matter.

An analysis that links voting behavior to the operation of the American party system is the Chambers, Burnham book cited above. Among those that relate voting behavior studies to the operation of the political system and democratic theory are Campbell, Converse, Miller, and Stokes, *Elections and the Political Order* (New York: Wiley, 1966), and Pomper, *Elections in America.*

Political Novels   How public opinion polling can be used to manipulate political candidates and voter behavior is described by Eugene Burdick in *The 480* (New York: McGraw-Hill, 1964). Burdick's story of a man's fast rise from unknown to presidential contender is a warning about the manipulation of voters through the use of computers, polls, and paid campaign consultants.

Norman Spinrad explores the use of television in elections as the means to political power in his science fiction novel *Bug Jack Barren* (New York: Avon, 1973). A telling point about voter manipulation and campaign dirty tricks is made by Isaac Asimov in his story about a political candidate accused of being a robot, "Evidence," in *I Robot* (New York: Fawcett, 1976).

GOVERNMENT DECISION
AND POLICY MAKING

Although democratic officials pay
heed to the attitudes of private citizens on political issues, they make the actual
decisions in the form of laws and decrees that bind the entire population. These
decisions are the product of a number of factors we will explore in this Part.

One major consideration is the *kind of people* who occupy important positions
in the government. The particular backgrounds and experiences of an officeholder shape his values and the attitudes he takes on public matters that
command his attention. Another related factor that affects his decisions in
his perception of his *role* in government—that is, what he thinks someone in his position should do in a given situation, as well as
what he believes others expect of him. These two sets of
expectations may differ: a congressman who has
studied a bill may feel that it is unwise legislation and
he should vote against it, and yet he may sense that his
constituents are for the bill and expect him to vote in accordance
with their wishes. Under such circumstances, he must decide which
course of action to follow.

While the attitudes of individual officials are important, decision making in all
three major branches of our national government tends to be a collective enterprise
in which many persons participate. It is, therefore, important to analyze both the
formal and the informal *structure* of each branch in order to determine the relationships that exist among its various officials. In particular, we need to know who exerts
the most influence on decision making and how that influence is exercised. Closely
related to structure is the *procedure* each branch uses to make its decisions, since
inevitably procedures favor certain persons and interests over others.

Finally, decision making in the American political system typically involves more than
one branch of government: our *separation of powers,* or more precisely, *separation
of processes,* is not a complete one. Therefore, it is important to understand the
powers each branch wields in the political process and the ways in which officials
of the three branches supple-
ment, modify, or nullify one
another's actions.

The ways in which these
various factors—personnel,
structure, procedure, and separation

of processes—affect the decisions made by the officials of our national government is best illustrated by studies of the formation of particular public policies. In the chapters that follow, four areas of public policy are explored: chapter 11, dealing with the Congress, treats energy policy; chapter 13, which analyzes the contemporary presidency, focuses on foreign policy; chapter 14, which treats the bureaucracy, outlines the regulation of cigarette advertising; and chapter 16, dealing with the federal courts, traces policy in the desegregation of public schools. Each of these four policies is thus associated with the particular branch of the national government that has been especially concerned with its formation—such as the courts and school desegregation policy. At the same time, as each of the case studies illustrates, no one branch alone is concerned with a particular issue; rather, public policies are generally affected by two or more branches of government as well as by outside influences, such as interest groups and political parties.

Senate Party Leaders: Republican Howard Baker
and Democrat Robert Byrd.

Chapter 11

Two years after Congress played a major role in forcing Richard Nixon out of office in 1974 for his misdeeds (we will examine his resignation in detail in the next chapter), a number of its own members became targets of criticism for unethical and illegal behavior. Most notorious was Democratic congressman Wayne Hays of Ohio, who was accused by Elizabeth Ray—a secretary working for the House Administration Committee, which Hays chaired—of keeping her on the committee's payroll for the sole purpose of serving as his mistress. (As Ray explained her official responsibilities, "I can't type, I can't file, I can't even answer the phone.") Soon other sex scandals involving members of the House of Representatives surfaced: Colleen Gardner also charged her boss, Texas Democrat John Young, with employing her primarily to have sex with him; Louisiana Democrat Joe Waggoner was arrested in Washington on charges of soliciting a police decoy for purposes of prostitution; and Utah Democrat Allan Howe was arrested in Salt Lake City on a similar charge.

Nor were criticisms of congressmen restricted to their sexual behavior; there were charges of improper financial activities as well. *Common Cause* filed an official complaint against congressman Robert Sikes (D. Florida) with the House Ethics Committee, charging him with using his position as chairman of the House Military Construction Appropriations Subcommittee to further the interests of companies in which he held stock. Gulf Oil Company reported that over the previous decade it had contributed more than $5 million in illegal corporate funds to dozens of congressmen, including Senate Minority Leader Hugh Scott (R. Pennsylvania). An aide of Senator Daniel Inouye (D. Hawaii) admitted that he had lied to authorities when he denied passing on $5000 of the Gulf money to the Senator. Even more shocking was the allegation that the "Seoul connection," South Korean businessman Tongsun Park, and his agents had dispensed between $500,000 and $1 million a year in cash and gifts to members of Congress to promote a "favorable legislative climate" for South Korea in Washington. And ironically, eighteen congressmen, including the chairmen of the House and Senate Ethics Committees—Representative John Flynt Jr. (D. Georgia) and Senator Howard Cannon (D. Nevada)—admitted going on unreported, free hunting trips in apparent violation of House and Senate rules.

CONGRESS

Some of the above matters did lead to prompt congressional action. The Democratic Caucus and House leadership kept pressure on Congressman Hays until he resigned the chairmanship of the House Administration and Congressional Campaign committees and, ultimately, his congressional seat as well. The House also reprimanded Sikes for conflict-of-interest activities and established a commission chaired by David Obey (D. Wisconsin) to develop a code of conduct for Congressmen. However, Congress refused to act on any of the other charges of unethical sexual and financial activities. As Flynt, chairman of the House Ethics Committee, put it, "It is never pleasant or enjoyable to sit in judgment on one's peers."*

'Take a letter, Miss Ray.'

Tongsun Park fields a reporter's question.

"COMPLIMENTS OF THE PEOPLE OF SOUTH KOREA, A SMALL DONATION TO AID YOU IN ANY INVESTIGATIONS YOU MAY BE UNDERTAKING..."

© 1976 Washington Star. Reprinted with permission. L.A. Times Syndicate.

Congressman Wayne Hays as he is about to announce his resignation from the chairmanship of key House committees.

* Nor were the constituents of most of the accused Congressmen very much concerned: of those who sought reelection (Congressman Hays resigned and Senator Scott retired), all were reelected except Howe, who lost in a Utah Democratic primary.

"UH — THE INVESTIGATORS ARE ONLY INTERESTED IN PAYMENTS TO WOMEN, AREN'T THEY?"

Copyright 1976 by Herblock in The Washington Post.

However, when Congressmen returned to Washington in early 1977, they began to respond to criticisms of unethical behavior by the press and the public. The House Democratic Caucus removed Congressman Sikes from his Appropriations Subcommittee chairmanship and the Obey Commission released the results of a survey of congressmen and of the American public, showing both groups to be critical of the ethical standards of congressmen and as favoring full disclosure of the financial holdings of all House members. In late January, the Senate followed the lead of the House by establishing a special committee, chaired by Gaylord Nelson (D. Wisconsin), to develop a comprehensive code of ethics for members of that chamber.

At this point an outside event intervened to hasten ethical reform in both houses of Congress. In his January budget message to Congress, outgoing President Gerald Ford recommended a pay raise of 29 percent for congressmen. Under the terms of a 1967 congressional law (the statute created a commission of private citizens to review the adequacy of salaries of executive, judicial and legislative officials every four years and to report to the President on the matter), the Chief Executive's recommendations were to take effect within thirty days unless either house of Congress vetoed his proposal within that period of time. In these circumstances, then, congressmen would receive a substantial salary boost on February 20, 1977 unless one of the two houses acted to nullify the former President's recommendation.

Congressmen found themselves in a difficult situation. On the one hand, they felt entitled to the raise, because except for a five percent cost-of-living raise in 1975, they had received no salary increase since 1969. (The Senate vetoed one recommended by President Nixon in 1974.) On the other hand, congressmen were sensitive to their low standing with the public (the survey undertaken by the Obey Commission showed that almost two-thirds of Americans regarded the Congress unfavorably) and to the resentment of many persons toward a system that allowed the legislature to receive a substantial raise simply by taking no action on the President's recommendation. The private commission on federal salaries itself made a suggestion (also endorsed by Presidents Ford and Carter) that Democratic congressional leaders seized on as a way out of the predicament: tie the pay raise to a new code of ethics for officials of all three branches of the federal government.

Moving to get its own house in order first, the lower chamber, under pressure from Speaker Thomas O'Neill, adopted a new code of ethics in early March. Included among its provisions was the requirement of a yearly report by all members disclosing full information on their personal finances, with the Clerk of the House authorized to make such reports public. The code also prohibited House members from accepting gifts of more than $100 a year from lobbyists or from foreign nationals or their agents; from using unofficial accounts raised by private funds to pay for office expenses (public funds were raised from $2000 to $7000 to cover such expenses); and, as previously indicated in chapter 9, from sending out franked mail sixty days before any primary or general election in which the member was a candidate. Also "lame duck" congressmen (those holding office after defeat in a primary or general election) were prohibited from traveling abroad. And most controversial of all was a limitation on earned outside income of congressmen to 15 percent of their salary ($8625 based on the 1977 salary of $57,500), with a top honorarium of $750 allowed for a speech or an article.

Representative Robert Sikes.

The following month the Senate followed suit by adopting its own code of ethics that included many of the same provisions as the one previously passed by the House. However, the Senate code went even further, prohibiting members from affiliating with a professional firm or practicing a profession during regular office hours of the Senate, and preventing those who leave the Senate from engaging in lobbying activities in that body for one year after they retire. The code also stipulated that employees could not be required to perform personal services (such as baby-sitting or errand-running) for senators; such employees were also forbidden to engage in any substantial campaign activities during office hours.

Thus both houses of Congress enacted ethics codes in early 1977, vesting the responsibility of enforcing such codes in their own ethics committees until such time as a statute could be enacted providing for standards of behavior for all federal officials. However, despite the restrictions spelled out in the codes adopted by the two houses, their members still enjoy many perquisites of office. Before turning to that topic however, we will examine the general functions that Congress performs in our political system.

FUNCTIONS OF CONGRESS

Congress undertakes a variety of functions in the American political system. Some are major tasks that Congressmen perform on a continuous basis and that consume the greatest share of their time. Other responsibilities are minor ones in the sense that they are handled on a sporadic basis and constitute a relatively small proportion of the legislator's heavy workload.

Major Functions of Congress

Legislating. One of the major responsibilities of Congress is to enact legislation designed to deal with the major problems of American society. For example, a number of years ago Congress passed a law requiring manufacturers of automobiles to install certain safety equipment (such as seat belts and head rests). The law stipulated that if the auto manufacturers failed to comply with its provisions, they could be fined or prevented from selling vehicles. As a result of the action of Congress, then, individuals and groups can be forced under pain of legal penalties to do what they otherwise could postpone or never do at all: despite the contentions of the automobile manufacturers that they would develop safety devices of their own and install them in all their motor vehicles, they did not do so until Congress forced them to take such actions.

There is, of course, nothing inevitable about Congress's recognition of a problem and decision to take actions to meet it. Americans had been killing and injuring each other on the highways for almost a half-century before the first congressional law was enacted in 1966 requiring safety equipment on motor vehicles. Until that time it had been assumed that the problem of vehicular accidents should be approached in other ways, such as constructing highways that were well designed and by regulating licenses to drive.

Contributing to the change in congressional thinking on the issue was Ralph Nader, a young lawyer whose best-selling *Unsafe at Any Speed* condemned the automobile industry for its failure to develop means of cushioning what he called the "second impact" (the one that occurs when drivers and passengers

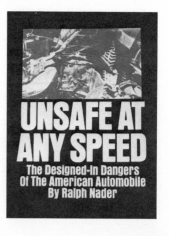

are thrown about inside the car after the initial impact with the other vehicle). Joining Nader as persons concerned with the issue were doctors who were on duty in emergency rooms of hospitals when accident victims were brought in; lawyers who represented injured persons in automobile accidents; and an important governmental ally, Senator Abraham Ribicoff, who had led a vigorous campaign for highway safety while he was governor of Connecticut. When the administration of President Johnson added its support to the idea by proposing legislation for federal automobile safety standards, Congress ultimately responded with the passage of the National Traffic and Motor Vehicle Safety Act of 1966.

In making its decisions on needed legislation, then, Congress responds to pressures from a variety of sources. Some are private groups and individuals who have a particular concern or interest in a problem and develop ideas about what should be done about it. A political party or candidate may propose legislative action to deal with a particular issue. Frequently the initiative comes from the executive branch. Indeed, it has been estimated that about 80 percent of all laws passed by Congress are originally proposed by the President or some administrative agency. Finally, congressmen themselves develop an interest in particular matters and become advocates of legislation designed to meet what they view as a major societal problem.

Although passing laws to meet societal problems continues to constitute an important function of the Congress, it is no longer as influential in legislation as it was earlier in the nation's history. Not only does Congress now tend to allow, and even to *expect,* the President to take the initiative in major legislative proposals (we will examine this matter in ch. 13), but it also is less inclined than in the past to make major changes in the content of those proposals.

In fact, Congress increasingly turns over to executive agencies the job of formulating precise rules and regulations for handling particular problems. Thus in the case of automobile safety standards, what Congress did was to recognize that standards were necessary, but it relinquished the responsibility of devising them. The language of the National Traffic and Motor Vehicle Safety Act of 1966 merely stated that the standards developed by executive officials should be "appropriate" and "practicable," "meet the need for motor vehicle safety," and "be stated in objective terms." Within these broad guidelines, the Federal Highway Safety Bureau, which was entrusted with the responsibility of administering the law, was granted authority to develop standards that it feels are necessary to make motor vehicles safe.

Congress takes this approach to public problems for two major reasons. One is that congressmen cannot be expected to have either the time or the expertise to deal with the intricacies of any of the broad variety of issues that they must be concerned with. They can only hope to identify some major problems and suggest general approaches for dealing with them, leaving particular policies to specialized agencies in the executive branch. Thus congressmen as generalists could determine that developing safety standards for automobiles was desirable without having special knowledge of what these standards should be.

The second reason is that congressmen often decide to leave the development of specific policies to executive officials for political considerations. Although everyone agreed on the need for safety devices on automobiles, they disagreed on which particular devices or on how long manufacturers should be given to

install them. Thus officials in the Federal Highway Safety Bureau were caught in the crossfire between the automakers, who wanted them to act cautiously in devising and implementing safety standards in order to allow the industry time to adjust to the new requirements, and critics like Nadar and Senator Ribicoff, who demanded that they act quickly to develop strict regulations. Quite naturally, congressmen typically prefer to allow others besides themselves to be exposed to such political pressures.

Controlling the Administration of Governmental Activities. The above developments reflect a shift in the major functions performed by the American Congress. Today it is less a body that develops specific rules regulating the actions of private individuals and groups than it is one that delegates to the executive branch the authority to develop rules under the supervision of Congress. In other words, Congress is not so much involved in directly controlling the activities of citizens through its own actions as in indirectly affecting the public through determining how administrative officials shall carry on that function. In the process, Congress has become less a body that legislates and more an institution that *controls the administration of governmental activities* performed by executive officials.

Besides establishing broad legislative guidelines for carrying out the programs it authorizes, Congress has a variety of other means of controlling the administration. These include such powers as creating the organization of the executive branch in which governmental programs are administered, providing (or *not* providing) moneys to carry on such programs, as well as confirming (or *not* confirming) presidential appointment of persons who occupy the major administrative positions entrusted with carrying out such programs. We will examine these powers in detail in chapter 14, dealing with the federal bureaucracy.

Informing and Educating the Public. A third function of Congress is what Woodrow Wilson, in his classic study *Congressional Government* (written in 1885*), referred to as the *informing* function. By this he meant that the national legislative body has the obligation of educating the general public on the major issues and on some of the basic approaches that can be taken to alleviate them. Thus when Congress holds hearings on automobile safety, pollution, or the control of drugs, it is trying to inform the American people (as well as its own members) about these problems and what steps might conceivably be taken to deal with them.

The major vehicle for the informing function of the Congress is an investigating committee, typically operating under either the House or the Senate, although in some instances both chambers create a joint committee to look into a matter. At times one of the regular committees or subcommittees conducts the investigation: the Senate Operations Subcommittee on Executive Reorganization, chaired by Senator Ribicoff, looked into the issue of auto safety. On other occasions a special committee is created to investigate a problem: in early 1973 the Senate established the Select Committee on Presidential Campaign

---

* Before going into public life Wilson was a professor of government. His study of Congress remains one of the most perceptive analyses of that institution ever written.

Activities under the chairmanship of Senator Sam Ervin to inquire into Watergate and related issues.

The size of the public affected by a congressional investigation depends on the innate interest created by the subject of the inquiry, the extent to which the hearings are covered by the media, and the skills of the committee members, particularly the chairman. All three of these factors converged to make the Watergate hearings one of the most dramatic incidents of recent years: the break-in and related scandals were intensely interesting to most Americans, particularly when leading administration figures like H. R. Haldeman, John Ehrlichman, and John Mitchell came to testify before the committee; the three television networks took turns covering the proceedings live in the daytime, and public television rebroadcast them at night; and chairman Sam Ervin with his droll humor and biblical quotations became a folk hero to many Americans.

While few congressional investigations are as dramatic or reach as broad a public as did the Watergate hearings, they all have two potential practical effects. One is that an aroused public will induce individuals and groups to change their past behavior. One of the purposes behind congressional inquiries into automobile safety was the hope that manufacturers would voluntarily inaugurate safety programs to protect the public against needless deaths and injuries. The hearings of the Ervin Committee were also designed to influence candidates for public office, as well as those serving in high government posts, to conduct themselves more ethically than those associated with Watergate had done.

"Its a television first. Two committees are investigating each other."

Generally speaking, however, voluntary actions alone are not sufficient to deal with major problems under investigation, and it is necessary to force persons to change their behavior under pain of legal sanctions. In this case the informing function serves another purpose: laying the groundwork for appropriate legislation. Concerned legislators hope that when enough groups are made aware of an issue and what might be done about it, they will put pressure on Congress to take action. When Senator Ribicoff conducted hearings on automobile safety, he was seeking to build public support for mandatory safety equipment for automobiles. Senator Ervin hoped that the Watergate hearings would lead to the passage of the kinds of remedial legislation recommended by his committee, including major changes in the financing of presidential campaigns, the establishment of a new Office of Public Attorney to investigate wrongdoing in the executive branch, and greater congressional review of federal intelligence and law-enforcement agencies.

In addition to educating the public in general on issues, many congressmen try to keep their constituents informed on a variety of problems, including those of special local interest. Such information typically goes out in the form of mass-produced newsletters, television broadcasts, and government publications. Although the primary motive behind such communications is often promotion of the congressman himself, nonetheless they do help to keep private citizens informed on matters of public concern.

Servicing Constituents. A final major function of Congress also pertains to relationships with constituents, namely, the *service* task that legislators perform for people in their state or congressional district who request assistance in dealing with practical problems involving the federal government. For instance, an elderly woman may inquire about her social security benefits or a father may seek help in clarifying his son's military status or his eligibility for a medical discharge. In performing this function, congressmen act as middlemen between private individuals and the administrative agencies in the executive branch. They help to get people in touch with the proper person to handle the problem, put in a good word on their behalf, and see to it that their constituents are well treated and receive benefits to which they are entitled. Indeed, much of the time of the average congressman is taken up with personal casework for the folks back home.

The legislative, administrative-control, informing, and service functions together constitute the major responsibilities of Congress. Of course, they are not entirely separable, and one frequently has important consequences for another. Overseeing the executive branch, for example, helps to make congressmen aware of additional legislation that is needed to make government more effective. Handling cases of constituents alerts legislators to defects in the procedures of executive agencies that require legislation or stricter administrative control by Congress.

The performance of these functions also has important by-products for society. By serving the needs of constituents, congressmen "represent" their interests and help develop the loyalty and allegiance of people to the political system. The give-and-take of the legislative process accommodates and compromises competing demands, and serves to help make the final decision acceptable to the parties concerned. This, in turn, helps to legitimize the political system so that citizens in general are willing to abide by the rules and regulations developed by Congress and executive agencies.

Minor Functions of Congress

In addition to its major responsibilities, the Congress performs other tasks on an irregular basis. Although not as vital to the overall functioning of the legislative body, on occasion they can become highly important to the operation of our political system.

In some instances, Congress acts like a *judicial* (rather than a legislative) body in resolving disputes involving individuals. An example of this type of function is the power to *remove executive and judicial officials of the national government from their positions.* The persons subject to removal include "The President, the Vice-President and all civil officers of the United States"; the grounds for removal include "treason, bribery or other high crimes and misdemeanors." The removal procedure involves the voting of an impeachment resolution by a majority of the members of the House of Representatives followed by a trial and vote of conviction by two-thirds of the members of the Senate.

We will examine the issue of impeachment and trial of the President in detail in the following chapter. It is sufficient to note for the moment that the general process has been rarely used. Impeachment proceedings have been initiated fifty times in the House, but only twelve cases reached the Senate for a trial. Of these twelve, four resulted in convictions. All the convictions involved federal judges (not executive officials); the last one occurred in 1936.

Each chamber also has power over the *seating and disciplining of its own members.* Thus both the House and the Senate have jurisdiction over disputed elections; they can also refuse to seat a person for failure to meet their qualifications for membership. While Congress has been asked often to determine the winner in contested elections, it has rejected the clear choice of the voters for lack of requisite qualifications in fewer than twenty cases since 1789. Both chambers have also been loath to discipline sitting members: seven senators and eighteen representatives have been formally censured by their colleagues for misconduct; fifteen senators and three House members have actually been expelled from their respective chambers.

The two houses of Congress are also involved on occasion in matters of *leadership selection for the executive branch.* As we saw in chapter 9, if no candidate for President or Vice-President receives a majority of the electoral votes, these matters are referred respectively to the House of Representatives and Senate for an ultimate decision. As we shall see in chapter 12, both houses may also become involved if the President is unable to carry on the duties of his office or if there is a vacancy in the vice-presidency. Congress also determines by legislation who will succeed to the nation's highest office if something happens to both the President and the Vice-President.

Congress also becomes involved on occasion in *specialized areas of public policy making.* As we have seen in chapter 2, both houses join in initiating constitutional amendments; they also have special powers in foreign and military policy that we shall examine in chapter 13. Finally, Congress has the constitutional power "to exercise exclusive legislation in all cases whatsoever" for the nation's capital. Thus residents of the District of Columbia find not only national policies but also their local concerns determined by the United States Congress.

Congress, then, performs a variety of specific functions in the political system that have important side effects for individuals, groups, and the larger society. The following section focuses on the individuals who perform those functions—the American congressmen.

CONGRESSMEN AND THEIR WORLD

Over the years our national legislators have ranked low in the estimation of many observers. They are common objects of derision for contemporary political cartoonists who picture them as bumbling, loquacious men of meager talent. Commentators in the past were often no kinder in their estimations. Alexis de Tocqueville, that perceptive French analyst of the Jacksonian period, referred to the "vulgar demeanor of that great assembly." He went on to describe its members as "almost all obscure individuals, village lawyers, men in trades, or even persons belonging to the lower class." To what extent do Tocqueville's comments accurately picture members who sit in Congress today?

Backgrounds of Congressmen

Contemporary congressmen resemble those described by Tocqueville in at least one important respect: they do tend to come disproportionately from the legal profession. Although *lawyers* constitute less than 1 percent of the adult population in the United States, about half of the members of the Ninety-fifth Congress (1977-79) are attorneys.

There are a number of reasons why attorneys dominate Congress. For one thing, the tools of the lawyer's trade—the ability to analyze statutes and administrative regulations, verbal and argumentative facility, and skills in negotiations—are precisely those that are needed by the men who perform the major functions of the Congress—legislating, controlling the administration, informing the public, and representing constituents. As a professional man, a lawyer enjoys prestige in his community. Moreover, his professional role is to provide help in various kinds of personal problems. People, then, regard lawyers as natural legislators.

Members of the legal profession themselves also seek legislative positions. In fact, some go to law school in the first place not just to practice but to prepare themselves for a political career. The law is also a "dispensable" profession, that is, it can be fitted in well with service in public life. Indeed, traditionally, many individuals continued to be associated with and to draw income from law firms while serving in Congress. However, as indicated at the beginning of the chapter, ethics codes adopted in early 1977 limit the amount of outside income members of the House can make and place limitations on senators' being affiliated with a professional firm or partnership at all. In any event, should a lawyer-legislator be defeated for reelection or decide to retire from Congress, he can return to his profession fairly easily, since law does not change as much as fields like medicine and engineering.

If by "men in trades" Tocqueville meant *businessmen,* then this characterization also applies today. Next to lawyers, businessmen and bankers constitute the most numerous group in both the House and Senate: they account for

Senator Mark Hatfield.

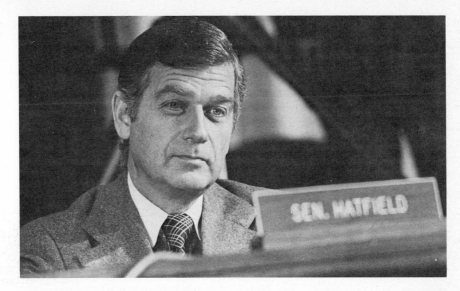

Senator Mark Hatfield.

about one-fourth of the members of the Ninety-third Congress. However, there were twenty fewer businessmen and bankers in the ninety-fifth Congress (1977–79) than there were in the ninety-fourth (1975–77).

The third most prevalent occupational group in today's Congress was not even mentioned by Tocqueville: *teachers.* This group has been increasing in recent years and today constitutes about one-seventh of the national legislature. Included are a number of former college professors, including senators Hubert Humphrey of Minnesota, George McGovern of South Dakota, Mark Hatfield of Oregon, Daniel Patrick Moynihan of New York, and S. I. Hayakawa of California.

Tocqueville's description of persons belonging to the lower class has limited application to the Congress today. In 1977 a Blue Collar Caucus was formed of House members who worked with their hands before going to Congress, but only fourteen congressmen—some 3 percent of the body's membership—could qualify on the basis of their previous occupation. Included among the group were a former professional heavyweight boxer, a one-time bartender, and a former riverboat captain.

In social background congressmen as a group fit the stereotype of the male white Protestant. Although more than half the population is female, only about 3 percent of the members of Congress are women; with the defeat of Margaret Chase Smith in 1972, the Senate was left without a single female member. Although blacks make up 11 percent of the American people, they constitute only 3 percent of the Congress, including one senator, Edward Brooke of Massachusetts. Finally, a nation that is just over one-half Protestant is represented by a Congress that is three-fourths Protestant.

Tenure and Career Patterns of Congressmen

As we saw in a previous chapter, incumbent congressmen have great advantages in political campaigns. Those advantages (assuming their desire to remain in office) are reflected in increasing tenure over the years. In the early years of

Congresswoman Barbara Jordan.

this century members of the House of Representatives averaged about six years in office; by the late 1960s the average tenure was some eleven years. The tenure of senators has also increased over the years since they became directly elected in 1914; by the latter part of the 1960s over three-fourths were beyond their first term in office.

As political scientist Samuel Huntington pointed out at that time, service in the national legislature had become increasingly professionalized and permanent over the years as more and more persons spent their entire working life in their congressional position. (The major exceptions were senators seeking the presidency and House members running for the Senate or the governorship of their own state.) Huntington emphasized in particular the decline in the movement of persons from Congress to a major executive position in the national government. From 1897 to 1940, one-fifth of Cabinet members had previously served in Congress; between 1941 and 1963 that ratio fell to one-seventh; and in the Johnson and Nixon administrations, only one Cabinet member in fifteen was an ex-congressman.

However, the situation described above changed greatly in the 1970s. A combination of early retirements and defeats of incumbents in congressional primaries and general elections (many of which occurred after the Watergate revelations) has resulted in a rapid infusion of new members into both houses of Congress. For example, by the Ninety-fifth Congress (1977–79), three-fifths of the members of the House and one-half the senators were persons who had been elected to those bodies since 1970. Moreover, there was some trend towards the selection of more ex-Congressmen to Cabinet posts by Presidents Ford and Carter: two of the nine appointments of the former Chief Executive, and a similar number of appointees among Carter's initial eleven choices for his Cabinet, had previously served in Congress.

Congressmen as "Local Boys"

Another important aspect of a congressman's life is his basic orientation to his local community and state. In a society in which more and more young people never return home after college and where workers and executives move around the country frequently as job opportunities dictate, Senate and House members retain deep roots in their home soil. Most of them return to their home towns—or at least their native states—after they finish their education, and they become immersed in political life. (The Robert Kennedys and Theodore Sorensons who seek public office in another state are the rare exceptions to the rule.)* And, of course, once elected, they remain residents as long as they stay in Congress.

In fact, congressmen are creatures of two worlds. One—Washington, D.C.— is the locale for two of their major functions, legislating and supervising the executive agencies of the national government. The other—their home area—is the focus of informing and servicing functions for constitutents.

Members of Congress retain close ties with their home areas in order to get reelected. To this end, senators and representatives find it wise to spend as much time "back home" as possible, particularly in an election year. For those

---

* The Constitution requires that senators and House members be inhabitants of the state they represent. By custom, the latter are also inhabitants of the district they serve.

who live in the East, not far from the nation's capital, extended weekends at home are the rule: many belong to what is known as the "Tuesday-Thurdsay Club"—that is, they are in Washington the middle three days of the week when the Congress customarily transacts its business and return to their local constituencies during the other four days. But even those from areas more remote from the District of Columbia find it advisable to make it home at least one weekend a month, and in those short periods when Congress is not in session, many of its members are on the road visiting in various parts of their constituency.

Living in two worlds is not an easy task for congressmen. It frequently means separation from their families to avoid taking children out of school. They face problems of allocating their time and that of their staff members between Washington and their home base. Increasing numbers of congressmen have home offices manned by permanent staff members to service the needs of their constituents. The double life of a congressman also calls for adjustment in interests and personal lifestyles. Back home they are expected to be "folksy," to demonstrate an avid interest in local events and in the progress of their constituents' children and grandchildren; in Washington they are called upon to evince a capacity to deal with domestic and foreign problems in a complex and sophisticated world.

A congressman's life and the way he spends his time reflect the demands of these two worlds in which he lives. A typical day, drawn from an account by the late Representative Clem Miller of California, goes as follows:

6:45 A.M.   Rise, read *Washington Post.*

8:00 A.M.   Breakfast with the British ambassador.

8:30 A.M.   Look over mail, dictate replies to important inquiries.

9:00 A.M.   Office appointment with business lobbyist to discuss trade legislation.

10:00 A.M.   Subcommittee hearings on depressed-area bill.

12:00 Noon   Attend debate on House floor.

1:00 P.M.   Lunch in office. Read state and local newspapers.

2:00 P.M.   Meeting with Harvard economist John Kenneth Galbraith to discuss tight money and economic policy.

2:45 P.M.   Listen to debate on floor of Congress.

3:30 P.M.   Meeting with a member of the House Appropriations Committee on public works in home district.

5:00 P.M.   Sign letters dictated in morning. Go over afternoon mail. Meet with constituents.

6:15 P.M.   Leave for home.

7:15 P.M.   Eat dinner.

8:00 P.M.   Read another newspaper from home district. Go through reports, speeches, and magazines. File material for future speeches.

A day in the life of
Congressman Max Baucus of
Montana.

Getting the word from
Speaker O'Neill (upper left).

'Sign right here,
congressman' (upper right).

Meeting with constituents
(lower left).

Committee hearing (lower
right).

11:00 P.M.   Read chapter from book.

11:45 P.M.   To sleep.

Thus a congressman's life is not an easy one. Neither is it boring, however. Moreover, as the following section indicates, a position in Congress is not without its privileges as well.

Congressional Pay and Perquisites

As we have already seen, in 1977 congressmen's salaries were raised to $57,500. In addition, the new codes of ethics of both houses permitted members to supplement that salary with an additional outside earned income of 15 percent of their congressional salary, or $8625. Thus the total earned income a congressman could make in 1977 was $66,125. This figure placed congressmen among the top 1 percent of Americans in income that year.

Even this figure, however, does not reveal the full story of a congressman's real income. The 15 percent limitation does not apply to unearned income derived from investments such as stocks or bonds or to the profits from a family business. Moreover, other types of income, such as that from royalties on books or from the sale of creative or artistic works, are also excluded from the limitation by the Senate code of ethics. Thus one may even assume that many congressmen have an annual income considerably in excess of $66,125.

Another major perquisite ("perk") enjoyed by a congressman is allowance for a *staff.* In 1977 members of the House were entitled to an allowance of more than a quarter of a million dollars to have some eighteen persons to work in Washington and their home district offices. For senators, the amount of money permitted for staff depended on the population of the state they represented, ranging from about half-million dollars for those from states with fewer than 2 million residents to just over $900,000 for those with more than 21 million residents. In addition, in 1975 junior senators won the right to appoint additional staff with salaries totaling just over $100,000 to help them with their committee assignments.*

In addition to staff, congressmen also receive *special allowances* for a variety of other expenses. Included are trips home—in 1977, twenty-six free round trips annually for House members; for senators, 40 or 44, depending on the size of the state they represent. There are also allowances for other expenses connected with communicating with constituents, including stationery, postage, telephone, telegraph, and newsletters. There is also free office space, together with an allowance for office equipment.

Another privilege, that of the *frank,* also enables members of Congress to mail letters and packages under their signatures without being charged for postage. Besides providing a major means for communication with their constituents on a variety of matters, as indicated by Figure 11.1, the privilege can also be used to mend political fences just prior to elections. However, as we have noted, in the ethic codes they adopted in 1977 both houses banned any

---

* Two of the major problems with respect to congressional staffs are preventing members from placing relatives in such positions and from using committee staff to do their own personal work.

Figure 11.1
House use of franking privilege, 1971–1974.
Source: Common Cause; reprinted in *Congressional Ethics* (Washington, D.C.:
Congressional Quarterly, Inc., April 1977), p. 41.

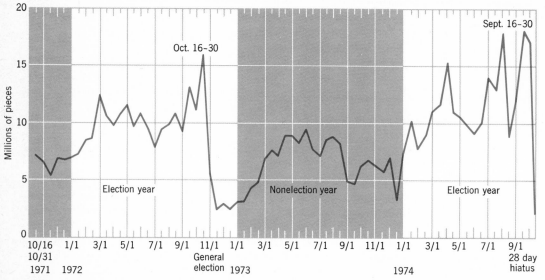

franked mass mailings within sixty days of a primary or general election in which a congressman is a candidate.

Finally, there are a number of other valuable "perks" enjoyed by congressmen. Included are traveling abroad at the taxpayer's expense (as noted earlier, however, "lame duck" congressmen can no longer have one last fling on their ungrateful constituents), free medical care and parking while at work, low-cost food, haircuts and gifts at government-subsidized establishments, and even plants and pictures with which to decorate their offices.

Thus a congressman's lot is not without its compensations. Indeed, a 1975 study by the *Americans for Democratic Action,* a liberal interest group, estimated the total value of a congressman's salary, staff and other allowances, and special privileges at nearly a half-million dollars a year. Recent wage and price increases in those items would set today's comparable figure at considerably above that amount.

At the same time, it should be realized that our national legislators have special demands placed on them. The cost of maintaining two homes (as many of them do), of travel between Washington and their home district (many make more than the authorized number of visits, and the travel allowance does not cover trips for family members), plus the expense of entertaining constituents while they are in Washington (lunch in the Senate dining room is not free, but goes on the congressman's bill); adds up to a heavy drain on the personal resources of members of Congress. Thus while congressmen live a busy and good life, it is not one that permits most to build up even a modest fortune.

BICAMERALISM IN THE AMERICAN CONGRESS

One basic and distinctive feature of the American Congress is that it has two separate and independent chambers. A number of factors contributed to the

decision of the Constitutional Convention to divide it so. One was the British legacy; the English Parliament was divided into two chambers, the House of Lords and the House of Commons. A second was the bicameralism of many of the colonial legislatures, where the upper chamber was composed of emissaries of the crown appointed by the king or his representatives and the lower consisted of individuals elected by the colonists themselves.

But these traditions were not determinative; after all, the legislature under the Articles of Confederation had been unicameral. Rather, the two-house legislature grew out of the conflicts described in chapters 2 and 3: the political struggle between large and small states and the legal battle over the issue of whether national legislators were to represent sovereign states or individuals. The "Connecticut Compromise" settled both arguments.

Bicameralism continues to have an effect on the workings of the American Congress. Most nations in the world today have two legislative chambers (two unicameral exceptions are Denmark and New Zealand), but in few places are they equally important. Rather, upper houses in nations like Great Britain and Italy are relics of the days of aristocracy; they are composed of persons who hold life tenure but who have little influence over the legislative process, which is controlled in reality by the popular, lower body. Only in countries like Australia and the United States does the upper house act as a coordinate legislative chamber. And of these few the United States Senate is preeminent, the most influential upper legislative chamber in the world.

The Founding Fathers had distinct purposes in mind for the Senate as compared to the House of Representatives. They created it to protect the interests of sovereign states, a function also served by upper legislative chambers in other federal systems, such as Australia, Switzerland, and West Germany. Beyond this, the Senate was expected to safeguard property interests: the prestigious nature of a Senate seat, it was thought, would attract an aristocratic elite, insulated from popular control by both indirect selection and a long term in office. In contrast, the directly elected House members with two-year terms were to reflect the interests of the many, those with little in the nature of worldly goods.

Linked to the protection of states' rights and property interests was the intention of using the Senate to check on hasty legislation passed by the House of Representatives. (As Washington explained the Convention's decision to the absent Jefferson, delegates provided for two houses to act on legislation for the same reason that they poured their coffee into a saucer—to let it "cool.") Thus the bicameral legislature was meant to serve two major purposes: the representation of different interests and deliberative, careful law making.

The Founding Fathers also had separate special functions in mind for the Senate and House. The Senate was to pass on the qualifications of the President's nominees to major positions in the national government, and it was to play a major role in foreign policy through the power to "advise and consent" on treaties negotiated by the President with other countries. The House was entrusted with the special and traditional prerogative of lower chambers: originating bills to raise revenue.

Having examined the reasons behind the Founders' adoption of a two-house legislature, we now turn to the ways in which the Senate and House carry on their business.

THE NATURE OF POWER IN CONGRESS

One of the most intriguing and controversial questions about any organization is, who controls it? Americans today seem preoccupied with this basic issue as it pertains to both private and public groups—universities, churches, and corporations, as well as all levels and branches of government. The standard answer, particularly with those who are unhappy with our basic institutions, is that the "establishment" an inner clique—determines the decisions of all of them.

When a political scientist examines the issue of organizational control, he tries to discover *who* has "power." And by power he means the ability of one person (A) to get another (B) to do his (A's) bidding. The political scientist asks, who can get others to do what he wants them to do even though they personally would prefer not to? Who are the leaders and who are the followers?

A related issue is the question of *how* power is exercised—whether through coercion or by persuasion. Another question is, what is the *source* of power? Does an individual have it because he occupies a particular position in an organization or because he has special skills in interpersonal relationships?

In Congress power involves the ability to shape major decisions. Thus legislators who successfully initiate, block, or make changes in legislative proposals through their ability to get other congressmen to go along with their desires exercise power. Power can be exerted in other functions of the legislature too. The senators who took the leadership in successfully defeating President Nixon's nominations of Clement Haynesworth and G. Harrold Carswell to the Supreme Court were also exercising power.

Who exercises power in the American Congress? As political scientist Randall Ripley suggests, there are various possibilities. It may be the persons who hold *elected positions* in the two chambers, such as the presiding officers of the two houses and the party officials chosen by the Democratic and Republican members. If so, we would say that power is *centralized*.

Another possibility is that congressional power is primarily exercised by chairmen of the various standing committees of the Senate and House. In such circumstances, power would be *decentralized*.

Power might not reside in those who hold official positions in the Congress, whether presiding officers, party officials, or committee chairmen. Rather, the organization may be controlled behind the scenes by an inner clique, some of whose members may not occupy any official post at all. Power in that situation would be *informal*.

Finally, there is the possibility that neither the official leadership of the Congress nor any informal group controls decisions but that rank-and-file members are to a great degree their own men. That power would be *individualized*.

With these general considerations in mind, in the following sections we will analyze the exercise of power in the American Congress. Because the situation differs somewhat in the two chambers, the Senate and the House will be examined separately. Attention will also be focused on the major changes that have taken place in the power structures of both bodies in recent years.

POWER WITHIN THE SENATE

There are two kinds of central leaders in the Senate. One is composed of those who preside over the body and exercise essentially ceremonial duties in that

chamber. Included in this group are the Vice-President of the United States and the Senate President Pro Tempore. The other type of central leader occupies a party position, such as a Majority Leader, Minority Leader, and party Whip. There are great differences in the amount and type of power that these two types of leaders exercise in the Senate.

Presiding Officers—Vice-President and President Pro Tempore

Under the Constitution the Vice-President of the United States is the President of the Senate. As such, he is entitled to preside over it and exercise such duties as recognizing speakers and ruling on points of procedure. He has no vote, however, unless there is a tie among the senators, in which case he can cast a ballot to break it. He can also assign bills to committee, a decision that can be important if a measure could be referred to more than one committee. One, for example, might speed it on its way to passage, while another might pigeonhole it, or bury it, a matter that we shall examine subsequently in the chapter.

The Vice-President is not an important figure in the Senate. Because he is not chosen by the senators themselves, they regard him as an outsider, especially when he is of the opposite political party from the one that controls the upper chamber—the fate of Republicans Richard Nixon and Spiro Agnew in Democratic Senates. Yet even when the Vice-President is from the party in control, he is still an outsider to some degree. Lyndon Johnson did not try to run the Senate when he was Vice-President from 1961 to 1963 as he had done as Majority Leader in the previous six years. Senate Democrats would have considered the attempt highly improper, even though he was an esteemed colleague whose leadership they had accepted in the immediately preceding period.

The President Pro Tempore who presides over the Senate in the absence of the Vice-President is not a powerful figure in the Senate either, even though he is selected by the members themselves. The choice is distinctly ritualistic: the party that controls the Senate nominates the person with the most seniority, and in a straight-line party vote he defeats the candidate of the minority party.

In early 1977 a new post of Senate Deputy President Pro Tempore was created for Hubert Humphrey, a long-time favorite of his colleagues who had unsuccessfully sought the majority leadership discussed below. Although the new post carried no meaningful powers, it did give Humphrey an additional salary, a chauffered limousine, an expanded staff, and the right to be included in congressional leadership meetings with President Carter. It remains to be seen whether the post will be continued after Humphrey no longer occupies it.

Since presiding over the Senate is generally unimportant, frequently none of the above officials does so. The role is rather assumed by freshman senators of the majority party who take a turn at exercising the responsibility.

Majority and Minority Leaders

The single most powerful person in the United States Senate is the *Majority Leader,* who is chosen by the members of the party in control. Although experience in the Senate is an important asset for a would-be leader, it is by no means determinative. Lyndon Johnson, considered by some observers to be the most influential Majority Leader (1955-61) in the history of the Senate, came to that position during his very first term in office. Democrat Mike Mansfield,

Johnson's successor, and William Knowland, the last Republican to sit in that post (1953–55), were both in the early years of their second term when chosen.

The Majority Leader has a number of rewards with which to affect the behavior of his fellow senators. He can use his influence with the committee that makes assignments to Senate standing committees. Lyndon Johnson's decision to allow freshmen senators to sit on one important committee (previously they had been placed only on obscure ones) helped build a base of political support on which he drew for a number of years. The Leader can also see to it that favored senators get appointed to select committees that take foreign "junkets," that they receive favorable office space, that some governmental installations (post offices, dams, federal buildings, air bases, and the like) are placed in their states, that grants are awarded to universities and local governments in their area, and that private bills they favor (such as allowing a relative of a constituent to come into the country under a special act of Congress) are given favorable consideration.

Even more crucial to the influence of the Majority Leader is his position in the center of the Senate's communications network. As the man responsible for legislative scheduling, he is in a position to know the status of bills: to which committee they have been assigned; what their chances are of being favorably reported out; which senators are for and against them; and when and under what conditions they will be ready for debate and voting on the floor of the chamber. In a confusing system of specialized committees and complex legislative procedures, the Majority Leader is the one man who sees the overall workings of the Senate. He thus possesses more information on more matters than any other senator, and he can use it to further his influence. Moreover, it is to him that the rank-and-file member must turn for knowledge and advice about particular concerns.

The Majority Leader also acts as the chamber's communication link with the President. The relationship is particularly close if, as is usual, both men are from the same party. Then he is regularly briefed by the man in the White House on the administration's programs and is expected to use his influence to get favorable Senate action on them. He thus becomes a source of intelligence on what the President wants, how keenly he wants it, and what compromises he is willing to accept to get some measure enacted. Information on presidential attitudes is sometimes important even when he and the Majority Leader are not from the same party. In developing Democratic legislative proposals in the late 1950s, Lyndon Johnson took into account what President Eisenhower would and would not accept (for example, how many units of public housing at what cost) and scaled down his party's bills to avoid a presidential veto.

The Majority Leader not only conveys presidential wishes to senators, but he also informs the Chief Executive of their attitudes. His colleagues thus expect him to be not just the President's man but theirs as well. Playing both these roles satisfactorily is not an easy matter, but the Majority Leader who does so can do much to cement good relationships between the legislative and executive branches of the national government.

In many respects, the *Minority Leader* parallels his majority counterpart: he is elected by his colleagues; he tends to have experience, but seniority alone is not determinative (Everett Dirksen of Illinois and his son-in-law, Howard Baker Jr. of Tennessee, both came to the post during their second term in the

Senate); and he serves as the focal point of communication among senators of the minority party. Because he works closely with the Majority Leader in legislative scheduling, he too is a source of information on the status of bills and their likelihood of being enacted into law.

The Minority Leader also has certain prerogatives that allow him political influence over his colleagues—he can influence committee assignments to some degree—but the rewards he can bestow are not as plentiful as those of the Majority Leader. For example, he has less to say about where governmental installations are to be located. He is also less likely to have the President's legislative program as a focal point for rallying his colleagues. Even when he does (Republican senators Robert Taft and William Knowland were Minority Leaders during the Eisenhower administration; Everett Dirksen held the post during the earlier Nixon years; and Hugh Scott was Minority Leader in the later years of Nixon's presidency and during the Ford administration), he has difficulty influencing a body controlled by the opposition party. The President may indeed find it politically more profitable to work with the opposition Majority Leader, particularly if the President's own party has relatively few senators compared to the majority party.

Whips

Both the Majority and Minority Leaders have assistants commonly referred to as *Whips*. The term came from the British Parliament, which borrowed it from fox-hunting: the Whip, or "whipper-in," was responsible for keeping the hounds from leaving the pack during the chase of the fox. By analogy, the Whip keeps the rank-and-file members from straying from the party fold; he sees to it that they are present to vote on key legislative measures and to cast their ballot as party leaders desire.

According to Senator Edward Kennedy, who served as Democratic Whip from 1969 to 1971, the name is a misnomer, for the Whip does not have the ability to bring his colleagues into line. He rather serves as a potential communication link between his Floor Leader (this is the term applied to either the Majority or Minority Leader) and the rank-and-file members of his party, letting each know what the other is thinking so that legislative strategy can be planned accordingly.

Even that function is not indispensable to the two Floor Leaders, since they can personally contact the limited number of senators from their party without too much difficulty. When Lyndon Johnson was Majority Leader, he was reputed to have talked daily with every Democratic senator.

To a considerable extent, the situation of a Whip under his Floor Leader is like that of a Vice-President under the President: frequently the two who are supposedly serving as a team come from the opposing factions of the party—Democratic Whip Alan Cranston of California, for instance, is much more liberal than the Majority Leader, Robert Byrd, with whom he serves. Personal relationships between the two may also be strained, as they were between former Democratic Whip Russell Long of Louisiana and his leader, Mike Mansfield of Montana. If so, the Floor Leader may simply work around his Whip, as Mansfield did when he appointed four assistant Whips to aid him in the Senate. Like the Vice-President's, the Whip's job is what his superior wants it to be: when Edward Kennedy replaced Long in 1969, Mansfield not only used the young senator (whom he admired) to gather information and get Democratic senators to the floor for crucial votes, but he also permitted Kennedy to share legislative scheduling and other leadership responsibilities. Mansfield also turned over many of the details of handling the legislative business of the Senate to his subsequent Whip, Robert Byrd.

The post of Whip also resembles the vice-presidency in that it may constitute a stepping-stone upward. Since 1949, four Democrats—Scott Lucas, Lyndon Johnson, Mike Mansfield, and Robert Byrd—and three Republicans—Kenneth Wherry, Everett Dirksen, and Hugh Scott—have been promoted to the Floor Leader's position by their party colleagues. Thus the position of Whip has recently become a training-ground for the top party post in the Senate.

Party Committees

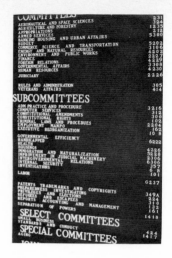

There are three major groups in each party. One is concerned with the assignment of members to standing committees (the Democrats call theirs the Steering Committee; the Republicans, the Committee on Committees). The second, the Policy Committee, is responsible for discussing the issues and helping to establish legislative agendas. The third, known as the Conference, to which all members of each party belong, serves as the major organizing body for each party. However as we shall see, the parties differ in the way in which they choose members of the first two committees as well as in the role the three groups play in party affairs. In addition, the particular style of the Floor Leader affects how the various groups operate.

The *Democratic Steering Committee* is chaired by their Floor Leader who also nominates all its members; such nominations are typically approved by the Democratic Conference. Its membership usually includes the Whip and many chairmen of standing committees as well. Although seniority in the Senate is a major factor in assignments and transfers, the Floor Leader can influence these decisions. As indicated previously, Lyndon Johnson initiated a rule that guaranteed even the most junior senator a major committee assignment, a tradition that was continued by his successor, Mike Mansfield. However, the operating styles and political preferences of the two majority leaders differed considerably. Johnson told the Steering Committee whom he wanted to see placed on various committees, while Mansfield generally permitted the Committee members to make their own decisions on such matters. Also, under Johnson the more conservative senators dominated the most important committees; in contrast, Mansfield used his influence with the Steering Committee to see to it that your liberal senators were assigned to such committees.

The *Republican Committee on Committees* is chaired not by the Floor Leader but by some other senior senator with good standing among his party colleagues. Except for the chairman, its members rotate every two years. The influence of the Floor Leader on the committee has also been lessened by the Republicans' tendency in assignments and transfers to standing committees to follow the seniority principle fairly strictly.

The Legislative Reorganization Act of 1946, which created the *Senate Policy Committees,* intended that they would be executive groups entrusted with the planning, development, and implementation of party programs. Under Lyndon

Johnson the seven-member Democratic group, composed largely of senior conservative senators from the South, was used to schedule legislation, with Johnson himself largely dictating its decisions. Under Mansfield, the Committee's size was expanded, junior liberal senators were added to the body, and the Majority Leader let the committee members play a larger role in determining which legislation should be brought to the floor and when it would be considered. The Republican Policy Committee is more independent of the party leadership, for it is chaired by someone other than the Floor Leader, and its members are nominated by the chairman of the Republican Conference and approved by the members of the Conference. It has also been of considerable service to rank-and-file Republicans in doing research, reporting on legislation, and providing them with material for use in their campaigns.

Finally, the *Conferences* of the two parties have also varied in recent years. Again the Floor Leader chairs the Democratic one, but how the Conference operates depends on the inclinations of individual leaders. Under Johnson, the Conference met only at the beginning of the legislative session for the limited purpose of organizing itself for the next two years; in contrast, with Mansfield at its head, the Conference met frequently and initiated many of the reforms discussed below dealing with the selection and staffing of committees as well as with the procedures used in committees and on the floor of the Senate. The Republicans again choose some senator besides their Floor Leader to chair the Conference; they meet frequently; and they occasionally even pass a resolution favoring a particular piece of legislation. Even so, like members of the Democratic Conference, they shy away from passing binding resolutions on controversial bills for fear that they will antagonize dissenting Republican senators and thereby jeopardize party unity.

Standing-Committee Chairmen

A second major source of power within the Senate lies with the chairmen of the permanent standing committees to which bills are referred for consideration prior to floor action. Over eighty years ago Woodrow Wilson referred to them as "little legislatures" in which the real work of Congress is accomplished. The greater volume of legislation that the Congress considers, plus the need for specialization in a more complex and technical society, has made the Senate—and the House as well—even more dependent on the committees today than they were in Wilson's time. Both chambers are inclined to accept the action (or inaction) of standing committees on most legislation.

The jurisdictions of committees are determined by the Senate itself. In 1946 that body, along with the House, passed the Legislative Reorganization Act, reducing the number of committees from thirty-three to fifteen. Over the years that number increased, and in early 1977 the Senate once again overhauled its committee structure, this time paring the number from thirty-one to twenty-five with a further reduction to twenty-one scheduled by the end of 1978. In the process, similar activities undertaken by separate committees were consolidated, including the concentration of energy legislation in one committee, headed by Senator Henry Jackson of Washington.

The standing committees of the Senate deal with a variety of subjects, including such divergent matters as agriculture, banking and currency, the armed services, and foreign relations. Two are concerned with money matters: the Finance Committee, which deals with raising it, and Appropriations, which decides how it shall be spent.

Not all standing committees, however, are of equal importance. The special role that the Senate plays in foreign affairs makes the Foreign Relations and Armed Services Committees particularly crucial to the Senate's work. Appropriations is a key committee because the level of expenditures allotted for various governmental programs reflects senatorial priorities and helps to determine how well each program operates. The Finance Committee is significant because it makes decisions about how the tax burden will be distributed among the population.

The committees' pecking order is reflected in their membership. Senior senators with high status among their colleagues are most likely to populate the key committees. Some freshmen senators manage to get on such committees early in their careers: one example is Harry Byrd Jr. of Virginia who sat on both the Armed Services and Finance Committees in his first term in office. More commonly, if a seat is open, a senior member is transferred to it from another committee; sometimes a senator gives up one committee chairmanship to accept another one, as Senator John Sparkman of Alabama did when he resigned the chairmanship of the Banking, Housing and Urban Affairs Committee to become chairman of the Foreign Relations Committee.

Traditionally both parties have followed a seniority custom of choosing the member with the longest continuous service on a committee as its chairman or ranking minority member. However, recently both parties have made it possible for members to overturn that custom: Republican committee members choose their own chairman, subject to the approval of the Republican Conference; Democratic members vote by secret ballot on a committee chairman if one-fifth of the Democratic senators request it. However, to date, neither party has used these new rules to deny a chairmanship to an individual entitled to one under the seniority custom.

As a result of the seniority system, senators from "safe," one-party states (which return them to office again and again) who choose to stay with a particular committee assignment move automatically up the ladder to the chairmanship when their party controls the chamber. When the Democrats exercise control (they have failed to control the upper chamber only four years since 1933), the chairmen of committees—particularly the important ones like Appropriations, Finance, Armed Services, and Foreign Relations—have come from the South. The ranking minority members of such committees, ready to take over the chairmanships if the Republicans once again gain control of the Senate, have tended to come from the area where the GOP has traditionally been strong—the Midwest. This situation is changing, however, for both Democrats and Republicans: senators from other areas of the country already occupy the chairmanships and ranking minority positions of many Senate committees and stand to take over those of the prestigious committees as well when some of the very senior Democrats and Republicans retire or are defeated for reelection in the future.

The power of the standing committee chairman in the Senate stems from two main sources. One is the preferments he has at his disposal vis-à-vis other committee members. The chairman can favor a colleague, for example, by

helping him become the chairman of an important subcommittee. The chairman can also see to it that a member gets to go on trips the committee makes in connection with its work. Moreover, he can allow a member to become the sponsor of an important piece of legislation, to lead the fight on the floor for its adoption, and to be included as a member of the conference committee assigned to work out any differences between the Senate and the House over the measure.

These activities also relate to the other major power base of a committee chairman: the ability to utilize the procedures of his own committee and the floor action of the entire chamber on legislation referred to it. As we shall see later in this chapter, the standing committee chairman looms large in the legal and political maneuverings of the legislative process.

An Inner Club or Establishment

Observers of the Senate in the 1950s like political scientist Donald Matthews and journalist William White contended that the body was controlled behind the scenes by a clique known as the "Inner Club" or "Establishment." Supposedly centered on senior Southern Democrats like Richard Russel of Georgia, Robert Kerr of Oklahoma, and Lyndon Johnson of Texas, the group was also thought to include Republicans like Everett Dirksen and liberal Democrats like Hubert Humphrey who followed certain "folkways" or customs required of "Club" types. Included were such norms as serving an *apprenticeship* before becoming actively involved in senate affairs; *specializing* so as to become an expert in a particular area of public policy; carrying one's share of the *legislative workload;* being *courteous* to other senators and avoiding personal attacks on political opponents; practicing *reciprocity* by honoring one's agreements and understanding other senators' problems and point of view; and remaining *loyal to the Senate* by not using it as a stepping stone to the presidency or vice-presidency.

Not all students of the Senate of the 1950s agreed with Matthews's and White's assessment of its power structure. Difficulties in agreeing precisely who was included in the "Inner Club" raised questions about its actual existence; also some doubted whether a group composed of men with such divergent political views as Russel and Humphrey could work together on vital legislation involving controversial issues of public policy. In any event, there is general agreement that even if such a group did control the Senate twenty years ago, it no longer does. Key figures like Russel, Kerr, Johnson, and Dirksen are gone, and a new breed of young legislators like Democrats Birch Bayh of Indiana and Thomas Eagleton of Missouri and Republicans like Mark Hatfield of Oregon and Charles Percy of Illinois have come into prominence.

The Power of Individual Senators

Attitudes of senators towards some of the folkways that guided their behavior in the 1950s have changed in the last twenty years. While the norms involving specialization, assuming a share of the legislative workload, and courtesy and reciprocity in dealing with one's colleagues are still respected, those preventing senators from seeking higher office and requiring them to serve an apprenticeship are not. A number of present-day senators including Democrats Birch

Bayh of Indiana, Lloyd Bentsen of Texas, Frank Church of Idaho, Hubert Humphrey of Minnesota, Henry Jackson of Washington, George McGovern of South Dakota, and Edwin Muskie of Maine, and Republican Barry Goldwater of Arizona, have unsuccessfully sought the presidency, yet have not been considered disloyal to the Senate or lost their influence in that body because of their presidential ambitions. Nor are new members now expected to sit back and wait until they have been in the Senate for a number of years before becoming actively involved in promoting legislation on important issues of public policy. For example, Bayh steered a controversial constitutional amendment relating to presidential succession (we will examine that amendment in ch. 12) through the Senate during his third year in that body, and during his first term in office Muskie took a leadership role on the issues of pollution and intergovernmental relations.

In fact, recent developments in the structuring and staffing of committees have significantly increased the power of individual senators, including those without much seniority in that body. The Legislative Reorganization Act of 1946 limited the number of standing Senate committees to fifteen, but over the years that number has been increased; even more significant has been the proliferation of subcommittees—smaller units into which parent committees subdivide to handle their ever-increasing work load. Even though the major committee reorganization in 1977 reduced the number of Senate committees and subcommittees, they still stood at over 20 and 100 respectively after the reorganization had taken place. Thus there are a large number of committee and subcommittee positions to be filled by the 100 members of the Senate.

Moreover, in recent years, the Senate has acted to limit the number of committee and subcommittee positions that an individual senator can occupy. Under the terms of the 1977 reorganization, for example, each senator is limited to membership on three committees and a total of eight subcommittees of those three parent committees. He is also prohibited from chairing a total of more than four committees and subcommittees, a figure that is scheduled to be further cut to three after 1978. The end result of these limitations is that committee and subcommittee posts and chairmanships are distributed widely among members of the Senate, including very junior members of that body.

Unlike the situation in the 1950s, a young senator today can begin to exercise influence in the Senate very early in his career. By becoming a member—and even more importantly, a chairman of a subcommittee—he can exert power that is felt up the line, for parent committees are inclined to accept the actions of their subcommittees, and the entire chamber often respects the decisions of the standing committees. Also contributing to the junior member's effectiveness is a 1975 Senate resolution that permits him to have additional staff to help him with his legislative duties.

Thus individual senators can today play a meaningful legislative role after a relatively short period of service. The newness of many of our national programs, the willingness of young legislators to educate themselves so that they become known as Senate "experts" on vital issues, and the availability of subcommittee chairmanship and staff with which to operate, all contribute to the legislative effectiveness of junior members of the Senate. Even members of the minority party can acquire reputations as specialists in a particular area, as Republican Charles Percy has done, for example, in the field of housing.

One other feature of the Senate allows individual members to be influential

Senate dissenters: William Fulbright, Wayne Morse and Eugene McCarthy.

Table 11.1
Power Structure of The
U.S. Senate, 95th
Congress (1977–79)

Ceremonial Offices

Vice-President of the U.S.	Walter Mondale (Minnesota)
President Pro Tem of the Senate	James Eastland (Mississippi)
Deputy President Pro Tem of the Senate	Hubert Humphrey (Minnesota)

Party Leaders

Majority Party (Democrats)		Minority Party (Republicans)
Floor Leader	Robert Byrd (West Virginia)	Howard Baker (Tennessee)
Whip	Alan Cranston (California)	Ted Stevens (Alaska)
Chairman of the Conference	Robert Byrd (West Virginia)	Carl Curtis (Nebraska)
Secretary of the Conference	Daniel Inouye (Hawaii)	Clifford Hansen (Idaho)
		(Committee on Committees)
Steering Committee Chairman	Robert Byrd (West Virginia)	Jake Garn (Utah)
Policy Committee Chairman	Robert Byrd (West Virginia)	John Tower (Texas)

Important Standing Committees

Chairman (Democrats)		Ranking Minority Member (Republicans)
Appropriations	John McClellan (Arkansas)	Milton Young (North Dakota)
Armed Services	John Stennis (Mississippi)	John Tower (Texas)
Finance	Russell Long (Louisiana)	Carl Curtis (Nebraska)
Foreign Relations	John Sparkman (Alabama)	Clifford Case (New Jersey)

in the affairs of that chamber: toleration of, and even respect for, the critic or dissenter. Included among senators who have played that role in recent years are Wayne Morse of Oregon, Ernest Gruening of Alaska, William Fulbright of Arkansas, Eugene McCarthy of Minnesota, and William Proxmire of Wisconsin. The Senate's tolerance of deviant views, plus the natural interest that unpopular views engender among the media, ensure that persons who disagree with their colleagues on major matters of public policy will find a ready outlet for their criticisms as indicated by the publicity given criticisms of the Vietnam war by Morse, Fulbright and McCarthy. Moreover, the eventual change that took place in our nation's handling of that tragic war attest to the fact that critics of traditional policies can ultimately be effective in the determination of public policy.

Power in the United States Senate is thus distributed broadly among a variety of persons. Before we analyze the major patterns of influence that prevail there, it would be instructive to compare and contrast the situation just described with that of the lower chamber of the United States Congress, the House of Representatives.

POWER WITHIN THE HOUSE OF REPRESENTATIVES

In some respects the sources and distribution of power within the House and the Senate are quite similar. Yet as indicated below, there are also some differences in the power structure of the two chambers.

Party Leaders

Unlike the Senate, the House has no purely ceremonial figure to preside over its deliberations. Rather, this function is handled by the body's most powerful figure—the *Speaker of the House of Representatives.* Theoretically chosen as an officer of the entire chamber, he is, in essence, selected by the caucus of the majority party, since this group nominates and then votes for him over the opposing party's candidate. Thus the Speaker is both a House and a party official.

Because this is so, the ceremonial duties of the Vice-President and the political powers of the Senate Majority Leader are combined in the office of Speaker. He has the power of recognition, rules on procedural questions, and refers bills to committees. But unlike the Vice-President, he is not a neutral figure with no vote except in a tie: not only can he vote, but he also can and does leave the chair to lead and participate in debate. Like the Senate Majority Leader he is the floor captain of his party who plans strategy and schedules measures for consideration and action.

The Speaker has generally the same rewards for exercising influence over his colleagues as does his Senate counterpart: assistance in obtaining a favorable committee assignment, appointment to select committees, help with favored private bills, invitations to serve as floor leader for a measure or to preside over the House, and help with a tough political campaign. Like the Senate Majority Leader, too, he is in the center of the internal communication network of the House as well as being its link with the White House.

In recent years the power of a Democratic Speaker has been increased considerably. As indicated below, a new Democratic Steering and Policy Committee was created in 1973 with the responsibility of nominating persons for committee assignments as well as helping to devise and direct the party's legislative program. These added responsibilities redounded to the benefit of the Democratic Speaker because he was made chairman of the Democratic Steering and Policy Committee and was also given a dominant role in choosing members of the Committee. Furthermore, the Speaker was granted additional powers to affect the procedures of the House that are described in more detail later in this chapter: he is now empowered to refer bills to standing committees and also to nominate the chairman and Democratic members of the House Rules Committee that plays such a major role in determining the scheduling and consideration of legislation on the floor of the House. Also redounding to the benefit of the Democratic Speaker is the recent increase in the number of assistant whips as well as in the financial and staff resources of the Whip's office.

Working with the Speaker of the House is the *Majority Leader.* Officially chosen by the majority party caucus, he is often the favorite of the Speaker himself. In any event, his influence in the House will be what the Speaker permits it to be. Generally he assists the Speaker in scheduling legislation, distributing and collecting information of concern to the majority-party members, and attempting to persuade the rank-and-file legislators to go along with the wishes of the legislative party leaders and also of the President, if he is from their party. As a subordinate, however, the Majority Leader frequently has a higher goal in mind: selection as Speaker when the incumbent dies or retires. For Democratic Majority Leaders of late this aspiration has been realized: five in a row—William Bankhead of Alabama, Sam Rayburn of Texas, John McCormack of Massachusetts, Carl Albert of Oklahoma, and Thomas O'Neill Jr. of Massachusetts—were all promoted to the top spot in the House.

The nominee of the minority party caucus who loses out in the election for the speakership becomes the *Minority Leader* of the House. His role is essentially the same as it is in the Senate: to work with the Majority Leader in scheduling legislation and to lead the opposition party. He has some influence over committee assignments and the like, but he suffers from the same frustrations of his Senate counterpart: fewer preferments than the majority party can offer and, except when his party controls the presidency, lack of an external program around which to muster the support of his House colleagues.

The *Majority* and *Minority Whips* have the same general function as they do in the Senate: to serve as a communications link between the party leadership and rank-and-file members and to see to it that the latter are there when crucial votes are taken. This function takes on far more importance in the House than it does in the Senate, however, because the greater number of members in the lower chamber makes it almost impossible for the party leaders themselves to reach them. (Whereas Lyndon Johnson could be in touch with all members of his party in the Senate in the 1950s, Sam Rayburn, serving as the Speaker of the House at the same time, could not.) Both parties have elaborate organizations composed of representatives (called *Assistant Whips*) from various areas of the nation who serve as liaison with colleagues from their regions.

There are, however, some differences in the parties' approach to the Whips. The Democratic Whip is appointed by their Floor Leader with the concurrence of the Speaker, while the Republican Conference (a body to which all House Republicans belong) chooses that party's Whip. As a consequence, the Democratic Whip is always part of the party team, a result that does not always occur in the G.O.P. (For instance, when Gerald Ford was chosen Minority Leader in 1965, he backed another candidate against the long-time incumbent Leslie Arends—who had served since 1943—but the Republican Conference continued Arends in office.) This difference in selection policy affects the pattern of succession to higher party offices in the House. Democratic Speakers John McCormack, Carl Albert, and Thomas O'Neill previously served as Whips (as well as Majority Leaders), but no Republican Whip in this century has been similarly promoted.

Party Committees

The functions of party committees in the House of Representatives parallel those in the Senate: assigning members to committees; taking the leadership in developing a legislative program; and establishing an overall group for party decision making in the House. However, as indicated below, the parties differ in how they handle such responsibilities; moreover, the Democratic party has made major changes in recent years with respect to such matters.

Traditionally, the Democratic party used its members on the House Ways and Means Committee (this committee is described in the next section) to serve as its Committee on Committees, which also included the Speaker, Majority Leader, and the Chairman of the Democratic Caucus (a body composed of all Democrats in the House). This group not only assigned members to standing committees but also followed the seniority custom in nominating the committee chairmen. While its nominees for chairmen had to be approved by the Democratic Caucus, there was no effective way for the Caucus to register its disapproval of a particular chairman because the nominees were all presented in a single slate. Moreover, if the entire slate were voted down, the Committee on Committees could resubmit a second slate also containing the objectionable chairman, but with the names of some favored chairmen removed. Faced with this situation, the Democratic Caucus automatically approved the recommendations of the Committee on Committees.

Beginning in 1971, however, the Democrats began to change their system so as to give the Caucus a more meaningful role in choosing committee chairmen. Initially, the Committee on Committees was required to present its nominees for chairmen one committee at a time, and upon the demand of ten or more Democratic members of the House, any nomination could be debated and voted upon. Later the system was changed so that all individual chairmen were voted on automatically and, if 20 percent of the members demanded it, the vote was by secret ballot. Ultimately, as we have seen, in 1973 House Democrats took the responsibility of nominating committee chairmen away from the Committee on Committees altogether and placed it in the newly created Steering and Policy Committee. New rules also provide for nominations to be made from the floor of the Caucus meetings in the event that an initial nomination of the Steering and Policy Committee is voted down.

The new system soon had an effect on the choosing of the chairmen of standing committees. In 1975 three standing committee chairmen—Bob Poage (Texas) of the Agriculture Committee, F. Edward Hebert (Louisiana) of the Armed Services Committee, and Wright Patman (Texas) of the Banking, Commerce, and Housing Committee—lost their positions as a result of action by the Democratic Caucus. In addition, Wayne Hays (Ohio), chairman of the Administration Committee, barely survived when Philip Burton (California), chairman of the Caucus, convinced its members to retain Hays in office even though the Steering and Policy Committee had not approved his nomination. However, as we saw at the beginning of the chapter, Hays finally lost his chairmanship in 1976 when he became involved in a sex scandal and, under pressure from the Caucus, resigned his position to avoid being voted out of it.

In addition to their new role in choosing chairmen of the standing committees of the House, both the Democratic Steering and Policy Committee and the Democratic Caucus have recently begun to play a more meaningful role in other business of the House. The Committee has taken the leadership in helping the Speaker of the House develop and implement the party's legislative program, thus serving as an executive committee for party policies and prac-

tices. The Caucus, which used to restrict itself to a short meeting at the beginning of a congressional session to choose its leadership and ratify committee assignments, now conducts its organizational meeting prior to the opening of the session and meets more regularly during the session on matters of public policy. Its most impressive recent demonstration of power was a vote taken in 1975 binding the Democratic members of the powerful Rules Committee (described below) to allow amendments to a tax bill to be made on the floor of the House removing special concessions for oil and gas interests.

The above events have thus made a substantial difference in the role that Democratic party committees play in House affairs. While not commanding the attention of recent activities of the majority party, House Republicans have also made some changes in the way they handle the choosing of ranking members of standing committees. In 1971 they changed their procedure so that all members of the House Conference (the counterpart of the Democratic Caucus) can vote by secret ballot on each nomination made by their Committee on Committees. The Republican Policy Committee (which unlike the Democratic one dates not just from 1973 but back to 1949) has been active since its creation in helping to develop a consensus of rank-and-file members on legislation and in communicating their attitudes to the party leadership. Most recently, however, this function has been assumed by the Republican Conference.

Standing Committee Chairmen

Traditionally, standing-committee chairmen have held a powerful position in the House. Protected by selection through the automatic system of seniority, they dominated the consideration of legislation by their committee, including the decision whether or not to utilize subcommittees, and if so, how these subcommittees should be staffed and financed. However, a number of recent reforms have drastically reduced the powers of committee chairmen in the House of Representatives.

As we have already seen, one major difference in the situation of House committee chairmen is that their tenure is no longer secure. Instead of automatic nomination by the Committee on Committees on the basis of seniority, followed by rubber-stamp approval by the party rank-and-file, chairmen and ranking minority members must now pass muster with the Democratic Steering and Policy Committee or its counterpart, the Republican Committee on Committees, and be individually approved by the members of the Democratic Caucus or the Republican Conference. The recent action of House Democrats in deposing three committee chairmen serves as a reminder that aspirants for that position must keep their fences mended both with party leaders in the House and with rank-and-file members.

The 1970 Legislative Reorganization Act passed by a coalition of Republicans and liberal Democrats also makes it much more difficult for chairmen to dominate the proceedings of committees as they once did. Included among the provisions of the Act are the requirements that members be given advance notice of committee meetings; that all its roll-call votes be made public; that committee members be given three days to file minority or supplementary reports on committee legislation; and that they be empowered to call up for floor action a bill being withheld by the chairman. In addition, the Act encouraged the holding of "open" meetings. In 1973 the House went further by providing that normal committee meetings be open to the public unless a majority of the committee members vote by roll call to close a particular meeting.

Finally, as a result of recent Democratic reforms, their committee chairmen have lost control over the operations of subcommittees. Chairmen no longer can decide unilaterally whether or not to have subcommittees; make discretionary decisions on which legislative matters to refer to them; and control their membership, staff, and budget. Now all committees with more than fifteen members must be divided into at least four subcommittees, and legislative hearings increasingly begin at the subcommittee level. Moreover, the choice of subcommittee chairmen now lies not with the standing committee chairmen but rather with the Democratic members of the committee,* and each subcommittee chairman and ranking minority member is guaranteed staff and a budget rather than having to depend on the committee chairmen for such matters.

Thus the days of the arbitrary House committee chairmen are past. This does not mean that chairmen are no longer influential figures in the House of Representatives. It rather means that they must now be more sensitive to the needs and desires of their committee colleagues and win their respect and support, rather than depending on an unresponsive system to perpetuate and justify their existence and actions.

Some of the same committees that are important in the Senate are also crucial to the operation of the House of Representatives. Appropriations is as important, if not more so, in the House (compared to the Senate) because of the political custom that spending measures originate in the lower chamber. Similarly, Ways and Means (the counterpart of the Senate Finance Committee) is vital because revenue measures *must* by constitutional edict commence in this chamber. In addition, the committee has jurisdiction over such vital subjects as health care, welfare, and foreign trade.

There are, however, differences in the committee pecking-order in the two chambers. Neither the Foreign Affairs nor the Armed Services Committee is as important in the House as its Senate counterpart. Yet the House Rules Committee is a key body because of the crucial role it plays in procedures for scheduling legislation; in contrast, the Senate Rules and Administration Committee (which concerns itself with such matters as supervising the Senate library and restaurant) is almost at the bottom of the priority list in the upper chamber.

Informal Leadership in the House

Observers of the House have been less likely than students of the Senate to impute influence to an inner "club" or "establishment." The most prominently mentioned clique of this type was Speaker Sam Rayburn's "board of education," an informal group of changing membership that is reputed to have made major decisions at certain times during the late Speaker's tenure in office. Little has been written about the actual composition of the "board," however, and no such group has existed under other party leaders.

One possible reason for the absence of a House "club" is that the sheer size of the body makes it difficult for a small group to control it from behind the scenes. While the formal and informal leaders of a small group may be different

* The exceptions are chairmen of subcommittees of the House Appropriations Committee, who are chosen by the Democratic Caucus.

persons, the more members an organization has, the more difficult contact between them becomes. As a result, only those in formal positions of authority have the visibility and communication ties with the general membership necessary to control the organization. These facts of organizational life may help to explain why party leaders and committee chairmen generally exercise influence in the House. Recently newer types of informal groups have been organized in the House such as the Black Caucus, the Women's Caucus, and the previously mentioned Blue Collar Caucus. However, the relatively small size of these groups (typically less than twenty) has limited their influence in the chamber.

Informal patterns of influence have not been totally lacking in the House. In the past, large state delegations frequently constituted important blocs of power that were frequently controlled by strong leaders like William Green of Pennsylvania and Charles Buckley of New York. However, the demise of local party organizations has eroded the political base of such individuals and broken up the bloc voting of states in the House.

The most significant unofficial organization in the House in recent years has been the Democratic Study Group. Established in 1959 by a relatively small bloc of liberal Northern and Western Democrats to research problems, to rally members to be present for crucial votes, and to help to finance liberal Democratic candidates, the group now numbers over half the membership and has taken the leadership in House reforms involving the seniority rule and establishment of the party's Steering and Policy Committee. The group was also instrumental in getting the Democratic Caucus to set a date for withdrawal from Vietnam and to oppose a constitutional amendment against busing to achieve racial balance in the schools. One indication of the group's growing influence in the House is the fact that one of its members, Thomas O'Neill, recently became, first, Majority Leader of the House, then its Speaker.*

The Power of Individual Representatives

The rank-and-file member of the House has less influence in the chamber than does an individual senator. Many representatives experience a real shock when they leave state and local political circles, where they have been influential figures, and are swallowed up in the anonymity of national politics. Typically in the early stages of a House member's career, he is an unknown, not only to the general and "attentive" publics but also to most of his colleagues.

Several factors help to explain this situation. One is the difference in the size of the two chambers. As one of 435 persons, the rank-and-file House member is simply less visible than a senator, who is one of a hundred. Consider particularly the representatives from populous states like California and New York, with congressional delegations of some forty members, compared to their two senators. In addition, congressmen have been less visible to the public because prior to 1970, House committee proceedings could not be televised as Senate hearings could be and were. It is also more difficult for the average representative to gain notoriety as a maverick or dissenter than for a senator. Few, if any, become "household names" in the same sense as a Fulbright or a Morse.

---

* A much smaller group of liberal Republicans has formed an organization called the House Wednesday Group, which has a staff to help its members formulate policy ideas.

Faced with these handicaps, the rank-and-file congressman has traditionally had to struggle to gain some visibility and influence in the chamber. Writing in the 1960s, one close student of the subject, Richard Fenno, suggested that the best way a young congressman could do that was to ingratiate himself with some senior party leader or committee chairman so as to become his protégé. The senior congressman would then see to it that his protégé got a good committee assignment, a subcommittee chairmanship, the opportunity to preside over the House, or other privileges. In turn, the dutiful protégé would serve his apprenticeship by specializing, doing his committee work, speaking only in areas of his speciality, and cooperating with party and committee leaders. If he performed these chores satisfactorily over a long period of time (and kept getting reelected), the principle of seniority would give him his eventual award: a place in the power structure of the House.

Congresswoman Elizabeth Holtzman of New York.

Both parties in the House, however, have recently begun to vest more power and responsibility in their junior members. Republicans were the first to do so, giving better committee assignments to freshmen and bringing them more into the decision-making process of the Republican Conference. Contributing to this development was the contest in 1965 in which congressman Gerald Ford utilized the support of younger Republicans in defeating the incumbent Charles Halleck, for the Minority Leadership and then subsequently rewarded his supporters with more influence in party affairs. Democratic leaders have not had to resort to such tactics because there have been no genuine contests for party posts in many years; however, recent majority leaders like Albert and O'Neill have seen to it that junior Democrats get better committee assignments and play a role in the expanded activities of the Democratic Caucus.

Another institutional development in the House has also contributed to the increased influence of junior House members, especially Democrats: the greater use of subcommittees to conduct legislative business. As in the Senate, the increase in the scope and complexity of legislative matters has forced the House to create more and more specialized subcommittees; in the Ninety-fifth Congress (1977–79) there were 152 of them operating within 29 parent committees. Moreover, recent actions of House Democrats in restricting the number of subcommittees on which an individual can sit has served to distribute such posts to a large number of members, including many freshmen. Possessed of such a subcommittee position, and with control over staff and budget for its operation, young members of the House no longer need to depend so heavily on the apprentice-protégé system to win visibility and influence in the lower House of the Congress.

The Distribution of Power: A Summary

This analysis indicates that power is not highly concentrated in either chamber of Congress. Although majority party officials such as the Speaker of the House and Majority Leaders in both chambers have important means of influencing their colleagues, persuasion is generally more effective than coercion (as Everett Dirksen put it some years ago, "the oil can is mightier than the sword"), particularly in dealings with individuals with seniority and power sources of their own. However, House Democrats have recently begun to vest more authority in the Speaker: as chairman of the newly created Steering and Policy Committee, he now has more influence over committee assignments, and his

Party Leaders

Majority Party (Democrats)

Speaker	Thomas O'Neill Jr. (Massachusetts)
Floor Leader	Jim Wright (Texas)
Whip	John Brademas (Indiana)
Chairman of the Caucus	Thomas Foley (Washington)
Secretary of the Caucus	Shirley Chisholm (New York)
Chairman, Steering and Policy Committee	Thomas O'Neill Jr. (Massachusetts)

Minority Party (Republicans)

Floor Leader	John Rhodes (Arizona)
Whip	Robert Michel (Illinois)
Chairman of the Conference	John Anderson (Illinois)
Vice Chairman of the Conference	Samuel Devine (Ohio)
Secretary of the Conference	Jack Edwards (Illinois)
Chairman, Committee on Committees	John Rhodes (Arizona)
Chairman, Policy Committee	Del Clawson (California)

Important Standing Committees

Chairman (Democrats)		Ranking Minority Members (Republicans)
Appropriations	John Mahon (Texas)	Elford Cederberg (Michigan)
Rules	James Delaney (New York)	James Quillen (Tennessee)
Ways and Means	Al Ullman (Oregon)	Barber Conable Jr. (New York)

new authority to name the Democratic members of the Rules Committee and to refer bills to committees strengthens his ability to affect legislation.

While committee chairmen remain as influential persons in both the House and Senate, they are not as powerful as they once were. Their selection is no longer automatic, as the deposing of three Democratic House chairmen reveals. In addition, more and more legislative activity is being decentralized in increasingly autonomous subcommittees.

Individual members of the Senate are more powerful than those of the House of Representatives. Their smaller number, plus the greater attention that the mass media focuses on members of the upper chamber, makes rank-and-file senators much more visible than their counterparts in the House. However, recent attempts of both parties to award junior members of the House more important committee assignments—together with the proliferation of subcommittees, many of which are chaired by such members—makes rank-and-file members of the House more important today than they were in the past.

Finally, the patterns of leadership differ between the two parties. In both chambers the Democrats concentrate almost all power in the hands of their Floor Leaders, who use other party officials and committees to further their purposes. The Republicans distribute influence among party officials more widely. It is difficult to determine the reason for this distinction. It might reflect the Republicans' general distrust of political power. It may also be related to a pragmatic feature of politics: the Democrats have controlled both houses of Congress, along with the presidency, for most of the last forty-five years and may have found it necessary to concentrate authority in their Floor Leaders in order to get legislative proposals of liberal Chief Executives enacted into law.

Closely related to the distribution of power in the American Congress is the question of how it is actually exercised in the course of the legislative process. The following section explores the basic procedures of the two chambers for considering legislation.

Only one of about 100 bills becomes law.

CONGRESSIONAL PROCEDURE: RUNNING THE LEGISLATIVE OBSTACLE COURSE

One outstanding characteristic of Congress is the tortuous process through which most proposals must pass. In a typical session only about one in a hundred proposed measures is finally enacted into law. The other ninety-nine fail to surmount some obstacle along the way.

The procedures of Congress are so complex and technical that only the parliamentarians of the two chambers, plus a few veteran congressmen, grasp their intricacies. Nonetheless, it is possible to outline in general terms the process through which legislative proposals are screened and the kinds of political, as well as legal, considerations that affect their ultimate disposition. There are some differences in detail between the Senate and the House, but the general stages are similar.

Introduction of Bills and Referral to Committees

The introduction of bills in either chamber is a simple matter: a member merely has a proposal drawn in proper form (a legislative counsel offers assistance with this chore) and introduces it in his name (the actual source of the bill may be the President, an administrative agency, or even an interest group). Since both chambers now permit cosponsors, frequently a measure bears the signature of a number of senators or representatives to indicate that it has considerable support. (Often members from both political parties, different regions of the country, or even different political philosophies—liberal, moderate, conservative—join together as sponsors for that reason.) Similar measures can be introduced simultaneously in the two chambers with the exception that revenue and appropriation bills originate in the House.

Naturally, some bills are more important and have a greater chance of passage than others; particularly successful are those that are suggested by, or have the backing of, the President or some executive agency (known as "administration" bills). Also, a major measure often bears the name of the chairman of the standing committee to which it is referred because its backers calculate that this will ensure sympathetic handling both in committee and on the floor.

Generally speaking, deciding which committee a bill should be referred to presents no great difficulty for the presiding officers of the Senate and the House. Even when a measure could be sent to several committees, the sponsor can have it drafted so that it is appropriate to one in particular. Previous decisions on similar bills provide precedents, so that only new types of legislation present any real problem.* In such circumstances, the discretion of the presiding officer is crucial and may help determine the ultimate fate of the bill.

Committee Consideration

One student has suggested that the standing committees are the kilns in which legislation is baked, where proposals are sorted, mixed, and molded into form. For most bills, however, they are more like Woodrow Wilson's description of them: "dim dungeons of silence" from which most measures never emerge. (Recent estimates indicate that, on the average, of ten bills referred to committee, only one is reported out favorably.)

In fact, standing committees do not even hold hearings on most bills referred to them. A chairman may simply not schedule any, a practice that used to effectively end the matter; however, recent reforms now make it possible for a majority of the committee members to force a chairman to hold hearings on a bill if they want to consider it. Even then, however, the hearings may have been so delayed that there is little chance of concluding them in time to get the bill reported out and passed before the end of the congressional session.

Bills that the chairman and most committee members favor are scheduled for early hearings by the committee or, even more often, by a subcommittee. A variety of witnesses appear at such hearings to give their views on a bill. Typically, these include: officials of the executive branch who have an interest in the legislative proposal (the Secretary of State or Defense will normally kick off hearings on matters of foreign policy); members of Congress from both houses; and finally, private citizens, particularly spokesmen for concerned interest groups. Both supporters and opponents are provided an opportunity to appear, although the chairman's own attitude on a bill often determines which side is favored in the scheduling of witnesses.

Witnesses generally read a prepared statement setting forth their views and supporting evidence for them, and then face interrogation from the committee members. The kind of treatment a person receives often depends on how his attitudes on the bill in question compare with those of the committee chairman. Sometimes, however, other committee members will come to the defense of a beleaguered witness, particularly if they are sympathetic with his stand on a matter.

Most analysts of congressional hearings agree that they reveal little factual information to determine how committee members vote. Indeed, most members have pronounced views on the matter before the hearings even begin. Why, then, are they held? Because they do serve other purposes. One relates to the informing function of Congress: media coverage of testimony given in hear-

---

* The Senate has a potential way around this problem, however, since a bill can be referred to more than one committee in that chamber.

ings alerts citizens to the bill and to the stands of various groups and individuals. Hearings thus widen the public concerned with the issue.* Hearings also act as safety valves for the losers. Legislative defeat is easier to accept if one has been given the opportunity to state his views, to feel that he has had his day in court.

At the conclusion of the hearings, the subcommittee or committee involved goes into session to reach a decision about the bill. (These sessions used to be held in private but in recent years are generally open to the public unless their disclosures would "endanger national security" or violate chamber rules.) The members may give it a favorable or unfavorable recommendation, suggest that it be tabled, or, more typically, amend it in any way they desire. The amendment process is usually referred to as the mark-up of the bill, since the committee members go over the measure line by line to rewrite it. When a subcommittee has completed the initial consideration of a bill, the parent committee is free to make changes. Generally, however, it tends to go along with the decisions of the subgroup. Bills that are favorably reported but do not receive unanimous endorsement are often accompanied by majority and minority reports setting forth the reasons why members favor or oppose passage.

Scheduling Bills for Floor Action

Senate. There is generally no problem in scheduling for floor action any bills reported by standing committees of the Senate. If a bill is noncontroversial, the chairman of the standing committee may ask for unanimous consent to hear the bill at once, and, if no one objects, floor action follows. If a bill is controversial, scheduling is left to the Majority Leader, who works it out with the Minority Leader and, if the Democrats control the chamber, with their Policy Committee as well. He also generally discusses the scheduling of administration bills with the President or executive-agency officials.

In the Senate there are even ways to get bills to the floor that have not been reported out of a standing committee. The most prevalent tactic is to move the bill as an amendment to a measure that is already on the floor for action. Since amendments need not be germane to the general measure to which they are attached (the one exception here is general appropriations legislation), almost any bill can be rescued from a standing committee. Liberals, for instance, used this technique to bypass the Senate Judiciary Committee chaired by Senator Eastland of Mississippi; one of the early civil rights measures was attached as an amendment to the foreign aid bill.

Another tactic is to place a House-passed measure on the Senate calendar for action without sending it to a standing committee, a maneuver that can be accomplished if a single senator objects to committee referral. It has been used frequently to get civil rights bills already passed by the House to the Senate floor for action without the necessity for having them considered by the Judiciary Committee.

Two other possibilities exist for bypassing Senate standing committees and bringing matters directly to the floor for action. One is suspension of rules, a method that is used primarily for amendments to appropriations bills to which

---

* Not all hearings are public, however. If testimony covers confidential matters (such as national defense) or may injure the reputations of third parties, it may be taken in private.

the rule of germaneness does apply. The other is a motion to discharge the standing committee from consideration of a bill already referred to it. Both motions, however, can be defeated fairly easily by a filibuster, a matter that we will explore below.

In fact, the possibility of a filibuster acts as a restraint on all four tactics, as does the informal courtesy of reciprocity among senators that standing committees should not generally be bypassed in the legislative process. Nonetheless, the availability of the nongermane amendment, consideration of a House-passed measure, and motions to suspend the rules and discharge a committee of a bill makes it likely that a measure favored by a majority of the Senate membership will not be blocked by a standing committee.

House. The relative ease of getting bills to the Senate floor for action is in sharp contrast with the situation in the House of Representatives. Some noncontroversial measures are scheduled in the lower chamber without too much difficulty: included are private bills—typically these involve special claims against the government—and public bills that are unobjectionable. Bills involving any degree of controversy, however, must generally clear the potent House Rules Committee. This group has the power to issue vital "rules" on the scheduling of a measure for floor action: whether it should be sent to the floor and, if so, under what conditions—that is, *when* debate should take place, *how long* it should last, whether the bill can be *amended* on the floor, and if so *by whom* (for example, only by the standing committee chairman).*

Because it makes such crucial decisions affecting floor action on controversial bills reported by standing committees, the Rules Committee is in a strong bargaining position. It can kill a bill altogether or insist that certain changes be made in its content as the price of scheduling it for floor debate. It has the power to hold hearings of its own on a bill and then to require its proponents on the standing committee to defend it before the House Rules Committee.

In the period from the late 1930s to the early 1960s, the Rules Committee was controlled, under the chairmanship of Howard Smith of Virginia, by a coalition of Southern Democrats and Northern Republicans who used it to kill, delay, and emasculate much liberal legislation. In 1961, at the urging of President Kennedy, Speaker Sam Rayburn succeeded in getting the House to change the size of the committee from twelve to fifteen; the appointment of two new carefully selected Democrats then gave the liberals a majority on the committee. This change; the defeat of Smith in a primary fight in 1966; the appointment of other liberals to the committee in 1967; and the adoption of rules denying the chairman the right to set meeting dates, requiring the consent of the majority of the committee to table a bill, and setting limits on proxy voting by members—all have served to diminish the committee's role in frustrating liberal legislative proposals. Other more recent developments contributing to that same result include the replacement of Smith's successor as chairman, William Coleman of Mississippi, with the more liberal Ray Madden of Indiana in 1973 and the assignment to the committee of three congressmen

---

* However, as previously indicated, the Democratic Caucus recently instructed the Democratic members of the Rules Committee to allow an amendment removing tax concessions to the oil and gas industry to come to the floor for discussion and debate.

sympathetic to the Speaker, Carl Albert, and the Majority Leader, Thomas O'Neill.

As in the Senate, there are ways that House members can circumvent a standing committee as well as the Rules Committee. For one, a bill can be discharged from a standing committee after thirty days if there is no report on it, and from the Rules Committee after only seven days of consideration without action. To rescue a bill under the discharge rule, a majority of the House members merely has to sign a petition. However, members are reluctant to use this device to enact legislation: between 1910 and 1971 only twenty-four bills brought to the House floor in this fashion passed the chamber. Discharge is much more effective as a threat. If the Rules Committee sees that a petition will probably be successful, it is inclined to release the bill in question. By doing so, the committee can exercise some control over the conditions of debate on the floor, whereas if a bill is discharged, no such control is possible.

Another procedure, known as Calendar Wednesday, can be utilized to free legislative proposals from the Rules Committee. Each Wednesday, under House regulations, standing committee names are read in alphabetical order; members can call up a bill that has been reported to the Rules Committee but has not been given a rule for floor action. This tactic, however, is generally ineffective and is used very infrequently. Indeed, Calendar Wednesday is usually dispensed with by unanimous consent of the House, and even if it is not, it is difficult to dispose of a measure within a single legislative day as required. Between 1950 and 1970, it was used on only two occasions.

Clearly, in the House—unlike the Senate—committees are generally formidable roadblocks to legislative action. In some instances, however, House members appreciate these barriers. Pressures may build up from powerful interest groups to pass legislative proposals the representatives do not actually favor; the chairmen of the standing and Rules committees (most of whom come from "safe" districts and hence are fairly invulnerable to such pressures) can then be blamed if the measures never come to the floor for a vote.

Congressman Richard Bolling of Missouri at House Rules Committee Meeting.

Floor Action

Senate. Debate on the Senate floor tends to be informal, and members are not inclined to adhere closely to even the limited number of rules that govern debates. For example, rules requiring that remarks be germane to the discussion are seldom enforced. Senators are not inclined to challenge a colleague who is speaking off the subject, and if he himself acknowledges that he is doing so, they will usually grant him unanimous consent to continue.

This tolerance for discussion makes the Senate a unique legislative body. It is the only one in the world that has the right of unlimited debate, whereby a senator can speak for as long as he wants to on a measure. On most occasions, however, members do not exercise that right, and debate terminates simply because senators voluntarily stop talking on a bill and proceed to vote on it.

There are ways in which debate may be closed involuntarily in the Senate. One is by a unanimous-consent agreement to terminate discussion. Even senators who oppose a bill may be willing to stop debating it because they concede that the majority should be able to work its will on the matter.

In some instances, however, feelings are so high against a particular bill (as on a highly emotional issue such as civil rights) that the minority is willing to use extraordinary means to prevent its passage. In this event members join together to filibuster it, that is, to keep discussing it so long that no vote can be taken on the measure. The participation of a number of senators is required since one or a few cannot talk continually for a long period. The technique is usually most effective at the end of a legislative session, when time is short and members have other business that they need to transact.

There are measures that can be taken to defeat a filibuster. One is to keep the Senate in continuous session so as to wear down the filibusterers. That tactic, however, is often subject to a counterploy: some years ago when Lyndon Johnson attempted to use this technique to break a filibuster against a civil rights bill, the minority retaliated by constantly calling for a quorum (the Constitution requires a majority of body membership to be present to do business), which necessitated many of those favoring the bill to get to the chamber at all hours of the night to keep the Senate in session. Meanwhile, only one of the minority's valiant band—the one talking—had to be there at any one time.

If all these tactics fail, a filibuster can be stopped by a cloture motion, which terminates debate. This method, which traditionally required a two-thirds vote for passage, was changed in 1975 so that three-fifths of the total membership of the Senate (60 if there are no vacancies in the 100-member body) can invoke cloture. If the motion is passed by that margin, each senator may speak for one hour on any one previously proposed amendment, after which time the bill must come to a vote.

At first blush it would appear that the cloture motion would be used frequently and, when attempted, would have a fair chance of succeeding. Yet from 1917 (when the cloture rule was first adopted) to 1974, it was tried on only seventy-nine occasions, and only fourteen of these were successful. In recent years, however, there has been a marked increase in the use of cloture. From 1917 to 1960 it was attempted twenty-two times and succeeded on four of those occasions; from 1960 to 1977 the Senate invoked cloture 105 times, and it was passed on thirty-two of those instances.

Several reasons explain why cloture has not been resorted to more often in the Senate. One is that members use the right of unlimited debate with considerable discretion, reserving it only for those measures to which they are violently opposed. Also, senators who are in the majority on an issue are reluctant to invoke cloture because they may want to filibuster future bills that are anathema to them. Then, too, traditions die hard in the Senate. But more importantly, many senators realize that the filibuster is a valuable weapon in thwarting what they feel are increasing encroachments of the President and the executive branch into their affairs.

After debate terminates in the Senate, whether voluntarily or by unanimous consent or through a cloture motion, the chamber moves to a vote on the bill. Prior to final passage, votes are taken on any amendments to the bill, some of which are designed to clarify a measure, others to defeat it. In addition, opponents move that the bill be sent back to committee, a tactic that is designed to kill it. In voting on motions as well as on the final amended bill, there are three possibilities: a voice vote, a division (standing) vote, or, if one-fifth of the members request it, a roll-call vote. The latter, which is reserved for controversial measures, requires each senator to answer yea or nay when his name is called; since the votes are recorded, the public can determine how each member cast his ballot.

House. The House of Representatives does not provide for unlimited debate. The chamber is able to move to a vote on a matter after members have had a reasonable time to deliberate its merits. On the other hand, controversial bills are dealt with in two steps—first by members sitting as the Committee of the Whole House and then as a regular chamber.

The Committee of the Whole device was borrowed from the seventeenth-century British practice of getting the Speaker (who was the king's man) out of the chair so that members of the House of Commons could act independently of his scrutiny. Although the original purpose is not applicable (the Speaker does, however, as a matter of custom vacate his place as presiding officer), the device is useful today for other reasons. When members are meeting as the Whole House, a quorum of 100 rather than 218 (the majority of the entire membership) is sufficient to do business. In addition, before 1970 actions of members while in the Committee of the Whole were protected from public scrutiny: no roll-call votes were possible and other votes—voice, division, and teller (under the teller arrangement, members favoring and opposing a bill pass through separate aisles)—were not recorded. As a result of a change in the House rules in 1970, however, one-fifth of the Committee quorum (twenty) can ask that clerks record how (as well as whether) members vote on teller tallies. Thus a relatively small number of House members can now force their colleagues to make their votes on measures a matter of public record. Some congressional observers credit this new procedure with contributing to the defeat of the funding of the supersonic transport plane (SST) in 1971 because members had to make their vote known on a measure that was unpopular with many of their constituents. Negative actions taken by the Committee of the Whole are final; affirmative decisions on bills and amendments to them are subject to overruling by the House when it reconvenes as a regular body.

The voting procedures of the House (as contrasted to the Committee of the Whole) are the same as those of the Senate, with the exception that yea and nay votes are now recorded electronically, which eliminates the need for time-consuming roll calls.

Resolving Differences Between Senate- and House-Passed Bills

Even if a measure has been able to get by the many roadblocks outlined above, unless it passes both chambers in identical form it still has one major obstacle to surmount: getting the two houses to agree on its content. For most bills this is no great problem. The differences are resolved by action of the chamber that first passes the bill, which simply agrees to changes made in its version by the second chamber.

On controversial measures, however, it is usually necessary to iron out the differences between Senate and House bills through the use of a Conference Committee composed of representatives from each chamber. Typically, the presiding officers of the two houses both appoint three to nine members—generally the chairman of the standing committee that considered the measure, the ranking minority member, and other prominent committee members. These individuals meet (such meetings were formerly held in private but recently they have been opened to the public) to resolve their differences and to recommend

This graphic shows the most typical way in which proposed legislation is enacted into law. There are more complicated, as well as simpler, routes, and most bills fall by the wayside and never become law. The process is illustrated with two hypothetical bills, House bill No. 1(HR 1) and Senate bill No. 2(S 2).

Each bill must be passed by both houses of Congress in identical form before it can become law. The path of HR 1 is traced by a black line, that of S 2 by a color line. However, in practice most legislation begins as similar proposals in both houses.

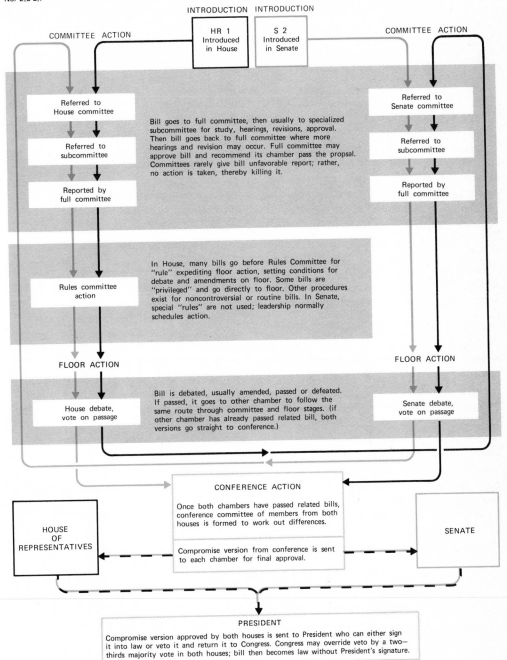

INTRODUCTION INTRODUCTION

COMMITTEE ACTION

HR 1
Introduced
in House

S 2
Introduced
in Senate

COMMITTEE ACTION

Referred to
House committee

Referred to
subcommittee

Reported by
full committee

Bill goes to full committee, then usually to specialized subcommittee for study, hearings, revisions, approval. Then bill goes back to full committee where more hearings and revision may occur. Full committee may approve bill and recommend its chamber pass the propsal. Committees rarely give bill unfavorable report; rather, no action is taken, thereby killing it.

Referred to
Senate committee

Referred to
subcommittee

Reported by
full committee

Rules committee
action

In House, many bills go before Rules Committee for "rule" expediting floor action, setting conditions for debate and amendments on floor. Some bills are "privileged" and go directly to floor. Other procedures exist for noncontroversial or routine bills. In Senate, special "rules" are not used; leadership normally schedules action.

FLOOR ACTION

FLOOR ACTION

House debate,
vote on passage

Bill is debated, usually amended, passed or defeated. If passed, it goes to other chamber to follow the same route through committee and floor stages. (if other chamber has already passed related bill, both versions go straight to conference.)

Senate debate,
vote on passage

HOUSE
OF
REPRESENTATIVES

CONFERENCE ACTION

Once both chambers have passed related bills, conference committee of members from both houses is formed to work out differences.

Compromise version from conference is sent to each chamber for final approval.

SENATE

PRESIDENT

Compromise version approved by both houses is sent to President who can either sign it into law or veto it and return it to Congress. Congress may override veto by a two—thirds majority vote in both houses; bill then becomes law without President's signature.

Figure 11.2 How a bill becomes law.

Source: *Congressional Quarterly Almanac*, 1976, p. xxv.

a report on a common bill. When agreement is reached (a majority of each chamber's representatives must approve it), it is sent to the respective houses for approval along with an explanatory statement. Neither house can change the Conference Committee version; they must accept it as it is, send it to the Conference Committee for further negotiations, or vote it down completely. As a rule, agreement is ultimately reached, and the report (and hence the bill) is ready for presidential action, a matter that we will examine in chapter 13.

VOTING IN CONGRESS

Congressman Richard Kelly of Florida voting in Committee.

Students of legislatures have long been concerned with the voting behavior of legislators. Traditionally the matter has been examined from a *normative* standpoint: what *should* guide a legislator when his own attitude on an issue differs from that of the majority of his constituents? One view is that, as an elected representative, he is obliged to carry out the wishes of the voters who put him in office regardless of his own outlook. In effect, he is to act as the agent, or instructed delegate, of the people. An opposing concept, most often associated with the eighteenth-century British statesman Edmund Burke, holds that the representative owes his constituents not blind obedience to their will but rather his own independent judgment.* The legislator is, in this view, a trustee whom the people elect because they have faith in his native capacities and in his ability to study matters and to arrive at judgments that are better informed than their own. Recent studies of legislative voting, however, have shifted their focus to what a legislator *actually does* and to the particular considerations he takes into account in deciding on bills.

One of the major findings of recent studies is that the traditional delegate-trustee dichotomy is far too simplified and fails to explain the complexities of legislative voting. For one thing, it exaggerates the interest in and information about legislative issues of both constituents and representatives. Most voters are not concerned with measures before the Congress, nor are they familiar with how their senators or representatives vote on such matters. On the other hand, congressmen are often unaware of the general sentiments of their constituents who do have attitudes on measures before the Congress. Letters from voters and even replies to questionnaires sent out by congressmen typically come from a relatively small number of individuals, whose views are not necessarily representative of those of all the voters. A 1958 study by the Survey Research Center at the University of Michigan comparing the attitudes of voters on major economic, civil rights, and foreign policy issues with what their congressmen *thought* their attitudes were revealed that the representatives misperceived their constituents' opinions, especially on the foreign policy and economic issues.

Moreover, the concept of the model congressman who carefully studies the facts and considerations behind each bill and, with this information in mind, rationally determines his vote is unrealistic. The tremendous volume of business that the Senate and House of Representatives have before them prevents a legislator from engaging in such a time-consuming task. Like the voter, the

---

* Burke delivered an oft-quoted speech to his constituents in Bristol setting forth his views to that effect. It is significant, however, that he subsequently withdrew as a candidate because he felt that he could not be reelected because of these views.

congressman is seeking shortcuts in the decision-making process and so he looks for certain cues, points of reference, to guide his actions.

Party affiliation has been the strongest influence in roll-call tallies in the American Congress over the years. Although senators and representatives do not vote the party line to the extent that legislators do in, for example, Great Britain, party is more closely associated with voting patterns on a wide range of issues than any other single variable. For example, on party votes (those in which a majority of Republicans voted on one side of the issue and the majority of Democrats voted on the other) in 1975, congressional Republicans voted with their party colleagues 70 percent of the time and Democrats with their fellow party members 69 percent of the time. The following year (1976), the comparable figures were 66 percent and 65 percent respectively. Party identification thus plays a major part in determining how congressmen vote on legislation, just as it does for many voters when they face a choice in a general election contest.

A related influence is the attitude of the *President* toward particular legislation. Congressmen from his party are obviously more inclined to support measures that he favors than are members of the opposition. In 1975, Gerald Ford's first full year in office, just over two-thirds of the Republican senators voted his sentiments on legislation, while just under one-half of the Democratic senators did. In 1965, after Lyndon Johnson's election when he was enjoying his greatest legislative successes, the situation was just reversed.* There are differences between freshman and veteran legislators in following the presidential lead. That same year, 1965, the seventy-one new Democratic members of the House of Representatives supported Mr. Johnson 82 percent of the time, compared to 74 percent for all House Democrats. Thus, ironically, Barry Goldwater's resounding defeat in the 1964 presidential contest helped carry into office a bumper crop of Democrats from politically competitive congressional districts, a bonus that contributed to Johnson's success with the "Great Society" programs.

Partisan differences within Congress, as well as between Congress and the President, by no means entirely determine the voting in the national legislature. For example, in 1976, an election year, there was a bipartisan majority on almost two-thirds of the roll-call votes: in other words, Democrats and Republicans voted on the same side of issues twice as often as on the opposite side. In addition, Mr. Ford's desires prevailed on about 54 percent of the measures on which he took a stand, even though the opposition party controlled both the Senate and House. Clearly, then, we must look to other considerations besides party to help explain the voting patterns in roll-call tallies.

One general influence to look at is a legislator's *constituency*. Senators and representatives from the *same state* tend to vote alike on many measures. Moreover, *region* helps explain congressional voting patterns. Over the last three decades, the major split among Democrats in both houses has been between

---

* Each year the *Congressional Quarterly* analyzes congressional voting along certain dimensions such as party and region. Included is a measurement of congressional support for the President on measures that he favors. To ascertain his attitudes on legislation, all his messages, press conferences, and other public statements are examined.

Northern and Southern states.† In 1976, this division was reflected in 32 percent of the votes in the Senate and in 24 percent in the House for an overall division of 28 percent in both houses. (This figure has generally been declining in recent years; for example, in 1972 it was 38 percent.) There has been less of a regional cleavage within the Republican party, but some division has existed between legislators from the coastal areas and those from the interior of the country, particularly on foreign policy. In addition to regional differences, some divisions have existed in both parties between members from *urban* constituencies and those from *suburban* and *rural* areas.

Thus constituency modifies party influences on voting in the American Congress, resulting in common interests across party lines. The most obvious example is the Conservative Coalition of Republicans and Southern Democrats that has formed against Northern Democrats on a variety of issues since the late 1930s. In 1976 this coalition formed on 24 percent of the roll-call votes and prevailed in 58 percent of those. Less well known, but still influential, is the liberal combination of Northern Democrats and Republicans, particularly from the New England and the Middle Atlantic states. Because of these coalitions, the outcome of many crucial votes in Congress turns on the extent to which the two minority groups in the two parties (the Southern Democrats and the Eastern Republicans) vote by party or by constituency.

The relationships that exist between these three factors (party, the President's attitude, and constituency) and congressional voting may well depend on the particular kind of public policy involved. The 1958 University of Michigan survey cited above showed, for example, that congressional voting was associated most closely with party positions on social welfare measures, with the President's views on foreign policy issues, and with constituency opinions on civil rights matters. Another more comprehensive analysis of congressional voting over the twelve-year period from 1953 to 1964 by political scientist Aage Clausen showed similar results: party was paramount on issues of "government management," such as the regulation of the economy, business-labor relations, and the like; both party and constituency affected voting on social welfare and agricultural assistance programs; constituency was the key factor relating to civil rights issues; and both constituency and presidential attitudes were associated with questions of international involvement.

While associations between party, presidential attitudes, and constituency on the one hand, and congressional voting on the other, are interesting, they do not indicate specifically which individuals or groups a congressman consults or defers to when he makes up his mind how to vote on a matter. For example, is the association between the party identification of congressmen and how they vote based on the fact that rank-and-file congressmen follow the wishes of their party leaders, or because congressmen of the same party have similar constituencies, or because they share the same general political philosophy? Only by asking congressmen in interviews to identify the particular individuals or groups that provide these "cues" on how to vote can answers to such questions be found. One political scientist, John Kingdom, did just that and reached

---

† The *Congressional Quarterly* classifies the following as Southern states: Alabama, Arkansas, Florida, Georgia, Kentucky, Louisiana, Mississippi, North Carolina, Oklahoma, South Carolina, Tennessee, Texas, and Virginia. The other thirty-seven states are designated as Northern.

some significant conclusions on who and what affects how members of the House of Representatives vote on the floor of that chamber.

Kingdom found that the two most important groups providing congressmen with cues on how to vote were their *fellow congressmen* and their *constituents*. The first are important because they are readily available at the time of the voting decision and are able to provide their colleagues with evaluations of both the merits (or lack thereof) of a particular bill and the probable political consequences of voting for or against the measure. Congressmen tend to defer especially to other congressmen who share their own general political views and to those who are considered expert on a particular bill, such as members of the standing committee that originally considered it. Congressmen look to their constituents for guidance on how to vote on issues that are of special relevance to people in their districts; they pay particular attention to the view of elites and of attentive publics in their constituency.

On the other hand, Kingdom found that neither congressional party leaders nor the President or top executive-branch officials are generally important sources of influence on congressional voting. However, in some circumstances these individuals can be effective in influencing how a congressman votes. Party leaders can use certain powers that they exercise over the fate of legislation in which a congressman is interested in order to induce him to follow their wishes. Moreover, a President can have an important effect on how junior congressmen from his party vote on issues in which the Chief Executive is interested.

Kingdom also discovered that three other groups had a limited effect on congressional voting. Interest groups are important only if they are closely connected with a House member's constituency. Only junior congressmen and those from highly competitive districts place reliance on the advice of the members of their staff, and even then, the staff is more influential before the bill has reached the stage of a final vote in the House.* The mass media also exert little influence over such congressional decisions, although they often affect which issues will be given serious consideration by the House of Representatives.

CONGRESSIONAL POLICY MAKING: THE ENERGY ISSUE†

The petroleum industry has long enjoyed a special relationship with the government. Recognized by public officials as the producer of an extremely valuable national resource upon which our industrial economy depends so heavily in time of war and peace, the oil companies have been the recipients of major government assistance and special benefits. Over the years since World War I, our State Department has helped American oil firms win concessions in foreign countries; this has included governmental involvement in Iran in 1951, which allowed American companies to operate in a country that had traditionally

---

* Students of Congress generally conclude that staff members are more influential in the Senate because legislators there have more committee assignments and hence have to rely more on staff for assistance. Moreover, the Senate offices are more amply staffed than those in the House.

† This account is drawn primarily from Harmon Zeigler and Joseph Olexa, "The Energy Issue: Oil and the Emergency Energy Act of 1973-74," which appears in Robert Peabody (ed.), *Cases in American Politics* (New York: Praeger, 1976), pp. 159-205.

been controlled by British oil interests. In addition, our tax policy has been designed to foster exploration for oil abroad: until 1975, companies were permitted to claim a special depletion allowance on foreign production that reduced their taxes; they could also deduct a portion of the taxes they pay to foreign countries from their federal tax liability. Further assistance to the oil industry included import quotas on foreign oil, designed to protect the domestic price of petroleum, and laws that allowed companies to restrict their production of oil if it appeared that the supply was going to exceed the demand for petroleum.

Beyond its special relationship with government, the oil industry is powerful in its own right. Although composed of some 10,000–12,000 oil producers operating in the United States, the industry is actually dominated by a relatively few companies. "Majors" (firms involved in all four levels of production—extraction, transportation, refining, and marketing) overshadow the thousands of "wildcatters" and independents; in fact, when people acquainted with the industry speak of the "majors," they typically have in mind eight giant, multinational firms—Exxon, (formerly Standard Oil of New Jersey), Gulf, Standard of Indiana, Texaco, Shell, ARCO, Mobil, and Standard of California—that were estimated in 1970 to control about two-thirds of our domestic reserves. The industry has also benefited from the fact that it has a monopoly of information on just what these reserves amount to and the probable costs of producing petroleum from them. Finally, oil companies have been politically powerful: the *American Petroleum Institute* (API), representing hundreds of firms and thousands of individuals, is generally conceded to be one of the nation's most powerful lobbying organizations; moreover, many presidential and congressional candidates have been recipients of sizeable (and sometimes illegal) campaign contributions from oil companies.

For a number of years the oil industry's special relationship with government, together with its own economic and political strength, enabled it to flourish and the nation's growing energy needs to be met. However, as the 1960s drew to a close, the industry began to develop some difficulties: an oil spill occurred off Santa Barbara, California, covering the beaches; concerned environmentalists initiated lawsuits to halt the construction of the Trans-Alaska pipeline until oil companies could guarantee that there would be no further disasters; the depletion allowance was reduced; and profits of all companies declined. Moreover, some elements of the industry began to warn in 1970 of probable shortages of oil in the very near future. That prediction came true in the winter of 1972–73, when heating-oil deficiencies first appeared, a development that led the Nixon administration to announce an increase in oil imports and the API to support the decision.

With the oil shortage now a fact of life, the issue shifted to the question of who was to blame for the situation. Democratic Senator Henry Jackson of Washington, Congress's leading spokesman on energy legislation, launched hearings of his Committee on Interior and Insular Affairs into the matter. Jackson himself focused attention on the oil companies, pointing to the industry's burgeoning profits and charged the major companies with using the shortage to eliminate their primary competitors—independent refining and marketing concerns. The industry responded by stepping up its advertising campaign in the media, blaming shortages on the mounting energy demands of the American consumer.

Senator Henry Jackson swears in executives of the major oil companies.

It was in this atmosphere that in early November 1973 President Nixon proposed legislation to the Congress establishing a broad energy conservation program. Warning that the recent Arab embargo on oil shipments made hopes of only temporary fuel shortages unrealistic, the Chief Executive asked congressmen to grant him authority to ration gasoline and fuel oil, reduce speed limits, exempt industries from environmental controls, and impose taxes on excessive use of energy. The President also requested that the emergency legislation he requested be on his desk by the time Congress recessed for the December holidays.

Meanwhile Senator Jackson's committee had already begun to draft a similar program even before the President's message was delivered. Heeding Nixon's call for speedy action, the Washington Senator prepared legislation embodying most of the President's recommendations and cleared a bill through his committee within a week after the President's message to Congress. The bill granted President Nixon broad authority to ration and conserve fuel, reduce speed limits, order industries using oil and gas to convert to coal, and allow power plants a variance from antipollution regulations. On the Senate floor Jackson introduced an amendment to the bill cleared by his committee to make rationing mandatory (rather than merely *authorizing* the President to impose it as the bill provided), but the Nixon administration opposed the amendment on the grounds that it destroyed the flexibility needed in the conservation program, and the amendment was defeated. Following that, the committee bill was passed by the Senate in mid-November, less than two weeks after the President's energy message was delivered.

While the energy legislation had smooth sailing in the Senate, it ran into major difficulties in the House. When its Interstate and Foreign Commerce Committee, under the chairmanship of Harley Staggers (D. West Virginia), opened hearings on a bill, Senator Lee Metcalf (D. Montana) appeared and charged that oil companies and banks were working together to dominate federal energy policy. Accusations were also made that the oil industry was holding back production in order to jack up prices, and the AFL-CIO called for the end of tax concessions to the industry on its foreign operations. The Staggers committee came under cross pressures by the AFL-CIO to recommend an excess-profits tax on oil companies; by the Nixon administration to relax environmental standards on industry operations; and by some Representatives to place more restrictions on executive authority over energy policy that they thought had been too freely granted by the Senate. The legislation that ultimately passed the House in mid-December 1973 was substantially different from the Senate version and contained two provisions that were particularly offensive to the oil industry and to the Nixon administration: energy plans were required to be submitted to Congress for approval (the Senate bill required congressional action only should it *disapprove* the President's program) and measures for dealing with excess profits by oil companies during the fuel shortage.

With the Senate and House unable to agree on how to deal with the emergency, their two versions of legislation were sent to a conference committee for resolution. Debate focused on the two controversial matters passed by the House: the necessity of congressional approval of presidential energy plans and the imposition of a tax on windfall profits of the oil industry. Ultimately, the conference committee in conjunction with the Nixon administration worked out a compromise: the requirement of congressional approval was eliminated and in return, the President was granted authority to set oil prices to permit "fair", but not excessive profits. The conference committee, however, added another troublesome provision from the industry's point of view which required oil companies to disclose their reserves.

The conference committee report was sent immediately on December 21 to the Senate and House, where it was expected to be approved quickly as the two chambers prepared to adjourn for the Christmas holidays. However, Republican Senator Clifford Hansen of Wyoming attacked the excess-profits and reserve-reporting requirement of the report, and Democratic Senator Long of Louisiana prepared to organize a filibuster because of his objections to the same two provisions. Faced with the prospect of seeing legislation he had worked so hard to promote defeated, Senator Jackson agreed to drop the two provisions (thus, in effect, rejecting the conference committee's report and going back to the original Senate legislation), and the new bill passed by a voice vote as the Senate adjourned for the holidays. On the House side, Representative Staggers tried to work out a compromise that would eliminate the windfall-profits section of the conference committee report and retain the reserve-reporting requirement, but House liberals refused to go along, and ultimately the members rejected the Senate version of the legislation. Thus Congress adjourned without passing the energy legislation President Nixon wanted by the end of 1973.

While the oil industry had staved off the attempts to impose a tax on its excess profits and the requirements to divulge its reserves, a climate of opinion

President Carter delivers his energy speech to Congress.

began to build against it. A Gallup poll showed that 25 percent of the public blamed the industry for fuel shortages; moreover, congressman Henry Reuss (D. Wisconsin) advocated legislation to roll back the price of oil to that in effect in May 1973. In late January 1974, President Nixon delivered a message to Congress, asking for the elimination of the depletion allowance on foreign oil and for a reduction of the amount of foreign income taxes companies could deduct from their federal taxes. Senator Jackson tried to get the previous conference committee report approved without having it recommitted to the committee, and when that effort failed, he urged the Senate-House conferees to substitute a "rollback" provision in place of the "windfall tax" proposal. The Conference committee report did so, providing for a rollback of domestic crude oil prices to $5.25 a barrel.

This time the conference committee report cleared both chambers. In addition to the rollback provision, the legislation that was approved authorized a rationing plan to be put in effect only after all other conservation measures had failed. It further provided that energy plans proposed after September 1974 be approved by Congress (prior to that date they had only to be *disapproved* by Congress). Finally, the legislation postponed until 1977 the implementation of automobile emission standards and waived through 1978 emission regulations for facilities converted to coal. However, President Nixon vetoed the legislation, and when four Southern Democrats in the Senate joined Republicans to uphold the veto, it prevailed.

Thus the long battle over the energy issue ended in the spring of 1974 with no major legislation enacted. In mid-March the Arab oil embargo ended and demands to do something about the fuel crisis diminished. In 1975 the new Congress, composed of a number of freshman legislators that were swept into office by the aftermath of Watergate, attached an amendment to a tax reduction bill eliminating the depletion allowance. However, no real progress was made on the enactment of a general energy policy. President Ford proposed to reduce dependence on foreign oil by raising import fees; some members of the Democratic Congress proposed instead that the President be authorized to ration fuel and Congress retain the right to review his decisions on that matter. However, the Congress was unable to come up with an overall energy policy, and the nation still had none when the Arab nations raised the price of oil again in December 1976.

An unusually severe winter caused a temporary fuel shortage in early 1977, and three months after he took office, President Carter took the leadership on the energy issue, which he described as "the greatest domestic challenge that our nation will face in our lifetime." First the President addressed the nation in what one aide described as his "the sky is falling" message, designed to impress on the American people the existence of a severe energy crisis that would become a disaster unless strong action were taken to meet it at once. Two days later in his first message before a joint session of Congress, the Chief Executive presented a comprehensive program that emphasized conservation of fuel. To accomplish that goal the President proposed increasing the tax on gasoline each year that the nation's consumption exceeded the previous year's target level. He also suggested that a special tax be levied on the purchase of gas "guzzlers" (cars that failed to meet certain fuel consumption standards). In turn, tax incentives would be granted purchasers of automobiles that saved fuel and to persons or businesses that saved fuel through conservation measures such as installing additional insulation or utilizing solar heating. Domestic oil would be taxed in successive stages until its price reached world levels in 1980 and federal control would be extended to the price of intrastate natural gas. In order to encourage a shift to coal, special taxes would be levied on industries burning oil or gas for boiler fuel, and the production of enriched uranium would be expanded.

Congressional leaders in both houses pledged their general backing of the President's program but warned that some parts of it, particularly the increased tax on gasoline, would run into severe opposition. In the Senate the program was referred to two committees in particular—the Finance Committee, chaired by Senator Long, and the newly formed Committee on Energy, presided over by Senator Jackson. No less than five House committees would deal with different aspects of Carter's energy program, and the chamber established a Select Energy Committee chaired by Representative Thomas Ashley (D. Ohio) to coordinate and merge the proposals of the five committees before they were brought to the floor for action. As this book goes to press, the Senate and House committees are beginning once again to deal with the energy issue. If past experience is any guide, their job will not be an easy one.

ASSESSMENT

Traditionally Congress has been an undemocratic body. It has been controlled primarily by committee chairmen from "safe" districts, chosen on the basis of seniority, who were to a great degree immune from influence by either the party leaders in Congress or by the rank-and-file members. Moreover, the closed nature of committee meetings and secrecy of voting in committee and in the House made it difficult for members of the public to know what their congressmen were doing on important issues and to hold them accountable for their actions. Also contributing to this latter problem was the lack of information about contributions of private individuals and groups to campaigns and other activities of congressmen.

The 1970s have brought a number of reforms designed to rectify the above abuses. As we saw in chapter 9, the campaign-spending legislation passed in recent years has done much to illuminate the financial situation with respect to elections. Also, the newly enacted codes of ethics by both houses of Congress—providing for full disclosure of congressmen's personal finances and for restrictions on their outside income and gifts to them by lobbyists and constituents—make it more difficult for individuals and groups to put congressmen in their debt as they were formerly able to do.

The procedures of both houses of Congress have also been opened up in the 1970s. Committee proceedings, including those used to "mark up" bills and, as well as meetings of conference committees, are increasingly conducted in open session. Moreover, roll-call votes of standing committees are more readily available for inspection, and the secrecy of teller voting in the House has been eliminated. Thus "sunshine" rather than shadow has come to characterize many of the procedures of Congress.

Individual congressmen, including rank-and-file members of the House of Representatives, have also gained more influence in recent years. The creation of additional subcommittees, plus rules limiting the number of such chairmanships and memberships an individual congressman can hold, has served to distribute more posts to junior congressmen; rules changes providing more staff and budget and greater autonomy for subcommittees from the chairman of the parent committee has also redounded to the benefit of rank-and-file members of Congress.

Finally, the situation of Democratic party leaders and committees in the House of Representatives has also been strengthened considerably in recent years. Additional powers granted to the Speaker of the House—including that of referring bills to committee, chairing and naming many of the members of the newly created Steering and Policy Committee, as well as choosing Democratic members of the Rules Committee—have added to the potential influence of the majority party's leader in the House. The role of the Steering and Policy Committee in helping to place congressmen on committees and in planning and steering the party program through Congress has added to the potential of congressional party government, as have the recent activities of the Democratic Caucus in committee assignments, and in playing a more significant part in the development of public policy.

There is no doubt that the changes outlined above have made the Congress potentially a much more responsive and accountable body than it used to be. It remains to be seen, however, how Congress will implement these changes. There is the danger that the wave of recent reforms resulted primarily from the Watergate and congressional scandals and that Congress will revert to "business as usual" when the public pressure growing out of these scandals recedes. Moreover, it will be difficult to reconcile different elements of some of the recent reforms. For example, the development of "subcommittee government" makes the House of Representatives even more decentralized than it used to be, and it is not certain that the additional powers granted to the Speaker and party committees will be sufficient to bring these subcommittees under centralized control. Thus Congress will have to balance two perennial aspects of democratic government: maximizing the role of individuals and at the same time permitting the majority to work its will.

SELECTED READINGS

The account of the 1976 congressional scandals and the development in 1977 of ethics codes by the House and Senate is drawn from *Congressional Ethics* (Washington, D.C.: Congressional Quarterly, Inc., April 1977), pp. 1–22.

A classic study of Congress is Woodrow Wilson, *Congressional Government: A Study in American Politics* (Boston: Houghton Mifflin, 1891). Two good recent treatments of the legislative process at both the national and state level are Malcolm E. Jewell and Samuel C. Patterson, *The Legislative Process in the United States* (New York: Random House, 1968), and William J. Keefe and Morris S. Ogul, *The Legislative Process: Congress and the States* (Englewood Cliffs, N.J.: Prentice-Hall, 4th ed., 1977). A good short treatment of Congress is contained in Nelson W. Polsby, *Congress and the Presidency* (Englewood Cliffs, N.J.: Prentice-Hall, 3rd ed., 1976). An excellent general study of Congress containing chapters on various topics by different authors is David B. Truman (ed.), *Congress and America's Future* (Englewood Cliffs, N.J.: Prentice-Hall, 2nd ed., 1971). The chapter entitled "Congressional Responses to the Twentieth Century," by Samuel P. Huntington, gives an excellent overview of the personnel, structure, and functions of the Congress. For an expanded analysis of the same general topics with particular emphasis on the latter, see John S. Saloma III, *Congress and the New Politics* (Boston: Little, Brown, 1969).

The world of a senator is graphically portrayed in Donald R. Matthews, *U.S. Senators and Their World* (Chapel Hill: University of North Carolina Press, 1960). Two excellent treatments of the life of a member of the House of Representatives are Charles L. Clapp, *The Congressman: His Work as He Sees It* (Washington, D.C.: The Brookings Institution, 1963), and Clem Miller (John W. Baker, ed.), *Letters of a Congressman* (New York: Scribner, 1962). Analysis of the tenure of House members over the years includes Huntington, op. cit., and Nelson Polsby, "The Institutionalization of the U.S. House of Representatives," *The American Political Science Review* 62 (1968): 144-68. The information on congressional pay and perquisites is taken from *Congressional Ethics,* op. cit., pp. 27-49.

A journalist's description of the Senate's inner club is William S. White, *Citadel, The Story of the U.S. Senate* (New York: Harper & Row, 1957); for one by a senator himself see Joseph S. Clark, *The Senate Establishment* (New York: Hill and Wang, 1963). Randall B. Ripley, *Power in the Senate* (New York: St. Martin's Press, 1969), is a balanced, scholarly treatment of the same topic. For an analysis of the role of the party in the House of Representatives see Ripley's *Party Leaders in the House of Representatives* (Washington, D.C.: The Brookings Institution, 1967).

Richard Fenno and Ralph Huitt treat the internal distribution of influence in the House and Senate in the 1960s respectively in Truman, op. cit. Excellent accounts of the changes in the 1970s are Norman Ornstein, Robert Peabody, and David Rhode, "The Changing Senate from the 1950s to the 1970s," and Lawrence Dodd and Bruce Oppenheimer, "The House in Transition," both of which appear in Lawrence Dodd and Bruce Oppenheimer (eds.), *Congress Reconsidered* (New York: Praeger, 1977), pp. 3-20 and 21-53 respectively. Nelson Polsby analyzes recent changes in the Senate in "Goodbye to the Senate's Inner Club," and Herbert Asher treats of those in the House in "The Changing Status of the Freshman Representative"; the two selections appear in Norman Ornstein (ed.), *Congress in Change: Evolution and Reform* (New York: Praeger, 1975), pp. 208-215 and 216-239 respectively.

An excellent comparative study of six House standing committees is Richard Fenno, *Congressmen in Committees* (Boston: Little, Brown, 1973). The Democratic Study Committee is analyzed in the Spring 1974 issue of *Current American Government,* pp. 88-93, and the House Wednesday Group is treated by Sven Groennings in a book edited by him and Jonathan Hawley, *To Be a Congressman: The Promise and the Power* (Washington, D.C.: Acropolis Books, 1973). Hawley has an excellent piece in the same volume dealing with the issue of seniority and committee leadership.

The best recent treatment of congressional procedure is Lewis A. Froman, Jr., *The Congressional Process: Strategies, Rules, and Procedures* (Boston: Little, Brown, 1967).

Two excellent analyses of voting patterns in Congress are Julius Turner, *Party and Constituency: Pressures on Congress* (Baltimore: Johns Hopkins University Press, 1951), and David Truman, *Congressional Party: A Case Study* (New York: Wiley, 1959). A good short treatment of the subject is continued in Lewis A. Froman, Jr., *Congressmen and Their Constituencies* (Chicago: Rand McNally, 1963). Two more recent studies of voting in the House of Representatives are David Mayhew, *Party Loyalty among Congressmen: The Difference between Democrats and Republicans* (Cambridge: Harvard University Press, 1966), and Wayne Shannon, *Party, Constituency and Congressional Voting: A Study of Legislative Behavior in the U.S. House of Representatives.* (Baton Rouge: Louisiana State University Press, 1968). An analysis based on survey data of attitudes of both congressmen and their constituents is Warren E. Miller and Donald E. Stokes, "Constituency Influence in Congress," which appears in Angus Campbell et al., *Elections and the Political Order* (New York: Wiley, 1966). Two excellent recent studies of congressional voting are Aage Clausen, *How Congressmen Decide: A Policy Focus* (New York: St. Martin's Press, 1973), and John Kingdom, *Congressmen's Voting Decisions* (New York: Harper & Row, 1973).

A major academic criticism of Congress is James MacGregor Burns, *Congress on Trial: The Legislative Process and the Administrative State* (New York: Gordian, 1966). Two congressmen most often associated with attacks on the two chambers are former Senator Joseph Clark and Representative Richard Bolling. The views of the former are set forth in *Congress: The Sapless Branch* (New York: Harper & Row, 1965) and of the latter in *House Out of Order* (New York: Dutton, 1965). A good defense of Congress is Ernest Griffith, *Congress: Its Contemporary Role* (New York: New York University Press, 5th ed., 1975). Thoughtful analyses of the issue of reform are contained in Froman's *The Congressional Process* and Saloma's work cited above. Recent interpretations of congressional reform in the 1970s include three excellent selections that appear in Dodd and Oppenheimer, op. cit.: Charles Jones, "Will Reform Change Congress?"; Richard Fenno, "Strengthening a Congressional Strength"; and Lawrence Dodd, "Congress and the Quest for Power." An overall analysis of Congress that evaluates the institution in terms of its responsibility, responsiveness, and accountability is Leroy Rieselbach, *Congressional Reform in the Seventies* (Morristown, N.J.: General Learning Press, 1977).

An excellent publication for keeping abreast of current developments in Congress and in American politics in general is the *Congressional Quarterly Weekly Report*.

Political Novels   In a Pulitzer Prize winning novel about Congress, Allen Drury, *Advise and Consent* (New York: Dell, 1961), tells of the traditions, trade-offs, and personalities that characterize the legislative branch of government. Another realistic treatment of how things are done on Capitol Hill is Drew Pearson's *The Senator* (New York: Avon, 1969), the story of a powerful senator unable to separate private gain from public trust.

Realistic and sympathetic descriptions of the daily life of a congressman are provided in two recent novels: Arthur T. Hadley, *A Life in Order* (New York: Viking Press, 1971), and John V. Lindsay (four-term Congressman, two-term mayor of New York City, and unsuccessful presidential candidate), *The Edge* (New York: Berkley, 1976). A story about raw corruption and influence peddling by the Speaker of the House of Representatives and other high government officials is told in *Conflict of Interest* (New York: Bantam, 1977) by Les Whitten. The author is the partner of well-known muckraker Jack Anderson and provides an educational—if exaggerated—look at investigative reporting in the nation's capital.

Abigail McCarthy (ex-wife of a former U.S. senator, Eugene McCarthy) in *Circles* (New York: Doubleday, 1977), and Gore Vidal (grandson of the first senator from Oklahoma, Thomas P. Gore) in *Washington, D.C.* (New York: Bantam, 1976), provide sobering accounts of the social swirl, interpersonal conflicts, and personality types that characterize the public and private lives of our lawmakers in Washington.

The transfer of power.

Chapter 12

No event in recent history has had as much significance for the American political system as the break-in of the Democratic headquarters in the Watergate Hotel apartment-complex on June 17, 1972. However, that significance was not immediately revealed. Although three of the men involved—James McCord, Howard Hunt, and G. Gordon Liddy—were associated with the Nixon administration, it appeared that only they and four Cubans who also participated in the break-in would be sentenced to jail by U.S. District Judge John Sirica and that no high administration officials would be implicated in the incident that was termed by some observers a "third-rate burglary."

But behind the scenes other forces were at work. After brilliant investigative reporting, Bob Woodward and Carl Bernstein of the *Washington Post* published accounts (for which they subsequently won a Pulitzer prize) revealing that the Watergate break-in was part of a massive campaign of political spying and sabotage directed against the Democrats by officials of the White House and the Committee to Reelect the President. Also important was the increasing suspicion of Judge Sirica, who said at the end of the trial in February 1973 that he was not satisfied that all the pertinent facts had been presented. Shortly thereafter the Senate appointed a seven-man bipartisan committee under the chairmanship of Sam Ervin of North Carolina (a former state supreme court judge and acknowledged expert on the United States Constitution) to inquire into illegal activities during presidential campaigns. Then in late March 1973 James McCord claimed that pressure was exerted on him and the other defendants to plead guilty and remain silent, and Judge Sirica postponed final sentencing to hear him and the others out. When that occurred, the lid blew off the Watergate caper.

In subsequent months the American public was bombarded by media accounts of legal investigations and proceedings into alleged illegal activities of high administration officials. A number of those officials resigned, including two of President Nixon's closest advisers, H.R. Haldeman and John Ehrlichman, along with White House counsel John Dean, Attorney-General Richard Kleindienst, and F.B.I. Director L. Patrick Gray. Kleindienst was replaced by Elliot Richardson, who, in turn, appointed Harvard law professor Archibald

Cox as Special Prosecutor to investigate possible criminal violations growing out of Watergate and related incidents.

Judge John Sirica.

In mid-May the Ervin Committee began television hearings into a broad range of administrative wrong-doing. Included were wiretaps and burglaries conducted by a special unit within the White House known as the "plumbers" (so called for their assignment to plug the alleged "leaks" of information important to the nation's security); sabotage and "dirty tricks" directed against the campaigns of leading Democratic presidential candidates in 1972; improper solicitation of—and failure to report—money raised by the Finance Committee to Reelect the President; and the compiling of an Enemies List of persons inimical to the Nixon administration who were to be "screwed" (as John Dean inelegantly put it) by the Internal Revenue Service and other government agencies. Appearing before the Committee in the hearings that lasted until the first week in August were a parade of witnesses, including such former administration luminaries as Dean, Ehrlichman, Haldeman, and two recent Attorneys-General—John Mitchell and Richard Kleindienst.

Meanwhile on July 31st, a House member from Massachusetts—Father Robert Drinan, a liberal Roman Catholic priest and an outspoken critic of the Vietnam War—introduced a resolution asking for the impeachment of President Nixon for "high crimes and misdemeanors". Considered premature by most House members, who said that they wanted to await the outcome of the Watergate Committee hearings, the measure drew little public attention. However, the situation changed suddenly the following October. President Nixon ordered Special Watergate Prosecutor Archibald Cox to cease attempting to obtain tapes, notes, and memorandums of presidential conversations pertaining to possible criminal activities of administrative officials (the details of this matter will be analyzed in ch. 16), and when the Special Prosecutor refused, the President ordered Cox's administrative superior, Attorney-General Elliot Richardson, to discharge him. Richardson refused to do so, and instead resigned himself, as did the Deputy Attorney-General William Ruckelshaus who had

Investigative reporters, Woodward and Bernstein.

Congressional investigators:
Baker and Ervin.

The investigated:
John Mitchell
John Erlichman
H.R. Haldeman

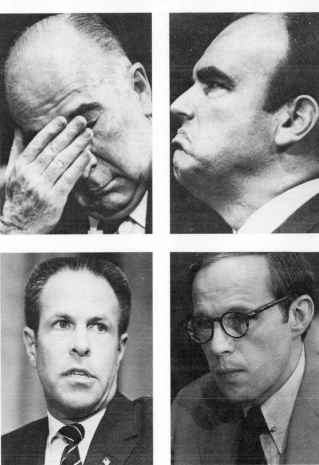

temporarily succeeded to the top law-enforcement post when Richardson vacated it. This series of dramatic events, tabbed the "Saturday Night Massacre" (for Saturday, October 20, 1973, on which the events occurred), set off a storm of public protest and led to the introduction of resolutions signed by eighty-four representatives calling for the impeachment of the President or for an investigation of impeachment procedures. Speaker Carl Albert immediately referred such resolutions to the House Judiciary Committee for investigation.

Delayed for a period by the task of inquiry for the House into the background of Gerald Ford, President Nixon's vice-presidential nominee, the committee began to get organized toward the end of 1973. Chairman Peter Rodino, a New Jersey Democrat, appointed John Doar, a nominal Republican who had served as Assistant Attorney-General for Civil Rights in the Kennedy and Johnson administrations, as the special impeachment counsel for the committee. In early January, Albert Jenner, a Republican trial lawyer from Chicago with ties to Adlai Stevenson, Jr., the Democratic senator from Illinois, was named the committee's chief minority counsel. In February, the House by an overwhelming 410-4 vote conferred broad investigatory powers on the committee, including the right to subpoena persons to appear before it as well as materials relevant to its inquiries.

In the months ahead, the thirty-eight-member body consisting of twenty-one Democrats and seventeen Republicans meticulously gathered evidence on various aspects of the President's activities. It subpoenaed forty-two tapes of conversations between President Nixon and his advisors; he refused to surrender them, arguing that because of their confidential nature they were protected from disclosure by the doctrine of executive privilege. The President did provide the committee with a 1300-page edited transcript of the taped conversations, but its members subsequently informed him that the transcripts did not comply with the committee's subpoena. Ultimately, however, the committee got a windfall of evidence when Judge Sirica ruled that it was entitled to have the Watergate grand jury report and related material dealing with the President's possible involvement in Watergate matters. The committee also heard testimony from a number of key administration officials. The end result was thirty-eight volumes of materials that the committee made available to the House and Senate for their consideration.

The Judiciary Committee also struggled with a number of legal problems involving matters of both procedure and substance. It debated whether to allow the President's attorney—James St. Clair, a Boston trial lawyer—to sit in on the committee's hearings, examine and submit evidence, and present and cross-examine witnesses; the members also argued over what was meant by the Constitutional language of "high crimes and misdemeanors," the kinds of violations that constitute impeachable offenses. Did the language refer only to criminal offenses or were presidential actions that involved abuse of power and violations of the public trust also "high crimes and misdemeanors"? Finally, members differed on how specific the articles of impeachment must be, whether they had to contain names, dates, and places to support charges of presidential wrongdoing. The committee ultimately settled such matters by according St. Clair the desired privileges, by including violations of both criminal offenses (specifically those relating to the obstruction of justice) and abuses of power in its articles of impeachment, and by allowing detailed information supporting

Special Prosecutor Archibald Cox.

the charges against the President to be included in its report and summary of evidence rather than in the articles of impeachment themselves.

For six days in late July the committee debated Mr. Nixon's fate before a nationwide television audience as pro- and anti-impeachment congressmen analyzed the evidence, voiced the arguments for and against Mr. Nixon's removal from office, and devised the specific articles of impeachment that should be recommended to the whole House for consideration. Ultimately all twenty-one Democrats and six of the committee's seventeen Republican members voted in favor of the first article, accusing the President of obstructing justice in connection with the coverup of the Watergate break-in. A second article, charging Mr. Nixon with abusing the powers of his office by attempting to improperly use such organizations as the Internal Revenue Service and the FBI, was supported by the same bipartisan coalition plus one more vote from Congressman Robert McClory of Illinois, the second-ranking Republican on the committee. A third article, involving contempt of Congress based upon the President's refusal to turn over tapes subpoenaed by the committee, passed by a narrower margin: 21–17. Two other articles, one relating to the secret bombing of Cambodia and the other based on Mr. Nixon's tax payments and improvements on his private properties, failed of passage by identical 12–26 votes. With the completion of the work of the Judiciary Committee, the entire House set aside the last two weeks in August for debate on the possible impeachment of Richard Nixon.

However, dramatic events intervened that made the House debate and subsequent impeachment actions unnecessary. On Monday, August 5, 1974 President Nixon made a public statement indicating that tapes he was furnishing to Judge Sirica as a result of a Supreme Court decision (this matter will be discussed in detail in ch. 16) revealed that he had known of the Watergate incident six days after it occurred and that he had ordered the FBI called off the case because the men involved had connections with the Committee to Reelect the President. This disclosure of vital information that the President had kept from the American public, the House Judiciary Committee, and even his own attorney set off a wave of anger, particularly among the ten Republican members of the Judiciary Committee who had supported him during that body's debate less than two weeks before. All ten soon indicated that they would now vote for impeachment.

In five tense days in early August, events moved to a dramatic climax. Republican Senators Barry Goldwater and Hugh Scott and House Minority Leader John Rhodes visited the White House on Wednesday to inform the President that his support had eroded so badly in both chambers that he would most certainly be impeached and convicted. The next morning, August 8th, Mr. Nixon told Vice-President Ford of his intent to resign and went before the nation's largest television audience—some 120 million—that evening (six years to the day from his 1968 nomination acceptance speech) to give the same message to the American people. At noon on Friday, August 9th, Gerald Ford was sworn in as the thirty-seventh President of the United States as Richard Nixon returned with his family to his home in San Clemente, California, once more a private citizen.

The political demise of Richard Nixon illustrates two circumstances that can end a President's term prior to its expiration: impeachment and resignation.

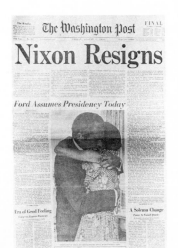

There are two other situations that can also terminate the tenure of a Chief Executive—namely, death and disability. Fortunately, as we will see later in this chapter, when any of the above four events creates a vacancy in the office, machinery exists for filling that vacancy with a successor, a process that ensures continuity in the American presidency.

TERMINATING PRESIDENTIAL TENURE

Impeachment

While a number of impeachment resolutions have been introduced in the House of Representatives against Presidents over the years, on only two occasions did that body formally authorize an investigation of grounds for impeachment. As we have just seen, one occurred in 1974 against Richard Nixon; the other took place in 1868 against Andrew Johnson.

Johnson, a Tennessee Democrat who was the only member of the United States Senate from a seceding state to remain loyal to the Union, was placed on the Republican ticket by Abraham Lincoln in the campaign of 1864. After the President was assassinated in 1865 and Johnson assumed the presidency, he soon found himself in direct conflict with congressional Republicans over the reconstruction of the South. Johnson favored a conciliatory policy that provided for the readmission of the South into the Union after such obvious steps as the nullification of secession, the repudiation of Confederate state debts, and the abolition of slavery had been taken. Many of the Republican congressmen—particularly those associated with the Radical wing of the party—demanded much more, including the creation of a Freedman's Bureau to protect exslaves from whites and to provide them with education and other services; they also favored the passage of legislation guaranteeing the civil rights of Negroes and the creation of military governments in the South to oversee the

Thaddeus Stevens gives the Senate formal notice of the impeachment of Andrew Johnson.

Facsimile of ticket of admission to the impeachment trial.

reconstruction process. Federal jobs also became a bone of contention between Johnson and Republicans: the President fired many executive officeholders during and after the election campaign of 1866, and the Congress responded with the Tenure of Office Act, forbidding the removal of officers appointed with the consent of the Senate without the concurrence of that body.

The battle between Johnson and congressional Republicans initially took the form of presidential vetoes of Reconstruction legislation followed by Congress's overriding such vetoes. However, the President dismissed Secretary of War Edwin Stanton, an ally of the Radical Republicans, on February 21, 1868 without senatorial approval, declaring the Tenure of Office Act to be an unconstitutional limitation on his removal power. Within a day, the House passed a resolution on impeachment and referred it to the Committee on Reconstruction, headed by Radical Republican leader Thaddeus Stevens of Pennsylvania. The next day the committee reported an impeachment resolution, and two days later the whole House concurred with the committee's action in a 126-49 straight party-line vote.

The House drew up eleven articles of impeachment (the main one based on the removal of Stanton in violation of the Tenure of Office Act) and appointed managers to argue the charges before the Senate. The trial began on March 30, 1968 with the Chief Justice of the United States, Salmon Chase, presiding. On May 11 the Senate took its first vote on the Eleventh Article (a summary of many of the charges in the previous articles), which ended with a vote of 35-19, one vote short of the necessary two-thirds majority needed to convict. The Radicals maneuvered a ten-day adjournment to try to line up more votes for Johnson's conviction, but when the senators reassembled and voted on two other articles, the same vote prevailed, and the President was spared removal from office.*

Death

The most prevalent circumstance that has terminated the tenure of American Presidents has been *death in office*. Eight Chief Executives have suffered this fate, four of them by the violence of assassination—Abraham Lincoln, James Garfield, William McKinley, and John Kennedy. The other four—William Harrison, Zachary Taylor, Warren Harding, and Franklin Roosevelt—died of natural causes. Thus of the thirty-eight Presidents (Grover Cleveland served two terms, with Benjamin Harrison's presidency intervening between them), eight—almost one in four—did not finish out their term of office.

Resignation

While most Presidents since George Washington have undoubtedly considered resignation from office, Richard Nixon, under great pressures from political friends and foes alike, is the only Chief Executive to have actually exercised that option. However, just prior to the 1916 election, Woodrow Wilson suggested in a letter to Secretary of State Robert Lansing that if he were defeated

---

* The key figure in the vote was Edmund Ross of Kansas, who, though a Radical Republican and under tremendous pressure to vote for conviction, voted not guilty. Six other Republican senators joined Ross in saving President Johnson.

for reelection, he would appoint his Republican opponent, Charles Evans Hughes, to Lansing's position; then he and his Vice-President, Thomas Marshall, would resign, and under the presidential succession law then in effect (we will examine that subject later in the chapter), Hughes would become President immediately rather than having to wait four months until his elected term was scheduled to begin. Fortunately for Wilson and for Marshall (who was not consulted on the matter), a Democratic election victory rendered the procedure unnecessary. When William Jennings Bryan asked Wilson to appoint Warren Harding Secretary of State immediately after his 1920 victory and then resign along with Marshall, Wilson ignored the advice. Harry Truman did the same when Senator Fulbright proposed after the Republicans won the 1946 congressional election that the President appoint a Republican to serve as Secretary of State and then resign.*

Disability

A fourth circumstance that can lead to either a temporary or a permanent termination of a President's term is his *disability* (sometimes called *inability*). Article II, Section 1 of the Constitution specifically provides that in case of the inability of the President "to discharge the duties of the said office, the same shall devolve on the Vice President." However, this terse language leaves a number of unanswered questions: (1) What, exactly, constitutes presidential disability—physical illness, mental illness, any disability that prevents his carrying out his duties? (2) Who, exactly, determines whether disability exists—the President himself, the Vice-President, Congress, the Supreme Court? (3) What is it that the Vice-President succeeds to—the powers and duties of the office or the office itself? If it is the latter, how can the President retrieve his office if he recovers from his disability? (4) Who is it that decides if and when the President has recovered from his disability—the President himself or the Vice-President who has taken over? If there is disagreement between the two—how is that resolved and by whom?

On several occasions, Presidents have been disabled, and because there were no definitive answers to the above questions, political leaders have had to improvise means of dealing with the immediate problem. On two occasions the results were most unfortunate. President James Garfield was confined to a bed for eighty days after being shot by an assassin, until he ultimately died. During that time he was able to fulfill only one official act (signing an extradition paper), yet Vice-President Chester Arthur declined to take any action to replace Garfield for two reasons: first, he was outside the President's inner circle, since he was from an opposite political faction of the Republican party (Arthur was a "Stalwart," a conservative-type Republican; Garfield was a "Half-Breed," a more modern-type Republican); second, some of the members of the President's cabinet thought that it would be legally impossible for Garfield ever to get the office back once Arthur had assumed it.

Even more serious was Woodrow Wilson's incapacity for 280 days following a stroke that he suffered on a speaking tour to win support for the League of Nations. During this long period when the Versailles peace treaty was before

---

* While there was no person serving as Vice-President to complicate the matter, Truman would, of course, have been giving up over two years of his term rather than only a few months.

DEATH

Claims our Beloved Ruler.

James Abram Garfield the 20th President of the United States of America,

Died Last Night at 10.34 o'clock.

the Senate and the nation was demobilizing with its economy in a state of transition, the President was completely shielded from all contact with the outside world with the exception of his wife and physician. Vice-President Thomas Marshall (like Chester Arthur) hesitated to act, and the overtures of Secretary of State Robert Lansing to get Marshall to take over the affairs of the nation were successfully opposed by close political friends of the President.

Once again the nation was faced with the problem of presidential disability when Dwight Eisenhower had a heart attack in 1955, an ileitis attack and operation in 1956, and a mild stroke in 1957. Although only the first incident was serious (and even that kept him totally removed from public affairs for only four days), the concern raised by the issue prompted Eisenhower, Kennedy, and Johnson to enter into agreements with their Vice-Presidents providing for the handling of the problem and also led Congress to make inquiries into the issue. Eventually the Twenty-fifth Amendment was ratified in 1967, dealing with most of the issues discussed above.

Specifically, the amendment provides that either the President himself or the Vice-President and a majority of his cabinet (or some other body designated by Congress) can declare that the President is unable to discharge the powers and duties of his office, in which case the Vice-President becomes *acting President* (not President). The President can also declare when his disability is over and resume the powers and duties of the office; however, if the Vice-President and cabinet (or other body designated by Congress) disagree with the President's judgment, Congress ultimately decides the issue. Thus the amendment treats the second, third, and fourth problems raised above, and leaves only the first (what constitutes disability) completely unanswered. Perhaps that issue is unanswerable and we should accept the definition of the leading scholar on the issue, Ruth Silva, that disability is "any de facto inability whatever the cause or the duration, if it occurs at a time when the urgency of public business requires executive action."*

Thus a President's term can be terminated by impeachment and conviction, death, resignation, or by disability.† As we have seen, provisions also exist for automatically filling presidential vacancies so that the continuity of the office is preserved.

PRESIDENTIAL SUCCESSION

Although Americans take for granted the Vice-President's succession to the office upon the death of the President, many political systems do not provide

The New York Times.   LATE CITY EDITION

KENNEDY IS KILLED BY SNIPER
AS HE RIDES IN CAR IN DALLAS;
JOHNSON SWORN IN ON PLANE

---

* During the course of the threatened impeachment and trial of Richard Nixon, the suggestion was made that he declare himself unable to carry on the duties of his office and allow Vice-President Ford to act as President until Mr. Nixon's fate was determined by the House and Senate.

† In addition to the termination of a presidential term prior to its expiration, the Twenty-second Amendment places a limitation on the number of times a President can serve. Under its provisions, no person can be elected to the office more than twice; moreover, if he has served more than two years of a term to which someone else was originally elected, then he can be elected only once. Thus the longest a person can serve in the office is ten years. There have also been suggestions made in recent years that a President be limited to one six-year term, a matter that we will assess at the end of chapter 13.

machinery to determine in advance who will become the leader of the nation if something happens to the incumbent. When Joseph Stalin suddenly died of a heart attack in March 1953, a power struggle ensued in the Soviet Union before Khrushchev eventually took over sole leadership of the nation. For over twenty-five years of communist control of China, speculation continued about who would become the political leader upon Mao Tse-tung's death. The succession to power is thus generally a major problem in totalitarian societies, but even democratic nations do not always take account of the problem: Great Britain, for example, has no official designated to succeed immediately to the prime ministership.

In contrast, the United States Constitution provides for presidential succession—a continuity of the presidential office if it is either permanently or temporarily vacant. Article II, Section 1 (as amended by Section 1 of the Twenty-fifth Amendment) provides for the Vice-President's taking over if a presidency is terminated for any of the four reasons discussed above; in addition, Section 3 of the Twentieth Amendment makes a similar provision in the event that a President-elect dies before taking office, or if a President is not chosen, or if one has failed to qualify for the office at the beginning of the term. These same constitutional sections empower Congress to provide by law who will succeed to the office or act as President if there is no Vice-President available or qualified to fill the Presidential office.

On three separate occasions Congress has enacted legislation to provide for presidential succession in the event of a double vacancy. A 1792 law tapped the legislative leadership by placing in line for the presidency first the President Pro Tempore of the Senate, then the Speaker of the House of Representatives; it also provided that if the double vacancy occurred in the first two years and seven months of the presidential term, Congress was required to call a special election to choose a new President and Vice-President. In 1886 Congress switched to the cabinet as a preferable source of presidential talent, beginning with the Secretary of State and on down the line in chronological order of the establishment of the executive departments; this law provided for the possibility of a special election but did not make it mandatory. Finally, in 1947 at the behest of President Truman (who argued that it was better to have an elected than an appointive official as President and that he ought not to be able to choose his successor by naming a Secretary of State), Congress went back to the legislative leaders as first in the succession line. This time, however, congressmen provided that the Speaker of the House precede the President Pro Tempore of the Senate, who, in turn, is to be followed by members of the cabinet; there is no provision at all for a special election under this most recent succession law.

The same amendment that provides for presidential disability—the Twenty-fifth—also contains provisions that affect executive succession. Section 2 states that if there is a vacancy in the vice-presidency, the President shall nominate a Vice-President who must be confirmed by a majority vote of both houses of Congress. This procedure was invoked twice within ten months' time—first in October 1973, when Vice-President Agnew resigned (after having been fined for federal income tax evasion) and President Nixon chose Gerald Ford as Vice-President; and later by Ford himself, when he succeeded to the presidency after Nixon resigned and then nominated Nelson Rockefeller as his Vice-Pres-

Former Vice President Nelson Rockefeller.

"Remember, in this great country, anyone—girl or boy—can grow up to be appointed President."

ident. Of course, this constitutional procedure not only permits the person ultimately selected as Vice-President to take over the duties of that office* but also puts him, rather than the Speaker of the House, first in line for the presidency. By providing machinery to rectify a double vacancy, the Twenty-fifth Amendment thus makes it less likely that presidential succession will ever reach the legislative leadership of the two houses of Congress.

Thus the continuity of the presidential office is much more assured today than it was earlier in the nation's history. The remainder of the chapter analyzes the kind of office that was originally established by the Founding Fathers, together with the changes that have occurred in it over the years.

THE ESTABLISHMENT OF THE PRESIDENCY

As we saw in chapter 2, the experiences under the Articles of Confederation had demonstrated vividly that the national government could not carry on executive activities through legislative committees. Therefore, those who gathered in Philadelphia were convinced that the new government required some kind of separate executive branch. They did not agree by any means, however, about what the nature and powers of the executive should be.

There was even some question of establishing a monarchy: as John Jay put it in a letter to George Washington, "Shall we have a king?" Of the fifty-five delegates at the Constitutional Convention, however, only Hamilton seemed willing seriously to consider the British model, which he considered the "best in the world." Others either opposed it on principle or recognized, as John Dickinson of Delaware put it, that a monarchy was "out of the question." The American experience under George III and the colonial governors sent as emissaries of the King had created a climate of opinion that excluded any kind of monarchy, however limited it might be.

There were, however, other American models to consider: the state governorships of the day. For the most part these were weak offices overshadowed by state legislatures, but there were two exceptions: New York and Massachusetts both provided for independent governors vested with important political powers. That the governors of these two states served effectively without endangering political freedom convinced many of the delegates that a strong Chief Executive accountable to the people was not to be equated with a tyrannical king or colonial governor.

Two disparate concepts concerning the nature and powers of the national executive emerged. One was the idea of a "weak" executive whose primary function would be to put into effect the will of the legislature. To this end, a plural executive would be established, or even if only one man headed the branch, a powerful council would share his powers and hold him in check. The Congress would choose the Chief Executive for a limited term; moreover, he could not be reappointed immediately and would even be subject to removal by the legislative body during his term of office. The powers of the executive would be limited and in essence delegated to him by Congress, which would also make appointments to the executive branch and exercise the treaty- and

---

* On no fewer than sixteen occasions prior to the enactment of the Twenty-fifth Amendment, the vice-presidential office was vacant due to the incumbent's succeeding to the presidency (8), dying (7), or resigning (1).

war-making powers. This concept of the office provided for no executive veto of laws passed by the Congress.

At the other extreme was the idea of a "strong" executive, independent of the Congress, exercising important functions in the new government. Under this concept a single Chief Executive, chosen by some means other than legislative appointment, would have no limit placed on his tenure. If he were to be removable at all, it would be only for certain definite, enumerated reasons, and then only after impeachment and conviction by a judicial body or the legislature. His powers would be derived from the Constitution and not be subject to legislative interference. He would appoint judicial and diplomatic officials and participate in the execution of foreign affairs, including the making of treaties. He would have a veto over legislation passed by Congress, a power that he would exercise either alone or in conjunction with the judiciary. Finally, either there would be no executive council at all, or, if one did exist, it would be merely an advisory body whose actions would not bind the Chief Executive.

In the initial stages of the Convention it appeared that the delegates would create an essentially "weak" executive. The New Jersey Plan called for a plural executive chosen by Congress; members would be eligible for a single term and be removable by the national legislative body on application of the majority of the executives of the states. Federal officials would be empowered to execute federal laws and to direct, but not take command of, military operations. The Virginia resolution provided for an executive (it was vague whether the executive was to be single or plural) chosen by the Congress and with no right to hold a second term. The powers were limited to executing national laws and implementing rights vested in Congress by the Confederation. Thus neither of the two major plans before the Convention envisioned a strong Chief Executive.

In the course of the Convention's deliberations, however, the office was strengthened. A decision made early by the Committee of the Whole to provide for a single executive was a major victory for the friends of a strong presidency. Subsequent Convention decisions—to which the work of the key Committees on Detail and on Style (James Wilson was an important figure in the former, and Gouverneur Morris in the latter) contributed—eventually led to an independent Chief Executive with considerable political powers.

The presidency created by the Convention resembles in many respects the strong-executive model described earlier. He is chosen by some method other than legislative appointment (electoral college), is eligible to succeed himself, and can be removed only for specific causes (treason, bribery, high crimes, and misdemeanors), and then only upon the bringing of an impeachment charge by the House of Representatives and conviction by the vote of two-thirds of the members of the Senate. He is not dependent on the Congress for his authority; rather, specific powers are granted to him by the Constitution. In addition, as a result of the efforts of Gouverneur Morris, he is given broad undefined authority by the opening sentence of Article II: "The executive power shall be vested in a President of the United States of America."

At the same time, the President does not enjoy all the prerogatives of the strong-executive model. Although he has the veto power, it is not absolute, since his action can be overridden by a two-thirds vote in each of the two houses of Congress. Moreover, his appointment power is subject to the approval of the Senate, as is his authority to negotiate treaties. Thus although the Founding Fathers did not create a council that shares all the Chief Executive's powers with him, they did grant the upper chamber of the national legislature a check on certain presidential actions.

Why did the Convention move from an essentially weak concept of the executive to a final version that closely fits the strong-executive model? Individual delegates certainly played a part in the outcome. The efforts of Pennsylvanians Wilson and Morris (who had also helped create the strong New York governorship), Rufus King and Elbridge Gerry of Massachusetts, Charles Pinckney and John Rutledge of South Carolina, Alexander Hamilton of New York, and others helped shape the Convention's decisions all along the way. George Washington, too, was a key figure in the process even though he never spoke to the issue personally. Pierce Butler, a delegate from South Carolina, described that contribution in a letter written after the Convention completed its deliberations: "Nor . . . do I believe that they [the President's powers] would have been so great had not many of the members cast their eyes toward George Washington as President, and shaped their ideas of the powers to be given to a President by their opinions of his virtue."

Other factors also played a role in the final decision. Because the powers of the Congress were increased as compared to those of the former Confederation legislature, some delegates came to the opinion that a strong executive was needed to counterbalance the new legislative body. As political scientist Joseph Kallenbach was pointed out, there is even some indication that during the course of the proceedings an alliance was formed between the supporters of a strong Chief Executive and delegates from the small states, an alliance that furthered the interests of both groups. Evidence of a coalition is particularly noticeable in the recommendations of the Committee on Postponed Matters and Unfinished Business granting the President and Senate joint responsibilities in the appointment of executive officials and the making of treaties, and making the Senate, rather than the Supreme Court, the trial body in impeachment cases. It is also worth noting that both the President and the small states benefit from the electoral college arrangement: the President is selected initially by a process that does not involve the Congress directly, but if no candidate receives an electoral majority, the House, voting by states, not individuals, chooses the Chief Executive.

Controversy over the executive continued after the convention adjourned. George Mason of Virginia, one of the delegates who refused to sign the Constitution, charged that the provisions relating to the presidency would prove to be a device for an "elective monarch"; this sentiment was shared by Luther Martin of Maryland, who also left the document unsigned. Moreover, some state-ratifying conventions proposed that the first Congress initiate amendments restricting the President's eligibility for reelection as well as limiting certain of his powers. Unlike the situation with respect to a Bill of Rights, however, Congress declined to act on any of these proposed amendments. Washington's presence in the highest office in the land undoubtedly helped to allay fears over the possible abuse of executive power.

Certain amendments to the Constitution, however, change the executive article somewhat: the Twelfth, on the choosing of the President and Vice-President; the Twentieth, pertaining to the beginning of their term; the Twenty-second, which limits the tenure of the Chief Executive; and the Twenty-fifth, about presidential disability and succession. Yet the essential constitutional framework of the presidential office remains as it was created almost two centuries ago. Most of the vast changes in the presidency since that time have arisen not from formal legal alterations in its structure but rather from informal political customs and precedents.

THE DEVELOPMENT OF THE PRESIDENCY

One of the dominant trends in American political life has been the growth of the presidency. The legislative and judicial branches of the national government have also increased in power and influence over the years, but not at the same pace. Thus the separation of powers is similar to the division of powers as described in chapter 3: all branches (like all levels of government) have augmented their political authority, but some have done so more than others.

Although the overall trend has been in the direction of a more powerful presidency, growth has not been constant. The office occupied by Grant was not as potent as that of Lincoln. Conditions in American society, the people's reaction to them, and the personal qualities of particular incumbents have affected the functions and influence of the presidency.

Conditions and Factors Affecting the Development of the Presidency

In defending a single Chief Executive in the *Federalist Papers,* Alexander Hamilton emphasized what he termed "energy" as a desirable characteristic of good government. He went on to suggest that energy was particularly associated with the executive, as compared to a legislative body. As he put it: "Decision, activity, secrecy and despatch will generally characterize the proceedings of one man in a much more eminent degree than the proceedings of any greater number; and in proportion as the number is increased, these qualities will be diminished."

More than any other single factor this axiom of human behavior so clearly put by Hamilton explains the growth of presidential power and influence. The need for "decision, activity, secrecy and despatch" has become increasingly necessary to a leading power in an interdependent world. If military action is contemplated, the President as Commander-in-Chief of the armed forces has a crucial role to play in decisions on committing American troops. As historian Arthur Schlesinger, Jr. suggests, it is the capture of "the most vital of decisions, the decision to go to war," that has led to the "Imperial Presidency," an office that has appropriated powers reserved by the Constitution and historical practice to Congress.

Even without military action, the President plays a dominant part in foreign affairs in general. As we shall see in chapter 13, he has a number of powers—such as the negotiation of treaties that require senatorial approval and of executive agreements that do not, the initiation as well as the breaking off of diplomatic relationships with foreign governments, and the choosing of representatives abroad—that make his voice the crucial one in foreign affairs. Moreover, as in military matters, diplomacy requires a certain amount of secrecy. As the late British scholar Harold Laski expressed it, "Diplomatic negotiations are like a proposal of marriage; they must be made in private even if the engagement is later discussed in public."

The President's role in crises, however, is not confined to military and foreign affairs. To an increasing extent the American people have demanded that the national government "do something" about economic depressions, social problems such as race relations, the plight of the cities, and other pressing concerns. Once again such expectations have enhanced the influence of the presidency, for a President can move swiftly and forcefully to help counteract mass unemployment, send troops to assist in integrating the schools, or deal with major riots such as the one in Detroit in 1967. Thus the presidency has grown in power and influence as the American people have accepted the concept of the positive state, that is, one in which the government—particularly the national one—plays a major role in meeting (and hopefully, on occasion, even preventing) the many crises of our troubled society.

Hamilton's conviction that a large assembly of men have trouble in taking decisive action has been borne out by the experience of the American Congress. As he suggested, the problem becomes greater as the number is increased; this is precisely what happened as the number of senators and representatives grew from 26 and 65 respectively in the first Congress to 100 and 435 today. The present American political system makes it especially difficult for legislators to move quickly on problems. The variety of viewpoints represented by congressmen from different kinds of constituencies in a large and diverse country prevents the national legislature from making the rapid decisions that are called for in a crisis. Also contributing to congressional sluggishness has been the way power has generally been distributed within the two chambers and the traditional predominance in positions of authority (especially the chairmanships of standing committees) of senior legislators from safe districts who are inclined to support the status quo rather than to respond to demands for change in society. Because the Congress often cannot, or will not, act decisively when the occasion demands, people turn to the President to do so.

Hamilton may not have foreseen another development that has led to the expansion of presidential power and influence: the democratization of the selection process for Chief Executive. (Given his distrust of the common man, he certainly would have disapproved the development.) The shift from choice by elites in the various states to a national popularity contest has given the President a nationwide constituency that no other officeholder (except his political inferior, the Vice-President) can claim. As a result, he is the most visible figure in American politics and the one official from whom the public expects action and leadership. Because the President is accountable at the ballot box to the American people as a whole, he can claim them as his following and as support for his policies.

All these conditions have contributed to the natural growth of the presidency, uninhibited by the constitutional provisions relating to the office. The indefinite phraseology of the opening sentence of Article II of the Constitution—"The executive power shall be vested in a President of the United States"—has been, in effect, a grant of broad authority for bold and innovative ventures. Supplementing this general grant of presidential power are other clauses—for instance, "he shall take care that the laws be faithfully executed"—on which Presidents can draw for legal justification of their actions.

Woodrow Wilson may have exaggerated the situation somewhat when he claimed in 1908 (five years before he occupied the presidency himself) that the Chief Executive "has the right in law and conscience to be as big a man as he can," but few students of the presidency would deny the great potential of the office.

Wilson's observation points up still another major factor in the development of the presidency: the important part that individual Presidents have played in the process. Neither the natural conditions conducive to the increase in presidential power and influence nor the legal potentialities of the office in themselves guarantee decisive actions. The crises that both James Buchanan and Abraham Lincoln faced were virtually identical. Buchanan, however, took the position that he was powerless to prevent secession, whereas Lincoln took bold steps to try to counter it.

Individual Presidents and the Development of the Office

The manner in which a particular President handles the powers and duties of the office naturally depends upon his own personality and character. His family background as well as the experiences he has as a young adult have a major effect on his sense or lack of self-confidence, his psychological needs, the kind of values he acquires, and the perceptions he has of himself and the world around him. They also shape his political philosophy and his view of how he should conduct himself as President. His performance in that role will also depend upon his verbal abilities, how effectively he works and interacts with others, and how much time and effort he is willing to put into the job.

Students of the subject like Erwin Hargrove and James Barber distinguish between Presidents "of action," or "active" Presidents on the one hand, and those of "restraint," or "passive" Presidents on the other. The former are persons who invest a great deal of energy in the presidency and whose personal needs and skills are translated effectively into political leadership; the latter are inclined to devote less time and effort to being President and have neither the inclination nor the ability to exercise political power effectively. Active Presidents exert leadership over Congress, chart new directions in public policy, and take actions that stretch the powers of the presidential office; passive Presidents respond to congressional initiatives, support the status quo, and do not use the full authority of their office.

Barber also makes another general distinction among Presidents that he refers to as the "positive-negative" dimension of their performance. Positive Presidents enjoy political life and derive a great deal of personal satisfaction from serving in the office. Negative Presidents do not experience pleasure from being President, but serve because of compulsion or out of a sense of duty to their country.

Barber suggests a typology of four types of President with varying motivations and purposes. Active-positive Presidents want to accomplish results, particularly changes in governmental institutions, procedures, and policies. Active-negative Presidents are preoccupied with acquiring and maintaining power for its own sake. The Passive-positive Presidents want most to be popular, to be loved and admired by others. Passive-negative Presidents have a deep sense of civic virtue and rectitude.

Presidential personalities:
Franklin Delano Roosevelt:
active-positive; Woodrow
Wilson: *active negative;*
William Howard Taft: *passive-positive;* Dwight Eisenhower:
passive-negative.

There are, of course, major problems in attempting to analyze Presidents in this way. It is very difficult to establish complex relationships between particular events and influences in persons' lives and their subsequent behavior, especially when the data consists of general biographical accounts rather than intensive personal interviews that psychologists use to explore specific matters. Therefore what has come to be known as psychohistory must be accepted with considerable caution. Moreover, individuals do not fit neatly into cubbyholes; it should be understood that in attempting to categorize Presidents, scholars must assess the overall tendencies of their character and behavior to determine which pure type they most closely exemplify.

With these reservations in mind, we shall examine four individual Presidents that Barber uses to illustrate each of the types of President he sees as having served in the nation's highest office. These include Franklin Delano Roosevelt, Woodrow Wilson, William Howard Taft, and Dwight Eisenhower.*

Active-positive. Franklin Delano Roosevelt exemplifies the active-positive President. Born in 1882, the only child of wealthy parents of Dutch background, he grew up on the family estate in the Hudson River Valley in New York state, not going to school until he was fourteen. Doted over by a mother who kept him in dresses until he was five years old, and by a father much older than his wife who introduced him to the joys of ice-boating and sailing, his childhood could only be characterized as serene and secure. He was the object of great affection from his family and friends and responded with a trust and love for others.

Franklin's education was what one would expect of a family with a patrician tradition. He went to a prep school (Groton) whose headmaster, Endicott Peabody, instilled in him "manly Christian character" and an upper-class sense of social responsibility for the less advantaged in society. Then on to Harvard, where he was editor-in-chief of the school newspaper, the *Harvard Crimson:* to Columbia law school; and, upon graduation, to a conservative New York law firm in 1907.

Bored with the law, Roosevelt announced to his fellow law clerks that he intended to go into politics, following a career ladder similar to that of another Roosevelt—his much-admired cousin, Theodore; the steps would be New York legislator, Assistant Secretary of the Navy, governor of New York, and, if luck shone on him, President of the United States. By 1910 he had reached the first office, and at age thirty-one he accepted Teddie's old job as Assistant Secretary of the Navy, in which capacity he served for seven years. After an unsuccessful race as the Democratic vice-presidential candidate in 1920 and a tragic bout with polio that he contracted in 1921, he eventually followed his political schedule, becoming governor of New York in 1929 and President in 1933.

Roosevelt's political life was one of action, but he had no consistent political philosophy beyond that of the patrician's sense of social responsibility for the

* It would be tempting to use Richard Nixon rather than Wilson to exemplify the active-negative President; however, we do not yet have the excellent scholarly studies or the perspective of history on Nixon that we do on Wilson. It also seemed better to use Taft rather than Warren Harding to illustrate the passive-positive President because the latter's extremely poor performance in office (he is generally rated as our worst President) might create the impression that all passive-positive Presidents are doomed to such abject failure.

disadvantaged, which he had acquired at Groton. He was pragmatic, willing to experiment, and, if a particular course of action were not productive, to try another. His view of public office also paralleled that of his cousin Teddie: it is preeminently a place of moral leadership.

Roosevelt left a legacy of action and innovation unmatched by any other Chief Executive. When he came into office in March 1933, business failures were legion, twelve million of his countrymen were unemployed, banks all over the country were closed or doing business under restrictions, and the American people had lost confidence in their leaders as well as in themselves. Counseling the nation in his inaugural address that "we have nothing to fear but fear itself," the new Chief Executive moved into action: a four-day bank holiday was declared, and an emergency banking bill was prepared within a day's time. During his first one hundred days in office, the nation was to witness a social and economic revolution in the form of Roosevelt's "New Deal" as Congress adopted a series of far-reaching governmental programs insuring bank deposits, providing crop payments for farmers, establishing codes of fair competition for industry, granting labor the right to organize, providing relief and jobs for the unemployed, and creating the Tennessee Valley Authority (a government corporation) to develop that region. With these measures and other programs that followed (Social Security, public housing, unemployment compensation, and the like), Roosevelt was to establish the concept of the "positive state" in America—a government that had the obligation to take the leadership in providing for the welfare of all the people.

Roosevelt did not ignore relations with other countries. Soon after he took office he recognized the Soviet Union diplomatically, embarked on a "Good Neighbor policy" toward South Americans, and pushed through a Reciprocal Trade Program lowering tariffs with other nations. In his second term FDR began the slow and difficult task of preparing the nation for its eventual entry into World War II by funneling aid to the Allies, trading fifty "over-age" destroyers to Britain for defense bases in this hemisphere, and obtaining the passage of the nation's first peace-time draft. As FDR himself put it, after Pearl Harbor "Old Dr. New Deal" became "Dr. Win-the-War," taking over the economic control of the war effort granted him by Congress and establishing the victorious strategy of concentrating on defeating Germany first (rather than Japan). And while the hostilities were still going on, he took the leadership in setting up the United Nations. (Unfortunately, he died before he could see the organization established in 1945.)

Roosevelt was also an innovator whose actions left a major impact on the presidential office itself. Not only was he an effective legislative leader, but he was also responsible for a major reorganization of the executive branch, including the creation of the Executive Office of the President, which we will examine in chapter 14. Most important of all, FDR was the most effective molder of public opinion that the nation has ever known. It was he who pioneered in the use of "fireside chats" over radio to explain his actions to the people. In addition, he raised the presidential press conference to new heights as a tool of public persuasion. As a man who could take idealistic goals, reduce them to manageable and practical programs, and then sell them to the Congress and the American people, Roosevelt had no peer.

Despite this record of achievement, however, Roosevelt made some mistakes, particularly after his smashing electoral victory in 1936. As we saw in chapter

8, he was unsuccessful in purging certain Southern congressmen in the Democratic primaries in 1938. When he tried to expand the size of the Supreme Court in order to add persons who shared his views, the public and Congress reacted against his "court-packing" plan. Thus active-positive Presidents in their zeal to accomplish results, sometimes underestimate the force of custom and expectations as to what is proper and improper in the realm of American politics.

Active-Negative. Thomas Woodrow Wilson epitomizes Barber's active-negative type of President. Born in Atlanta, Georgia the son of a Presbyterian minister with a large congregation, Tommy had the benefit of a rich intellectual background. However, he was slow to learn: he was nine years old before he learned his alphabet and eleven before he could read. He was also frail and wore glasses in marked contrast to his father, a tall handsome man with a commanding physical presence. Tommy was loved; but he was also dominated by a father who expected much of him and ridiculed him when he did not live up to the expectations. Surrounded early in life by girls and intimidated by the rough play of boys, Tommy retreated to the protection provided by his mother, a quiet, gentle woman.

At sixteen, young Wilson went off to Davidson College, a small Presbyterian school in North Carolina. He experienced homesickness, his health failed, and he came home where he stayed for over a year until he entered Princeton at eighteen. There his shyness initially prevented his acquiring many friends, but by his sophomore year he found a niche for himself: he organized the Liberal Debating Club, wrote its constitution, and became its most prominent member. Eventually, like Roosevelt, he went on to become the editor of his school paper, the *Princetonian*. He also wrote an outstanding paper on cabinet government in the United States, which was published by the *International Review,* then edited by his enemy-to-be, Henry Cabot Lodge.

Later Wilson graduated from the University of Virginia Law School, but after practicing for only one year in his hometown of Atlanta, he returned to school to attend John Hopkins University, from which he received a doctorate in political science. Continuing his scholarly career, he returned to teach at Princeton, where he became one of the outstanding lecturers on the campus. Eventually, he became president of his alma mater.

Wilson made an auspicious start as president of Princeton by taking the leadership in developing a new curriculum, reorganizing academic departments, and modifying its tutorial system. However he met his first defeat when he tried to abolish the traditional undergraduate eating clubs and replace them with residential quadrangles. Subsequently he got into a bitter struggle with Andrew West, the dean of the graduate school, over the development of a graduate center; when Wilson refused to compromise on that issue, he lost it as well. At this point he decided to abandon academic life for a public one by running for, and winning, the governorship of New Jersey in 1908, from which post he went to the presidency four years later.

Unlike Roosevelt, Wilson suffered from insecurity, which biographers Alexander and Juliette George attribute primarily to the overwhelming domination of his father, whom he could not please but would not oppose. The result was a displacement of his hostility on male figures like West and Lodge, who became his mortal enemies. Character traits associated with Wilson's sense of personal inadequacy included an unwillingness to compromise and a compulsion to work, coupled with a lack of satisfaction with his considerable achievements.

Wilson's values and world view reflected his Calvinistic background. He believed that God ordained him to be President of the United States and that his own causes were those of the Almighty. His political philosophy was a kind of Jeffersonian faith in smallness (the government should regulate large corporations) and the innate wisdom of the common people. As we have seen, Wilson's concept of the presidency was one of unlimited potential (the President has "the right in law and conscience to be as big a man as he can"), coupled with a desire to convert it into a kind of prime ministership similar to that of the British, whose political and social institutions he so much admired.

Wilson used various techniques in implementing his prime-minister concept of the presidency. A skilled public speaker, he was the first President since John Adams to go before the Congress in person to give his State-of-the-Union message. He held frequent meetings with legislative leaders both at the White House and at a previously seldom-used President's Room in the Capitol. Like Jefferson, he was a powerful party chief who worked through congressional leaders and the Democratic Caucus to influence legislative decisions. He also did not hesitate to take his case to the people: on one occasion when special-interest spokesmen made concerted efforts to defeat a low-tariff bill he favored, Wilson made a public statement decrying the fact that "the people at large should have no lobby and be voiceless in these matters, while great bodies of astute men seek to create an artificial opinion and to overcome the interests of the public for their private profit."

These techniques were highly successful as Wilson took the leadership in both domestic and foreign affairs. In his first term in office he pushed through a vast program of economic reform, which included major measures lowering tariffs, raising taxes for the well-to-do, creating a central banking system, regulating unfair trade practices, providing cheap loans to farmers, and establishing an eight-hour day for railroad employees. When the United States became involved in World War I during his second term, rather than prosecute it through unilateral executive action as Lincoln did, Wilson went to the Congress and obtained authority to control the economic, as well as the military, aspect of the war. He was thus granted the power to allocate food and fuel, to license trade with the enemy, to censor the mail, to regulate the foreign language press of the country, and to operate railroads, water transportation systems, and telegraph and telephone facilities. At the end of the war, he made a triumphant trip to Europe, where he assumed the leading role in the writing of the Versailles peace treaty.

Eventually, however, Wilson's sense of moral righteousness and his unwillingness to compromise proved to be his downfall. Conceiving the League of Nations as his contribution to a practical implementation of the teachings of Jesus Christ, he adamantly refused to accept any reservations proposed by the Senate for the League of Nations Covenant of the Versailles treaty. In the process he played into the hands of his archenemy, Henry Cabot Lodge, who calculated that Wilson's intransigence and personal hatred of him would be so intense that the President would reject all compromises. In the end Lodge proved to be right: spurning the advice of close friends like Colonel House as well as his wife's pleas, Wilson claimed it "better a thousand times to go down fighting than to dip your colors to dishonorable compromise." A trip to win popular support for the League ended in failure, and as a result the country whose leaders proposed the League of Nations ended up not belonging to the organization at all.

Passive-positive. An example of the passive-positive President is William Howard Taft. Like Roosevelt and Wilson, he had a doting mother who showered him with love. His father, seventeen years older than his mother, was a lawyer who was given to preachments on discipline but not inclined to follow his own advice as far as Willie was concerned. Taft's boyhood was a pleasant one; unlike Wilson, he liked physical combat and was not a stranger to an occasional fight. But most of all he was a friendly lad with a perennial smile and sunny disposition.

Taft's romance with life continued when he left home to attend Yale University. There he was taken into the exclusive Skull and Bones Club and was considered to be the most popular boy in the entire school. While his extensive social life seemed to his father to be inconsistent with high scholarship, Taft graduated second in a class of 132. Following that, he attended the University of Cincinnati Law School.

Back home in Southern Ohio, Taft served a short stint as a reporter covering the courts and then began a career in law and politics that eventually resulted in his being appointed a state—and later, a federal—judge. He enjoyed the role of referee rather than of advocate in legal proceedings and set a goal for himself of appointment to the United States Supreme Court. But his ambitious wife, Nellie, whom he dearly loved, steered his career away from the judiciary towards the active political arena.

In 1900 Taft complied with President McKinley's request to head a comission to govern the Philippines. Ultimately McKinley's successor, Theodore Roosevelt, called him home to be his Secretary of War, where he served as a diplomatic trouble-shooter and domestic peacemaker for the President. Taft fell under the President's spell and at his urging allowed himself to be nominated for the presidency in 1908, when Roosevelt retired from the office.

Taft had an engaging personality and found it difficult to say no to anyone, including his ambitious wife and a wide host of friends. Most of all in life he wanted approval and to be loved. While he flirted with the Progressive ideas of his hero, Roosevelt, at heart Taft was a conservative with a great admiration for existing institutions and a fear of radicals and militants. He needed order and reason in his life and found them in the law. In contrast to his predecessor, who argued that he could take any action not expressly forbidden by the Constitution or the laws, Taft held that the President possessed only those powers specifically delegated to him from those two sources.

When Roosevelt left for a trip to Africa in 1909, all was well between him and the new President. However, Taft soon began to disappoint his mentor. After making tariff reductions his first objective, he finally signed a bill giving generous concessions to domestic producers. He also was unable to arbitrate a fight between Gifford Pinchot, the conservation-minded chief of the Forest Service, and his boss, Richard Ballinger, Secretary of the Interior, whom Pinchot accused of giving away public lands to private profiteers. Respecting the authority of the superior officer, Taft ultimately accepted Pinchot's resignation.

These and other incidents led the Progressive wing of the Republican party and Roosevelt to conclude that Taft was not the man to whom they could entrust their leadership. He, in turn, was horrified when Roosevelt proposed that the voters had the right to overturn judicial decisions. Ultimately Roosevelt opposed Taft for the Republican nomination in 1912 and, when he failed, ran on the Progressive ticket. The resulting split in the Republican party helped put Woodrow Wilson into the White House.

After he left the presidency Taft was appointed to the post he had wanted all along: the Chief Justice of the United States. He worked harder and longer in that position than he ever did as President. In the structured judicial environment removed from the pressures of the political arena, Taft found peace with his first love, the law.

Passive-negative. Dwight Eisenhower typifies the passive-negative President. Unlike Roosevelt, Wilson, or Taft, Ike was not born of a rich or prominent family; his father was a mechanic in a creamery who moved his family from Texas to Abilene, Kansas when Ike was six. Their home was only 800 square feet, into which the family of eight was jammed. Ike enjoyed physical activities, particularly sports, and seems to have been influenced primarily by his mother, a woman with a fundamentalist religious background who managed with some success to calm Ike's considerable temper.

Naturally the family's meager resources would not permit Ike to go off to an Ivy League college like Harvard, Princeton, or Yale. He managed to get into West Point (after being turned down at Annapolis because he was too old) with the primary aim of continuing the athletic career he had begun in high school. Unfortunately he injured his knee badly in a football game and was forced to give up not only that sport but baseball, track, and boxing as well. Following that incident he fell into despondency and his grades suffered. He graduated from the Point sixty-first in a class of 164, hardly a promising prospect for playing a leading role in the nation's military establishment.

Subsequently Ike redeemed himself in the Army, graduating first in a class of 275 from the Command and General Staff school, served on General Douglas MacArthur's staff in the Philippines, and shortly after the attack on Pearl Harbor was assigned to the War Plans Division with the job of preparing a blueprint for the cross-channel invasion of Europe. In that capacity he came to the attention of Army Chief of Staff George Marshall, and at Marshall's suggestion he was placed by President Roosevelt in command of the invasion of Africa and eventually of the victorious Allied forces in Europe.

As the nation's number-one war hero, Ike was subjected to pressures to run for President in 1948 by many persons, including some Democrats who were disillusioned with Harry Truman. He declared that he had no interest in a political career and instead became Army Chief of Staff and then president of Columbia University, a position for which he was ill suited. Subsequently, and against his wishes, he accepted President Truman's request in 1950 to become Supreme Commander of the North Atlantic Treaty Organization. Persuaded by Republican politicians to run for President in 1952, he won easily over the Democratic candidate, Adlai Stevenson.

Eisenhower's major personal assets were an extremely pleasant personality that radiated optimism, unusual organizational abilities, and a happy facility for getting people with differing viewpoints to work together. He had little ambition and accepted positions not for his own personal aggrandizement but out of a deep sense of duty to his country. His primary values were a belief in individualism and voluntary action and a marked dislike for the coercion of big government. His conception of himself as President was that of a nonpartisan leader bringing unity to the nation.

Eisenhower's performance in office reflected his background and values. He refused to play the role of party leader, assigning that task to his Vice-President, Richard Nixon. He sought both to make Congress a coequal branch of government rather than the inferior institution that he felt it had become under Roosevelt and Truman, and to return powers to the states that the national government had assumed. As an administrator of the executive branch, Eisenhower implemented methods that he had learned in the military: an extensive delegation of authority to others and a rigid chain of command.

In keeping with his conservative political philosophy and passive conception of the presidency, Eisenhower did not attempt new ventures in public policy. On the other hand, he made no effort to turn back the clock by eliminating the major features of Democratic rule of the previous twenty years. He rather moved cautiously within the established framework, proposing an increase of social security benefits, eliminating segregation in the nation's capital, and adding to the country's military commitments around the world.

These then are examples of the different types of President who have served in the nation's highest office in this century. As Barber suggests, there is a connection between the climate of public expectations and the kind of person that is chosen as President. In times of crisis, the American people turn to an activist like Roosevelt or Wilson to do something about their mounting problems; when the public tires of effort and sacrifice, it prefers a passive type such as Taft or Eisenhower to restore a sense of national unity and calm. There is also a cyclical pattern to presidential types: activists inherit problems that passive executives ignore; the latter slow down the excesses of the former.

Thus a variety of influences have contributed to the development of the American presidency: the press of foreign and domestic events, the inability and unwillingness of Congress to assume leadership, and the actions of strong Chief Executives that established precedents for their successors to draw on. Increasingly, however, the public has come to expect all Chief Executives to exhibit the initiatives of Presidents of "action." In the process, the office has become more and more complex and demanding. The kinds of varied responsibilities that contemporary Presidents face, as well as the methods they utilize to discharge those responsibilities, are examined in the following chapter.

SELECTED READINGS

Two recent studies of impeachment are Michael Benedict, *The Impeachment and Trial of Andrew Johnson* (New York: W.W. Norton, 1973), and Raoul Berger, *Impeachment: The Constitutional Problems* (Cambridge: Harvard University Press, 1973). A short book written by a Yale law professor to help laypersons understand the impeachment process is Charles Black Jr., *Impeachment: A Handbook* (New Haven: Yale University Press, 1974). A helpful compendium of materials on the subject are contained in *Impeachment and the U.S. Congress* (Washington, D.C.: Congressional Quarterly Inc., 1974).

There are several excellent general treatments of the presidency. Two of the best recent ones are Joseph Kallenbach, *The American Chief Executive: The Presidency and the Governorship* (New York: Harper & Row, 1966), and Louis Koenig, *The Chief Executive* (New York: Harcourt, Brace, rev. ed., 1975). Earlier studies included Edward Corwin's legalistic treatment of the office, *The President: Office and Powers, 1787–1948* (New York: New York University Press, rev. ed., 1948), and two highly readable analyses: Sidney Hyman, *The American President* (New York: Harper & Row, 1954), and Clinton Rossiter, *The American Presidency* (New York: Harcourt, Brace, 1960).

Two studies treating of the problem of presidential disability are Ruth Silva, "Presidential Succession and Disability," in *Law and Contemporary Problems* (Autumn 1956): 646–63, and Richard Hansen, *The Year We Had No President* (Lincoln: University of Nebraska Press, 1962).

The best analysis of the establishment of the presidential office is contained in chapter 1 of Kallenbach's book.

Analyses of the reasons for the growth of the presidency, along with the contributions of individual Presidents, include chapter 1 of Corwin, and chapters 3 and 5 of Rossiter. Two very good studies of the psychological aspects of presidential performance are Erwin Hargrove, *Presidential Leadership: Personality and Political Style* (New York: Macmillan, 1966), and James Barber, *The Presidential Character: Predicting Performance in the White House* (Englewood Cliffs, N.J.: Prentice-Hall, 1972). An excellent psychological treatment of an individual President is Alexander and Juliette George, *Woodrow Wilson and Colonel House* (New York: John Day, 1956).

Political Novels   Several political novels deal with termination of presidential tenure. The impeachment process as a weapon of unscrupulous partisans is the focus of Irving Wallace's story of the first black President, *The Man* (New York: Fawcett, 1964), and of Drew Pearson's *The President* (Garden City, N.Y.: Doubleday, 1970). Written some time before Watergate, these novels preview many of the arguments against impeachment later used by the White House during the impeachment hearings of 1974.

The traumatic effect of sudden presidential death and the danger of succession by an unprepared Vice-President are drawn clearly by Robert J. Serling in *The President's Plane is Missing* (New York: Dell, 1967).

Fletcher Knebel, *Night of Camp David* (New York: Bantam, 1965), deals with presidential disability (here, insanity) and highlights the inadequacy of present procedures. Randall Garrett conceives of an unusual use of disability and thereby teaches a lesson about placing the national interest before personal ambition in his science-fiction story "Hail to the Chief," in J. Olander, M. Greenberg, and P. Warrick (eds.), *American Government through Science Fiction* (Chicago: Rand McNally, 1974).

Traditionally the vice-presidency has been a much-neglected office, but the controversial tenure and later resignation of Spiro Agnew cast new interest on it. Agnew has written a novel about the vice-presidency that provides an insider's glimpse of the pressures, temptations, and people around the V.-P.: *The Canfield Decision* (New York: Berkley: 1977).

The scandals of Grant's second administration, and the way in which the Republicans virtually stole the election for Rutherford B. Hayes from Democrat Samuel Tilden, is described by Gore Vidal in *1876* (New York: Bantam, 1977). For those unaware of the very real dangers of abuse in the electoral college system, Vidal's novel is a disturbing introduction.

Chapter 13

In a very real sense the American President stands at the center of the American political system. As the prime elected official, he is the head of his political party. At the same time he is expected to be the President of all people, including those who voted against him. As such, he acts as the ceremonial head of the government; in addition, as a leader of a democratic nation, he both reflects and molds public opinion. Moreover, he must not only head the executive branch but also provide legislative leadership. Finally, he plays a dominant part in policy making in both domestic and foreign affairs. In this chapter we will examine various features of the contemporary presidency. We first analyze the Chief Executive's relationships with two major forces outside the government—his own political party and the general public. Next we focus on his connection with the Congress (the President's interrelationships with the members of the executive branch will be treated in ch. 14; his association with the courts, in ch. 16). Finally, we analyze the role that the Chief Executive plays in foreign and military policy.

THE PRESIDENT AND HIS PARTY

Of the various activities of the President, that of party leader would have been least appreciated by the Founding Fathers, who visualized him as a neutral figure standing above conflict and promoting unity and justice in society. Yet it is expected today that the Chief Executive will be the avowed chief of the party that put him in the White House. It was, indeed, while President Kennedy was conducting party business—trying to restore some semblance of unity to the Texas Democratic organization—that he was struck by an assassin's bullet.

The President's role as partisan leader involves him in all the major political activities of his party. He is expected to play some part in the election contests for various offices in our political system. As party chief, he also has the responsiblity for identifying problems and for formulating programs to deal with them. Finally, the President has a major role in organizing and managing the government as a means of implementing his programs.

The President and Electoral Activities

Naturally the President's part in electoral activities is most pronounced as far as his own office is concerned. If a President decides to seek reelection, the renomination is normally his for the asking; he dominates every aspect of the convention—location, choice of major officers, party platform, and selection of his running mate—and makes strategic decisions regarding the general election campaign. The Chief Executive may choose, for example, to have little to do with congressional candidates of his own party running in a presidential year, a strategy that Nixon followed in 1972 in his quest for traditionally Democratic voters.

American Presidents have also come to play an important part in midterm congressional elections. Even Dwight Eisenhower, who did not enjoy playing the role of partisan leader, gave some forty speeches in the 1954 campaign. President Kennedy took an active part in the 1962 congressional elections until the Cuban missle crisis forced him to cancel speaking engagements and return to Washington. And although Lyndon Johnson did not go on the campaign trail in 1966 (in part because the Vietnam war had made him so unpopular that many congressional candidates preferred that he stay away), the pattern of presidential involvement was restored (in fact, expanded) by Richard Nixon in 1970 when he traveled to more than twenty states on behalf of Republican candidates. His successor, Gerald Ford, visited a similar number of states in 1974 to try to help congressmen and governors running on the Republican ticket.

A popular President who decides to campaign in the midterm elections has the difficult decision of determining which candidates he will work for. Should he concentrate on crucial competitive contests, or should he also assist close political friends who seem to be in no appreciable danger of being defeated but who seek his assistance anyway? Should he campaign in favor of important party figures even though they voted against him on a number of major legislative measures? If the President does not, and an ignored man wins anyway, the latter may retaliate with even less support in the future; moreover, if his party's candidate loses, the opposition replacement may be even more opposed to the President's programs.

Because of such unattractive possiblities, a President may be tempted to try to pick his party's nominees for Senate and House seats. As we saw in chapter 8, however, this course of action violates the political custom of local determination. If there is local opposition, the President who gambles on intervention, only to have his protégé lose in a primary fight, risks a decline in political prestige and also the enmity of the winning candidate. For these reasons Presidents typically avoid overt involvement in spirited nomination contests.

If the battle lines in a congressional nomination have not been drawn, however, a President can influence the selection of congressional candidates by taking early action in support of certain persons. President Kennedy, for example, encouraged certain people, such as Joseph Tydings Jr. of Maryland, to seek a seat in Congress, and President Nixon persuaded some ten Republican members of the House to give up their seats to run for the Senate, where they would be more important politically to him. Thus Chief Executives attempt to build a base of support in Congress by personally recruiting men who share their general views on public affairs. Presidents also work discreetly behind the scenes

through sympathetic state political leaders to interest certain people in running. They may also use their influence to funnel needed funds to candidates whom they favor.

A President's ability to affect the persons who are selected for Congress is limited, however. The large number of elections for the House of Representatives (435 every two years) precludes any significant presidential involvement in them. Even Presidents as popular as Dwight Eisenhower find it difficult to transfer popularity to others, especially in a nonpresidential election. In addition, an incumbent congressman is in a very strong electoral position: as long as he keeps his political fences mended with state and local party leaders and with his constituents, he has little to fear from presidential opposition. The difficulties that a President faces in midterm elections is reflected in Mr. Nixon's experience in 1970: of the twenty-one Republican senatorial candidates for whom he campaigned in the general election, only eight won. Gerald Ford's record was even more discouraging in 1974: of the thirty-three candidates he tried to help in Senate, House, and gubernatorial races, there were five senate winners, two governors, and no winners in the House of Representatives.

Yet it would be a mistake to write off the President's role in congressional campaigns as meaningless. In competitive states (as well as some congressional districts) a visit by the Chief Executive, a special endorsement, or a channeling of funds to his party's candidate may provide the margin of victory. Moreover, as we have seen in chapter 9, the President can now help raise money for congressional candidates in presidential election years since he receives public funds for his own general campaign. Furthermore, there is some evidence that national issues (as compared to state and local ones) are becoming more important, even in midterm elections, and that the fate of both Senate and House aspirants in many areas may turn on voters' regard for the current administration. Thus even if the President does not become directly involved in a congressional race, his conduct in office may indirectly affect its outcome.

Despite the potentialities of the President's role as party leader, however, there are considerations that deter him from playing it on all occasions. Voting in the American Congress, as we found in chapter 11, does not follow strictly partisan lines. President Eisenhower was dependent on votes from Democratic congressmen for many of his programs, particularly in foreign policy. Presidents Kennedy and Johnson also received crucial Republican support on civil rights legislation as a result of the efforts of the Republican Floor Leader in the Senate, Everett Dirksen. The Minority Leader also defended Johnson's Vietnam policies more vigorously than did many Democrats. In such circumstances, it was hardly surprising that neither Democratic President expended any genuine effort to get Dirksen defeated in Illinois. Richard Nixon treated some of his Democratic supporters the same way: his Attorney-General, Richard Kleindienst, told Mississippians in the 1972 campaign that if he lived there, he would vote for Senator James Eastland.

Other factors also prompt some Presidents to play down their activities in midterm elections. If their party's candidates do not do well, the election may be interpreted as a repudiation of their administration. Campaign rhetoric can also be taken personally by members of the opposition party, making it more difficult for the President to get their furture support for his legislative program. The Chief Executive may also be concerned that too much time spent on the campaign trail will create the impression in people's minds that he is not exerting enough effort on the more important duties of his office; it may also detract from his image as the leader of all the American people.

Presidents resort to certain tactics to overcome these disadvantages. One is to schedule foreign visits (which emphasize the Chief Executive's nonpartisan role as the entire nation's representative) to coincide with congressional elections: Richard Nixon visited the Middle East and Mediterranean areas in early October 1970. Another is to make use of the Vice-President: Spiro Agnew campaigned longer and in more states that year than Nixon did, and it was he, rather than the President, who attacked the opposition candidates in personal terms.* This practice permitted Nixon to take the "high road" in the campaign by stressing issues rather than personalities.

Developing Party Programs

One area of partisan activity that the President clearly dominates is the preparation of party programs for dealing with major national problems. An incumbent President has the biggest hand in the writing of the party platform at the national convention. He also has the opportunity to identify party issues and programs during the course of the campaign. He may choose to emphasize certain parts of the platform, ignore others, or even take stands at variance with those contained in the document.

Traditionally, students of American politics have concluded that party platforms and presidential campaign speeches are not to be taken seriously. (The former are for candidates to "run" on, not to "stand" on; the latter are merely rhetoric and do not involve commitments on the candidate's part.) However, recent studies by two political scientists have called into question these somewhat cynical views. Gerald Pomper's analyses of the party platforms of the Republican and Democratic parties over the period from 1944 to 1964 revealed that pledges made in such platforms were taken seriously by Presidents who worked with the Congress, as well as by means of their own executive orders, to get most of them enacted into law. Similarly, Fred Grogan found that both Lyndon Johnson and Richard Nixon acted on more than half of the promises they made in campaign speeches in 1964 and 1968 respectively. The former, whose party controlled the Congress, acted more fully on campaign promises requiring legislative action; the latter, facing an opposition-dominated Congress, was more inclined to carry out those pledges that required executive action alone.

Partisan Influences in Organizing and Managing the Government

The extent to which presidential programs actually get implemented depends to a considerable degree on the President's influence over the party within the government. This group is composed of officials in the legislative and executive branches who are either elected under a partisan label or appointed primarily

---

* Nixon also let the Vice-President handle the sticky job of criticizing Republican Senator Charles Goodell of New York, who voted against the President on a number of key issues such as Vietnam. Agnew even helped raise money for the victorious Conservative party candidate, James Buckley.

because of their party activities or because it is expected that they will implement party views on public-policy matters.

The President's control over his party in the legislature is distinctly limited. He has little to do with its composition, since most senators and congressmen are elected independently of him. Moreover, he has comparatively little influence over the organization of his party in Congress. Although some Presidents have played a major role in determining their party's legislative leadership (Thomas Jefferson did, for example), for the most part American Chief Executives have been chary of interfering with the right of Congress to choose its own men. Dwight Eisenhower was forced to work with Senate Republican Leader William Knowland whose views on foreign policy were quite different from his own. During part of John F. Kennedy's administration the Democratic Speaker of the House was John McCormack, a political enemy from Kennedy's home state.

The President has more influence over the party in the executive branch, a matter that we will examine in detail in the next chapter. The only other elected official, the Vice-President, is his man, to be used or not as he sees fit. In addition, the President can make appointments to policy-making posts that both reward individuals for their service to the party and permit him to influence the administration of government programs. In particular, his closest political advisers on the White House staff constitute what is, in effect, the President's personal party: persons who have labored in his presidential campaign continue to protect his interests and promote his policies after they assume top governmental posts in his administration.

THE PRESIDENT AS HEAD OF STATE AND LEADER OF PUBLIC OPINION

As we saw in chapter 5, private citizens have general attitudes about the nation, its form of government, and major public officials, as well as particular views of specific political matters, such as social problems and policies for dealing with them.

To a considerable extent, the American President is the major focus of each of these kinds of public attitudes. Like the British monarch, our Chief Executive is the symbol, the personification, of the nation and the state. It is the President who inspires feelings of loyalty and patriotism, particularly in times of crises, when he becomes the rallying point for national efforts. Thus both political friends and foes of Franklin Roosevelt turned to him for leadership when the Japanese attacked Pearl Harbor in December 1941.

Even though this is a democratic nation, the presidency is surrounded with the trappings of ceremony and pomp. The inauguration of a President bears certain resemblances to the coronation of a king, complete with the taking of an oath in the midst of notables and the multitudes. Ceremonial aspects of the office have generally included the display of the presidential seal and the playing of "Hail to the Chief" when the President arrives at an event, along with a round of traditional duties: visiting other nations and entertaining foreign heads of state when they visit Washington, D.C., lighting the giant Christmas tree on the White House lawn, throwing out the first ball at the opening of the baseball season, proclaiming a variety of "weeks" devoted to a host of good causes, and the like. All such activities emphasize the role that the Chief Executive plays in embodying the nation, its government, and its ideals.

Unlike the British monarch, however, the American President not only "reigns" but also "rules." As the nation's leading political figure, he is expected to develop and put into effect controversial policies that are binding on the entire populace. In doing so, he must lead public opinion on vital public issues; at the same he must respect the broad limits that public attitudes (particularly those of interest groups) place on his actions.

The size and composition of the President's "public" varies with circumstances. He may have almost the entire nation as an audience for his inauguration or a major speech in time of crisis. But his target may be much smaller, as for an address on a current issue to the annual meeting of a major interest group such as the NAM or the AFL-CIO. The President must even take into account the attitudes of foreign publics on certain matters: one of the considerations that led President Kennedy to stop the shipment of Russian missles into Cuba by blockade rather than by invasion was his assessment of foreign reactions, particularly in Latin America.

As the most visible political figure in the nation, the President is constantly in the public spotlight. Almost everything about him—including his golf or tennis game, favorite foods and songs, health, and reading habits—becomes a matter of intense interest. In fact, public attention focuses on his entire family. Yet a President cannot depend on public curiosity alone (much of which is trivial) for success in wielding political power. He must establish close ties with a variety of publics in order to convert personal popularity into political effectiveness. Such ties enable him to help mold public opinion while informing himself about the attitudes of citizens.

Personal Trips

One of the earliest means developed for communicating with the American public was the "Grand Tour," first used by George Washington in a two-month trip through the South in 1791. Enduring both the rigors of travel and a

President Carter meets with foreign leaders.

surfeit of wining and dining by citizens eager to please the new Chief Executive, Washington found value in the trip. According to his own account of the venture, it both reassured him that the new Federalist government was popular in the South as well as in New England and enabled him to learn with more accuracy than he could have gained by any other means the "disposition" of the people.

Modern Presidents have continued the Washington tradition: Johnson and Nixon both spoke of the invigorating feeling they experienced in getting away from Washington, D.C. and establishing contacts with the people in other parts of the country. (Smarting from the political in-fighting in the nation's capital, Presidents find the adulation of crowds a good tonic; it also reassures them that the popularity they enjoyed on the campaign trail has not disappeared.) Many Presidents today find it helpful to extend their travels abroad as evidenced by Eisenhower's trip to eleven nations, Kennedy's tour of Europe with his wife, and Nixon's visits to China, the Soviet Union, and the Middle East. In his early months in office, Jimmy Carter went to Great Britain to meet with leaders of the major western industrial nations. Such ventures capture the attention of a variety of publics, including the people of the countries visited, ethnic groups at home (Irish-Americans, Italian-Americans, English-Americans, and the like) with ties to those nations, and the general American populace.

Not all presidential trips, however, turn out to be triumphant. The most notable failure was Woodrow Wilson's ill-starred attempt in 1919 to take his case for the Versailles peace treaty and the League of Nations to the American people when these proposals ran into political difficulties in the Senate. He collapsed near the end of the tour and was disabled for a long period. He was particularly discouraged because his efforts went completely for naught: the American people failed to respond to his pleas, and some historians have concluded that not a single senator's vote was changed by this difficult journey.

Presidents contemplating trips, for whatever purpose, face the possibility not only of failure but also, even when successful, of draining away valuable time from other facets of their demanding job. Because of these hazards Presidents in recent years have commissioned Vice-Presidents to make journeys for them both at home and abroad. Moreover, leading cabinet members are also frequently dispatched to explain administration policies to interested publics and to get their reactions to such policies.

White House Visits, Mail, and Public Opinion Polls

In most personal contacts between a President and other citizens, they come to him. Along with meeting public officials, a Chief Executive spends much of his day in the White House receiving individuals and group representatives in connection with a variety of matters. (Harry Truman, for example, averaged about 100 such visits a week.) The activities include holding sessions with interest group representatives pertaining to public policy concerns, welcoming delegations of young people who are visiting the capital, and honoring persons receiving the Congressional Medal of Honor as well as those singled out for achievement in letters, the arts, or sports. Such visits enable the President to creat a favorable impression upon his flattered guests, and they also provide him with clues to what is on the minds of a variety of Americans.

The public reacts! Telegrams and mailgrams relating to President Ford's pardon of President Nixon.

Another source of information is the letters, telegrams, and telephone calls that pour into the White House from the American people. The volume has varied with the incumbent: after Jimmy Carter initiated his program to encourage citizen involvement in government, the White House was flooded with 70,000 letters a week, three times the amount under Ford. Particular events, such as the "incursion" into Cambodia in 1970, swell the flood. Although the views expressed give the Chief Executive some idea of public reactions to vital issues (his staff compiles the number registering pro and con attitudes and analyzes the major reasons behind them), letter-writers, telegram-senders, and long-distance callers do not necessarily constitute a cross-section of the American people. Typically, they have intense feelings one way or the other on an issue, and they come disproportionately from the more educated and/or articulate segment of the citizenry.

A more reliable barometer of attitudes of the general population is provided by public opinion polls taken by private firms such as the Gallup, Harris, and Roper organizations. Since the days of Franklin Roosevelt, Presidents have had an avid interest in such polls because they provide various kinds of useful basic information. One is the attitude of the public toward specific issues of public policy, such as the pace of school integration or the percentage of people who are unemployed. Another is the degree of approval or disapproval of his handling of a particular situation, such as the war in Vietnam. Still another is the public estimate of his overall handling of his job, a question that is periodically put to the American people by the pollsters.

A close student of public opinion polls, John Mueller, analysed the polls taken on presidential performances from the beginning of the Truman administration in 1945 to the end of the Johnson administration in early 1969 and concluded that certain basic factors affect the popularity Chief Executives enjoy with the American public. One general pattern is for that popularity to decline over a period of time. Presidents typically start with a high standing in the polls, but as they undertake various actions, they antagonize more and more groups. Mueller labels this the "coalition of minorities" factor by which he means that different minorities react unfavorably to specific presidential decisions, as businessmen did when President Kenney forced them to roll back a steel price rise in 1962 and as Southerners did when Chief Executives enforced the Supreme Court decision on school desegregation. These different groups become unhappy with the President for different reasons, but the end result is a progressive decline in presidential popularity.*

In addition to this overall downward trend, Mueller determined that public opinion on the presidency reacted to certain kinds of events. A downturn in the economy, particularly as reflected in an increase in the rate of unemployment, harmed presidential popularity. International events cut both ways. At the time of a dramatic event involving national and presidential prestige, a "rally-round-the-flag" phenomenon results, with Americans supporting their Chief Executive. This occurs even if things turn out badly, as they did, for example, at the Bay of Pigs in 1961 when the United States effort to help ex-Cuban forces invade the island and overthrow Fidel Castro ended in a fiasco. On the other hand, wars like those in Korea and Vietnam ultimately harm the President's popularity.

The Press

Historically the most important medium linking the President to the American public has been the press. In the early years of the republic there was a partisan press similar to what prevails in many European countries today. The Federalists had their party organ, the *Gazette of the United States,* while the *National Gazette* spoke for their Republican opponents. The partisan press reached its apogee during the presidency of Andrew Jackson when federal officeholders were expected to subscribe to the administrative organ, which was financed in part from revenues derived from the printing of official government notices.

In the latter part of the nineteenth century, however, the partisan press began to disappear in the United States, largely because of two developments. One was the invention of the telegraph, which led to the formation of wire services that distributed news to all parts of the country; the information transmitted tended to be standardized and politically fairly neutral to avoid antagonizing the diverse readership of the various newspapers in the country. The other factor was the increased use of the press for advertising by business concerns; this innovation provided newspapers with a secure financial base and lessened their dependence on official notices and other types of party largesse.

The modern press in the United States is nonpartisan in the sense that newspapers are not overtly affiliated with particular parties. There is little question, however, that most of today's newspapers have distinct partisan preferences that they disguise thinly, if at all. The *Chicago Tribune* speaks distinctly for the more conservative elements of the Republican party, while the *St. Louis Post Dispatch* clearly represents the views of the liberal Democrats.

It is important, however, to distinguish between the owners and editors of newspapers on the one hand and the members of the working press—reporters

---

* One exception to this principle was Dwight Eisenhower, whose popularity continued to remain high during his stay in office. One possible explanation (among others) that Mueller suggests for this phenomenon is that Eisenhower didn't do much in domestic policy and so did not antagonize groups as much as other Presidents did.

and commentators—on the other. Most of the former, representing the interests of management and business in general (on whom they depend for advertising revenue) tend to defend the *status quo* and favor the Republican party. The latter, interested in the world of ideas, are more inclined to want change in American life and are more often attuned to the general philosophy of the Democratic party.

A President must take these realities into account in utilizing the press to further his influence over public opinion. Each has sought to establish useful relationships with reporters who can help or hinder his efforts. Theodore Roosevelt initiated the practices of providing working quarters in the White House for reporters and of granting personal interviews to some of them. Woodrow Wilson later established the regular press conference to which all Washington correspondents were invited.

Over the years the press conference has become a major tool used by Presidents both to influence public opinion and to gauge the public mind as revealed by the questions put to them by reporters from all parts of the country. Each President has used the institution in his own way. Some, like Harding, Coolidge, and Hoover, have required that questions be submitted in advance. (This practice began when Harding was unprepared for a question involving a treaty and gave an erroneous and damaging interpretation of it.) Others, like Franklin Roosevelt, have permitted spontaneous questioning. The frequency of press conferences has also varied widely among Presidents; FDR held as many in his first three months in office (28) as Richard Nixon did in his first four years. Moreover, in times of crisis Chief Executives have tended to hold few press conferences, in part because they have little time for them, in part because they wish to avoid divulging sensitive information.

The success of a press conference depends on the skills of the President. Harry Truman, who enjoyed the give-and-take of exchanges with the reporters, nonetheless performed poorly in formal encounters: he tended to answer questions quickly rather than thoughtfully, and he was unable to envision just how his words would look in print or how they might be interpreted. Dwight Eisenhower also came across badly. Not only did he have trouble expressing himself clearly and grammatically, but he also displayed meager knowledge about many vital issues of the day. In contrast, Franklin Roosevelt and John Kennedy were masters of the press conference. The former had a keen sense of what was newsworthy and even suggested reporters' headlines for them. He also prepared members of the press for actions he took on controversial problems by educating them initially with confidential background information; consequently reporters tended to support Roosevelt's ultimate decisions because they understood the reasons behind his actions. Kennedy, who served a brief stint as a newspaper man and enjoyed the company of reporters, used his press conferences to great advantage; his ability to field difficult questions impressed not only the members of the press involved, but also the American public who viewed the proceedings on live television.*

Presidential contacts with the working press have thus changed over time. Today it is expected that the Chief Executive will conduct some formal press

---

* While it is too soon to judge President Carter's overall performance in press conferences, his early ones were generally considered to be highly successful ventures in which he came across as calm, well prepared, frank, and articulate.

President Carter fielding
questions from the press.

conferences attended by hundreds of Washington reporters and watched simultaneously by millions on television. Not all Presidents feel at ease in that situation, however, President Johnson, who preferred to converse with small groups of reporters, also experimented with informal, hastily called conferences held in a variety of settings; at times, he led the assembled press on a brisk walk around the White House. Even Kennedy did not confine his meetings with reporters to formal press conferences; he also gave exclusive stories to special reporter friends of his, a practice that was naturally resented by many other members of the working press. Jimmy Carter granted his first press interview three days after he took office; he met with four reporters for the Associated Press and the United Press International.

Presidents also attempt to work through other elements of the press besides the Washington reporters and correspondents. President Kennedy invited newspaper editors and owners to White House conferences at which he discussed major public issues. President Nixon, wary of the Washington press corps, chose to experiment with a number of approaches for establishing contacts with sympathetic elements of the medium—for example, holding briefings before selected editors and executives of news organizations around the country with key officials like Henry Kissinger on hand to discuss foreign policy problems and decisions, and furnishing editorial writers around the nation with transcripts of his speeches and comments on issues.

Other Mass Media

Television and radio are, of course, available to a President who wants to address the American people directly without having his remarks filtered through reporters or editorial writers. While holding relatively few press conferences, Richard Nixon appeared more often on prime-time television broadcasts during his first eighteen months in office than did Presidents Eisenhower, Kennedy, and Johnson combined during comparable periods. Franklin Roosevelt made effective use of radio for his famous "fireside chats." His resonant voice and effective timing were the envy of professional broadcasters; his facility for discussing complicated social problems in understandable terms won the confidence of the American people in difficult times. He made the first of his chats at the end of his first week in office and continued to utilize them effectively during his twelve years in the White House. At the same time, he was careful not to overuse the technique because, as he put it, ". . . individual psychology cannot, because of human weakness, be attuned for long periods of time to a constant repetition of the highest note in the scale."

Television required new techniques and formats. Dwight Eisenhower hired movie and television star Robert Montgomery to coach him on methods of projecting a favorable image. On one occasion he appeared with cabinet members to convey the idea that his administration was a "team" in which individual specialists joined efforts in the common cause of "good government." Nixon announced the appointment of his cabinet on television as a means of dramatizing the event and introducing the appointees. And John Kennedy, searching for an equivalent of FDR's fireside chat, had major television commentators come to the White House for personal interviews in which he fielded spontaneous questions from the informal comfort of his favorite rocking chair. In his first address to the nation, Jimmy Carter used Roosevelt's format; seated in an easy chair before an open hearth and wearing a cardigan sweater, the new President sought to project an image of informality and also to underscore his concern with the nation's energy crisis.

Today's President can utilize a variety of media in his efforts to shape public opinion. How effectively he does so will depend on his own communication skills as well as his ability to gauge when and how far he should go in trying to alter public sentiments on controversial matters. To some extent there is a built-in conflict between the President and the media representatives. The former often wants to suppress information that he feels will endanger the nation's security, or at least put his administration in a bad light; the latter, in turn, are eager for news, however sensitive it may be, and have a vested interest in criticizing the President and his associates as a means of stimulating public interest and thereby creating a demand for their services. Almost every President has complained of unfair treatment by the media, while newsmen have often charged that the President and his team are "managing" the news to further their own political purposes. The situation became exacerbated during Richard Nixon's presidency: convinced that media representatives were personally prejudiced against him, the administration responded with presidential denunciations of television commentators, attacks by Vice-President Agnew against the liberal bias of the Eastern press, threats not to renew licenses of stations that carried "ideological payola" and failed to provide a "balanced" treatment of public affairs, and the wire-tapping of telephones of some newsmen considered to be hostile to the administration.

Recent Developments in Presidential Public Relations

While all Presidents have tried to win the support of the American people, none has approached the task more systematically and imaginatively than Jimmy Carter. Even before he took office, his political pollster, Patrick Caddell, prepared a fifty-one page memorandum suggesting public relations goals for the new President and means of accomplishing these goals. Emphasizing that "governing with public approval requires a continuing political campaign," Caddell suggested a number of actions be taken to demonstrate that Carter is an "open man," and "different from other politicians."

Fireside chat, Carter style.

Inaugural walk down Pennsylvania Avenue.

Some of Carter's early moves were designed to show that he was a "People's President" who had no use for the trappings of the "Imperial Presidency" that had characterized the office during the Nixon adminstration. At the swearing-in ceremony at the Capitol, the President wore a dark blue business suit rather than the traditional formal morning coat, then walked down Pennsylvania Avenue to the White House rather than riding at the head of the inaugural parade as his predecessors had done. In the days that followed, the new President continued to cut down on presidential pomp, abandoning the playing of "Hail to the Chief" by the Marine Corps band when he arrived at ceremonies, eliminating the use of chauffeured limousines by members of the White House staff, and reducing drastically the number of television sets in the White House. He also enrolled his nine-year-old daughter, Amy, in a public school rather than send her to a private school, as all Presidents since Theodore Roosevelt had done.

President Carter also initiated a number of new approaches to the American people. As we saw in chapter 1, he participated in a telephone call-in show and visited a New England community for a mock town-meeting, staying overnight with a family that had supported his presidential campaign. Later he visited Los Angeles, where he fielded questions from a public audience. He even had his energy adviser, James Schlesinger, send letters to 450,000 citizens, soliciting their views on ways to handle the energy problem. Thus President Carter sought to sensitize himself to the views of his fellow citizens and to convince ordinary Americans that he cared about them and their problems.

A President's relations with his party colleagues and with the American people create the potential for the public support required of the leader of a democratic nation. However, the decisions he makes either on his own or in conjunction with other public officials depend on the legal powers of the presidency and on his ability to convince other officeholders to act as he desires. (Political scientist Richard Neustadt suggests that the essence of presidential leadership is that of persuading others that what he wants them to do is not only in the President's interest but in theirs as well.) Among such officeholders are the members of the United States Congress.

THE PRESIDENT AND CONGRESS

Although the primary responsibility for making the laws is vested in the Congress, the Founding Fathers clearly intended the President to play a vital role in influencing legislation. To that end they granted him certain powers through which he might affect legislative decisions, among them giving messages and recommendations to Congress, calling it into special session, and vetoing bills. In some instances, the use of these powers is mandatory: as discussed in detail below, even President Eisenhower, who was not inclined to exercise strong leadership over the Congress, remarked that "the Constitution puts the President right square into the legislative business."

Beyond the legal powers vested in the President, however, certain practices that have developed over the years have increased his influence over the making of the laws. These practices were initiated by individual Presidents who wanted to exercise strong leadership over legislation. But over the years Con-

"MR. PRESIDENT, YOU JUST DON'T UNDERSTAND HOW CONGRESS WORKS!"

Distributed by Los Angeles Times SYNDICATE

gress and the American people have come to expect that all Presidents will follow them as part of the political, if not legal, duties of the office.

Messages and Recommendations

Article II, Section 3 of the Constitution is specific in its language that the President "shall from time to time give to the Congress information on the State of the Union and recommend to their Consideration such Measures as he shall judge necessary and expedient." Chief Executives since Washington have generally followed his practice of presenting an annual message to the Congress at the beginning of each regular session, but the method of delivery has changed over time. Washington and Adams gave their messages in person, but Jefferson (a notoriously poor public speaker) dispatched a written message, giving as his reasons that such a speech intruded on the privacy of the legislature and that the practice smacked too much to the royal prerogative from which it developed.* This practice continued until Woodrow Wilson surprised Congress and the nation by delivering a message in person shortly after he was inaugurated. Since Wilson's time all presidents (no matter how meager their speaking skills) have generally appeared before Congress to deliver the annual State-of-the-Union Message.

Although the assembled senators and congressmen are the immediate target of the speech, the President has other audiences in mind as well. In a sense, the message is addressed to all the American people, who today can watch the proceedings on television. In fact, the State of the Union Message is beamed to nations around the world via satellite and becomes a matter of interest to political friends and enemies alike. For through this general pronouncement the President indicates the problems that he feels are of concern to American society and suggests policies to mitigate them.

Typically the State-of-the-Union Message contains far more concerns and proposals than the President expects the Congress to deal with; twenty-five or thirty separate matters may be treated in the speech. (Covering a wide variety of topics is designed to appeal politicially to a broad range of interest groups.) Moreover, the President seldom attempts to distinguish among the problems on the basis of their relative importance. Finally, the policy proposals made in the message are usually couched in very vague terms. Thus the State-of-the-Union Message is somewhat like a party platform in its comprehensiveness and generality, yet it does represent some screening of policy proposals made in the platform.

Modern Presidents, however, do not restrict their recommendations to Congress to those contained in this message. Instead they adopt the practice, initiated by Woodrow Wilson, of following up this general pronouncement with a series of specially written messages focusing on specific problems and outlining in detail proposals for dealing with them. In 1973 Richard Nixon abandoned the idea of a single message altogether by giving an initial "overview" statement and then following it with five other messages devoted to natural re-

---

* The message followed the British tradition whereby the king delivered a "speech from the throne" to Parliament. This custom was carried to the New World in the form of pronouncements by colonial governors to the legislatures of the day.

President Ford delivers a
State-of-the-Union message.

sources and the environment, the economy, human resources, community development, and crime and law enforcement.

A final presidential step in spelling out precisely what should be done about a particular issue is the development of a specific bill. Even though Congress may (and usually does) make changes in the "administration" proposal, the bill enables the Chief Executive to affect ultimate legislative actions by forcing senators and congressmen to focus initially on what the President thinks should be done about a given problem.

Congress itself has come to realize that large assemblies cannot establish a legislative program that reflects an overall system of priorities. The program must come from an outside source—the President. (This is true even when different parties control the presidency and the Congress: rival legislative leaders made it clear to Presidents Truman, Eisenhower, Nixon and Ford that they expected them to propose specific programs, including administration bills.) When Congress passed the Budget and Accounting Act of 1921, requiring the Chief Executive to present a comprehensive plan of suggested expenditures by the various executive agencies (we will examine this matter in the following chapter), it indirectly placed in his hands of job of establishing priorities among governmental programs, since success depends on financing. In recommending expenditures, the President is forced to express his preferences among programs. Thus the annual Budget Message is a much better indication of which policies and programs in particular the President favors, and how much so, than is his annual State-of-the-Union Message. (Unlike the latter, the Budget Message forces him, as the saying has it, "to put his money where his mouth is.") As a result of the passage of the Full Employment Act of 1946, the President must also give an annual Economic Message to the nation in which he estimates, among other matters, how much money the government may expect to take in from existing revenue measures and how additional moneys might be raised should they be needed.

Today's Presidents are thus expected to develop both a comprehensive legislative program reflecting overall priorities and concrete proposals for dealing with specific problems. Following a practice first developed in the Truman administration, Presidents now have departments include, with their estimates of financial expenditures, information on legislative matters of interest to them. Such information contains actual drafts of bills and the names of other executive agencies interested in the matter. With this systematic inventory of proposals at his disposal, a President can better screen and coordinate the legislative concerns of the many agencies of the executive branch.

Calling Congress into Special Session

The President has the constitutional prerogative to convene the Congress—both houses or either one—on "extraordinary occasions." (For example, the President might want to bring only senators together for the purpose of confirming an executive appointment or approving a treaty.) Unlike many state governors, however, he has no power to restrict the agenda of the special session. He thus runs the risk not only that congressmen may ignore what he wants them to do but also that they may decide to take actions that he considers peripheral or even opposes.

The use of the power to call Congress into special session has varied. The practice became particularly prominent in the first third of this century, as Presidents (beginning with Taft) called special sessions shortly after they took office in March of the year in order to get the Congress busy immediately rather than waiting for the then-appointed time of December. The highly productive congressional session held during the first year of the Wilson administration (1913–14) and the famous "Hundred Days" under Franklin Roosevelt were both specially convened by the Chief Executives.

Since the passage of the Twentieth Amendment in 1933, the President's power to call the Congress into special session has become less important as a tool of legislative leadership. He is inaugurated on January 20, but the two houses assemble on January 3; therefore, there is no necessity for convening them as did Wilson and FDR when they first took office. Since Congress begins each annual session on January 3, it is ready to receive the President's various messages later in the month. Beyond this, Congress now meets almost year-round (exceptions are holiday recesses, breaks for national conventions, election-year campaigns, and the immediate postelection period in November and December), so there is relatively little time when the law makers are not available for hearing presidential legislative requests.*

Even so, the power to call Congress into special session is still potentially useful as an electoral tactic when one party controls the presidency and another the Congress. Harry Truman used it effectively in the summer of 1948 when he convened the Republican-controlled Congress after the party's national convention was held and a platform adopted; in so doing, he challenged the GOP legislature to enact the platform's policy proposals into law. He used its failure to do so to great effect in his fall campaign.

---

* The President's discretion *not* to convene Congress is also less important than it once was. Lincoln's tactic of acting on his own in the early months of the Civil War would not be available today.

Legislative leader: Franklin Delano Roosevelt signs a major piece of New Deal legislation, the Emergency Banking Act. Below are facsimiles of other important New Deal programs: Agricultural Adjustment Act, Reforestation Unemployment Act, and the Tennessee Valley Authority.

THE NEW DEAL LEGISLATION was enacted at great speed. As soon as the special session of Congress passed a bill, Roosevelt signed it. President and a harmonious Congress acted hand in hand. Here March 9, 1933—FDR puts his name to the Emergency Banking.

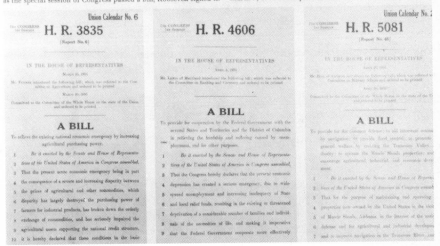

The Veto Power

More important than the authority to call Congress into special session is the President's veto power, which gives him three options with respect to a measure passed by Congress: (1) he may sign it, thereby making it a law; (2) he may veto the measure by withholding his signature, in which case it (together with an explanatory message) is returned to the chamber in which the measure originated; this nullifies the measure unless each house, by a two-thirds vote, repasses it over his veto; and (3) he may take no action, so that it becomes a law within ten days unless Congress is no longer in session; if that is the case, the measure is said to have been "pocket vetoed."

Conceived originally by the Founding Fathers as a defensive weapon for the President to protect himself against encroachments into his domain by a powerful legislature, the veto developed into a tool that he can use to shape public policy. Franklin Roosevelt vetoed over 600 measures—a record—partly because he was in office longer than any other President, partly because he had strong views on public policy and was willing to use the prerogative to demonstrate his political power; he was known to tell his aides, "Give me a bill I can veto," in order to let congressmen know that they had a President to deal with.

"They can't say I'm not doing anything"

Copyright 1975 by Herblock in The Washington Post.

The most important single factor affecting the use of the veto has been political conflict between the Congress and the Chief Executive. The control of the presidency and the Congress by opposite political parties tends to create the kind of conflict that gives rise to frequent vetoes, as evidenced by the number of times Harry Truman (250) and Dwight Eisenhower (181) exercised the prerogative.*

Actual use is not the only gauge of the veto power's value, for the mere *threat* to use it can be a valuable weapon for a President who wishes to shape pending legislation. By passing the word on which features of a particular bill he finds objectionable and what must be done in order to make it acceptable to him, the President can affect the content of any measure that is sent to him. This tactic does not always work, however. Congressmen may not be willing to scale down measures that they favor; moreover, if the Congress is controlled by the opposite political party, its leadership may accept the presidential challenge and force him to veto what they believe is a popular measure. The Democrats in Congress in 1970 sent President Nixon a bill for hospital construction that he vetoed for economy reasons. Not only did they successfully override his veto, but they also charged in the congressional campaign that year that his veto indicated his lack of concern for the health needs of the citizens.

The mere possession of these several legal powers does not, of course, ensure presidential success with the Congress. Political factors play a major part in determining how effective his use of his powers will be.

Conditions Limiting Presidential Influence with Congress

Every President faces certain basic conflicts with Congress that were built into the constitutional system by the Founding Fathers. Operating on Madison's advice that "ambition must be made to counteract ambition," they deliberately created rivalry between the executive and the legislature by assigning important constitutional powers to each, thus inviting them to compete for political leadership. By granting the rivals independent bases of political power, they ensured that each would be capable of protecting its interests.

Their expectations have proved to be very accurate. Since the days when some members of the first Congress began to withstand the attempts of Alexander Hamilton (and indirectly of Washington) to push an economic program, senators and House members have resisted presidential efforts to dominate their affairs as well as those of the nation.

Of course, the conflict between the presidency and the Congress is likely to be even more pronounced if the two are controlled by opposite political parties:

* While Congress can override a presidential veto, over the years only about one in twenty have met that fate. This tendency even prevailed during Nixon's difficult year of 1973, when Congress overrode only one of his nine vetoes. However, his successor, Gerald Ford, was overriden twelve times (he vetoed a total of sixty-one bills), which made him the most overridden President since Andrew Johnson.

added to the natural rivalry between the branches of government is the competition between parties for political leadership. Still, congressmen from a President's own political party frequently engage him in political battle. In fact, as the late British scholar Harold Laski suggested, some members, particularly those in the House of Representatives, have a vested interest in doing this as a means of gaining publicity. So long as the press plays up conflict because it is more newsworthy than cooperation, a congressman who opposes a President will find public attention focused on him. He can then appeal to his constituents by claiming that he is no rubber stamp for the President, that he is battling to protect their interests. Of course, a congressman takes into account the popularity of the President: few Republican senators or representatives picked a fight with Dwight Eisenhower.

Conflicts also reflect differences in constituencies. Since the President has a nationwide vote, he tends to look at public policy issues from a national perspective. A senator or member of the House of Representatives is necessarily concerned with how a matter affects residents, particularly the "attentive publics," of his state or district. The careers of John Kennedy and Lyndon Johnson gave vivid evidence of the different attitudes appropriate to different offices. As a representative and then a senator from Massachusetts, Kennedy voted to protect key industries in that state (watchmaking, textiles, and the like) from the economic effects of foreign competition. When he became President, the first important piece of domestic legislation that he helped steer through Congress was a Reciprocal Trade Act designed to promote commerce between the United States and other countries. Similarly, when Lyndon Johnson represented Texas in the House and Senate, he was not a strong advocate of civil rights; when he assumed the presidency, however, he successfully promoted several major statutes protecting minority rights and appointed Negroes to major governmental positions, including Thurgood Marshall, the first black to sit on the United States Supreme Court.*

President Johnson's increased concern with the problems of the Negro stemmed not only from the national perspective of his office but also from a keen appreciation of the number of blacks in the populous states with many electoral votes. The large-state bias built into the election of the President tends to make Democratic candidates solicitous of groups (blacks, "ethnics," labor-union members) that are concentrated in urban areas. But this concern produces political conflicts between these Presidents and Southern congressmen whose constituencies contain fewer voting members of such groups. Southern dominance of important standing committees (when the Democrats control the Congress) makes effective legislative leadership particularly difficult for Democratic Presidents.

Constituency differences also result in conflicts between Republican Presidents and congressmen. Even though Eisenhower's popularity enabled the Republican party to capture the presidency in 1952, he immediately ran into political difficulties with Daniel Reed and John Tabor (representing rural areas in New York and Illinois respectively) who, as chairmen of the House Ways and Means and Appropriations Committees, sought to cut taxes and reduce his budget requests for mutual security. Richard Nixon, who pursued a "South-

---

* When Johnson was the Majority Leader of the Senate, he did assist with the passage of the Civil Rights Act of 1957, but it was a conservative measure compared to the legislation of the 1960s.

ern" strategy in his quest for votes in 1968, saw his nominations of South Carolinian Clement Haynsworth and Floridian G. Harold Carswell to the Supreme Court opposed by a number of Republican senators from the North, who differed with them over racial matters.

Thus the influence of constituencies underlie certain basic executive-legislative relationships. Liberal Presidents, of whatever party, have generally encountered major political problems when they have tried to steer legislation changing the status quo through the House of Representatives, many of whose members have reflected the conservative values of rural and small-town America. They have had less difficulty with the upper chamber, because senators from the large states articulate the interests of urban Americans, who tend to be somewhat more liberal in their political views than are people from less populated areas. However, as was suggested in chapter 9, the reapportionment of Congress has had the effect of replacing legislators from rural areas with those from the burgeoning suburbs. As a result, the House of Representatives has become more liberal in the 1970s, so that it is no longer possible to distinguish its general political orientation so clearly from that of the Senate.

Informal Methods of Influencing Legislation

Such political realities make it difficult for a President to make effective use of his constitutional tools (messages, special sessions, and vetoes), but there are informal methods for influencing Congress. Two sources have already been dicussed: party loyalty and public opinion. A President can appeal to his colleagues in Congress to follow the party program and, with senators and representatives who are vulnerable politically, he can threaten to withhold political backing. He can also cultivate the support of the people—particularly "attentive publics"—for his legislative programs and depend on them to exert pressure on congressmen to enact those programs into law.

Personal persuasion is another valuable technique, one with a variety of manifestations: wooing individual congressmen with personal flattery and invitations to them and their wives to social affairs at the White House; making phone calls to key senators and representatives (particularly those who are not publicly committed on an issue) immediately preceding a crucial roll call; and for the President whose party also controls the Congress, holding periodic conferences with the leadership of the House and Senate as well as with major standing committee chairmen. At times Chief Executives even meet with members of the opposition party as President Ford did with the freshmen Democrats who took office in January 1975. Although personal contacts do not necessary bring a President all the results he desires, they do often win some immediate congressional support for his programs and may also create a reservoir of good will upon which he can draw in future attempts at legislative leadership.

Beyond personal persuasion, a President has a certain amount of patronage to use as a bargaining point with recalcitrant congressmen. Franklin Roosevelt deliberately postponed filling government positions in which congressmen were interested until major portions of his legislative program had been enacted into law. Even though fewer public jobs are at the disposal of Presidents today (over the years more and more have come under Civil Service regulations requiring competitive examintions), modern patronage exists in the form of government contracts, grants, and defense installations. Recent Presidents have seen to it that major military bases have been located in the home states of principal congressional leaders and committee chairmen, particularly those from Southern states like Texas, Georgia, Alabama, and Florida. Chief Executives have also seen to it that legislators from their party are given advance notice of these government contracts, grants, and defense installations and the opportunity to publicly announce such awards through their congressional offices.

Recent Presidents have also developed systematic lobbying efforts on behalf of their legislative programs. Included in such efforts are persons handling legislative liaison from various executive departments, a central liaison unit within the White House Office, and, in some instances, the Vice-President (Lyndon Johnson, for example, used Hubert Humphrey in that capacity). Such individuals typically divide their responsibilities so that some concentrate on the Senate and others on the House; in addition, some are assigned to particular groups of legislators—such as Southerners, liberal House members who belong to the Democratic Study Group, or congressmen from the big-city delegations.

These executive-branch lobbyists use the same general techniques as representatives from private interest groups do. They are thus involved not only in direct contacts with senators and representatives but also employ indirect lobbying to reach legislators through intermediaries, such as congressional staff, campaign contributors, defense contractors, newspaper editors, and other politically important persons from legislators' constituencies. The executive-branch lobbyists also join forces with private interest groups to work on legislation of common interest to both kinds of organizations.

Presidents who want to exercise strong legislative leadership and who are skillful in utilizing the tools to do so can often persuade congressmen to enact their programs into law. Particularly successful legislative leaders in this century have been Woodrow Wilson, Franklin Roosevelt, and Lyndon Johnson. Yet each of them benefited from particular conditions of the time that favored their efforts. In Wilson's case there existed a sentiment for progressive domestic legislation among political leaders and "attentive publics" alike when he came to office; moreover, he had large Democratic majorities in the House, and in the Senate a number of liberal Republicans supported his social and economic legislative programs. Roosevelt was elected in a time of crisis, when the nation and the Congress turned instinctively to the President for leadership; he also enjoyed large congressional majorities. When Johnson took office, major social and economic legislation delayed for a quarter-century was ripe for enactment; to get it passed he asked Congress to honor John Kennedy's memory by acting speedily on measures that the late President had initiated, and he counted on the bumper crop of freshman congressmen elected in 1964 to support his (Johnson's) proposals. Thus the general climate of the times and the specific situation in Congress constitute major factors in a President's legislative success.

Of course, other Presidents besides those who have unusual success with Congress also play a part in the development of public policy. As political scientist Erwin Hargrove suggests, there is a cyclical pattern to such activity. Some Presidents such as Theodore Roosevelt and John F. Kennedy, who were not able to get Congress to enact many of their legislative proposals, nonetheless helped *prepare the way* for the legislative achievements of their successors (here, Wilson and Johnson). Others such as Hoover and Eisenhower were primarily interested in *consolidating* past legislative gains by means of effective administration rather than in new legislative ventures. In ignoring the need for legislation to meet new problems in American society, such Presidents, in turn, lay the groundwork for the eventual preparation and *achievement* phases of policy making.

There is also a time dimension to legislative accomplishments of individual Presidents. Generally speaking, these accomplishments come early in a President's term (Wilson's major legislative achievements occurred in 1913-14; Franklin Roosevelt's particularly in his first 100 days but throughout his first term in office; and Lyndon Johnson's in the period 1964-66). Figure 13.1 illustrates the highs and lows in the legislative records of recent Presidents.

PRESIDENTIAL POLICY MAKING: FOREIGN AND MILITARY AFFAIRS

Harry Truman once told a group of Jewish War Veterans that he "made" foreign policy. Although this statement is a bit exaggerated, it is fair to say that the Chief Executive dominates foreign policy in a way that he does not dominate the making of domestic policy. As political scientist Aaron Wildavsky put it, we have one President but two presidencies—one for domestic affairs and the other for foreign and military policy.

The difference between the roles that the President plays in foreign and domestic policy stems from several sources. One is the fact that as the sole representative of our nation in foreign affairs, it is the President who speaks officially for the nation in matters of international concern. He is thus in a position to affect the general goals and approaches the nation will pursue in international affairs. Moreover, the legal powers granted to the President over foreign and military affairs are much greater than they are in domestic affairs,

Figure 13.1
Presidential success on congressional votes, 1953–1976. Percentages based on votes on which Presidents took a position.
Source: *Congressional Quarterly Almanac*, 1976, p. 991.

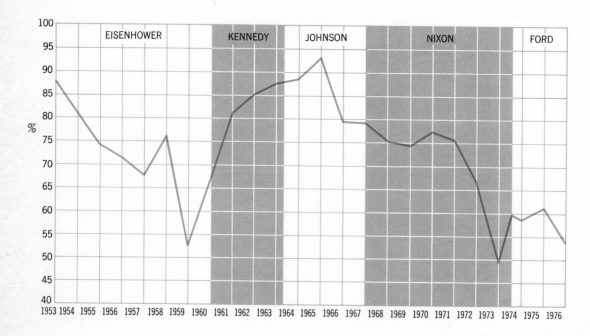

while the reverse is true as far as the Congress is concerned: its authority in international affairs is considerably less than it is in domestic policy. Finally, the very nature of foreign and military policy is such that the President enjoys natural political advantages in this area over the Congress and the courts as well as such traditional elements of poular control as public opinion, interest groups, and political parties.

Presidential Influence on General Approaches to Foreign Policy

The United States, like other nations, pursues a variety of *goals* in foreign affairs. Like individuals, the nation has been motivated in international relations by two general purposes: *ideals* and *self-interest*. The former has led us to seek moral goals that transcend national boundaries. The latter has caused us to pursue our own selfish concerns, or what is generally referred to in foreign affairs as the "national interest." While Presidents have generally been concerned with achieving both general types of goals, they have differed in the amount of emphasis they have given to each.

The Chief Executive that is most clearly associated with the idealistic approach to foreign affairs is Woodrow Wilson. In his speech to Congress on April 2, 1917, asking for a declaration of war on Germany, he explained that the nation was fighting "for the rights of nations great and small and the privilege of men everywhere to choose their way of life and of obedience. The world must be made safe for democracy." At the same time, Wilson assured the legislature: "We have no selfish ends to serve. We desire no conquest, no dominion. We seek no indemnities for ourselves, no mutual compensation for the sacrifices we shall freely make."

While not aspiring to as lofty goals as Wilson, early in his administration Jimmy Carter made it clear that a matter of central concern of the United

President Carter delivering "human rights" speech at the United Nations.

The Weather
Today—Variable cloudiness, windy, chance of precipitation near zero tomorrow tonight; high from 45 to 50. Low in the 20s. Wednesday — Fair, cooler. Temperature range: Today, 25°. Yesterday, 20-45. Details C5.

The Washington Post
Times Herald

Index		60 Pages
Amusements B 6	Metro	C 1
Classified C 7	Obituaries	C 6
Comics B 8	Outdoors	D 7
Crossword B 4	Sports	D 1
Editorials A16	Style	B 1
Financial D 8	TV-Radio	B 5

95th Year   No. 79   © 1972, The Washington Post Co.   TUESDAY, FEBRUARY 22, 1972   Phone 223-6000   Circulation 223-6100 Classified 223-6200   The Beyond Washington Maryland and Virginia   10¢

President Nixon meets with Chinese Communist Party Chairman Mao Tse-tung. Others, from left, are Premier Chou En-lai, interpreter Tang Weng-shen and Presidential adviser Henry Kissinger.

Nixon Sees Mao, Chou in Day of Cordiality

States would be the state of "human rights" not just in this country but in other nations as well. He repeatedly made public statements expressing concern over violations of human rights in nations like the Soviet Union, Cuba, Uganda, and South Korea. The President also announced cutbacks in foreign aid for Ethiopia, Argentina, and Uruguay for failing to live up to internationally recognized standards of human rights. Carter also addressed a personal letter of support to Soviet dissident Andrei Sahkarov, assuring him of our government's firm commitment to human rights not only in this country but also abroad. And when Soviet leader Leonid Brezhnev accused the United States of using the issue of human rights to interfere with the internal affairs of the Soviet Union, the President said that he would not back down on human rights, adding, "Some people are concerned every time Brezhnev sneezes."

President Carter's two predecessors, Richard Nixon and Gerald Ford, pursued a foreign policy that placed great emphasis on our nation's self-interest and security. Working closely with Secretary of State Henry Kissinger, who served with both Chief Executives, Nixon and Ford stressed the importance of maintaining a balance of power among the major nations of the world, including such traditional ideological foes of our country as the Soviet Union and China. In reestablishing relationships with Communist China and developing a policy of " détente" involving increased trade and arms limitations agreements with the Soviets, Nixon and Ford sought to avoid a nuclear threat to our nation's security.

Human rights were not entirely ignored in the Nixon-Ford-Kissinger foreign policy. The 1975 Helsinki agreement settling the post-World-War-II boundaries of Europe—signed by thirty-three European nations as well as by the United States, Canada, and the Soviet Union—pledged the signatories to respect human rights and to allow freer exchanges and travel by each nation's citizens. However, the Ford administration was not inclined to challenge the Soviet Union on violations of the agreement, such as its failure to allow Sakharov to travel to Norway to receive his Nobel Peace Prize in 1975. Ford was also opposed to legislation cutting off trade benefits for the Soviet Union if that nation interfered with the rights of its Jews to emigrate. Moreover, when Soviet

"HE WAS TAKEN FROM US BEFORE WE REALLY KNEW HIM"

DÉTENTE 1972(?)-1976

Copyright 1976 by Herblock in The Washington Post.

author and dissident Alexander Solzhenitsyn visited the United States, at Kissinger's urging President Ford refused to meet with him. In each case the Ford-Kissinger rationale was that while they were concerned with human rights within the Soviet Union, they felt that there were practical limits on the ability of the United States to press its moral values on other countries, and that confronting the Soviet Union on such matters could interfere with the policy of détente on which our nation's security and that of the world depend.

Presidents also differ on the *style* that they employ in the area of international affairs. Again, a comparison of the Carter and Ford administrations is instructive. The former seems to take pride in what he terms "open diplomacy," frequently speaking out publicly on rather delicate matters as Carter did at an early press conference in which, as a possible solution to the Middle East controversy, he proposed the use of the "defensible borders"* of Israel. In contrast, the Ford administration was very cautious about making premature statements on international affairs, depending instead on the "shuttle diplomacy" of Henry Kissinger, a procedure in which the Secretary of State conducted separate, secret conferences with all parties to a dispute, withholding public statements on such matters until the negotiations were completed.

Thus Presidents have considerable discretion in the emphasis they give to different goals and approaches in international affairs. Moreover, as the following section indicates, they have broad constitutional powers to implement these goals and approaches.

Presidential Authority in International Affairs

The great influence of the Chief Executive in foreign affairs stems in part from certain broad legal powers. He has a number of constitutional prerogatives that enable him to play the role of the nation's *chief diplomat*. He can, for example, negotiate agreements with foreign countries, either by a formal treaty, for which he must receive Senate approval by a two-thirds vote (and usually does),† or by an executive agreement. Of the latter, some he negotiates under legislative authority (for instance, reciprocal trade agreements adjusting tariffs within limits set by Congress) and some he can exercise entirely on his own (for a notable example, the Yalta agreements Franklin Roosevelt entered into in 1945 with the Soviet Union affecting developments in Central Europe and the Far East).

Aside from his agreement-making authority, the President determines formal diplomatic relationships with other nations. He has the prerogative to recognize foreign countries diplomatically. When rival groups purport to represent a nation, as has been the case with China for over twenty-five years, the President's decision regarding the diplomats he receives determines which government we regard as the legitimate one. The Chief Executive can also break off diplomatic

---

* The term *defensible borders* is a controversial one in Middle East politics because it implies that Israel need not return all the lands it seized from the Arabs in the 1967 War since the previous borders do not provide sufficient security for Israel.

† The Senate has turned down or refused to act on only about 10 percent of the treaties negotiated over the years. It can, however, indirectly defeat a treaty through attaching reservations to it that are unacceptable to the Chief Executive or foreign country involved. President Wilson's opponents used this technique to defeat the Treaty of Versailles.

relationships with a nation by asking that its representatives be withdrawn as President Wilson did a few weeks before the declaration of war against Germany in 1917; he can also reestablish such relationships, as Jimmy Carter appeared to be preparing to do with Cuba in the early months of his administration.

The President also chooses, and can dismiss as well, the major officials involved in the making of foreign policy. Although he must seek Senate approval for his nominees for cabinet positions, such as the Secretary of State, and for diplomatic representatives abroad, he is seldom turned down. Moreover, the Chief Executive can avoid this possibility altogether by appointing personal envoys to conduct diplomatic activities. Thus Franklin Roosevelt used Harry Hopkins to handle delicate matters with our allies in World War II, although the latter held no official diplomatic post in FDR's adminstration.

Finally, the President can employ "personal" diplomacy. Woodrow Wilson, for example, attended the Paris Peace Conference as the head of the United States delegation. Richard Nixon's dramatic visits to China and the Soviet Union are other examples of personal diplomacy, a technique generally employed by Presidents since World War I.

If anything, the powers that the President exercises over *military matters* are even more awesome than those that he wields over diplomacy. Many Chief Executives have claimed the authority to send American troops anywhere in the world, including into actual combat if they so desired. Recent major commitments of American troops to battle were made by executive action alone: President Truman's decision to order American forces into Korea in 1950, along with presidential actions with respect to the use of Americans in Vietnam. These current examples have many precedents. For the century after 1815, historian Arthur Schlesinger Jr. counted no fewer than forty-eight separate occasions of the use of armed forces abroad without formal declaration of war by Congress.

As Commander in Chief of the armed forces, the Chief Executive possesses other major powers that enable him to dominate military policy. He chooses, with Senate approval, the major functionaries, both civilian and military, such as the Secretary of Defense, the Joint Chiefs of Staff, and other highranking officials. He can also remove them. Thus Abraham Lincoln went through a series of commanders of the Northern forces in the Civil War until he found a man to his liking, Ulysses S. Grant; President Truman eventually decided to relieve General Douglas MacArthur from his command in Korea when the general persisted in advocating policies (such as bombing Red China) that Truman did not favor; and President Carter relieved Army Major General John Singlaub from his command in South Korea for suggesting that Carter's plan to withdraw American troops from that country would lead to war.

The Truman-MacArthur incident points up another prerogative of the President as Commander in Chief: determining major strategic decisions governing the conduct of hostilities. Truman decided to fight a "limited" war in Korea because he was concerned about drawing the Soviet Union into the war on the side of mainland China (the two at that time were partners in a defense pact) and because he did not want to involve the United States in an all-out war in Asia at a time when it had major military commitments in Europe. Franklin Roosevelt also made a number of strategic decisions that affected how World

President Nixon meets with Chairman Mao.

War II was fought, including giving the war in Europe initial priority over the one in Asia.

Basic decisions involving weapons are also up to the President. Thus Truman proceeded with Roosevelt's initial commitment to the development of the atomic bomb and then made the awesome decision to use it against the Japanese in the closing days of World War II. He also decided later to go ahead with the manufacture of the hydrogen bomb, even though some of his advisors opposed this course of action. On the other hand, President Kennedy terminated the development of the Skybolt missile (to be launched from highspeed bombers) in favor of the Minuteman and Polaris weapons, which could be fired from the underground silos and submarines.

As Commander in Chief the President even has the authority to make tactical military decisions. Although they generally leave such matters to professional officers, Chief Executives have been known to enter into the details of military operations. At the time of the Cuban missile crisis in 1962 President Kennedy insisted on planning the position of American ships off Cuba. Lyndon Johnson not only decided to bomb North Vietnam in 1965 but also chose the targets. Richard Nixon determined that the harbors of key ports of North Vietnam should be mined and ordered the resumption of bombing of that country at Christmas in 1972 after peace negotiations appeared to be breaking down.

Thus the President has a wide range of powers affecting foreign affairs that he can exercise in the manner contemplated by Hamilton in the *Federalist Papers*—with "decision, activity, secrecy and despatch." For his preeminence in this area of public policy stems both from the breadth of his prerogatives and from his ability to take decisive initiatives that others find it difficult to counter or reverse. Although the Congress has the power to refuse to appropriate funds for military ventures such as those in Korea and Vietnam, it is reluctant to exercise its authority when the lives of Americans fighting there depend on supplies and equipment. Another advantage that the President enjoys over the Congress (and over other participants in foreign-policy making) is the superior information about international developments that executive-branch members located here and abroad provide him.

Major Executive-Branch Personnel

The wealth of resources available to the President in foreign affairs is reflected in the size of the two major departments involved: Defense and State. As of February 1977, the former had almost 1 million *civilian* employees, the latter just under 30,000. In addition, other departments, such as Commerce, Labor, and Agriculture, have people assigned to international affairs.

The three top presidential advisors in foreign affairs are the Secretary of State, the Secretary of Defense, and a member of the White House Staff, currently designated as the Assistant to the President for National Security Affairs. (At times a single individual may hold two positions simultaneously: from 1973 to 1975 Henry Kissinger served as Assistant to the President for National Security Affairs and as Secretary of State.)

The first official is expected to bring a political perspective for foreign policy, the second offers a military view, and the third presumably takes both these

The intermediary: Henry Kissinger with Golda Meir and Anwar Sadat.

interests into account in counseling the Chief Executive. Of course, the division between the Secretaries of State and Defense is by no means complete: each is expected to appreciate the perspective of the other. At times, persons holding these positions have appeared to reverse roles. Secretary of State Dean Rusk was considered by many observers to have adopted an essentially military stance towards the problems of the Vietnam war, while Secretary of Defense Robert McNamara (particularly towards the end of his term) and his successor, Clark Clifford, were supposedly convinced that the conflict there was essentially political and could not be won on the military battlefield.*

* This assessment is by no means unanimous: some analysts believe it was Rusk, rather than Clifford, who convinced Lyndon Johnson to stop the bombing of the North in the spring of 1968.

The relative influence that each of these three exercises in foreign-policy making depends on the relationship he enjoys with the President. Dwight Eisenhower had great admiration for, and confidence in, John Foster Dulles and gave him broad discretion in handling a variety of matters: conducting high-level negotiations with foreign leaders, representing the American position on issues before the United Nations, and the like.

The importance of Dulles in the Eisenhower administration is to be contrasted with the part assigned to the Secretary of State in the administration of John Kennedy and during Richard Nixon's first term. Kennedy chose Dean Rusk, a low-key figure from a private foundation with no political support of consequence, and so limited Rusk's role in foreign affairs that the Chief Executive, in effect, became his own Secretary of State. Richard Nixon followed a similar course of action by iniatially appointing William Rogers, a close personal friend with very limited experience in foreign affairs. Secretary Rogers seems not to have been briefed ahead of time on the Cambodian invasion and to have played no role in helping to work out the arrangements for the most dramatic diplomatic event of recent years: President Nixon's announcement of his contemplated trip to Communist China to confer with leaders there.

The man who did play a major part in both of these latter decisions was Henry Kissinger, who served initially only as Assistant to President Nixon for National Security Affairs. The fact that McGeorge Bundy, who held that same post under Kennedy (as well as under Johnson for a period), was also an important figure suggests that Presidents (especially those who want to take a major leadership role themselves) want the advice of strong figures who are knowledgeable about foreign affairs. At the same time there are advantages in having such advisors on the White House staff, where they can be controlled and where they are also free from questioning by congressional committees and members of the press that might lead to disclosures of vital information.*

The role of the Secretary of Defense in foreign policy also varies with the incumbent and his relationship with the President. Robert McNamara, a highly competent, forceful figure who advised both Kennedy and Johnson, had a major impact on policies during his six years in office. In contrast, of the three secretaries who served in that post in the eight years of the Eisenhower administration (Charles Wilson, Neil McElroy, and Thomas Gates), only the first appears to have had much say in major foreign-policy decisions. President Nixon also appeared to pay relatively little attention to the advice of James Schlesinger as compared to that of Kissinger. President Ford followed the same practice until he ultimately removed Schlesinger from office because of his inability to get along with Kissinger.

Although the Secretaries of Defense and State and the President's Assistant for National Security Affairs are generally the key figures in foreign-policy making, the Chief Executive depends on other top-ranking officials for advice and recommendations. He may, for example, look to other members of the White House staff for assistance in special areas of concern as Kennedy did to Arthur Schlesinger Jr. on Latin-American Affairs, or the President may seek

---

* When Kissinger eventually was nominated as Secretary of State, some senators expressed concern that he would use his other position as Assistant to the President for National Security to shield himself from questioning that a departmental secretary alone would have to face.

the counsel of second- or third-level officials in executive departments. Thus Franklin Roosevelt completely bypassed his Secretary of State, Cordell Hull, and dealt with Under Secretary of State Sumner Welles on a range of foreign-policy issues. Assistant Secretaries of State with expertise in a certain region (Europe, Africa, East Asia and the Pacific, and so on) and the director assigned to a specific country are also important sources that Chief Executives can tap for information and advice. Thus John Kennedy placed great faith in the counsel of G. Mennen Williams, Assistant Secretary of State for African affairs.

As a result of experiences in World War II, a number of official organizations have been created through statute (primarily by the National Security Act of 1947) to assist the President in foreign and military affairs. One is the National Security Council (composed of the President, the Vice-President, and the Secretaries of State and Defense), which operates as a kind of miniature cabinet to advise the President on the integration of domestic, foreign, and military policies relating to national security. But like the larger cabinet, it operates at the sufferance of the President. Truman and Eisenhower convened it regularly, whereas Kennedy preferred to utilize ad hoc groups such as the one he assembled at the time of the Cuban missile crisis. Even if a President presents a problem to the NSC, he need not accept its recommendations: Eisenhower declined to do so when that body recommended intervention in Indochina in 1954 on the side of the French against the Vietnamese forces.

Reporting to the NSC is another body of considerable significance in foreign and military policy: the *Central Intelligence Agency.* Developed from the Office of Strategic Services (OSS) during World War II, in 1947 this agency was entrusted with coordinating the intelligence work (gathering and interpreting information about other nations) carried on by units operating under the Army, Navy, Air Force, and State Department. The CIA was also given a monopoly on espionage and other covert activities undertaken in foreign countries. Over the years since that time, the agency has reportedly undertaken a wide variety of activities, including successful ventures, such as helping rebels to overthrow the leftist Arbenz government in Guatemala in 1954, and fiascos, such as training Cuban exiles to invade their island in 1961 at the Bay of Pigs where they were slaughtered by Castro's forces. Despite the imposing nature of the CIA (its exact budget is secret but it has been estimated at about $2 billion a year) and the scope of its operations (it has sometimes had closer diplomatic relations with foreign governments than the State Department), like all agencies in the executive branch its influence ultimately depends on the President. After the CIA mistakenly assured Kennedy that if we helped the Cuban exiles invade the island there would be internal uprisings against Castro, the President had all overseas operations placed under the ambassadors concerned. He also ordered the entire range of intelligence activities to be reexamined by a special board reporting to him and asked the director of the CIA, Allen Dulles, to resign. The CIA ran into difficulties again in the 1970s for its alleged role in helping to overthrow the Marxist government of President Allende of Chile and also for spying on Vietnam war protesters; as a result, director William Colby was forced to resign.

The President's major professional military advisers are the *Joint Chiefs of Staff.* Created by Franklin Roosevelt in World War II and placed on a per-

"WHERE BUT IN AMERICA COULD A POOR FARM BOY WORK HIS WAY UP, IN FOUR SHORT YEARS TO BECOME THE HEAD OF A SMALL BUT IMPORTANT FOREIGN COUNTRY?"

Joint Chiefs of Staff.

manent statutory basis by the National Security Act of 1947, the Joint Chiefs presently include a chairman and the military chiefs of the three services (Army, Navy, and Air Force). Their expertise puts them in a position to exercise a major influence on military policy. Like other executive agencies, however, they are under the President's control. Almost as soon as he took office, Dwight Eisenhower inaugurated a "new look" in military policy, which emphasized nuclear "massive retaliation" as provided by the Air Force over conventional warfare as favored by the Army. The President, who placed great stress on obtaining unanimous recommendations from the Joint Chiefs, maneuvered the then Army Chief of Staff, Matthew Ridgeway (who naturally opposed the new policy), into appearing publicly to endorse it. President Kennedy also used his power effectively over the Joint Chiefs. Angered by the bad advice he got from them on the Bay of Pigs operation, the Chief Executive replaced the chairman, General Lyman Lemnitzer, with a military man more to his liking—General Maxwell Taylor.

These, then, are the major agencies of the executive branch that are involved in foreign and military policy.* Of course, as we have already noted, others such as the Departments of Commerce, Agriculture, and Labor, which are primarily concerned with domestic matters, engage in some activities relating to foreign affairs. Moreover, those agencies concerned with the financial and budgetary control of government operations (such as the Treasury and the Office of Management and Budget) play a role in establishing limits on, as well as the direction of, the activities undertaken in international affairs. Both these agencies, for example, had an important part in developing and implementing the "new-look" military policy of the Eisenhower administration, which was designed to produce "more bang for the buck" than conventional weaponry.

Checks on Presidential Policy Making

Congress. Congress has much less influence in foreign and military affairs than it has in domestic matters. As we have seen, concern for the attributes of

---

* Other units that play a part in the day-to-day operation of our foreign policy include the Foreign Service, the Agency for International Development, the Arms Control and Disarmament Agency, and the United States Information Agency.

"decision, activity, secrecy and despatch" prompted the Founding Fathers to grant the President, rather than the Congress, the more important constitutional powers in the field of national security. For example, he can officially recognize a foreign government diplomatically; Congress can only pass resolutions in favor or opposition. Even where the national legislators do have prerogatives, they are often placed in a position of having to react to presidential initiatives. He negotiates the treaties and makes the diplomatic and military appointments that senators must then consider. And although Congress alone has the formal power to declare war, the President can render that power almost meaningless by committing troops to battle on his own, as was done in both Korea and Vietnam.

In the period from the end of World War II until the mid-1970s, Congress was not disposed to use its traditional powers effectively in dealing with matters of national security. While it exercised its power-of-the-purse prerogative vigorously in cutting domestic programs proposed by the President, for much of the post-World-War-II period it gave the Chief Executive all he requested in the way of military funds—usually more, in fact. Major conflicts between Congress and the President in the 1950s and for most of the 1960s occurred because the legislators wanted to spend more money and maintain higher levels of military force than the President did. While this situation began to change, especially in the Senate, in the late 1960s, the House (which traditionally is more tightfisted with money that the upper chamber) was more reluctant to use its power of the purse to reduce military expenditures or even to alter the conduct of war in Vietnam.

Nor has the congressional power of investigation been as potent in foreign and military affairs as it has been in domestic policy. Such investigations suffer because they often occur considerably after major executive actions have taken place: the inquiry into the events at Pearl Harbor in 1941 took place five years later, after the war was over. Even when investigations are held at a time when they could have influence on the administration's course of action, they often seem not to have much effect: the series of hearings that the Senate Foreign Relations Committee held on Vietanm in 1966 appeared to have limited consequences (if any) on the conduct of the war there.

Studies point up the inferior part that the legislative branch has generally played in foreign and military affairs compared to the executive. Aaron Wildavsky's analysis of congressional voting on executive proposals from 1948 through 1964 indicates that, including refugee and immigration bills, Presidents prevail about 70 percent of the time on defense and foreign policy, compared with 40 percent in the domestic sphere. Similarly, James Robinson's study of foreign and military policy issues from the late 1930s to the early 1960s shows that the executive rather than the Congress had more to do with almost all the major decisions reached during that period. Congress must be considered a very junior partner to the executive in the making of foreign and military policy during that time.

After the termination of American involvement in the Vietnam War and the Watergate experience, Congress began to assert itself more in the area of foreign and military policy. It exercised its power-of-the-purse prerogative in refusing President Ford's request for additional military aid to Cambodia and South Vietnam when the two countries were on the brink of military collapse in early 1975. Congress also rejected Ford's plea in 1976 for financial assistance to anti-Communist forces engaged in a civil war in Angola. Both the Senate and House also launched investigations into the activities of the CIA; the upper chamber subsequently created a committee to exercise oversight over intelligence activities of the United States. Congress also sought to involve itself directly in decisions involving the use of American troops by passing the War Powers Bill, limiting the President's commitment of American troops abroad to sixty days (thirty additional days if American troops are in danger) without Congressional approval; the legislation also provided that Congress could terminate the commitment prior to the sixty-day deadline through the passage of a concurrent resolution (not subject to presidential veto).

It is too early to determine just how significant these recent actions of Congress will be. It is possible that as the memories of Vietnam fade, legislators will be less cautious about providing military assistance to countries that appear to be threatened by Communist forces. It is also difficult to determine as yet just what effect congressional committees will have on the activities of our intelligence agencies. Finally, the actual significance of the War Powers Act is still in doubt: as previously suggested, congressmen typically rally round the flag in the early stages of military crisis and so are likely to support the President's actions during the initial sixty-day period provided for by the legislation.*

The Courts. If Congress is a junior partner to the Executive in foreign and military policy, the Supreme Court is for all practical purposes not a member of the firm at all. Throughout American history the Court has declined to intervene in international affairs on the grounds that they constitute "political" matters that are better left to the popular branches of government. Judges are also reluctant to substitute their judgment for that of the President on foreign and military affairs because they realize that they do not have the sources of information and expertise on such matters that the Chief Executive has. Thus a number of legal challenges were lodged against actions taken by public officials during the Vietnamese hostilities on the grounds that Congress had not officially declared war, but none of these challenges was ever heard by the Supreme Court.†

Popular Control. Generally speaking, Americans are not as well informed about foreign-policy issues as they are about domestic concerns. (As one close student of the subject, Bernard Cohen, suggests, most of the time the real problem is finding more than a handful of people who know what the foreign-policy issues *are*—much less what they are *about*.) For one thing, such issues

---

* The only military incident to occur since the passage of the 1973 Act was President Ford's sending marines to rescue the men of the merchant vessel *Mayaguez,* seized by the Cambodian navy in May 1975. Most congressmen supported the President's action, but the incident was over so quickly that Congress had no time to take formal action on the matter.

† The Court in a 1952 decision, *Youngstown Sheet and Tube Company* v. *Sawyer,* did invalidate President Truman's seizure of the steel industry (where a strike was, in the President's judgment, imperiling our situation in Korea), but that action occurred after a ceasefire had been declared. The Court also heard cases involving military matters after the conclusion of the Civil War and World War II. Thus judges are inclined to intervene in such matters only after military crises are past.

usually have less *immediacy* for them. If the President orders a temporary freeze on prices and wages, the average citizen can appreciate the impact that the policy has on his own life. It is much less clear how he is affected by a change in the government of Chile. Moreover, a great deal of *secrecy* necessarily surrounds our relationships with other countries, and thus the public is not privy to information that would enable it to make informed judgments about international developments. Furthermore, foreign and military affairs are often so *complex* and *technical* that the average citizen would have trouble comprehending them even if he had the necessary information.

To compound the problem for the average citizen, the ordinary reference groups that help to guide his opinions on domestic concerns are not as meaningful for foreign-policy issues. A person who is not conversant with the advantages and disadvantages of a national health insurance program, for example, may get some clues from how business or labor leaders feel about it. His party affiliation, too, may help him make up his mind on the matter if one candidate favors the plan and another opposes it. However, because different social and economic groups, as well as political parties and candidates, have been less likely in recent years to be lined up on one side or the other of foreign and military concerns, helpful clues are missing.

Lacking guidelines to judge foreign policy matters, most Americans adopt a rather permissive attitude toward the actions that the government takes in international affairs. When Presidents have involved the nation in the world's problems (as all of them have since World War II), the public has been willing to support their efforts. As previously suggested, in time of crisis, Americans "rally round the flag" (and thus their leader) as evidenced by the increased ratings President Kennedy received in public-opinion polls even at the time of the Bay of Pigs fiasco. The same reaction occured when President Truman first sent American troops into Korea in 1950 and President Johnson extended commitments in Vietnam in 1965.

At the same time, however, public support for particular military ventures (as contrasted to a general policy of involvement in world affairs) erodes when they run into difficulties. As John Mueller has pointed out, after the Chinese entered the Korean war in late 1950, and our casualties began to mount and hopes for a short war were dashed, support for the war dropped significantly. The same thing began to occur (though at a slower rate) in Vietnam in mid-1966 after the Buddhist crisis, increased casualties, and a public perception developed that we were in for a long, bloody war. Moreover, public disenchantment with this latter war continued even after casualties declined: in May 1971 a Gallup poll showed that 61 percent of the public thought that we had made a mistake in sending our troops to Vietnam.

While public opinion is thus slow to react to international affairs, once formed, it establishes an outer limit on presidential actions. The isolationist mood of the country growing out of the experiences of World War I was such that Franklin Roosevelt had to carefully bring the American public around to supporting his goal of involving the nation in the allies' struggle against the Axis powers, a policy that ultimately succeeded only after the Japanese attack on Pearl Harbor. It is probable that the public reaction to the Vietnamese war will act as a similar restraint for a number of years on presidential attempts to involve our nation in hostilities abroad.

Although the general public's interest in foreign affairs is sporadic, responding mostly to dramatic events (such as military encounters), there is an "attentive public" that follows a range of international developments with some regularity. These are the persons who pride themselves on having a cosmopolitan outlook on the world. They keep informed on what happens in world politics by reading books, articles, and editorials on the subject, attending lectures and debates dealing with such matters and discussing current events with one another. Composed primarily of professionals such as academics, lawyers, bankers, newspaper editors, and schoolteachers, this group also constitutes an important source of information on foreign developments for members of the general public who may look to them for advice and clues.

Joining this group from time to time are those who develop a particular interest in a specific issue. Thus individuals with a Jewish background are likely to be concerned about events in the Middle East that affect Israel. Economic considerations also play a part in stimulating interest in certain issues: businessmen who are threatened by competition from Japanese imports respond to actions the government takes affecting foreign trade.

In many instances these attentive publics organize themselves into *interest groups* to try to influence foreign policy. They may take the form of a general-purpose organization (such as the *Foreign Policy Association*) or they, may adopt a particular approach or point of view (like the *Committee for Nuclear Responsibility*). They may reflect ethnic (*Zionist Organization of America*) or economic (*American Tariff League*) concerns. Also active in trying to influence American foreign policy are other governments, such as that of Taiwan trying to prevent our recognition of Communist China.

Another general type of lobby that has been given great attention in recent years is the so-called military-industrial complex. This is the general name given to the combination of professional military men, defense contractors, and their congressional allies (who want military installations and defense industries in their districts), who are said to exert tremendous pressures to keep military spending at a high level and to further a "hard-line" policy with communist nations. Although there is no overall formal organization that speaks for all these groups, they coordinate their efforts through such interest groups as the *American Security Council*.

"PRIORITIES SHOULD BE GIVEN THEIR DUE, IT'S TIME THE MILITARY-INDUSTRIAL COMPLEX BECAME THE INDUSTRIAL-MILITARY COMPLEX."

It is difficult to determine just how much influence attentive publics and organized interest groups actually have on foreign and military policy because of the secrecy and complexity of the decisions involved. Those decisions that are made in a short period of time, which affect all the members of American society fairly equally, and about which private groups have no presumed expertise (for example, the decision in the Cuban missile crisis), are unlikely to be much influenced by interest groups. On the other hand, long-term policies that have a particular impact on certain segments of the population and that concern matters about which such groups are considered to possess special knowledge (such as businessmen are thought to have about foreign trade) presumably reflect a higher degree of group influence. In any event, most students of interest groups attribute less influence to them on foreign affairs than in domestic policy.

The same generalization applies to *political parties.* The necessity of presenting a united front to the world and the desire to achieve continuity in our policies toward other nations means that party leaders and candidates are less likely to take opposite stands on foreign than on domestic affairs. Even when they do (as when the Republican party in the 1952 presidential campaign called for the "liberation" of Eastern European countries behind the Iron Curtain), the policies that the new administration actually follows when it comes to political office tend to parallel those of the former party in power. Thus partisan factors that characterize so much of domestic policy making are much less important in foreign and military affairs.

The President, then, has a much freer hand to operate in foreign and military affairs than he does in domestic policy. Not only are such matters dramatic and crucial (as President Kennedy remarked a few years ago, if one makes a mistake in domestic policy, it costs money; but in foreign affairs, it may mean the survival of the nation or the world), but Presidents engaged in such activities are not as beleaguered by Congress, the courts, contending interest groups, the opposition party, or the general public, as they are when they are dealing with domestic matters. This may help to explain why many of our recent Chief Executives have devoted so much time to international affairs. True to form, immediately upon assuming office, Jimmy Carter plunged into a round of foreign and military policy making even though his presidential campaign, as well as American public opinion at the time, was focused primarily on domestic concerns.

ASSESSMENT

Generally speaking, most Americans, particularly those of a liberal persuasion, have applauded a strong presidency. As Thomas Cronin has suggested, the model for the textbook view of the presidency has been Franklin Delano Roosevelt, a bold innovator who seized the leadership of Congress and the American people in the nation's battles first against economic depression and next against the Axis enemies—Germany, Italy, and Japan. Other Chief Executives like Wilson, Truman, and Kennedy—who took the lead in proposing "New Freedom," "Square Deal," and "New Frontier" programs benefiting social, political and economic underdogs in American society and who involved the nation in world affairs—have also been highly rated by political scientists, historians, and journalists.

Recently, however, many persons—including those who have traditionally supported a strong presidency—have begun to have sober second thoughts on the subject. American involvement in the Vietnam war, President Nixon's vetoes as well as the Watergate and related scandals have alerted people (particularly liberals) to the fact that vast presidential powers that can be utilized for ''good'' purposes are also available for ''bad'' ones. What concerns scholars like Arthur Schlesinger Jr. is that we now have not a ''strong'' presidency but an ''imperial'' one.

This realization has led to a host of recent proposals for reforming the presidency by reining in occupants of the office. One general approach is to place limitations on the term of an incumbent. For example, during his presidency, Richard Nixon suggested that the Commission on Federal Election Reform that he appointed give particular attention to the possibility of limiting the President to one six-year term. The theory behind this proposal is that since Chief Executives will not have to worry about being reelected, they will pursue objective policies that are best for the country rather than those that will help them get reelected.

Such a suggestion is highly undemocratic. As we saw in chapter 1, democracy deliberately creates insecurity for officeholders by requiring them to go before the electorate periodically to have their terms renewed. Such a process is specifically designed to make them receptive to the views of the people whom they represent, to make them accountable to the public. Democracy is not ''efficient'' or ''objective'' government, but *responsible* government. The Twenty-first Amendment, which generally limits a President to two terms, is itself unwise; a single term is even more objectionable.

The Watergate affair and the difficulties that it has presented for the nation have also stimulated proposals for some means besides impeachment for removing a President who has lost the confidence of the American people. The argument is that impeachment is too long and drawn-out a process and produces too much division in the country to be effective as a weapon against a President who should not be permitted to stay in office. What is rather needed is some other method of dealing with the problem such as a vote of no confidence by both houses of Congress, which will spare the nation the trauma of impeachment and still remove the incumbent of the office.

Such a proposal, of course, is the method used in countries with a parliamentary system of government such as Britain and France. Transposing it to our presidential system based upon the concept of the separation of powers could create major problems. For example, it would make it possible for legislators to remove a President whose policies were not currently popular with the Congress, a body which might be controlled by the opposition party. Moreover, if one went this route, it would probably be necessary to allow the President to dissolve a Congress that was not following his policies and to call for new elections. Such procedures would create the potential for great political instability in the country; moreover, given our lack of disciplined political parties, there is no guarantee that the problem would be resolved, since the same President and a similarly-constituted Congress could conceivably be returned to office.

Another increasing concern of students of the American presidency in recent years has been the growing isolation of incumbents of the office from the harsh realities of political life. Originally noted by a former White House aide, George Reedy, who served under Lyndon Johnson, the tendency of the President to surround himself with a protective staff became even more pronounced during the Nixon administration. The unfortunate result of utilizing advisors that court favor by telling the President what he wants to hear rather than what he should be told is to desensitize the Chief Executive to the facts of political life and what he can realistically do about them.

Various proposals have also been made for trying to counteract this growing isolation of the presidency. One suggestion is to require the Chief Executive to have an official advisory body drawn from the Congress that might also include members of the opposition party. While such a group would help ensure that he would receive a variety of information and viewpoints, there is no way to guarantee that he would take these considerations into account when making decisions. In fact, there appears to be no good way to force a President to consult certain persons if he is not disposed to do so. After the revelations about the Watergate incident, President Nixon promised a more "open" presidency, but, if anything, he seemed subsequently to further constrict his circle of advisors until it included only two regulars, General Haig and Ronald Ziegler, with periodic conferences on foreign affairs with the peripatetic Henry Kissinger.

Another more promising possibility for keeping the President in touch with reality would be to have him hold press conferences periodically. This situation would be a vast improvement over the practice of Chief Executives (like Mr. Nixon) of going for long periods of time with no contact at all with the media, followed by a spate of meetings that overlap each other in subject matter and for which the President cannot adequately prepare. Again the problem is one of practicality: can one force a President to hold press conferences if he does not want to? Perhaps not, but if it were known that the American public expected such conferences periodically, this might induce reluctant Presidents to accede to its wishes.

The role of the President in foreign and military affairs does not appear to be as "imperial" as it was at the time that Arthur Schlesinger, Jr. wrote on the subject in the early 1970s. Congress has begun to play a more meaningful role in checking presidential initiatives in international affairs. However, as previously suggested, it is difficult to determine at this point whether the resurgence of congressional activity represents merely a reaction to Vietnam and Watergate or whether legislators will continue to assert such prerogatives as the power of the purse and investigations to affect foreign policy. In any event, considerations of secrecy, dispatch, and expertise are such that one may expect decisions involving foreign and military affairs to continue to be made primarily by the President and his advisers in the executive branch.

Given these facts of life, it is particularly important that vital checks and balances be built into the system by which the Chief Executive reaches the awesome decisions regarding foreign and military policy. As this process operates, the presidential advisers structure the situation and shape the options from which he chooses; the prize in the political struggle thus becomes not the public's mind, but that of the President. Each participant has the goal of convincing the Chief Executive that his concept of political reality (the intentions of other nations, our own capacities, the significance of a particular event) is the *true* one. If the process is to operate as it should, the President must be exposed to as wide a range of views and proposals as possible so that he can choose intelligently from among them.

One possibility for effecting better executive policy making in foreign affairs is to employ what political scientist Alexander George refers to as a system of "multiple advocacy." This system would use the Special Assistant to the President for National Security Affairs as a "custodian" to organize competing information, views, and options on how to handle particular matters from a variety of presidential advisers; the President would serve as the "magistrate" of the process, making the final decision on the course of action to be pursued. These procedures might well broaden (as well as refine) the advice and options that a President receives on foreign policy matters. As George suggests, such a system would not guarantee "good" decisions in every instance, but it might help prevent some very "bad" decisions. Given our experience in Vietnam, that in itself would be no small accomplishment.

SELECTED READINGS

The problems that the President faces as party leader are analyzed by James Burns in *Deadlock of Democracy: Four-Party Politics in America* (Englewood Cliffs, N.J.: Prentice-Hall, 1963). Lester Seligman treats the President's personal party in "The Presidential Office and the President as Party Leader," *Law and Contemporary Problems* (Autumn 1956): 724-35. Gerald Pomper's study of the relationship between party platforms and legislative and executive policies appears in his *Elections in America* (New York: Dodd, Mead, 1968), and Grogan's analysis of presidential campaign statements and similar policies is set forth in "Candidate Promise and Presidential Performance, 1964-1972," a paper delivered at the meeting of the Midwest Political Science Association, April 21-23, 1977.

For an excellent analysis of the President's role as leader of public opinion, see Elmer Cornwell, *Presidential Leadership of Public Opinion* (Bloomington, Ind.: Indiana University Press, 1965). The Chief Executive's relationships with the press are treated by Douglass Cater, "The President and the Press," *The Annals of the American Academy of Political and Social Science* (September, 1956): 55-66. Two more recent analyses of the relationship between the President and the mass media are Daniel Moynihan, "The Presidency and the Press," *Commentary* 51 (March 1971): 43-50, and Newton Minow, John Martin and Lee Mitchell, *Presidential Television* (New York: Basic Books, 1973).

Wilfred Binkley's revised edition, *The President and Congress* (New York: Vintage Books, 1962), chronicles the relationships that have prevailed between the two over the course of our history. Lawrence Chamberlain's analysis of the respective parts that the President and Congress have played in the formulation of major legislation is dealt with in *The President, Congress, and Legislation* (New York: Columbia University Press, 1946). A recent study of presidential-congressional relations is Louis Fisher, *President and Congress: Power and Policy* (New York: Free Press, 1972). Alexander Holtzman treats executive-branch lobbying in his *Legislative Liaison: Executive Leadership in Congress* (Chicago: Rand McNally, 1970). Erwin Hargrove explains his concept of the cyclical nature of policy making in chapter 6 of *The Power of the Modern Presidency* (New York: Knopf, 1974).

Two valuable books that treat the general process by which foreign and military policy are made are Roger Hilsman, *The Politics of Policy-Making in Defense and Foreign Affairs* (New York: Harper & Row, 1971), and Kenneth Waltz, *Foreign Policy and Democratic Politics* (Boston: Little, Brown, 1967). The President's role in foreign affairs is treated by Sidney Warren, *The President as World Leader* (Philadelphia: Lippincott, 1964), and in military affairs by Ernest May (ed.), *The Ultimate Decision: The President as Commander-in-Chief* (New York: Braziller, 1960). Arthur Schlesinger Jr.'s *The Imperial Presidency* (Boston: Houghton Mifflin, 1973) analyzes changes in that office brought about by recent developments in foreign and military affairs. Aaron Wildavsky compares the President's role in foreign and domestic affairs in "The Two Presidencies," *Transaction* (December 1966): 7-14. Graham Allison's "Making War: The President and Congress," which appears in Thomas Cronin and Rexford Tugwell (eds.) *The Presidency Reappraised* (New York: Praeger, 1977), analyzes the subject since the passage of the War Powers Act of 1973. The best treament of defense policy is Samuel Huntington, *The Common Defense* (New York: Columbia University Press, 1961). For an analysis of the way that the American administrative structure shapes foreign policy, see Henry Kissinger, "Domestic Structure and Foreign Policy," in his book *American Foreign Policy: Three Essays* (New York: Norton, 1969). An excellent study of the role of executive agencies in foreign affairs is Morton Halperin, *Bureaucratic Politics and Foreign Policy* (Washington: The Brookings Institution, 1974).

For a treatment of the role of Congress see James Robinson, *Congress and Foreign Policy Making* (Homewood, Ill.: Dorsey, 1962). For a discussion of the role that the Supreme Court has played in foreign policy, see chapters 5 and 6 of Edward Corwin, *The President: Office and Powers* (New York: New York University Press, 3rd ed., 1948).

An insightful discussion of the role of public opinion in foreign policy is Gabriel Almond, *The American People and Foreign Policy* (New York: Harcourt, Brace, 1950). An historical analysis of the subject is Frank Klingberg, "The Historical Alteration of Moods in Foreign Policy," *World Politics* (January 1952): 239-73. Three studies of the attitudes of the American people on foreign policy and recent wars are William Caspary, "The Mood Theory: A Study of Public Opinion and Foreign Policy," *The American Political Science Review* (June 1970): 536-47; Sidney Verba et al., "Public Opinion and the War in Vietnam," *The American Political Science Review* (June 1967): 317-34; and John Mueller, *War, Presidents and Public Opinion* (New York: Wiley, 1973). Bernard Cohen's *The Public's Impact on Foreign Policy* (Boston: Little, Brown, 1973) provides needed clarity in relating public opinion to decisions involving foreign affairs.

The role that interest groups play in the making of foreign policy are analyzed in Bernard Cohen, *The Role of Non-Governmental Groups in Foreign Policy Making* (Boston: World Peace Foundation, 1959); Raymond Bauer et al., *American Business and Public Policy* (New York: Atherton, 1963); and Lester Milbrath, "Interest Groups and Foreign Policy," in James Rosenau (ed.), *Domestic Sources of Foreign Policy* (New York: Free Press, 1967). Two selections in that same volume that deal with the part that elections play in foreign policy are Warren Miller, "Voting and Foreign Policy," and Kenneth Waltz, "Electoral Punishment and Foreign Crises." Bernard Cohen, *The Press and Foreign Policy* (Princeton: Princeton University Press, 1963), is the best treatment of that subject.

Alexander George's prescription for executive foreign policy making appears in his "The Case of Multiple Advocacy in Making Foreign Policy," *The American Political Science Review* 66 (September 1972): 751-785.

A very good overall analysis of the presidency that favors a "strong" Chief Executive is James Burns, *Presidential Government* (Boston: Houghton Mifflin, 1965). George Reedy, *The Twilight of the Presidency* (New York: World, 1970), expresses a fairly pessimistic view of the ability of the presidency to cope with the current problems of our society.

Political Novels   The myth as compared to the reality of the presidency is aptly illustrated by Sam Sackett's science-fiction story about the *real* President—and he's not the one the people thought they elected—"Hail to the Chief," in J. Olander, M. Greenberg, and P. Warrick (eds.), *American Government Through Science Fiction* (Chicago: Rand McNally, 1974). Several former assistants to ex-President Richard M. Nixon have written novels about the presidency: John Erlichman, *The Company* (New York: Pocket Books, 1977), writes about a President being blackmailed by the Director of Central Intelligence; William Safire, *Full Disclosure* (New York: Doubleday, 1977), tells of a blind President struggling to hold his office while being hounded by a vicious news media; and Herbert Stein (former chairman of the Council of Economic Advisors) with Benjamin Stein in *The Brink* (New York: Simon and Schuster, 1977) recounts the dramatic efforts of the Council of Economic Advisors to avert impending financial disaster for the nation.

Misbehavior in the executive branch of government and White House "cover-ups" are themes developed by Patrick Anderson, *The President's Mistress* (New York: Pocket Books, 1976), and Ben J. Wattenberg (famous pollster and election expert), *The West Wing* (New York: Doubleday, 1977).

The fragile relationship between national security and civilian control of the military rests at the heart of *Seven Days in May* (New York: Bantam, 1969) by Fletcher Knebel and Charles W. Bailey. These novelists conceived the inconceivable—a military coup against the President. Pierre Salinger (Press Secretary to President Kennedy) provides an insider's view of White House decision making during crisis in his novel about an international confrontation suspiciously similar to the Cuban Missile Crisis of 1962, *On Instructions of My Government* (New York: Dell, 1972). The case for presidential deception in the national interest is made by Fletcher Knebel in *Vanished* (New York: Avon, 1969).

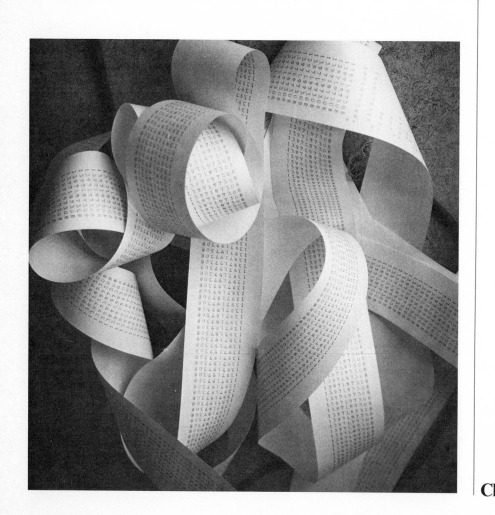

Chapter 14

In 1976 the pre-convention presidential contenders differed widely on how best to deal with such problem areas as unemployment and inflation, détente with the Soviet Union, the busing of school children, and abortion. But each in his own way took aim at a common foe: the federal bureaucracy. Leading the charge was Republican challenger Ronald Reagan, who complained that "Thousands of towns and neighborhoods have seen their peace disturbed by bureaucrats and social planners, through busing, questionable educational programs, and attacks on family unity." To remedy the evils of "Big Brother government," the former Governor of California proposed a bold measure: to transfer responsibility and funds for social programs—welfare, education, housing, food stamps—back to the states, thereby reducing federal spending by some 90 billion dollars a year.

The incumbent, Gerald Ford, branded Reagan's proposal "impractical" and "irresponsible" but did not come to the defense of the federal bureaucracy that he himself headed. Instead the Chief Executive leveled a broadside of his own against the bureaucracy. He accused it of concocting a "Mulligan stew of government rules and regulations" resulting in "red tape, paper shuffling, and new heights in counter-productivity." He noted that the bureaucracy employed "over 100,000 persons whose primary responsibility is to regulate some aspect of our lives" and pointed to the creation of over 230 new departments, agencies, bureaus, and commissions in the period 1960-75. The President's proposal would therefore be to trim back the number of federal programs and employees and to guarantee that "government policies . . . not infringe unnecessarily on individual choice and initiative nor intervene needlessly in the market-place."

Even the Democratic candidates—generally considered more sympathetic to a powerful federal government—zeroed in on Washington officialdom. George Wallace, a long-time foe of "pointy-headed intellectuals and theoreticians who can't even park their bicycles right," continued his assaults on big government and the "Eastern Establishment." In fact, Wallace charged that other Democratic candidates "done stole my water—they're drinking out of my dipper,"

THE BUREAUCRACY

497

President Carter signs reorganization bill.

claiming his familiar stands on bureaucrats, welfare, busing, and federal guidelines as their own.

Among these candidates was the eventual Democratic nominee, Jimmy Carter, who made reorganization of the federal bureaucracy one of his major campaign promises. He pointed to his record while governor of Georgia, where he consolidated 300 state agencies, boards, commissions, and departments into 22 major departments. Now he would pledge to reduce 1900 similar units of the executive branch in Washington to 200. He would further reform budgeting techniques, as he had done while Chief Executive of the Peach State.

What accounts for this great animosity toward the federal bureaucracy? How justified are the criticisms leveled against it? How realistic are proposals for reforming it? To try to answer such basic questions, we must first understand what the federal bureaucracy *is* and what it *does;* how it is *organized* and *operates;* the kinds of *persons* who staff the bureaucracy and how they are chosen; and what *means* exist to check its possible abuses and to make it responsive to popularly elected officials and to the general public as well.

THE NATURE OF BUREAUCRACY

The scorn for the federal bureaucracy expressed by the presidential candidates is not a new or unique reaction to the activities of government and its officials. According to a leading scholar of the subject, Reinhard Bendix, the word *bureaucracy* can be traced to eighteenth-century France: the term *bureau,* referring to a cloth covering the desk of public officials, was combined with *cracy* (rule) to suggest an autocratic type of government. During the following century this unflattering sense of the word spread to other European countries where critics of absolutist governments employed it to describe the complex procedures and high-handed manner of autocratic public officials. Today the term retains its unfavorable meaning. It summons up the image of a blundering petty official—called a *bureaucrat*—who spends his time developing meaning-

UNITED STATES DEPARTMENT OF JUSTICE
LAW ENFORCEMENT ASSISTANCE ADMINISTRATION

WASHINGTON, D. C. 20530

DATE: March 31, 1972
REPLY TO
ATTN OF: OGC
SUBJECT: Office of General Counsel

TO: All Employees

Efffective today, the name change of the Office of General Counsel to the Office of Legal Counsel is rescinded and the current Office of Legal Counsel is redesignated Office of General Counsel.

JERRIS LEONARD
Administrator

less forms with which to torment innocent citizens, applying rules and regulations rigidly with no concern for the specific case before him. He is also seen as building a personal empire composed of ever-increasing numbers of subordinate employees, all at the expense of the state treasury and the tax-paying citizenry.

While this hostile use of the term *bureaucracy* remains a popular one, political scientists and sociologists employ the term in a more neutral sense to describe a large-scale organization with certain common features.* Prominent among these is the handling of complex tasks through a *divison of labor* that allows persons with various kinds of skills to concentrate on different aspects of the total operation. Another feature is a *hierarchical* form of organization in which authority flows downward from superiors to subordinate employees. Modern-day bureaucracies recruit persons for their *technical expertise* and expect them to be *politically neutral*—that is, to make decisions based only upon their expertise and not on partisan or personal considerations. For a bureaucrat to meet these expectations, he is protected from arbitrary dismissal and also given incentives to remain as a permanent employee of the bureaucracy.

It is precisely these characteristics of bureaucracy that explain its prominence today at all levels of government, including the federal. As we have seen in chapter 11, Congress has neither the expertise nor the time to deal with the intricacies of all the various issues facing the nation. At best, it can *identify* a problem such as pollution, *suggest* some basic approaches for dealing with the problem, and *leave it to the experts* in a specialized agency to grapple with the issue on a day-to-day basis. (Meanwhile, Congress moves on to other matters.)

As the federal government has intervened more and more in the economic and social life of the nation, the federal bureaucracy has become increasingly important as nonelected officials make decisions that vitally affect the lives of citizens. For example, agencies help to determine who is entitled to certain *benefits*. Recently, the Department of Agriculture issued new regulations concerning food stamps that had the effect of removing 5 million persons from the program, at the same time increasing the amount of stamps to which eligible persons were entitled. Federal agencies also *regulate* economic activities. Thus, all mobile homes must meet new federal construction safety standards set by the Secretary of the Department of Housing and Urban Development with the assistance of the Consumer Product Safety Commission.

In determining the distribution of benefits and regulations, the federal bureaucracy acts in various capacities. Some of these are primarily *executive* or managerial in nature, as in the hiring of qualified personnel and the allocation of funds so that it does not run out of money before the end of the fiscal year. In other instances, the bureaucracy's functions are more *legislative* in nature, as when it develops general rules and regulations that govern, for example, the kinds of safety equipment that must be installed in automobiles or aircraft. Moreover, in some instances agencies undertake *judicial* functions, deciding which applicant for a television franchise should receive it, or whether a given person is entitled to receive a veteran's disability pension.

* Several of these features apply to private organizations as well as to public ones. A bureaucracy exists in General Motors just as it does in the federal government. However, this discussion will concentrate on public bureaucracies.

It would thus be a mistake to think of the federal bureaucracy as performing essentially routine clerical tasks. While some of them are of this character—as when an agency simply enforces a provision of a law that is clear-cut and has specific application,—many of the activities involve great discretion. Congress may provide only broad guidelines in stating that freight rates set by the Interstate Commerce Commission must be "just" and "reasonable," or that in assigning radio frequencies and television channels, the Federal Communications Commission must take into account the "public interest, convenience, and necessity." Thus federal agencies deal frequently with vague and essentially unfinished laws which they must interpret, supplement, and apply to a variety of individuals, groups, and circumstances.

The federal bureaucracy has thus come to constitute a major force in our national government making not only executive decisions but also those of discretionary nature more typically associated with legislatures and courts. Moreover, its activities dwarf those of the older, more traditional bodies. As a former Commissioner of the Federal Communications Commission put it: "While the courts handle thousands of cases a year and Congress produces hundreds of laws each year; the administrative agencies handle hundreds of thousands of matters annually." Another measure of comparative activity demonstrates that fact even more clearly. Currently some 2.8 million persons are employed in the federal bureaucracy compared to 38,000 by Congress and some 11,00 by the fedeal courts.

But while the bureaucracy is an increasingly important component of our national government, it is by no means an autonomous body. Rather, as the following section demonstrates, it is the *legal creature* of two of the traditional branches—the President and the Congress. Together they determine *what* the bureaucracy does, *how* it goes about its work, and *who* is in charge of its operation.

THE PRESIDENT, CONGRESS AND THE BUREAUCRACY

Since the bureaucracy is entrusted with administration of the laws, it is natural to expect that the President, vested by broad constitutional language (Article II, Section 1) with the "Executive Power," should play a major role in its functioning. Indeed, further language in Section 3 of that same Article charges the Chief Executive with the duty to ". . . take care that the laws be faithfully executed." At the same time, however, Article I, Section 8, grants Congress the authority to make all laws "necessary and proper" not only for implementing its own delegated powers, but also for carrying out ". . . all other powers vested by this Constitution in the Government of the United States, or in any department or officer thereof." Thus the Founding Fathers intended that the President and Congress should share the responsibility for the functioning of the bureaucracy.

This joint responsibility is implemented by specific powers shared by President and Congress that affect the operation of the bureaucracy. As the following discussion indicates, the *structure* for carrying out the activities of the bureaucracy is today created by action of both the Chief Executive and the Congress. Together they also determine the amount and allocation of *moneys* that are expended by the bureaucracy. And finally, both the President and the Congress influence the *appointment and removal* of the men and women who occupy the major positions in the federal bureaucracy.

The Structure of the Bureaucracy

While at first one might expect that the President possessed the power to determine the organization and internal operation of the executive branch, as a matter of fact it is the Congress that is granted this constitutional authority. Since 1789, when the national legislature first created the departments of State, War (and Navy), and Treasury, along with the Office of the Attorney General and the Post Office, the executive structure that has evolved has been primarily a product of congressional action. Such action has determined not only the general nature and scope of government programs, but also the specific organizations in which they are administered. In some instances Congress has placed new programs within existing organizations; in other cases it has created new entities to handle them. It has also shifted programs from one unit to another.

Congressional control over the organization of the executive branch goes beyond the matter of its general structure. National legislators can also determine the internal operation of executive agencies by deciding the subunits into which they are to be divided as well as the different ranks of officials who carry out various aspects of their programs. Congress has also legislated on even more detailed internal matters, determining how executive agencies shall enter into contracts, issue publications, purchase supplies, or use the mails and means of travel.

The development of a broad variety of New Deal programs in the 1930s created a burgeoning bureaucracy. In 1936 President Roosevelt appointed a Committee on Administrative Management chaired by Louis Brownlow, a distinguished former city manager, to analyze and make suggestions concerning the management of the executive branch. The major recommendation of the group was that the President "needs help" in administering the bureaucracy and that some of this help should be provided by presidential assistants with a "passion for anonymity." In 1939 Congress granted President Roosevelt the authority to reorganize the executive branch subject to some restrictions (for example, certain agencies were exempted from being reorganized), and he responded that same year with an executive order creating the Executive Office of the President, a highly important unit that we will examine in detail later in the chapter.

This pattern of joint executive-legislative involvement in executive reorganization has persisted over the years since 1939. Congress has periodically granted the President the power to reorganize the executive branch but has kept for itself the right to veto the reorganization plans. Since 1949 that veto has taken the form of a resolution passed by either house within 60 days of the issuance of a presidential reorganization plan; if neither chamber takes any action to nullify such a plan within that period, it automatically goes into effect. (Since 1964, the authorizing legislation has also prohibited the creation of cabinet-level departments by executive order, reserving to Congress alone the power to take that action by statute.)

In early 1977, in response to a request by President Carter, Congress once again enacted such a statute granting the Chief Executive the authority to reorganize the federal bureaucracy for a three-year period. However, this particular statute requires that when the President submits a reorganization plan, a resolution of disapproval is automatically introduced in Congress; such a resolution is referred to the Senate Governmental Affairs and the House Gov-

ernmental Operations Committees, and if not reported within forty-five days, the resolution is automatically discharged from committee and can be called up by any member. This provision is designed to make it easier to obtain congressional floor action on reorganization plans.

Armed with this statutory authority to reorganize the executive branch, and frequently fortified with suggestions by outside commissions composed of prestigious private citizens,* Chief Executives have taken the leadership in making some major changes in the bureaucracy. These include the addition of a Department of Health, Education, and Welfare during the Eisenhower administration, and two additional cabinet-level units during Lyndon Johnson's presidency, the Department of Housing and Urban Development and the Department of Transportation. President Nixon reorganized the Bureau of the Budget during his first term, giving it a new title of Office of Management and the Budget, and also created the Domestic Council to help coordinate various domestic programs of the federal government. In the first year of the Carter administration, a new Department of Energy was created.

However, a number of major presidential reorganization proposals have *not* been approved by the Congress. President Truman was unsuccessful in upgrading the Federal Security Agency (in charge of the Social Security programs) to departmental status, and President Kennedy met defeat in his effort to create a Department of Urban Affairs. Congress refused to approve Lyndon Johnson's proposal for merging the Commerce and Labor departments; it also declined President Nixon's bid to combine seven existing departments (Agriculture; Commerce; Health, Education, and Welfare; Housing and Urban Development; Interior; Labor; Transportation) into four (Community Development; Economic Affairs; Human Resources; Natural Resources).

Typically, presidential reorganization plans are proposed on the grounds that they will prevent duplication of work, group agencies with similar functions together, and save the taxpayers money. However, there is little evidence that they actually accomplish these managerial goals; for example, only 4 of the 92 reorganization plans submitted to the Congress from 1949 through 1973 were supported by precise dollar estimates of savings. Rather, as one veteran observer of the Washington scene, Harold Seidman suggests, such plans are highly *political* in nature. The method of organization determines priorities among governmental programs (a new program may be placed in a specially-created unit to prevent its being slighted by an existing agency with other ongoing programs.) The organization in which a program is administered also affects the kind of access that interest groups have to the bureaucracy. Thus President Johnson's proposed merger of the Departments of Commerce and Labor was opposed by both business and labor because each feared a loss of the influence it enjoyed in the department with which it had established relationships over the years.

One other major factor greatly impedes executive reorganization: the committee structure of Congress. Under the Legislative Reorganization Act of 1946, each standing committee of the Congress exercises legislative oversight over certain executive agencies. Therefore, if such agencies are reorganized, that action affects the activities of the corresponding congressional committees.

---

* In the late 1940s and early 1950s, two separate bodies chaired by former President Herbert Hoover reported their recommendations to Presidents Truman and Eisenhower.

As Seidman puts it: "The key to rationalizing executive branch structure lies in the reorganization of Congress, not the reverse." And, as we have seen in chapter 11, traditionally the national legislature has shown little inclination to fundamentally change its committee organization for *any* purpose, let alone for accommodating its major constitutional rival, the President.

Money

Like the creation of the structure of the bureaucracy, the provision of money for its operations is a joint responsibility of both the President and Congress. The process involves three basic steps: (1) the requesting of funds for the operation of the executive branch—a procedure that is today controlled by the President; (2) the authorization of government programs and the appropriation of funds for them—two separate procedures, both of which are carried out by the Congress; and (3) the actual spending of the money—a decision in which both the President and the Congress share.

Requests for Funds. Initially the Congress granted the first Secretary of the Treasury, Alexander Hamilton, the authority to "prepare and report estimates of the public revenues and the public expenditures." In this way it provided for some executive control over agency requests for funds. However, this practice was later abandoned in favor of a process in which the Secretary of the Treasury simply passed on to the Congress the departments' own estimates of expenditures without making any changes. The end result of this lack of executive authority to examine and revise department estimates—and to relate them to revenues—was a growth of government spending and the incurring of large deficits. Eventually Congress became concerned with these deficits and passed the Budget and Accounting Act of 1921, placing responsibility for the preparation of a budget for government expenditures on the President. To assist him in this responsibility, the Bureau of the Budget was created and placed in the Department of the Treasury. When the Executive Office of the President was established by executive order in 1939, the Bureau was transferred from the Treasury Department to the Office; since 1970 it has been known as the Office of Budget and Management (OBM).

The preparation of the presidential budget today is a lengthy and complicated process. In the spring (some ten months before the President's budget is presented to the Congress the following January), the Treasury, the OBM, and the Council of Economic Advisers (this body will be discussed in the next section) develop the administration's economic projections of overall spending and tax policies for the next fiscal year. At the same time, executive agencies are requested to submit estimates of their financial needs for the next year.

During the summer months, the annual budget battle shifts to the departmental level. The head of a bureau (or other subunit of a department) proposes estimates of his needs for the coming year. The departmental budget staff screens these requests and makes recommendations to the departmental secretary concerning them. That fall, after the departmental secretary makes his decision on the total department figure to propose for the coming year, the process moves upward again. The OBM examines each departmental budget and holds hearings at which agency heads are required to justify their estimates. Following this procedure, the OBM makes recommendations to the

President on expenditures, and each agency is later notified of the amount the President allows it. If an agency feels that the Chief Executive has trimmed its budget too much, it can appeal its case—if the departmental secretary is willing to do so. Ultimately, the President makes the final decision on all requests, and all budget materials are combined in a single document and submitted to Congress. In his Budget Message that same month the President presents this information to the national legislators in summary form.

Authorizing Programs and Appropriating Funds. Traditionally, this exclusively congressional phase of the total money-providing process has been a highly decentralized one as agency heads knock on the doors of a variety of groups in presenting their case for funds. Initially they must receive congressional authorization for their programs from the appropriate substantive committees (Agriculture, Armed Services, Labor, and the like) of both the House and Senate. These authorizations may provide a maximum dollar figure that can be expended for such programs, but as political scientist Aaron Wildavsky, a close student of the budgetary process, explains, these are only "hunting licenses" which the two congressional Appropriations committees (House and Senate) are under no obligation to recognize or honor. For it is these latter committees, operating through subcommittees (each of which has jurisdiction over one or more executive agencies) that have traditionally made the final decisions on how much money is actually appropriated for the various executive agencies. The recommendations of these subcommittees are generally adopted by their parent Appropriation Committee and the entire chamber (House or Senate), with a conference committee ultimately settling House-Senate differences on appropriations.

This highly fragmented process has proved over the years to be most unsatisfactory. There has been no way to ensure that the funds Congress appropriates for expenditures are related to the amount of money it raises through revenue measures. Nor has the legislature been willing to set an overall figure for expenditures in a given fiscal year and see to it that its appropriations for various programs stay within that total figure. Finally, Congress has often failed to complete the appropriation process before the end of the fiscal year on June 30, with the result that it has had to pass supplemental appropriations to permit government agencies to carry on activities at previous levels of expenditures until the legislators can reassess their needs.

Faced with these problems, Congress passed a major budget reform act in 1974 providing for a Congressional Budget Office as well as new budget committees in each chamber to study and recommend changes in the President's budget. New procedures have also been established that require Congress to develop an alternative congressional budget relating appropriations and spending to taxes and the federal debt and requiring that appropiations stay within an overall spending figure authorized by the two chambers. The reform measure also seeks to remedy Congress's failure to complete its appropriation process on time by establishing a new fiscal year (running from October 1 to September 30, rather than July 1 to June 30) that gives the legislators three extra months to act upon budget proposals made by the President the previous January.

After experimenting in 1975 with the new procedures established by the Act, Congress placed the system in full operation in 1976. In mid-September, a budget resolution was passed for the fiscal year beginning October 1, setting a $413.1 billion ceiling on outlays and a $362.5 billion floor under revenues, with a resulting deficit of $50.6 billion. The measure, which did not require the President's signature, also set the level of the public debt at $700 billion. Under the terms of the resolution, any legislation deviating from these levels would be ruled out of order unless Congress adopted specific revisions under a new budget resolution.

Spending. Most moneys appropriated by the Congress are spent by the executive branch without question. However, in some instances Presidents have impounded funds—that is, refused to spend them—for various reasons. In some instances, Chief Executives have merely deferred spending because of changing circumstances; Jefferson did this when the settlement of differences with the French concerning the Mississippi made the moneys appropriated for gunboats unnecessary. In some cases, Congress itself authorizes the withholding of funds, as happened in 1967, when Congress directed a spending cut in which the President was expected to participate. A number of recent Chief Executives, including Truman, Eisenhower, Kennedy, and Johnson, have invoked their authority as Commander-in-Chief to justify refusing to spend moneys for military forces and weapons that they did not think were necessary for the nation's defense.

The most dramatic use of impoundment, however, was that practiced by Richard Nixon. Not only did he refuse to spend large sums of money appropriated by Congress (some $40 billion in his first four years in office alone), but his impoundments were directed at a broad range of domestic, not national defense, programs. (Singled out as particular targets were programs in agriculture, housing, and water-pollution control.) Moreover, the reasons Nixon invoked for his actions—that he had the constitutional right to impound funds when spending of moneys would cause inflation of require an increase in taxes,—involved major financial issues that have traditionally been left to the Congress. The fact that the President directed many of his impoundments at legislation be personally disapproved (and had unsuccessfully vetoed) also indicated that he was utilizing the weapon to affect particular public policies rather than to impose financial control over the total level of government spending.

Nixon's use of impoundment was soon challenged on two fronts. Some impoundments were struck down by the federal courts, including a $9-billion impoundment—this one, of federal water-pollution control money—that was nullified by the Supreme Court. In addition, when Congress passed the law reforming its budgeting procedures, it also included provisions limiting presidential impoundments. The Act, known as the Congressional Budget and Impoundment Control Act of 1974, stipulates that if the President *defers* the expenditure of funds, either house can pass a resolution forcing him to release them. If he believes certain moneys should not be spent at all, he may propose a *rescission* of them; however, both houses must approve this rescission within 45 days or he must release the funds at the end of that period. Thus Congress must take positive steps to prevent the deferring of the expenditure of funds but need take no action to eventually release moneys that Presidents refuse to spend at all.

Despite the passage of the 1974 law, presidential impoundments have continued. To date, Congress has been more willing to allow deferrals of expenditures to stand—by not passing resolutions against them—than it has been to approve of rescissions within the forty-five-day period. In the early months of the Carter administration, a spending issue emerged as the first major controversy between the Congress and the new President. Carter proposed that funds be cut off for certain water-resource projects, and angry legislators expressed their intention to use the powers granted Congress under the 1974 Act to see to it that funds that might eventually be appropriated for such projects would be spent.

Thus the provision of money for the activities of the bureaucracy is a process shared by both Congress and the President. While one may think of budgets, appropriations, and expenditures as dull, bookkeeping kinds of operations, in reality they are the stuff of which public policy is made. For the allocation of money reflects decisions involving priorities, preferences, and values; as political scientist James Davis Jr. suggests, it "converts hopes and symbols into reality."

This being the case, the process by which funds are allocated to various governmental programs is a highly *political* one. As Aaron Wildavsky describes the process, it involves a number of persons who assume different roles and employ various calculations and strategies. Department heads serve as *advocates* of their agencies and programs, calculating the amount of their requests on the basis of how much the OBM and the Congress are likely to cut from their budget; the OBM, acts *to protect the President* against an overweening budget, but at the same time attempts to increase spending for the Chief Executive's favorite programs; the House Appropriations Committee adopts the role of *guardian of the Treasury* against raids by overambitious bureaucrats and selfish interest groups; its Senate counterpart conceives of itself as a *Court of Appeals* for groups whose essential programs have been emasculated by the niggardly House; and finally, the Chief Executive, strives to *protect the financial stability* of the nation, while also supporting the favored programs of a variety of groups that helped to put him in office.

Personnel

As we have already seen, Congress has the ultimate authority in determining the structure of the executive branch, including the major positions in the departments and subunits, through which a broad range of governmental programs is administered. The Constitution also grants the national legislature broad authority over appointments to such positions. Article II, Section 2, does provide that the President shall appoint, *with the "advice and consent of the Senate,"* ambassadors, consuls, other public ministers, and Supreme Court justices), as well as "all other Officers of the United States whose appointments are not herein otherwise provided for, and which shall be established by law." However, that same section also empowers Congress by law to vest the appointment of "such inferior Officers as they think proper in the President alone, in the Courts of Law, or in the heads of departments."

Thus Congress generally controls how appointments in the bureaucracy are to be made. Only major diplomatic and judicial appointments specifically require presidential nomination and senatorial confirmation; otherwise, it is up to Congress to decide whether the appointment to a particular position it creates (or allows the President to create with its permission) must follow the same nomination-confirmation procedure, or whether the President or some department head can make the appointment alone.

The general pattern is for Congress to allow the President alone to appoint persons with whom he works most closely on a personal basis, such as those who are in the White House Office. (We will examine this unit in the next section.) Other major officials in policy-making positions must be approved by the Senate. Finally, those in lesser or "inferior" positions are appointed by department heads rather than by the President.

Within this broad legal framework, political aspects of appointments to the bureaucracy have evolved over the years. The custom of "senatorial courtesy," which has been in effect since the Washington Administration, means that the Chief Executive must clear appointments to federal positions within a particular state with the senators of his own party from that state.* If the senator or senators involved do not approve the person nominated or have nominees of their own, as a matter of courtesy the entire Senate will refuse to confirm the appointment.

Senators are inclined to allow the President to have his way, however, in appointing officials whose offices have "national" jurisdiction or scope. For example, only eight times in the nation's history has the Senate refused to confirm a President's nominee for a cabinet post. The most recent occurrence of this was during the Eisenhower administration: the Senate voted against confirming Lewis Strauss as Secretary of Commerce, primarily because while serving as head of the Atomic Energy Commission, he incurred the wrath of Clinton Anderson of New Mexico, a powerful and respected member of the Senate. However, sometimes the President or the nominee himself will withdraw his name from consideration for a post, as Theodore Sorensen (a close presidential aide of President Kennedy) did when his nomination by Jimmy Carter as Director of the Central Intelligence Agency (CIA) ran into difficulties with many conservative senators in early 1977.

The Senate has been less deferential to the Chief Executive in appointments to the independent regulatory commissions, which are considered to be less close to the President than cabinet-level departments and more aligned with Congress. The Senate has also been more inclined to look into the particular qualifications of persons serving on such commissions and to be less tolerant of the use of such appointments for strictly political purposes. When President Ford nominated Warren Radman, former Attorney General of New Hampshire, as Chairman of the Interstate Commerce Commission just twenty days before the 1976 presidential primary in that state, the appointment was attacked by both Democrats *and* Republicans as a tactic to boost the President's chances in that primary; ultimately, because of this opposition, the nominee asked that his name be withdrawn.

In some instances, individual senators can be very influential in appointments to the bureaucracy. Several of the officials on independent regulatory

---

* Woodrow Wilson even consulted with senators of the opposite political party (Republican). However, more typically, if there are no senators of the President's party from a state, he will consult with the chairman of the state organization or with other persons prominent in state-party affairs.

commissions owed their appointments to the support of the late Senator Dirksen of Illinois, who, as Minority Leader, also forced President Nixon to withdraw the nomination of Dr. John Knowles as Assistant Secretary of Health, Education, and Welfare, even though he was the first choice of the departmental secretary, Robert Finch.

The other major power affecting the staffing of the bureaucracy, namely, the ability to *remove* persons from office who are not performing satisfactorily, is not provided for at all by the Constitution. Three of the Founding Fathers had differing views on the subject. James Madison took the position that removal was part of the executive power, while Thomas Jefferson said it was a matter that Congress had the authority to determine. Alexander Hamilton took an intermediate position, arguing that removal was linked to appointment: the same person or persons who were involved in the process of choosing an appointee should also be entitled to participate in his removal. If he were appointed by the President alone, the Chief Executive could remove him from office; if he had been confirmed by the Senate, then that body would have to consent to his removal.

Generally speaking, the Congress has been willing to allow the President alone to remove officials from office. However, as we have noted in chapter 12, the Tenure of Office Act of 1867 forbade the removal of officers appointed with the consent of the Senate, unless the Senate also agreed to the removal, and President Andrew Johnson's defiance of the Act in removing Secretary of War Stanton was made a major ground of the impeachment action initiated against him. The failure of the Senate to convict the President left the issue unresolved, as no case challenging the Act was brought before the Supreme Court.

Ultimately, however, the Court became involved in the issue. President Wilson removed a Postmaster General from office, and some years later, in *United States* v. *Meyer* (1926), the Court—speaking through Chief Justice Taft, himself a former President—upheld Wilson's action as an executive prerogative, thus supporting the view of Madison on removal. However, when Franklin Roosevelt later removed a member of the Federal Trade Commission not for the reasons set forth in the governing statute ("malfeasance" and "misfeasance" in office) but because his political philosophy regarding the governmental regulation of business differed from Roosevelt's own, the Court struck down FDR's action as unconstitutional in *Humphrey's Executor* v. *United States (1935)*. The Court distinguished the latter case from the former one on two grounds: (1) unlike the Post Office Department, the FTC "occupies no place in the executive department" (the justices did not say, however, what "place" the Commission *did* occupy), and (2) the Commission exercises not only executive but also quasi-legislative and quasi-judicial functions. Thus, officials of regulatory commissions and other agencies involved in such activities, can be removed from office only for the reasons set forth by Congress.

It should be understood, however, that the removal of government officials involves not only *legal* but highly *political* considerations as well. Even when Chief Executives possess the power to remove a person from office, they may be reluctant to do so because of his political popularity. Thus a number of Presidents of both political parties tolerated a variety of independent actions by the former head of the Federal Bureau of Investigation, J. Edgar Hoover, primarily because they feared that his dismissal would hurt them politically. Conversely, a number of years ago a member of the Federal Communications Commission, accused of favoring the awarding of a television franchise to a station in which he had a financial interest, resigned voluntarily in order to save President Eisenhower (who had appointed him) from political embarrassment.

Frequently it is the Congress rather than the President that is actually responsible for officials leaving office. For while the national legislature does not have the *direct authority* to remove such officials, congressional investigations can have the *indirect effect* of accomplishing that purpose. Thus both Dwight Eisenhower and Richard Nixon had their closest political associates (the former, Sherman Adams; the latter, H.R. Haldeman and John Ehrlichman) driven from office against their will because of the heat generated against them by congressional committees. Congress can also financially starve agencies headed by officials whom they disapprove or have the officials' functions transferred to another unit. Such actions led Harold Seidman, a veteran of the Washington bureaucracy for almost a quarter-century, to conclude that, "Probably more executive-branch officials have been fired or reassigned as a result of pressure from Congress than by the President."

Thus the President and Congress jointly determine the operation of the bureaucracy, providing it with the structure, the funds, and the staff needed to carry out a wide variety of governmental programs. The following section focuses on the first aspect of that operation—the organization of the bureaucracy.

THE ORGANIZATION OF THE EXECUTIVE BRANCH

We have already seen that one of the hallmarks of bureaucracy is a division of labor that facilitates specialization by function or task. Nowhere is that principle more evident than in the organization of the executive branch as represented in Figure 14.1. As the figure shows, a great variety of units dealing with different types of matters are included within the executive arm of the national government. It is possible, however, to place these units into several broad categories based on the essential functions and tasks they perform, as well as on the legal and political relationships that they enjoy with the President, the Congress, and with interests outside the government itself.

The White House Office

Closest to the President are the members of the White House Office, a part of the larger Executive Office of the President. They are, in the phrase of Patrick Anderson, "The President's men": he appoints them without the necessity of senatorial approval, assigns them whatever duties he deems appropriate, and removes them when they no longer serve his purposes. (The election of a new Chief Executive generally means a complete turnover in the composition of the White House Office.) Moreover, as the President's men, they are not subject to interrogation by Congressional committees.

The White House Office is organized to assist the President in his numerous tasks. Included are those assistants who write his speeches, arrange his appointments, plan his trips, facilitate his relationships with the press and other media, and smooth his way in dealings with Congress, with other executive branch officials, with political-party officials, and with interest-group representatives. Others advise him on matters of public policy, such as national security and

Figure 14.1
The executive branch of the U.S. Government.
Source: National Archives and Records Services, General Services Administration.

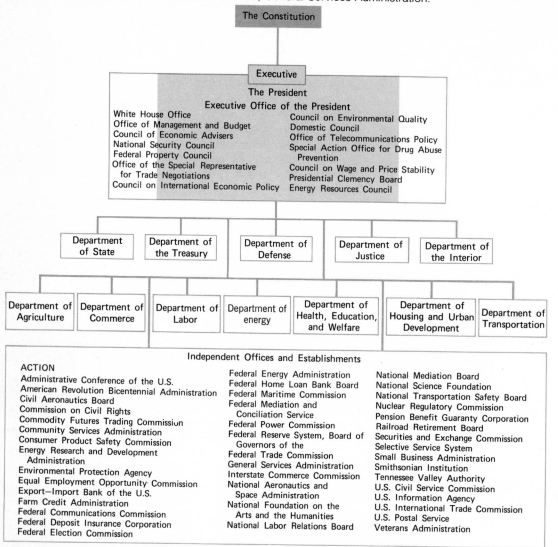

economic and domestic affairs. Although their tasks vary, they share a common concern: the welfare of the President. As Theodore Sorensen, a former aide to President Kennedy, described their responsibilities: "We were appointed for our ability to fulfill the President's needs and talk the President's language. We represented no man but John Kennedy."

The White House staff is populated with people whom the President knows well personally and in whom he has great trust and confidence. During the Kennedy administration, men like Sorensen (who was formerly on Kennedy's Senate staff), were much in evidence, along with Arthur Schlesinger, Jr., with whom the President had close intellectual ties. Also represented were political

President Carter meets with James Schlesinger, Secretary of Energy and Jim Fallows, Chief Speechwriter.

campaign associates like Lawrence O'Brien. Nixon also appointed to his White House office people he knew intimately, including Robert Finch and H.R. Haldeman, long-time friends from California politics; Bryce Harlow, who served in the Eisenhower White House Office while Nixon was Vice-President, and Leonard Garment, a former New York law partner, who was also a major figure in the 1968 presidential campaign. Gerald Ford's White House Staff included Philip Buchan and William Seidman from his home state of Michigan; Donald Rumsfeld and Rogers Morton, former associates in the House of Representatives; and Robert Hartman, who served as his Chief of Staff when he was Vice-President. Of the seven highest-level aides of Jimmy Carter, six were Georgians, including Presidential Assistant Hamilton Jordan, director of his 1976 presidential campaign, and Press Secretary Jody Powell, who had worked with Carter since his 1970 gubernatorial campaign. The importance of these two individuals in the Carter administration is indicated by Figure 14.2, showing their White House office locations along with those of other key Carter aides.

Figure 14.2
Carter's White House.
Source: *Newsweek* (17 Jan. 1977), p. 12.

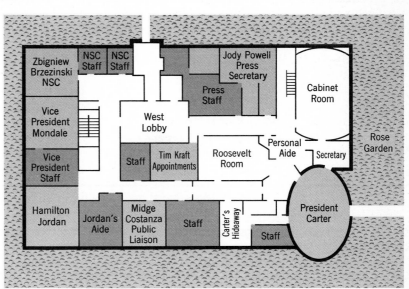

Flexibility is the major characteristic of the White House Office organization. Presidents Kennedy and Truman had relatively few persons in major positions in the Office—on the average, about fifteen; Eisenhower and Nixon generally used more than twice that number.* Positions also change. For the one traditional press secretary, Nixon substituted two: Ronald Ziegler was made special assistant for press relations, and Herbert Klein, who was made director of communications for the executive branch, was responsible for supervising and coordinating public statements made by units throughout the branch.

Presidents feel free to use a single person in a variety of capacities, switching him from assignment to assignment as they see fit. Theodore Sorensen was a jack-of-all-trades for John Kennedy (who referred to him as his "intellectual blood bank"): he wrote the President's speeches, helped formulate his legislative program, and acted as his trouble-shooter on a variety of public-policy issues. William Moyers performed a similarly broad array of duties for Lyndon Johnson, including a short stint as his press secretary. In making decisions about the internal organization and operation of the White House Office, the President applies a single criterion: "What is likely to serve my personal political interests most effectively?"

Other Units in the Executive Office of the President

The other units shown in Figure 14.1 that are located in the Executive Office of the President also have close relationships with him, but their personnel are not so much "the President's men." For example, their appointments must be confirmed by the Senate. Moreover, while the top officials in these units leave with a change in administration, many lower-level employees remain. Persons who serve in these posts tend to be specialists in their particular areas of responsibility, not generalists who occupy the positions in the White House Office. (Members of the Council of Economic Advisers are unlikely to be switched to another position in the Executive Office as are White House aides.) The President is less likely to be personally familar with them and frequently accepts recommendations from others about who would, for example, make a good chairman of the Council of Economic Advisers. Symbolically, White House staff men are generally located in the White House itself while others in the Executive Office are housed in a separate building across the street.

Most important of the units located in the Executive Office of the President is the Office of Management and Budget. Known as the Bureau of the Budget prior to its reorganization by President Nixon in 1970, the agency concentrated its efforts on helping the Chief Executive prepare his budget and legislative recommendations. It also assisted him in making decisions on whether or not to veto a bill: the agency's procedure was to get the reaction of executive-branch units to the bill in question. Nixon extended the organization's responsibilities to include other aspects of executive management, including the evaluation and coordination of existing governmental programs, improvement of executive-

---

* The White House Office staff mushroomed during the first Nixon administration: the total number of employees was 311 in 1970; one year later it was 600. It remained close to that level after Gerald Ford assumed the presidency and actually increased during the early months of the Carter administration despite the President's vow to reduce its size.

branch organization, the devising of information and management systems, and the development of executive talent.

Three other units in the Executive Office are especially important in providing advice and helping the President coordinate a wide variety of governmental activities. The Council of Economic Advisers (created by the Full Employment Act of 1946) is composed of three professional economists who advise the Chief Executive on his annual Economic Report to the nation and on the economic policies that his administration should pursue. As indicated in the previous chapter, the National Security Council advises the President on foreign, military, and domestic policy aspects of the nation's security. A comparable body, the Domestic Council (created by executive order of Richard Nixon in 1970), composed of various officials concerned with the country's internal problems, performs a similar integrating function for the President. Thus the Executive Office includes agencies responsible for initiating and coordinating programs in three broad areas of public policy with which the President is concerned—the economy, national security, and domestic affairs.

Also included in the Executive Office of the President are agencies to deal with problems that are thought to require special presidential attention. Thus the *Office of Economic Opportunity* was originally located in the Office, reflecting President Johnson's particular concern with his major Great Society programs. During the Nixon administration, special units were created to concentrate on environmental quality, consumer affairs, telecommunications policy, and drug-abuse prevention. Gerald Ford added a *Council on Wage and Price Stability* and another on *Presidential Clemency*. Frequently, however, such specialized agencies are favorites of a particular Chief Executive and may not be so highly regarded by his successor: President Nixon first transferred some operations of the OEO—an agency he inherited—to other units in the bureaucracy and then tried to kill the OEO altogether; in turn, Nixon's own agencies on drug-use prevention and telecommunications policy were deemphasized by Gerald Ford.

The Cabinet Departments

The next general category of units in terms of closeness to the President is the twelve departments granted cabinet rank by Congress. The heads of these departments (called *secretaries*) are appointed by the President with the consent

President Carter meets with Cabinet members and advisors.

of the Senate. As previously suggested, however, only rarely does the Senate refuse to confirm a President's nominee for a cabinet post; it is his right to choose cabinet officers and to remove them if he is dissatisfied with the way they are performing. When a new President comes into office, an entirely new cabinet team generally comes in with him.*

Although Congress does not generally interfere with the President's selections for the cabinet, other factors place some real limitations on his choices. For one thing, some cabinet posts require special experience and expertise: the Secretary of the Treasury, for example, must have a broad knowledge of financial affairs. The President is also expected to introduce some partisan balance into the makeup of the cabinet. The losing faction at the previous national convention is often permitted to name some cabinet officials: several "Taft men," for instance, were included in Eisenhower's initial cabinet. Similarly, both liberal and conservative elements of a party are usually represented. If a national crisis exists or an election is close, the President may even include members of the opposition party in his cabinet: Franklin Roosevelt's wartime cabinet included two Republicans; John Kennedy, and eventually Richard Nixon, chose persons of the opposite party for cabinet posts.

A former congressman is usually included, presumably to help the President establish good relationships with that body. Most Chief Executives (including Nixon) have considered it politic to include a Southerner in the cabinet; traditionally the Secretary of Interior comes from the western part of the United States, where most of the vast public lands under the department's jurisdiction are located. In fact many of the departments have a "clientele"—that is, particular groups that they serve:† thus the Commerce Department caters to business and the Department of Labor to the working man. In making appointments to these cabinet positions, the President takes into account the attitudes of interest groups toward the man who is to head the department: he would not, for example, appoint a Secretary of Agriculture who is unacceptable to the farmers of the country.

Four of the twelve departments, however—State, Defense, Treasury, and Justice—do not have as specialized a clientele as the other eight departments. The first departments to be established in the federal government, their functions relate to general problems of governance rather than the needs of a particular segment of our society. Because their activities are so basic, Presidents typically pay more attention to these four departments and are inclined to place "strong" men in such positions. Thus the two most prominent men in the Eisenhower cabinet were Secretary of State John Foster Dulles and George Humphrey, the Secretary of the Treasury; Robert McNamara, the Secretary of Defense, and Attorney-General Robert Kennedy were the most powerful members of the Kennedy administration; and Attorney-General John Mitchell and

---

* A Vice-President who succeeds to the office of President is likely to keep the same team for the transition period, as Lyndon Johnson did after John Kennedy's assassination and Gerald Ford did after Richard Nixon's resignation.

† The composition of the cabinet reflects the political power of various interest groups: one sign that a group has arrived politically is the establishment of a cabinet-level department to serve its needs.

Secretary of State Henry Kissinger were the leading figures in the Nixon administration.

One close student of the subject, Thomas Cronin, suggests that the Secretaries of State, Defense, Treasury, and the Attorney-General constitute an "inner" cabinet in contrast to the "outer" cabinet (i.e. the heads of the other eight departments). The former are closer to the presidential orbit in terms of sharing his general perspective on problems; because of this, they have a "counseling" role with the Chief Executive. In contrast, the latter represent special interests that the President would like to subordinate to general concerns of his administration; as a result of this basic conflict, members of the outer cabinet are more likely to adopt an "advocate's" (rather than a "counseling") role with the President.

The Independent Agencies

The independent offices and establishments listed in Figure 14.1 are all "independent" in the sense that they are not part of any cabinet department, but their degree of independence from the President and the Congress varies. There are four major types of these independent agencies.

One type performs a specific function and is headed by *one administrator;* examples are the *National Aeronautics and Space Administration* and the *Veterans Administration.* Their relationships with the President parallel those of cabinet departments.* Major administrators are appointed by the Chief Executive with the consent of the Senate and are removable by his action alone. Even so, the heads of these independent agencies frequently stay in office after a new President takes over; the late General Lewis Hershey, for example, served as head of the Selective Service System for a succession of Presidents of both political parties until he retired because of age. Seidman describes the administrations of such agencies as occupying a "no-man's land" between the "President's men" and "agencies of the Congress."

Included in the latter type by Seidman are the seven *independent regulatory agencies,* which are administered through boards rather than through single administrative heads.† This general group of agencies includes the Civil Aeronautics Board (CAB), Federal Communications Commission (FCC), Federal Maritime Commission (FMC), Federal Power Commission (FPC), Federal Trade Commission (FTC), Interstate Commerce Commission (ICC), and the Securities and Exchange Commission (SEC). The members of these boards are less subject to presidential control because they have fixed terms (five to seven years) and cannot be removed by the President except for causes set forth in the statute creating each agency. Moreover, the commissioners' terms are usually "staggered" (that is, overlapping) so that few (if any) expire simultaneously. This combination of lengthy, staggered terms and removal only for cause makes board members relatively free from presidential control and influence.

* Some cabinet departments were originally independent agencies that acquired cabinet status when they became more important politically.
† It is considered to be easier for a President to influence the thinking of a single administrator than to affect the attitudes of a multimember board.

The rationale for insulating these commissions from presidential control is that they are concerned with regulating activities of major private industries and so should be free of partisan politics that might interfere with their objectivity and fairness. (Most boards are required to be composed of members of both major parties.) The result of this policy, however, is to create a political vacuum into which other forces rush, including not only congressmen, but also groups supposedly regulated by the agencies. Thus the railroads take a great interest in the Interstate Commerce Commission, which regulates the fares that they charge and the routes that they follow, and television-station owners exert influence over the Federal Communications Commission, which determines the conditions that they must meet to obtain and retain their licenses. As a result, the special interests that are supposedly regulated by governmental agencies frequently end up controlling the regulators.

Included in the third major category of independent agencies are the government corporations, exemplified by the *Tennessee Valley Authority* and the *United States Postal Service*, agencies which are relatively free of control by either the President or the Congress. Because these agencies perform commercial functions (the TVA builds dams and channels, and produces and sells electrical power, while the Postal Service distributes mail), they are organized along the lines of a private corporation, with a governing board that makes policy for the unit. Like the commissioners of the independent regulatory agencies, the board members of government corporations are appointed by the President with the consent of the Senate and serve long, staggered terms to prevent any one President from controlling the activities of those units. Furthermore, the corporations are less subject to financial control by the President or the Congress than are other executive departments and agencies because they are not dependent on annual appropriations for their operations. Rather, long-term appropriations are provided (Congress, for example, is committed to a fifteen-year funding program for the Postal Service); in addition, corporations furnish some of their own financing (the Postal Service uses revenues that it generates from its own activities and is also empowered to borrow money by issuing bonds). Government corporations are therefore free of the usual process

The Federal Reserve Board.

of defending their estimates for the coming fiscal year before the Office of Management and Budget, the President, and the Congress. Although their operations are reviewed annually by all three, since the corporations are not requesting funds, the scrutiny tends to be less severe than it is for other executive units.

The final type of independent agency includes those providing *central services and controls* such as the *Civil Service Commission* and the *General Services Administration*. The former establishes overall policies and guidelines governing such matters as the recruitment, classification, evaluation, promotion, and termination of all employees covered by the Civil Service Commission system described in the following section. The latter controls buildings, supplies, transportation and communications facilities, and records utilized by all agencies. The CSC and the GSA provide services to, and regulate the activities of, other governmental units rather than the private individuals and groups with which most public agencies are concerned.

Thus, as political scientist Stephen Bailey has suggested, the executive branch is a "many-splintered" thing, comprising a variety of organizations with different functions and different legal and political relationships with the President, Congress, and outside groups. The employees of these organizations collectively constitute the executive-branch personnel, the bureacrats.

THE BUREAUCRATS

As we have seen, federal bureaucrats have become an inviting target of criticism for politicians and citizens alike. For one thing, their numbers are thought to rise dramatically every year. For another, a popular stereotype exists of the federal bureaucrat as a petty clerk employed by the *Department of Health, Education, and Welfare* and who is located in Washington, D.C.

As a matter of fact, the realities of public employment contradict both of the above assumptions. Rather than burgeoning in numbers, the size of the federal bureaucracy has been comparatively stable in recent years. In 1955 some 2.4 million civilians worked for the national government; by 1969 that figure has grown to 3 million; in 1976 it was at 2.8 million.* Measured as a proportion of the total U.S. work force (which grew considerably over the period of two decades), the percentage of federal employees actually declined from some 4 percent in 1955 to 3 percent in 1976.

Nor does the stereotype of the clerk square with the great variety of occupations in the federal service. Employees of the national government represent a great variety of skills, similar to those possessed by persons who work in private enterprise. White-collar employees run the gamut from professionally trained doctors, lawyers, and engineers to persons involved in more traditional clerical and general office duties. Moreover, almost 600,000 federal employees (about one-fifth of the total) are blue-collar workers who operate mobile industrial equipment, do manual labor, repair aircraft, and engage in other trades.

As Table 14.1 indicates, it is *not Health, Education, and Welfare* that harbors the most federal employees; it is *Defense*. The latter, with almost one million

---

* This situation is to be contrasted with the rapid growth of public employees at the state and local level from some 4.5 million in 1955 to over 10 million in 1976.

Who says government workers are all paper-pushers?

civilian employees, has almost seven times as many persons working for it as does HEW, which does not even have as many employees as two of the major independent agencies, the Postal Service and the Veterans Administration. These three largest units of the federal government (Defense, Postal Service, and the Veterans Administration) together employed almost 1.9 million of the some 2.8 million civilians that worked for the national government in 1976.

Nor are federal civilian workers concentrated in the area of Washington, D.C., as is commonly supposed; 300,000 (or one in nine) lived there in 1974. The rest were located in every state in the country. Almost as many resided in California as in the nation's capital; over 100,000 lived outside the United States.

Thus the federal bureaucracy is composed of persons with a wide variety of occupational skills who work in diverse agencies (see Fig. 14.1) and are located in every state of the Union as well as abroad. The compensation they receive for their services also varies greatly: cabinet members in 1976 received $63,000 a year, while persons at the lowest levels of the pay scale earned only about $6000. Thus the federal bureaucracy represents a broad economic cross section of the American people.

The question remains how well the federal bureaucracy represents women and minority groups in the United States. A 1974 survey by the U.S. Civil Service Commission showed that women (who at that time were 51 percent of the population) held about one-third of the white-collar jobs in the federal service. However, the proportion of women who served in different types of federal employment varied greatly. Almost half of the clerical workers were women, as compared to fewer than one in five who served in an administrative capacity. Over 70 percent of employees in lower grades of the federal bureau-

Table 14.1
Number of Civilians
Employed by Cabinet
Departments and Selected
Independent Agencies,
February 1977

Unit	Employees
Cabinet Departments	
Agriculture	111,247
Commerce	38,352
Defense	993,767
Health, Education, and Welfare	156,527
Housing and Urban Development	16,573
Interior	77,649
Justice	53,249
Labor	16,509
State	29,895
Transportation	74,853
Treasury	134,382
Independent Agencies	
U.S. Postal Service	652,745
Veterans Administration	223,261

Source: U.S. Civil Service Commission, Monthly Release of Federal Civilian Workforce Statistics.

cracy (G.S.* 1 through G.S. 6, earning from $5500 to $13,000) were women; in the middle-grade positions (G.S. 7 through G.S. 12—$11,000 to $25,000) that figure fell to 25 percent; while the proportion of employees occupying the highest levels of the federal bureaucracy (G.S. 13 through G.S. 18—$23,000 to $38,000) dropped drastically to less than 5 percent. However, there were some federal agencies that did employ a fairly high percentage of women in such top-level positions: leading the list was the National Foundation on the Arts and Humanities with over one-third of its G.S. 13-G.S. 18 positions occupied by women.

The general record of federal employment for minorities is clearly better than it is for women. Another 1974 survey by the CSC showed that blacks constituted 16 percent of all federal employees, whereas they were 11 percent of the total U.S. population. Persons with Spanish surnames were slightly under-represented (3.3 percent of all federal employees as against 5 percent of the national population), while American Indians and Asian Americans each constituted 1 percent of the federal bureaucracy even though their total proportion of the nation's people was 2/5 and 3/5 of 1 percent respectively.

As with women, however, most of these minority groups were concentrated disproportionately in the lower levels of the federal service. Most affected were blacks, who held 28 percent of the jobs in the low G.S. 1-G.S. 6 category; 8 percent of those in the middle range (G.S.7-G.S. 12), and only 3 percent of those in the upper grades (G.S. 13-G.S. 18). However, the situation was quite different for Asian Americans. Their proportion in each of the three general grades was the same: 1 percent of the total.

Why should Americans of Asian ancestry fare comparatively better in obtaining prestigious federal jobs than do members of other minority groups? One possible explanation is their higher level of education. As Figure 14.3 indicates, Asian Americans employed by the federal government are not only better educated than their counterparts of other minority groups; they also have more education than *non*-minority men and women who work in the federal bureaucracy. The figure also indicates that women may possibly be disadvantaged in federal employment by their level of education: women from the various social groups listed in the figure all have less schooling than males of similar backgrounds.

Thus diversity is the hallmark of the national bureaucracy as a broad range of persons with different occupational, educational, and social backgrounds fill its various positions. However, it is possible to place these various types in two broad categories. One is composed of those who dedicate themselves to public service (career service) and enjoy security of tenure in their job. The other comprises persons in political posts in the bureaucracy who typically come into office for a limited period and then generally move on to positions in private enterprise or to other jobs in public life.

The Career Service

The principle that federal employees should hold positions on the basis of merit rather than as a reward for their political activities first became established as

Woman near the top: Dr. Marjorie Berlincourt, Head, Summer Fellowship Program, National Endowment for the Humanities.

---

* G.S. stands for General Schedule, a system developed by the Civil Service Commission for classifying all merit positions in the federal service.

Figure 14.3
Educational attainment of men and women employees by minority (and nonminority)
group, August 1974.
Source: U.S. Civil Service Commission, *Federal Civilian Manpower Statistics*, p. 39.

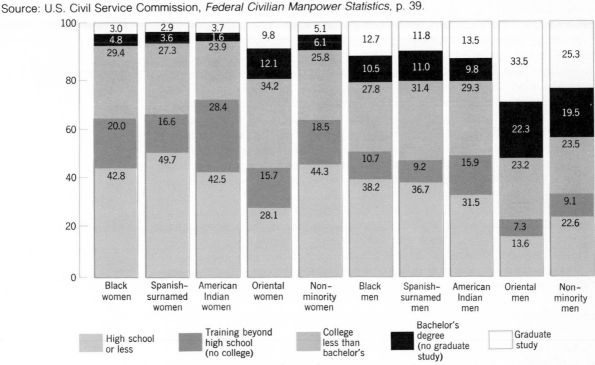

a matter of law with the passage of the Pendleton Act in 1883. Over the years this principle has become so accepted that today almost all employees of the executive branch are under one or another kind of merit system for selection and tenure. Over two million are governed by the rules of the United States Civil Service Commission regulating entrance requirements and general working conditions. In addition, some federal agencies, because of their special needs, have their own merit systems. Included in this group are such well-known organizations as the Federal Bureau of Investigation, the Central Intelligence Agency, the Atomic Energy Commission, the Tennessee Valley Authority, the U.S. Postal Service, and the Foreign Service.

These various merit systems operate on similar principles. Persons are hired on the basis of their abilities. Generally, this means performing well on a competitive examination: agencies are typically authorized to fill a vacancy from among the three candidates scoring highest on the test. Not all examinations are competitive, however; if a job calls for professional or technical skills that are in relatively short supply, it may be filled by someone who gets a minimum score on the examination. And some positions that involve policy-making or confidential relationships with high governmental officials may require no examination at all.

Working conditions are governed by definite rules and procedures. Positions and pay are ranked on the basis of difficulty as reflected in the General Schedule (G.S. classifications 1 through 18 referred to above) that govern all organizations coming under the jurisdiction of the Civil Service Commission. (Agencies with their own merit systems use similar methods for classifying positions.) In-service training is provided for employees,* and promotions are based on performance on the job. A career employee can be dismissed only for "cause" after procedural safeguards (hearings and the like) have been satisfied.

Critics of the merit system charge that it is essentially a negative one that rewards docile functionaries who carefully fulfill its numerous requirements (including filling out countless forms and reports) rather than imaginative persons who relish innovation and experimentation in the public's business. While such a blanket charge against all public servants is undoubtedly exaggerated, the fact remains that the civil service system does seem to appeal to persons concerned with job tenure and security. The turnover rate for federal employees is much lower than it is for persons working in private industry. Moreover, there is a tendency for employees to stay in the same agency and to rise in its hierarchy through seniority rather than transferring to better positions in another organization in the executive branch.

Traditionally, federal employees have been expected to give up certain *economic and political liberties* enjoyed by persons working in the private sector. One is the right to join unions and to engage in collective bargaining over compensation and working conditions, a matter already discussed in chapter 6. Another is the right to engage in political activities. In recent years, however, federal employees (like their counterparts at the state and local levels) have become much less willing to accept such restrictions and have made concerted efforts to get them lifted.

Restrictions on political activities of federal career employees have been imposed under the rationale that such restrictions are necessary to preserve a neutral civil service, free from partisan influences. Regulations of the Civil Service Commission, together with the Hatch Act passed by Congress in 1939, protect federal employees from being coerced into making financial contributions or working in a partisan campaign. They also prohibit employees from voluntarily participating in many political activities. At the same time, federal employees do retain certain rights, including that of voting and expressing their opinions on political matters.

In recent years some career service employees have taken the position that limitations on their political rights interfere with their First Amendment freedoms. However, their attempt to have existing restrictions declared unconstitutional on that ground was rejected by the Supreme Court in *U.S. Civil Service Commission* v. *National Association of Letter Carriers* (1973), upholding the Hatch Act. Subsequently, they turned to the legislative arena to accomplish their purposes. In 1976, the Democratic Congress passed legislation that would have allowed public employees to participate in partisan campaigns and run for office, but President Ford successfully vetoed the bill. However, with Ford's successor, Democratic President Jimmy Carter, recommending such legislation to the Congress in 1977, it stood a good chance of eventually being enacted into law.

---

* One notable example is the Federal Executive Institute, which conducts intensive eight-week sessions led by academic and career professionals for upper-level executives (those in G.S. 16–G.S. 18 positions).

Political Executives

"Political Executives" are those who hold policy-making positions, among them officials of the Executive Office of the President, secretaries of cabinet departments, and the heads of independent offices and establishments. They also include second- and third-level officials, such as assistant and under secretaries of departments and heads of certain subsidiary "bureaus," "administrations," "divisions," and "services." All told, only a few thousand persons serve as federal political executives.

Recruiting and retaining capable persons for these positions constitutes one of the major personnel problems faced by the federal service. Typically, a newly-elected President chooses some knowledgeable person to lead a talent search for able men and women in private industry, state and local government, or academe to fill the 200 or so top posts in the bureaucracy. While many are flattered by such requests, they must obtain leaves of absence from their present positions and, if they are persons employed by industry, generally take a cut in salary as well. Moreover, even if such persons agree to come to Washington, they often leave subsequently, because of financial reasons, to accept better-paying positions in private industry or even, in some cases, in state or local government.*

Such losses have severe consequences because while political executives are relatively few in number, they are vital to the functioning of the government. They bear the responsibility of converting political goals into concrete programs and results. Because of their role, they are seldom technicians or specialists; rather, they are "politicians" who spend most of their time dealing with individuals and groups, both inside and outside government, that can help or impede their mission.

The single most important official to a political executive is, of course, the President, to whom in most instances he ultimately owes his appointment. In turn, the executive's own power to appoint and remove major political officials under him is dependent on support from the President. How his unit stands within the executive branch also frequently depends on the actions taken by the President under a reorganization statute authorized by Congress. The executive also depends on the President's recommendations for financing and legislative proposals.

Given the vast responsibilities of the President, it is natural that a political executive has relatively few, if any, direct contacts with the Chief Executive. Accordingly, he must spend time cultivating the men around the President, particularly those on the White House staff and in the Office of Management and Budget. And because the operations of executive units are not autonomous but instead are closely related to those of other organizations, political executives spend time "touching base" with their counterparts in other agencies of the federal government.

However, as we have seen, Congress shares with the President all the major powers that affect the bureaucracy. Senators can block presidential appoint-

---

* A recent case in point is that of Terrell Bell, who was reported to have resigned his $37,800 position as U.S. Commissioner of Education to become Commissioner of Education and head of the Board of Regents of Utah at a salary of $48,600.

ments and, in some instances, themselves determine who will be placed in charge of government agencies. Congressmen can also force executive officials out of office through investigations. While the Chief Executive can propose the budget for each agency, the Congress ultimately determines the moneys that will actually be appropriated for its operations. And under the Congressional Budget and Impoundment Control Act of 1974, Congress can force the President to spend those moneys. Finally, the Congress has the final say over which agency will administer a particular program as well as over the internal operation of that agency.

While the entire Congress ultimately affects how an agency fares, a political executive is most concerned with the committees and subcommittees that have special power over his organization. Included are those that deal with the substantive policy area in which the agency operates, pass on its budget requests, and oversee its administration. A political executive must establish good relations with particular committee and subcommittee chairmen as well as with key members of congressional staffs, on whom the chairmen depend heavily for information and advice.

Thus the political executive is subject to the actions of both the President and the Congress. In a very real sense, he must serve two political masters. Further, he finds himself competing with his counterparts in other executive agencies over scarce funds and over jurisdiction. Thus for many years the Forest Service in the Department of Agriculture and the National Park Service in the Department of the Interior have vied for the control of vacant lands, particularly in the western part of the United States. Similarly, the Defense Department's Army Corps of Engineers and the Interior Department's Bureau of Reclamation have battled for the right to develop the waterways of the nation.

Under such circumstances, a political executive finds it necessary to secure political allies outside as well as inside the formal structure of government. One natural outside source is his "clientele." Thus the *Veterans Administration* establishes close relationships with the *American Legion* and the *Veterans of Foreign Wars,* and the *Office of Education* does the same with the *National Educational Association,* the *American Federation of Teachers,* and other professional educators. The support of such interest groups can prove to be very useful in the political process.

Many political executives also seek to build a broader basis of outside support than that provided by special interest groups; they look to the general public as well. Perhaps best known for its activities in this regard is the *Federal Bureau of Investigation.* As many visitors to Washington, D.C. know, the most interesting tour of governmental agencies is provided by the Bureau. It has also succeeded in making itself the subject of many magazine articles, books, movies, and even television series, which extol the virtues of the "G-men." In the process its former director, J. Edgar Hoover, became a Washington legend, virtually immune from control not only by the Attorney General of the United States, of whose office the Bureau is a part (witness the difficulties between Hoover and recent Attorneys-General Robert Kennedy and Ramsey Clark), but also by the President of the United States.

While a political executive spends most of his time courting outside individuals and groups, he has another important constituency he must also cultivate: *the employees of his own agency.* Particularly important are senior civil servants who generally have served a long time in the organization. With their superior knowledge of the agency's internal operations—as well as of the personnel and procedures of other executive agencies, key congressional committees, and concerned interest groups—these permanent employees are in a position either to facilitate or to impede the policies and desires of the political executive under whom they serve. Lower-level employees also look to the political executive for leadership and expect him to protect the agency's interests in perennial battles involving adequate funding for, and jurisdiction over, important governmental programs.

Maintaining good relations with all these individuals and groups is a difficult and delicate task for a political executive. In many instances he is subject to competing demands. The President may cut his agency's budget, while the chairman of a key congressional committee or subcommittee may advise the political executive to work behind the scenes with him to help get the cut restored. The Chief Executive may advise him to tone down efforts to enforce rules and regulations against business concerns, while senior civil servants and other employees of the agency urge him to step up enforcement as necessary to preserve the essential mission of their organization.

Political executives placed under such cross pressures must decide how to deal with the situation. With skillful maneuvering they may be able to steer a compromise course of action that will satisfy the contending parties. However, in some cases compromise is not possible, and they must favor one side over another. An executive's loyalty to, or shared political philosophy with, the President—or his ambition for other more important assignments in the executive branch—may lead him to throw his lot in with the Chief Executive. Conversely, a calculation that a powerful committee chairman will be around longer than the President—or an executive's conversion to the values and mission of the agency as seen by its permanent employees—may result in his deciding to go against the wishes of the President who appointed him.

If the political executive chooses the latter course of action, he will generally find ready allies outside his own agency. One source of support is the congressional committees and subcommittees that tend to favor his agency's programs. Another is the interest groups that stand to benefit from such programs.

These three-way alliances of executive units, congressional committees and subcommittees, and interest groups have been called "whirlpools of power" and "subsystems" operating within the larger political system. However described, they point to the existence of enduring political relationships that advance common interests. For example, expanding and improving the services provided by the Veterans Administration increases the prestige and influence of its director and raises the morale of the agency's permanent employees; a program of better benefits for veterans also naturally pleases the American Legion and the Veterans of Foreign Wars. By the same token, such a program is usually favorably regarded by congressional committees and subcommittees involved with veterans' affairs, since senators and representatives generally seek assignments to committees that deal with matters in which they have a personal interest and sympathy.

One of the major problems in controlling the bureaucracy is to prevent these three-way alliances or subsystems from dominating the making of public policy. The following section analyzes some of the major techniques that have been utilized to try to exercise control over these alliances and over other aspects of bureaucratic activities as well.

ATTEMPTS TO CONTROL THE BUREAUCRACY

We have seen that both the President and the Congress possess constitutional powers over the structure, financing, and personnel of the executive branch. By using these weapons judiciously, and with an appreciation of the complexity of bureaucratic politics, both branches are in a position to exercise some control over the bureaucracy.

Presidential Attempts to Control the Bureaucracy

While the President is the Chief Executive and Administrator under our constitutional system, he experiences great difficulties in making members of the bureaucracy responsive to his wishes. Franklin Roosevelt, the epitome of a strong President, experienced great frustration in influencing administrators. Bemoaning his inability to get action and results from the Treasury and State Departments, he went on to exclaim:

> But the Treasury and State Departments put together are nothing compared with the Na-a-vy. The admirals are really something to cope with—and I should know. To change anything in the Na-a-vy is like punching a feather bed. You punch it with your right and you punch it with your left until you are finally exhausted, and then you find the damn bed just as it was before you started punching.

A generation later another ambitious Chief Executive experienced similar difficulties. Arthur Schlesinger Jr. reports in his biography of John Kennedy that the resistance Kennedy encountered from executive officials was almost as great as the opposition he received from the members of the rival constitutional branch, the Congress.

A number of factors contribute to the President's inability to control the bureaucracy. He can hardly be expected to supervise the activities of the almost 3 million persons who have been on the executive-branch payroll in recent years. Moreover, he has no say at all in the appointment or the removal of the overwhelming number of them who come under one or more of the merit systems utilized for permanent civil servants. And while in theory he exercises such prerogatives over political executives, in reality his lack of first-hand knowledge of personnel matters is such that he must depend upon others for recommendations for appointments to high posts and for removing individuals who do not perform well in their jobs.

Adding to the problem of presidential control over the bureaucracy is the fact that the Congress shares all his major powers over that body. The national legislators are in a position to thwart his reorganization plans, starve his favorite programs while taking good care of their own, investigate an agency he supports, and even to have some influence on who occupies the major policy-making posts in the executive branch.

Finally, and perhaps most important, is the conflict that exists between the values and perspectives of the President as compared to those of what Schlesinger calls the "permanent government." The Chief Executive typically takes a broad view of the nation's needs and is interested in fitting the activities of individual executive organizations into his overall political program. In doing so, he must establish a system of priorities that gives precedence to some governmental programs and agencies over others and that also limits total governmental expenditures. His time frame is also shaped by the realities of electoral and congressional politics: he wants to implement his campaign promises before the next presidential election, when the voters will pass judgment on his performance in office, and he also knows that his best chance for success with the Congress is during the honeymoon period just after he is inaugurated.

Members of the "permanent government" typically look at matters very differently from the President: their world is smaller than his. They are interested in their own agency and its programs and are unwilling to see them cut back in the interest of the President's overall system of priorities, economy, and efficiency. They are also less sensitive to political constraints and realities than the President and operate on a calendar different from his. While the Chief Executive thinks in terms of presidential terms and congressional sessions, they look at more long-range considerations, such as the past history and long-term future of a program, or the political lifespan of an agency head or congressional chairman.

All Presidents face these same basic problems in controlling the bureaucracy. However, they react differently to such problems and develop diverse techniques to deal with them. The following discussion focuses on the methods employed by four recent Presidents—two Democrats and two Republicans—in attempting to tame the bureaucracy and convert it to their own purposes and goals.

Franklin Roosevelt. While Roosevelt is normally remembered as a powerful legislative leader and masterful manipulator of the press and public opinion, he was also an innovative administrator. He handled bureaucratic leaders essentially by playing them off against each other. FDR created overlapping responsibilities among different administrative units: work-relief programs came under the joint jurisdiction of Harry Hopkins, head of the Works Program Administration, and Harold Ickes of the Public Works Administration. Termed the competitive theory of administration, his policy was deliberately designed to create rivalries between individuals, a practice that he justified on the basis that each person would therefore try to do a better job than his counterpart. (This technique also provided FDR with more information than he would have gained from any one person alone and so enabled him to stay on top of situations.) Roosevelt also frequently bypassed the chain of administrative command by dealing directly with assistant secretaries and bureau chiefs without informing cabinet officials (their superiors) of such actions.

Harry Hopkins, Head of Works Program Administration.

Roosevelt's use of his cabinet reflected his general philosophy of administration. His cabinet was made up of persons representing a broad spectrum of political persuasions, from the conservative Secretary of the Treasury, Will Wooden, to the liberal Frances Perkins (the first woman ever appointed to the cabinet), who served as Secretary of Labor. Given this diversity of political views, Roosevelt made no effort to utilize the cabinet as a policymaking or coordinating body. He rather used it as a sounding board to test how actions he considered taking would be received by the various clientele groups represented by department heads sitting in the cabinet.

During the early years of World War II, FDR tried to do what no previous President had ever done: give important administrative responsibilities to his Vice-President. Henry Wallace was made chairman of a succession of economic boards entrusted with overseeing the production of war material. However, Wallace soon became embroiled in a series of battles with Secretary of State Cordell Hull, and Secretary of Commerce Jesse Jones, and Roosevelt ended the conflict within his administration by abolishing a key Wallace-headed board and transferring its responsibilities to a new agency under another chairman. So ended a noble experiment in making a Vice-President an important administrator, a practice that neither Roosevelt nor his successors would repeat.*

A more successful tactic that FDR used to control the bureaucracy was to develop *his own counterbureaucracy.* Included in that latter category were heads of newly created agencies operating outside traditional departments, such as the Securities and Exchange Commission (SEC) and the National Labor Relations Board (NLRB), which regulated the stock exchange and labor-management relations, respectively. Roosevelt also utilized free-wheeling "trouble-shooters" like Thomas Corcoran and Harry Hopkins who, as the President's personal representatives, were given *ad hoc* assignments to cut red tape and overcome obstacles to the settlement of disputes in both domestic and foreign policy. And, as previously indicated, in 1939 another form of FDR's personal bureaucracy became institutionalized with the creation of the Executive Office of the President.

Dwight Eisenhower. Directly opposed to the unstructured, competitive system of administration employed by FDR was the systematic *staff approach* followed by President Eisenhower. Based upon methods he learned as a career military man, Ike's administration was characterized by an extensive delegation of authority to subordinates and a strict adherence to a chain-of-command principle. Thus unlike FDR, Eisenhower clearly delineated responsibilities so as to minimize overlapping responsibilities. He also dealt only with the top man in an agency and expected subordinates to take their orders from their superiors.

Presidential Assistant, Sherman Adams.

The man that made Ike's staff system operate was Assistant-to-the-President Sherman Adams. All memoranda were funneled through Adams and personally analyzed by him; the familiar notation "O.K. S.A." had to appear on a paper before Eisenhower would look at it. Ike also expected Adams to summarize the pro and con arguments on a particular matter and reduce them to a one-page memorandum that the President could examine in a short period of time. Beyond this, Adams became the doorkeeper of the Oval Office: no individual or group could see the President without the permission of the Assistant to the President. Because Adams conceived his job as protecting Ike from unnecessary distractions and intrusions, that permission was frequently denied, which led some frustrated persons to tab Adams as "the abominable No-man."†

* A possible exception is President Carter's early assignment of important administrative responsibilities to his Vice-President, Walter Mondale. It remains to be seen whether this practice will continue.

† Adams's preeminence also led to a joke that made the rounds in Washington during Ike's administration. One person commented: "Wouldn't it be terrible if Eisenhower died and Nixon became President?" The counterploy followed: "It would be even worse if Sherman Adams died and Eisenhower became President!"

Eisenhower even applied his staff system to the operations of the cabinet. Instead of allowing that body to meet infrequently and with little advance planning as most Chief Executives do, Ike appointed a secretary to facilitate the work of the cabinet. Papers outlining various arguments and options for handling matters were circulated among cabinet members and their assistants prior to cabinet meetings; further, a formal agenda also circulated in advance that put members on notice of the business to be discussed at the proceedings.

Eisenhower's systematic approach to administration also permeated other aspects of his dealings with the bureaucracy. He frequently convened the National Security Council—a kind of mini-cabinet—to discuss matters involving foreign and military policy. He also used interagency committees to resolve disputes within the executive branch, expecting them to develop consensus policies with which all the contending parties could agree. Finally, Ike was a believer in "follow-through" and obliged cabinet subordinates to monitor the results of decisions reached in the cabinet and National Security Council to see that departments and lower-level agencies actually implemented such decisions.

John Kennedy. In administrative style, JFK was much closer to his fellow Democrat, FDR, than to Dwight Eisenhower. Like Roosevelt, he gloried in convening a group of intelligent, articulate spokesmen of various political persuasions and letting them go at a dispute, reserving for himself the right to make the final decision. Unlike Ike, Kennedy wanted to be in on the details of decision-making, even at its earliest stages, rather than wait for others to resolve differences through a committee decision emphasizing the importance of consensus.

For the most part, JFK ignored or abolished the institutions upon which his Republican predecessor depended for the administration of the bureaucracy. Kennedy seldom convened the cabinet, and when he did, its meetings were unplanned and, for the most part, unimportant. The same was true of the National Security Council: when the Cuban missile crisis developed in the fall of 1962, JFK bypassed the Council in favor of an *ad hoc* committee composed of persons inside and outside the government to analyze the crisis and to give him advice on how to deal with it. He also abolished the Planning Board, which Eisenhower had developed to serve as an executive unit for the NSC, as well as the Operations Coordinating Board, created to implement the Council's decisions.

Kennedy also followed and even augmented Roosevelt's technique of developing a counterbureaucracy. The White House Office became the primary site for the President's personal bureaucracy. McGeorge Bundy, the President's Assistant for National Security Affairs, was permitted to develop a "little State Department" to replace the traditional department in which Kennedy had so little confidence. JFK also appointed task forces composed not only of regular agency heads but also of members of the White House staff to develop new approaches and policies for dealing with troublesome problems. He also used White House staffers like Bundy to analyze proposals of agency heads and to alert him to administrative and political difficulties created by such proposals.

Richard Nixon. Of all our Presidents, Richard Nixon made the most concerted attempt to establish firm control over the bureaucracy. As he considered it an enemy camp populated by liberal Democrats who fostered expensive social-service programs for the unworthy, Nixon determined to thwart the bureaucracy in every way possible. In the process he waged war against it on many fronts, utilizing the full range of his presidential powers and, in some cases, exceeding those powers.

In the initial stages of his presidency, Nixon gave lip service to the idea of a strong cabinet. Even before his inauguration, he went on television to present his cabinet choices to the nation, claiming that the persons designated for specific positions were all-around individuals who could have served in other cabinet posts as well. Like Eisenhower, he emphasized the idea that the cabinet was made up of "team" players who would work together harmoniously. Nixon also gave the cabinet secretaries a free hand in choosing second- and third-level political executives to work in their departments.

However, the President soon became disillusioned with his cabinet members because, as White House aide John Ehrlichman put it, "They went off and married the natives." (That is, they became too cozy with the career bureaucrats whom they supposedly supervised). Nixon's close personal friend Robert Finch was removed as Secretary of Health, Education, and Welfare and brought into the White House Office, where he could remain isolated from departmental bureaucrats. Independent popular political figures like Walter Hickel, George Romney, and John Volpe (all three former governors) were eased out of the cabinet, their places taken by political unknowns (many of them from the business world) who were chosen for their concern with efficiency and their fierce loyalty to the President. Nixon also withdrew the right of the cabinet members to pick their own subordinates and insisted that their appointments be cleared with the White House, a practice that led to the placement of Nixon loyalists in second and third-level positions as well.

In addition to subverting the traditional bureaucracy, Nixon also set out to create his own counterbureaucracy. We have already noted that the functions of the traditional Bureau of the Budget were broadened and its staff increased under the name of the Office of Management and Budget. Moreover, a new agency—the Domestic Council—was created and placed under John Ehrlichman. Operating under the Council were a series of working groups dealing with a variety of domestic issues; heavily staffed by members of the White House Office, these groups soon preempted policy-making activities that had traditionally resided in the "outer" cabinet departments.

Eventually the President tried still another tactic to control these latter departments and their congressional and interest-group allies as well. As we have seen, one of the reorganization plans he proposed was that the seven domestic departments be consolidated into four, dealing with Economic Affairs, Community Development, Human Resources, and Natural Resources. When the Congress refused to go along with that proposal, the President designated three of his cabinet members, the secretaries of Housing and Urban Development, of Health, Education, and Welfare, and of Agriculture—as "Counselors to the President" for the latter three policy areas respectively, and named the secretary of the Treasury as Assistant to the President in charge of Economic Affairs. While this concept of "Super Secretaries" was abandoned after the problems associated with Watergate began to overwhelm the President, units dealing with the above four broad areas of public policy were organized within the OBM and were represented in the White House Office as well.

After his overwhelming electoral victory in 1972, Nixon resorted to other, more extreme measures to tame the bureaucracy. He required that all persons occupying top positions submit their resignations, a number of which he accepted. He placed persons unsympathetic to certain departments in charge of their activities. Casper Weinberger (known as "Mac the Knife" for his propensity to wield that instrument against budgets and programs) was appointed Secretary of Health, Education, and Welfare, while Howard Phillips, a founder of the conservative organization *Young Americans for Freedom,* was made Director of the Office of Economic Opportunity with instructions to dismantle the agency. Meanwhile the President stepped up his impoundments of funds for programs he opposed.

Ultimately, of course, Nixon's plans to take over the "permanent government" and subordinate it to his political goals foundered as the Watergate revelations destroyed the men around him and ultimately Nixon himself. Dependent upon H. R. Haldeman and John Ehrlichman, key members of "the Berlin Wall" who sheltered the President from unpleasant realities, Nixon found it increasingly difficult to function after being forced to accept the resignations of "two of the finest public servants" he claimed he had ever known. Ironically, career employees in the Department of Justice, the Federal Bureau of Investigation, and the Central Intelligent Agency, who refused to go along with the Watergate cover-up, helped to bring down the President who had tried so hard to best them and other agencies in the jungle warfare of bureaucratic politics.

Congressional Efforts to Control the Bureaucracy

Congress experiences some of the same difficulties in controlling the bureaucracy as the President does. One of these is the sheer size of the establishment. For the national legislators, this fact of life is most graphically reflected in the difficult task of assessing the relative needs of hundreds of agencies with a combined annual budget of some four hundred billion dollars. The fact that the appropriation for each agency is made each year results in Congressmen being overwhelmed by a task that is constantly with them.

Moreover, as previously suggested, Congress must share its powers over the bureaucracy with the President. Just as it may thwart his efforts, so he too may frustrate congressional attempts to control the executive branch through its authority over the structure, funding and the personnel of the bureaucracy. This sharing of powers by the Congress and the President enables members of the bureaucracy to play off the constitutional rivals against one another.

Finally, Congress, like the President, faces the problem of controlling the triangular alliances of government agencies, interest groups, and congressional committees and subcommittees. Although these last are created by, and subject to, the authority of the entire body, the decentralized nature of congressional decision-making is such that the committees are granted considerable autonomy. As Herbert Kaufman, a student of legislative-executive relations suggests, the substantive and appropriations committees and their staffs typically develop "possessive and protective attitudes" towards government agencies with which they are associated. In return for the protection they provide for such agencies, Congressmen receive reciprocal benefits: the location of facilities and programs in states and congressional districts of committee members; considerate treatment of their constituents who have business with the agencies;

and influence over the hiring of job applicants by the bureaucracy.

Recently, however, the entire Congress has begun to make some efforts to establish better control over the bureaucracy and its interest groups and committee allies. One important move in that direction was taken with the passage of the budget reform legislation of 1974. If Congress continues to discipline itself to stay within its overall budget limit, and to require its appropriations committees to respect that total figure, this procedure should serve to restrict the budgets of individual agencies.

Other proposals currently before Congress would establish still further controls on the bureaucracy. One is the establishment of "zero-base" budgeting— a system under which agencies would be required to justify every dollar they plan to spend during the next fiscal year rather than simply to apply for an increase over the previous year's appropriation, the procedure that is presently followed. Another proposal is a "sunset" law that would place all government programs on a five-year schedule of congressional consideration: unless the Congress specifically reauthorized a program at the end of the allocation period, it would automatically be terminated.* Patterned after similar laws already in effect in several states, zero-base budgeting and sunset provisions represent new approaches to the congressional problem of taming the bureaucracy.

Thus the American political process is characterized by a perennial battle for influence and power between the bureaucracy and other formal institutions of our national government as outside interests seek to accomplish their purposes through one or more of these institutions. The following section illustrates the interplay of political forces surrounding an increasingly salient issue in American politics: the regulation of cigarette advertising in the United States.

BUREAUCRATIC POLICY-MAKING: REGULATING CIGARETTE ADVERTISING†

By any definition, the cigarette industry is Big Business in the United States. In 1963 smokers spent over $7 billion for cigarettes, a figure that contributed to the financial well-being of a variety of Americans. A share of it went to 600,000 farm families in 26 states that grew tobacco, another to the 34,000 persons who worked in cigarette factories. Also benefiting from the multi-billion-dollar industry were advertising firms, television and radio stations, and newspapers and magazines carrying cigarette advertisements, as well as the federal, state, and local governments receiving revenues from cigarette taxes.

As might be expected, these interests were well represented in Washington. In fact, the familiar triangular alliance was much in evidence. Included were officials within the Department of Agriculture involved in various programs benefiting the tobacco industry as well as congressmen sitting on the subcommittees that handle authorizations and appropriations for the tobacco industry. Outside the government, lobbyists for tobacco-growers, cigarette manufactur-

* A recent study by Herbert Kaufman showed that of a sample of 175 federal executive organizations in existence in 1923, 148 (85%) were still in operation in 1973. Moreover, in most cases the activities of the 27 units that did not survive were taken over by other agencies that did.

† The account of this battle is taken from the excellent case study on the subject by A. Lee Fritschler, cited in the *Selected Readings*.

ers, and advertising media and other marketing firms carefully nurtured the political interests of their employers.

Arrayed against this powerful political alliance were some individuals and groups that had become increasingly concerned with the effect of smoking. In 1939 the first major health study based upon medical records was released, showing that more cigarette-smokers than nonsmokers contracted lung cancer. Some fifteen years later, a series of studies based not only on records, but also on the results of autopsies, concluded that smoking caused lung cancer. The Public Health Cancer Association and the American Cancer Society adopted resolutions supporting the 1954 studies' conclusions linking lung cancer to cigarette smoking, a conclusion shared by the British Ministry of Health.

Facing a challenge from these health groups, the tobacco "subsystem" took action to preserve its interests. Arguing that the health studies had not produced any medical evidence demonstrating that smoking actually *caused* cancer (as compared to being merely *correlated* with it), the tobacco industry created a Research Committee (now called the Council for Tobacco Research—USA) to distribute moneys for scientific research on the subject. A separate organization, the Tobacco Institute, Inc., was established to lobby and handle public relations work on behalf of the industry. Ultimately, former Tennessee Senator Earle Clements was hired to direct the activities of the latter group.

Initially the tobacco interests and their allies were successful in blocking the health groups on a variety of fronts. A Congress dominated by representatives of the six major tobacco states (their congressmen controlled one-third of the committee chairmanships in the House and one-fourth in the Senate) prevented meaningful legislative action from being taken on smoking. Smokers' lawsuits against manufacturers (on the grounds that cigarette promotion implied that smoking was healthful) were successfully defended by the industry's lawyers. Nor did the health interests find sympathetic allies in certain quarters of the bureaucracy: the Department of Agriculture supported the continuation of price supports for tobacco and the Secretary of Health, Education, and Welfare prevented both the Food and Drug Administration and the Public Health Service from initiating any action to regulate cigarette advertising.

Eventually, however, the health interests found important allies for their cause. Senator Maureen Neuberger of Oregon introduced a resolution in March of 1962 calling for the establishment of a presidential commission on tobacco and health. Spurred by the suggestion, a reporter at a press conference asked President Kennedy what he intended to do about the issue of smoking and health; caught unawares by the question, the ordinarily well-briefed Chief Executive asnwered that he would look into the matter and respond to it the following week. He asked the Public Health Service to report on what it had been doing in the field of smoking and health, and the Surgeon General of the United States seized on the opportunity to establish an advisory committee to study the effect of smoking on health.

With these forces set in motion, the battle for the regulation of cigarette advertising picked up momentum. In early 1964 the Surgeon General's Advisory Committee—a prestigious committee composed of eight physicians, a chemist, and a statistician—issued a report stating that cigarette smoking was causally related to lung cancer in men and, although the data on women were

less extensive, they pointed in the same direction. The Public Health Service accepted the report and ordered its own hospitals to stop distributing free cigarettes to patients. Moreover, within a week after the issuance of the report, the Federal Trade Commission, entrusted with protecting the public against "unfair and deceptive trade practices", issued an official notice of its intention to hold public hearings on the question of requiring a warning to appear on all cigarette packages and advertising that smoking is dangerous to health. After three days of hearings involving witnesses from both the health and tobacco interests, in June 1964 the Commission promulgated rules requiring such a warning to appear both on the package and in advertisements of cigarettes.

However, the victory of the health groups was to be short-lived. The tobacco and allied interests turned to the Congress for support in the battle over the regulation of cigarette advertising. Following a brilliantly orchestrated lobbying effort led by former Senator Clements, the Congress passed the 1965 Cigarette Lobby and Advertising Act that suspended the rule-making powers of the FTC in the area of cigarette advertising until 1969.* While the Act constituted a major victory for the tobacco interests, it was not complete. The Commission requirement that a health warning appear on cigarette packages (as contrasted to advertising) was retained, and $2 million was appropriated to establish the National Clearing House for Smoking and Health, which would carry on educational campaigns and collect data on smoking and health research.

Moreover, the congressional victory of the tobacco interests proved to be a temporary one. Bureacratic allies joined the FTC in the battle over the regulation of cigarette advertising. One task force appointed by the Public Health Service reported that lower tar and nicotine content in cigarettes reduced their harmful effects, and another adopted the previous FTC regulation that health warnings appear on advertising. In 1967 the Federal Communications Commission joined the fray by ruling that under its "fairness doctrine", television and radio stations carrying cigarette ads were required to provide health groups free time to present the other side of the issue. The Commission later proposed a rule prohibiting cigarette advertising on radio and television altogether.

Eventually the tobacco interests lost their influence in Congress as well. In 1970 the national legislature passed a new law adopting the FCC proposal for a complete ban on cigarette advertising on radio and television, and also agreed to allow the FTC to consider requiring warnings on printed advertising after July, 1971. (Seven of the nine major cigarette companies subsequently agreed voluntarily to include such warnings.) Two years later the Congress passed legislation which included "little cigars" in the cigarette advertising ban.

The tobacco interests thus fought a series of unsuccessful battles over the regulation of advertising of their products. However, the end result of such battles appears not to have hurt them economically. After dropping slightly in the period from 1966 to 1970, the per capita consumption of cigarettes began rising again in 1971. Moreover, that latter year (the one following the TV and radio ban on advertising cigarettes), the advertising budgets of cigarette manufacturers fell an estimated 30 percent. Ironically, despite government regula-

---

* Another major contribution of Clements to the legislation was his close political friendship with President Johnson; because of this friendship, the Chief Executive stayed out of the battle and signed the bill.

tion, or perhaps because of it, the tobacco industry appeared to be selling more cigarettes with fewer promotional costs.

ASSESSMENT

As we saw at the outset of this chapter, the federal bureaucracy has recently become the favorite target of politician and citizen alike: both blame it for almost all the nation's ills. Yet ironically it is these same persons who have been primarily responsible for the development of the bureaucracy. The former have passed the laws authorizing governmental programs and providing the funds and creating the organizations to carry them out. The latter have used their political influence, typically organized through interest groups, to see to it that federal programs are created to meet needs they conceive to be important to their well-being.

In fact, a good case can be made for the fact that our diverse and "many-splintered" bureaucracy is not a catastrophe but rather a generally healthy development. Given the pluralistic nature of American society composed of a broad variety of social and economic groups, it is natural that the bureaucracy should reflect and be receptive to such diverse interests. The growth in the number of governmental agencies and programs over the years has occurred because formerly disadvantaged groups have developed the political influence to have their interests represented in the executive branch of government along with more powerful economic interests that have traditionally been well-represented there.

There is, of course, a danger that special interests will become so well ensconced in the bureaucracy that they will be almost immune from effective control. There are, however, two major types of safeguards that serve to lessen that possibility. One is the fact that executive agencies and their congressional and interest-group allies are typically opposed by rival alliances, and the competition prevents any of them from becoming all-powerful. In Madison's terms, "ambition is made to counteract

ambition." The case study of regulating cigarette-advertising reflects the ways in which the tobacco interests on one side, and health interests on the other, frustrated each other's demands and conducted their ongoing battle on a variety of bureaucratic, as well as legislative and judicial, fronts.

The other major control over the bureaucracy exists in the form of the legal powers that elected officials possess over its activities. If disposed to exercise it, both the President and the Congress can utilize their authority over executive-branch organization, funding, and staffing to rein in a too-powerful bureaucracy. Moreover, recent developments indicate that both the Chief Executive and the national legislature have begun to exert concerted efforts to accomplish that purpose. Not all these efforts, however, have been salutary, and this is particularly true of recent presidential actions. Centralizing policy-making in the White House staff at the expense of the regular departments has some obvious disadvantages. One is the fact that members of that staff are often appointed for their contribution to presidential electoral politics and are inexperienced and lack knowledge about substantive policy issues as well as about the governmental process in general. There is also the simple problem of manageability: trying to run the government almost entirely from the White House overloads the system at the center and strains the capacities of even the most able individuals. Downplaying the role of cabinet secretaries and other major political executives also makes it difficult to recruit able persons for such positions. Finally, excessive centralization in the executive branch means that the advice of experienced and knowledgeable senior civil servants who are familiar with the day-to-day operation of government programs is ignored or discounted when important public-policy decisions are made.

Recent congressional attempts to establish better overall control of the executive budget are generally encouraging. It remains to be seen, however, whether legislators can handle this task effectively, along with their new responsibilities in reviewing presidential impoundments. Even more questionable are proposals for zero-base budgeting and the periodic reauthorization of all governmental programs under the provisions of sunset laws. While certainly commendable in theory, they call for a kind of exhaustive scrutiny of the bureaucracy that may well be beyond the capacities of Congress. It would, indeed, be ironical if Congress in its zeal to control the executive-branch bureaucracy ended up creating its own unwieldy counterbureaucracy.

SELECTED READINGS

Reinhart Bendix's general treatment of the concept of bureaucracy appears under that title in the *International Encyclopedia of the Social Sciences*, 2nd ed. Vol. 2, pp. 206-19. An analysis of bureaucracy emphasizing technical expertise is given in Francis E. Rourke, *Bureaucracy, Politics, and Public Policy* (Boston: Little, Brown, 2nd ed., 1976). Peter Woll, *American Bureaucracy* (New York: Norton, 1963) focuses on the legal aspects of bureaucracy, while Emmette S. Redford approaches the subject from the standpoint of democratic theory in *Democracy in the Administrative State* (New York: Oxford University Press, 1969).

The best overall treatment of the relationship of Congress to the bureaucracy is Joseph P. Harris, *Congressional Control of Administration* (Washington, D.C.: The Brookings Institution, 1964). For an insightful analysis of the political aspects of governmental reorganization, see Harold Seidman, *Politics, Position, and Power*, 2nd ed. (New York: Oxford University Press, 2nd ed., 1975). Louis Fisher, *Presidential Spending Power* (Princeton: Princeton University Press, 1975) emphasizes the historical development of that power. A political analysis of budgetmaking is given in Aaron Wildavsky, *The Politics of the Budgetary Process*, 2nd ed. (Boston: Little, Brown, 1974). *Current American Government* (Washington, D.C.: Congressional Quarterly, Inc., Fall 1975), pp. 56-60, analyzes the effects of the 1974 law on presidential impoundment; and the same publication for Spring 1976, pp. 5-8, discusses congressional experiences with budget control under the provisions of the same law.

Two excellent analyses of the organization of the executive branch are contained in chapter 4 of James W. Davis Jr., *An Introduction to Public Administration: Politics, Policy, and Bureaucracy* (New York: The Free Press, 1974), and chapters 2 and 3 of Seidman, cited above. A classic study of the cabinet is Richard Fenno, *The President's Cabinet* (Cambridge: Harvard University Press, 1959). For a historical analysis of Senate action on presidential nominations, see Joseph Harris, *The Advice and Consent of the Senate* (Berkeley: University of California Press, 1952). Excellent studies of close presidential advisors are found in Louis Koenig, *The Invisible Presidency* (New York: Holt, Rinehart and Winston, 1960) and Patrick Anderson, *The President's Men* (Garden City: Anchor, 1969).

John W. Macy Jr., former Chairman of the U.S. Civil Service Commission, gives his insights into the federal bureaucracy in *Public Service: The Human Side of Government* (New York: Harper & Row, 1971). An analysis of unionization of federal employees appears in chapter 16 of Ivan L. Richardson and Sidney Baldwin, *Public Administration: Government in Action* (Columbus: Charles E. Merrill Publishing Company, 1976). Studies of high-level civil servants and political executives include John Carson and R. Shael Paul, *Men Near the Top* (Baltimore: Johns Hopkins University Press, 1966), Dean Mann, *The Assistant Secretaries* (Washington, D.C.: The Brookings Institution, 1965), and Marver Bernstein, *The Job of the Federal Executive* (Washington, D.C.: The Brookings Institution, 1958).

The best overall treatment of the President's relationship to the bureaucracy is Thomas E. Cronin, *The State of the Presidency* (Boston: Little, Brown, 1975). Chapter 8 of Louis W. Koenig, *The Chief Executive* (New York: Harcourt, Brace, Jovanovich, 3rd ed., 1975) and chapters 2 through 7 of Stephen Hess, *Organizing the Presidency* Washington, D.C.: The Brookings Institution, 1976) contain excellent analyses of the administrative styles of a number of recent Presidents. Robert P. Nathan's *The Plot that Failed: Nixon and the Administrative Presidency* (New York: Wiley, 1975) and Dan Rather and Gary Paul Gates, *The Palace Guard* (New York: Harper & Row, 1974) are accounts of President Nixon's attempt to control the bureaucracy. A systematic analysis of the Domestic Council under President Nixon is given in John H. Kessel, *The Domestic Presidency* (North Scituate, Mass.: Duxbury Press, 1975). Herbert Kaufman, *Are Government Organizations Immortal?* (Washington, D.C.: The Brookings Institution, 1976) is a study of the longevity of federal executive agencies.

An excellent in-depth case study of the battle over the regulation of cigarette advertising is A. Lee Fritschler's *Smoking and Politics: Policy Making and the Federal Bureaucracy* (Englewood Cliffs, N.J.: Prentice-Hall, 2nd ed., 1975).

Political Novels   A major problem for public organizations is the recruitment of persons with sufficient skills in governing, especially in view of the American practice of making many high-level appointments on the basis of political loyalty. One solution to this problem is proposed by Raymond E. Banks in a science-fiction story about a test, involving life and death for the participants, to which all prospective government leaders must be put *before* they can assume authority, "The Short Ones," in M. Greenberg and P. Warrick (eds.), *Political Science Fiction* (Englewood Cliffs, N.J.: Prentice Hall, 1974).

For Lawrence Sanders, *The Tomorrow File* (New York: Berkley, 1976), American Government in 1998 is little more than a bloated bureaucracy in which administrators are preoccupied with jockeying for power, bugging one another's offices, and indulging in plots and counter-plots.

Andrew Tully, a veteran Washington correspondent, provides a colorful behind-the-scenes examination of the burning ambitions and petty politics that characterize the scramble for Cabinet appointments in a presidential election year, *Capitol Hill* (New York: Simon and Schuster, 1962).

Three novels that raise especially troubling questions about the nature of bureaucracy in an age when mass destruction is a constant threat are: *The Andromeda Strain* (New York: Dell, 1971) by Michael Crichton, in which a government-sponsored biomedical team desperately battles a deadly space microbe. Crichton's novel powerfully illustrates the limits of science, technology, and modern administrative management in the face of imperfect knowledge and human fraility. The risks inherent in blind reliance on technology and bureaucratic procedures leads to nuclear disaster in *Fail Safe* (New York: Dell, 1969) by Eugene Burdick and Harvey Wheeler. This novel provoked an outcry from the Pentagon, which resented its accusations, but is reputed to have stimulated a high-level review of our safeguards against accidental nuclear war. Leonard C. Lewin, *Report From Iron Mountain on the Possibility and Desirability of Peace* (New York: Dell, 1969), presents a bureaucratic fantasy in which a select committee of government experts, in the unique language of bureaucracy, concludes after detailed study that peace is far too dangerous a policy to pursue in modern America. This savage satire on bureaucratic thinking raises many profound questions about the nature of modern society and government's role in providing security.

Chapter 15

In January 1962 the Clerk of the United States Supreme Court received a petition from Clarence Earl Gideon, a prisoner serving a five-year term in the Florida State Prison for breaking and entering a pool hall and stealing coins from a cigarette machine. In the petition Gideon asked that the Court get him out of jail because during his trial in the county court in Panama City, Florida his request for a lawyer (he was too poor to hire one himself) had been refused initially by that court and later by the Florida Supreme Court. Gideon contended that the failure to provide him with an attorney when he was being tried for a felony crime* violated the provisions of the Fourteenth Amendment of the Constitution guaranteeing that "no state shall deprive any person of life, liberty or property without due process of law."

Gideon, a poorly educated man who had been in and out of jails most of his life, could hardly have been expected to understand the subtleties of the law bearing on his case. Although the Supreme Court had previously ruled in a 1938 case, *Johnson* v. *Zerbst,* that defendants who could not afford an attorney in criminal trials in federal courts were entitled to have one appointed for them, it had refused to apply the same ruling to state criminal proceedings. Instead, in a 1942 case—*Betts* v. *Brady*—the Court had formulated the rule that a defendant had the right to counsel in a noncapital state criminal case (one not involving the death penalty) only if it could be demonstrated that "special circumstances" prevailed, such as the defendant's illiteracy, ignorance, youth, or mental incapacity; or that the charge was complex; or that there was community hostility; or that the conduct of the prosecutor or judge at the trial was improper. Yet Gideon's petition contained no indication that any of these circumstances was present in his trial before the county court in Florida. If the Supreme Court were to follow its former ruling, it would refuse to hear Gideon's case, and he would remain in the Florida jail.

Fortunately for Gideon, the *Betts* v. *Brady* ruling was unpopular with many persons, including three justices of the Supreme Court who had refused to go

* A *felony* is a serious crime; a minor one is a misdemeanor. A felony ordinarily has a potential penalty of imprisonment for at least a year and a day.

Clarence Earl Gideon reading a law book. It was in the prison library that he researched the possibility of his right to counsel, an inquiry that led to a landmark Supreme Court decision.

along with majority. Moreover, the courts had experienced difficulties in deciding cases under the "special circumstances" rule. In a number of decisions prior to 1962 (including all those in the past twelve years), the Supreme Court had reversed state criminal convictions on the grounds that "special circumstances" unacknowledged by state officials warranted the appointment of counsel. Several new justices had also joined the Court in the twenty years since the *Betts* decision. All these factors contributed to the Court's decision in June 1962 to hear the Gideon case for the purpose of reconsidering the *Betts* v. *Brady* decision.

The Supreme Court appointed an eminent lawyer, Abe Fortas, to represent Gideon in the case. Fortas (later to become a Supreme Court justice himself) was widely respected as one of the finest legal minds in the nation; at fifty-one a senior partner in a prominent Washington law firm, he was an experienced advocate who had successfully argued major cases before the Supreme Court. To assure a thorough preparation of the *Gideon* case, he assigned young men in his firm to research the problem. In addition, amicus curiae briefs were filed in Gideon's behalf by the attorneys-general of twenty-three states and by *the American Civil Liberties Union.**

In contrast, the task of persuading the Supreme Court to retain the *Betts* v. *Brady* ruling fell to Bruce Jacob, a twenty-six-year-old inexperienced lawyer from Florida who had never even seen the Supreme Court, let alone tried a case before it. Originally assigned to the case in the spring of 1962 while he was a member of the state attorney-general's office, by the following fall when the brief for the State of Florida was due to be filed with the Supreme Court, Jacob had entered private practice. He prepared the case entirely on his own, working on it over weekends, when he drove 250 miles to use the facilities of the Florida State Supreme Court library. Although Jacob wrote to the attorneys-general of all fifty states to solicit *amicus curiae* briefs on behalf of Florida's side of the

---

* A brief is a written statement setting forth the facts of the case and the arguments for a particular finding that a party to litigation files with a court to persuade it to rule in his favor. An *amicus curiae* (literally "friend of the court") brief is one filed by some individual or group that is not a direct party to the suit but has an interest in its outcome.

case, only two—in Alabama and North Carolina—responded to his request. (Ironically, it was Jacob's letter that stimulated the *amicus curiae* briefs favoring Gideon's side of the case to be filed by the attorneys-general from twenty-three states.)

The following January, a year after Gideon originally filed his case before the Supreme Court, oral arguments were heard. Jacob and an assistant attorney-general of Alabama argued that the *Betts* v. *Brady* ruling should be followed by the Supreme Court because it was consistent with the principle of federalism that states should be free to experiment with the use of counsel in criminal proceedings so long as defendants' interests were not harmed by "special circumstances." They also cautioned that if the *Betts* case were overruled, prisoners in Florida and other states who were convicted in proceedings in which they were not represented by counsel would suddenly be released into society en masse. Fortas's major contentions were that the *Betts* v. *Brady* ruling was unworkable and that it did a disservice to the principle of federalism by requiring the Supreme Court to intervene in state criminal proceedings to determine whether or not "special circumstances" were present in each individual case. A representative of the *American Civil Liberties Union* who joined Fortas in the oral argument made another basic point: a man cannot get a fair trial when he represents himself.

Two months later, in mid-March, 1963, the Court handed down a decision in favor of Gideon that specifically overruled the *Betts* v. *Brady* case. Delivering the decision for the Court was Justice Black; joining in with him in the unanimous ruling were the other eight members of the Court. (Three, however—Douglas, Clark, and Harlan—filed separate opinions in which they concurred with Black's result but set forth different reasons for reaching it.) A few weeks later Black, who had been in the minority twenty years before, confided to a friend: "When *Betts* v. *Brady* was decided, I never thought I'd live to see it overruled."

Subsequently, Gideon was tried again before the same county judge who had been involved in the first proceeding against him. A stubborn man, Gideon initially contended that he could not get a fair trial—"It's the same court, the same judge, everything"—and refused the assistance of counsel provided by the *Florida Civil Liberties Union.* (Ironically, this time Gideon wanted to plead his own case.) The judge subsequently appointed a local attorney to represent him, and in the subsequent trial the jury found Gideon not guilty. Later a newspaper reporter asked Gideon if he thought that he had accomplished anything. "Well I did," he replied.

Relatively few of the millions of cases tried in the courts at all levels of our political system are as dramatic and far-reaching in their impact as the Gideon one. Yet the law, and the various courts in which the law is enforced, play a major part in regulating the activities of individuals and groups in American society. We first examine the basic elements of our legal system; the next chapter concentrates on the federal courts, including the one in which Gideon's case was ultimately decided—the United States Supreme Court.

THE NATURE AND PURPOSES OF THE LAW

Law is a term that is used in various ways. It refers to personal authority, as in the phrase "so-and-so's word is law," meaning that what he says goes, as far as his associates are concerned. In some societies, the father of a family makes the major decisions, which the remainder follow with little or no question. The word also describes certain basic immutable principles governing human behavior—that is the sense of "natural laws," or the "laws of nature," which are held to be rational and applicable to all individuals and societies. The problem is to discover what natural laws are and how to utilize them in governing human affairs.

Here we will use "laws" to mean the rules and regulations that a government imposes on individuals or groups. (In the United States, laws can emanate from national, state, or local governments.) These rules differ from those made by other individuals or other social institutions: only the government can enforce its regulations through its monopoly of legitimate force. Thus a father's command is not "law" in the sense in which we are using the term, because it does not apply generally. Indeed, the government places limits on the sanctions that a father is permitted to impose on his children: he cannot legitimately imprison them or take their lives for disobeying his commands. Nor is natural law the law we are talking about: it refers to general principles that *should* regulate human affairs, not necessarily those that *actually do*. Only if enacted into governmental rules and regulations would such principles constitute laws in the sense meant here.

Every organized society must resort to law to govern the behavior of its members, primarily to avoid or resolve *conflicts* over a variety of matters: sexual rivalry, distribution of material goods, what use should be made of the resources of the society, and so on. Some means have to be developed to settle such conflicts. One possibility, of course, is force: the stronger claimant prevails. But that approach leads to chaos and destruction.

Another possibility is for antagonists to turn to a third party to settle the conflict. In a dispute between two persons over, say, a piece of land, a disinterested party could hear the facts of the case and the reasons why each party feels that he is entitled to the land. *A* may say that he is entitled to the property in question because the former owner made an oral promise to give it to him; *B* may, in turn, produce a piece of paper signed by the owner that describes the land and details the terms of sale to *B*. The person deciding the dispute might rule that *B* has a better claim to the land because he has specific written evidence of the former owner's intentions. The arbitrator has thereby developed a rationale for his decision, and such a rationale constitutes a principle of law. Assuming that *A* accepts the principle, the "law" will serve its major purpose: *to settle disputes peacefully.*

Principles of law also provide persons with *advance notice of their rights* by letting them know ahead of time what they must do to accomplish a certain result. A person wanting to lay claim to a piece of land might deduce from the dispute between *A* and *B* that he had better get a written statement of transfer from the former owner. Thus the law introduces an element of certainty and predictability in human affairs and thereby serves *to prevent future disputes:* someone without written evidence of his right to a piece of land might not think it worthwhile to contest the claim of another person who has such evidence.

Another function of the law is to *render justice in society*. It is admittedly difficult to define *justice* precisely, but generally it refers to the idea of giving every man "his due"—what he is entitled to in life. Basically, then, justice is fairness in deciding disputes between individuals, and fairness means that the

results of a dispute ought not to depend on who the parties to it are: the same principles of law should be applied to all individuals regardless of their background or station in life. The belief that this is so does much to ensure that decisions in disputes will be accepted by the losing party and by other persons as well. Thus the contribution of the law to just decisions not only serves the interests of the immediate parties concerned but also fosters a peaceful society.

SOURCES OF AMERICAN LAW

American principles of law evolved from certain developments in England in the eleventh and twelfth centuries, when its monarchs gradually developed a central system of courts to administer justice. The rules of law developed to decide disputes came to be known as the "common customs of the realm," or more simply common law. What was "common" to the law was that it was applied throughout the country so that the same general legal principles governed disputes in the various local units.

Common law was "judge-made" law, developed on a case-by-case basis by representatives of the king hearing disputes. In determining what principles to apply, the judges sometimes drew upon customs that had been followed in the community, and sometimes they derived their own notions of sound, commonplace principles of fairness that would help prevent similar disputes in the future.

To avoid deciding each individual case anew, and also to give some certainty to the law, judges followed the general principle of *stare decisis,* which means literally "to adhere to the decision." That is, they looked at what judges in the past had done in similar situations and applied the earlier results and rationale to the immediate case before them. Out of this practice there developed a body of common-law principles that were utilized to settle disputes throughout England.

The Development of "Equity"

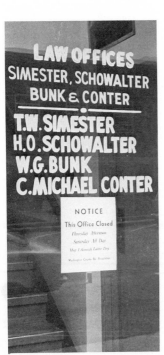

Although the common law thus provided continuity and certainty in the handling of legal matters, it also became exceedingly rigid. Unless a person could fit his particular grievance and the relief he sought within the special categories of common-law actions that the courts recognized, he could receive no redress for his difficulty. In time, aggrieved persons began to petition the king to hear their cases "in the interests of justice and charity." He, in turn, referred such matters to his chancellor, the most important figure in his executive council. Separate courts of chancellery were developed to hear such cases; in time they came to be known as courts of "equity," because they were based on general principles of fairness and conscience.

Equity thus developed as a distinct type of law. Although still "judge-made," it was based less on the principle of *stare decisis* and more on the merits of each particular case. In time, however, precedents developed for deciding these matters also. Nonetheless, equity retained two special characteristics that differentiated it from ordinary common law. One was the type of relief it granted: courts of equity were not restricted to compensating an aggrieved party for past damages; they could also issue decrees preventing future wrongs. (Thus a person who was concerned about his neighbor's plans to build a dam on adjoining property that would serve to flood his land could ask a court of equity to grant an injunction forbidding its construction rather than wait for the flooding to occur and then seek compensation.) The second distinction was that courts of equity did not use juries (bodies of lay persons) to find the facts in the case as common-law courts often did; the judge performed this function, along with developing and applying rules of law as in common-law courts.

The principles of common law and equity law, together with dual courts to administer them, were brought to the New World by the English colonists in the seventeenth and eighteenth centuries. After the American Revolution the states adopted them as the foundation for their own law and court systems. Later, in the nineteenth century, states began to abolish separate courts of common law and equity (there never have been separate courts at the federal level), and today in almost all states the same judges administer both types of law, with their distinctive remedies and procedures.

The development of the English common law and equity law had certain far-reaching consequences for American society. For one thing, as in England, it produced a special group trained in developing and applying the complexities of law on a case-by-case basis: the legal profession,* including both judges and attorneys. (Judges were selected from the ranks of practicing attorneys rather than constituting a group set apart by special training as in some countries.) Both the judges and the attorneys tended to be conservative in their social and economic views. Often drawn from upper-class families, they were also exposed to the common law's solicitude for the property rights of individuals as well as its concern for precedent in deciding present cases on the same basis as those of the past.

Statutory Law

Although Americans tend to think of legislatures rather than courts as the primary source of law, in fact legislative statutes did not take on much significance in the United States until the second quarter of the nineteenth century. The change was linked with the spread of the franchise and the Jacksonian Revolution, which resulted in the election of legislators with different views from those of the judiciary. In time legislative bodies began to pass laws that modified those previously developed by the courts. For example, although common-law rulings provided that an employee who was injured because of the carelessness of a fellow employee could not receive damages from his employer if the latter were not at fault, eventually legislation made the employer liable as a means of protecting workers against the dangers of industrial employment.

Today statutes enacted by legislative bodies are a major source of laws—statutory laws—at all levels of government. Americans are governed by acts of Congress and state legislatures as well as by regulations of local bodies such as city councils. These statutes spell out in detail the rules governing a great variety of human relationships in our increasingly complex and interdependent society.

---

* Traditionally, lawyers received their training in the law office of a practicing attorney, but since the end of World War I attendance at a law school (typically associated with a university) has replaced the apprenticeship method.

Administrative Law

The increasing complexity of American society has resulted in still another major source of law: rules and regulations of administrators in the executive branch of government; these are known as administrative law. As we have seen in chapter 11, Congress no longer has the time, expertise, or political inclination to deal with all the varied problems in society, so it delegates authority to executive agencies to fix regulations within broad guidelines. To refer to an earlier example, Congress has entrusted the Federal Highway Safety Bureau with developing automobile safety standards that are "appropriate" and "practicable," "meet the need for motor vehicle safety," and are "stated in objective terms." State legislatures make similar authorizations to agencies in the states' executive branches.

Constitutional Law

One final source of American law is the national Constitution and the constitutions of the fifty states; yielding constitutional law. Constitutions differ from other sources of law in that they are adopted through extraordinary processes. The national Constitution was originally written by the delegates to the Constitutional Convention and then ratified by action of conventions called in the various states. State constitutions were also framed by delegates to special conventions and then ratified by the voters. Changes in constitutions also typically require extraordinary procedures: extramajority votes of legislatures, special constitutional conventions, and actions of the voters.

Interrelationships among Laws from Different Sources

American law thus stems from a variety of sources—all three branches of the government, special conventions, and the public. Out of this mixture comes a wide variety of rules and regulations that govern the activities of individuals and groups in society.

Because of potential conflicts among the various sources of law, priorities among them are required. Statutory law takes precedence over common law and equity law; thus legislators can change judges' rules, as in establishing the liability of employers for injuries suffered by their employees. Legislatures also have the power to change regulations developed by administrative agencies; Congress could enact automobile safety regulations of its own if it were dissatisfied with those developed by the Federal Highway Safety Bureau. Finally, common law, equity, and statutory and administrative regulations must all give way to constitutional provisions.

In actuality, of course, the legal regulations of one branch of government are affected by those of the other branches. Although legislators can change common-law rulings and overrule administrative regulations, the wording of statutes that they pass is interpreted initially by executive officials and, in many instances, later by the courts. As we shall see in the next chapter, the courts also have the power in the United States to determine whether statutes or executive actions violate the national or state constitutions. But not even the judiciary has the final say, for the Congress can change judicial rulings through constitutional amendments—which, in turn, are subject to interpretation by the courts. Thus the law is a seamless web subject to actions and counteractions of various public officials as well as the people themselves.

APPLICATIONS OF LAW

Law can be analyzed in terms not only of its sources but also of its applications. One important distinction is between private law and public law. Regulations regarding contractual agreements, marriage and divorce, wills, deeds of land, and the like determine the legal rights and obligations among individuals and nongovernmental groups. Much of the law (derived in this instance primarily from common law, equity, and statutes) is of this nature. Although public officials develop, apply, and enforce legal regulations on private individuals and groups, the officials themselves are not directly affected by them.

Legal rules and regulations that apply to government officials are known as *public law*. They define the rights and obligations that exist among the officials themselves as well as those that govern relationships between them and private citizens and groups. For instance, the power of the President to veto acts of Congress is governed by public law, as is the right of a private individual to criticize actions of public officials. The primary sources of public law are constitutional provisions, administrative regulations, and statutes, but common law also plays some role. Judges too shape the public law through their power to interpret and apply constitutional, administrative, and statutory provisions.

JUDICIAL PROCEDURES FOR ENFORCING LAW

The hallmark of a law, as compared to an informal custom or a moral principle, is that it can be enforced through sanctions that are considered legitimate by affected parties and that can actually involve the use of physical force. Thus the means by which laws are enforced and the purposes of enforcement are central to a legal system.

The two major means to enforce laws are civil and criminal procedures. The former has as its major purpose the personal interest of the individual whose rights have been violated by others. In a civil proceeding the affected party brings a legal action to compensate him for some unjustified loss that he has suffered because of the activities of the individual or group he is suing. A may bring an action against B for injuring him in an automobile accident, for breaking an agreement to sell him goods, for trespassing on his property and damaging it, or the like. In such circumstances A seeks money damages to reimburse him for a wrong that he has suffered at the hands of B.

Civil proceedings can also be instituted to prevent threatened actions that would harm A's interests if they occurred. Thus A might ask a court to issue an injunction (a remedy in equity) forbidding B to build a manufacturing plant next to his private home that would interfere with A's rights to clean air and a pleasant view. Or A might ask the court to order B to take some action to protect A's interests. For example, B might be permitted to build the plant, provided he used a certain kind of "clean" fuel and built a fence around the property.

For the most part, civil procedure is utilized to enforce the rights of private individuals and groups against other private groups and individuals; however, public officials can also be parties to a civil proceeding. The Commissioner of Internal Revenue, for instance, can bring a civil action against a person who fails to pay his taxes in order to recover the moneys owned to the federal government. Also, in some instances, public officials can be sued by private individuals. For example, if a public official mistakenly computes a person's income tax with the result that he is required to pay more than he actually owes, the taxpayer can sue the official for the amount that he is overcharged if the official refuses to return the money to him.*

A criminal procedure involves the rights of society in general, not merely those of the particular person wronged. For example, in the *Gideon* case it was the state of Florida, not the owner of the pool hall into which Gideon was alleged to have broken, that brought the criminal suit. The actions of the state were based on the premise that Gideon's alleged action was of legitimate concern to others besides the pool-hall owner.

One reason for employing criminal procedures is the basic idea that a person who commits a serious wrong must be punished for it: justice requires that he pay—by a fine, by imprisonment, or in extreme circumstances with his life—for the harm that he has done his fellow man. Another purpose of criminal proceedings is to deter future wrongdoing by establishing the expectation of punishment. Finally, there is the motive of protecting society. If a convicted criminal is imprisoned or put to death, he has been removed as a potential threat to society, and during imprisonment he may be successfully rehabilitated so that he can be safely returned to society. (Frequently, however, rehabilitation efforts fail because few prisons have adequate programs or facilities and also because a released prisoner often finds it hard to find a job and so returns to crime to sustain himself.)

An act that gives rise to a criminal proceeding can generally give rise to a civil suit as well, since it involves harm to property or persons. Thus in the *Gideon* case the owner of the pool hall could have brought a civil proceeding against Gideon to recover the money that he allegedly stole from the cigarette machine. However, both the small amount of money involved and the unlikelihood that it could be collected from Gideon made the step impractical.

COURTS FOR CONDUCTING JUDICIAL PROCEDURES

In the American legal system there is a variety of courts in which judicial procedures are conducted. One basic distinction is between trial courts, which hear cases originally, and appellate courts, to which cases are taken on appeal from the decisions of the trial tribunals.

It is in the trial court that the excitement and drama of the judicial process occur. Attorneys argue their cases, using witnesses to testify to various facts that are important to the case; the judge referees the spirited contest, indicating what kind of evidence can be introduced by the two sides to the case. The jury, composed of laymen, hears the evidence and decides what facts are true, guided by the judge who advises them on points of law. The final outcome of the case depends on the decisions made by the judge and the jury. The overwhelming share of cases that courts hear (most disputes are settled out of court by the parties) end in the trial court.

In some cases, however, the losing party seeks a reversal of the decision of the trial court by filing an appeal in a higher, or appellate, court. In such a

---

* Under the doctrine that the king can do no wrong, governments cannot be sued without their permission. However, legislative bodies generally grant individuals and groups the right to bring certain types of actions (such as those growing out of a breach of contract) against public officials.

tribunal the only participants are the opposing attorneys and the judges (most frequently more than one), who read the written briefs and hear the oral arguments of the attorneys. In hearing appeals the court determines whether any errors of law occurred in the trial court that operated against the interests of the losing party. If the appellate court finds that errors did occur, it either reverses the decision of the lower court outright or sends the case back to that court for a new trial.

Another important division in American courts exists between the *states* and the *national government.* As we saw in chapter 3, one feature of the federal system is that each level of government has its own distinct political institutions, including separate systems of courts. Each state provides, through its constitution and laws, for its judiciary; but there is a fairly standard system that includes general trial courts at the county level and state courts of appeal.* As we shall see in detail in the following chapter, there are also federal trial and appellate courts. Despite our dual-court system in the United States, state and federal courts are not entirely separate. As chapter 16 will show, some kinds of cases can be tried originally in either state or federal courts, depending on the wishes of the parties. Moreover, as exemplified by the *Gideon* case, some litigation that begins in a state court is eventually appealed to a federal one.

With this basic information on the law, judicial procedures, and the courts in mind, we can turn to more specific aspects of the American legal system.

CRIMINAL PROCEDURE

It has long been a central feature of Anglo-American legal systems that the serious sanctions available in criminal procedures cannot be invoked against an

---

* States also have special courts at the local level to hear certain kinds of cases, such as traffic violations and other misdemeanors, small civil claims, and juvenile matters. In addition, the larger states have intermediate courts of appeal, as well as a final one (usually called the State Supreme Court).

accused person arbitrarily. As early as the fourteenth century, English courts provided that no man could be imprisoned or put to death except by "due process of law." English settlers in America brought with them a concern for the rights of the accused and a determination to protect those rights in criminal procedures. This solicitude for the rights of the accused in criminal cases has continued to be a hallmark of the American legal system. The late Supreme Court Justice Felix Frankfurter observed that "the history of liberty has largely been the history of the observance of procedural safeguards."

This concern derives from a number of fundamental beliefs. The rights of a person to privacy and to freedom from arbitrary governmental action are basic values in democracies in general and the American society in particular. Justice, or giving every man his due, is also a major purpose of the law. Finally, democracy attempts to protect the citizen from the state. Government is a powerful institution, and in a criminal case the parties are seldom of equal strength. The state can marshal its vast resources against a single person, who must struggle to defend himself against charges that he has committed a wrong against society.

These considerations are reflected in the American system of criminal justice. The government is forbidden to violate the privacy of the individual through unreasonable searches and seizures of his home or person. Nor may it arrest him for arbitrary reasons. In the trial, the state must prove its charge "beyond a reasonable doubt." Such prohibitions and requirements are deliberately designed to favor the accused by making it difficult for the government to succeed in its attempt to deny him his property, his freedom of movement, or his right of life itself.

Sources of Criminal Procedure and Rights of the Accused

The dual legal system in the United States has resulted in separate lists of criminal offenses and trial procedures for the nation as a whole and for the fifty states. The overwhelming proportion of criminal acts violate state rather than federal laws and are tried in the state courts. Included are such major crimes as auto theft, burglary, rape, and murder. There are criminal offenses against the national government, however: for example, assassination of the President and taking a stolen automobile across state lines violate federal criminal laws and are subject to prosecution by federal officials in federal courts.*

There are several sources for rules governing criminal procedure and the rights of the accused in federal cases. The principal source is the United States Constitution, particularly the Fourth, Fifth, Sixth, and Eighth amendments, which spell out certain prohibitions and procedural methods that must be respected. Specifically, the Fourth Amendment protects an individual against unreasonable searches and seizures of his person or his property; the next two amendments detail how he must be charged and tried for a federal offense; while the Eighth Amendment restricts the severity of sanctions that can be

---

* Since a single act can violate both state and national criminal laws, the accused can be prosecuted by both jurisdictions. Such dual prosecutions do not violate the double jeopardy prohibition of the Fifth Amendment because under our federal system two separate levels of government are involved.

imposed upon him as well as the amount of the bail that he must post in order to gain release from custody pending trial.

In addition to the specific procedural protections spelled out in these four amendments, the Fifth Amendment contains the historic English guarantee that a person cannot be denied his life, liberty, or property, without due process of law. The federal courts have interpreted that broad clause to mean that a person is entitled to a hearing before a fair and impartial tribunal. In the process, they have held that a person is entitled to other protections besides those specifically spelled out in the Fourth, Fifth, Sixth, and Eighth amendments—for example, that a plea of guilty or not guilty must be made before a trial proceeds and that the defendant must be personally present at every stage of the trial where his substantive rights may be affected.*

In addition to national constitutional provisions, acts of Congress also govern the rules of the federal criminal process. As we shall see below, the Omnibus Crime Control and Safe Streets Act of 1968 spells out the conditions under which confessions can be introduced in federal courts. Moreover, the federal courts themselves also issue certain rules pertaining to their handling of criminal matters. Each of the fifty states also has its own constitution, and state legislatures and courts develop rules for criminal procedures. Federal and state criminal processes are thus based on separate and distinct sources, but there is one provision of the national Constitution that has served to link them, namely the provision of the Fourteenth Amendment, which declares that a state cannot "deprive any person of life, liberty, or property, without due process of law"— an extension to the states of the restriction on the national government in the Fifth Amendment.

The due process clause of the Fourteenth Amendment is open to various interpretations. One is to equate it with the same clause in the Fifth Amendment. Under this interpretation the accused in a state criminal procedure, as in a federal court, is entitled to a hearing before a fair and impartial tribunal with the protection of specific safeguards (such as the right to be present at every stage of the trial). This is an interpretation of minimal procedural protection.

The interpretation of maximum procedural protection would construe the clause to include all the specific prohibitions and procedural methods spelled out in the Fourth, Fifth, Sixth, and Eighth amendments. This is the interpretation favored by the late Supreme Court Justice Hugo Black: the clause incorporates every safeguard mentioned in these four amendments.† By this reasoning, the accused in a state criminal case should enjoy all the procedural rights that he has in federal proceedings (plus any other protections granted by a particular state's constitution or laws).

---

* Although this is the general rule, the courts have recently been faced with the problem of how to deal with defendants who deliberately try to disrupt their trial. In *Illinois* v. *Allen* (1969) the Supreme Court upheld the right of a judge to remove a defendant from the courtroom who used vile and abusive language.

† Black's incorporation theory covers not only the procedural safeguards spelled out in these four amendments but also other rights included in the first ten amendments. It would have the effect of making all such rights a person enjoys vis-à-vis the federal government also available in relation to the states.

The Supreme Court has followed a middle ground in its interpretation of the matter by including within the coverage of the clause the general concept of a hearing before a fair and impartial tribunal along with certain of the specific procedural matters spelled out in the four earlier amendments. In choosing among such safeguards the Court has applied a general test first enunciated by Justice Benjamin Cardozo in a 1937 case, *Palko* v. *Connecticut:* is the particular procedural right at issue "of the very essence of a scheme of ordered liberty"? Is it "so rooted in the traditions and conscience of our people as to be ranked as fundamental"?

For a number of years the Supreme Court was rather selective about the procedural safeguards it was willing to bring under the due process clause of the Fourteenth Amendment. For example, in the *Palko* case it refused to consider the double jeopardy prohibition of the Fifth Amendment as "fundamental" so as to prevent the state of Connecticut from appealing cases in which an accused person was acquitted in a lower court as a result of errors of law. Subsequently the Court refused to transfer other federal procedural rights to the states, including the right to a jury trial and—the issue in the *Gideon* case— the right to counsel in all criminal cases.

In so refusing, the Court took the position that Bruce Jacob argued in the *Gideon* case: under the federal system of government, states ought to be free to experiment with different criminal procedures so long as they do not violate the nation's fundamental traditions or "a scheme of ordered liberty." Just because the Founding Fathers reacted to particular circumstances of their time and provided specific safeguards in federal criminal cases, the justices held, it does not follow that identical procedures need be followed by all the individual state governments 200 years later.

Gradually, however, the Supreme Court has read more and more of the specific provisions of the Fourth, Fifth, Sixth, and Eighth amendments over into the due process clause of the Fourteenth Amendment. In *Benton* v. *Maryland* (1969) the same right at issue in the *Palko* case was extended to the states: the Fifth Amendment prohibition against double jeopardy. In the decision specifically overruling that earlier case, Justice Thurgood Marshall stated that the prohibition "represents a fundamental ideal in our constitutional heritage." Today as a result of a series of such decisions, of all the safeguards spelled out in the four amendments, only the ones requiring grand jury indictment and prohibiting excessive fines and bail remain outside the coverage of the due process clause of the Fourteenth Amendment.

What has happened is that the Supreme Court has maintained the same test first developed in the *Palko* case; however, it has come to regard more and more procedural rights as "traditional," "fundamental," or as "of the very essence of a scheme of ordered liberty." Although the test applied is still Cardozo's, the results now approach Black's preference for the wholesale application of federal rights in criminal cases to the states.

A by-product of this trend in the Court's attitude has been the convergence of the rights of the accused and of court procedures in federal and state criminal actions. As a result, today there is a substantial similarity in the criminal procedures of both types of jurisdiction.

General Procedure in Criminal Cases

Criminal procedures in the American dual legal system are complex and detailed, but it is possible to get a general overview of them.

The initial step is the apprehension of the suspect—either through voluntary surrender or by swearing out a warrant empowering a police officer to arrest him. A police officer can also arrest a person without a warrant if an offense is committed in his presence or, in the case of a felony, if he has good reason to believe that the person did commit it.

Within a reasonable time after the suspect has been taken into custody, authorities must take him before a magistrate for a preliminary hearing to determine whether there is probable cause to believe that a crime has been committed and that the arrestee committed it. The hearing is designed to protect the accused against hasty or malicious action and the state against useless expense of subsequent proceedings if it does not have sufficient evidence to convict him. The magistrate examines the government's evidence, not to decide whether the accused is guilty or innocent but to determine whether further proceedings are justified. If the evidence is insufficient, the accused is released; otherwise he is held to answer the allegations against him.

Jurisdictions differ in handling the next step. Cases in federal (and many state) courts are taken before a grand jury, a group of citizens who hear the evidence against the accused to decide whether it is sufficient to warrant further proceedings. If they decide that it is, they return a true bill, or indictment, against him; if they decide it is not, they return a no bill and charges are dropped.

Because the Supreme Court has held that indictment by a grand jury is not included within the due process clause of the Fourteenth Amendment, states can use some other method at this stage. About half the states, particularly those west of the Mississippi, permit the prosecutor to file an information consisting of charges supported by sworn statements of evidence against the accused.

The accused is next brought before the court for arraignment and pleading. The former is an official reading of the terms of the indictment or information by the court, after which the accused is given the opportunity to plead guilty or not guilty. In most criminal cases the parties engage in a process known as plea bargaining whereby the prosecutor agrees to reduce the charges against the accused in return for his pleading guilty to the lesser charges. If a guilty plea is entered, the judge decides on the sentence. (Usually he will accept the prosecutor's recommendations.) If the accused pleads not guilty, then the case must go to trial.

A person accused of violating a serious federal or state crime is entitled to have his case heard by a jury of citizens.* Federal court rules provide for a jury of twelve, but some states use smaller juries; in *Williams* v. *Florida* (1970) the Supreme Court upheld Florida's use of six-man juries.

Choosing a jury can be a long and tedious process. Both the government and defense attorneys interrogate prospective jurors (called veniremen) to deter-

---

* In *Baldwin* v. *New York* (1970) the Supreme Court ruled that a defendant is entitled to a jury trial if the offense carries a potential sentence of six months or more in prison.

"Crime does not pay at your level"

Drawing by Handelsman; © 1975 The
New Yorker Magazine, Inc.

mine whether they have prejudices that may interfere with their ability to hear the case objectively. Both sides are entitled to challenge veniremen for "cause," that is, to ask the judge to dismiss them for certain reasons, such as personal acquaintance with persons involved in the case or the fact that they have already formed a judgment about the case. Both sides also have a certain number of "peremptory" challenges for which they need give no reasons.

When the composition of the jury is set, the trial itself begins. Both sides make opening statements setting forth the general nature of their case and the evidence that they plan to introduce to support it. Witnesses testify about the events in question, and each side has the right to cross-examine the other's witnesses. The judge acts as the referee of the contest, ruling on what kinds of evidence are admissible and the propriety of the questions put to the witnesses. At the end of the trial he also gives the jury instructions on questions that they have to consider and what matters they may legitimately take into account in answering the questions.

The jury then retires to deliberate and reach a verdict. In federal courts the verdict must be unanimous, but the Supreme Court has upheld guilty verdicts in state criminal cases based upon the votes of as few as nine of the twelve jurors (*Johnson* v. *Louisiana,* 1972). However, jurors must find the defendant guilty "beyond a reasonable doubt," which frequently means that the jury is "out" for a considerable period of time. If the jury is "hung"—that is, unable to reach agreement—it is necessary to choose a new one and begin the trial all over again.

Proceedings that follow the jury verdict include the *sentencing* of guilty defendants, the *appeal* of some cases to higher courts, and the final execution of the sentence.

Recent Trends and Controversies in Criminal Procedure

The Supreme Court has been very much concerned in recent years with the protection of the accused in criminal cases. Not only has it extended more and more procedural rights from federal courts to state tribunals, but it has also liberalized its interpretation of a number of basic rights so as to benefit accused persons. The Court's aim has been to extend the concept of equal justice under the law to the poor and uneducated, who so often get into difficulty with legal authorities.

The Right To Counsel. One area in which this is particularly apparent is *the right to counsel.* The *Gideon* case, described at the beginning of this chapter, established a basic principle: every person accused of a serious crime (felony) is entitled to have the assistance of an attorney. If he cannot afford to have one himself, then the government is obliged to provide one.

Gideon was a landmark case in that it opened the door to a series of specific questions involving the right to counsel. One concerns the kind of criminal cases to which it applies. Initially it was thought that the right to counsel might be restricted to felony cases, but in *Argersinger* v. *Hamlin* (1972) the Supreme Court ruled that any deprivation of liberty is a serious matter, and therefore the right also applies to misdemeanor offenses that carry a potential prison or jail sentence.

Another question involves the particular stages of the criminal process to which the right to counsel applies. The Supreme Court has extended the right to proceedings before and after the actual trial. It thus ruled in an important 1964 case, *Escobedo* v. *Illinois,* that the accused is entitled to the assistance of an attorney when an investigation is no longer a general inquiry into an unsolved crime but has begun to focus on a particular suspect, taken into custody, whose statements under interrogation will be used at his trial. At the same time, the Court ruled in *Kirby* v. *Illinois* (1972) that the right to counsel does *not* apply to a confrontation between a recently arrested suspect and the victim of the crime held at the police station-house two days after the crime and before any formal charges have been brought. A year later in *United States* v. *Ash* (1973), the Court held that the constitution does not require that an attorney be present at a pretrial photographic lineup. At the other end of the process, the Court ruled in a 1963 case, *Douglas* v. *United States,* that defendants are entitled to an attorney when their lower-court conviction is appealed to a higher court; however, it has denied such a right in a prison disciplinary hearing (*Wolff* v. *McDonnell,* 1974) and in a parole violation hearing (*Morrissey* v. *Brewer,* 1972).

Since the *Gideon* case, the federal government and the states have wrestled with the problems of who should act as attorneys for the accused and how they should be compensated for their services. In 1966 the national government passed legislation providing funds for attorneys appointed by federal courts to assist defendants in criminal proceedings. States have handled the matter in different ways. Some have provided public defenders, attorneys paid by public funds who concentrate on providing a legal defense in criminal cases for all persons who cannot afford an attorney of their own. Others have provided funds to compensate attorneys appointed in individual cases. Still others have refused to face up to the problem at all, with the result that lawyers have had to provide their services free of charge.

Confessions. The Supreme Court has also been concerned about *confessions.* It has utilized its powers to supervise the administration of justice in federal cases by imposing strict limitations on the interrogation of suspects by federal agents. For example in a 1957 case *Mallory* v. *United States,* the Court ruled that a confession obtained during a ten-hour questioning of the accused between arrest and arraignment was inadmissible at the defendant's trial because the delay gave the opportunity for the extraction of the confession.

The Supreme Court has also become increasingly vigilant about the use of confessions in state proceedings. Not only has it invalidated those involving physical force or the threat of such force; it has also shown increased concern about the use of psychological pressures. In this connection the Court has looked at the "totality of the circumstances" surrounding a confession to determine whether it was voluntary or involuntary. Under that test the Court has balanced the pressures exerted against the ability of the defendant to resist them, taking into account such factors as the kind and duration of the interrogation, and the age, intelligence, and literacy of the accused.

The Supreme Court has also changed its rationale for excluding involuntary confessions. Formerly they were excluded because they were likely to be unreliable. In a 1961 decision, *Rogers* v. *Richmond,* the Court suggested another reason: that because ours is an accusatory—not an inquisitorial—system, the state should be required to prove the guilt of the defendant by evidence other than that which it obtains by coercion out of his own mouth. Since the Supreme Court subsequently held in a 1964 decision, *Mallory* v. *Hogan,* that the Fifth Amendment privilege against self-incrimination expressly applies to state proceedings, confessions extracted by state officials can be invalidated on that basis rather than merely on the grounds that they may be unreliable.

Thus the Supreme Court has increasingly expanded the right to counsel and prohibitions against incriminating confessions so as to protect accused persons. Moreover, it has linked the two in a way that provides even further safeguards. The classic instance, with respect to state proceedings, was a 1966 case, *Miranda* v. *State of Arizona,* the crux of which was that after a two-hour questioning by police officers the accused had confessed to kidnapping and rape. In overturning his conviction the Court ruled that once he had been taken into custody or deprived of his freedom of action in any significant way, law enforcement officials should have informed him that he had the right to remain silent and

that anything he said could later be used against him. They had the additional obligation to tell him that he had the right to an attorney at the questioning and that if he lacked funds to hire one, he would be provided one by the state. Since officials had not complied with these procedural requirements, the Court ruled that the defendant's confession was illegally introduced into evidence and his conviction was invalid.

Few Supreme Court cases have evoked the storm of protest that followed the announcement of the *Miranda* decision. Law enforcement officials complained that it would handcuff their efforts to deal with criminals, and that in its zeal to protect the rights of the accused the Court had forgotten that the real victim was the person against whom the offense was directed, not the one who committed it. Some critics even went so far as to link the nation's mounting crime rate with the permissive attitude of the Supreme Court.

Eventually this sentiment was found in many members of Congress, and when that body passed the Omnibus Crime Control and Safe Streets Act of 1968, it included a provision that sought to prevent the application of the *Miranda* ruling in federal criminal proceedings. The act stated that if a judge, after looking at all the circumstances surrounding a particular confession, found it to have been given voluntarily, then it would be admissible in evidence even though each procedural requirement established in the *Miranda* decision had not been met. In addition, the law sought to alter the effect of the *Mallory* decision by providing that delay in bringing a person before a federal magistrate would not invalidate a confession if it were found to be voluntary and were given within six hours after the arrest of the accused.

In recent years the Court has had to deal with a number of cases raising issues relating to the *Miranda* decision. Some of its subsequent rulings have qualified the broad principles set forth in that Opinion. Thus the Court held in *Harris* v. *New York* (1971) that an unwarned defendant's confession can be admitted for the purpose of discrediting his testimony if he takes the witness stand (but it cannot be used as *evidence* in the prosecution's case). In *Michigan* v. *Tucker* (1974)—a case in which an unnotified defendant named a friend who later incriminated him—the Court ruled that the friend's testimony could be used in the trial because *Miranda* only bars the defendant's own statements, not those of other persons. The Court also held in *Michigan* v. *Mosley* (1975) that if a defendant exercises his right to be silent when questioned about a crime, but at a second interrogation voluntarily makes statements about a different crime, the latter statement is not protected by his original decision to remain silent and can be used as evidence against him. The Court also refused in another 1975 decision, *United States* v. *Mandujano,* to extend the principle of the *Miranda* case to witnesses who appear before grand juries.

While some of the recent Supreme Court decisions have thus restricted the application of the *Miranda* decision, others have extended its principles. In *Doyle* v. *Ohio* and *Wood* v. *Ohio* (1975), the Court ruled that a defendant's remaining silent after being advised of his right to remain so during interrogation could not be used against him in a trial. Moreover, in a highly controversial 1977 decision, *Brewer* v. *Williams,* the Court ruled that a police officer's statement to a defendant accused of the rape and murder of a 10-year-old-child that it would be hard to find her body after more snow had fallen and that the girl's parents deserved to be able to give her a "Christian burial" constituted an

INTERROGATION WARNINGS TO PERSONS IN POLICE CUSTODY:

THE FOLLOWING WARNINGS MUST BE GIVEN TO THE SUBJECT BEFORE THE INTERROGATION BEGINS:

1. "You have the right to remain silent and refuse to answer questions." Do you understand? Subject replied _____.

2. "Anything you do say may be used against you in a court of law." Do you understand? Subject replied _____.

3. "You have the right to consult an attorney before speaking to the police and to have an attorney present during any questioning now or in the future." Do you understand? Subject replied _____.

4. "If you cannot afford an attorney, one will be provided for you without cost." Do you understand? Subject replied _____.

5. "If you do not have an attorney available, you have the right to remain silent until you have had an opportunity to consult with one." Do you understand? Subject replied _____.

6. "Now that I have advised you of your rights, are you willing to answer questions without an attorney present?" Subject replied _____.

Directions to police officer:

A. If the subject indicates that he does not understand any portion of the instructions, they may be explained to him further in substantially similar language.

B. If the subject does not understand English, the statement and any explanations shall be given in whatever language he does speak or understand.

C. If the subject states he wants an attorney, he may not be interrogated until an attorney is present. If the subject states he wishes to remain silent and make no statement, he must not be interrogated. If the subject is talking to the police and then indicates his desire to stop, the interrogation must cease and he must not be interrogated further.

D. If the person in custody indicates he has an attorney and wants to consult with him, the officer conducting the interrogation shall ascertain the identity of such attorney and make every reasonable effort to contact him.

E. Custodial interrogation means questioning begun by police or law enforcement officers after a person has been taken into custody, or otherwise deprived of his freedom of action in any significant way.

2

The "Hot Seat."

interrogation even though the officer did not actually ask the defendant where the body was. When the defendant responded by showing the officers the location of the body and that evidence was introduced at the trial, the defendant's lawyer objected on the grounds that the evidence was obtained on a trip on which the attorney was not permitted to accompany the defendant and against the attorney's explicit instructions that the defendant not be questioned during the trip. The Supreme Court ruled that the trial court's admission of the evidence violated the defendant's right to counsel and ordered the defendant to be retried, a result that Chief Justice Burger called "intolerable in any society which purports to call itself an organized society."

The Death Penalty. Another subject of current controversy in criminal law is the *death penalty.* In a 1972 case, *Furman* v. *Georgia,* the Supreme Court ruled against such a penalty as it is currently applied by the states. Two justices, Brennan and Marshall, felt that it is inherently unconstitutional because it violates the "cruel and unusual punishments" clause of the Eighth Amendment; but others who joined in the opinion place emphasis on the fact that it is applied so rarely, "so wantonly and freakishly," particularly against disadvantaged persons in society, that it serves no valid purpose. The decision thus left open possibility that states could pass new death penalty statutes that would avoid the imposition of that severe sentence in a capricious way. Between 1972 and 1975 some thirty states did enact new death penalty laws containing various provisions such as making the penalty mandatory for certain offenses (such as the murder of a police officer) or establishing separate procedures for determining the guilt of the defendant and for deciding what sentence he should receive.

In 1976 the Court heard five related cases involving the constitutionality of the death penalty laws of Georgia, Texas, Florida, North Carolina, and Louisiana.* It upheld the laws of the first three states and invalidated those of the latter two. While there were a number of differences among the five death penalty laws, all three of those that were upheld contained the two-part procedure providing for the separate determination of guilt and sentencing, and required those making decisions (on whether to impose the sentence of death) to take into consideration the character and record of the defendant and the circumstances of the particular offense involved. In contrast, the invalidated North Carolina and Louisiana statutes provided for a mandatory death sentence for first-degree murder, departing from what the judges regarded as standards of contemporary society that consider such a mandatory sentence as unduly harsh and rigid. At the same time, the Court left open the possibility that a law providing for a mandatory death penalty for a narrowly defined offense—such as the killing of a prison guard by a person sentenced to life imprisonment—might be upheld.

Wiretapping and Other Electronic Surveillance. Perhaps no area of law enforcement has been more controversial and confusing than that involving the use of wiretaps and electronic devices to gather evidence on suspected crimi-

Justice Louis Brandeis.

* The five cases were *Gregg* v. *Georgia, Jurek* v. *Texas, Proffitt* v. *Florida, Woodson* v. *North Carolina,* and *Roberts* v. *Louisiana.*

nals. An early judicial decision, *Olmstead* v. *United States* (1928), approached the matter on the basis of the literal language of the Fourth Amendment protecting "the right of the people to be secure in their persons, houses, papers, and effects against *unreasonable searches* and *seizures.*" Under this approach the Court held that wiretapping of telephones was not unconstitutional because the device used did not involve a physical intrusion into the suspect's premises; nor was any material thing seized. Filing dissents in the *Olmstead* case were Justice Holmes, who called wiretapping a "dirty business," and Justice Brandeis, who made his famous statement that the Constitution grants individuals "the right to be left alone—the right most valued by civilized man."

The Court later abandoned the literal approach to the issue, ruling in a 1967 decision, *Katz* v. *United States,* that the Fourth Amendment "protects people, not places," and that therefore whether a physical intrusion of the premises takes place or whether any material thing is seized is irrelevant. At the same time, the Court held in that decision that the Constitution does not forbid electronic surveillance, provided authorities obtain a valid warrant authorizing the eavesdropping, as required by the Fourth Amendment for searches and seizures. In that case, however, the justices actually extended the protection of the Amendment by holding that police officers must obtain a warrant to eavesdrop on persons in a semipublic place, such as a telephone booth.

With the *Katz* decision as its guide, the Congress enacted Title III of the Omnibus Crime Control and Safe Streets Act of 1968, which permits *court-approved* wiretaps and electronic surveillance in the investigation of a number of crimes. The statute also provides certain exceptions to the necessity of obtaining a court order in order to eavesdrop, for example, in the case of conspiratorial activities threatening the national security or those conspiratorial activities characteristic of organized crime. If an activity is so classified by the Attorney-General of the United States or the principal prosecuting attorney of any state or its subdivisions, the surveillance can proceed *without* a court order, provided an application for an order is obtained within forty-eight hours after the surveillance has occurred or begins to occur. In addition, the 1968 statute also states that its provisions do not "limit the constitutional power of the President to take such measures as he deems necessary to protect the nation against actual or potential attack or other hostile acts of a foreign power. . ."

In recent years the Court has been faced with a series of cases involving the interpretation of the 1968 statute, as well as the general provisions of the Fourth Amendment to the Constitution. In a 1972 decision, *United States* v. *United States District Court for the Eastern District of Michigan,* the Court ruled that the wiretapping of radical domestic groups without prior judicial approval was unauthorized under the 1968 statute as well as being a violation of the Fourth Amendment to the Constitution. Two years later in *United States* v. *Giordano* and *United States* v. *Chavez,* the justices invalidated the evidence obtained from the intercepted conversations of two accused criminals on the grounds that the approval of wiretaps relating to their activities came not from Attorney-General John Mitchell or one of his assistants specially designated for that purpose, but from a minor aide and sometimes from the latter's secretary. Finally, in a 1977 decision, *United States* v. *Donovan,* the Court interpreted the 1968 statute to require that applications for Court orders for wiretaps or electronic surveillance identify all individuals who are suspected of criminal ac-

James McCord, convicted Watergate participant, educates Senate Investigating Committee on a bugging device.

Attorney General Robert Kennedy.

tivity under investigation and who are expected to be overheard, rather than just the principal target of the surveillance. The justices also stated that the 1968 law requires that after the surveillance is completed, the judge who issued the order be furnished with a list of all persons overheard so that he can decide who, in addition to those named as targets in the order, should be informed that they were overheard. However, the Court ruled that in this case the failure to meet these procedures did not invalidate the otherwise legal wiretap.

The relationship of the rights of persons accused of crimes and the rights of society in protecting its members against dangerous individuals remains a major issue in a democracy. Drawing the line between these competing values is a difficult and perennial test in a free but orderly society.

CIVIL JUSTICE AND THE POOR

Along with the increased concern for "equal justice under the law" in criminal matters has come a realization that the poor also need assistance in their civil problems. As Robert Kennedy, while Attorney-General, put the case some years ago:

We have secured the acquittal of an indigent but only to abandon him to eviction notices, wage attachments, repossession of goods and termination of welfare benefits. To the poor man, "legal" has become a synonym simply for technicalities and obstructions, not for that which is to be respected. The poor man looks upon the law as an enemy, not as a friend. For him the law is always taking something away.

Kennedy's statement points up the kinds of legal problems that poor people encounter in their everyday lives and their experience that the law is what other people use to take away their meager possessions. A classic case of this sort occurred some years ago in Washington, D.C., where an appliance store sold a mother of seven children who was on relief $1800 worth of merchandise on an installment contract, whereby she made payment over a long period of time. Five years later, when she had only $170 more to pay, the same firm sold her a $515 stereo set. When she was unable to pay for this, the firm repossessed not only the set, but all the other merchandise that she had been paying for over the years. The company's justification was an obscure provision in fine print in the sales contract to the effect that unpaid balances on any item could be distributed among all prior purchases so as to make her liable for all of them.

The poor have become prey to unscrupulous companies that have not hesitated to extend them credit for goods despite their inability to pay for them. Not only have they become the victims of repossession (frequently without notice), but they also find their wages garnisheed—that is, attached through legal orders served on their employer, a practice that not only denies them the fruits of their labor but also frequently gets them discharged by employers who dislike the inconvenience. The poor are at the mercy of landlords who force them to sign thirty-day leases (typically for dilapidated, crowded quarters) and then evict them without notice for any default in rent.

The poor also suffer at the hands of government agencies, particularly those concerned with welfare and public housing. Traditionally, they have found their benefits cut off without any hearing being held or even any reasons being given for the action. Even when they do receive governmental services, they do so at the price of an invasion of their privacy on such matters as where they live and with whom, what they spend their money for and at which stores, and where they go when they are sick.

Because the poor have so few possessions, it is important they be able to keep the little they have. Yet their usual lack of education and ignorance of their rights makes them vulnerable to persons who take unfair advantage of them. Thus poor people need the assistance of the one individual in society who can make them aware of their rights and how to protect them: the lawyer.

Providing Legal Services For The Poor

Although the *Gideon* decision and others that followed have extended the right to counsel in criminal cases, the Supreme Court has not been disposed to extend the right to civil matters. Even if it did, such a ruling probably could not be implemented. Estimates of the number of poor people needing subsidized legal services have been set as high as forty million. This fact of life has led some urban law experts to suggest that if all the lawyers in the United States did nothing but help poor people with their legal problems, they still would be unable to meet the need. Nonetheless, there has been a marked improvement in the situation since the mid-sixties.

Traditionally, servicing the legal problems of the poor in the United States has been the responsibility of the legal aid societies that first came into existence at the turn of this century. These societies have been supported through local charitable organizations, such as the United Fund or Community Chest; in some instances, local bar associations also provided free legal service to needy persons. Even so, the aid extended through voluntary programs has always been sparse: in 1949 there were only thirty-seven legal aid offices and twenty local bar associations in the United States where the poor could obtain legal assistance. The case loads of these agencies have always been heavy. They

have also been accused of not being aggressive enough in fighting for the rights of the poor for fear of antagonizing private contributors as well as leaders of the bar.

The most significant development in the provision of legal services for the poor was the establishment in 1965 of the Legal Services Division of the Office of Economic Opportunity, a part of the Executive Office of the President. Its approach has been the funding of law offices in ghetto neighborhoods and of traveling attorneys in rural areas. The emphasis has been on taking legal services to the poor in their own locales rather than expecting them to travel to the usual locations of law offices—central-city business districts, suburban areas, and small towns. The Legal Services Program has also dispensed justice in untraditional surroundings such as storefronts.

The Legal Services Program has grown over the years since its establishment in the mid-1960s. By the end of the decade it had a full-time staff of more than 1800 lawyers and operated through 850 neighborhood offices in 265 communities located in forty-nine states, the District of Columbia, and Puerto Rico. It has also handled a large volume of work with good success: in 1968 its lawyers processed 800,000 cases, winning 70 percent of its court trials and 60 percent of its appellate cases.

While the Legal Services Program has placed its primary emphasis on the neighborhood law office, it has also experimented with other methods of providing legal services for the poor. One, known as Judicare, patterned after legal aid in Britain, permits the indigent person to choose his own lawyer, whose services are subsidized by the government. Tried in rural counties in Wisconsin and in New Haven, Connecticut, it has been found to be more expensive than dispensing legal aid through neighborhood law offices but more acceptable to the organized bar. Some students of the problem have also concluded that the quality of legal services dispensed through these law offices tends to be better than that provided by Judicare because the storefront lawyers specialize in the problems of the poor while the individual practitioners must handle them as only a part of their general practice.

In recent years private groups and individuals have also contributed increased legal assistance to the poor. Law schools have made it possible for their students to work with indigent clients and to receive academic credit for the experience, and private foundations have provided fellowships for young lawyers who want to specialize in the legal problems of the poor. Large law firms have also opened branch offices in ghetto areas where they have handled legal matters at fees far below their standard charges; they have also permitted their members to devote a certain portion of their time (for which the firm pays them) to assisting the poor. (This practice has helped such firms to recruit bright, idealistic young lawyers.) Some "public interest" law firms have also concentrated a significant portion of their practice on matters concerning broad societal interests rather than on the problems of individual private clients.

Thus, providing legal services for the poor has undergone a revolution in recent years as a number of groups have contributed toward the goal of equal justice under the law. The entire movement has been strengthened by the substantial endorsement and support of the organized bar in the United States. Yet as the following section shows, there have been controversies over its objectives, particularly as these have been reflected in the activities of the Legal Services Program of the Office of Economic Opportunity.

Objectives and Controversies in the
Legal Services Program

One of the major controversies in the Legal Services Program has been the question of its major goal. Some observers have taken the position that those assisting the poor should concentrate on servicing their needs as they exist within the present structure of law. In other words, poor people should be informed what their legal rights are in dealing with merchants, landlords, spouses, welfare agencies, and public housing authorities, and what they need to do to protect such rights. This concept of helping the poor with their legal problems (often referred to as "Band-Aid" law) has traditionally been pursued by legal aid societies.

In contrast, some experts, including many who have occupied high positions in the Legal Services Program, have argued that much of the present common, statutory, and administrative law discriminates against the poor and in favor of merchants, landlords, and the government itself. Helping the poor, therefore, means more than just protecting their present rights; it also involves helping to establish new rights for them through a reform of the law. And reform involves encouraging clients to challenge present legal rules through test cases taken to the appellate courts with the purpose of getting them to overturn past decisions. It also means helping the poor to organize themselves politically so that they can get Congress and state legislatures, as well as administrative agencies at both levels, to enact laws and regulations favoring the poor.

As might be expected, that approach has not been popular with a number of groups. Some elements of the bar, representing merchants and real estate interests, credit companies, and other commercial concerns, have sought to maintain the status quo in their relationships with consumers, tenants, debtors, and the like. Many public officials have not taken kindly to suits brought against the government itself that seek to establish new rights for welfare recipients or those who live in public housing. What they have particularly resented is that public funds have been channeled through the Legal Services Program to lawyers who have proceeded to challenge many aspects of government programs affecting the poor. Some public officials have also charged that Program funds have been used to provide assistance to militant groups who resort to violence to achieve their goals.

Beginning in 1971 there was general agreement on the part of supporters of legal services in Congress and President Nixon on the desirability of creating a government corporation to handle such matters. However, there was considerable controversy over the composition and method of appointment of the governing body of the corporation and the extent to which it should undertake political and social causes or legal reform activities. The differences were ultimately reconciled in 1974 when legislation was passed establishing the Legal Services Corporation with an eleven-member bipartisan board of directors, all appointed by the President with the consent of Congress. A number of limitations were placed on the kinds of functions the organization can perform, including a curb on political activities, a ban on lawsuits aimed at desegregation of the schools or at obtaining nontherapeutic abortions, and on awarding grants and contracts to outside centers doing research on poverty law or to "public interest" law firms.

Many of the initial disputes involved in the federal government's legal services program for the poor have subsided in recent years. However, it took almost a year after the establishment of the Legal Services Corporation in 1974 for its bipartisan board of directors to be selected: President Ford did not submit his list of nominees for several months, and some senators considered two of Ford's original nominees to be unsympathetic to legal-aid programs, and they had to be replaced. In 1976 the House voted to lift the ban on the corporation's funding outside research centers specializing in poverty law, but the Senate took no action on the measure, and it died at the end of the Ninety-fourth Congress.

Meanwhile, the reform efforts have begun to bear fruit in a number of areas affecting the legal rights of the poor. Courts have declared that grossly exorbitant interest rates and unfair repossession clauses make contracts "unreasonable" and hence unenforceable; they have also recognized tenants' rights against landlords who fail to keep their properties in proper repair or who try to evict them for reporting housing code violations to public officials. Test cases have also established rights for the poor against the government: state residency requirements for welfare benefits have been invalidated; hearings must now be provided both before a person's welfare rights can be terminated and before he can be evicted from public housing; welfare inspectors cannot invade recipients' privacy at any time; benefits cannot be cut off simply because a mother is living with or seeing a man other than her husband; and urban renewal projects cannot proceed until adequate provision is made for relocating residents of the area affected. These and other matters have continued to engage the efforts of those interested in providing equal justice under the law in civil, as well as criminal, cases.

ASSESSMENT

American law as it has evolved over the years consists of a vast body of legal rules and regulations that has served two major purposes: peacefully settling disputes and giving people advance notice of their rights. However, it has been less successful in another goal of the law: rendering justice to all persons equally. The most flagrant violation of the principle of equality under the law was Gerald Ford's pardoning of former President Nixon for any and all crimes he may have committed during his more than five years in office. Such a procedure flies in the face of the democratic concept that the law should be applied impartially without regard to the identity or the status of the individual involved. Particularly unjust was the fact that many persons who had worked for President Nixon, including John Dean and others who

helped to expose the Watergate wrongdoings, served time in jail while the top man went unpunished. President Ford's use of the pardoning power also was premature and lacked legal precedent; typically, a pardon is granted after a person has been tried and found guilty of a crime. Ford's misuse of his prerogative prevented our system of justice from determining what crimes the former President may have committed, a valuable piece of information for those seeking to prevent future Chief Executives from abusing the powers of the office.

Beyond this instance of the special treatment of former President Nixon, there has been a tendency for our legal system to favor the more affluent elements of American society. The development of the legal profession composed of persons from socially advantaged backgrounds, a preoccupation with property values, and the use of *stare decisis,* have all combined to make the law generally a conservative force in society, primarily committed to protecting the status quo and hence the interests of the "haves."

Recent developments, however, have generally led to better protection of the rights of "have-nots" in American society. Supreme Court decisions have created greater procedural safeguards for those accused of crime and have also granted them the right to an attorney to assist in the protection of their rights. Governmental and private efforts have also led to better representation for the poor in civil cases and to the reform of civil law in the direction of better protection for the interests of debtors, tenants, wage earners, and welfare recipients. Although the poor still do not receive the high quality legal service that is available to the affluent, and although they are more likely to be detained pending trial and to receive longer sentences than the socially advantaged for similar offenses, our legal system has made substantial progress toward the goal of "equal justice under the law."

The issues raised by cases involving the right to counsel, confessions, the death penalty, and the use of wiretapping and electronic surveillance pose difficult dilemmas for American society. With our crime rate increasing several times faster than our population growth, it is easy to see merit in Justice Cardozo's observation that "justice is due the accused, but also the accuser" as well as in Justice Stanley Reed's statement that the "purpose of due process is not to protect an accused against a proper conviction, but against an improper conviction." Permitting potentially dangerous persons to go free because of mistakes made by well-meaning but harried police officers operating under extreme pressures raises the distinct possibility that we have overemphasized the rights of the accused at the expense of his victim and society in general.

On the other hand, it is difficult to argue that the end justifies the means in a free society, that police officers should be able to violate the law in order to enforce it. As Justice Brandeis put it so well a number of years ago: "Crime is contagious. If the government becomes a lawbreaker, it breeds contempt for the law; it invites every man to become a law unto himself; it invites anarchy." With the experience of Watergate so close at hand, we should carefully consider the essential wisdom of Brandeis's observation.

There are some possibilities for helping to deal with the problem. One is to make a major investment in more and better-trained police officers, prosecutors, public defenders, and judges. The other is to help the victims of crime by providing them with financial assistance and services designed to mitigate the trauma and difficulties they encounter as a result of their unfortunate experience.

SELECTED READINGS

The information on the Gideon case is taken from the highly readable account of it by Anthony Lewis, *Gideon's Trumpet* (New York: Random House, 1964).

An excellent overall analysis of the law and the judicial process written for students of political science (rather than law students) is Henry J. Abraham, *The Judicial Process* (New York: Oxford University Press, 3rd ed., 1975). Another brief general treatment of the American legal system prepared by members of the Harvard Law School faculty for broadcasts to foreign audiences is Harold J. Berman (ed.), *Talks on American Law* (New York: Vintage, 1961). Both these books contain basic information on the development of law, the various types of laws and judicial procedures, and the kinds of courts that exist for enforcement of the law.

Both the above books also treat of various aspects of the criminal process, as does Henry Abraham's excellent book, *Freedom and the Court: Civil Rights and Liberties in the United States* (New York: Oxford University Press, 3rd ed., 1977). A general analysis of the subject is contained in David Fellman, *The Defendant's Rights* (New York: Holt, Rinehart and Winston, 1958). A critical account of the criminal process is Arnold S. Treback, *The Rationing of Justice* (New Brunswick: Rutgers University Press, 1964). Chapters 19 and 20 of James S. Campbell, Joseph R. Sahid, and David P. Stang, *Law and Order Reconsidered* (New York: Bantam, 1970), analyze recent developments and problems in criminal procedure (this is a Report of the Task Force on Law and Law Enforcement to the National Commission on the Causes and Prevention of Violence). An interesting attack on the *Miranda* decision is Fred Graham, *The Self-Inflicted Wound* (New York: Macmillan, 1970). An excellent summary of recent Supreme Court decisions prepared by the editors of *The Criminal Law Reporter* is *The Criminal Law Revolution and Its Aftermath* (Washington: Bureau of National Affairs, 1973). Chapter 3 of the Report of the Task Force analyzes recent developments and problems in providing civil justice for the poor.

Political Novels   A government-sponsored program ostensibly dedicated to saving America from crime and civil disorder, but secretly designed to establish a police state, is described in *The R Document* (New York: Bantam, 1977) by Irving Wallace. Robert Ludlum, *The Chancellor Manuscript* (New York: Dial, 1977), traces the consequences of abuse of power in a novel about a Director of the Federal Bureau of Investigation (FBI) who used official files for political blackmail.

A variety of competing federal, state and local law-enforcement agencies document, through dozens of wiretaps (not all of them legal), the planning of a major crime in *The Anderson Tapes* (New York: Dell, 1971) by Lawrence Sanders. Because of intergovernmental jealousy and bureaucratic narrow-mindedness, however, these agencies collectively fail to prevent the crime and later cover up their ineptitude.

The crushing brutality of crime and the inadequacies of our criminal-justice system are portrayed by Edwin Torres (a former Assistant District Attorney and presently a judge of the New York County Criminal Court) in his novel *Q and A* (New York: Dial Press, 1977). James Mills, *One Just Man* (New York: Simon and Schuster, 1975), presents a stirring portrayal of contemporary American jurisprudence in a novel about a young public defender who, weary of incessant plea bargaining, sets out to change the system. Anyone who doubts the debilitating effect of crime upon all it touches need only read of its impact upon the police officer who must face it daily. A ferocious novel describing the dangerously dehumanizing effect of urban police work by Joseph Wambaugh, *The Choirboys* (New York: Dell, 1976), reveals frightening aspects of America's least understood public profession.

Though not a work of fiction, a very unique book about the jury system with rare insights into the precarious nature of this process (and its often tenuous relationship to justice) is *Call the Final Witness* (New York: Harper & Row, 1977) by Melvyn B. Zerman. The author served on the jury in a murder trial and offers some disturbing observations as to how a real jury reaches its verdict.

Chapter 16

In his opening statement before the Senate Watergate Committee on June 25, 1973, former presidential counsel John Dean stated that at the end of one of his conversations with the President he had been taken to the side of the room and been addressed by Mr. Nixon in a very low voice, actions Dean interpreted as meaning that the conversation was being recorded. Following that lead on July 13, 1973, the deputy minority counsel of the committee, Donald Sanders, asked Alexander Butterfield, former deputy assistant to the President, if he knew of any basis for Dean's suspicions. "I was hoping you fellows wouldn't ask me that," Butterfield responded and then went on to declare that the President had a taping system installed in the White House in 1970 for historical purposes.

No other aspect of the entire Watergate proceedings had as far-reaching effects as did disclosure of the existence of tape recordings of conversations between high administration officials, including many involving the President himself. Soon both the Watergate Committee and the Special Prosecutor, Archibald Cox (who was exploring possible criminal violations by such officials) sought a number of the taped conversations. As we have seen in chapter 12, the House Judiciary Committee later tried to obtain some of these tapes in connection with its investigations into the possible impeachment of the President. To all three types of investigations Mr. Nixon made the same response: his duty to protect the independence of the presidency under the separation of powers doctrine, as well as the confidentiality of presidential communications with advisers, required him to say no to such requests.

The tales of the tapes had three different endings. The Watergate Committee failed to acquire them because Federal District Judge John Sirica ruled that he had no jurisdiction to enforce the committee subpoena. The House Judiciary Committee declined such a judicial remedy for Mr. Nixon's non-compliance with its subpoenas; it rather made the President's refusal the basis of an impeachment article that it reported to the House of Representatives. But the Special Prosecutor's Office carried the issue to the courts for resolution.

Legal skirmishing over the presidential tapes began in late August of 1973 in the courtroom of Judge Sirica. The President's attorney, Charles Wright, a professor from the University of Texas Law School, argued that the nine tapes sought were immune from disclosure under the doctrine of executive privilege protecting confidential presidential conversations with advisors and that the President is the sole judge of the privilege. Special Prosecutor Cox, at the time on leave from Harvard Law School, countered that such a privilege could not protect specific evidence needed by a grand jury investigating criminal matters and that the courts, not the President, should determine whether the privilege applies to the tapes in question. Sirica ruled in Cox's favor and ordered the President to turn over the tapes to be examined by the judge in the privacy of his office to determine whether they were protected by executive privilege or whether all or portions of them should be turned over to the Special Prosecutor. Sirica's ruling was appealed by the President to the United States Court of Appeals for the District of Columbia; in mid-October the decision of the lower court was affirmed. Thus the stage was set for the last step in the proceedings: an appeal to the United States Supreme Court for a final judicial resolution of the issue.

As the nation waited for a possible confrontation between the President and the Supreme Court, administration spokesmen indicated that Mr. Nixon would obey a "definitive" order of the Court but refused to say specifically what was meant by that term. However, the President decided not to appeal to the highest tribunal, proposing instead a compromise whereby he would release to the grand jury not the tapes themselves but a transcript of them validated by Democratic Senator John Stennis of Mississippi. Special Prosecutor Cox refused the compromise, and the chain of events previously described as the "Saturday Night Massacre" ensued: Cox, Attorney-General Richardson and Deputy Attorney-General William Ruckelshaus were "out" of office, and the public outcry created by the scandal led to the beginning of the congressional impeachment investigation.

Subsequent developments turned from bad to worse for the President. He decided to turn over the tapes after all to a newly appointed Special Prosecutor—Leon Jaworski, a trial lawyer from Houston—but two of the nine subpoenaed tapes were found to be missing, and an 18½-minute gap, considered by some the crucial portion of that conversation, existed on a third one. A panel of experts appointed by Judge Sirica concluded that the gap was the result of deliberate erasure. Moreover, Jaworski himself pushed forward vigorously with his investigation into the Watergate developments and petitioned Sirica for tapes and documents of sixty-four presidential conversations. When the judge again ruled that the President must turn over the subpoenaed materials to

Former Presidential Assistant, Alexander Butterfield, revealer of the White House taping system.

Special Watergate Prosecutor, Leon Jaworski.

Jaworski, the second judicial battle of the tapes was ready for resolution by the appellate courts.

The President once again appealed Judge Sirica's ruling to the United States Court of Appeals. However this time the Special Prosecutor filed a petition of certiorari asking the Supreme Court to take the case directly (without going through the circuit court) in order that a ruling could be made in time for the possible use of the tapes in criminal litigation against some of Mr. Nixon's key advisers set for September. To the surprise of many who expected the justices to duck the controversial issue, the Court granted certiorari in early June and set the date of July 8 for argument of opposing counsel on the case. The Court again confounded many observers by not deferring its decision until after the House Judiciary Committee completed its work; instead, the justices handed down their decision on July 24, 1974, the very day the committee began its televised debates on whether to recommend impeachment of the President to the House of Representatives.

The momentous decision, described by some as a civics lesson for the President, dealt with some of the most fundamental issues of the American constitutional system. A unanimous 8-0 opinion (Justice William Rehnquist withdrew from the case because of his previous service with former Attorney-General John Mitchell) delivered by President Nixon's first appointee to the Court, Chief Justice Burger, ruled on three major issues of the case. First, the Court pushed aside the argument that the Special Prosecutor could not sue the President because he was the Chief Executive and his superior in the executive branch, holding that regulations issued by the Attorney-General establishing the unique authority of the Special Prosecutor's office explicitly granted him the power to contest the President's claim of executive privilege. Second, the Court invoked the language of *Marbury* v. *Madison* (1803)—to be discussed later in the chapter—that "it is emphatically the province and duty of the judicial department to say what the law is." The Chief Justice held that the Court, not the President, is the final judge under our constitutional system of the proper use of executive privilege. Finally, the justices dealt directly with the nature of the privilege itself and how it applied to the facts of the case. The Court explicitly recognized for the first time the general principle of executive privilege as having "constitutional underpinnings"; however it ruled that the general claim of the privilege when unrelated to military, diplomatic, and national security issues, must give way to the more immediate need for evidence in a criminal case and the fundamental principles of due process of law and the fair administration of justice.

While the President had refused to say this time whether he would even obey a "definitive" Court decision, within eight hours after the opinion was handed down he announced through his attorney, James St. Clair, that he would turn over the tapes. Within a week, the President began to examine the materials for national security matters that he would ask Judge Sirica to withhold from the Special Prosecutor.

Few cases take on the historical significance of *United States* v. *Richard Nixon* and have such a major impact on the basic operation of our political system. Nonetheless, federal courts play a major role in resolving a variety of disputes in American society.

THE JURISDICTION OF FEDERAL COURTS

The general jurisdiction of the federal courts is set forth succinctly in Article III, Section 2 of the Constitution. Two words used there, cases and controversies, have been construed by the federal courts to mean that the litigation they hear must involve an actual dispute. Two parties cannot trump up a lawsuit merely to have the Court interpret a federal statute or determine its constitutionality. Nor will federal judges render advisory opinions about how or whether a particular law should be enforced. Only a party that has actually been adversely affected by the provisions of a law can obtain an interpretation or test its constitutionality.

Assuming an actual case brought by a legitimate plaintiff, it can be heard by federal courts only if its falls within one of two broad categories. One concerns the *subject matter* of the suit, which is limited to litigation involving the federal Constitution, a federal law, a treaty, or admiralty and maritime matters.

The other category relates to the *particular parties* to the suit. If the United States is suing or being sued, the federal courts can hear the case. They have jurisdiction over cases affecting ambassadors and other agents of foreign governments, disputes between a state or one of its citizens and a foreign government or one of its citizens. Interstate conflicts can also come to the federal courts. These include litigation between states, between citizens of different states, between citizens of the same state who claim lands under grants of different states, and between a state and a citizen of another state (but only if the state is bringing suit).

The jurisdiction of federal courts is established by the Constitution, but the way they exercise it is for the most part determined by Congress. The only constitutional provision that restricts its discretion is the stipulation in Article III, Section 2 that in cases involving ambassadors, other public ministers, and consuls, and those in which a state is a party, the Supreme Court has original jurisdiction (the power to hear the case for the first time).

With this exception, Congress can make what rules it wishes. For example, it may forbid the federal courts to handle a particular kind of case. Indeed, a suit between citizens of different states must involve $10,000 or more before a federal court will hear it; Congress has turned over to the state courts controversies involving lesser amounts of money. Or Congress may allow both federal and state courts to hear a particular type of case—in other words, to exercise concurrent jurisdiction. Suits between citizens of different states involving more than $10,000 are in that category: if both parties desire, they can litigate the matter in a state court. Finally, Congress has the power to assign exclusive federal jurisdiction; for instance, cases involving alleged violations of a federal criminal statute must be heard in a federal court, not a state one.

In addition to its power to allocate cases between federal and state courts, Congress can also decide at which level in the federal judiciary a matter will be heard. The only judicial tribunal specifically mentioned in the Constitution is the Supreme Court; Article II, Section 1 empowers Congress to create "inferior" (that is, lower) courts to assist with the processing of federal litigation. The following section of that same article also empowers Congress to regulate the appellate jurisdiction of the Supreme Court, determining what matters it will review that have initially been tried in lower courts. The federal judicial system today, as developed through statutes passed by Congress over the years since the initial Judiciary Act of 1789, includes, in addition to the United States Supreme Court, the United States district courts and the United States courts of appeals.*

MAJOR FEDERAL COURTS

The District Courts

The United States district courts are primarily courts of original jurisdiction. Although they get some cases from state courts and review some actions of federal administrative agencies, for the most part the district courts are the trial tribunals of the federal judiciary. It is here that spirited battles occur, involving opposing attorneys, witnesses, a jury (though often, particularly in civil cases, the parties waive a jury trial), and a single presiding judge (however, when an injunction is sought to declare federal or state statutes or the order of a state administrative agency unconstitutional, three judges sitting as a group hear the case). The overwhelming proportion of federal cases—some 90 percent—begin and end in the district courts.

District courts concern themselves with a wide variety of matters. The most prevalent is bankruptcy, which cannot be heard in a state court. It is there, too, that the federal government brings antitrust suits and prosecutes persons who steal automobiles and take them across a state line. Cases involving citizens of different states are much like those that fill the dockets of state courts: automobile accidents, breaches of contract, and labor cases. Over 300,000 cases, about two-thirds of them bankruptcy proceedings, are filed annually in federal district courts; of these some 15,000 actually go to trial.

This flood of cases is heard by some 400 judges located in ninety-four district courts.† In size they range from one to twenty-seven judges. They are national

---

* In addition to the federal courts of general jurisdiction authorized by Article III there are special federal courts that handle disputes arising from particular functions of Congress under powers granted by Article I. Included are United States Customs courts, the United States Court of Custom and Patent Appeals, the United States Court of Military Appeals, territorial courts, and the United States Court of Claims, which hears claims brought against the national government.
† Legislation introduced in the Senate in early 1977 would add over 100 new federal district judgeships; at the same time the House was considering similar legislation. Given the fact that no new federal district judgeships have been created since 1970, and a Democratic President—Jimmy Carter—would have the power (along with the Senate) to choose such judges, the legislation was given a good chance of passage.

courts, but they are oriented to a considerable degree to states and localities. Each state has at least one federal district court, and no court jurisdiction crosses state lines. And although district court judges occasionally are assigned to hear cases in other districts (for example, a visiting North Dakota district court judge issued the famous injunction in 1957 prohibiting Governor Faubus and other Arkansas officials from interfering with the integration of the Little Rock schools), for the most part they preside over disputes arising in their own area.

The United States Courts of Appeals

The United States courts of appeals serve as the major appellate tribunals in the federal court system. They review principally the civil and criminal decisions in cases initially heard in federal district courts and the orders and decisions of federal administrative units, particularly the independent regulatory agencies. Over 90 percent of the approximately 13,000 cases heard annually by the courts of appeals end right there; only a small proportion go to the United States Supreme Court for final disposition.

Figure 16.1

The U.S. Courts of Appeals and the U.S. District Courts. The large numerals indicate the various Courts of Appeals, and the heavy lines represent the jurisdictional boundaries of each circuit. The broken lines represent jurisdictional boundaries of District Courts in states having more than one district. *D.C.* indicates the "eleventh" circuit court, situated in the District of Columbia and titled *U.S. District Court for the District of Columbia.*
Source: Administrative Office of the U.S. Courts.

As indicated by Figure 16.1, there are ten regional courts of appeals located in various parts of the United States, plus one in the District of Columbia.* The size of the courts varies from three judges in the First Circuit in the New England area to fifteen in the Fifth Circuit in the South. In some instances judges sit in different cities located within a court's jurisdiction.

To expedite their considerable case load, courts of appeals are divided into panels of three judges. The Chief Judge of each court determines the composition of the various panels, which are changed from time to time so that a judge does not always have the same colleagues. On application of the parties or the judges themselves, a case can be heard *en banc*—that is, by the entire court. The procedure is fairly rare, being restricted to legal questions of exceptional importance or cases in which the court feels that a full tribunal is necessary to secure uniformity in its decisions or compliance with a controversial decision.

Courts of appeals judges tend to be less closely tied to particular states and localities than their counterparts in district courts. Thus Fifth Circuit judges have been more likely to vote in favor of blacks in civil rights cases than have their brethren in the Southern federal trial courts, and they have overruled a number of lower court decisions that originally favored white litigants.

The United States Supreme Court

Attorneys frequently assure clients who have lost cases in state or lower federal courts that they will take the matter to the United States Supreme Court, where it will be settled in their favor. Designed as a tactic to console clients and to convince them that their attorneys will stand by them, the promise is seldom realized. For one thing, most people lack the financial resources needed to carry legal battles to the highest tribunal. Costs naturally vary with the nature of the suit and the court level at which it is first tried, but at a minimum, tens of thousands of dollars will be involved in court and attorneys' fees, and in many instances the figure will be in the hundreds of thousands.† For another, even if a person has the money to fight his case to that level, he may not be willing to take his chances on the decision.

Besides, there is a great difference between taking a case to the United States Supreme Court and getting the justices to hear it. In recent years several thousand cases have been filed annually, but the Court generally takes on only a few hundred. Over 90 percent of those who seek the assistance of the Court have come away disappointed.

In fact, the Supreme Court has almost complete discretion over the cases it will hear. Litigation that comes within the *original jurisdiction* of the Court (cases involving foreign ambassadors, ministers, and consuls, and those in

* The legislation referred to in the previous footnote would add thirty-five new court of appeals judges to the present number of ninety-seven. It would also create an additional circuit by splitting off a portion of the Fifth Circuit, which presently handles the most cases. The new circuit would include Texas and Louisiana, while Alabama, Mississippi, Georgia, Florida, and the Canal Zone would remain in the Fifth Circuit.

† It has been estimated that the litigation that eventually resulted in the 1954 school desegregation decision, *Brown v. Board of Education,* cost the National Association for the Advancement of Colored People over $200,000.

The Supreme Court.

which a state is a party) may come to it for initial consideration. But even here there is some leeway since Congress has granted to district courts *concurrent jurisdiction* over controversies pertaining to foreign diplomatic personnel and some involving a state. As a result, most cases heard for the first time before the Supreme Court involve two states. In any event, cases of original jurisdiction constitute a very minor part of the case load of the Supreme Court, typically amounting to only a few cases each year. For all practical purposes, then, the Supreme Court is an appellate body.

Congress, which regulates the appellate jurisdiction of the Supreme Court, has established two major sources of cases: the United States courts of appeals and the highest courts of the various states.* Yet the Court is granted discretion over which cases it will actually review. Typically, it chooses only those that involve a "substantial federal question" or that for "special and important reasons" the Court feels it should deal with. The Court chose to hear Gideon's controversy, for instance, because it felt that the right to counsel in state criminal cases was an important constitutional issue and that the previous ruling in the 1942 *Betts* v. *Brady* decision had not dealt with the matter satisfactorily.† In other instances the Court may choose a case because it involves the interpretation of an important federal statute or because it raises a legal issue on which various district courts or courts of appeals have ruled differently. It is not

---

* Certain cases, such as those involving challenges to state or federal statutes, come directly to the Supreme Court from the federal district courts, as do some from special federal courts like the United States Court of Claims or territorial courts. The Court also allows major cases like *United States* v. *Richard Nixon,* for which there are compelling reasons for an immediate decision, to be heard without going through a court of appeals.

† Gideon's case was considered by the Supreme Court under special rules that permit it to review appeals filed by indigents (designated as "paupers") even though they do not satisfy requirements such as the filing of forty copies of a typewritten petition in proper form and the paying of court costs.

Supreme Court Justices.

enough that members of the Supreme Court believe that the wrong party won in the lower court or that a legal injustice has been done. Before they accept a case (four justices must agree to do so), they must also feel that it raises important issues transcending the particular parties and case involved, with important consequences for the American political system or society in general.

The most important factor affecting decision making by the Supreme Court is that it is a *collegial* body. Unlike the courts of appeals, it does not divide itself into separate panels to hear different cases. Members have taken the position that the Constitution refers to one Supreme Court, not several, and therefore all judges should normally participate in each case. (The fact that the Court has almost complete discretion over the cases it will hear enables it to concentrate its attention on relatively few; otherwise, the Court could never employ collective decision making.)*

The annual session of the Supreme Court is spread over a thirty-six-week period from October to June, although on occasion the court issues decisions after that time, as it did in *United States* v. *Richard Nixon.* During this period the Court sets aside about four days a week during two weeks of each month to hear oral arguments of opposing counsel on cases that the Court has chosen for a full hearing. Typically, the time is divided between the two sides, with each attorney having a half-hour to an hour to present and defend his case. The justices feel free to interrupt attorneys for questions at any point: interrogation by Justice Frankfurter was considered a harrowing experience, not unlike a searching oral examination of a graduate student. Contributing to the tension for many, if not most, attorneys is the fact that this may be their first and last appearance before the Court. Only the Solicitor-General, who presents cases in

* Recently a suggestion was made by a group appointed by Chief Justice Burger that a National Court of Appeals be created to screen cases for the Supreme Court to hear. However, the proposal drew opposition from former Justices Douglas and Brennan, as well as by the late Chief Justice Earl Warren.

which the United States is a party (about half of all those argued before the Court), gets extensive experience in the nation's highest Court.

The overwhelming proportion of the work of the Supreme Court, however, takes place behind the scenes, or behind the "purple curtain" (which forms the backdrop for the public appearances of the Court). The justices spend most of the time individually reading and studying cases and discussing them with their law clerks (recently graduated students of the nation's top law schools)* as well as some of their colleagues. However they come together as a single group for conferences, held on Friday (increasingly supplemented by post-3:00 P.M. Wednesday meetings) to make joint decisions on certain matters.

One major matter settled in conference is the choice of cases that the Court will hear that term. Another is the way cases already heard by the Court should be decided. In both matters the Chief Justice gives his views first, then the associate justice with the longest service on the Court speaks, and so on to the most junior man, who speaks last. The voting on both issues proceeds in reverse order with the Chief Justice voting last.

After the case is decided, it must be determined who will write the opinion setting forth the decision of the Court and the reasons behind that decision. If the Chief Justice votes with the majority, he decides who should write the opinion. If the case is a major one, he will probably assume the responsibility himself, as Chief Justice Warren did in the *Brown* v. *Board of Education* decision in 1954 and Chief Justice Burger did in the *United States* v. *Richard Nixon* case in 1974. Most opinions, however, are assigned so as to spread the work load of the Court among its nine members. If the Chief Justice is not on the prevailing side, the most senior justice who is writes the opinion himself or assigns it to one of his colleagues.

The assignment of an opinion is a delicate decision. An opinion is often assigned to the justice whose views are closest to those of the minority, the idea being that he may be able to win them over to the majority's side. This tactic is often pursued when a premium is placed on getting a unanimous or nearly unanimous opinion by the Court, a particularly desirable goal in controversial decisions when the justices want maximum public acceptance, as they did in the *Brown* and *Nixon* cases. For the same reason, an opinion may be assigned to a justice with personal or background characteristics that help to make the result more palatable: Chief Justice Warren assigned the controversial opinion outlawing the reading of the Bible and the repeating of the Lord's Prayer in the public schools to Justice Tom Clark, a Southern conservative, who was a deeply religious man.

The assignment of an opinion to a justice, however, does not necessarily end the collegial process. Negotiation may continue as he strives to write the opinion so that a maximum number of the justices join with him in it. He may even adopt suggestions and reasoning of other justices in order to dissuade them from writing opinions of their own. (Separate opinions may be either concurring ones, in which the writer agrees with the result reached by the majority opinion but not for the same reasons, or dissenting opinions—those reaching the opposite result.) It is often not possible to settle differences: because most cases heard by the Supreme Court are controversial and because the justices

---

* Associate Justices are entitled to three, the Chief Justice to five, such clerks.

"WHEN IT'S 6-TO-3, YOU'RE ONE OF THE THREE. WHEN IT'S 7-TO-2, YOU'RE ONE OF THE TWO. WHEN IT'S 8-TO-1, YOU'RE THE ONE. SIR, YOU ARE AN INCORRIGIBLE SPOILSPORT."

are typically men with strongly held views, a great number of divided opinions result.

Getting nine men with strong, diverse views to work together well as a group is not an easy feat. One close student of the subject, political scientist David Danelski, has pointed out that it calls for both "task" leadership, or expediting the work of the Court, and "social" leadership, or helping establish good interpersonal relationships among the justices. The key part that the Chief Justice plays in conference discussions and in the assignment of opinions furnishes him with the opportunity to provide both types of leadership. How well a given Chief Justice performs, however, depends on his personality and skills in interpersonal relationships. Danelski feels that former Chief Justice Hughes was successful in providing the Court with both "task" and "social" leadership, whereas Chief Justice Stone failed on both counts. Chief Justice Taft performed the social role effectively but let his good friend Justice Van Devanter become the task leader during his tenure.

The final stage in the decision-making process of the Supreme Court is the announcement of its decisions and the reasons for them in open session on "opinion day," typically held on two or three Mondays each month while the Court is in session.* The justices present their opinions orally: some read them verbatim, others merely summarize their major points. These sessions are frequently enlivened by caustic comments and even verbal exchanges between judges who differ strongly on cases under discussion.

The operation of the federal courts, of course, depends not only on their jurisdiction and their customs but also on the individual judges. The following section explains how judges are chosen and describes the kinds of persons who become judges at all three levels of the federal judiciary.

THE SELECTION AND BACKGROUNDS OF FEDERAL JUDGES

Unlike most state judges, who are elected by the people, federal jurists are appointed. The Constitution specifically states that the President shall nominate and, by and with the advice and consent of the Senate, appoint Supreme Court judges. Congress provides for the same process to be used for staffing the lower federal courts, so the President and the Senate are partners in the appointment process for all federal judges.

The Politics of Selection

Both the President and the Senate have sought the assistance of other officials to help them carry out their responsibilities of appointment. The Attorney-General's office recommends judicial candidates to the President. And the Senate Judiciary Committee considers the nominees and votes as a group recommending confirmation or rejection. Although neither the President nor the entire Senate is obliged to accept the advice of the Attorney-General's office or the Senate Judiciary Committee, both are generally inclined to do so.

* By delivering all its opinions on Monday, the Court creates problems for the mass media, which frequently must report and comment on a variety of cases at one time. Former Chief Justice Warren initiated a practice of releasing some opinions on other days, but most are still delivered on Monday. The *Nixon* decision, however, came on Wednesday, July 24, 1974, the very day on which the House Judiciary Committee began its historic impeachment debate.

The selection of federal judges involves many other persons and groups, both inside and outside the government. Their interests are different, and their influence is felt at different stages of the selection process.

The earliest and perhaps the most important part of the process is the *recruitment* of candidates. Senators (of the President's party) from states in which district courts and courts of appeals appointees are to serve are a major source of suggestions. State and even local party officials are sometimes drawn into the process, especially if the state has no senators of the President's political party. The President himself, as well as his representatives in the Attorney-General's office, also recruits judicial candidates, especially for the Supreme Court and the United States courts of appeals.

Other persons and groups involved in the process do not belong to either the party in the government or the party organization. A prime example is a lawyer who is a self-starter—that is, one who promotes his own candidacy for the federal bench and lines up influential support. Sitting federal judges may also become involved, although most of them are inclined to wait for others to seek their advice on prospective nominees rather than advance candidates of their own. Although they are important on occasions, neither judicial self-starters nor sitting judges are as significant in the recruitment process as are public and party officials.

The second stage is the *screening* of candidates. It is here that the President and the senators scrutinize one another's nominees. The analysis of the various candidates by the Attorney-General's office includes a check into their backgrounds and activities by the Federal Bureau of Investigation.

Interest groups also enter the process at this juncture. In particular, the Committee on the Federal Judiciary of the American Bar Association evaluates persons being considered for nomination to the federal bench. It has customarily used the ratings "exceptionally well-qualified," "well-qualified," "qualified," and "not qualified." Although Presidents are not required to refer prospective nominees to the committee for consideration, they have generally done so since 1946. Other interest groups (including state and local bar associations, labor unions, and business groups) may also play some part in evaluating nominees, but their role in the process is not as institutionalized or considered as legitimate as that of the Committee of the American Bar Association.

After the President makes his nomination for a federal judgeship, the Senate must act to *confirm* or *reject* it. The Senate Judiciary Committee, operating through subcommittees, conducts hearings and invites testimony. Interest groups, including nonlegal ones, often become involved at this point. Those that have been unable to prevent the President from nominating a person they do not favor may carry the fight against him to the committee. The Senate committee gets the view of the American Bar Association and gives any senator of the President's party from the state concerned a chance to indicate approval or opposition by the use of a "blue slip" (a standard blue form) or by invoking the informal rule of "*senatorial courtesy*," declaring that the nominee is "personally noxious" to him. This merely means that the senator opposes him for political reasons or has a candidate of his own whom he prefers to the President's man; when this occurs—rarely of late—the Senate may refuse to confirm the nomination as a matter of political custom. Unless the nomination is withdrawn by the President, the Judiciary Committee makes a recommendation on the nomination, but the final decision is up to the entire Senate.

Patterns and Trends in the Selection of Federal Judges

The variety of persons and groups that participate in the selection of federal judges makes the process a complex one. Those who are especially influential in the choice of one judge may not be nearly so important in the selection of another. The eventual outcome depends on a number of factors: the level of federal court involved, the attitudes and political skills of the President and particular senators involved, the characteristics of the candidate, and the general political tenor of the times. Nonetheless, it is possible to discern certain basic patterns and trends in the selection of federal judges.

Although the Constitution clearly provides that the President is to nominate and, by and with the advice and consent of the Senate, to appoint all federal judges, the process for the district courts typically works in reverse. The initiative comes from the Senate, or more precisely the senator or senators of the President's party from the state concerned. The President has a veto power over those who are offensive to him politically or who fail to meet the minimum qualification standards of the organized bar, but the rule of senatorial courtesy, which has been in effect since the Washington administration, is a powerful weapon for use against the President. Moreover, few Chief Executives are willing to risk the loss of political support in the Senate over a district court judgeship, since the work of such a tribunal is seldom crucial to his own political goals or programs.

The President is generally more influential in the selection of judges to the United States courts of appeals. He takes more of a personal interest in them than in district court appointments for two reasons. First, the courts of appeals handle matters of more importance to him. For example, their review of actions of the independent regulatory commissions can affect his overall economic program. Second, courts of appeals judgeships are less numerous and more prestigious, inviting the interest of his major political supporters. Furthermore, with the courts of appeals appointments, senators are in weaker bargaining positions. Since these courts encompass several states, no senator (or pair of senators) from any one state can lay a special claim to name an appointee that is recognized by the entire Senate. By political custom these judgeships are apportioned among the various states involved, but the President and his advisors determine how and in what sequence to do so.

The President clearly dominates the selection process for the Supreme Court. He is, of course, vitally interested in the decisions reached by that tribunal since they affect the operation of the entire political system and the functioning of American society in general. Since a Supreme Court judgeship is so prestigious, few, if any, lawyers would be inclined to turn down the post. And with the entire nation as the Court's geographical jurisdiction, no senator, or even group of senators, has a special say over the allocation of judgeships. Only the entire Senate can thwart the President's wishes.

The historical record of Supreme Court appointments is that about one in five presidential nominations has either been rejected outright or not acted on by the Senate, a far higher proportion of failure to confirm than for any other federal office. There has been considerable variation in the fate of nominees at different times. Bitter political battles led to a number of failures to confirm in the period from 1829 when Andrew Jackson took office until Grant left the presidency in 1877. At the other extreme, from 1894 (when two of President

Cleveland's nominees were rejected) until 1968 when the Senate failed to act on Lyndon Johnson's nomination of Associate Justice Abe Fortas to the chief justiceship, and the nomination of Homer Thornberry to take Fortas's place, only one nominee—a Southern court of appeals judge, John J. Parker—failed to be confirmed. The Fortas matter was soon followed by the outright rejection of two of President Nixon's nominees, Clement Haynsworth and G. Harrold Carswell, courts of appeals judges from South Carolina and Florida respectively, within a few months' time in late 1969 and early 1970.

An analysis of the circumstances surrounding the four incidents in this century reveals the factors that contribute to the Senate's failure to confirm presidential nominees. Perhaps the most basic is the presence of major political differences between key senators and the President. Democrats joined with progressive Republicans of the day in defeating the nomination of Judge Parker by Republican President Herbert Hoover. The same type of coalition of Northern Democrats and liberal Republicans formed to defeat Haynsworth and Carswell. On the other hand, prominent Senate Republicans allied themselves with conservative Democrats from the South to filibuster successfully against Justice Fortas.

These four failures to confirm also reflected broader political divisions in the nation. All three of the rejected Republican nominees—Parker, Haynsworth, and Carswell—were Southerners who were bitterly opposed by black and liberal interest groups for their rulings on civil rights cases. The former two were also considered antilabor. Fortas, in turn, had incurred the enmity of a number of conservative groups through his liberal decisions in obscenity cases and suits involving the rights of the accused in criminal proceedings.

Other issues have played a role in the three most recent incidents. Several senators who had originally supported Fortas's elevation subsequently joined with others in urging that he resign from the Court when his acceptance of a fee from a family foundation become known. Some senators were also opposed to Fortas's continuing to advise President Johnson on political matters while he was serving on the Court. Judge Haynsworth was criticized for ruling on cases involving companies in which he had a financial interest, while Judge Carswell's role in helping incorporate a segregated social club in his hometown in Florida contributed to the defeat of his nomination. While the political infighting in these three nomination battles was particularly vicious, and although these issues represented outward manifestations of deeper partisan and philosophical differences between the contending parties, it is very possible that the financial affairs of Supreme Court nominees, as well as their off-the-bench activities in general, may in the future come under closer scrutiny.

The opposition to Judge Carswell's nomination by members of the bar, particularly law professors who claimed that his opinions were mediocre, may indicate that the legal qualifications of Supreme Court nominees will also be analyzed more carefully in the future. This development would suggest an increased role for the American Bar Association's Committee on the Federal Judiciary in future appointments.* The fact that the committee found Carswell to be qualified for the position may lead it to analyze candidates more thor-

---

* Republican Presidents have been more inclined than Democratic ones to pay heed to the Committee's ratings; it has also played a more important role in the selection of lower federal judges than of Supreme Court justices.

oughly in the future and to check their legal credentials with both the academic segment of the bar and practicing attorneys.

Characteristics of Federal Judges

The characteristics of federal judges reflect a number of the considerations that bear on their appointment. The most basic qualification is membership in the *legal profession*. Although this is not a legal requirement, it is an informal custom: no nonlawyer has ever been appointed to a federal judgeship. Moreover, in keeping with contemporary preparation of lawyers, almost every judge appointed to the federal bench since the end of World War II has been a graduate of a law school.

Another common attribute of federal judges is *public experience*. All except one of the 102 judges who have served on the Supreme Court previously engaged in public service at some level of government or participated in political activities. Lower federal court judges also have political backgrounds; in fact, they are frequently described as "lawyers who knew a United States senator," particularly those on district benches. Attorneys who refrain from any type of participation in public affairs are not likely to be as visible to senators or to Presidents or their advisors as are lawyers who are active in public life.

As might be expected, the most prevalent kind of previous public office is one connected with the *courts*. Judges have often been city, county, or state prosecutors, or district attorneys. Some have also served as United States attorneys or their associates, while a few have been Solicitor-General or Attorney-General of the United States.

Previous *judicial experience* is also common among federal judges, although not as common as might be supposed. About one-third of the present district judges have previously been state judges; two in five judges on courts of appeals have been on the bench previously, most of them as federal district judges. The Supreme Court draws its appointees from both pools: of the 102 justices in the nation's history, twenty-two came from an inferior federal court, and twenty-one from a state bench.*

Whatever the particular public experience of potential judicial appointees has been, they tend to be affiliated with the *same political party* as the President who appoints them. As indicated by Figure 16.2, recent Chief Executives have all overwhelmingly favored members of their own party as appointees to lower federal courts. Presidents also tend to stay within party ranks when making appointments to the Supreme Court: only thirteen of the 102 justices have been named by a President of another party.

When a President does cross party lines, it is likely to be because he has a high regard for the person concerned and a conviction that the nominee, while affiliated with the opposition, shares the President's *general political philosophy* and views on public policy issues. A vivid statement of this consideration is contained in a letter Republican President Theodore Roosevelt once sent to his

---

* Extensive judicial experience among Supreme Court justices is not common: of the 102 justices, only twenty-four had ten or more years' experience on some court. Although the lack of such experience has been criticized, some of the most eminent jurists, including John Marshall, Roger Taney, Louis Brandeis, Felix Frankfurter, and Earl Warren, had no prior judicial experience at all.

Figure 16.2
Appointments to Federal District Courts and Courts of Appeals, 1933–1976.
Source: Data from *Congressional Quarterly Almanac*, 1976, p. 969.

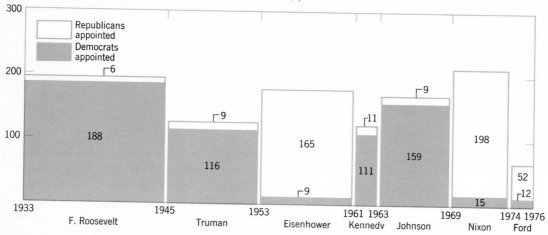

good friend Senator Henry Cabot Lodge of Massachusetts explaining a nomination:

. . . the nominal politics of the man [Horace H. Lurton, a Democrat] has nothing to do with his actions on the bench. His real politics are all important. . . . . He is right on the Negro question; he is right on the Insular business; he is right about corporations; and he is right about labor. On every question that would come before the bench, he has so far shown himself to be in much closer touch with the policies in which you and I believe.*

Although Presidents attempt to choose men for the Supreme Court who share their general political views, they are not always successful in doing so. Justices often behave in ways not anticipated by their benefactors. Immediately after he was appointed to the Court by Theodore Roosevelt, Oliver Wendell Holmes, Jr. voted on the side of private enterprise and against the administration in a famous antitrust case, *Northern Securities* v. *United States* (1904). And President Eisenhower had little reason to suspect that his nominee for Chief Justice, Earl Warren, would become one of the most liberal, "activist" jurists in the history of the Supreme Court. Yet once the Chief Executive has placed a man on the Court, there is little he can do about his appointee's decisions since for all practical purposes, he is there for life.†

A Supreme Court appointment is so important because many social, economic, and political issues of the day become involved in litigation that comes to the Court for a decision. Most of these decisions require the Court to interpret major congressional statutes. Some, however, involve the justices of the Supreme Court in an even more demanding and controversial task: interpreting the Constitution itself.

* Lodge replied that a Republican with similar views could be obtained and persuaded Roosevelt to nominate William Moody, the Attorney-General of Massachusetts. Lurton was subsequently appointed by Roosevelt's successor, another Republican, President William Howard Taft.
† All federal judges hold office during "good behavior" or until they die or choose to retire voluntarily. They can also be impeached, but only four have been removed in that manner, and none of them was a Supreme Court justice.

JUDICIAL REVIEW

Although the expression judicial review might conceivably be applied to a court's reexamination of any matter already handled by a lower tribunal, it has a much more precise meaning. It refers to the power of a court to review the actions of all public officials—legislative, executive, and judicial—to see whether they are inconsistent with the governing constitution and, if the court finds that they are, to declare them unconstitutional and hence unenforceable.

In exercising judicial review, a court thus regards a constitution as being superior to ordinary laws or executive and judicial decrees; in determining that an official action is unconstitutional and therefore invalid, the court must find that a legislator, an executive, or a judicial official has done something that he has no authority to do under the constitution or that he has taken some action that is forbidden by the constitution.

Judicial review exists at various levels of our political system. For example, state courts have the power to determine whether actions of state legislators, executives, or judicial officials violate the state constitution and to render invalid those that do. On such matters the decision of the highest state court is final. State courts also have the power to interpret the national Constitution as it applies to state actions. It can also decide whether a federal law or treaty is in violation of the national Constitution. But the rulings of state courts are not final on these issues; they may be appealed to the federal courts for final disposition.

The federal judiciary has the final say on whether actions of state or national officials violate the national Constitution. In the *Gideon* case the Supreme Court ruled that state judicial officials in Florida violated the due process clause of the Fourteenth Amendment when they tried and convicted Gideon for a state felony offense without providing legal counsel for him. In an earlier case, *Johnson* v. *Zerbst* (1938), the Court had decided that the Sixth Amendment granted indigent persons accused of violating federal crimes the right to counsel and that therefore the defendant's trial by a lower federal court without the assistance of an attorney was unconstitutional.

Some aspects of judicial review are more controversial than others. The right of a court to set aside actions of political officials—that is, legislators and executives—has been of more concern to students of the democratic process than its power to invalidate what other judges have done. The power of the federal courts to review the actions of national officials has been more seriously questioned than their authority to render unenforceable the activities of state officials. And it is the combination of these two most criticized aspects of judicial review, the power of federal courts to invalidate actions of legislative and executive officials of the national government, that has provoked the greatest controversy.

Very few nations grant courts the power of judicial review as it is exercised in the United States. Typically, in countries with a federal form of government the power is granted to judicial tribunals, as in Australia, Canada, India, and West Germany. Even in these nations, however, the role of the courts in invalidating actions of political officials has never taken on the significance that it has in the United States. It would, therefore, be instructive to examine how our courts acquired the power of judicial review and the ways in which they have used it over the years.

The Establishment of Judicial Review in the United States

Ironically, judicial review is not specifically provided for in the Constitution. Nowhere does it expressly grant federal courts the right to nullify actions of public officials. The power has been derived by implication from certain wording in the Constitution and from interpretation of the intentions of the Founding Fathers. Article V, Section 2, which provides that the *national* Constitution, law, or treaties shall be "supreme" over state constitutions or laws, has been used to justify the power of federal courts to invalidate state actions. The clause itself, however, does not state that national courts should pass on such conflicts; in fact, it specifically mentions state judges and provides that they shall be bound by the supremacy clause, which might be construed to mean that state, rather than federal, judges should have the power of judicial review. The argument for federal courts' invalidating actions of the other two branches of the national government is even less supported by the wording of the Constitution.

Nonetheless, most historians agree that the Founding Fathers favored judicial review and expected the federal courts to exercise it over both state and national actions. Why, then, did they not provide for it specifically in the Constitution? One theory is that everyone took the power for granted anyway, since most of the state courts of the time were exercising judicial review over the actions of state officials. Another is that the delegates were aware that owing to the secrecy of the Convention and to constitutional provisions for a Senate and a President that the people did not elect, many citizens would view the new government as too elitist. Specifically granting to appointed judges with life tenure the power to overrule actions of popularly elected officials would make matters even worse and almost ensure that the Constitution would not be ratified. Therefore, for reasons of political expediency the delegates may have deliberately omitted any reference to judicial review.

Hamilton, however, was not so cautious or discrete. In *Federalist Paper* 78 he specifically stated that the federal courts possess the power of judicial review and gave justifications for it, some of which are legalistic. He held that a constitution is a type of law and that, since it is the province of the courts to interpret laws, they necessarily interpret the Constitution. He also pointed out that the Constitution is a fundamental law, which means that if judges find ordinary legislation in conflict with it, the Constitution prevails and the legislation is invalid.

Hamilton also drew on his views of human nature to justify judicial review. Legislators cannot be trusted always to respect the limitations placed on them by the Constitution; when they do not, the courts must intervene to protect the rights of the people. Nor are the people themselves to be entirely trusted; they too will suffer "the effects of ill humor" on some occasions and threaten the minority party or the rights of particular classes of citizens. Again it is the judges, trained in settling controversies growing out of "the folly and wickedness of mankind," who can be counted on to protect the rights of minorities.

Although Hamilton's views were thus set forth in a frank and bold fashion, they were simply his own and not binding on anyone else. The issue could only be settled ultimately by public officials. It remained for the Supreme Court itself to establish its power of judicial review through actual exercise of that

Chief Justice John Marshall.

prerogative. This it did in the famous case of *Marbury* v. *Madison*, decided by Chief Justice John Marshall in 1803.

Whereas Hamilton had based his case for judicial review on legalistic arguments, the circumstances of the *Marbury* decision could hardly have been more political. After the Federalists were defeated in the election of 1800, they labored in the interval until the Republicans assumed control of the presidency and the Congress to retain a foothold in the one remaining branch still open to them: the judiciary. The lame-duck Congress passed legislation creating a number of new circuit judgeships along with justiceships of the peace in the District of Columbia. In the waning days of his administration, President Adams appointed Federalists to these new judicial posts (they became known as "midnight" appointments because they were accomplished shortly before that hour on March 3, 1801). In the last-minute rush, however, John Marshall, who was then Secretary of State (and at the same time also serving as Chief Justice of the Supreme Court) did not get all the necessary commissions of office signed; included among them was one making William Marbury a justice of the peace in the District of Columbia. The new Republican Secretary of State, James Madison, who, along with the new President, Thomas Jefferson, resented the Federalists' attempt to pack the bench, refused to deliver the commission to Marbury or otherwise honor his appointment.

Frustrated in his attempts to obtain his commission, Marbury turned for help to the Supreme Court, over which John Marshall presided as a result of his appointment by President Adams. Marbury asked that the Court issue a writ of mandamus (an order requiring a public official to perform an official duty over which he has no discretion) compelling Madison to deliver the commission. As his authority for the suit, he invoked a provision in the Judiciary Act of 1789 granting the Court the power to issue such writs.

Marbury's case placed Chief Justice Marshall (who should have disqualified himself from hearing it, since he was the one who failed to deliver the commission while he was still Secretary of State) on the horns of a dilemma. If he (and the rest of the Federalist judges on the Court) ruled that Marbury was entitled to the commission, his political enemy, President Jefferson, could simply order Madison not to deliver it, which would serve to demonstrate that the judiciary could not enforce its mandates. On the other hand, to rule that Marbury had no right to the commission would seem to justify Jefferson's and Madison's claim that the midnight appointments were improper in the first place.

But the Chief Justice was up to the challenge. He slipped off the horns of the dilemma by ruling that, while Marbury had the right to the commission and a writ of mandamus was the proper remedy to obtain it, the Supreme Court was not the tribunal to issue it. In reaching this result, he reasoned that the original jurisdiction of the Supreme Court is provided for in the Constitution, and Congress cannot add to that jurisdiction. Therefore, the section of the Judiciary Act of 1789 granting the Supreme Court the power to issue writs of mandamus in cases it hears for the first time is unconstitutional and, hence, unenforceable.

The ruling extricated Marshall from an immediate difficulty; it had other effects as well. It created the possibility that the Federalists could use this newfound power to check actions of the Republican Congress and President. And most crucial of all from a long-term standpoint, it established the power of the courts to declare acts of public officials invalid.

Crucial as the *Marbury* v. *Madison* ruling was, it did not settle all the aspects of judicial review. For one thing, it applied only to the actions of the national government. Not until seven years later, in the case of *Fletcher* v. *Peck* (1810), did the Court invalidate a state law on the grounds that it violated the national Constitution. Moreover, the *Marbury* case did not define the scope of judicial review. As some persons, like Jefferson, reasoned, the ruling merely meant that the Court could strike down laws that affected the judiciary itself (as the Judiciary Act of 1789 did), but that it had no power over matters pertaining to the other two branches of government because each was the judge of the constitutionality of matters within its own province. Indeed, not until the *Dred Scott* case (1857), in which the Court invalidated Congress's attempt to abolish slavery in the territories, did the Court lay that theory to rest by striking down a law that had nothing to do with the courts.

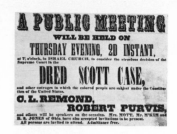

The Supreme Court's Use of Judicial Review

Although judicial review puts a powerful weapon in the hands of the Supreme Court, for the most part the power has been used with considerable restraint, particularly with respect to federal laws. In the some 175 years since *Marbury,* the Court has invalidated some 136 provisions of national laws, an average of less than one a year. In the same period of time, it has declared close to 800 state laws unconstitutional, or about four per year.

The Court's use of judicial review has not been uniform over the years, however. After all, fifty-four years transpired between the *Marbury* v. *Madison* decision at the beginning of the nineteenth century and the *Dred Scott* case decided on the eve of the Civil War. In contrast, the Court declared unconstitutional no fewer than thirteen New Deal laws during the period from 1934 to 1936.

The types of issues of concern to the Supreme Court have changed over the years. Subject matter has naturally varied from case to case, but different basic themes have dominated the Court's attention in different eras of our constitutional history. The issues have reflected both the major problems of American society at the time and the justices' own conceptions of the values that they should protect through the power of judicial review.

The major issue facing the Court from 1789 until the Civil War was nation-state relationships. As we saw in chapter 3, Chief Justice Marshall took the leadership in providing support for a strong national government. The constitutional basis for its expansion came in the form of a broad interpretation of both the interstate commerce power and the "necessary and proper" clause. At the same time, state activities that affected the powers of the national government were invalidated. Toward the end of the era, when Marshall died and was replaced by Roger Taney, the Court moderated its stand on nation-state relationships. For example, it ruled that states could regulate interstate commerce, provided that the regulation concerned local matters and did not affect a subject requiring uniform treatment throughout the United States. As a whole, however, the era was clearly a time of general support for the nation over the states in constitutional conflicts.

The pre-Civil War period was also characterized by judicial protection of private property. In fact, there was a connection between the nation-state and property-rights issues: for the most part, the federal government was promoting business and commercial interests, while the states were more involved in trying to regulate them. Thus judicial support for a strong national government dominant over the states favored commercial interests. Furthermore, Chief Justice Taney's decision in the *Dred Scott* case invalidating Congress's attempt to abolish slavery in the territories showed the Court's solicitude for another type of property-holder: the large landowner in the South.

The Civil War settled the nation-state problem, and the courts became preoccupied with one overriding issue in the period that followed: *business-government relations.* Unlike the earlier era, however, now both the national government and the states were involved in regulating burgeoning industrial empires along with smaller commercial enterprises. Therefore, favoring one level of government over the other would not accomplish the goal of many justices of the day: protecting business against what they conceived to be improper governmental interference.

The Court thus embarked upon a two-pronged judicial attack on governmental regulation of business by the two political levels. It frustrated the national government's control of industry by limiting the scope of the interstate commerce power so as to cover only businesses that were actually involved in interstate commerce (such as railroads, shipping companies, and the like) and those that directly affected that commerce; this approach freed concerns involved in agriculture, mining, and production from control by the federal government. Similarly, the taxing power of the national government was contracted through judicial rulings inquiring into congressional motives behind the use of that power: for instance, a special tax on businesses using child labor was invalidated on the grounds that the purpose of the tax was not to raise money but to discourage the use of child labor. State regulation of business was also thwarted through a novel interpretation of the due process clause of the Fourteenth Amendment. Although, as we have seen, historically that clause had always referred to procedures of public officials, the Supreme Court now gave it a substantive meaning by holding that what the justices considered to be unreasonable regulation of private interests denied persons their property without due process of law.*

This dual approach served to protect business against regulation by government, both national and state. It dominated the Court's thinking in the early part of this century, continuing into the 1930s when it was utilized to strike down many New Deal laws. President Roosevelt, following his reelection in 1936, sought to curb the Court's power over his programs by introducing legislation permitting him to appoint additional justices equal to the number sitting on the Court who had reached the age of seventy and had not retired. This proposal provoked a storm of protest from critics who charged that FDR was trying to pack the Court, and it ended in a congressional defeat for the President on the issue. Although FDR lost the battle in the Congress, he won the war in the courtroom: Justice Owen J. Roberts, who had, to that point, gener-

---

* Another tactic that the Court used to protect business was to interpret the word *person,* which appears in the Fourteenth Amendment, to include *corporations.* Thus the Court utilized an amendment that was designed to safeguard the civil liberties of individuals to protect the property rights of business interests.

ally been aligned with the four justices on the Court invalidating social and economic legislation, began in 1937 to vote with the four on the other side. With this change (a satirical description was "a switch in time saves nine"), the era of the Court's preoccupation with property rights came to an end.

Since 1937 the Supreme Court has focused almost all its attention on protecting the *personal liberties of individuals* against infringement by either the national government or the states. The Court has been very active in the last thirty years, voiding fifty-nine federal laws from 1943 until, in recent times, *Buckley* v. *Valeo* (1976), previously described in chapter 9. (This compares with just 77 federal laws invalidated in the century and a half from 1789 to 1937.) Included in the Court's concerns have been violations of First Amendment freedoms, along with procedural rights of the accused spelled out in the Fourth, Fifth, Sixth, and Eighth amendments. In addition, the due process clause of the Fifth Amendment has been utilized to invalidate criminal statutes for the vagueness of their language and to outlaw the segregation of the schools in the District of Columbia.* The Court has also been vigilant against infringements of personal liberties at the state level, relying on the due process and equal protection clauses of the Fourteenth Amendment to protect individuals against actions violating freedom of expression and religion, denials of procedural safeguards in criminal cases, and racial discrimination.

This brief review of the uses to which the Court has put judicial review over the years raises the issue of how individual judges conceive of the power of judicial review. What is the nature of the process? That is, what specifically does a judge do when he goes about deciding whether a law or executive or court order is unconstitutional? What role does he think judicial review should play in the political process?

Justice Owen Roberts.

Concepts of Judicial Review

Former Supreme Court Justice Owen Roberts is more closely associated with the legalistic concept of judicial review. He once described the process as a rather simple one: all a judge does is to lay the constitutional provision involved beside the statute being challenged and decide whether the latter squares with the former. According to Justice Roberts, judges do not "make" law; they "find" it.

Another former Associate Justice of the Supreme Court, Felix Frankfurter, had a much different concept of judicial review. According to him many of the key words and phrases that appear in the Constitution, such as "due process of law" and "equal protection of the law," are so vague and undefined that they compel a judge to read his own views into them. Those views, in turn, depend on the judge's own personal philosophy and scheme of values, which he acquires from his particular background and experiences in life. Since matters of discretion are involved, judges, in Frankfurter's view, *do* "make" law rather than simply "find" it.

---

* While many students of the Court have branded the Burger Court as a very "conservative" one (as compared to its "liberal" predecessor, the Warren Court) or as being liberal only on procedural due-process issues, Professor P. Allen Dionisopoulos points out that in the period from 1969 to 1976, the Court under the Chief Justice Burger voided twenty-seven federal laws, including many for violations of the First Amendment as well as of equal-protection freedoms read into the due-process clause of the Fifth Amendment.

Few students of the judicial process, including judges themselves, would agree with Justice Roberts's simplistic concept of judicial review. If deciding whether a law is constitutional or not is as simple as he claims, why is there so much disagreement among justices hearing the same case? Or why does the Court overrule its former decisions, as it has done on many occasions over the years? Frankfurter's concept of the process of judicial review is much more realistic.

But even if a judge concedes that values play a part in his thinking, he still has the problem of deciding the extent to which he will allow his values to affect his rulings on constitutional issues. Perhaps because Frankfurter was so sensitive to how an individual's background and experiences shape his personal values, he is generally identified as a *"nonactivist"* judge, one who was hesitant to substitute his constitutional values for those of legislators and executives. For example, in a 1940 decision, *Minersville School District* v. *Gobitis,* Frankfurter, in upholding the right of a school board to expel students who refused to salute the flag as required by Pennsylvania state law, took the position that the courts have no competence to tell political authorities that they are wrong to use this method of instilling patriotism in children.

The *"activist"* attitude concerning the role that judges feel they should play in constitutional issues is exemplified by Justice Robert Jackson's opinion in *West Virginia State Board of Education* v. *Barnette,* decided three years later, which specifically overruled the *Gobitis* case. In declaring a similar West Virginia flag-salute law unconstitutional, Jackson reasoned that the law interfered with a child's freedom of speech because he had the right to be silent and not be obliged to utter what was not in his mind. The justice went on to assert that the right of legislative discretion to which Frankfurter referred should be more restricted when it affects civil liberties than when property rights are involved.

This last comment of Justice Jackson points up another important aspect of the concept of judicial review: how activist or nonactivist a judge is may well depend on the particular value that is at stake in a given case. Thus Justice Jackson was less willing to defer to the judgment of political authorities on civil liberties than he was on those affecting property rights. Other judges, like Frankfurter, may be unwilling to permit freedom of speech or racial tolerance to occupy a higher place in their scheme of values than do property interests.

Analysis of Supreme Court decisions over the years reveals the attitudes of individual justices that underlie the positions they take in a series of cases reaching the Supreme Court. Some, for example, consistently vote on the side of the individual in civil liberties cases; others tend to favor economic have-nots in litigation against affluent interests; still others generally prefer one side in litigation between certain kinds of individuals; and federalism is also an issue that some justices respond to in a fairly consistent manner.

Of course, discerning the factors that dispose a judge to vote the way he does is a difficult task, particularly since he is frequently faced with deciding between competing values. For example, had Justice Frankfurter still been on the Court at the time of the *Gideon* case, he would have faced such a problem. As we have seen, he considered procedural safeguards basic to liberty, so he would have been disposed to favor furnishing the accused the assistance of counsel so that he could take full advantage of such safeguards. On the other hand, the former justice was a strong advocate of federalism and the right of the states to experiment with their own legal and political processes; also, as a nonactivist he was hesitant to have a Supreme Court justice substitute his judgment for that of other public officials. Those attitudes would have inclined him toward allowing Florida to decide how it should handle its own criminal proceedings. He thus would have had to do what he conceived the major function of a judge to be: balance the interests and values involved in each case and decide which should prevail.*

Personal values are not always controlling in a case. A judge sometimes puts other considerations ahead of them. He may, for example, respect the views of an influential colleague on a case or decide to go along with his fellow judges in order to present a unanimous decision to the public. He may also respect the principle of *stare decisis* and so refuse to overrule a former precedent; nonactivist judges also hesitate to invalidate actions of other public officials.

There is little question, however, that in exercising the right of judicial review, Supreme Court justices have considerable discretion in deciding cases on the basis of their own value systems. (As Max Lerner commented some years ago, "Judicial decisions are not babies brought by constitutional storks.") Unlike many cases at the lower levels of our judicial system, those that reach the Supreme Court do not typically involve technical legal issues but rather broad philosophical questions for which there are no easy or automatic answers. In passing on such matters, justices of the Supreme Court, then, like legislative and executive officials, make public policy.

Judicial review is certainly an important feature of American democracy, but its role in public policy making must be kept in perspective. For one thing, most of the work of the Supreme Court consists of the interpretation of statutes passed by Congress, not in determining whether they are constitutional. Moreover, as the following section indicates, even when the Supreme Court does decide a constitutional issue, the controversy is not necessarily ended.

THE SUPREME COURT IN THE POLITICAL PROCESS

Even though the life tenure of Supreme Court justices protects them from the kinds of pressures that elected officials face, they are not totally insulated from the political process. In particular, the two coordinate branches of the national government are in a position to check the Court's actions in a number of significant ways. Included are direct checks involving specific judicial decisions and indirect methods designed to affect general activities of the Supreme Court.

The Court and Congress

Congress has the power to affect Supreme Court decisions by passing laws that reverse or modify what the Court has previously done on an issue. Examples of this technique, already referred to in chapter 3, are the enactment of legislation deeding tideland oil properties to the states after the Court had ruled that the national government, not the states, owned such lands, and the passage of legislation permitting states to regulate insurance companies following a Court decision holding that they fell under the control of the national government through its interstate commerce power. Another instance previously cited was

---

* Justice Frankfurter is reported to have told Justice Black that if he had still been on the Court at the time, he would have voted to grant counsel to Gideon.

the enactment of the Omnibus Crime Control and Safe Streets Act of 1968, which limited the effect of the *Mallory* case by allowing up to six hours for prearraignment questioning of suspects in federal criminal proceedings.

Some reversals of Supreme Court decisions cannot be accomplished through ordinary legislation, and Congress must initiate constitutional amendments to achieve its purposes. When the Court ruled in *Chisholm* v. *Georgia* (1793) that a state could be sued in a federal court by a citizen of another state, the Eleventh Amendment was enacted to deny jurisdiction in such cases. The *Pollock* v. *Farmers' Loan and Trust Company* decision (1895), which invalidated a national income tax, was ultimately reversed through the passage of the Sixteenth Amendment granting Congress the power to enact such a tax without apportioning it among the various states. More recently, when the Supreme Court ruled in 1970 that Congress could not grant eighteen-year-olds the right to vote in state and local elections, the Twenty-sixth Amendment was enacted in 1971 to achieve that result.

In addition to reversing specific judicial decisions, the national legislature can affect the Court's consideration of particular kinds of issues through its power to determine the Court's appellate jurisdiction. A famous example of the use of this power is the passage in the immediate post-Civil War period of legislation that had the effect of denying the Court appellate jurisdiction over certain cases in which the constitutionality of the Reconstruction Acts was at issue. The tactic was particularly effective in that instance because the Court bowed to Congress's will by dismissing a case on which it had already heard arguments but had not yet ruled.

Taking away the Court's jurisdiction over a case it has already heard is rare; trying to prevent the justices from deciding certain issues in future litigation is much more common. This was the approach used by Senator William Jenner of Indiana in the late 1950s when he introduced legislation that would have denied the Court appellate jurisdiction over a number of issues on which he felt that the Court had unduly favored the rights of individuals at the expense of internal security. Included in the statute's coverage were the rights of witnesses before congressional committees, the removal of federal employees for reasons of national security, state antisubversion laws and regulations regarding the activities of school teachers, and state statutes pertaining to admission to the bar. Although the Jenner bill failed to pass, it constituted one of the major threats to the independence of the Court in recent years.

Control over Court personnel is still another power whereby Congress can affect the actions of the tribunal. Thus the number of justices is determined by legislation, and this number has varied from five to ten over the years since 1789. An example of the use of this power for political purposes was the enlargement of the Court by the Radical Republicans in 1869 after President Johnson left office so that President Grant (whom they controlled) could appoint an additional justice. Franklin Roosevelt tried a similar technique in 1937 with his Court-packing bill. The number of justices has remained at nine since 1869, however, which may mean that manipulating the size of the Court is now considered improper and will be, as in Roosevelt's case, unsuccessful.

The concern of Congress with Court personnel can also be directed at particular persons. As we have already seen, the Senate can interject constitutional issues into its consideration of nominees to the Court. In recent years nominees have frequently been questioned by the Senate Judiciary Committee about their judicial philosophy and "activist" or "nonactivist" views; at the time of his nomination for the chief justiceship, Associate Justice Fortas was criticized by Senators Eastland and McClellan for his rulings in obscenity cases. Nor do attacks on judges necessarily cease once they are confirmed. Justice William Douglas, who went on the Court in 1939, was on two occasions—the first in 1953 and the second in 1970—the object of impeachment resolutions in the House of Representatives. Neither attempt was successful.

Thus the Congress has a number of weapons that it can use to affect the activities of the Supreme Court. For the most part it has used the less drastic of these measures, such as reversals or revisions of Supreme Court decisions and the failure to confirm nominees, rather than more severe anti-Court actions, such as altering the appellate jurisdiction of the Court, tampering with its size, or impeaching sitting judges.*

The Court and The Presidency

Like the Congress, the President has several powers at his disposal that can have major effects on the actions of the Supreme Court. One such power has already been discussed: the appointment of justices. As Robert Dahl has pointed out, over the years one new justice has been appointed on the average of every two years; a President, then, can expect to appoint two judges for each term he has in office. Thus a Chief Executive can, through judicious choice of persons with policy views similar to his own, influence the general direction of the Court's thinking, as Franklin Roosevelt did through his nine appointments. If the Court is a divided one, even a smaller number of appointments can be crucial: immediately after President Nixon chose Chief Justice Burger and Associate Justice Blackmum,† the Court began to modify the general tenor of its previous rulings, particularly with respect to procedural rights of the accused in criminal proceedings.

The President also shares with Congress the power to enact legislation affecting the Court. In fact, the initiative for such legislation may come from the Chief Executive, as it did in the Court-packing plan of 1937. Even when this is not the case, however, the President's veto power means that legislation affecting the Court will probably not be successful unless it meets with his approval.

Finally, the President has the ability to affect Supreme Court decisions that require his action for implementation. Recall one of Chief Justice Marshall's problems in the *Marbury* v. *Madison* decision: if he ruled that the former had a right to his justice-of-the-peace commission, President Jefferson might tell Madison not to deliver it to him. Just such an eventuality later occurred when Marshall ruled in two separate decisions, *Cherokee Indian* v. *Georgia* (1831) and *Worcester* v. *Georgia* (1832), that the state had no legal authority over land

---

* There are other potential weapons that Congress could use against the Court, but past experience demonstrates that they have little chance of passage. Included are requirements that Court decisions invalidating national laws be either unanimous or by extra-majorities, that Congress be empowered to overrule Supreme Court decisions by extra-majority votes, and that the electorate be given the power to overturn such decisions. Attempts to require that Supreme Court justices have previous judicial experience have also failed to gather sufficient congressional support to pass.
† During the October 1970 term Justices Burger and Blackmum disagreed in only four of some 120 decisions, which led Court observers to label them the "Minnesota Twins."

occupied by the Cherokee Indian tribe, and President Jackson refused to take steps to implement either ruling. On the other hand, the positive effect that a Chief Executive can have on a Supreme Court ruling is demonstrated by President Truman's order to Secretary of Commerce Charles Sawyer to return the steel mills to their private owners after the Court's decision in *Youngstown Sheet and Tube Company* v. *Sawyer* (1952) that the Chief Executive had no authority to seize them. Further evidence of the key role that the President plays in implementing Court rulings is provided by the actions of Presidents Eisenhower and Kennedy in sending federal troops and marshals to enforce school desegregation decisions. President Nixon's compliance with the Court's decision that he turn over tapes subpoenaed by the Special Prosecutor led to disclosures of the President's involvement in the Watergate cover-up that ultimately forced him to resign his office.

The combination of powers of the Congress and the President with respect to the Supreme Court means that they can have a major effect on its actions. Robert Dahl, who some years ago analyzed the ultimate outcome of Court decisions declaring acts of Congress unconstitutional, concludes that legislation reversing and revising such decisions and new presidential appointees to the Court who vote to overrule them, mean that if the two political branches are agreed on a matter of public policy, they will eventually get their way. Dahl contended that the most that the Court can do is delay the application of a policy for a number of years, as occurred, for example, between the 1895 ruling in the Pollock case and the passage of the Sixteenth Amendment in 1913.

While congressmen and the President have positive powers that they can use to check the Supreme Court, other public officials are frequently able to have a negative effect on its actions through delaying, or even avoiding, the execution of its orders. For just as some Supreme Court decisions require the President to enforce them, others depend for their ultimate effectiveness on what individuals in various political positions do about implementing them.

Lower Courts and Supreme Court Decisions

Typically, a Supreme Court decision does not end a legal controversy; rather, it remands the case to a lower court which is entrusted with proceeding further on the matter in light of the Court's opinion. One might assume that inferior tribunals would promptly carry out the orders of the highest Court; as a matter of practice, lower courts frequently delay or modify the upper Court's wishes in significant ways.

The possibilities of lower courts' altering the intentions of the Supreme Court are particularly promising when the highest Court's order itself is uncertain and vague. The classic instance was the Supreme Court's directive following the 1954 desegregation decision to the federal district courts to supervise the integration of the public schools in their areas so that it occurred with "all deliberate speed." The exceedingly slow pace of integration in parts of the South led some critics to charge that many judges emphasized the "deliberativeness" of the process to the exclusion of its "speed."

But even when the Court does not grant the lower federal tribunals such broad discretion in implementing its decisions, judges are frequently able to avoid the Court's rulings by distinguishing them in subsequent cases—that is, drawing distinctions between the facts of the cases in which these rulings were originally made and those present in the litigation before them. This occurred in the aftermath of the *Mallory* decision, which provided that defendants in federal criminal cases must be arraigned a short time after they are arrested. Studies of subsequent proceedings in both federal district courts and courts of appeals indicate that judges avoided the *Mallory* doctrine by distinguishing it from cases before them.

State tribunals, like lower federal courts, can also obstruct Supreme Court decisions. After the Court ruled in 1958 that Alabama could not require the *National Association for the Advancement of Colored People* to furnish copies of its membership lists as a condition for operating in the state, a prolonged legal battle was carried on at the state level. Through a combination of delays and avoidances with respect to the upper Court's rulings, Alabama was able to keep the NAACP from operating in the state for over six years after the 1958 decision was handed down.

State and Local Officials and Supreme Court Rulings

The dramatic events following the 1954 school desegregation decision attest to the role that state officials can also play in obstructing rulings of the Supreme Court. As indicated below, Governor Orval Faubus intervened after a federal district court approved the decision of the school board in Little Rock, Arkansas to integrate the schools of that area in the fall of 1957 and it became necessary for President Eisenhower to send federal troops to enforce the district court's order. As we shall see later in this chapter, the legislature of Virginia tried to avoid the integration of the public schools by repealing compulsory school attendance laws and permitting students to attend private schools subsidized by the state. (As with the Faubus incident, however, the Supreme Court's will eventually prevailed as it invalidated Virginia's attempt to circumvent its rulings in this way.)

In many instances the effectiveness of Supreme Court rulings depends on local officials. Studies have indicated, for example, that despite decisions outlawing Bible reading and prayers in the public schools, boards of education still permit such practices in some communities, particularly in rural areas. Similarly, the effect of cases like *Miranda* and *Mallory* turn on the actual interrogation practices of local law-enforcement officials, while book and magazine dealers determine the consequences of the host of obscenity cases with which the Court has dealt in recent years.

Even though the Supreme Court must depend on others to effect compliance with its rulings, for the most part compliance does occur. Attempts to delay and avoid its edicts are reserved to the more controversial areas of public policy in which the Court's opinions run counter to traditional practices and beliefs.

Even then, however, the Court's will eventually prevails in most cases. Despite the unpopularity of school desegregation decisions in the South, the general opposition to the outlawing of prayers and Bible reading in the schools, and the natural reluctance of legislatures to reapportion themselves along the lines required by the Court, the fact of the matter is that many schools did become integrated, religious exercises did disappear from most schools, and state legislatures all over the nation have redistricted themselves as well as the House of Representatives. Such sharp departures from former practices in controversial areas of public policy testify to the major influence that the Court continues to exercise on American life.

JUDICIAL POLICY MAKING: THE DESEGREGATION OF THE PUBLIC SCHOOLS

In the early 1950s the battery of lawyers for the *National Association for the Advancement of Colored People* headed by Thurgood Marshall made a strategic decision regarding the "separate but equal doctrine"—a principle adopted by the Supreme Court in the case of *Plessy* v. *Ferguson* (1896) that separate public facilities for persons of different races are constitutional provided that they are equal. Instead of continuing to chip away at the doctrine on a case-by-case basis by demonstrating that black schools are really not equal to white ones (a tactic that the NAACP successfully adopted for a number of years), the organization would make the legal argument that separate facilities in and of themselves violate the "equal protection of the laws" clause of the Fourteenth Amendment.

Having decided to directly challenge the "separate but equal" doctrine, the NAACP lawyers had no difficulty in finding the proper means to get the issue to the Supreme Court. Five separate suits were filed involving segregated schools in Delaware, Kansas, South Carolina, Virginia and the District of Columbia. As might be expected, the lower federal courts that initially heard the various suits generally upheld the doctrine. However in 1952 the Supreme Court granted *certiorari* and in December of that year heard arguments on the cases. Assisting Thurgood Marshall through *amicus curiae* briefs were other lawyers, including President Truman's Attorney-General, James McGranery, and some thirty distinguished social scientists who contended that segregation was harmful psychologically to both black and white children; heading the segregationist side of the case was John W. Davis, one of the nation's foremost constitutional law experts and former Democratic candidate for President in 1924.

Aware of the great significance of the issue, the Supreme Court bided its time. In June of 1953 it rescheduled the cases for reargument and asked both sides to be prepared to analyze the historical meaning of the Fourteenth Amendment with respect to segregation as well as the practical problems that the desegregation of the schools would present. The new Republican administration of Dwight Eisenhower had its Attorney-General, Herbert Brownell, file an *amicus curiae* brief on the desegregation side of the cases that were reargued in December of 1953.

Five months later on May 17, 1954 the Supreme Court in a unanimous decision—*Brown* vs. *Board of Education*, written by Chief Justice Earl Warren—struck down the "separate but equal doctrine" as applied to the public schools as a violation of the "equal protection clause" of the Fourteenth Amendment.* Claiming that the historical meaning of the amendment is ambiguous as far as its relevance to public education is concerned, Warren instead based his decision on the findings of sociologists and psychologists that segregation creates a sense of inferiority that affects the motivation of a child to learn. As the Chief Justice put it, to separate children "from others of similar age and qualifications solely because of their race creates a feeling of inferiority as to their status in the community that may affect their hearts and minds in a way unlikely ever to be undone."

Concerned with the practical problems involved in implementing the decision, the Court delayed its immediate enforcement and ordered reargument of all five cases for April of 1955. The following month, a year after the original *Brown* decision, the Court entrusted the federal district courts with requiring local school boards to make "a prompt and reasonable start toward full compliance" with the 1954 ruling and with seeing to it that desegregation proceed "with all deliberate speed."

The Supreme Court's concern with the problems involved in desegregating the public schools proved to be fully justified. In the fall of 1957 a federal district court ordered the desegregation of the schools of Little Rock, Arkansas; despite the fact that only nine black children were involved, Governor Orval Faubus called out the National Guard to prevent the enforcement of the order. Ultimately, President Eisenhower had to send federal troops into the area to enforce the court decree. Subsequently President Kennedy was forced to dispatch federal troops to Oxford, Mississippi and to Tuscaloosa, Alabama to overcome the resistance of Governors Ross Barnett and George Wallace to the attendance of black students at the two state universities.

Southern states and communities also resorted to legal maneuvering to try to avoid integrating their schools. Prince Edward County in Virginia (the site of one of the original cases that led to the *Brown* decision) closed its public schools and with state assistance provided tuition money for students to attend private nonsectarian schools. Other communities devised "freedom of choice" laws (permitting children to choose the school that they wanted to attend) and manipulated pupil placement to avoid the effects of desegregation. The Supreme Court voided such actions as interfering with the elimination of segregated "dual" school systems in favor of integrated "unitary" ones mandated by the *Brown* decision. Some fifteen years after that decision, the Court held in *Alexander* v. *Holmes County Board of Education* (1969) that "All 'deliberate speed' for desegregation is no longer constitutionally permissible. . . . The obligation of every school district is to terminate dual school systems at once."

At the beginning of the 1970s the problems of desegregating the nation's schools became more complex. The major issue shifted from how to deal with obstructive tactics designed to perpetuate dual schools to the question of what

---

* The four state suits were consolidated under the Brown case that arose in Kansas. The fifth suit involving the District of Columbia was handled as a separate case, *Bolling* v. *Sharpe,* because the Fourteenth Amendment does not apply to the federal government, and it was necessary for the Court to declare that segregation of schools under its jurisdiction violates the due process clause of the Fifth Amendment.

Busing in Louisville.

positive steps should be required to bring about a greater degree of racial integration in the classroom. The nature of the problem also changed from segregation in Southern schools caused by legal discrimination (*de jure* segregation) to separation of the races in schools in all parts of the country, including the North, brought out by residential living patterns (*de facto* segregation).

In a 1971 case, *Swann* v. *Charlotte-Mecklenburg Board of Education,* the Court approved a variety of measures ordered by the federal district court to bring about a greater degree of integration in the schools of Charlotte, North Carolina. Included were the use of racial quotas, the pairing or grouping of noncontiguous attendance zones, and even the busing of children beyond their immediate neighborhoods. (As Chief Justice Burger put it, "Desegregation plans cannot be limited to the walk-in school.") At the same time, the Court was careful to point out that it was dealing with *de jure,* not *de facto,* segregation, and that it was not requiring the total elimination of all-black or all-white schools or expecting each school to reflect the racial composition of the school system as a whole.

The first Supreme Court case involving a large non-Southern city was *Keyes* v. *School District # 1, Denver, Colorado,* decided in 1973. While there was no evidence of statutorily-authorized segregation in the city's schools, the Court found that the Denver school board had brought about segregation in some areas of the city through the creation of school attendance zones and the location of school sites. According to the justices, this *de jure* segregation in one part of the district established a presumption of intentional segregation in all of Denver's core-city schools, which could only be rebutted by direct evidence to the contrary. In the absence of such proof, the Court held that the Denver school board had a duty to desegregate the entire school system "root and branch."

The Denver case, however, involved only a single school district. A suit was instituted in 1970 by the executive board of the Detroit NAACP that ultimately tested the Court's attitude on *de facto* segregation in a large, northern, metropolitan area (Detroit) consisting of both central-city and suburban schools.

During the course of the protracted litigation, the federal district court turned down plans proposed by the Detroit Board of Education on the grounds

Anti-busing demonstration.

that while they would bring about better racial balance in the schools of the city, Detroit's schools would still be identifiably black, a situation that would increase the flight of whites from the city to the suburbs. The district court concluded that "it must look beyond the limits of the Detroit school district for a solution to the problem" and subsequently ordered that fifty-three of the eighty-five suburban school districts be included within the area designated for desegregation. The Court also instructed the Detroit School Board to acquire at least 295 buses to provide the necessary transportation under its plan. The court of appeals upheld the district court order and the Supreme Court granted *certiorari*. On July 25, 1974, almost four years after the NAACP filed the original suit and twenty years after the first *Brown* decision, the Supreme Court handed down its opinion in the landmark case of *Milliken* v. *Bradley*. Unlike the unanimous *Brown* decision, however, the justices divided 5-4, with Justice Potter Stewart joining the four Nixon appointees, Burger, Blackmun, Powell, and Rehnquist, in striking down the district court plan as unconstitutional.

The majority opinion written by Chief Justice Burger held that since none of the fifty-three suburban school districts operated segregated schools or contributed to the discrimination that was found to exist in the Detroit city school district, it was improper to include them within the desegregation plan. The Chief Justice stressed the fact that substantial local control of public education is a deeply rooted tradition in this nation and therefore concluded that school district lines may not be treated as mere administrative conveniences that can be casually ignored. Chief Justice Burger raised the specter that the district court plan would create logistical problems involving large-scale transportation of students and would also establish a new super school district over which the district court would have to preside as a "school superintendent."

Justice Thurgood Marshall (who had argued the *Brown* case for the NAACP) wrote a vigorous dissent in which Justices Brennan, Douglas, and White joined. Pushing aside the argument of local control of schools, Justice Marshall held that the state of Michigan clearly has the power to require suburban school districts to participate in a metropolitan remedy to the segregation of the races; he also contended that the number of children and distances involved in busing children under the district court plan compared favorably with the existing arrangements for the transportation of school children in the Detroit area. Marshall's dissent also expressed his own personal frustrations with the majority:

"After 20 years of small, often difficult steps towards the great end (equal educational opportunities for all), the Court today takes a great step backward. . . .

Our nation I fear will be ill-served by the Court's refusal to remedy separate and unequal education, for unless our children begin to learn together, there is little hope that our people will ever learn to live together. . . .

In the short run it may seem to be the easier course to allow our great metropolitan areas to be divided up each into two cities—one white, the other black—but it is a course I predict our people will ultimately regret."

The two decades between the *Brown* and *Milliken* decisions were thus marked by constant conflict over the issue of segregated schools in the United States. The *Milliken* decision represents the current (1977) thinking of the Supreme Court. It will not order busing unless it can be established that there has been intentional segregation. In 1976 the Court set aside a wide-ranging busing

*"I say to hell with racial imbalance—
I'm through being bused in every day!"*

plan for the Austin, Texas schools because there was no evidence of discriminatory motivation on the part of school officials. The Court also ruled in another 1976 case, *Pasadena City Board of Education* v. *Spangler,* that if school authorities initially comply with a court-ordered busing plan, they cannot be required to readjust busing zones each subsequent year to reflect changing population patterns.

Executive and Legislative Action on School Desegregation

As in most public-policy areas, school desegregation has not been shaped entirely by one branch of government. While the Courts have been the agency that has been most involved in desegregation policy over the years, the executive and legislative arms of our national government have also played a role in efforts to integrate the public schools.

For the first ten years after the *Brown* decision, the judiciary dominated school desegregation policy. Presidents were involved sporadically as Eisenhower was when he sent troops to Little Rock, Arkansas in 1957 to enforce a court desegregation order; so was Kennedy, when he dispatched federal law-enforcement officials to protect blacks entering the state universities of Mississippi and Alabama. However, it was not until 1964 that legislative and and executive branch officials assumed a significant role in the struggle to integrate the public schools.

The Civil Rights Act of 1964 became the vehicle by which the Congress authorized the federal bureaucracy to become heavily involved in school desegregation. Title IV authorized the Office of Education to provide technical assistance (information, personnel, and grants) to local education agencies to facilitate school desegregation and also empowered the Attorney-General to file suits for the desegregation of the schools. Title VI of the law authorized the Department of Health, Education, and Welfare to cut off federal funds to local school districts that did not comply with the law to desegregate schools. In addition, Title X created the "Community Relations" Service to provide technical assistance to local communities in mediating desegregation disputes. Thus the 1964 legislation contained a combination of inducements and penalties for local school districts concerned with school desegregation.

Operating under the provisions of the 1964 legislation, the federal bureaucracy of the Johnson administration soon assumed a major role in school desegregation. The Justice Department became aggressive in filing suits, and by 1969 the HEW had cut off federal funds for some 123 school districts, almost all of them in the South. Moreover, the mere *threat* of withdrawal became a potent weapon in the hands of HEW against local school boards that did not meet departmental guidelines on desegregation. Indeed one student of the subject, Thomas Dye, concluded that the threat of the loss of funds did more to bring about desegregation than all of the previous actions of the federal courts.

With the advent of a Republican administration, however, the approach to school desegregation changed markedly. Rather than continue the coercive tactics of HEW under the Johnson administration (i.e. terminating or threatening to terminate federal funds to school districts), President Nixon ordered his administration to pursue integration in the courts or through encouraging local school districts to comply voluntarily with desegregation guidelines. To facilitate the latter course of action, the Nixon administration asked Congress to provide federal grants to assist school districts involved in desegregation. The Congress responded initially by establishing a short-term assistance program to facilitate desegregation and in 1972 passed the Elementary and Secondary School Act, which included funds for that purpose. Gerald Ford essentially continued the administrative policies of his predecessor on school desegregation after he took over the Presidency from Nixon in 1974.*

As far as busing itself is concerned, it is fair to say that the political officials of our national government are even less enthusiastic about it than Supreme Court judges have been. Both Presidents Nixon and Ford strongly opposed busing. While Jimmy Carter opposed mandatory busing in his 1976 campaign, his administration, after six months in office, indicated that it might be more aggressive in pursuit of school desegregation than its Republican predecessors. A memorandum issued by Attorney-General Griffin Bell (at the request of HEW Secretary Joseph Califano) asserted the legality, in some circumstances, of the government's withholding funds from school districts that refuse to merge black and white schools to facilitate desegregation. (Such a merger of two or more schools—called *pairing* or *clustering*—usually requires some busing.)

In 1974 Congress attached an amendment to the Elementary and Secondary School Act prohibiting the busing of children beyond the school nearest to their homes unless a court determined that more extensive busing was necessary to guarantee a student his civil rights under the Constitution. Moreover, in 1976 an amendment was introduced by Senator William Roth (R., Virginia) to a Senate bill increasing federal judgeships, which would have taken away the authority of the federal courts altogether to order the transportation of students or teachers in order to carry out a plan for the desegregation of any school. However, the amendment was defeated.

Thus public policy on school desegregation appears to have reached a stalemate in the United States. While officials in all three branches of government of the national government are committed to ending *de jure* segregation, they do not favor a policy of extensive mandatory busing to overcome *de facto* segregation in large metropolitan areas in the North occasioned by housing patterns involving the concentration of blacks in the central cities and whites in the suburbs.† Yet at the same time, neither the Supreme Court nor most executive and legislative officials want to forego the use of busing altogether as a weapon in the continuing battle against segregation in the public schools.

* How the Carter administration may approach the issue of school desegregation has begun to emerge. In February 1977, the new Secretary of HEW, Joseph Califano, pledging to restore the integrity of the department's civil rights programs and to execute civil rights laws with "energy and compassion," ordered the review of six cases involving alleged discrimination by school districts in Arkansas and Texas.

† Public opinion polls consistently report the fact that most Americans are opposed to the policy as well. Recently James Coleman, a University of Chicago sociologist who has studied the problem of school desegregation over a number of years, concluded that mandatory busing of school children in the large metropolitan areas is driving whites to the suburbs, resulting in increased segregation of the races. Coleman suggests that a more effective policy would be to allow any child in a metropolitan area to attend any school he chooses, providing that school does not have a higher proportion of his race than his neighborhood school does. Such a policy would permit blacks and the economically disadvantaged of all races to benefit from a better education if they and their parents want to exercise that voluntary option.

ASSESSMENT

It is difficult to reconcile judicial review with some of the major principles and assumptions of democracy. Granting to nine men (or more precisely, five, since that constitutes a majority of the Court), who are appointed and who serve for life, the power to overturn the actions of elected legislative and executive officials violates the idea of majority rule. It also is at variance with the democratic assumption that there are no elites who are intelligent enough or unselfish enough to make decisions that vitally affect the interests of the remaining members of society.

As indicated in chapter 1, however, democracy does not always trust the majority; it also seeks to protect certain fundamental rights of minorities. In passing on constitutional questions, the Supreme Court is in a position to safeguard fundamental rights with which democracy has traditionally been concerned: freedom of speech, the press, and religion; social equality; procedural due process in criminal proceedings; and private property. Thus Supreme Court justices can act, and have acted, under the power of judicial review to protect both rights "in" government and rights "from" government.

But assuming that such minority rights should be safeguarded, there still remains the question of why Supreme Court justices should be granted that power: what is special about their training and/or position in the political system that qualifies them, rather than legislative or executive officials, to protect the rights of minorities?

If the major issues that came to the Supreme Court for decision were narrow legal ones, it could be argued that the training of the justices gave them a special expertise to pass judgment on such matters. But as previously suggested, this is not so: the issues that are resolved there are mostly broad philosophical ones involving basic values such as racial equality, the separation of church and state, and freedom of speech and the press. There is nothing in his

law school education that specifically prepares a judge to deal with such matters; indeed, students of sociology, religion, and communication are probably better qualified than jurists to deal with these three issues. (One area where Supreme Court justices do have special training, and sometimes experience as well, is in dealing with the procedural rights of accused persons, but even then they are not necessarily familiar with the practical consequences their rulings have on the work of policemen, prosecutors, defense counsels, and trial judges.)

A more valid argument for the Court's prerogative in protecting the rights of minorities is the rather unique political situation that justices enjoy compared to elected legislative and executive officials. It is unrealistic to expect the latter to fully protect the rights of minorities when they are elected by majorities, particularly in times of emergency and stress when the general public is likely to show little concern for the rights of unpopular minorities. A classic example is the "law and order" issue, which has led many congressmen and executive officials to advocate stricter policies towards persons accused of crime. Only officials who enjoy life tenure could afford to take the position that some Supreme Court judges have with respect to the procedural rights of the accused.

Whether judicial review is consistent with democracy or not, it will in all probability continue to be a part of our governing process. It has some 175 years of tradition behind it. Moreover, persons of all different political persuasions support judicial review when it favors values that they cherish. Thus conservatives in the 1930s applauded the Court's role in seeking to protect property interests from the incursions of Franklin Roosevelt's New Deal; in the last several decades liberals have praised Supreme Court judges for their role in the desegregation of public schools, the reapportionment of state legislatures, and the provision of additional procedural safeguards for persons accused of crime.

Judicial review will also survive because it is not an absolute power. Judges are sensitive to public attitudes, as was indicated by Justice Roberts's switch in voting on New Deal issues after the 1936 presidential election that Franklin Roosevelt won by a landslide. Furthermore, the Congress and the President have important powers by which to affect decision making by the Supreme Court. That body is very much a part of the democratic process.

SELECTED READINGS

Henry J. Abraham, *The Judicial Process* (New York: Oxford University Press, 3rd ed., 1975), contains basic information on all the subjects treated in this chapter. A recent compilation of materials that also bear on such subjects is *The Supreme Court: Justice and the Law* (Washington, D.C.: Congressional Quarterly, Inc., 1973).

A recent analysis of the lower federal courts written from a political, rather than a legal, standpoint is Richard J. Richardson and Kenneth N. Vines, *The Politics of Federal Courts* (Boston: Little, Brown, 1970). A similar approach to all the federal courts, including the Supreme Court, as well as to the judicial process in general, is Herbert Jacob, *Justice in America* (Boston: Little, Brown, 2nd ed., 1975). Two good general treatments of the Supreme Court are John R. Schmidhauser, *The Supreme Court* (New York: Holt, Rinehart and Winston, 1960), and Glendon A. Schubert, *Constitutional Politics* (New York: Holt, Rinehart and Winston, 1964). David Danelski analyzes the role of the Chief Justice in "The Influence of the Chief Justice in the Decision Process," which appears in Walter F. Murphy and C. Herman Pritchett (eds.), *Courts, Judges, and Politics* (New York: Random House, 1961).

Chapter 4 of Richardson and Vines analyzes judicial selection and the backgrounds of judges of the lower federal courts. A historical account of the Senate's role in the selection of federal judges (as well as executive officials) is Joseph P. Harris, *The Advice and Consent of the Senate* (Berkeley: University of California Press, 1953). For an excellent analysis of the role that the Federal Judiciary Committee of the American Bar Association plays in the selection of federal judges, see Joel B. Grossman, *Lawyers and Judges: The ABA and the Politics of Judicial Selection* (New York: Wiley, 1965). Chapters 2 and 3 of Schmidhauser's book discuss the selection and backgrounds of Supreme Court judges.

A general treatment of judicial review is Robert K. Carr, *The Supreme Court and Judicial Review* (New York: Farrar and Rinehart, 1942). A historical analysis of the subject is Robert G. McCloskey, *The American Supreme Court* (Chicago: University of Chicago Press, 1960). For an analysis of judicial review from the standpoint of democratic theory, see Howard E. Dean, *Judicial Review and Democracy* (New York: Random House, 1967). P. Allan Dionisopolous analyzes the Supreme Court's use of judicial review to invalidate many federal laws since 1943 in "Judicial Review in the Textbooks," *DEA News*, no. 11 (Fall 1976), pp. 1, 19-21. Henry Abraham's *The Judiciary: The Supreme Court in the Governmental Process* (Boston: Allyn and Bacon, 4th ed., 1977) is an excellent overall analysis of that subject.

For a book favoring judicial activism, see Charles L. Black, Jr., *The People and the Court: Judicial Review in a Democracy* (New York: Macmillan, 1960). Another, counseling judicial restraint, is Alexander M. Bickel, *The Least Dangerous Branch: The Supreme Court at the Bar of Politics* (Indianapolis: Bobbs-Merrill, 1962). Two early studies of attitudes of Supreme Court justices are C. Herman Pritchett, *The Roosevelt Court* (New York: Macmillan, 1948), and his subsequent *Civil Liberties and the Vinson Court* (Chicago: University of Chicago Press, 1954). A more recent and more sophisticated analysis of the same subject is Glendon A. Schubert, *The Judicial Mind* (Evanston: Northwestern University Press, 1965).

An early study urging that the courts be viewed within a political framework is Jack Peltason, *The Federal Courts in the Political Process* (New York: Doubleday, 1953). Two recent books analyzing the consequences of Supreme Court decisions are Theodore Becker (ed.), *The Impact of Supreme Court Decisions* (New York: Oxford University Press, 1969), and Stephen Wasby, *The Impact of the United States Supreme Court: Some Perspectives* (Homewood, Ill.: Dorsey, 1970). Two good studies of conflicts between the Supreme Court and the Congress are Walter F. Murphy, *Congress and the Court* (Chicago: University of Chicago Press, 1962), and C. Herman Pritchett, *Congress versus the Supreme Court* (Minneapolis: University of Minnesota Press, 1961). Jack Peltason, *Fifty-eight Lonely Men* (New York: Harcourt, Brace, 1961) treats of the pressures that federal judges in the South face in the enforcement of Supreme Court decisions on school desegregation. Chapter 6 of Robert Dahl, *Pluralist Democracy in the United States* (Chicago: Rand McNally, 1967), analyzes the extent to which the Court has been able to check actions of the Congress and the President over the years.

For an excellent account of legal developments in school desegregation over the years, see Henry Abraham, *Freedom and the Court: Civil Rights and Liberties in the United States* (New York: Oxford University Press, 3rd ed.; 1977). Alfred Kelly and Winifred Harbison, *The American Constitution: Its Origins and Development* (New York: Norton, 1976) contains a very good analysis of recent developments in the Burger Court, including its role in school desegregation.

Political Novels For some reason, the federal judiciary has rarely been a subject for novelists. An important exception is Andrew Tully who has written of a Supreme Court Justice trapped between political loyalty to the President who appointed him and his responsibilities as a member of the Court, *The Supreme Court* (New York: Simon and Schuster, 1963).

Finley Peter Dunne, a journalist whose fame at the turn of the century made him a public figure and a confidant of President Theodore Roosevelt, created an Irish bartender whose satiric observations about politics continue to capture the absurdity of American institutions. In *Mr. Dooley on the Choice of Law* (Charlottesville, Va: The Michie Company, 1963), compiled by Edward J. Bander, some of the bartender's choicest conversations concerning the Supreme Court and the Constitution are to be found. For those who might doubt the value of listening to this fictional character as he discourses about the Supreme Court, it should be pointed out that among Mr. Dooley's long list of admirers were Chief Justice Charles Evans Hughes and Justice Oliver Wendell Holmes. Even more impressive is the fact that Justice Felix Frankfurter actually cited Mr. Dooley in the Supreme Court case of *A.F.L.* v. *American Sash Door* (1949)!

STATE AND LOCAL GOVERNMENT

The essential promise of American democracy is that of political equality not as an end in itself but as the instrument through which each citizen seeks the equality of opportunity necessary to control his own life. As sites of extensive political authority, our state and local communities significantly condition the prospects for achieving political equality. Their broad role in the provision of important public services directly affects the improved quality of life we expect to accompany equal opportunity. In this way state and local government in the nature and conduct of their responsibilities play an important part in defining the performance of American democracy.

In Part Four the position of subnational government within the federal system as well as its formal structure and practices are described. Although state and local units are usually less visible than the national government, they are nonetheless important political bodies. They have constitutional status (under the Tenth Amendment) and are assured political significance by tradition and popular attitudes. These governments provide important services to citizens, create essential sources of political competition with national leadership, and are frequently irreplaceable reservoirs of governmental innovation and experimentation.

Chapter 17 is divided into two major sections. Section one describes the constitutions and major governmental institutions at the state level. The important similarities and differences between the structure and performance of these state institutions and their national counterpart are emphasized. Section two describes the charters and major governmental institutions at the local level. This includes consideration of the four basic types of local government: (1) municipal, (2) county, (3) special district, (4) township. In this section the extent to which the structure and performance of local units meet their public responsibilities is emphasized.

The theme of Part Four is that state and local governments are important parts of the federal system. Although frequently overshadowed by the national level, subnational governments continue to play a critical role in determining how far toward the promise of democracy this nation progresses.

Sign of the times: the web of government.

Chapter 17

A SEPARATION OF GOVERNMENTS AND A SHARING OF AUTHORITY

Government in the United States, the promise and performance of American democracy, is not defined solely by the national government in Washington, D.C. As we have seen in chapter 3, the Constitution established a federal system in which the tasks of government were divided between—or, in many instances, shared by—subnational as well as national units of government. At the heart of this federal system is the principle that each level of government maintains a degree of legal autonomy from the others. That is, the subnational units of government (state and local) under the Constitution have substantial independent authority to make and implement public policy. At the very least, federalism means two levels of government—state as well as national—both having a constitutional status that guarantees their continued existence. Under the basic law of the land, the national government may not abolish the states, nor may the states abolish the national government, even indirectly by withdrawing from the federal union.

The Constitution does not specify what the states may actually undertake as units of government. Primarily this is because the states, unlike the national government, were not created by the Constitutional Convention of 1787. The framers understood that, subject to the specific prohibitions and limitations stated in the Constitution, and given the supremacy of the national government, each state would continue to exercise essentially the same general powers under the new federal arrangement as it had wielded under the Articles of Confederation. The authority of the states was considered as *reserved* in nature and not requiring specific enumeration anew in the Constitution. The states derived their authority from the people, as did the national government, and were understood to be relatively autonomous political units—even if the new Constitution did impose national supremacy in principle. The Philadelphia delegates apparently assumed that the states under the new federal arrangement would be legally free to exercise any powers that were not expressly prohibited by the new Constitution or exclusively delegated to the national

**THE
SUBNATIONAL
DIMENSION OF
AMERICAN
DEMOCRACY**

government. It became apparent, however, during the ratification campaign that many citizens preferred to have this assumption spelled out explicitly in the Constitution. Thus the reserved powers of the states were specifically recognized with the addition of the Tenth Amendment in 1791. It provided that:

> *The powers not delegated to the United States by the Constitution, nor prohibited by it to the States, are reserved to the States respectively, or to the people.*

Generally this provision has been taken to mean that the states have the power to tax and spend for the general welfare of their citizens. Specifically, the reserved powers have been taken to include state authority to (1) regulate the ownership and use of property as well as the offenses against persons and property; (2) administer records and otherwise regulate birth, death, marriage, and divorce; (3) provide for public education, welfare, health and hospital services, as well as for the provision of highways, roads, canals and other forms of public transport; and (4) wield almost exclusive authority over the creation, organization, and conduct of local units of government.*

A Multiplicity of Governments

The sheer number of state and local units of government within the federal system suggests their potential significance in the performance of American democracy. As Table 17.1 shows, in 1972 there were a total of 78,269 governments in the United States, of which the national government is just one. American citizens are subject each day to the authority of—and are affected by—the state, county, town or city, school district, (and perhaps special district or townships) within which they are located. Each of us is at once subject to the costs as well as the benefits of several political units. These units in turn exercise a wide variety of responsibilities and broad powers that also extend to each of us in the conduct of his life. Subnational government, financed by public revenue spent for public purposes, regulates much of our business and social relationships, as well as many of the more private aspects of our lives. This level

---

* Though unmentioned in the Constitution, local governments are considered the legal agents of the states and in this capacity possess similar authority under the Tenth Amendment—insofar as the state chooses to delegate such authority.

Table 17.1
The Number of
Governments in the
United States,
1962–1972

	1972	1967	1962
National Government	1	1	1
State Governments	50	50	50
Local Governments	78,218	81,248	91,186
Total	78,269	81,299	91,237

Source: U.S. Bureau of the Census, Census of Governments: 1972, vol. 1, *Governmental Organization* (Washington, D.C.: U.S. Government Printing Office, 1973).

of government is composed of hundreds of agencies employing thousands of officials, from the motor vehicle licensing agent to the neighborhood policeman or the county agricultural agent. If we are truly to enjoy the fruits of liberty and good government it is not enough to look to the national government alone. The performance of the over 70,000 other political units that exercise authority must also be taken into account.

It is clear that the Constitution provides a system of multiple government, and it is obvious that a large number of governments in fact exist. It is much less clear just how significantly these governments relate to the promise and performance of American democracy, for it is beyond dispute that the national government is the senior partner in the federal partnership. In our century this seniority has grown to firm dominance, and the dominance appears to grow ever more extensive, to the degree that many have come to question the importance of subnational governments, especially the states.

National Dominance

Many factors have led to the contemporary dominance of national government over state and local units. National supremacy as a legal principle was of course established under the Constitution, but the *fact* of this supremacy developed over an extended period. Foreign and domestic crises since the inception of the Republic have consistently resulted in wider national activity, while the federal tax system has produced a wealth to sustain this activity beyond the dreams of any subnational unit of government. The development of national news media devoted largely to national and international affairs, coupled with the development of a political system with a single national official, the President, as its focus has increased public perception of the role and scope of the national government. These forces have tended to diminish the relative visibility and importance of subnational levels of government in the public mind. It would be a mistake, however, to attribute national expansion in performance and perception simply to factors outside state and local government. These units themselves have contributed to the diminishing of their political role relative to that of the government in Washington.

As critics have been quick to point out, much of the expansion of federal activity in domestic affairs may be attributed to the unwillingness or inability of lower levels of government to meet the needs of their citizens. Restrictive state constitutions; fragmented units of local government; feuding institutions; regressive and rigid tax systems; inept, corrupt, or simply unresponsive public

officials at these levels— all to some degree have contributed to a growing public sense that only the national government could assume the initiative in providing vital services as well as social justice in this country. If the national government has come to dominate our federal system, it is due, in some measure, to the lackluster performance of state and local governments in the past. While unwilling—and, under the present Constitution, unable—to abolish these lower levels of government, we have often simply gone around them and looked to Washington to fulfill our public needs.

Government Pluralism

Yet state and local governments continue to contribute to the performance of American democracy despite national dominance by the federal system. The existence of state and local units automatically distributes governmental power more widely among different sets of leaders. This distribution of power may be considered an important safeguard from central tyranny or an abusive national majority. A state governor or the mayor of a city may not be the political equal of the President, but every President must deal with many such public officials in the conduct of his office. Often the President's immediate success—and political future—depends upon obtaining the cooperation of governors, mayors, and other subnational officials. Certainly the extent to which a single national social or political group can dominate our politics and government is limited by the existence of state and local leadership. This plurality of leadership, guaranteed by both Constitution and custom, is a critical aspect of American democracy.

Further, state and local governments provide a political base from which electoral minorities may work to become national majorities. When unsuccessful in national elections, the opposition party can bide its time and rebuild for the future while holding power in state and local government. In this way, the loss of a national majority in any given election does not deny a political party all seats of governmental power. The thousands of subnational offices in this country assure a party denied national office a base from which to challenge those in power in Washington. Third parties, unsuccessful at winning much in the way of national offices (the presidency, or seats in Congress), nevertheless have been able to sustain themselves as a political alternative by using state and local office as a power base. Thus, state and local governments play an important role in assuring the party competition upon which American democracy so heavily depends.

Similarly, individuals and groups in our society that are unable effectively to transmit their demands at the national level, or who have perhaps lost their battle before the national government, can pursue their interests in the arena of state and local governments. The multitude of governmental offices below the national level offers access to authority that would otherwise be unavailable.

Ultimately, democracy depends upon the involvement of individual citizens in public affairs. State and local government offers expanded popular participation in politics and government. There are many more state and local offices to fill than national. The proximity of these governments to their citizens does not assure their responsiveness, but it at least makes them more immediately accessible than the federal government. Also, subnational government in many cases offers greater opportunity for public service because holding national elective

Mayor Beame of New York reminds Jimmy Carter that a President's success will often depend on local officials.

office means leaving home and usually foregoing any other career, whereas many state and local offices can be filled without such personal disruption. It is often possible to serve while pursuing one's original career. The national government itself is improved and benefited by the participation of persons originally introduced to public service and gaining valuable ability and experience at the subnational level who later move on to national office.

Attitudes Toward State and Local Government

State and local governments constitute an important part of American politics if for no other reason than because of the attitude about them held by many citizens. While popular attachment to state and local government remains quite strong in some regions of the country, especially in the South and Southwest, national expansion and population mobility have generally weakened such loyalties. The pre-Civil War attitude of being a citizen of Virginia first, and a citizen of the United States second, has given way to the tide of nationalism that has characterized twentieth-century America.

Fewer people tend to vote in state and local, than in national, elections, as chapter 5 showed. Usually we may expect 20 to 30 percent fewer eligible voters to turn out in state and local elections than in national. Research conducted by Robert R. Alford and Eugene C. Lee, for example, found that local voting turnout in American cities in the early sixties ran at only about 31.2 percent of the adult population on the average when the election was not held concurrently with state or national elections. And the evidence is strong that citizens are more knowledgable about national than subnational politics.

But these facts do not necessarily render state and local governments insignificant or expendable in the public eye. In an important study of the prominence of the states in American politics, Jennings and Zeigler found that "while the states may not be uppermost in the political thought of their residents, they do occupy a secure niche." In that study a national sample of citizens was asked to rank how closely they followed public affairs at the international, national, state, and local levels. The results, summarized in Table 17.2, indicate that almost one in five Americans place state affairs above those of all other levels, and about one in three do so for local affairs. Thus, the first-rank atten-

Table 17.2
Rank Order
Distribution for
Attention to
Governmental Affairs
at Four Levels

Level of Governmental Affairs	Rank of How Closely Followed				Total*
	First	Second	Third	Fourth	
International	20%	16%	22%	42%	100
National	32	31	26	10	99
State	17	33	27	22	99
Local	30	20	25	25	100
	99%	100%	100%	99%	

* Total percentages do not equal 100% due to rounding.

Source: M. Kent Jennings and Harmon Zeigler, "The Salience of American State Politics," *The American Political Science Review* 64 (June 1970).

tion paid to *both* state and local government is certainly substantial; just under half of those surveyed were most closely attentive to one of those levels. Further, when asked to rank which level they followed second most closely, one in three citizens mentioned state affairs, and over half selected state or local governments as their second choice for attention. These figures reflect a public reasonably attentive to subnational units of government, leading Jennings and Zeigler to conclude:

> *It is apparent that the States still loom large in the perspectives of the American public. Any attempted juggling of political units involving the states would probably confront a reservoir of mass attachments to the historic traditions, legal preserves, and political utility of the states, this salience helps assure the continued prominence of the several states within the federal system.*

Other public opinion surveys reinforce the findings of Jennings and Zeigler. For example, public attitudes toward state and local government also reflect an important degree of confidence in the performance of these units. A 1972 survey reported by the U.S. Advisory Commission on Intergovernmental Relations (ACIR)* showed that when citizens were asked which level of government delivered the most for the taxes it collected, state and local governments received a more favorable response rate than that of the national government— 44 percent for state and local compared to 39 percent for the national level. An earlier survey, reported in the Congressional Record in 1967, showed that more Americans (49 percent) believed that state governments spent taxpayers' dollars "more wisely" than did the federal government; only 18 percent held the opposite view.

A national survey of citizen attitudes toward American government, sponsored by the U.S. Senate Subcommittee on Intergovernmental Relations in 1973, found that public confidence in most governmental institutions had declined dramatically in recent years, although the ratings of local governmental units fared relatively better than those of state and national governments. As Table 17.3 shows, a majority of the public then felt that both state and local governments were about as trustworthy as had been true earlier—although it must be noted that about twice as many felt *less* confidence in these levels in 1973 than felt *more* confidence. Most striking, of course, was the very serious relative decline in public confidence in the national level of government, in which over half of the citizens surveyed felt *less* confidence than had been true five years earlier. Obviously each level of government in contemporary America has problems keeping in the public esteem, but the problem for the national level appears presently more severe. These surveys suggest that the affection and respect of the American people has by no means been completely forfeited to the national level of government.

More striking still is the opinion of state and local officials concerning their own levels. Again based on the 1973 Senate Subcommittee study, Table 17.3 shows that state and local government officials themselves have actually grown

---

* The ACIR is a permanent national advisory body created by Congress in 1959 to provide continuing systematic attention to intergovernmental problems in federal-state, federal-local, state-local, as well as interstate and interlocal problems. It periodically studies specific intergovernmental problems and issues reports with recommended solutions.

Table 17.3
General Public
Confidence in Levels
of Government, 1973
Compared to 1968

Public Officials'
Confidence in Levels
of Government, 1973
Compared to 1968

	More	Less	Same	Not Sure
National	11%	57%	28%	4%
State	14	26	53	7
Local	13	30	50	7
State Govt.				
State Officials	61%	10%	29%	—
Local Officials	20	36	43	1%
Local Govt.				
State Officials	25	6	69	—
Local Officials	48	18	34	—

Source: Committee on Government Operations United States Senate, *Confidence and Concern: Citizens View American Government* (Washington, D.C.: Government Printing Office, 1973), 42–43.

more confident in these levels. While few have *less* confidence in their own level of government, many (almost two out of three in the case of state officials judging state government) feel *more* confident about the institutions within which they serve than was true five years earlier. This provides some indication of the continuing perceived vitality these political units have.

In summary, contemporary attitudes toward state and local governments suggest that these units continue to hold an important place in the opinion of many Americans. The preeminence of the national government may be generally recognized, yet at the same time few citizens or public officials seem prepared to condemn subnational units of government to the political scrap heap. This attitude of support for state and local units defines the political environment within which the institutions and officials of the national government must operate.

Innovation and Experimentation

State and local governments are significant units within the framework of American government due to the *opportunity* they create for innovation and experimentation in both government structure and public policy. In this way, they contribute to the quality of the entire system by fostering the gradual improvement of government throughout the nation. These units are often free to pursue new or different ideas about government, to test them on a limited scale, and in so doing to provide examples that may later be emulated by their neighbors as well as by the national government. Our history is replete with instances of state and local innovation that stimulated national emulation.

For example, several of our Western states provided the vote for women nineteen years before the national government took this step in 1920 with the Nineteenth Amendment. Agricultural measures pioneered by North Dakota in the 1920s were adopted by the national government a decade later during the Depression. Louisiana developed a public system of medical assistance for the elderly decades before the Congress made this a matter of national policy. New York began a statewide program to encourage the construction of sewers and

	Federal	State and Local
1902	35%	65%
1927	31	69
1936	50	50
1944	91	9
1950	64	36
1960	62	38
1970	64	36
1975	61	39

Table 17.4
Public Expenditures
in the United States
by Level of
Government,
1902–1975: National
as Compared with
State and Local
(Expressed in
percentages)

Source: Thomas R. Dye, *Politics in States and Communities* (Englewood Cliffs, N.J.: Prentice-Hall, 3rd ed., 1977).

sewage treatment plants in local communities three years before national action was taken in this area.

At present, state and local governments are experimenting with stringent antipollution and environmental protection measures; decriminalization of certain drugs; no-fault auto insurance; hand-gun control; welfare reform; and a host of political reforms designed to make government more open and accountable. It is likely that, based on these experiences, the national government will undertake similar programs. This process affords citizens an opportunity to shape their states and communities in ways a national majority may not be prepared to accept. At the same time, it provides the entire national experience a chance to develop and, in the long term, to institute better government at all levels.

Provision of Vital Services

There has been a dramatic change in the locus of governmental activity in the United States since the inception of the federal system, and this shift has tended to make the national government more prominent in the minds of most Americans. The figures in Table 17.4 indicate that in the early 1900s state and local governments together accounted for about two out of every three dollars spent by government in this country. Most of that money was devoted to supporting local activity. As the century has progressed, the national government has become increasingly active, until by 1970 its expenditures—including grants-in-aid, which are actually spent by subnational units—amounted to almost two out of every three dollars spent by government in the United States. This is obviously an important change. But the extent of national intervention into affairs earlier considered the exclusive responsibility of state and local governments depends on the type of activity involved. A substantial amount of the dramatic increase in the national share of public expenditures has been concentrated in three policy areas: national defense, space research, and the postal service. In the remaining areas of public expenditure, state and local governments continue to *share* financial responsibility with Washington. They still expend the majority of public funds devoted to education, highways, as well as health and hospitals, and they provide between 18 and 45 percent of the money allocated for the remaining domestic services.

The future quality of our lives
depends on environmental
protection measures taken at
the local level.

Despite the extension of national government activity in domestic areas previously the exclusive domain of state and local governments, this has not resulted in the withering of our states and communities. Quite the contrary; as the national government has increased its activity, so too have state and local governments increased theirs. These units are taxing, spending, and borrowing more than ever before in order to meet their still heavy responsibilities. This growing relative effort of state and local governments is apparent in the summary provided in Table 17.5. Public fiscal activity of every type (revenue and borrowing) has increased dramatically in the past quarter-century. What is most striking, however, is that in each instance the growth of state and local activity has been relatively greater than the increases in the comparable national activity. These figures demonstrate that state and local government in the last twenty-five years has increased, at an even greater rate than the national growth, its financial support for public services.

Another important indication of the vitality of state and local government—and of the recent expansion in its activity—is public employment levels. Here too it is apparent that, in the domestic sphere, state and local units play a continuing role. The top one-half of Table 17.6 reveals that it has been states and communities, not the national level, that have most substantially increased their share of public employment in the last quarter-century. In 1950 about 67 percent of the government workers in this country were state or local employees. By 1974, national expansion notwithstanding, the subnational share of the public employment had actually increased significantly—to 80 percent. This increase occurred because, while federal employment has grown by about 36

Table 17.5
Percentage Increase
in Public Fiscal
Activity, 1950–1974

	Revenue % Increase
National	+464
State and Local	+674
Total Public	+536

	Expenditure % increase
National	+440
State and Local	+632
Total Public	+519

	Debt Outstanding % increase
National	+ 78
State and Local	+683
Total Public	+130

Source: U.S. Bureau of Census, *Statistical Abstract of the United States: 1976* (Washington, D.C.: U.S. Government Printing Office, 1976).

Essential public services provided by local units include health care, hospitals, police and fire protection.

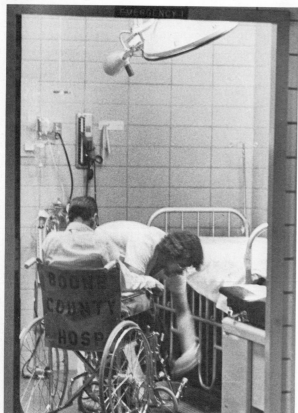

	National	State and Local
1950	33.1%	66.9%
1960	27.5	72.5
1967	25.2	74.8
1970	22.1	77.9
1974	19.6	80.4

Table 17.6
Public Employment,
1950–1974

	National	State and Local
National Defense*	100.0%	0.0%
Postal Service*	100.0	0.0
Education	.4	99.6
Highways	.8	99.2
Health & Hospitals	16.6	83.4
Police Protection	8.3	91.7
Fire Protection	0.0	100.0
Sanitation and Sewerage	0.0	100.0
Parks & Recreation	0.0	100.0
Natural Resources	55.0	45.0

Public Employment
by Function, 1974

* Note that in 1974 fully 71% total national government employment was in these two areas.
Source: U.S. Bureau of Census, *Statistical Abstract of the United States:* 1976 (Washington, D.C.: U.S. Government Printing Office, 1976).

percent over 1950 levels, the number of state and local workers had increased 175 percent for this period. The implications of this dramatic subnational growth become clearer when we realize that the bulk of national employment (about 71 percent in 1974) was devoted to national defense, international relations, and the postal service. But as the lower portion of Table 17.6 shows, state and local employment was exclusively devoted to domestic activities of the type that immediately touches our day-to-day existence: education, health, welfare, police and fire protection.

Summary: The Subnational Role in American Democracy

State and local units of government in the United States are not presently as visible as the national government. While it is not difficult to understand why this has come about, it would be a serious error to conclude that low visibility has rendered them unimportant as political units. These subnational governments continue to enjoy constitutional status as well as a political position buttressed by tradition and public attitudes. They continue to provide vital services to citizens and afford vital sources of potential competition with the national leadership. This competition in principle assures citizens a degree of protection from an overly powerful, coercive national government. Finally, state and local governments serve as sources of important policy innovation and experimentation that later may be adopted nationally. As one noted state-and-local scholar, Thomas R. Dye, has observed:

Despite the glamor of national politics, states and communities carry on the greatest volume of public business, make the majority of policy decisions, and direct the bulk of public programs. They have the major responsibility for maintaining domestic law and order, for educating the children, for moving Americans from place to place, and for caring for the poor and the ill. They regulate the provision of water, gas, electric, and other public utilities, share in the regulation of insurance and banking enterprise, regulate the use of land, and supervise the sale and ownership of property. Their courts settle by far the greatest number of civil and criminal cases.

In short, contemporary American government still depends in large measure on the performance of state and local units as it strives to realize the promise of democracy.

STATE GOVERNMENT WITHIN THE UNITED STATES

The American states are a fascinating mixture of similarity and difference. Each operates under a written constitution that divides authority between an executive, legislative, and judicial branch of government. The general structure and processes that define these branches of government are quite similar from state to state. And the states share the same national language as well as a common national political tradition and history.

Yet beneath these fundamental similarities can be found fifty separate political systems embedded in what usually prove to be very different environments. The states differ in the actual nature and detail of their constitutions and in the patterns of authority distribution between their three-branch governments. The executive, legislative, and judicial branches of state government usually exhibit varying styles of operation from state to state. As a result the same branch of government is likely to behave much differently in one state from the way it does in another. Moreover, the nature and design of the public policy produced by state government is itself likely to vary substantially across the nation. Despite having essentially the same fundamental political responsibilities, the policies pursued by decision makers in separate states are often very different. Further, the states also diverge at the level of economic development, since not all have attained the same level of industrialization, urbanization, wealth, or standards of education. The discrepant level of economic development between the states in turn conditions the nature of demands and supports that later become incorporated in the political system. Because of the presence of great differences amidst basic similarities, it is impossible to provide a comprehensive explanation of contemporary state government in a single chapter. What follows is designed merely to accentuate the most important similarities and differences found among the American states.

THE STATE CONSTITUTION

The formal structure and responsibilities of the government, as well as the fundamental civil rights of citizens, are delineated for each of the fifty states in its written constitution. The constitution is the formal "rules for rule making" and expresses both the basic responsibilities *to,* as well as the responsibilities *of,* political authority within the state. The written constitution serves the following functions for each state political system: (1) it establishes the basic protections afforded the people in the exercise of their civil liberties; (2) it defines the powers of the government; and (3) it creates methods appropriate for changing the basic law itself should the need arise.

It has often been argued that these functions are best served by a short, general document that vests broad powers in the representatives of the people and holds these officials responsible through the political process. Such an approach to constitution writing maintains that the interests of society are best served when government is afforded considerable discretion in the exercise of its authority, and that the prerogatives and responsibilities should be spelled out in direct, simple, language. Such constitutions are not to be legal codes (statutory law) themselves. The details that make up statutory law are later written into specific legislative enactment.

As Justice Benjamin Cardozo once wrote, "A constitution states or ought to state not rules for the passing hour but principles for an expanding future." The flexibility inherent in such a broad declaration of principles should reduce the need for formal constitutional alteration. As the need arises, reinterpretations of general provisions can be made and these should usually suffice to keep the constitution timely. Perhaps the best example of this view as to the "proper" constitutional format is the national Constitution. Only around 6700 words long, it has been amended only sixteen times since the Bill of Rights was added to correct several original defects. Its grants of power have been sufficiently generous to allow the national government to adjust to changing needs without having very often to resort to formal alterations of the fundamental law of the land. This exercise of national authority is left in very large measure—subject to the specific restrictions in the Bill of Rights—to the discretion of those charged with the responsibility to govern. Moreover the amendment process is somewhat arduous and this reduces the likelihood of frequent amendment.

The earliest of our state constitutions served as excellent examples of the philosophy that constitutions ought to be *brief, general, flexible,* and *relatively difficult to amend.* In usually fewer than 10,000 words the state constitutions framed between 1776 and 1800 established the basic state and local institutions of authority, outlined their powers, and specified political and personal liberties. In reaction to the colonial experience, the moving principles behind the governments they established were: (1) separation of powers; (2) legislative supremacy; (3) appointed executive and judicial departments; and (4) limited suffrage. These early documents established state governments with extensive insulation from the electorate and granted policymakers substantial freedom of operation. Moreover, they were often adopted by less than entirely democratic means. Only Massachusetts and New Hampshire, for example, placed the question of constitutional ratification before the electorate; the other states merely ratified through legislative endorsement.

Movement From Early Patterns

Because of a long era of extensive constitution writing between 1850 and 1920, the contemporary state constitutions bear little resemblance to the model criteria discussed above. During this middle period of state history constitutional framers were guided by a very different conception of what made a "good" constitution. Rather than considering a simple, direct outline of government as the best format for a constitution, the philosophy dominating the middle period held that these documents best served the people when they were *restrictive, comprehensive,* and *specific.* That is, rather than as general "rules for rule making," constitutions increasingly came to be thought of as the best place for the rules themselves. This shift in constitutional philosophy was the result of four important nineteenth-century forces: (1) the movement that was called "Jacksonian Democracy"; (2) the deterioration of public faith in the state legislature as a representative institution; (3) the development of deep conflicts between strong interests within states; and (4) general popular attitudes toward state constitutions.

"Jacksonian Democracy." The Jacksonian movement to "democratize" state government led to the addition of a host of new procedural details and constitutional offices. The intention was to make electoral majorities more influential in determining the structure, procedures, personnel, and even policies of state and local government. Thus constitutions began to be filled with new, detailed suffrage materials; executive and judicial offices previously appointive were made elective; and, to increase their prestige (thereby inviting greater citizen interest in holding them), many new public offices were given constitutional status. To make the constitution itself more "democratic," procedures of revision and amendment were simplified and the role of the electorate expanded.

Loss of Faith. Because legislatures in particular and other state agencies in general were increasingly viewed as corrupt, incompetent, and unresponsive to the needs of the people, there occurred a severe loss of faith in representative government in the second half of the last century. This decline of faith in representative institutions strongly affected constitution makers, and the opinion became generally accepted that public officials could no longer be held sufficiently accountable through periodic elections. So constitutions increasingly came to be filled with provisions that severely restricted the discretion and power of public officials to make and implement public policy.

For example, detailed constitutional limits were placed on the type and level of taxes that could be levied by state and local governments. Fearful of irresponsible borrowing for unwise or corrupt purposes, framers added stringent debt limitations to state constitutions, as well as restricting the purposes for which such debt could be incurred. Spending limits were imposed in many cases, and often the purposes for which state moneys could be allocated were enumerated in detail. Further, it became popular to make the detailed organization of the executive and judicial departments the subject of technical, restrictive constitutional provisions.

In some states citizens were extended the constitutional power to *directly* propose (and later at a statewide election vote up or down) legislation as well as constitutional amendments without any action on the part of the state legislature.* This initiative device was thought to ensure that government would truly

---

* There are two basic types of initiative: the "constitutional initiative" (18 states), whereby a specified number of voters can by petition propose an amendment for popular consideration without any action by the legislature; and the "legislative initiative," which allows a specified number of voters by petition to propose the adoption of new laws or the repeal of old laws without any action by the legislature (16 states).

☐ ☐

YES   NO

**PROPOSED AMENDMENT
NUMBER FIVE
PENSION BENEFITS OF WIDOWS
AND WIDOWERS OF RETIREES**
Shall the proposed amendment
to Article seven, Section eight, subdivision two of the Constitution in
relation to the increasing of pension benefits payable to widows and
widowers of retired members of a retirement system of the State, or of a
subdivision of the State, be approved?

☐ ☐

YES   NO

**PROPOSED AMENDMENT
NUMBER SIX
FILLING OF VACANCIES ON
BOARDS OF EDUCATION**

Shall the proposed amendment to
Article thirteen, Section three of
the Constitution in relation to the
filling of vacancies on boards of
education, be approved?

be responsive to the people or at the very least would give them the power completely to circumvent unresponsive legislatures and act directly in their own interest. Similarly, the referendum device was added to constitutions in which voters were given the opportunity to approve or disapprove constitutional amendments, and in some states even laws previously approved by the state legislature.*

Some states took the additional step of giving citizens the power of the recall.† This device permits voters, once a specified number of signatures are obtained on a recall petition, to vote a public official out of office prior to the normal expiration of his or her term.

With the onset of the decline of faith in representative democracy, state constitutions began to contain lengthy, detailed, and restrictive provisions that sought to narrow the prerogatives of public officials and thus limit the amount of damage that they could do to the body politic. And, in many states, the constitutions added provisions for initiative, referendum, and recall as means of further overcoming the perceived shortcomings of representative institutions.

Conflict of Interests. The tremendous economic expansion, urbanization, and population growth of the post-Civil War era precipitated a great clash of social and economic interests within the states. Fierce group competition for social, economic, and political advantage inevitably had a deep and lasting effect on state constitutions. The new economic order brought powerful industrial and labor interests into the political arena to challenge the traditional political power of agricultural and small-business interests in state government.

Taking full advantage of the numerous ongoing special conventions and legislative deliberations devoted to constitutional revision,‡ the competing interests devoted vast amounts of energy and resources to bend the state constitutions into just another instrument of their influence. Fearful that state government would be unduly responsive to those with whom they were in competition—or simply mindful of protecting their own particular sphere of influence—these groups sought to build advantage for themselves into the basic law. Failing in that, they sought at least to build in disadvantages for those with whom they were in competition.

The addition of specific constitutional provisions earmarked for their benefit was especially attractive to these groups because it increased their prestige by winning constitutional recognition of their positions at the same time as it created protections that were more difficult than regular legislative enactment to change later. Although almost every state during this period made it easier

---

* There are two basic types of referendum: the "constitutional referendum" (49 states), whereby constitutional amendments must be approved by the voters before taking effect; and the "legislative referendum", in which certain acts of the state legislature can become law only after being approved by the voters (38 states).

† The recall may apply to all, or only some, public officials depending upon the state concerned. Some form of recall for state level officials is presently available in only twelve states.

‡ Between 1870 and 1910, forty-two states established new, or revised old, constitutions in an incredible flurry of activity. Many of these documents remain in effect or have only recently been replaced. During this great era of constitution making, the states held 128 constitutional conventions!

than before to amend the constitution, it remained more difficult to achieve amendment than to alter a legislative statute. Accordingly, constitutions were soon replete with lengthy and detailed provisions designed to assure constitutional advantage to one interest or another.

Popular attitudes. The final major force leading state constitutions away from the ideal model of broad, general, and short documents, was popular attitudes toward them. It was commonly believed at the time that the best available protection against bad government, and the most dependable assurance of good government, was to write a rule about it. This naive faith in the power of written rules led many citizens to view political reform as largely a matter of simply developing the proper set of rules. And it was natural, in the pursuit of "good government through good rules," to begin with the state constitution— the source of all the state rules. As state governments fell more and more into disrepute, the impulse to write additional rules "governing the government" rose accordingly.

Since state constitutions never enjoyed the high popular esteem accorded the national Constitution, it was not a difficult matter to pursuade voters that constitutional tinkering was a reliable approach to reform. Thus popular attitudes toward state constitutions were such that constitutional revision to suit passing fashion or immediate need was never considered the drastic political act at the state level that it would have been at the national. These attitudes led to amendment after amendment, revision after revision. Eventually, any sense that the constitution was something more fundamental than other state laws was largely lost.

Contemporary State Constitutions

The typical state constitution today is heavily influenced by the philosophy and events of the middle historical period (1850-1920). Thirty of our states continue to live under documents originally framed then, while several others with older constitutions were heavily amended at that time. Thus the contemporary state constitution is usually characterized by (1) extreme length; (2) excessive detail; (3) frequent amendment; and (4) a restrictive approach to government. Georgia has the longest constitution (over a half-million words in length despite the fact that it was rewritten as late as 1945), and eight other states (Alabama, Arkansas, California, Colorado, New York, Oklahoma, South Carolina, and Texas) have documents with more than 40,000 words. Nor have the states been shy about amending their already lengthy constitutions: thirteen states have amended these documents 100 times or more. In this, Georgia is the leader again, having amended its 1945 constitution some 767 separate times. (Remember that the national Constitution runs only about 6700 words and has been amended only 26 times.)

Extreme length and frequent amendment have produced constitutions replete with *details*. In its constitution, Delaware specifies the entire judicial procedure, step by step, for the prosecution of election offenses. The Missouri constitution details the structure of its state and local judiciary, including the exact wording to be used on the ballot for judicial elections. Illinois devotes an entire article of its constitution to public warehouses, while Michigan provides for an executive mansion. The detailed rules for the regulation of lobbying are a part of the California constitution, as well as are such details as the exemption from taxation of "fruit and nutbearing trees under the age of four years." South Carolina used the constitution to define the age of consent in explicit terms, while Colorado, Utah, and Wyoming go so far as to forbid the State Board of Education to prescribe the textbooks used in public elementary schools. California and New Mexico, on the other hand, require the state boards to make such a prescription.

The practical consequences of detail, amendment, and restriction have been severe. A constitution that has become essentially a statutory code is usually too rigid to cope successfully with emerging problems in a changing world, and the ability of the government itself becomes impaired. Insofar as public officials may be kept from doing harm by detailed restrictions on the exercise of their power, they are also denied the opportunity to do good. Limiting the power of government to very narrow functions, which in turn are spelled out in every detail, leaves officials little room to expand or otherwise alter public policy as public needs change. Length and detail breed rigidity, which in time requires specific constitutional amendment, which eventually leads to further amendments still. Only those state constitutions that were confined to fundamentals have been spared unending amendments.

Richard H. Leach has observed that "State constitutions, in sum, work to slow the rate at which states can meaningfully adjust to altered circumstances; to render adaptation and change difficult; to inhibit performance—in short, to reduce the flexibility and dynamism of state government to the vanishing point." Most students of state politics share that view. The basic consequence of lengthy, detailed, and negative constitutions has been to obstruct state government in the performance of its duties, rather than to facilitate it.

The shape of the state constitution continues to be an important question in state politics. Albert L. Sturm has estimated that since midcentury more official attention has been given to revising and modernizing state constitutions than during any comparable period since before the Civil War; in the last twenty years almost a third of the states have undertaken effective constitutional reform. Citizens have approved new fundamental charters in Michigan (1963), Connecticut (1965), Florida (1969), Illinois (1970), Virginia (1970), North Carolina (1970), and Louisiana (1974), and these have tended to be shorter, more general, and less restrictive than those written in the middle era. Still, constitutional revision stirs much opposition, particularly when the proposed changes are extensive, and voters have turned down proposed new constitutions in New York (1967), Rhode Island (1968), Maryland (1968), New Mexico (1969), and Arkansas (1970). The primary emphasis of constitutional revision has tended to be on institutional reform proposals directed at strengthened executive leadership, judicial reorganization, and bureaucratic professionalization.

In most cases, however, constitutional development in the states continues to reflect the same penchant for piecemeal alteration that characterized the 1850-1920 period. On any given election day it is common to find one or more proposed constitutional amendments on the ballot in most states. During the recent 1970-1975 period for example, forty-eight of the fifty states considered altogether a total of 1288 separate constitutional amendments, of which 849 were actually adopted. These proposals tended to be most often concerned with issues of local taxation and finance, although a large number were specifically directed toward the state legislature (usually providing for open legislative meetings, new apportionment, and the alteration of sessions).

THE LEGISLATIVE PROCESS AMONG THE STATES

The legislative process at the state level is similar in many ways to that at the national. The legislative function is in every state performed by a representative assembly that is directly elected by the people and that enjoys independent constitutional standing. These representative bodies, variously styled *legislature, general assembly, legislative assembly,* or *General Court,* are divided into two separate chambers. The only exception to the two-house (bicameral) rule is that of Nebraska, which has a one-house (unicameral) legislature. The upper house in these legislatures is called the *Senate* while the lower house is usually known as the *House of Representatives.* *

Seats in the legislature must be assigned on the basis of population in accordance with the one-person, one-vote principle explained in chapter 9, and the size of these bodies varies widely from fewer than 60 to more than 400 members. Typically, the lower house has more members than the upper house, although that is not always the case at the state level. In the majority of states, members of the Senate are elected for four-year terms. All house members face reelection at the same time in these bodies, while in about one-half of the states, senators serve staggered terms in which only 50 percent of the membership faces reelection every two years. Thus, with the important exception of unicameral Nebraska, the structural arrangements for the state legislatures rather closely approximate that of the national Congress.

Legislative procedures and organization at the state level also tend—at least superficially—to resemble the Congress. With the exception of Nebraska, which elects members without any party affiliation, legislators are identified by political party and organized into majority and minority segments in much the same way as Congress, with formal positions of legislative leadership being accorded on the basis of the distribution of party strength. To facilitate the business of the legislature, permanent committees have developed with jurisdiction being divided roughly into functional areas such as education, highways, commerce, and natural resources.

The formal lawmaking procedure itself is virtually identical to that of the Congress: a legislative proposal is formulated, introduced, and referred to the appropriate committees—which may hold hearings in both houses of the legislature. After the proposal is reported out of the committees it must be approved by a majority of both houses. If there are any differences between the versions approved in the separate houses, a conference committee must reconcile them before final approval of the bill can be given. The bill is then forwarded to the state governor for signature or veto.† Further, as has proven to be the case at

Caught in the act: the Wisconsin Legislature in session.

---

* In some states the lower house is known as the *House of Delegates* or simply as the *Assembly.*
† Nebraska again is an exception to the rule. Since there is only a single house in the legislature, action need be taken only by a single committee, and a single vote of approval won prior to sending the bill to the governor. Also, the veto power of governors varies from state to state. The governor in North Carolina is denied the veto.

the national level, the chief executive has become increasingly active in this process in the states. An increasing volume of legislative activity is devoted to consideration of policy programs or budgets developed by the governor rather than initiated by the legislature.

Most of the major and minor functions that define the legislative task of the national Congress discussed in chapter 10 are also the responsibility of the state legislatures. Thus their major responsibilities would include making statutory law, controlling the administration of governmental activities performed by executive officials (executive oversight), informing the general public on major issues and the alternative approaches to resolving them (the information and investigation function), and providing assistance in dealing with problems individuals may have with the government (constituent service). In addition each state legislature exercises certain *executive* functions by reviewing gubernatorial appointments, a few *judicial* functions by having the power—in limited circumstances—to remove executive and judicial officials from their positions in state government, and some important intergovernmental functions in making decisions concerning proposed amendments to the national Constitution, considering interstate compacts and agreements, as well as deciding whether or not to sanction state participation in certain federal programs.

Differences Between State Legislatures and Congress

It would be a serious distortion to assume that the similarities discussed make the state legislatures simply fifty local versions of the Congress. In fact, there are a variety of very important differences between these representative bodies and the national legislature that tend to affect their relative performance in significant ways. Thus, whereas being a member of Congress is a full-time occupation, with salary and benefits commensurate with the responsibilities, in only a few states does the legislature require the full-time attention of its members.

For example, as of 1976, fourteen states still limited their legislatures to a single session every *other* year, while fewer than one-half empowered these bodies to call themselves into special session. Furthermore, direct and indirect limitations on the length of sessions continue to be imposed in thirty-three states. Only four states currently approximate the congressional practice of a continuous two-year legislative session that meets virtually year-round with bills that carry over from one session to the next.* While the trend is in the direction of annual sessions (in 1963 only twenty states had annual sessions, but by 1976 this had increased to forty-two) and longer ones, the large majority of legislators still consider themselves to be amateurs and maintain other primary occupations.†

Despite major similarities as to function, state legislatures differ from Congress in that they do not have to deal with foreign policy and instead concentrate exclusively on domestic affairs. This makes their legislative task less difficult perhaps, but also tends to reduce the visibility of these bodies relative to

* These states are California, Michigan, New Jersey, and Pennsylvania.
† Between 1972 and 1975, annual session proposals were rejected by voters in Alabama, Kentucky, Texas, and New Hampshire. During the 1973-74 session, voters in Montana approved the return from annual to biennial sessions.

the Congress. The dramatic foreign policy issues that attract such widespread media attention, and on which so many congressional careers have been based, are not available for legislators at the state level—thereby reducing the attractiveness and prestige of long-term careers within the subnational assemblies.

It has been suggested by Kenneth T. Palmer that the most important contrasts between Congress and state legislatures tend to make the local assemblies much less *institutionalized* than their national counterpart.* Thus the Congress—which has come to be very highly institutionalized in recent decades—has a membership that remains within the organization longer than its state counterparts and consequently becomes more professional and expert in performing legislative duties. Further, congressional committees exhibit greater internal complexity, with a greater division of labor, than is true of committees in state legislatures. Finally, Palmer views Congress as more institutionalized because of the training, experience, and skill of its personnel as compared with the states.

The critical barrier to the institutional development of the state legislatures has been their relative inability to develop the type of stable, experienced, dedicated membership that is available to Congress. Turnover of membership in the state legislatures has consistently exceeded that of Congress in this century. As late as 1974, over half of the states turned over 27 percent or more of their state senators and over 33 percent of the members of their lower house, between sessions. In studying legislative turnover between 1963 and 1971, Alan Rosenthal found that the overall rate at each election for the fifty states ran at about 30 percent for the upper, and 36 percent for the lower, house of the assembly. The turnover figures for the Congress for the same period show a much more stable membership: in the Senate, only 10 percent of the seats were changed, and in the House, about 15 percent. In other words, at any given time in the past decade we would expect that roughly one out of every three members of the typical state legislature would be new to the institution, whereas only about one in ten members of the Congress would be a novice.

This institutionally damaging rate of turnover in state legislatures appears to be the product of several factors: (1) low compensation for legislative service, which renders membership in some cases a matter of severe financial hardship and thereby induces some representatives to quit prematurely; (2) psychological reasons, which lead some new members of the legislature to retire voluntarily after one or two terms simply because they prove to be poorly adapted to legislative life; and (3) political factors, in which the most skilled and ambitious legislators regard their state service merely as a stepping-stone to higher political position.

These factors, cited by Palmer—in addition to the fact that incumbents in the state legislature are usually unable to command the kind of political advantage from their office that is more typical of the resources available to a sitting member of Congress—results in relatively unstable, short-term membership in the typical state legislature. Thus state legislatures most especially differ from

---

* Institutionalization according to Palmer refers "mainly to the degree of professionalism, stability, or permanence that a political organization exhibits." It is generally thought that the greater the level of institutionalization attained by an organization, the more effective it will be in maintaining its independence and ensuring that it will effectively perform its functions.

The increasing number of black state legislators such as Carl McCall of New York has been one tangible product of reapportionment.

the Congress in their relative inability to attract and maintain a permanent group of first-rate career members. Cumulatively, the institutional differences that characterize the state legislative assemblies as compared to the national legislature have made them tend to be less effective and enjoy less political status in the pursuit of their responsibilities.

Legislative Performance at the State Level

In addition to the problems inherent in the relatively low levels of institutionalization attained by state legislatures (Palmer says that state legislatures seem to reflect today about the same degree of institutionalization present in the U.S. House of Representatives in the early nineteenth century), these bodies have typically been charged with other performance shortcomings. Among the more common significant complaints would be that the legislature is not sufficiently responsive to the majority will within the electorate or within the legislature itself; that special-interest groups at the expense of the "public interest" dominate legislative politics and policy making; and that institutional arrangements in the legislature obscure the public's view of the decision making process, thereby making it difficult to ascribe responsibility for actions taken by the representative assembly. These are serious charges and their accuracy is likely to vary from state to state. But, they would seem to summarize feelings about the state legislatures that can probably be found nationwide.

Reapportionment. The most significant development in recent years aimed at meeting these criticisms has stemmed from legislative reapportionment. Efforts to make legislatures more responsive to electoral majorities have been assisted by the reapportionments made in every state since the 1970 decennial census. At present, in only sixteen lower houses and fourteen senates is there a deviation of greater than 10 percent between the smallest and the largest population per seat. This represents a very substantial improvement over previous levels of legislative malapportionment.

In reviewing the consequences of bringing state legislative districts into "reasonable conformity" with the one-person, one-vote standard, Samuel C. Patterson found that the number of state legislators from urban and suburban areas within states has increased, and the number from rural areas has declined. Further, in those states previously the most seriously malapportioned, this shift in membership has produced a higher proportion of "younger, better-educated legislators, and a marked increase in the representation of ethnic minorities, notably blacks." Patterson reports that reapportionment has also tended to stimulate party competition for legislative seats as well as a greater degree of party voting within the state legislatures. Finally, reapportionment appears to have contributed to greater legislative responsiveness in terms of substantive policy decisions. The changes in state apportionments that occurred in the 1960s have, according to Patterson's survey, "been related in a significant way to changes in public policy," especially in respect to liberal and urban-oriented policy.

Special-interest domination. The problem of special-interest domination of legislatures is likely to be most severe when the legislative decision-making process is obscure, closed, and dependent on lobbyists for information and staff assistance. A variety of steps are being taken in the states to reduce the susceptibility of the legislature to undue special-interest influence: in many states major reductions in the number of committees have been made, several often being consolidated into one. Before consolidation, legislators were assigned to too many separate committees; the wide range of unrelated subjects covered in these separate assignments made it virtually impossible for a legislator to become knowledgeable in more than a few of the many subjects for which he or she was responsible in committee work. Because committees under consolidation are reorganized by *subject area,* legislators can concentrate on, and develop, specialized knowledge about legislation in a reduced number of subject areas. This committee consolidation potentially improves the ability of the individual legislator to concentrate on a few specialized areas and in so doing to develop an expertise necessary for dealing with, and often challenging, special-interest efforts. Consolidation also allows for better allocation of legislative staff and facilities, thereby reducing institution-wide the dependence upon special interests for information and manpower.

Openness. Other reforms of a procedural nature are also being undertaken to make the decision-making process more open and subject to public scrutiny. Advance notice of committee hearings and of bills to be considered is now the practice in the majority of states. Formal rules of committee procedure are now in effect in over two-thirds of the states, thus reducing the danger of unfair or arbitrary tactics being used to frustrate majorities within the legislature. By 1975 in all but about eight states legislative hearings had to be open to the public and the media, further reducing the obscurity in the legislative process that was previously so conducive to special-interest manipulation.

This openness, in conjunction with the formal recording of all roll-call votes in committees (now required in the majority of legislatures), makes it difficult for special interests to subvert the public interest behind closed doors, beyond the view of the public. These reforms, in the direction of a more open, integrated committee system within the various state legislatures, do not guarantee that the representative assembly will not be unduly responsive to special-interest groups. But they do make it more difficult for such behavior to go unno-

Telling it like it is at a legislative committee hearing.

ticed. Further, these changes appear to enhance the development of the institutional strength of these bodies, whereby their ability to resist undue outside interests is improved.

Evaluation of State Legislatures

It is very difficult to come to an evaluation of the state legislative process that is fair and applicable to every state. Certain general conclusions are possible when these institutions as a whole are considered. First, almost all state legislatures are better than they used to be. The effects of legislative reapportionment and piecemeal reforms have tended to increase the quality of these institutions. But none of these representative bodies presently enjoys high public visibility or substantial popular confidence.

Second, few state legislatures, if any, are as good as they *could* be. In 1971, the Citizens Conference on State Legislatures (CCSL) released a critical study of the fifty state legislatures that measured the extent to which each met the basic needs of its state. This nonpartisan, reform-oriented group measured each legislature by its capacity to perform as "a genuinely democratic decision-making body, reflecting the various views and values of its citizenry on the one hand and responding effectively and authoritatively to their needs and problems on the other." The basic conclusion of the CCSL was that, as of 1970, *"in no state does such a legislature exist."* That study was concerned with determining the institutional capacity of the legislatures to perform their basic functions (and not concerned with the quality of the individual members or the wisdom of their decisions). Figure 17.1 provides a representation of how each state ranked within this study and provides some idea as to which were found to be the most and the least developed.

Reapportionment in conjunction with recent trends in legislative compensation, standards, organization, and procedures has undeniably brought some improvement in state legislatures since 1970. There is, for example, strong evidence that the overall quality of the individual legislator is improving and that the composition of the entire legislature is becoming more representative in almost every state. Whether or not these developments will also lead to improvement in actual legislative performance is still uncertain. Significant gains in performance will be possible only if these representative assemblies are able to keep the most dedicated, talented, and politically astute of their lawmakers as a corps of career members. It is in this way that the continued *institutionalization* of the legislature remains a critical question within every state. If these bodies are to practice effective control of our burgeoning state executive bureaucracies, the luxury of an *amateur* legislature in feeble competition with a professional executive is probably one that we can no longer afford.

But where does the responsibility for the present state of the subnational legislature rest, and wherein lies the hope for the future? John Gardner has observed that

> *The grave shortcomings of state legislatures as instruments of a responsive and honest government must be laid squarely at the door of the American citizen. . . . If the American people can be said to own their legislatures in any sense, they most certainly have been absentee landlords. Few institutions in our national life have been as consistently ignored and neglected by the average American.*

Figure 17.1

The pattern of state legislative rankings on institutional capacity.

Source: Data from the Citizens Conference on State Legislatures, *State Legislatures: An Evaluation of Their Effectiveness* (New York: Praeger Publishers, 1971).

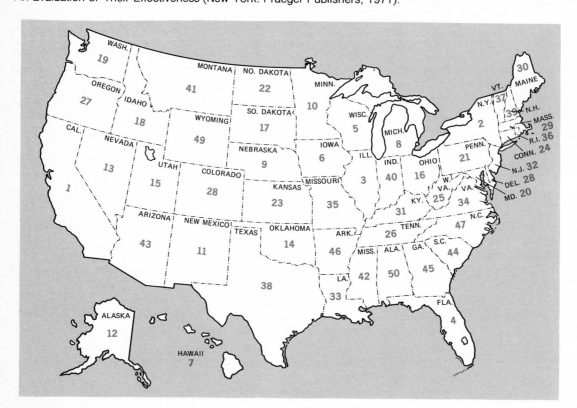

The future development of the fifty state legislatures depends primarily upon the extent to which citizens in the states demand better performance and are willing to provide the support, political as well as financial, that is necessary to provide greater institutionalization. Without sustained public interest in, and demand for, the constitutional and statutory reorganization necessary to upgrade our legislatures, it is unlikely that the necessary steps will be taken. The record is quite clear: in state politics the effective impetus for reform rarely comes from within the institutions of government alone and is unlikely to emerge from whatever powerful special interests benefit from the status quo. At work here is a basic democratic principle: the future of our political institutions rests in the hands of any citizen who cares enough to act.

THE EXECUTIVE PROCESS AMONG THE STATES

In every state the executive function is performed by a separate branch of the government formally headed by a directly elected chief executive called the governor. The governor, variously elected to terms of two or four years, is the single state official the people hold most generally responsible for the constitutional task of taking care that the laws are faithfully executed. The extent to

"Hi—we're your neighborhood petition people, and we wonder if you'd care to sign petitions against the noise of overhead jet flights, unsanitary streets, the rising school budget and food additives, and for playground renovation, more traffic lights, a new branch library. . ."

which the governor is in effective control of the administration of state government has shifted throughout history and today varies considerably from state to state.

The Development of the State Executive

In colonial America the governor, except in Rhode Island and Connecticut, was responsible directly to the British Crown (rather than to the people in the colonies) and enjoyed extensive authority. The Crown governors had the power to appoint civil officers, enforce all laws as well as grant pardons and reprieves, and served as commanders-in-chief of the colonial militia. In addition to these prerogatives (which have traditionally accrued to powerful executives), the governors also exercised considerable judicial and legislative powers: they appointed judges and served as head of the highest colonial court and had the authority to call, adjourn, or dissolve colonial representative assemblies, in addition to having the power to recommend and veto legislation.

This powerful governor was in fact the local representative of an absentee government—a political arrangement that did not prove to be popular. The deep conflicts between the colonial legislatures and the executive had two important long-run consequences for subsequent state government: (1) Americans became extremely suspicious of executive power, viewing executive authority as inherently corrupt and suspect. This created a strong impetus for decentralizing and limiting executive power. (2) The conflicts established a strong belief that executive and legislative departments were inevitably opposed in both nature and interest so that only the separation of powers could ensure proper government.

Between 1776 and 1789 the first state governments reacted strongly against their colonial experience and replaced executive with legislative supremacy. This shift was ensured by extending broad grants of authority to the legislature at the same time that the governor was provided with almost no independent political or administrative power. In many states "executive councils" were created within the legislature to maintain control over the governor, while all but two states provided for selection of the chief executive by the assembly rather than by the people directly. To further reduce the independence of the governor, states usually limited his term to one year without eligibility for reelection. To keep the legislature independent of gubernatorial influence, most states denied the governor any veto power and reduced the power of the chief executive further by having key executive and judicial appointments made by the state assembly. In this way our earliest state governors were reduced to little more than figureheads.

The adoption of the national Constitution provided states with an example of balanced government with a strong executive and was eventually influential in bringing most governors into a more powerful position. During the period 1789–1850 the governor in most states became popularly elected, terms of office were increased, the executive councils were abolished, and the veto power was reestablished.

Although by 1850 the governor was able to escape the domination of the state legislature, the reforms known as *Jacksonian Democracy* prevented the governor from asserting real control of the executive branch itself. The advent

Speaking out at a community meeting—"The Voice of the People."

of the direct election of numerous executive and judicial officers, designed to make state government more responsive to the people, established a government largely beyond the effective control of the governor. The power of appointment to key state offices was taken from the state legislature and transferred to the electorate directly, rather than to the governor. The practical effect of this change was to create a state government staffed with popularly elected officials such as the secretary of state, state treasurer, attorney general, auditor, superintendent of public instruction, and others who were very independent of *both* the legislature and the governor.

Eventually the general unsuitability of the legislature as an instrument of effective leadership in state affairs was unmistakable. For lack of any other practical alternative the common post-Civil War solution to this leadership problem was to increase the political and administrative power of the chief executive. Rarely, however, did the expansion of gubernatorial power prove sufficient to assure the effective control of the entire state government.

In reaction to the problems of industrialization and urbanization, the states assumed a variety of new functions between 1850 and 1920, for which numerous additional executive agencies were created. In this post-Jacksonian era, some of the new offices were elective, but most were appointive by the governor with the consent of the state senate. At the same time, governors were growing more powerful as legislative and political leaders. By obtaining the power to formulate and submit the state budget and policy packages, to call the legislature into emergency session, and to item-veto appropriation bills,* governors became formidable legislative actors. Informal gubernatorial power was increased due to the development of strong political parties in which the state governor was often an important leader. By virtue of influence within the political party, and with the decline of the prestige and power of the legislature, the governor during this period tended to become the most visible single political actor within a state.

While the legislative and political power of most governors grew, their capacity to govern effectively through control of the executive branch did not. The unplanned spread of numerous state agencies usually meant overlapping, duplication, and interagency rivalries that resulted in great waste. In most instances these agencies were beyond the effective control of the governor because officers within them enjoyed a tenure of office independent of the chief executive and could be removed only with great difficulty. Those who were not directly elected themselves, and who were therefore immune from gubernatorial influence through "hiring and firing," were usually appointed to terms of office much longer than that of the governor. This led to situations in which governors were saddled with executive officers appointed by a predecessor, perhaps from the other political party, who were unsympathetic to the views of the new chief executive.

The latter half of the nineteenth century produced governors who were increasingly powerful in comparison to other political figures or to the state legislature, but who were still incapable of exerting strong direction over the executive branch itself. Since 1920 an administrative reorganization movement

---

* The power to veto sections or items of an appropriation bill while signing the remainder into law. In a few states governors can also item-veto nonfinancial bills.

devoted to increasing the central responsibility of the governor—functionally integrating executive departments and eliminating independent regulatory boards—has sought to strengthen the "weak-governor" administrative system produced between 1850 and 1920. But the typical state continues strongly to resemble the patterns set in the earlier era.

Similarities and Differences Between the Governor and the President

The offices of state governor and President of the United States bear fundamental similarities as to structure and purpose. By law and custom, the role of the chief executive at both levels involves leadership responsibility in several functional areas. Today, for his respective government each is expected to perform as (1) the administrative leader with certain legislative and judicial functions; (2) a political and public opinion leader; (3) a ceremonial and diplomatic leader; and (4) a civilian leader of the military.

At the same time, although executives at both levels are charged with very similar responsibilities, the governors are most definitely not "little presidents." Their position in state government and politics is only *roughly* analogous to that of the President in the national government, and the differences between executive power at the two levels prove to be most revealing.

Administrative leader. Their respective constitutions assign the chief executives at the state and national level the power to execute public policy. Toward that end the structure of the executive throughout the United States appears remarkably similar: the chief executive is placed atop an administrative structure that is roughly hierarchical in organization and divided into an array of functional departments, agencies, boards, and commissions. Under the nominal coordination and supervision of the chief executive, these various executive agencies are expected to implement the public policy developed by the legislature. In their capacity as chief executive or administrative leader, both the governor and the President are expected to assume responsibility for the performance of the entire branch and to some degree to answer for the behavior of their subordinates in that organization.

Very few governors have anything approaching the authority of the President of the United States when it comes to the direction of administrative activities. Typically, the governor must share supervisory authority with a number of other directly elected officials with divided executive authority in a way unknown at the national level. A President, through extensive appointment powers, can soon place his own stamp on the national executive, and if appointees prove uncooperative, he can demand their resignation (and if that is not forthcoming, he has the power to dismiss them). State governors are typically in a much less advantageous position since only the electorate can remove directly elected state officials.*

As the only elected executive official (with the exception of the Vice-President), a President can lay special claim to being the spokesperson of the entire

---

* While in most states such officials could be impeached and later removed from office, this is a cumbersome procedure and holds little scope for gubernatorial influence.

American people, and he can convert this symbolic authority into definite authority over other executive officials. Governors, sharing executive power with many elected officials who have essentially the same broad electoral base, can thus lay no such special claim to superior legitimacy. The other state officials can assert an equal right to speak for the people in resisting the governor's policy since they too were directly elected. In short, because of a President's "monopoly" in being the only directly elected officer in the executive branch, and due to extensive presidential appointive powers, the national chief executive is in a better position to exercise administrative leadership than is the typical state governor.

Legislative and Judicial leader. Governors have tended to become important legislative leaders by virtue of their right to propose comprehensive executive budgets and policy programs, as well as due to their formal powers to exercise the veto and summon the representative assembly into special session. In much the same way as the President, governors today typically deliver a "state of the state" message at the beginning of the regular legislative session in which they outline the legislative actions that should have priority. Thus the governor is expected to set the legislative agenda, and later—through messages, expert testimony by executive branch personnel, and meetings with key legislative leaders—to influence legislative outcomes. Moreover, to some extent in every state the governor enjoys certain judicial prerogatives that have been traditionally associated with the head of state: the power to issue pardons, commutations, and reprieves for offenses against the state.

Political and public opinion leader. Because the office of chief executive at both levels is viewed as the most powerful and prestigious political position in the government, it has tended to become the focus of politics and public opinion. A governor is the single state official most visible to the state electorate during and after the election, and accordingly he has come to serve as the major state public opinion leader. Although they command only a small portion of prestige

The Chief Executive is also the Chief Legislator. Governor Byrne of New Jersey presents his "State of the State" address to a joint session of the state legislature.

At a town meeting Governor Dukakis of Massachusetts attempts to assume leadership in public opinion.

The energy crisis is but one of many problems likely to invite the attention of the annual National Governors Conference.

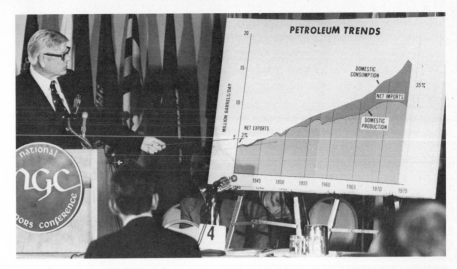

and attention compared to the President, governors are expected to speak out on vital public issues of the day and to lead in the formulation of state solutions of important problems. Toward that end the state media concentrate on the governor and extend broad coverage to gubernatorial news conferences, meetings, and public appearances.

Since he is the state's single most visible political actor, his support is likely to be actively sought by groups with demands to make upon state government. Even with the decline in the strength of political party organization in the last generation, governors continue to be the head of the political party and devote a substantial amount of time to attending party activities and trying to settle disputes between rival factions within the party organization and within the legislature. Governors typically have available some state patronage to dispense, and are expected to use it to some extent as a reward for the party faithful. Again, however, few governors are able to exert the kind of public-opinion and political-party leadership that typically is exerted by the President. The low visibility of state government as compared to the national reduces the power of any governor as a public opinion leader. Further, the amount of party activity within a single state, and the amount of patronage available to a single governor, pales in comparison to the potential party influence and patronage available to a President.

Ceremonial and Diplomatic Leader. As the ceremonial and diplomatic leaders of their states, governors perform as the official spokespersons for the people and the government. In much the same way that the President is the head of the American state, a governor presides at official gatherings, receives visiting dignitaries, and issues proclamations in the name of the people. In a fashion roughly similar to the way in which the President is responsible for our national relations with other nations, a governor is expected to assume responsibility for relations between his state and the others within the federal system. By attending national conferences and appearing in Washington before various federal agencies and the Congress, the governor represents the views and interests of his state as we expect our President to do for the United States in the international arena. In this era of intergovernmental federalism, the role of diplomatic leadership has become increasingly important in state government.

Civilian leader at the military. Every governor serves as commander-in-chief of the National Guard, except when it is called into national service. Although typically this role does not assume high priority and receives little attention from most governors, it has from time to time proved to be extremely important. Since World War II the Guard has largely been an instrument of rescue and relief in times of natural disasters and emergencies, although during the 1960s and early 1970s it assumed an important role in police work in cities and on college campuses. When the Guard has been called out during such an emergency and has performed well, the governor's nominal role as commander-in-chief has been a most valuable political resource. But in some instances—for example during the Detroit riots in 1967 and at Kent State in 1970—the performance of the National Guard was a source of political controversy and embarrassment to the governors involved. Of course, no governor enjoys the awesome power, status, or potential influence over the economy that accrues to the President as Commander-in-Chief of our national military, but in the hands of a skillful governor it may prove an important, if somewhat risky, political resource.

Executive Performance at the State Level

The capacity of the governor to effectively perform the executive functions outlined above varies substantially from state to state. Although none is likely to exert as much control in state affairs as the President is in national, in some states the governor is a more powerful chief executive than in others. Whether or not a state is likely to have strong gubernatorial leadership is conditioned by the extent of formal power given the chief executive as well as by the administrative organization with which a governor must contend.

Joseph A. Schlesinger has extensively studied formal gubernatorial power among the states and found that executive power is a combination of (1) tenure potential; (2) appointive power; (3) budget authority; and (4) the veto.

Tenure. Tenure is important because the possibility of reelection to another relatively lengthy term makes the governor a more formidable political and administrative adversary. In states with a longer tenure and the potential for reelection to another term of office, a governor has a chance to make a mark on the state administration over time.

Appointive power. With extensive appointment power a governor may more effectively influence the conduct of administration, as Schlesinger puts it, because "if a person can name an official, not only is the official beholden to him, but that person can also name someone whose values are close to those he wishes to implement."

Budget authority. Budget authority means the power to determine revenue and expenditure priorities for the state. Providing the governor firm control over how money is allocated makes the chief executive a more formidable actor in government. If the governor has extensive budget authority, then those who depend on state expenditures may ignore gubernatorial policy only at their potential hazard.

The Veto. Finally, the veto power gives the governor an effective means through which the decisions of the legislature may be influenced. The threat of a veto alone may induce legislators to alter key policy decisions more in accord with gubernatorial wishes. Through the use of the item-veto, a governor may strike appropriations sections without rejecting the entire law. This will usually prevent agency heads from going around the governor to friendly legislators for appropriations in excess of the governor's recommendation and is an important way of keeping these officials cooperative.

As Table 17.7 indicates, the formal powers allocated to state governors vary considerably. Schlesinger's research suggests that large, urban, more industrial states are more likely to furnish their governors with extensive formal powers than are the relatively small, rural, less industrial states. This, says Schlesinger, is because "as the complexity of a state increases, the governor's need for explicit means of control over his administration also increases." More powerful gubernatorial systems also are more likely to develop in highly competitive states where active political parties and interest groups demand effective executive leadership in politics.

Gubernatorial influence in state affairs is also a function of the type of administrative organization that has been created. As we saw earlier, the typical state executive department created in the late 1900s consisted of a plural executive in which administrative power was dispersed and the authority of the governor was restricted. Figure 17.2 illustrates two basic types of state administrative organization, the weak and the strong executive.

"Weak" Executive. In the weak executive type of state administration, represented by the top half of the illustration, the governor shares authority with several other directly elected officials. This assures the various department heads electoral independence of the governor and may well mean that a governor must have influence with members of the opposite party or with members of rival factions within the same party. The gubernatorial focus of most state elections often results in competitive races for that office, leading to the relatively frequent turnover of the chief executive. At the same time, the other important elected state officials tend to face less stiff electoral competition and are frequently returned to office term after term. This usually results in governors having a less dependable electoral base than do other state officials, as well as less experience in office. Obviously this situation is not likely to lead to effective gubernatorial control of these other executive offices.

Further, in the weak governor system many of the appointed public officials have longer terms of office than the governor. In this way a new governor, elected under a program of changing the state government, is usually unable to effect such change because many important officials appointed by a predecessor continue to serve unexpired terms and are not subject to removal except for serious misconduct. In short, the weak executive type of state administrative organization assures more or less frequent turnover in the chief executive but

Table 17.7
State Differences in Schlesinger's Index of Formal Power of Governors

High Power Index	Medium High Power Index	Average Power Index	Medium Low Power Index	Low Power Index
New York	Utah	North Dakota	Arizona	New Mexico
Illinois	Washington	Kentucky	South Dakota	North Carolina
Hawaii	Ohio	Virginia	Maine	Mississippi
California	Massachusetts	Montana	Vermont	Indiana
Michigan	Wyoming	Nebraska	Kansas	Florida
Minnesota	Missouri	Connecticut	Arkansas	South Carolina
New Jersey	Alaska	Delaware	Iowa	West Virginia
Pennsylvania	Tennessee	Oklahoma	New Hampshire	Texas
Maryland	Idaho	Alabama	Rhode Island	
		Wisconsin		
		Colorado		
		Louisiana		
		Georgia		
		Oregon		
		Nevada		

Source: Joseph A. Schlesinger, "The Politics of the Executive," in Jacob and Vines, *Politics in the American States* (Boston: Little, Brown, 2nd ed., 1971).

Figure 17.2
Weak and strong types of state organization.
Source: Frederic A. Ogg and P. Orman Ray, *Introduction to American Government*, 13th ed. by William H. Young (New York: Appleton-Century-Crofts, 1966), pp. 772–73.

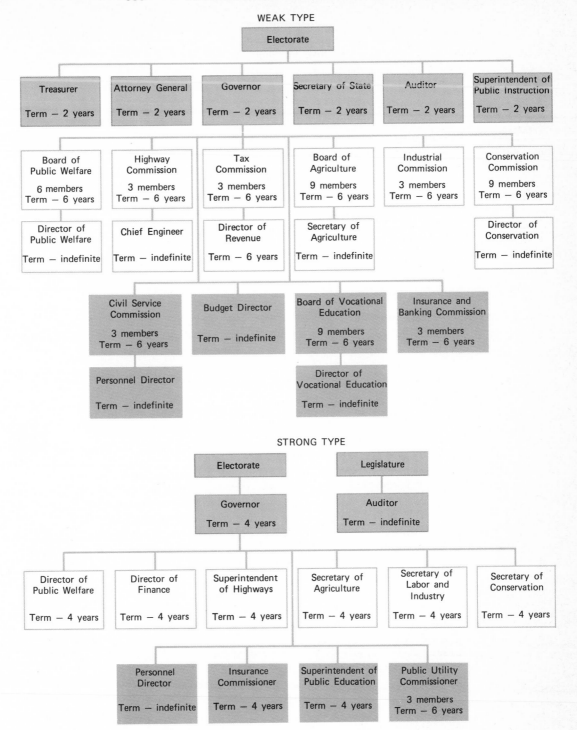

relatively limited change potential in the other executive offices. Those upon whom any governor must depend for policy implementation remain largely independent of formal gubernatorial control, reducing the governor in such cases to a position of one among equals.

"Strong" Executive. By way of contrast, in the strong executive type of administration, illustrated in the lower portion of Figure 17.2, the governor is provided with a relatively long term of office, the right to seek reelection, extensive appointment authority, and direct or indirect control of almost all key executive personnel. The department heads and other important executive officials are appointed to terms of office coterminous with that of the appointing chief executive. In this system, the governor heads the administration not only in name but by virtue of his appointment power and sole executive right to speak for the people as the only popularly elected administrative officer.

Actual adherence to one or the other type of executive organization varies from state to state, although most states fall closer to the weak executive system than to the strong. Only three states* limit direct election to that of the chief executive, while forty others continue to directly elect six or more separate state officials in the executive branch. Almost half of the states still elect the governor and lieutenant-governor separately—providing the opportunity for members of different parties to hold the first and second state offices at the same time, while nineteen states still restrict the governor to two consecutive terms of office.

The gradual trend is clearly in the direction of the stronger executive system. As state bureaucracies have continued to expand in size and influence, it has become apparent that popular control of these organizations through the governor is increasingly important. Thus in recent years the four-year term for governor has become widely accepted: Iowa, Kansas, South Dakota, and Texas moved from two- to four-year executive terms in 1972.† In the past four years an additional six states have changed to the team election of governor and lieutenant-governor, bringing the total number of "team executive" states to twenty. The gradual movement to stronger gubernatorial systems has also been apparent in some recent reductions in the number of directly elected state officials as well as in the removal of some state offices from independent constitutional status: since 1972 both Kansas and Oklahoma have taken steps in that direction.

Another important tendency is toward the reorganization of state agencies to increase gubernatorial control and facilitate administrative coordination. Since 1965, for example, nineteen states have undergone comprehensive executive reorganization and a number of others have accomplished more limited administrative changes. Typically, the comprehensive reorganizations involve the consolidation of various departments, agencies, and commissions into fewer, more manageable and functional departments that are more readily susceptible to gubernatorial direction.

---

* New Jersey and Maine elect only the governor and have no lieutenant-governor, while Alaska elects only the governor and lieutenant-governor.
† The states maintaining two-year executive terms are Arkansas, New Hampshire, Rhode Island, and Vermont.

Evaluation of State Executives

In this era of expanding governmental activity, one of the crucial issues before the states is the accountability of those who wield authority. The overwhelming majority of officials who staff our state governments are not elected to their office and are thus insulated from direct citizen control. These thousands of anonymous officials are not expected to make public policy, only to administer it. But the fashion in which a public law or service is implemented carries fully as much importance as—if not more importance than—how it was made or the intentions of the original policymakers. The significance of the implementation process in government is now commonly acknowledged and has led to an executive focus in much of our state politics.

In all states the governor is a more powerful figure than was true in the past, and with the growing executive power goes an increased danger that such authority may be abused or that public resources will be wasted. To avoid this, our states have erected a system of executive accountability based upon the principles of *separation of powers,* which involves legislative oversight of the executive department and the popular election of the chief executive to superintend the execution of the laws.

In the typical state it is apparent that the legislature is not in a position, largely due to institutional weakness, to exercise effective control of the executive branch of government. This leaves the people dependent primarily on popular election of the chief executive as a means of assuring executive responsibility. Our review of the executive at the state level, however, provided little comfort in this direction. In the typical state the governor simply does not wield formal authority commensurate with his or her political and administrative responsibility. The two essential devices of popular control of state government—the representative assembly and the popularly elected chief executive—have commonly been rendered so institutionally weak as to compromise both the effectiveness and the accountability of the bureaucracy. The separation of powers, sharing of responsibilities, and popular-election scheme of democratic government requires strong elected officials who can reasonably meet their responsibilities and be held accountable for the behavior of nonelected subordinates.

THE JUDICIAL PROCESS AMONG THE STATES

The judiciary at both the state and national level serves as the department of government charged with the constitutional responsibility of interpreting the law, and as such serves as the rule-adjudicating branch of the political system. In both structure and purpose the state courts bear a close resemblance to the federal judiciary: as the basic governmental agency charged with the rule-interpretation function, these courts are expected to resolve legal and political disputes by providing a forum for testing the meaning and applicability of the law. The courts set legal right and wrong and establish the situations in which the penalties of the law shall be applied. To some degree in every state, the courts provide judicial review for the policies set by the other institutions of government and, in providing the constitutional standards to which all institutions must adhere, establish the guidelines for law enforcement. Finally, the state judiciary serves as a symbol of the law and community virtue through

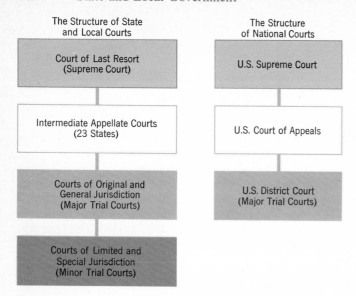

The Structure of State
and Local Courts

- Court of Last Resort
  (Supreme Court)
- Intermediate Appellate Courts
  (23 States)
- Courts of Original and
  General Jurisdiction
  (Major Trial Courts)
- Courts of Limited and
  Special Jurisdiction
  (Minor Trial Courts)

The Structure
of National Courts

- U.S. Supreme Court
- U.S. Court of Appeals
- U.S. District Court
  (Major Trial Courts)

Figure 17.3
Judicial organization in the
United States.

which the principle of equal justice is supposedly applied. Together these functions define a state institution with essentially the same mission as the judiciary at the national level. The performance of these functions creates within state government a sense of legitimacy that extends eventually to all of the branches of state government.

As is illustrated in Figure 17.3, state court systems are organized in a hierarchical fashion quite similar in structure to that of the federal judiciary. There are usually four important levels: two divisions are appellate, one has general original jurisdiction, and a fourth (for which there is no national equivalent), has limited or special jurisdiction.

Limited and special jurisdiction. At the first level of the state court hierarchy are the courts of limited and special jurisdiction. This is where the vast majority of legal actions begin and end. These courts constitute about 78 percent of the total number of courts in the United States and tend to be the judicial bodies with which the average American is most likely to have contact. Courts of limited and special jurisdiction are restricted as to the type of cases they are authorized to hear and by the nature of the remedial action they may order. Usually these courts can hear cases concerning only less serious criminal offenses, misdemeanors, and traffic violations. Often they are not even required to maintain verbatim records of proceedings.*

General jurisdiction. At the second level of state courts are those of general jurisdiction. These are the major trial courts, and they enjoy jurisdiction that is

* Additionally, the law typically sets the maximum fine or sentence such a court may impose—most limited courts cannot set fines above $1000 in criminal cases or impose jail sentences in excess of one year, and they cannot hear civil suits involving amounts in excess of $1000, according to a recent Department of Justice study. Criminal and traffic cases constitute most of the workload for this level of court, with probably less than 10 percent of judge-time devoted to civil cases.

unlimited as to the civil or criminal cases they are authorized to hear. It is at this level that the majority of serious criminal offenses and major civil suits are tried. This judicial level is equivalent to the federal district courts, which are the major trial courts for the national government. As is true of the U.S. District Courts, the state courts of general jurisdiction are divided into judicial districts or circuits based on geography. In thirty-nine states the courts of limited and general jurisdiction have overlapping jurisdiction, and in about 75 percent of the states the second-level courts have appellate jurisdiction over first-level court decisions.

Intermediate appellate jurisdiction. The third level of state court organization consists of the courts of intermediate appellate jurisdiction. These are roughly equivalent to the U.S. Courts of Appeals. Not all states have an intermediate appellate structure; some instead consolidate the entire appellate jurisdiction into a single court of last resort. In the twenty-three states with intermediate courts of appeals these bodies have the authority to review decisions made already by lower state courts. They basically serve to settle specific questions of law pertaining to whether lower courts correctly observed statutory and constitutional procedures in rendering their decisions, and they are not supposed to settle questions of fact. Thus the intermediate courts of appeal sit without jury and do not conduct a trial, which is the responsibility of lower courts. Original jurisdiction—the right to hear arguments about a case first without having to wait for an appeal from a lower court—is extended to intermediate appeals courts only in very special circumstances, usually involving a constitutional, intergovernmental, or procedural dispute.* States have added this intermediate level of court to relieve the supreme courts of heavy case burdens; thus they are designed to serve as a buffer between the major trial courts and the court of last resort to expedite the appeals process.

Final Jurisdiction. At the fourth level of the state court system may be found the courts of last resort or *supreme courts*. These courts have the final appellate jurisdiction (within the state judicial system) from either courts of original jurisdiction or intermediate courts of appeals, although in a limited number of cases the final decisions of these courts may be appealed to the United States Supreme Court. In many states the highest court is expressly delegated responsibility for establishing judicial rules and administrative procedures for the entire court system, including the establishment of limits on the types of cases that may be heard by the intermediate courts of appeals. As is true of the U.S. Supreme Court, the courts of last resort are the most important, prestigious, and visible judicial bodies within their respective states. Headed by a chief

---

* The 1973 survey of court organization in the United States conducted by the Department of Justice found that appellate judges spent between 90 and 100 percent of their time on appellate cases, and that time not spent on appeals was devoted to original proceedings such as writs of habeas corpus, mandamus, and administrative review. Further, it was found that time spent on juvenile or traffic cases was negligible, while criminal matters typically took the majority of appellate judge-time in only about 19 percent of these courts. That is, "civil matters" (expressed in judge-time as distinguished from number of cases) composed the bulk of the workload in most courts of appellate jurisdiction.

justice, each of these supreme courts publishes and distributes decisions, and these are taken as important guidelines for the legal system as a whole. Their decisions are taken, short of later action by the U.S. Supreme Court, to be the final word as to the meaning of the state's constitution and laws.

Basic Differences Between the State and National Judiciary

Although the fundamental judicial functions performed by tribunals at the state and national level in the United States are roughly equivalent, there are certain important differences. The power of judicial review, while general to some extent in all American courts, has had variant consequences depending on the level of court involved. At the national level, the courts continue to play a widely recognized significant role in expanding the power of the national government by giving a broad interpretation to the Constitution. The state courts, heavily involved in constitutional interpretation because of the long, detailed, and technical state documents, have tended to be more restrictive in interpreting state power. This is largely because the constitutions, in their specificity and length, give the state judiciary considerably less latitude in making broad reinterpretations of governmental power than is true at the national level. As a consequence, the state courts have tended not to assume the active policy role that has often characterized the federal judiciary.

Despite the superficial correspondence between the federal and state judicial systems as hierarchical structures, important differences continue to exist. The state systems are more oriented toward the trial level than is the national. In the federal judiciary only one level—the District Court—is devoted to conducting trials. In the typical state, however, two separate and large types of court are devoted to such activities—both the limited and the general courts. This difference is primarily due to the larger volume of judicial business that the states must handle. David R. Berman has estimated that the state court systems process some three million cases a year compared to only about 140,000 by the federal courts.

A major state-national difference with respect to judicial organization not immediately apparent in the organization charts is that—unlike the national system, in which the courts are well coordinated, procedures are uniform, and professionalism is high—state courts are typically uncoordinated, unstandardized as to procedure, and less professional. The lines of judicial authority in practice at the state level are often confused, overlapping, and tenuous. Rarely does the state supreme court enjoy the effective control over judicial administration and procedure that characterizes the U.S. Supreme Court. More often it is local politics and tradition, not the highest state court, that sets court procedures and conditions judicial behavior. As Kenneth T. Palmer has observed:

> Although state supreme courts are equipped with both a reviewing power and a power to command lower tribunals to take certain actions . . . the highest courts exercise nothing like day-to-day supervision over their local courts. Viewed as a whole, the typical state court system seems to manifest a fairly low degree of institutionalization.

By way of contrast, the federal court system has developed a structure of authority relationships that are highly conducive to professional, standardized, coordinated judicial processes.

As Table 17.8 shows, the states employ a variety of methods of judicial selection, most of which give voters a far greater amount of direct influence than is true for the national system. And the various selection procedures vary as to the extent to which judicial selection is susceptible to the influence of political parties and the legal profession itself. Over half of the states provide for some form of direct election of some or all of their appellate or major trial-court judges. But direct voter influence on judicial selection is also assured under the Missouri plan used by fifteen states.* As a result, the voters at the state level, unlike the national electorate, have some direct voice in whether or not a judge should continue to hold office. The more limited tenure of state judges, as well as the more direct role of the electorate in judicial selection and retention, tends to render the state judiciary more "democratic" than its national counterpart.

Judicial Performance at the State Level

The performance of the state judiciary, while difficult to determine accurately for every state, generally appears to be a function of the extent to which the courts are capable of administering justice in an equal, expeditious, and professional fashion. Critics of the state judiciary have for years argued that these court systems are compromised in the performance of their duty by fragmented administrative authority and low levels of professionalism (legal competence). The large number of lower courts with extensive autonomy and overlapping jurisdictions get in the way of providing equal justice and they waste resources. As the Advisory Commission on Intergovernmental Relations observed in 1971:

---

* In that procedure, judges are initially appointed by the governor from a list submitted by a nominating commission. After a specified period of time, these judges are then required (if they wish to continue to hold office) to go before the statewide electorate for popular election. Any judge under the Missouri plan who fails to get majority approval is removed from office and a replacement is appointed by the governor, subject to later approval by the electorate.

Much party influence and little bar influence			Little party influence and much bar influence	
Partisan election	Election by legislature	Appointment	Nonpartisan election	Merit plan
Alabama	Connecticut	Delaware	Arizona	Alaska
Arkansas	Rhode Island	Hawaii	California*	California†
Georgia	South Carolina	Maine	Florida	Colorada
Indiana*	Vermont	Maryland	Idaho	Indiana*
Kansas	Virginia	Massachusetts	Kentucky	Iowa
Illinois		New Hampshire	Michigan	Kansas
Louisiana		New Jersey	Minnesota	Missouri*
Mississippi		New York†	Montana	Nebraska
Missouri*			Nevada	Oklahoma*
New Mexico			North Dakota	Tennessee*
New York†			Ohio	Utah
North Carolina			Oregon	Wyoming
Pennsylvania			Oklahoma*	
Tennessee*			South Dakota	
Texas			Washington	
West Virginia			Wisconsin	

Table 17.8
Methods of Judicial Selection in the States (Appellate and Major Trial Courts)

* Judges of some courts selected by merit plan, others by election.

† Judges of some courts elected, others appointed.

Source: Kenneth N. Vines and Herbert Jacob, "State Courts and Public Policy," in Jacob and Vines, *Politics in the American States* (Boston: Little, Brown, 3rd ed., 1976).

Proliferation of lower courts and overlapping of jurisdiction leads to uneven administration of justice. The treatment an offender receives depends in large part on which of the several available courts he is tried in. Moreover, the taxpayer has to pay for maintaining two or more parallel sets of courts.

In addition, the quality of justice dealt out in the court systems is seriously affected by the extent to which judges and support personnel are well trained in the law and are subject to professional standards of conduct. As Table 17.9 indicates, there is a considerable degree of difference among the states in their organizational systems, with only a half-dozen having fully modern, simple judicial structure. David R. Berman has estimated that only about 18 states have fully or "substantially integrated" court systems capable of maximizing judicial coordination and enhancing judicial performance.

It is well to remember that the separation of powers that characterizes each state constitution requires, if it is to function as intended, three strong, independent, and effective branches of the government. Yet, in a recent review of the state of the subnational judiciary, Frank H. Bailey and Jag C. Uppal warned that

There is a growing feeling among state jurists that the separation-of-powers doctrine is being eroded. This erosion has occurred slowly, but occurred nevertheless, because the

Table 17.9
Differences in State
Court Organizations

Simple and modern ———————————→ Complex and traditional

Arizona	Alabama	Connecticut	Arkansas
California	Alaska	Idaho	Delaware
Illinois	Colorado	Iowa	Mississippi
North Carolina	Florida	Kansas	Virginia
Oklahoma	Georgia	Kentucky	
Washington	Hawaii	Maine	
	Indiana	Massachusetts	
	Louisiana	Minnesota	
	Maryland	Montana	
	Michigan	Nebraska	
	Missouri	New Hampshire	
	Nevada	North Dakota	
	New Jersey	Rhode Island	
	New Mexico	South Carolina	
	New York	South Dakota	
	Ohio	Tennessee	
	Oregon	Utah	
	Pennsylvania	Vermont	
	Texas	West Virginia	
	Wyoming	Wisconsin	

Source: Henry Robert Glick and Kenneth N. Vines, *State Court Systems* (Englewood Cliffs, N.J.: Prentice-Hall, 1973), p. 30.

courts, concerned with their primary responsibility for settling legal issues, have often turned to other branches of state government for assistance in performing administrative functions and securing funds.

In consequence the independence of the judicial branch of government has tended to weaken. Such an erosion is most likely to be checked only through the development of a state judiciary that manifests a high degree of institutional strength and development. Clearly, such strength is not the product of a fragmented, diffused, unprofessional court system. Thus the improvement of judicial performance has come to be closely associated with the institutional development of that branch of the government. In this way the dominant recent trend in judicial development at the state level has taken the form of intense, although not entirely successful, efforts toward structural and administrative improvement in conjunction with growing legal professionalism.

The development of a more *institutionalized* state judiciary has involved efforts to bring a variety of reforms: The structural reorganization of state courts to create a single unified system continues as seven states in the past three years have, through constitutional or statutory provision, moved toward establishing an integrated system. Improved means for financing, budgeting, and obtaining appropriations for the judiciary are being developed. For example, total state responsibility for judicial expenditures (undertaken by only six states as late as 1968) is now assumed by thirteen states. The judicial branch may now request appropriations directly from the legislature in ten states, rather than having to rely on the governor's intercession. These financial arrangements enhance unification of the courts, equalize judicial financial support throughout the state, and promote judicial independence of local politics or the governor, on which they were previously dependent for funding.

The goal of these recent changes toward a more institutionalized state judiciary has been to render lower courts less dependent on local politics in small substate areas and more subject to statewide standards. This has required increasing the authority of the state's highest court to develop and enforce comprehensive rules of judicial standards and procedure that are applicable throughout the state court system. Further, judicial professionalism at all levels within many states is beginning to improve through the promulgation of rules concerning relationships between judges and other members of the legal community, appellate procedures, codes of professional responsibility, and standardized lower-court procedures.

Judicial professionalism, so important to the development of institutional strength and performance, is also being improved through comprehensive judicial education programs now available in fifteen states. Pressure is growing in most states to copy the example of California in establishing a judicial qualifications commission to maintain professional standards. To assist the state courts develop administrative procedures and process judicial statistics, almost all states now employ court administrative officers who collect information on caseloads and assist in the supervision of budgets and judicial personnel.

In summary, the typical state court system remains one of uncoordinated, overlapping, complex judicial organizations. It has seen its independence, so important to the proper operation of the separation-of-powers principle, eroded to a substantial degree. Yet at the same time, important efforts are being made within most states, with varying degrees of success, to develop the judiciary into a fully *institutionalized* branch of the state government.*

LOCAL GOVERNMENT WITHIN THE STATES

Unmentioned in the Constitution, local government has been assumed to possess neither an inherent legal right to exist, nor reserved powers of authority. Whatever political authority is possessed by local government must first be delegated to it by the state through the constitution or appropriate legislative enactment.† Local governments have traditionally been extremely dependent upon the state government and subject to its close supervision. For most of the nineteenth century, local governments were kept in a condition of what Charles R. Adrian has called "perpetual infancy," as the state legislature exercised direct supervision over local affairs.

---

* For example, in 1976 Kansas adopted a unified court system, Kentucky continued work on a new court system, Missouri approved the consolidation of its lower courts by 1979, New York assumed lower-court costs, California reorganized its lower courts, and Connecticut merged its trial courts. Georgia reorganized its judicial districts, South Carolina moved toward a unified court system, and Iowa created a new appellate court.

† The courts have consistently held a very narrow construction on these delegations of state authority, usually ruling that unless a power were expressly granted by the state, or was indispensable to the declared purpose of the local unit, the local government must not be allowed to exercise the power in question. In many instances where the delegation was ambiguous, courts have usually ruled *against* the exercise of the power by the local government. In other words, the courts have tended to rule that, if in doubt, the local unit does *not* get to exercise the disputed power.

Direct legislative oversight declined in this century when most local governments became too complicated to be adequately supervised by amateur, part-time legislators. The need for continuous, professional oversight led most legislatures to transfer primary responsibility for local supervision to the executive branch of state government. Because of the detailed, technical, and restrictive provisions concerning local government that usually characterize the state's constitution and laws, the state judiciary also tends to be heavily involved in local supervision. As a result of their status as the legal creatures of the state, and because their delegated powers have traditionally been so narrowly construed, local governments are constantly having to prove in court that they actually have the power to do what they seek to do.

Today, local governments exercise more control over their own affairs than was true a hundred years ago, but the gain is only relative. Communities still possess no constitutional right to self-government, and this makes local governments the legal offspring of the state, subject to whatever limitations the parent government may impose. Through the constitution or legislative enactment, the state continues to possess the legal power to create, alter, or abolish any unit of local government. In this sense, the local government tends to be a political unit incapable of completely controlling its own present or future.

BASIC FUNCTIONS AND STRUCTURES OF LOCAL GOVERNMENT

Originally, local agencies within the state were developed to provide essential public services at the community level. Their basic functions were to provide for the protection of life and property, administer justice, provide education, collect taxes, maintain public roads, administer elections, maintain vital records, and administer state programs. With the emergence of the social service state,* a number of other functions have been assumed by local governments

---

* The social service state concept refers to the view that the government should assume responsibility for employment security, compensation payments in the event of unemployment or industrial accident, and, in those instances when individuals cannot provide them for themselves, health care, retirement income, and housing. This view of the role of government has taken hold in the United States only since the late 1920s and has led to a dramatic growth in local responsibilities.

An annual town meeting in New England—many are not even this well attended.

such as the provision of public welfare, administration of recreation programs, institution of land-use control through planning and zoning, operation of public utility services, and administration of federal programs. Not every type of local government within a state provides all of these functions. The division of local responsibility is likely to differ somewhat from state to state, and the emphasis placed on performing these functions tends to vary from local unit to local unit even within the same state.

In the United States there are four basic types of local government. Table 17.10 shows how many of each type may be found. Municipalities, or cities, are general-purpose units of government that are organized by charters granted by the state government. Counties are general-purpose governments that tend to be the most important local unit in rural areas and may be found in all but two states.* Townships are unincorporated units of government that have a multipurpose character but are usually found in rural areas only. Only about half of the states have townships. Special districts, unlike the local governments mentioned earlier, are not general-purpose units. They tend to perform only a single, special function, usually by providing services across already established

	1972	1967	1962
Municipalities	18,517	18,048	18,000
Townships	16,991	17,105	17,142
Counties	3,044	3,049	3,043
Special Districts	39,666	43,046	43,001
Local Governments—Total	78,218	81,248	91,186

Table 17.10
Type and Number of Local Governments in the U.S., 1962–1972

Source: U.S. Bureau of the Census, *Census of Governments:* 1972, vol. 1, *Governmental Organization* (Washington, D.C.: U.S. Government Printing Office, 1973).

* Connecticut and Rhode Island do not utilize counties as independent units of local government.

political boundaries. The most common type of special district is the school district.*

MUNICIPAL GOVERNMENT

Cities in the United States are incorporated under state charters that provide for municipal boundaries, governmental powers and functions, methods of finance, as well as the procedures for the election or appointment of public officials and employees. Some of the provisions of a city charter simply authorize the city to act as an agent of the state government, while others grant the municipality the right to act as the agent of the local inhabitants. Rarely is the city charter a single document; it also includes all state laws and court opinions that serve to define the structure, powers, and procedures of the municipality.†

There are three basic forms of municipal government in the United States: (1) the mayor-council; (2) the commission; and (3) the council-manager plans. Approximately half of all American cities have the mayor-council form of government, while about 40 percent use the council-manager and 6 percent the commission plans.

The Mayor-Council Plan

The earliest form of city government in the United States was the mayor-council plan, and during the nineteenth century nearly all American cities operated under this system. As Figure 17.4 shows, there are two types of mayor-council plan: the weak-mayor and the strong-mayor systems.

Weak-Mayor System. Municipal government during most of the nineteenth century was dominated by the weak-mayor system, in which the directly elected city council serves as both a legislative and an executive agency. Council members are ordinarily elected from separate constituencies within the city, called *wards,* and run for office on a partisan ballot. The council is extended extensive executive functions: it appoints many important administrative offi-

---

* In a few states, including Connecticut, New Jersey, and Pennsylvania, small incorporated places are called *boroughs.* Within New York City, certain general administrative responsibilities are delegated to districts designated as boroughs. These units perform such tasks as the laying, construction, and maintenance of streets and sewers.

† Municipal incorporation is accomplished through four basic methods: (1) *Special Act Charter,* in which the legislature specifically draws up a charter for the cities named in them. This was once the most common method of incorporation but has now been largely abandoned because of its restriction on local initiative and overdependence on legislative supervision. (2) *General Act Charter,* in which cities are classified according to size, after which municipal laws are developed that apply to an entire class of municipalities. (3) *Optional Charter,* in which cities are provided with some choice in the structure and organization of their governments. It is still the state legislature or the constitution that sets the options from which a municipality must choose. (4) *Home Rule Charter,* in which cities are authorized to adopt municipal government forms and services as they see fit, without the involvement of the state legislature. These methods of incorporation thus range from those in which the municipality falls most subject to direct state legislative control (special act charter) to those in which it is subject to the least direct state control (home rule charter).

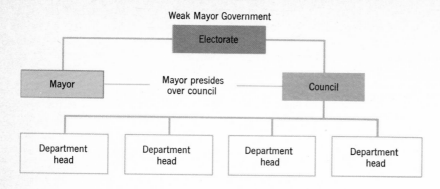

Weak Mayor Government

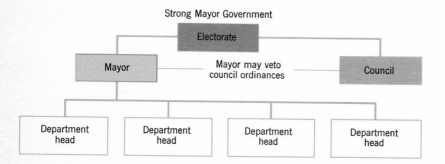

Strong Mayor Government

Figure 17.4
Weak and strong mayor forms of government.
Source: John J. Harrigan, *Political Change in the Metropolis* (Boston: Little, Brown, 1976).

cials, prepares the city budget, and may even appoint the administrator who directs city expenditures. The mayor is little more than a presiding officer for the council and is considered *weak* because the office lacks formal administrative power.

The weak-mayor system reflects the traditional American suspicion of executive authority: the mayor is denied the formal power to act as the chief executive, many of the executive departments are headed by directly elected officials who then are able to dispense considerable patronage independent of the mayor, and no single official is charged with overall supervision of the bureaucracy. As a result, it is extremely difficult for the public to know which officers are responsible for various municipal policies. This wide division of authority also tends to inhibit the coordination of municipal policy, so that the provision of governmental services is usually hindered.

As long as the need for cities to provide many public services was relatively limited, the weak-mayor system presented no serious difficulty; however, the development of large cities in the late nineteenth century brought demands for significant expansion in municipal activity. For a long time, the political machines that developed in many weak-mayor cities were able to compensate for the inherent incapacities of that system, but eventually its inadequacies for modern municipal government led reformers to seek alternative structures. Today the pure weak-mayor system tends to be found most often in relatively small cities, although a few major cities continue to have weak-mayors, especially in the South.

The weak-mayor system facilitated the development of the great political machines of the last century. This form of municipal government was especially conducive to machine politics because its many elective offices offered a series of very valuable prizes that could be won at city elections. This invited the development of powerful party organizations that were capable of amassing the requisite resources to assure electoral success. Well-organized political parties in our largest cities were able to convert the votes of the new immigrant populations into formidable electoral blocks capable of controlling the outcomes of municipal elections. The party faithful, once in office due to the efforts of the machine, used their public position to directly reward voters and friends with special favors that further consolidated party loyalty, discipline, and strength.

The excessive number of elected offices tended to present voters in large cities with many individual candidates with whom they were completely unfamiliar. Political parties simplified voting choices in this situation by providing an easily recognizable label to guide otherwise uninformed voters. The importance of party loyalty and identification in organizing voting was particularly enhanced within the weak-mayor system because these elections lacked focus; since the mayor was little more than a figurehead, in most of these cities the candidates as individuals tended to become unimportant; only their party mattered. The political party machine thus served to bring order out of an electoral system that otherwise tended to be exceptionally unruly in the big-city context.

The confusing and uncoordinated dispersion of authority within the weak-mayor system became especially troublesome when municipal governments were forced to greatly expand services. The lack of clear lines of responsibility and the complete absence of administrative coordination in this structure created governments that, left to their own devices, were incapable of managing the large cities. In practice, the informal coordination of municipal services provided by the political party organization, especially through the executive leadership of the "boss," enabled municipal government, in spite of its structural flaws, to operate at acceptable levels.

The political machine flourished in the weak-mayor environment because of the inability of the public to fix responsibility for municipal performance. Once in power, the machine, so long as it operated the city at a minimal acceptable level, could easily and flagrantly use the offices of government to reward its friends and punish its enemies. For a considerable period of time the political machine was able to compensate successfully for the basic inadequacies of the weak-mayor system. Because the machine was less interested in improving the public policy than in controlling the patronage and government contracts that assured its political power, it did not prove to be a long-term solution to the fundamental inadequacies of the weak-mayor system: public accountability for municipal government and the coordination of municipal administration were not enhanced. Eventually, abuses of the public policy and the misuse of the city treasury became so blatant and expensive that even the confused lines of responsibility within the weak-mayor structure could not hide the scandal.

Strong-Mayor System. Many reformers felt that the establishment of a system with a strong mayor, independent of the political "boss," would suffice to overcome the defects of the machine-ridden weak-mayor cities. In the strong-mayor-council system, administrative responsibility is concentrated in the office of the mayor, and policy making responsibility is shared by the mayor and the city council. The voters directly elect only the council members and the mayor. City department heads are appointed by the mayor, who is thereby responsible for

Baltimore: urban crisis and renewal.

the preparation and administration of the city budget.

The mayor's extensive formal powers in this system allow not only for the exertion of strong executive direction but also for political leadership. Exclusive responsibility for the administration of the city places the mayor in the advantageous political position of being the official spokesperson for the city. Control of the municipal budget and influence over the day-to-day affairs of the government can prove formidable weapons of mayoral influence in city politics. At the very least they enhance the bargaining position of the chief executive as compared to other city officials.

The city council in the strong-mayor system usually plays a subordinate role in the city government. It shares its legislative functions with the mayor and is given only limited administrative authority. Because this system is conducive to strong political leadership, it appears suitable for use in larger cities where the complexities of government and the rigorous demands of a diverse environment require initiative and focus. A few cities have provided mayors with a *chief administrative officer* (CAO) to assist in the administration of city government. The CAO plan enables the mayor to select a professional deputy trained in

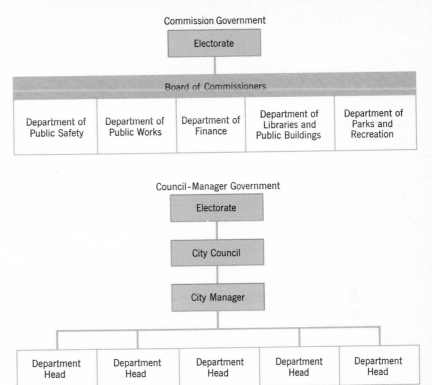

Figure 17.5
Manager and commission
forms of government.
Source: John J. Harrigan,
*Political Change in the
Metropolis* (Boston: Little,
Brown, 1976).

municipal finance and administration who can coordinate and supervise the actual operation of the government. This leaves the mayor free to assume the role of ceremonial head of the city and political leader, in which matters of broad policy are likely to be settled.

In the extremely diverse social and economic climates that define our largest cities we might expect to find the greatest need for government structures that emphasize representation and political accommodation. Thus the mayor-council plan is found in *all* of our cities with a population of over 1,000,000, in three-quarters of the cities between 500,000 and 1,000,000, and in just under one-half of the cities between 250,000 and 500,000 in population. Further, in the very smallest of our cities, where low demands for city services place little strain on the lack of administrative coordination in the mayor-council plan, this system appears well suited: almost 60 percent of the cities between 5000 and 10,000 in population, and nearly 70 percent of those between 2500 and 5000, have this system.

The Commission Plan

The *commission plan* for municipal government, shown in Figure 17.5 provides for the direct election of a limited number of officials who collectively serve as the policy making council for the city and who individually serve as the head of one of the city's administrative departments. The city commissioners perform both legislative and executive functions. The commission is always small (typi-cally between three and seven members) and is usually elected on a nonpartisan ballot, at-large, to four-year terms. In many cities, to assure a degree of continuity in the administration of the city, the terms of the city commissioners are staggered so that only two or three members are elected at the same time.

The mayor under the commission plan is usually directly elected by the people; the International City Management Association (ICMA) has estimated that the mayor specifically appears on the ballot in 78 percent of the commission cities over 5000 in population. Otherwise the mayor is selected by the commission from among its membership (around 21 percent of commission cities), while a few (less than 1 percent) designate the commissioner receiving the highest number of votes in the previous election as mayor.

The mayor in commission cities is little more than a ceremonial figure for the city as a whole. Typically, the mayor's chief task is to act as presiding officer at commission meetings. The mayor usually lacks the veto power and is unlikely to exert any more influence over city affairs than any of the other commissioners.

The commission plan was originally developed in Galveston, Texas in 1900 when the regular city government failed miserably to cope with the devastating effects of a hurricane. In the face of this emergency the state legislature suspended the local government and replaced it with a temporary government composed of five local businessmen. The "Galveston Commission" accomplished so much more than its predecessor government that the plan was retained permanently in that city. This unusual reform and its surprisingly good results attracted such interest that within ten years another 107 cities had copied it. By 1917 the number of commission cities had grown to about 500. The plan was initially welcomed by reformers as a more modern approach to municipal administration than the usual machine-ridden weak-mayor systems of the times. It concentrated executive responsibility and authority in a few officials so that voters could more easily familiarize themselves with those whom they had to judge come election time. Further, this "businessman's government" was thought to offer a more efficient, less political approach to city management that would thereby reduce municipal corruption and waste.

However, despite its tremendous initial popularity, the commission plan soon became outdated. Most municipal reformers lost interest in it and began, instead, to push for an even newer innovation, the *council-manager plan*. Moreover, an inability to attract qualified administrative personnel to run for the commission frequently produced an amateur commission incapable of managing municipal responsibilities. The lack of administrative leadership to coordinate these separate, independent commissioners made it difficult to integrate municipal policy. Each department of the government was free to pursue its own direction. As a result of these structural flaws, the commission plan was soon outdated with the development of the *strong-mayor* system and the council-manager plan, and the number of cities using the commission plan has steadily declined since 1920.

The Council-Manager Plan

The basic principle behind the council-manager plan for municipal government, shown in Figure 17.5 earlier, is that an elected council shall hold policy making responsibility and an appointed professional administrator shall have responsibility for policy implementation as well as for overall supervision. The council is small (usually five to nine members), and is ordinarily elected at-large on a nonpartisan ballot to four-year terms of office. It is legally responsible to the electorate for the conduct of all city government, since it officially sets municipal policy and determines the selection, as well as direction, of the appointed professional administrator. Under the model city charter for the council-manager plan, as developed by the National Municipal League, only city-council persons are directly elected. In this way responsibility is concentrated on a limited number of individuals who, because of their small number, can be reasonably well known and fairly judged by the public at large.

Thus in this system there is no formal separation of powers; there is no independent executive. The mayor normally performs only ceremonial functions and presides over council meetings. As was true of the commission plan, the mayor lacks real administrative power and usually has no veto. According to the ICMA, around 50 percent of the manager-council cities with more than 5000 population directly elect the mayor. About 49 percent of such cities allow the council to select the mayor from among its own members, and the remaining communities (less than 1 percent) designate the candidate receiving the highest number of votes for the council at the previous election as mayor.

The actual responsibility for the administration of the city government under this system rests with the professional manager. The manager is hired by the council and serves for no definite term of office. A city manager's tenure is subject to the will of the elected city council and it may fire the manager at any time that a majority so decides. Accordingly, the manager is expected to function as the administrative arm of the council itself and not as an independent executive. The city manager is expected to hire other professionally competent technicians who will manage the departments of city government. Administrative positions below department heads are also supposed to be staffed with persons who are technically competent, and these are usually selected by civil-service merit examination. Thus the manager-council plan places a premium on technical competence in the management of city government, from the professional city manager on down, and is designed to bring expertise to bear upon municipal administration.

The council-manager plan had its roots in the early writing of Havan A. Mason, who as early as 1899 urged that there should be "a distinct profession of municipal managers," and in the design of Richard S. Childs, whose basic plan largely defines today's manager system. The first appointment to a position similar to that of a city manager occurred in Staunton, Virginia in 1908, when a "general manager" was employed to oversee municipal administration. Childs's manager plan was itself adopted by Sumter, South Carolina in 1912. The council-manager plan grew steadily after 1912; by 1918 there were 100 manager cities, by 1930 there were 400, and since 1945 the annual rate of adoption has increased by about 65 to a 1975 total of 2356 cities.

This structure, probably less attractive in the large cities that possess deep social conflicts and highly politicized environments, seems particularly suited to communities sufficiently large to demand high levels of municipal service that require professional coordination, but small enough to possess some consensus as to their own "public interest." Accordingly, none of our very largest cities (over one million in population) have the council-manager plan, and only about 25 percent of cities with a population between 500,000 and 1,000,000 have it. But almost half of the cities between 250,000 and 500,000, and over half of the cities between 25,000 and 250,000, are council-manager cities.

Reformism and Public Policy in City Government

In comparison with other municipal structures, the mayor-council plan is usually considered *more* political, or *unreformed,* because of its past association with machine politics, its emphasis on selecting some or all of its relatively large council from smaller constituencies within the city at partisan elections, and its reliance on the combination of policy making and administrative authority placed directly in the hands of political figures. The plan is based on the idea that city policy making and administration are inseparable and ought to be performed under the control of directly elected officials who are responsive to separate constituencies within the city. Emphasis is placed on representation and political accommodation of these separate constituencies, rather than on the city as a whole, efficiency, or professionalism in administrative decision making.

Because the council-manager plan originally developed as an alternative to the use of the political machine to operate the city government, and because of its emphasis on selecting all council members from a single citywide constituency at nonpartisan elections and its reliance on the strict separation of political and administrative leadership, the plan is usually considered a *less* political, or *reformed,* municipal structure. The plan is based on the idea that by eliminating the representation of small separate constituencies in favor of the city electorate as a whole, and by keeping political parties out of municipal elections, decision makers are left more free to rule in the public interest without regard to party gain or to the interests of one section of the city over another. The separation of policy making and administrative responsibility is supposed to provide for governmental operation that is businesslike, professional, and dedicated to efficiency, rather than being based on accommodation to political groups. With its emphasis on professional, disinterested administration, the council-manager plan is explicitly designed to make the city government less responsive to the social, economic, and political environment.

The basic difference between reformed and unreformed municipal structures directly relates to whether or not the government is designed to be immediately responsive to the socioeconomic and political conflicts that may emerge within a city. Unreformed structures facilitate the extension of these conflicts into the government itself; the structures thus presumably produce public policy that reflects the conflicts as well. *Reformed* structures are designed to insulate the government from these conflicts so that the whole "public interest" can be efficiently and professionally pursued; these structures presumably produce public policy that is independent of the conflicts as well. To what extent do these different structures actually result in distinctive public policies in American cities?

Although the evidence is far from conclusive, there is an important body of research suggesting that in fact the *mayor-council* plan is more responsive to social, economic, and political differences within its environment than is true of its reformed *council-manager* counterpart. George S. Duggar reports that mayor-council cities are quicker to apply for, and actually to begin work on, federal urban renewal programs than are council-manager cities. Research by Albert K. Karnig found that council-manager cities were less responsive to civil rights groups, in policy areas of concern to the poor and blacks, than were mayor-council cities. An important study of the relationship between reformism and city taxing and spending conducted by Robert L. Lineberry and Edmund P. Fowler revealed important differences between mayor and manager cities. They found that reformed cities (council-manager, at-large constituencies, and nonpartisan elections) appeared to be unresponsive in their taxing and spending policies to differences in income, education, occupation, religion, and ethnicity within the city population. Unreformed cities, on the other hand, (mayor-council, ward constituencies, and partisan elections) reflected class, racial and religious differences in their taxing and spending decisions. Thus Lineberry and Fowler were led to conclude that:

Political reforms may have a significant impact in minimizing the role which social conflicts play in decision making. By muting the demands of private-regarding groups, the electoral institutions of reformed governments make public policy less responsive to the demands arising out of social conflicts in the population.

These findings suggest that council-manager cities have moved toward the reformist goal of insulating city government from the social cleavages and political conflicts that have tended to importantly affect the mayor-council form of government significantly.

COUNTY GOVERNMENT

Counties are an extremely common form of local government in the United States and are found in almost every state. But these units are not identical everywhere: states employ a variety of structures and delegate varying amounts of responsibility in establishing the jurisdiction of their county governments. Over time, the role of the county government within the states has significantly altered. In the past, when the United States was basically a rural nation, counties were a vital link between citizens and their state government.

Today, in the South, county government continues to play a vital role in political activities and social development, but in New England it has been largely deemphasized as a local unit. Outside of our cities, in those areas of the nation that are least urbanized, the county remains the most important substate unit of government. While many counties have enough population to be considered *urban,* most counties are rural or small-town in character and continue to reflect government structures appropriate to nonurban lifestyles and needs. The rural tradition in county government often leads to a reliance on part-time and amateur public officials.

Although 300 urban counties (comprising only 10 percent of the total number of county governments) serve more than two-thirds of the nation's citizens, even these units tend to continue to reflect a sustained rural outlook and tradition in government. The growing presence of city-dwellers within the jurisdiction of county governments creates understandable tensions: urban and suburban demands for services from the county government are likely to be strongly resisted by rural residents—especially since the provision of such municipal-like services inevitably means new and higher taxes for all county residents.

Urban-rural tensions within counties are also likely to be reflected in the structures of government that appeal to these differing sectors: urban dwellers concerned with efficient and comprehensive provision of services are somewhat less likely than their rural counterparts to look with favor upon the traditional, unprofessional structures of the typical county government. The play of urban-rural tensions within counties has resulted in recent modifications in the structure of county government in some counties, but changes have been slow in developing.

The Structure of County Government

Until quite recently, the unfailing pattern of county government was a plural executive akin to the weak-mayoral system of municipal government. Thus in almost every state the main governing authority for the county is an elected body that exercises both legislative and executive powers. Variously styled the *Board of Commissioners, Board of Supervisors, County Court,* or some other similar title, these representative bodies are typically composed of three to five members selected from the county as a whole. Selected by other members of the governing board, or sometimes directly by the county electorate, the presiding officer of the county government has little power. Usually this officer lacks even a regular vote on the governing board, let alone a veto. It is the county board that is the policy making and administrative authority for the jurisdiction, while the presiding officer is simply expected to implement the decisions it makes.

Among the fundamental responsibilities before the county board and its presiding officer would be construction and maintenance of county buildings and roads, management of county equipment and property, and negotiation of contracts in the name of the county. Subject to the constitutional and statutory limitations imposed by the state—which are often very restrictive—the county board has taxing and spending authority within its jurisdiction.

In addition to the county board, which exercises the fundamental authority for executive and legislative functions, most counties also depend on a plural executive organization along the lines represented in the top third of Figure 17.6. Since the functions delegated to the county tend to vary from state to state, the executive offices within these governments tend to be different as well. But, among the county offices found in most states would be: sheriff, tax collector, tax assessor, treasurer, coroner, road commissioner, county clerk, and perhaps school board. The county may also provide for other agencies that—always subject to the supervision of the county board—are designed to serve specialized functions. For example, they may administer state and federal programs, supervise elections, and undertake land use planning. The plural executive structure is currently used by approximately 90 percent of American counties.

As a result of the demands of urban-dwellers, and reflecting efforts to reform and modernize county government, a single-executive form of county government has emerged. As illustrated in the middle third of Figure 17.6, some counties have moved to a form of government roughly analagous to the strong-mayor system in which the executive authority is made somewhat independent of the county board, centralized in a single elected executive official, and responsibility is fixed for county administration.

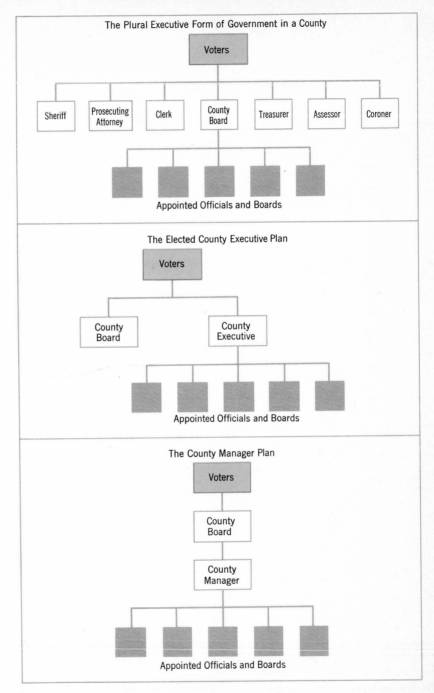

Figure 17.6
The forms of county
government.

A third variation on county government form is the county-manager system represented in the lower third of Figure 17.6. The rationale behind this plan is the same as that for the council-manager form of urban government: to facilitate efficient, professional administration through the separation of policy making and policy implementation. Thus under the county-manager plan, the administration of policy is delegated by the county board to a professional manager who directs the executive branch of the county government.

The introduction of the county-manager or the single-executive forms of county government has been undertaken in only about 10 percent of American counties. Usually these are the most urbanized counties for which the rural-based plural executive plan proved inadequate for the needs of the population. Although many more counties might prefer to move toward either the county-manager or the single-executive plan, constitutional barriers in many states make this difficult, if not impossible. States have as a rule proven quite hesitant about giving counties the authority to reorganize their structures; home rule, for example, has been extended to only about 2 percent of all counties.

Counties over the years have drawn growing criticisms as units of local government, and some critics have urged their complete abolition. But the county endures, largely because it performs many functions that other existing governments are incapable, or unwilling, to assume. County elective offices continue to be valued political prizes; office holders at that level usually have considerable minor patronage to dispense, and thus party organizations are often constructed around the county offices. It should not therefore be surprising to discover that state legislatures (which would have to act before abolition, consolidation, or any other significant reorganization could occur) are reluctant to reorganize these units. Many legislative careers were built around previous county service, and many political futures depend upon the county political organizations.

SPECIAL DISTRICTS

A large amount of local government activity in the United States is performed by special districts, which include independent school districts. According to the U.S. Bureau of the Census, there were about 39,600 total special districts in 1972, of which school districts were the most common type—comprising around 40 percent of these local units. School districts are formed for the express purpose of providing education for the children within their jurisdiction and are usually organized in a manner similar to the council-manager form of government. A small elected school board exercises policy making responsibility for the district and appoints a superintendent who administers the system. The trend in school district organization in recent years has been toward the consolidation of these units to achieve financial and administrative efficiency; since 1962, the number of independent school districts have decreased by almost 66 percent; that is, there were about half as many school districts in the United States in 1972 as could be found just ten years earlier.

Nonschool special districts are established to provide a single service. About half of these districts are devoted to fire protection, soil conservation, water, and drainage. Among the other common types of special districts would be those that provide for transit, sewer, housing, mosquito abatement, and cemetery services. Most of these special districts are relatively limited and small units, but some are very large: the Port Authority of New York and New Jersey, for example, was organized as a special district to construct, purchase, lease, and operate transportation and terminal facilities in the New York City region (which includes portions of New Jersey as well as New York state). It now owns port and terminal facilities in the two states worth more than $1 billion and leases other properties. It has responsibility for the operation of tunnels, bridges, dock and port facilities, a railroad system, and all of the major New York area airports.

Special districts are usually created to deal with problems that transcend the boundaries of other units of local government or to circumvent taxation and debt restrictions imposed upon already existing local units by state law. Moreover, these districts are considered an effective means for removing the provision of certain services from politics by giving them to units beyond the control of city or county officials. The popularity of this device has continued to grow; between 1962 and 1972—when the number of most other types of local government was stable or actually decreasing—the number of special districts in the U.S. increased by about 30 percent.

TOWNSHIP GOVERNMENT

The township is a political unit most commonly found in northern states between New York and the Rocky Mountains.* Established by state action, the township is simply a square subdivision of a county, usually six miles long and six miles wide. Today these units exercise jurisdiction only over the rural,† unincorporated regions within states, and tend no longer to be important units of government. Always limited, their usefulness has diminished further in the modern age. In actuality the townships were never more than agents of the county, exercising only those functions delegated to them, and increasingly these services are being reassumed by the counties themselves. Although the township government is not likely completely to disappear in the foreseeable future, the trend is in the direction of their elimination: between 1932 and 1972, the number of these local units decreased nationally by about 15 percent.

* The township as *governmental unit* should not be confused with the township as a simple *geographic subdivision*. In some states such geographic divisions are found but, unlike township government, they exercise no political authority and perform no public services.
† Unincorporated regions are those land areas within a state that are not within the boundaries of a chartered town or city.

ASSESSMENT

For the most part our state and local governments remain strong, vital units within the larger framework of the federal system. Undoubtedly these governments continue to face a very large number of extremely difficult problems. It is, after all, at these levels that citizens expect to see such perplexing conditions as poverty, crime, pollution, and drug abuse controlled—if not solved. We do as a nation continue to rely on state and local governments to bear the heaviest share of the public burden for the provision of education, welfare, health care, hospitals, as well as police and fire protection. If we are less than satisfied with the performance of these governments— and there are many who are—we are not at present prepared to see the national government assume their functions entirely; and voices calling for the abolition of state and local government are seldom heard.

Most of the expansion of national-government domestic activity in this century has been explicitly designed to enhance, rather than replace, state and local efforts. It is true that much of this national effort has been devoted to establishing new social programs according to national standards and goals. But these programs have typically depended heavily on state and local cooperation; in many instances it is still the state and local governments that implement the program. In this way, even in the face of expanding national domestic activity, we have become increasingly dependent on the performance of subnational units of government.

Therefore the central question concerning contemporary state and local governments is not whether they have a political future. The national constitution and laws, the nature of the federal system, our political culture and traditions—all combine to guarantee the continued existence of these jurisdictions. What is at issue today, however, is the capacity of state and local governments to meet their expanding responsibilities efficiently and democratically. It is not the government in Washington alone that conditions our lifestyles, provides our security, and assures (or threatens) our personal and political liberty. The plethora of state and local governments in this country—each exercising rather extensive political authority—in the day-to-day conduct of their business touch the lives of Americans in ways that significantly affect the extent to which these citizens enjoy, or are denied, the fruits of liberty.

Recognizing the potential threat to individual freedom inherent in such awesome state and local power, architects of these governments have tended to seek protection in the strict division of authority and the creation of intrinsically weak institutions. The practical result has often been not only that citizens have lost the ability clearly to fix political responsibility, but that public officials are denied the authority needed effectively to meet their public duties. Much of the foregoing chapter is devoted to explaining how state and local reformers seek, with mixed results, to overcome this debilitating approach to popular government.

The dilemma is easily enough stated: how do citizens at the state and local level provide public officials with sufficient independence and power to meet the demands of government in a modern society and at the same time keep government responsive to the people? The solution to this basic democratic dilemma remains essentially the same today as it was at the beginning of the Republic: the responsibility of political authority (national, state, or local) can best be assured only when the people are informed and involved in public affairs. Our rather naive traditional reliance upon long, restrictive constitutions, fragmented authority, and the amateur public official has usually proved a poor substitute for an alert, attentive public.

Democracy at every level requires strong, competitive institutions of government that are subject to the periodic review of an informed citizenry at regular elections. And it requires officials who, once elected or appointed to public office, have sufficient independence and authority to effectively act in the interests of the people. As this chapter points out, the performance of state and local government is vital to American democracy, and the best assurance of an effective, responsible performance remains dependent on the collective intelligence and vigilance of the citizens within these jurisdictions.

SELECTED READINGS

There are a number of excellent general texts on state and local government; among the very best would be: Charles R. Adrian, *State and Local Governments* (New York: McGraw-Hill, 4th ed., 1976); David R. Berman, *State and Local Politics* (Boston: Holbrook Press, 1975); Thomas R. Dye, *Politics in States and Communities* (Englewood Cliffs, N.J.: Prentice-Hall, 3rd ed., 1977); Daniel C. Grant and H.C. Nixon, *State and Local Government* (Boston: Allyn and Bacon, 3rd ed., 1975); Duane Lockard, *The Poli-*

tics of State and Local Government (New York: Macmillian, 1968); and Murray S. Stedman Jr., *State and Local Governments* (Cambridge, Mass.: Winthrop, 1976). Of the volumes exclusively devoted to state politics and government, three are particularly outstanding: though dated, V.O. Key's *American State Politics* (New York: Knopf, 1956) remains unexcelled for insight; and Kenneth T. Palmer's *State Politics in the United States* (New York: St. Martin's, 2nd ed., 1977) is clearly the best short work on the subject available today. Though considerably more sophisticated than the other general treatments of state politics and government, Herbert Jacob and Kenneth N. Vines, *Politics in the American States* (Boston: Little, Brown, 3rd ed., 1976) stands out as an introduction to the subject.

Frank C. Trippett has offered an especially critical view of the role and performance of the states in contemporary America in *The States—United They Fell* (Cleveland: World Publishing, 1967). A considerably more sympathetic, though hardly less critical, treatment of the states is Terry Sanford, *Storm Over the States* (New York: McGraw-Hill, 1967); the author is the former Governor of North Carolina and offers some constructive suggestions concerning state government in the future. Ira Sharkansky in *The Maligned States* (New York: McGraw-Hill, 1972), has made a strong defense of the performance of the states, in refreshing contrast to much of the other literature on the subject. Reflecting the continuing concern for state and local performance, the Committee for Economic Development has recommended blueprints for action to improve government at these levels: *Modernizing State Government* (New York: Committee for Economic Development, 1967), and *Modernizing Local Government* (New York: Committee for Economic Development, 1966).

State constitutions are comprehensively discussed in a variety of works. The National Municipal League has been particularly interested in this subject, having issued: *The Model State Constitution* (New York: National Municipal League, 6th ed., 1968); Robert B. Dishman, *State Constitutions: The Shape of the Document* (New York: National Municipal League, 1960); and John P. Wheeler Jr., *Salient Issues of Constitutional Revision* (New York: National Municipal League, 1961). A comprehensive collection of essays concerning constitutional issues at the state level is available in David R. Morgan and Samuel A. Kirkpatrick (eds.), *Constitutional Revision: Cases and Commentary* (Norman, Okla.: Bureau of Government Research, 1970).

The legislative process at both the state and national level is treated comprehensively in William J. Keefe and Morris S. Ogul, *The American Legislative Process* (Englewood Cliffs, N.J.: Prentice-Hall, 4th ed., 1976), as well as in Malcom E. Jewell and Samuel C. Patterson, *The Legislative Process in the United States* (New York: Random House, 1968). Very useful treatments of the legislative process with an exclusively state focus may be found in Malcom E. Jewell, *The State Legislature: Politics and Practice* (New York: Random House, 2nd ed., 1973), and John C. Wahlke et al., *The Legislative System* (New York: Wiley, 1962). The best brief treatment of state legislatures is Samuel C. Patterson, "American State Legislatures and Public Policy," in Jacob and Vines, op cit.. The most comprehensive survey of state legislative practices in the fifty states available is the Citizens Conference on State Legislatures, *State Legislatures: An Evaluation of Their Effectiveness* (New York: Praeger, 1971).

The standard work on the Governor remains Coleman B. Ransome Jr., *The Office of Governor in the United States* (Birmingham, Ala.: University of Alabama Press, 1956). The important comparison between the governorship and the presidency is drawn especially well by Joseph E. Kallenbach, *The American Chief Executive* (New York: Harper & Row, 1966). An outstanding collection of essays and research articles on the state executive is provided in Thad Beyle and J. Oliver Williams (eds.), *The American Governor in Behaviorial Perspective* (New York: Harper & Row, 1972); included among these excellent articles is an especially thoughtful analysis by Deil S. Wright entitled "Executive Leadership in State Administration." The most influential recent study of gubernatorial power is Joseph A. Schlesinger, "The Politics of the Executive," in Herbert Jacob and Kenneth N. Vines (eds.), *Politics in the American States* (Boston: Little, Brown 2nd ed., 1971). No better summary of the guiding principles of state government organization can be found than in the chapter entitled "The Architecture of State and Local Governments," in Herbert Kaufman, *Politics and Policies in State and Local Governments* (Englewood Cliffs, N.J.: Prentice-Hall, 1963).

A most comprehensive introduction to the role of the judiciary in the political process is provided by Herbert Jacob, *Justice in America* (Boston: Little, Brown, 2nd ed., 1972). Thomas R. Dye's chapter on "Courts, Crime, and Correctional Policy," op cit., is an excellent overview of judicial policy making and problems at the state and local level. A very good survey of the courts in all fifty states is made in Henry R. Glick and Kenneth N. Vines, *State Court Systems* (Englewood Cliffs, N.J.: Prentice-Hall, 1971); while the most comprehensive brief analysis of the state courts is Kenneth N. Vines and Herbert Jacob, "State Courts and Public Policy," in Jacob and Vines, op cit. Two excellent basic sources of information about state and local courts are the Council of State Governments, *State Court Systems* (Lexington, Ky.: Council of State Governments, 1974); and the U.S. Department of Justice, *National Survey of Court Organization* (Washington, D.C.: Government Printing Office, 1973).

An overwhelming amount of literature is available concerning urban politics and government in the United States. Among the better recent introductory treatments would be: Charles R. Adrian and Charles Press, *Governing Urban America* (New York: McGraw-Hill, 5th ed., 1977); Edward C. Banfield and James Q. Wilson, *City Politics* (New York: Vintage Books, 1966); John J. Harrigan, *Political Change in the Metropolis* (Boston: Little, Brown, 1976); Eugene Lewis, *The Urban Political System* (Hinsdale, Ill.: Dryden Press, 1973); Robert L. Lineberry and Ira Sharkansky, *Urban Politics and Public Policy* (New York: Harper & Row, 2nd ed., 1974); and Murray S. Stedman Jr., *Urban Politics* (Cambridge, Mass.: Winthrop, 1975). The abundant literature on urban reform and public policy is summarized very well by Brett W. Hawkins, *Politics and Urban Policies* (Indianapolis, Ind.: Bobbs-Merrill, 1971), and by Thomas R. Dye in chapter 9, op cit. Two collections of essays and research articles stand out in this area: David R. Morgan and Samuel A. Kirkpatrick (eds.), *Urban Political Analysis: A Systems Approach* (New York: Free Press, 1972); and James Q. Wilson (ed.), *City Politics and Public Policy* (New York: Wiley, 1968). Urban problems are given outstanding general attention in several important works such as Edward C. Banfield, *The Unheavenly City Revisited* (Boston: Little, Brown, 1974); Anthony Downs, *Urban Problems and Prospects* (Chicago: Markham, 1970); Bryan T. Downes, *Politics, Change, and the Urban Crisis* (North Scituate, Mass.: Duxbury Press, 1976); and most recently by the Advisory Commission on Intergovermental Relations, *Improving Urban America: A Challenge to Federalism* (Washington, D.C.: Government Printing Office, 1976). The best available analysis of suburban politics and government is Frederick M. Wirt et al., *On the City's Rim: Politics and Policy in Suburbs* (Lexington, Mass.: D.C. Heath, 1972).

A variety of excellent and invaluable sources of information about state and local government are readily available. The U.S. Bureau of the Census provides a vast array of statistical data in both the *Statistical Abstract of the United States* (Washington, D.C.: Government Printing Office, published annually), and the *Census of Governments* (Washington, D.C.: Government Printing Office, published every five years). The Council of State Governments publishes the *Book of the States* (Lexington, Ky.; biennially), which is unrivalled as a source of data and scholarly summaries of recent developments in state government. Information on city government is provided by the International

City Management Association, *The Municipal Yearbook* (Washington, D.C.; annually); and the National Association of Counties produces *The County Yearbook* (Washington, D.C.; annually). Each of these organizations also from time to time publishes reports of special interest to those concerned with state and local affairs, as does the National Governor's Conference (headquarters in Washington, D.C.) and the National Municipal League (headquarters in New York City).

Political Novels   Because much of contemporary state government reflects reforms initiated by the populists, an appreciation of the forces behind that movement is essential to understanding politics at the state level. Frank Norris in a classic novel about the battle between farmers and railroads in nineteenth-century California provides a vivid account of these forces in *The Octopus* (New York: Bantam, 1971). The class struggle, social unrest, and ethnic bigotry that resulted from tensions between the "old" and "new" immigrants and so strongly colored state politics in the last century are shown by Howard Fast in a biographical novel, *The American* (New York: Duell, Sloan and Pearce, 1946).

Several novels provide graphic accounts of Southern state politics. The political dynasty created by Huey Long in Louisiana has served as a model for both John Dos Passos, *Number One* (Boston: Houghton Mifflin, 1943), and Adria Langley, *A Lion Is in the Streets* (New York: Sun Dial Press, 1945). Wirt Williams, a former political reporter in New Orleans, describes the Louisiana political machine while telling the story of a ruthless female politician who becomes governor of that state, *Ada Dallas* (New York: McGraw, 1960). In *The Shad Treatment* (New York: Putnam, 1977) Garrett Epps traces modern Virginia politics and politicians through a novel about a contemporary southern governor. William Brammer (a former aide to Lyndon B. Johnson) tells of politics in a southwestern state in a series of characterizations of legislators, administrators, and assorted politicos in his book *The Gay Place* (New York: Bantam, 1961).

A first-rate novel about city government in times of crisis is *Rulers of the City* (New York: Doubleday, 1977), in which Thomas Fleming recounts the struggle of a conscientious mayor to deal with the Boston busing controversy. William Manchester, *City of Anger* (New York: Ballantine, 1953), offers a powerful novel about political corruption and racketeering in a large northern seaport city.

The classic novel about machine politics in our cities remains Edwin O'Connor's *The Last Hurrah* (New York: Bantam, 1957). Although not strictly fiction, two unusual approaches to explaining the workings of the old city machines would be: William O. Riordon, *Plunkitt of Tammany Hall* (New York: E. P. Dutton, 1963), in which the philosophy and political wisdom of one of the bosses of the Tammany machine of New York City is reported; and Leo Hershkowitz, revising history's conclusions about "Boss" Tweed of New York City and arguing that the famous scoundrel was actually framed by political opponents and a hostile press, *Tweed's New York: Another Look* (Garden City, N.Y.: Doubleday, 1977).

Local public officials, confronted by a natural disaster and initially more concerned with business and the next election than with public safety, are described by Peter Benchley in *Jaws* (New York: Bantam, 1974).

GLOSSARY

"ACCESS" The opportunity of private persons and groups to present their views on political matters to government officials with the understanding that such views will be considered.

ACCUSATORY SYSTEM A criminal law system in which the government is required to prove the guilt of the defendant by evidence other than that provided by the defendant himself.

"ACTIVE-NEGATIVE" PRESIDENTS Those who invest a great deal of energy in the office but who do not derive personal satisfaction from serving, and who are preoccupied with acquiring and maintaining power for its own sake.

"ACTIVE-POSITIVE" PRESIDENTS Those who invest a great deal of energy in the office, derive personal satisfaction from serving, and who want to accomplish results, particularly changes in governmental institutions, procedures, and policies.

"ACTIVE" PRESIDENTS Those who invest a great deal of energy in the office, exerting leadership over Congress, charting new directions in public policy, and stretching the powers of the presidential office.

"ACTIVIST" JUDGE A judge who closely scrutinizes the actions of legislative or executive officials and who is willing to invalidate those actions which he believes violate constitutional principles.

ADMINISTRATION BILL Bills introduced into Congress that have the backing of the President or some executive agency.

ADMINISTRATIVE LAW Rules and regulations developed by executive agencies within broad guidelines established by the legislature.

ADVISORY OPINION Legal opinion given by a court to a government official advising in advance of actual litigation how or whether a particular law should be enforced.

AFFIRMATIVE ACTION PLANS Plans that attempt to encourage organizations (such as political parties and public and private employers) to take positive action to involve and hire members of traditionally disadvantaged groups, such as blacks, women, and Chicanos.

AGENT The concept of a legislator as one who votes on legislation as his constituents want him to vote.

"ALL DELIBERATE SPEED" The phrase used by the Supreme Court in its 1955 order implementing its 1954 school desegregation ruling. The order entrusted the federal district courts with requiring local school boards to make "a prompt and reasonable start toward full compliance" with the 1954 ruling and with seeing to it that desegregation proceed "with all deliberate speed."

"AMATEURS" Persons who participate in party activities primarily out of a concern for the public interest and the desire to see basic principles and values they espouse implemented in public programs and policies.

AMICUS CURIAE BRIEF A brief filed by some individual or group who is not a direct party to the lawsuit but who has an interest in its outcome.

"ANTI-FEDERALISTS" Subsistence farmers, small businessmen, artisans, mechanics, and debtors who were generally satisfied with the economic and political conditions during the Articles of Confederation period. This group, which had few national leaders, unsuccessfully opposed the ratification of the Constitution.

APPELLATE COURT A court in which only the attorneys appear and the judge or judges involved decide whether any errors of law occurred in the trial court that merit a reversal of its decision or a new trial.

APPORTIONMENT OR REAPPORTIONMENT (LEGISLATIVE) The process of allocating or reallocat-

ing seats in the House of Representatives among the various states on the basis of population.

APPREHENSION The gaining of custody of an alleged perpetrator of a crime through his voluntary surrender, by arrest while he is committing a crime, or pursuant to a warrant.

APPROPRIATION The actual amount of money that Congress authorizes to be spent for a given purpose.

ARRAIGNMENT A proceeding before a court at which the terms of the indictment or information are read and the accused is given the opportunity to plead guilty or not guilty.

ARTICLES OF CONFEDERATION The framework that determined the governance of the United States in the period following American independence from Great Britain and prior to the adoption of the present Constitution. The Articles vested most important powers in the states rather than in the national government. Under the Articles the legislature was the preeminent branch of the national government.

"AT LARGE" DELEGATES Convention delegates chosen not to represent a particular political unit, such as a congressional district, but the entire state.

AUTOMATIC PLAN Plan proposed for changing the present Electoral College system that would eliminate the presidential electors and automatically cast a state's electoral votes for the popular-vote winner in that state.

"BAD TENDENCY" TEST The judicial test that permits restrictions on freedom of expression if it can be demonstrated that the utterance involved might tend to bring about an evil sometime in the future.

"BALANCING" APPROACH The concept associated with the late Justice Frankfurter that calls for a case-by-case weighing of values in deciding when restrictions on freedom of individual expression are warranted in order to protect society's interest in order and authority.

"BAND-AID" LAW The concept of helping the poor within the present structure of the law rather than trying to reform the law so as to better protect their rights.

"BANDWAGON" TECHNIQUE A strategy used by the frontrunning candidate at a presidential nominating convention to persuade delegates that he is going to win the nomination and that if they are politically smart, they will support him while he still needs their help and is willing to reward them for such support.

BICAMERAL LEGISLATURE A legislature divided into two separate chambers—usually called the House of Representatives and the Senate. Of the American states, only Nebraska does not have a two-house legislature.

BIFACTIONALISM A system in which there are two major factions in the dominant political party that contest politically over a series of elections.

BLACK CAUCUS Unofficial organization of black members of the House of Representatives who confer and plan political strategy on matters of common concern.

"BLACK POWER" A vague term associated with greater economic and political power for blacks along with the idea of black consciousness.

"BLOCK" GRANTS Grants by the national government (usually funneled through state governments) for general purposes such as health, education, and welfare, rather than for specific, limited programs. (See Special Revenue Sharing)

BLUE-COLLAR CAUCUS A recently formed unofficial organization of members of the House of Representatives who prior to becoming congressmen were in occupations in which they worked with their hands.

BRIEF A written statement setting forth the facts of a case and the arguments for a particular finding designed to persuade the court to rule in the brief-filer's favor.

BUDGET MESSAGE Annual message required by the Budget and Accounting Act of 1921 in which the President proposes suggested expenditures for the various executive agencies during the next fiscal year.

BUREAUCRACY A large-scale organization subdivided into specialized units with a hierarchical chain of command that employs persons who are expected to make decisions on the basis of technical expertise rather than for partisan or personal reasons.

CABINET A body composed of the heads of the twelve executive departments granted cabinet rank. Presidents can, and do, invite other officials, such as the Director of the Office of Management and Budget, to join in cabinet meetings.

"CALENDAR WEDNESDAY" A seldom-used procedure in the House of Representatives under which members can bring to the floor for action bills that have been reported by standing committees to the Rules Committee but have received no rule from that Committee.

"CAMPAIGNERS" The term used by Verba and Nie to describe the persons in their study who concentrated their efforts on participating in political campaigns but who had little to do with "communal" activities. (See "Communalists")

CAREER SERVICE The category of public service that employs persons on a merit rather than a political basis and which provides them with security of tenure.

"CASE AND CONTROVERSY" Litigation involving an actual dispute that is required to give a federal court jurisdiction over a case.

CATEGORICAL GRANTS Grant programs restricted to specific, limited purposes such as aid to dependent children.

CAUCUS Body consisting of all the members of the Democratic party in the House of Representatives that performs its organizing function and is its ultimate decision-making group.

CERTIORARI A writ issued by a higher court calling up a record of a proceeding in a lower court for review.

"CHECK AND BALANCE" The theory that by giving each of the other branches of the government the right to participate in a process that is the primary responsibility of one of them (such as the President's power to veto laws passed by Congress), each branch can assert and protect its own rights by withholding its support for the essential activities of a coordinate arm of the government.

CIVIL DISOBEDIENCE The deliberate violation of a law to protest its immorality or the immorality of other laws, coupled with the willingness to accept the consequences of one's disobedience.

CIVIL LIBERTIES The freedoms that individuals enjoy in such diverse matters as religion, speech, press, assembly, and petition; the rights of the accused in criminal cases; the protection of private property and other forms of privacy; the right to vote; and lack of discrimination in political, economic, and political matters.

CIVIL PROCEDURE A procedure that enforces the rights of private individuals or groups through compensation for past wrongs or the prevention of future ones.

CIVIL RIGHTS The rights or liberties of minority groups in general or of blacks in particular.

"CLEAR AND PRESENT" DANGER The test proposed by Justice Holmes under which restrictions on freedom of expression are invalid unless they are necessary to prevent the imminent occurrence of an evil that will probably result from the utterance in question.

"CLOSED" PRIMARIES Those in which only persons affiliated with a political party can participate, such affiliation to be evidenced by a declaration when they register to vote, or by pledging that they have supported the party's candidates in the past or that they will do so in the future.

CLOTURE A method of terminating debate in the Senate under which 60 percent of the total membership can bring a bill to a vote.

"COINCIDENT" ISSUES Issues such as social programs for the poor that run parallel to traditional New Deal economic issues.

COMMISSION PLAN This plan provides for the direct election of a limited number of city officials who collectively serve as the policy-making council and individually serve as the head of separate administrative departments. Due to its emphasis on nonpartisan administration and businesslike practices, this plan is considered more "reformed" than the mayor-council plan.

COMMITTEE OF THE WHOLE HOUSE A device under which the House of Representatives goes into a special procedure for initially discussing and debating legislation that has different rules (such as a quorum of 100 instead of 218) from those that apply when it is meeting as a regular chamber.

COMMITTEE ON COMMITTEES The committee used by Republicans in both the Senate and the House of Representatives to assign their members to standing committees.

COMMON LAW Law made by judges in the process of deciding specific cases as contrasted to statutes passed by legislative bodies.

"COMMUNALISTS" The term used by Verba and Nie to describe persons in their study who were active in cooperative ventures in community affairs but who avoided the conflict of political campaigns.

"COMPETITIVE THEORY OF ADMINISTRATION" Term applied to Franklin D. Roosevelt's idea of creating overlapping responsibilities among different administrative

units so as deliberately to create rivalries among administrators—rivalries that made each administrator try harder and that also provided FDR with more information than one administrator alone would provide.

"COMPLETE ACTIVISTS" The term used by Verba and Nie to describe persons in their study who participated in all types of political activity with great frequency.

CONCURRENT JURISDICTION The power of two courts (such as federal and state) to hear the same kind of case.

CONCURRENT POWERS Powers possessed jointly by the national and the state governments, such as the power to tax.

CONCURRING OPINION An opinion written by a justice who agrees with the result reached by the justice writing the majority opinion, but who does not agree with the reasons for that result.

CONFEDERATION OR CONFEDERATIVE SYSTEM A political system in which the people grant broad power over certain matters to the governments of the component parts of the system, and those governments, in turn, grant power over a narrow range of those matters to the central government.

CONFERENCES The bodies, consisting of all Democrats and Republicans (separate bodies) in the Senate, and Republicans only in the House of Representatives, that perform the organizing function for the party and are its ultimate decision-making group.

CONFERENCE COMMITTEE A committee consisting of members of both the Senate and House of Representatives that is appointed by the presiding officers of the two chambers to iron out differences between bills passed by the two houses on a common subject matter.

CONFERENCE (SUPREME COURT) The meetings at which the members of the Supreme Court

collectively make decisions on which cases to hear and how those cases they have already heard should be decided.

CONGRESSIONAL AUTHORIZATION Congressional approval of a proposed governmental program, together with a maximum expenditure for that program.

"CONNECTICUT COMPROMISE" The plan favored by the delegates at the Constitutional Convention from that medium-sized state that resolved the conflict between the "large-state" Virginia Plan, which based representation in the national legislature on state populations or financial contributions to the national government, and the "small-state" New Jersey Plan, which provided for equality of state representation. The compromise provided for a House of Representatives based on the size of state populations and a Senate in which each state has two members.

CONSTITUENCY The persons to whom a public official is politically responsible because such persons choose him or because he is chosen by someone else to look after those persons' interests.

CONSTITUENT SERVICE An important function of legislatures at the state and national level, in which individual legislators provide citizens with assistance in dealing with problems they may have with the government.

CONSTITUTION The basic framework that determines the functions, procedures, and structure of the government. In a democratic system, the constitution both grants and restricts the exercise of political power.

CONSTITUTIONAL DEMOCRACY A system of democracy that emphasizes placing limits on government through legal means.

CONSTITUTIONALISM The concept that those in positions of political authority should be responsible to the mass of the people for their actions, and that government, even when acting with the support of the majority, should not interfere with the rights of minorities in such matters as religion, the ownership of private property, freedom of speech, and the like.

CONSTITUTIONAL LAW Law emanating from the national constitution or from state constitutions.

"CONSTRAINT" The term used to describe a low level of consistency on political issues such that a person is inclined to take a "liberal" position on one issue and a "conservative" position on another.

"COOPERATIVE" FEDERALISM Sometimes referred to as the "new" federalism, the term suggests that the national, state, and local governments are "partners" that do not operate independently of one another but rather cooperate in carrying out various public functions.

COUNCIL-MANAGER PLAN A plan for city government with an elected city council for policy making and an appointed, professional, manager to administer the city government. This plan developed as an alternative to the highly political mayor-council plan and is generally considered a more reformed municipal structure.

COUNCIL OF ECONOMIC ADVISERS A group of three professional economists, located in the Executive Office of the President, that advises the President on his annual Economic Report to the nation and on the economic policies that his administration should pursue.

COUNTY GOVERNMENT A general-purpose unit of government including such offices as commissioner, sheriff, treasurer, and clerk. Counties are found in all but three states and are especially important units in rural areas.

COUNTY-MANAGER SYSTEM A relatively new form of government roughly analogous to the council-manager plan, in which administrative power is delegated to a professional manager appointed by the county board.

"COURT-PACKING" PLAN A term given to Franklin Roosevelt's proposal that if sitting justices of the Supreme Court reached age 70 and did not retire, he, as President, be authorized to nominate additional justices to the Court.

CRIMINAL PROCEDURE A procedure that enforces the rights of society against violators, such enforcement taking the form of a fine, imprisonment, or, if the violation is serious enough, death.

CRITICAL OR REALIGNING ELECTION An election in which there is a major realignment of blocs of voters who switch their traditional party affiliation, and/or a significant number of new voters who cast their votes disproportionately for one party's candidate, the end result being a permanent change in the social support provided the respective parties.

"CROSS-CUTTING" ISSUES Issues such as race, law and order, and Vietnam, that do not divide the electorate along the same lines as do the traditional New Deal economic issues.

"CUSTODIAN" Role proposed by Alexander George for an official such as the Special Assistant to the President for National Security Affairs, who would organize, for the Chief Executive's consideration, competing information, views, and options on how to handle particular matters in foreign and military policy.

DECOMPOSITION OF PARTY (also PARTY DECOMPOSITION) The idea that the two major American political parties are losing their traditional ability to serve as rallying points for majorities of individually powerless citizens.

"DE FACTO" SEGREGATION Segregation caused by residential living patterns rather than by intentionally discriminatory legal action or inaction.

"DE JURE" SEGREGATION Segregation caused by intentionally discriminatory legal action or inaction.

DELEGATE (see AGENT)

"DEMANDS" Claims that individuals or groups place on political leaders.

DEMOCRACY A system of government in which a large number of people enjoy the right to have some voice in important decisions that seriously affect their lives.

"DEMOCRATIC" STUDY GROUP An unofficial organization of Democratic members of the House of Representatives that has recently taken a major role in reforming the practices of the Democratic party in that chamber.

DEPUTY PRESIDENT *PRO TEMPORE* A newly created ceremonial post in the Senate that includes the right to be included in leadership meetings with the President.

"DÉTENTE" The term applied to improving relations between our country and the Soviet Union through increased trade, cultural exchange, and the negotiation of arms limitation agreements.

DEVIATING ELECTION One in which a short-term force such as an appealing candidate or some salient issue or event sufficiently benefits the minority party that it overrides the long-term preferences of the electorate.

DIRECT DEMOCRACY A system of government in which citizens personally participate in the making of governmental decisions.

DIRECT LOBBYING Communicating directly with political decision makers to try to influence what they do about a political matter.

DIRECT POPULAR ELECTION A proposal for abolishing the Electoral College system in favor of one under which the presidential candidate receiving the largest popular vote nationwide would be declared the winner, provided he received a minimum percentage of the vote (such as 40 percent). If no candidate did, there would be a runoff election between the two top candidates, or

Congress would choose from the front-runners.

DIRECT PRIMARY A system under which the voters themselves nominate their party's candidates for elective office.

DISABILITY A condition leading to a temporary or permanent termination of a President's term. One scholar, Ruth Silva, suggests that it covers "any inability, whatever the cause or the duration, if it occurs at a time when the urgency of public business requires executive action."

DISCHARGE RULE A rule permitting a majority of the members of the House of Representatives to discharge a bill from a standing committee or the Rules Committee.

DISSENTING OPINION An opinion written by a justice who disagrees with the result of a decision reached by the majority of the justices of a court.

DISTRICT PLAN Plan proposed for changing the Electoral College so that the presidential candidate receiving the plurality of popular votes in a congressional district would receive its electoral vote, with the winner of a plurality of the statewide popular vote receiving the remaining two electoral votes of the state.

DIVISION OF POWERS The allocation of powers between the national government and the governments of the states (or other subunits of the national government).

DOMESTIC COUNCIL A group of officials located in the Executive Office of the President who advise the Chief Executive on the nation's internal problems.

DOUBLE JEOPARDY A constitutional provision prohibiting the federal government (and by judicial interpretation also the states) from trying a person more than once for the same criminal offense.

"DUE PROCESS OF LAW"
A term that has traditionally meant that the government cannot deprive a person of his life, liberty, or property

without observing certain procedural safeguards designed to protect such interests.

ECONOMIC EQUALITY A concept subject to different interpretations. A literal interpretation would hold that all persons should receive the same amount of worldly goods regardless of their individual contributions to society. Western democracies, however, while favoring a fairly wide distribution of wealth, emphasize equality of opportunity, not of results.

ECONOMIC MESSAGE Annual message required by the Full Employment Act of 1946 in which the President reports to the Congress on general economic conditions in the nation, including, among other matters, how much money the government may expect to take in from existing revenue measures and how additional moneys might be raised, should they be needed.

ELECTORAL COLLEGE The system whereby electors chosen in the various states (and equal in number to the senators and representatives from that state) choose the President and Vice-President.

ELITE POLITICAL CULTURE OR OPINION Basic political beliefs of political leaders as compared to those of ordinary citizens. (See Political Culture and Public Opinion)

ELITIST POLITICAL SYSTEM
A system in which political, economic, and social resources are concentrated in the hands of a relatively few individuals and groups.

EN BANC A court sitting with all its members rather than only a portion of them.

EQUALITY Equality has several meanings. See Economic Equality, Equality of Opportunity, Social Equality, and Equality under the Law.

EQUALITY OF OPPORTUNITY
The right of all persons to develop themselves to the fullest extent of their capabilities. Some persons believe that government only has the

obligation to guarantee that formal opportunities are open to all persons, while others contend that government should equalize actual opportunities by providing basic services (health care, education, and the like) that are vital to individual self-development.

EQUALITY UNDER THE LAW
The concept that the law is to be applied to persons impartially without regard to the identity or status of the individual involved.

"EQUAL PROTECTION OF THE LAWS" CLAUSE A provision of the Fourteenth Amendment that forbids states from denying equal protection of the laws to any person within their jurisdiction. In recent years courts have utilized this clause to protect blacks and women from discrimination by state or local governments and also to prevent malapportionment of legislative bodies.

EQUITY A special type of "judgemade" law in which the judge can issue orders (typically injunctions) to prevent future wrongs and in which no jury is utilized in the legal proceeding.

EXCLUSIVE FEDERAL JURISDICTION The power that only federal, not state, courts have to hear a particular type of case.

EXECUTION The carrying out of the judgment or verdict of a court.

EXECUTIVE AGREEMENT An agreement entered into by the President with a foreign nation or nations either under the authority and within limitations established by Congress, or by the President acting on his own.

EXECUTIVE OFFICE OF THE PRESIDENT An Executive branch unit consisting of a variety of agencies (such as the Council of Economic Advisers, the National Security Council, and the Domestic Council) that assist the President on major problems in public policy.

EXECUTIVE OVERSIGHT A major function of legislatures at both the state and national level, in which the representative assembly checks on how executive agencies are interpreting and applying public policy.

EX OFFICIO CONVENTION DELEGATES   Delegates to the national convention who serve automatically as a result of holding another political office, such as a governor or state party chairman.

"EXPRESSED" POWERS   Those specific, enumerated powers set forth in Article I, Section 8 of the Constitution that are granted to the Congress.

"EXPRESSIVE" MOTIVES   Psychological motives for political participation based upon an individual's personal satisfaction in doing the "right" thing, even though he sees no real chance that his candidate will be elected or a favored bill enacted.

"FACTION"   A term used by James Madison in *Federalist Paper* No. 10 to describe "a number of citizens, whether amounting to a majority or minority of the whole, who are united and actuated by some common impulse of passion or of interest, adverse to the rights of other citizens, or to the permanent and aggregate interests of the community." Madison considered the most common and durable source of factions to be the uneven distribution of property. Today the term is used to designate groups that are part of a larger body, such as the conservative faction of the Republican party, or the Southern faction of the national Democratic party.

FEDERALISM OR FEDERAL SYSTEM   A political system in which political power is divided between the central government of a country and the governments of its component parts so that each level is legally independent of the other within its own sphere of activity.

"FEDERALIST" (APPROACH)   An approach to dividing political power between the national and state governments represented by the New Jersey Plan at the Constitutional Convention. Although it granted the national government authority over commerce and taxes along with the power to act against states that failed to meet their requisitions or to obey national laws, no national powers could be exercised without the consent of an indefinite number of states.

FEDERALIST PAPERS   A series of newspaper articles authored by Alexander Hamilton, James Madison, and John Jay that explained and defended the Constitution. They appeared during the battle over the ratification of the Constitution and are credited with influencing persons in key states like New York to vote in favor of ratification.

"FEDERALISTS"   Persons in commerce and finance, as well as the professions, who felt aggrieved by the economic conditions during the Articles of Confederation period and who favored a strong national government with power over commerce and taxation. This group, which contained most of the national leaders of the day, successfully campaigned for the ratification of the Constitution.

FELONY   A serious crime usually carrying a potential penalty of imprisonment for at least a year and a day.

FILIBUSTER   The technique of discussing a bill so long in the Senate that no vote can be taken on it.

"FIRESIDE" CHATS   Radio talks addressed to the American people by Franklin Roosevelt in an informal, intimate tone, designed to acquaint them with problems facing the nation and to explain his actions in dealing with them.

FLOOR LEADER   Either majority or minority party leader in the Senate or House of Representatives.

FRANCHISE   The right to vote that in the United States has been extended to more and more groups over the years (non-property owners, blacks, women, eighteen-year-olds).

"FRIENDS AND NEIGHBORS" SUPPORT   Electoral support for a candidate based on his appeal as a "home-town" boy rather than on his stand on issues.

GARNISHMENT   A court order seizing the property of an individual (usually in the form of wages) for money he owes.

GENERAL JURISDICTION (COURTS)   The second level of the state court hierarchy, in which the majority of *serious* criminal and important civil suits are heard. These are the major trial courts in the states.

GENERAL REVENUE SHARING   The distribution of a portion of the resources of the national government to states and localities with few or no restrictions on how the money should be spent.

GENERAL SCHEDULE   A system developed by the Civil Service Commission for classifying all merit positions in the federal service.

GERRYMANDER   The drawing of legislative district lines so as to favor certain political interests such as the majority party or incumbent legislators.

GOVERNMENT CORPORATIONS   Government agencies that undertake commercial enterprises (such as the Tennessee Valley Authority) and are governed by boards of directors who serve long, staggered terms and who are less subject to annual financial control by the President and Congress than are other public agencies.

GRANTS-IN-AID   Grants by the national government to the states, usually of cash, but in some instances involving things such as agricultural commodities.

GRAND JURY   A group of citizens that hears the evidence against the accused and decides whether it is sufficient to warrant further proceedings against him.

"GRAVITY OF THE EVIL" OR "SLIDING SCALE" TEST   The judicial test under which the type of restriction permitted on freedom of expression depends on the seriousness of the evil to be prevented. If the evil is grave enough, then one need not demonstrate that the expression to be regulated will probably result in the immediate occurrence of the evil. But if the evil is not so grave, then one must demonstrate the probability of its immediate occurrence.

"HIGH CRIMES AND MISDE-MEANORS" Grounds for impeachment along with treason and bribery. A question exists whether the term refers only to criminal offenses or whether abuse of power and violation of the public trust are also included within its meaning.

HOUSE RULES COMMITTEE Committee of the House of Representatives that possesses the power to issue "rules" on the scheduling and terms of debate of legislation on the floor of the chamber.

HOUSE WEDNESDAY GROUP A group of liberal Republicans in the House of Representatives that has a staff to help its members formulate public policies.

IMPEACHMENT The bringing of a charge by a majority of the House of Representatives against the President, Vice-President, or any U.S. civil officer (such as a judge), accusing him of treason, bribery, or "high crimes and misdemeanors" justifying his removal from office.

"IMPERIAL PRESIDENCY" The term used to describe the situation in which the Office of the President has become more and more powerful and irresponsible, primarily as a result of incumbents' appropriating the decision to go to war that the Founders intended be shared with the Congress.

"IMPLIED" POWERS All those powers that are "necessary and proper" for carrying into effect the expressed powers of the national government.

IMPOUNDMENT The temporary or permanent refusal of the President to spend moneys appropriated by the Congress.

INABILITY See Disability

"INACTIVES" The term used by Verba and Nie to describe persons in their study who did not participate in any form of political activity.

INCORPORATION THEORY The idea that the due process clause of the Fourteenth Amendment that applies to the states includes all the procedural safeguards spelled out in the Fourth, Fifth, Sixth, and Eighth Amendments that apply to the national government.

INDEPENDENT AGENCY One not part of any cabinet-level department. Included are agencies headed by one administrator, such as the Veterans Administration, independent regulatory commissions, government corporations, and those providing central services and controls such as the Civil Service Commission and the General Services Administration.

INDEPENDENT REGULATORY AGENCY An Executive unit headed by a bipartisan, multimember board that regulates activities of major private industries and whose members serve long, staggered terms and who can be removed only for cause.

INDEPENDENTS Persons who do not identify with a particular political party.

INDICTMENT A grand jury determination that the evidence against the accused is sufficient to justify further proceedings against him.

INDIRECT LOBBYING Working through intermediaries to try to influence political decision makers on a political matter.

"INFERIOR" FEDERAL COURT All federal courts below the U.S. Supreme Court.

INFORMATION The charge or charges against the accused filed by the prosecutor that also contains sworn statements of evidence against the accused supporting the charge or charges. Many states, particularly those west of the Mississippi, substitute this procedure for the grand jury proceeding used by federal and other state courts.

INITIATIVE A system that permits citizens (not legislators) to propose that certain laws be enacted.

INJUNCTION A court order requiring an individual or group to do something or not to do something; it is designed to prevent future wrongs, as compared to compensation for past wrongs.

"INNER" CABINET The Secretaries of State, Defense, and Treasury, and the Attorney General, all of whom share the broad perspectives of the President and have a "counseling" role with him.

"INNER CLUB" OR "ESTABLISH-MENT" A term used to describe the informal group of senators—mostly Southern Democrats—who supposedly controlled the Senate in the 1950s from behind the scenes.

INQUISITORIAL SYSTEM A criminal law system in which the government depends on evidence obtained from the defendant himself in establishing his guilt.

"INSTITUTIONAL" ADVERTISING Advertisements that carry essentially a political point of view rather than merely a commercial message.

INSTITUTIONALIZATION The degree to which a political organization exhibits professionalism, stability, and permanence in its operations. The greater the level of institutionalization attained by an organization, the more effective it is likely to be in performing its basic functions and maintaining its independence.

"INSTRUMENTAL" MOTIVES Psychological motives for political participation based on a specific goal such as a victory for a particular candidate or the passage of a certain bill.

INTEREST GROUP Any group of persons, having a shared attitude on a matter, that makes claims or demands on others in society with respect to that matter.

INTERMEDIATE APPELLATE JURISDICTION (COURTS) The third level of state courts, in which the authority to hear appeals from lower courts is vested. Used in twenty-three states to reduce the workload of the supreme court, these bodies settle specific questions of law pertaining to lower-court procedures and do not settle questions of fact.

ITEM VETO   A special type of veto given the governor in many states—though denied to the President—in which the chief executive may refuse to approve a portion of an appropriations bill (or other law in some cases) without rejecting the entire piece of legislation.

JUDICARE   A system patterned after legal aid in Britain, which permits indigent persons to choose their own lawyer, whose services are subsidized by the government.

JUDICIAL REVIEW   The power of a court to review the actions of all public officials—legislative, executive, and judicial—to see whether they are inconsistent with the governing constitution, and, if the court finds that they are, to declare them unconstitutional and hence unenforceable.

JURY (PETIT JURY)   The body of citizens that hears the evidence and decides on the facts in a civil or criminal proceeding.

JUSTICE   The traditional idea that each person should receive what is "due" him in life.

"KICKBACK"   A political contribution to a political party by a government contractor consisting of a portion of the money paid to the contractor by the government.

"LAME DUCK" CONGRESS   The term used to designate the former Congresses (since changed by the Twentieth Amendment) in which members defeated in November of even-numbered years remained in office until the following March.

LAW   Rules and regulations issued by national, state, or local governments that can be enforced through the legitimate use of force.

LAWS OF NATURE   Immutable principles governing human nature that should be followed by persons in all societies at all times.

LEGAL AID SOCIETIES   Organizations (typically supported through local charitable groups such as the United Fund or Community Chest) that provide free legal service to needy people.

LEGISLATIVE CAUCUS   A system used early in our history in which party members in the state legislature and the House of Representatives nominated candidates for statewide office and for President and Vice-President respectively.

LIBERAL DEMOCRACY   A system of democracy that is concerned primarily with the liberty of the individual.

LIBERTY   The right of individuals to select their own purposes in life together with the means to accomplish those purposes provided those choices do not unduly interfere with the rights of other persons.

LIFE CYCLE   The various stages of one's life—early family relations, school, college, work—through which an individual passes and which have separate kinds of influence on his political attitudes.

LIMITED AND SPECIAL JURISDICTION (COURTS)   The first level of the state court hierarchy, in which the majority of all legal actions begin and end. These courts usually hear cases concerning less serious offenses.

"LITTLE STATE DEPARTMENT"   A term frequently given to the staff of the President's Assistant for National Security Affairs because of the staff's tendency to duplicate some of the functions traditionally undertaken by the State Department.

LOBBYING   Communicating with political decision makers to try to influence them on a political matter.

LOGROLLING   A process whereby legislators or interest group representatives exchange support for measures in which they are separately concerned.

"LUG"   A financial contribution by a public employee to a political party, usually based on a certain percentage of his salary.

"MACHINE"   A party organization, run by a "Boss," that provides material and social benefits for persons in return for their vote.

"MAGISTRATE"   Role proposed by Alexander George for the President in weighing various information, views, and options provided him on foreign and military matters on which he makes the final decision.

MAINTAINING ELECTION   An election in which the long-term partisan orientation of the electorate results in keeping the traditional majority party in power.

MAJORITY LEADER   The leader of the majority party in both the Senate and the House of Representatives.

"MARK UP"   The procedure under which legislative committees or subcommittees go over a bill (often line by line) to amend and at times almost to rewrite it.

MATERIAL BENEFITS   Tangible rewards, often monetary, that persons seek to gain through membership in an organization.

MAYOR-COUNCIL PLAN   A plan for city government with an elected mayor as the chief executive and an elected council as the legislature. This plan is considered unreformed because of its past association with machine politics, a reliance on partisan elections, and its placement of policymaking power in the hands of political figures.

"MIDNIGHT" APPOINTMENTS   Appointments made by Federalist President John Adams to judicial posts, just prior to his leaving office, that were designed to give his party, defeated in the presidential and congressional elections of 1800, a foothold in the judicial branch of the national government.

MILITARY-INDUSTRIAL COMPLEX   Name given to the combination of professional military men, defense contractors, and congressional members (who want military installations and defense industries in their districts) who are said to exert tremendous pressures to keep military spending at a high level and to further a "hard-line" policy with communist nations.

MINORITY LEADER   The leader of the minority party in the Senate or the House of Representatives.

MISDEMEANOR   A minor crime usually carrying a penalty of a fine or imprisonment of a year or less.

"MIXED" GOVERNMENT   A system of government favored by John Adams that provides for representation of both property and numbers of people in the political structure. Thus the Founders expected the Senate to represent primarily persons of economic substance from the upper social classes while the House of Representatives would represent the interests of the many in society, the common people who owned no private property of any consequence.

MULTIFACTIONALISM   A system in which several factions (often existing for only a short time) contest politically for control of the dominant party.

MUNICIPALITY   A general-purpose unit of local government organized by charters by the state government.

"NATIONAL INTEREST"   The self-interest of a nation, including such matters as maintaining its territorial integrity, basic governmental institutions, access to foreign markets, honor, prestige, and "way of life."

"NATIONALIST" (APPROACH)   Approach to dividing political power between the national and state governments represented by the Virginia Plan at the Constitutional Convention. It proposed allowing the national government to legislate when the states were "incompetent" to do so or when their individual legislation would interfere with the "harmony of the United States."

NATIONAL PARTY CONVENTION   The system that developed in the 1830s and that still exists today under which citizens from the various states choose delegates to the national convention who, in turn, nominate the party's candidates for President and Vice-President.

NATURAL LAWS   See LAWS OF NATURE

"NECESSARY AND PROPER" CLAUSE   The clause in Article I, Section 8 of the Constitution that grants Congress the power to make laws "necessary and proper" for carrying into execution its specific, enumerated powers previously set forth in that section. This clause is the basis of the "implied" powers of the national government.

"NEGATIVE" PRESIDENTS   Those who do not experience pleasure from being President, but serve because of compulsion or out of a sense of duty to their country.

NEW DEAL COALITION   The blacks, Southerners, members of organized labor, ethnic groups, intellectuals, and urban political bosses that together supported Franklin Roosevelt.

NEW JERSEY PLAN   The plan introduced at the Constitutional Convention favored by the small states that provided for a one-house national legislature with each state having the same number of representatives.

NO BILL   A grand jury determination that the evidence is not sufficient to warrant further proceedings against the accused.

"NONACTIVIST" JUDGE   A judge who presumes that actions of legislative or executive officials are constitutional and who seldom substitutes his constitutional judgment for that of such officials.

OFFICE OF MANAGEMENT AND BUDGET   A unit in the Executive Office of the President that provides the Chief Executive with advice on budgetary and legislative matters, the coordination of governmental programs, executive branch organization, information and management systems, and the development of executive talent.

OLIGARCHY   A system of government in which political authority is vested in a few persons who are not accountable or responsible to the mass of people.

"ONE MAN-ONE VOTE"   The phrase used to summarize the Supreme Court ruling in *Wesbury* v. *Sanders* (1964) that House members must represent approximately equal numbers of people because ". . . one man's vote in a congressional election is to be worth as much as another's."

"OPEN DIPLOMACY"   The term applied to conducting diplomatic relations in public view rather than secretly behind the scenes.

"OPEN" PRIMARIES   Those primaries in which a voter may choose to participate in whichever political party's primary he chooses regardless of his own affiliation.

"OPINION" DAY   The day (usually Monday) on which the Supreme Court announces in open session its decisions on various cases and the reasons for them.

ORIGINAL JURISDICTION   The power of a court to hear a case for the first time.

"OUTER CABINET"   Secretaries of the eight departments that have a special clientele (such as agriculture and labor) and who have an "advocatory" role with the President.

"PAROCHIAL" PARTICIPANTS   The term used by Verba and Nie to describe the persons in their study who participated in political activities by initiating particularized contacts with government officials on matters that affected their personal lives, but who did not engage in "campaign" or "communal" activities. (See "Campaigners" and "Communalists")

"PARTICIPATORY" DEMOCRACY   The concept that ordinary persons should play a greater part in making decisions that vitally affect their lives and that democracy should have as its major purpose the full development of an individual's personality and character through participation in the political life of the community.

PARTISAN IDENTIFICATION OR AFFILIATION A favorable psychological attitude that a person develops towards a particular political party, which inclines him to vote for that party's candidates.

PARTY IN THE ELECTORATE Those persons who are supporters of, voters for, and identifiers with, a political party.

PARTY IN THE GOVERNMENT Those persons who hold official positions in the legislative or executive branch and are either elected under a party label or are appointed to a position primarily because of their relationship to a particular party. Moreover, in the discharge of their official duties, they are expected to reflect the views of their party.

PARTY ORGANIZATION Those persons active in party affairs whether they hold an official party post or not.

"PASSIVE-NEGATIVE" PRESIDENTS Those who do not have the inclination or ability to exercise political power effectively, do not experience pleasure from being President, and who serve out of a sense of civic duty and rectitude.

"PASSIVE-POSITIVE" PRESIDENTS Those who do not have the inclination and ability to exercise political power effectively, but who do enjoy serving in the Office, primarily because they want to be popular, to be loved and admired by others.

"PASSIVE" PRESIDENTS Those who do not have the inclination or the ability to exercise political power effectively and who tend to respond to congressional initiatives and support the status quo, and who do not use the full authority of their Office.

PEERS Contemporaries of an individual as contrasted to authority figures such as parents, teachers, and the like.

PERIOD EFFECTS Salient political events that have a similar impact on the political attitudes of persons of all ages.

"PERMANENT GOVERNMENT" The term applied to members of the federal bureaucracy who remain in their positions rather than change from one presidential administration to another and who are primarily concerned with the activities of their own agency rather than with an overall presidential program.

"PERSONAL" DIPLOMACY The carrying on of diplomacy, particularly handling major treaties and agreements, by the President rather than by lower-level officials.

"PICKET FENCE" FEDERALISM The symbol of present-day federalism, with the "pickets" representing the close relationships that exist among officials of national, state, and local governments engaged in the same functions (highways, welfare, and the like), and the crossrails depicting the horizontal relationships among legislators and chief executives who as generalists try to regulate and integrate the activities of the specialists engaged in the various functions.

PLEA BARGAINING A process by which the prosecutor in a criminal case agrees to reduce the charges against the accused in return for his pleading guilty to a lesser charge.

PLEADING The declaration by the accused in a criminal case as to whether he is guilty or not guilty.

PLURALISTIC POLITICAL SYSTEM A system in which political, economic and social resources are distributed widely among a large number of individuals and groups.

"POCKET" VETO A veto that occurs when the President takes no action on a bill when Congress is no longer in session at the end of the ten-day period after he receives the measure.

"POLICE POWER" The power granted to the states to pass laws for the "health, safety, and morals" of the people.

POLICY COMMITTEE The committee used by both parties in the Senate, and by the Republicans in the House of Representatives, to plan and develop party programs.

POLITICAL AVAILABILITY The characteristics and experiences that supposedly make particular persons politically attractive to party activists and regular voters as candidates for political office.

POLITICAL CULTURE The fundamental beliefs of citizens concerning the ends or purposes of political activity; the general nature of the political process; and the part that individual citizens play in the process.

POLITICAL EQUALITY The equal right of persons to participate in the political process through voting, joining interest groups, serving in political office, and the like.

"POLITICAL EXECUTIVES" Persons who hold top policy-making positions in the executive branch, including officials of the Executive Office of the President, secretaries of cabinet departments, heads of independent offices and establishments, as well as second- and third-level officials in such agencies.

"POLITICAL GENERATION" A group of age cohorts who share salient political experiences during pre- and early adulthood as exemplified by the "Depression generation," who were 17-25 years old in the period 1929-1935.

POLITICAL GENERATION INFLUENCES The salient political events that a person experiences during his pre- and young-adult years (17-25) that help to shape his political attitudes.

POLITICAL PARTY An organization that runs candidates for public office under its label.

POLITICAL SETTING The general political environment of an

area—relating to such matters as whether politics has traditionally been an important activity or whether political contests are close—which affects the general level of political participation by residents of the area.

POLITICAL SOCIALIZATION The process by which persons acquire political attitudes over the course of their lifetime.

POLITICAL "SUBCULTURE" The distinctive political beliefs of members of certain social groups such as blacks, Chicanos, southerners, easterners, and the like.

"POSITIVE" PRESIDENTS Those who enjoy political life and who derive a great deal of satisfaction from serving in the office.

"POSITIVE" STATE The concept that government, and particularly the national government, should play a major role in dealing with major economic and social problems of society.

"PREFERRED POSITION" APPROACH The concept that First Amendment freedoms enjoy a special status in our constitutional system and that therefore judges should carefully scrutinize the actions of legislative or executive officials that relate to such freedoms even though they presume that such officials' actions in other matters (such as regulating economic affairs) are constitutional.

PRELIMINARY HEARING A hearing before a magistrate to determine whether there is probable cause to believe that a crime has been committed and that the person before the magistrate committed it.

PRESIDENTIAL PRIMARY A system under which voters choose delegates from their state to represent them at the national presidential convention.

PRESIDENTIAL SUCCESSION The provisions for determining who will succeed to the presidency if his tenure is terminated. Presently it is the Vice-President, Speaker of the House, President Pro Tempore of the Senate, and then cabinet officials in

chronological order of the establishment of the executive departments.

PRESIDENT PRO TEMPORE The chief ceremonial officer of the Senate who presides over the chamber in the absence of the Vice-President.

PRESSURE GROUP The older term for interest group that implies that the group is selfish and that it uses improper means—force, bribery, and threats—to achieve its purposes.

PRIVATE LAW Rules and regulations that govern relationships between private individuals and groups on such matters as contractual agreements, deeds of land, marriage and divorce, and the like.

"PRIVATE-REGARDING" GROUPS Groups that hold values placing their short-term benefit before the welfare of the city as a whole. Such groups view city politics as another means of group advancement, in contrast to "public-regarding" groups, which are willing to forego immediate group advantage for the benefit of the entire city.

"PROFESSIONALS" Persons who are active in party affairs because they want some tangible, material benefit, or because they enjoy the "game" of politics for its own sake.

"PROJECT" GRANT-IN-AID Grants that require the specific approval of the national government (such as moneys for municipal waste-treatment plants) rather than being automatically provided to all communities that apply for them.

PROPORTIONAL PLAN A plan proposed for changing the present Electoral College system so that a state's electoral votes would be divided in proportion to the division of the popular vote in that state for presidential candidates.

PROPORTIONAL REPRESENTATION A system of allocating delegates to a convention, or seats in a legislative body, that takes into account the proportion of the popular vote cast for the various candidates.

PSYCHO HISTORY The use of psychological factors in explaining the behavior of individuals and the way such behavior affects events.

PUBLIC DEFENDER An attorney paid by public funds who concentrates on providing a legal defense in criminal cases for all persons who cannot afford an attorney of their own.

"PUBLIC INTEREST" GROUPS Interest groups with the goal of bringing improvements in society as a whole rather than just for their own membership.

"PUBLIC INTEREST" LAW FIRMS Law firms that devote a significant portion of their practice to matters concerning broad societal interests rather than just on the problems of their individual clients.

PUBLIC LAW Rules and regulations that apply to government officials controlling their relationships to other government officials as well as to private individuals and groups.

PUBLIC OPINION Attitudes of citizens towards matters that affect the day-to-day operation of the political system, such as important issues facing the nation, policies to be followed in dealing with such issues, and candidates and persons who hold public office.

PUBLIC POLICIES Decisions made by public officials that affect the distribution of benefits and the incidence of burdens among individuals and groups in society.

"PUBLICS" Separate groups of persons with distinctive views on different political matters.

"PURPLE CURTAIN" The curtain that forms the backdrop for public appearances of the justices of the Supreme Court. Most of the work of the Court occurs behind the scenes (hence, behind the "Purple Curtain").

"PURPOSIVE" BENEFITS Benefits that transcend one's own personal interests and that are associated with other individuals or groups or with society as a whole.

QUOTA SYSTEM   The system developed by the Democratic Party in 1972 under which some states selected as delegates to the national convention members of minority groups, women, and young people, in proportion to their numerical presence in the state population.

"RALLY-'ROUND-THE-FLAG" PHENOMENON   The tendency of the American people to initially come to the President's support at a time of international crisis.

RANDOM SAMPLING   A technique of eliciting information from a small number of persons (the sample) which is representative of the views of a larger group (the population) from which the sample is drawn. The important statistical principle involved is that each person in the population must have an equal chance of being chosen in the sample.

RECALL   A system that permits citizens to oust officeholders between elections.

REFERENCE GROUPS OR SYMBOLS   Groups or symbols that a person identifies with, either affirmatively or negatively, even though he is not personally associated with them.

REFERENDUM   A procedure for referring proposed laws to the voters for an ultimate decision.

REINSTATING ELECTION   Following a deviating election, an election in which long-term partisan factors operate so that the traditional majority party is returned to office.

REORGANIZATION PLANS   Plans proposed by Presidents to the Congress for changing the organization of the executive branch of the government.

REPRESENTATIVE DEMOCRACY   A system of government in which ordinary citizens do not make governmental decisions themselves but instead choose public officials (usually through elections) to make decisions for them. This system is used in political units that are too large to employ direct democracy.

REVENUE SHARING   The distribution of a portion of the resources of the national government to states and localities. (See General Revenue Sharing and Special Revenue Sharing)

RULE-ADJUDICATING BRANCH   The judicial department of state or national government. This is another way of expressing the rule-interpretation function of the courts.

"SELECTIVE BENEFITS"   Benefits that accrue only to members of an organization, such as low-cost insurance, health benefits, malpractice insurance, and the like.

"SENATORIAL COURTESY"   The custom that senators will refuse to confirm presidential nominations to executive or judicial positions if a senator from the state concerned opposes the nomination.

SENIORITY CUSTOM   The custom typically followed by both parties in the Senate and House of Representatives of choosing the member with the longest continuous service on a standing committee as its chairman or ranking minority member.

SENTENCE   The penalty assessed in a criminal case.

"SEPARATE BUT EQUAL" DOCTRINE   The doctrine enunciated in *Plessy* v. *Ferguson* (1896) that separate public facilities for persons of different races are constitutional provided they are equal.

SEPARATION OF POWERS (PROCESSES)   The concept borrowed by the Founding Fathers from the French political thinker Montesquieu, that the liberties of the people are best protected by a system in which political power is distributed among the three branches of the government so that the legislature has the primary responsibility for making the laws, the executive for putting them in effect, and the judiciary for interpreting them.

"SHUTTLE DIPLOMACY"   The type of procedure used in international negotiations (particularly associated with former Secretary of State Henry Kissinger) in which separate, secret conferences are held with all parties to a dispute and public statements on such matters are withheld until negotiations are completed.

"SILENT" GERRYMANDER   The technique of failing to redraw legislative districts to reflect changes in population within a state.

SOCIAL CLASS STATUS   The social position one enjoys as a result of his educational, occupational, or economic background.

SOCIAL EQUALITY   The concept that persons should be free of class or social barriers and means of discrimination. Disagreement exists on the role (if any) that government should play in trying to ensure social equality.

"SOCIAL ISSUE"   The collective term used to describe issues other than traditional economic and foreign policy matters, and including such matters as race, crime, and disorder.

"SOCIAL" LOBBY   Trying to keep communication channels open to political decision makers by entertaining them socially.

SOCIAL SERVICE STATE   A view of government in which the public sector is expected to provide employment security and other forms of social welfare service for individual citizens.

"SOLIDARY BENEFITS"   Intangible benefits such as friendship and fellowship that people seek from belonging to an organization.

SPEAKER   The major officer of the House of Representatives, who is theoretically chosen by the entire membership of the House, but who in reality is selected by the members of the majority party in that chamber.

SPECIAL DISTRICT   A unit of local government created to perform only a single function or provide a particular service, usually across already established political boundaries.

SPECIAL REVENUE SHARING   The distribution of a portion of the resources of the national government to states and localities, with the latter authorized to spend the moneys for certain broad purposes. (See Block Grants)

"SPECIAL SESSION" POWER The power of the President to call one or both Houses of Congress into special session at times other than when they are in session.

SPLIT-TICKET VOTING Voting for candidates of more than one party for different offices at the same election.

STANDARD METROPOLITAN (STATISTICAL) AREA A central city with a population of 50,000 or more, together with the county in which that city is situated and other counties that are economically and socially integrated with the county in which the central city is situated.

STARE DECISIS A term whose literal meaning is "adhere to the decision," which means that in the process of deciding a case, a judge will look to see what judges in similar situations have done and then apply the earlier results and rationale to the immediate case before him or her.

STATE CONVENTION CHOICE OF DELEGATES A system under which delegates to the national presidential convention are chosen by state convention delegates who themselves are elected at lower geographical levels, such as precincts, wards, counties, and congressional districts.

"STATE OF THE UNION" MESSAGE The annual message mandated by the Constitution in which the President reports to the Congress on conditions in the nation and recommends measures that he thinks are necessary and expedient for dealing with such conditions.

STATUTORY LAW Rules and regulations enacted by legislative bodies at various levels of the political system.

STEERING COMMITTEE The party committee used by Senate Democrats to nominate persons to be assigned to standing committees.

STEERING AND POLICY COMMITTEE Party committee of Democrats in the House of Representatives that nominates members for assignments to standing committees and that also devises and directs the party's legislative program.

"STRONG" EXECUTIVE SYSTEM A state government administration in which the governor is the only directly elected state official and is granted very extensive formal authority.

"STRONG" MAYOR SYSTEM A version of the mayor-council plan in which the mayor is granted extensive formal authority, often including a veto over council decisions.

"SUBSYSTEM" Three-way alliances of executive agencies, congressional committees and subcommittees, and interest groups, combining efforts in various areas of public policy in order to advance their common interests.

"SUNSET" LAW A law that would place all government programs on a limited schedule (such as five years) of legislative consideration and would have programs terminate automatically at the end of that period unless the legislature specifically reauthorized them.

"SUPPORTS" The cooperation and assistance that individuals—and particularly interest groups—provide to political leaders.

"SWITCHERS" A term for persons who vote for one party's candidate for an office (such as the presidency) one year and for another party's candidate for that office in the following election.

SYMBOLIC SPEECH Political views expressed through conduct rather than words.

TENURE OF OFFICE ACT An act passed by Congress shortly after the Civil War that prohibited the President from removing persons appointed with the consent of the Senate from office without the consent of that body.

THIRD PARTIES The term applied to all minor parties in the United States, that is, all parties except the Democrats and Republicans.

"TOP-BOTTOM" COMBINATION A combination of highly educated professionals and economically disadvantaged persons that some have suggested is the future basis of support for the Democratic Party.

TOWNSHIP An unincorporated unit of local government with a general-purpose character. Found only in a limited number of states, the township is today important only in rural areas.

TRIAL The stage in judicial proceedings in which both sides present their case to the judge and/or jury.

TRIAL COURT The court in which a case is originally heard where witnesses testify on the facts of the matters involved and the jury determines what the facts are.

TRUE BILL (See INDICTMENT)

TRUSTEE The concept that a legislator should vote on legislation on the basis of his own independent judgment rather than how his constituents want him to vote.

UNICAMERAL LEGISLATURE A legislature in which the entire membership is contained in a single house. Nebraska is the only state at present with a one-house legislative assembly.

"UNIONISTS" The group at the Constitutional Convention that compromised the differences between the "Nationalist" and "Federalist" approaches to representation by proposing the "Connecticut Compromise," which provided for a two-house legislature, with the Senate representing the states and the House of Representatives representing individuals.

"UNIT" OR "GENERAL TICKET" SYSTEM The system, presently used by all states except Maine, of awarding all the state's electoral votes to the presidential candidate who wins a plurality of the popular votes in the state.

UNITARY SYSTEM   A political system in which the people grant broad power over their activities to the central government, which, in turn, delegates authority over a limited number of those activities to the governments of the component parts.

UNITED STATES COURT OF APPEALS   The major appellate courts of the federal judicial system that principally handle cases that begin in the U.S. District Courts as well as appeals from orders and decisions of federal administrative units, particularly the independent regulatory agencies.

UNITED STATES DISTRICT COURT   A trial court in the federal judicial system that hears such matters as bankruptcy cases, anti-trust prosecutions, and suits involving the interstate theft of automobiles.

UNITED STATES SUPREME COURT   The highest court in our federal system, consisting of nine justices who have original jurisdiction over cases involving foreign ambassadors, ministers and consuls, and those in which a state is a party, but who hear most cases on appeal from lower courts.

UNREASONABLE SEARCHES AND SEIZURES   Invasions of privacy of one's person or property forbidden by the Fourth and—through judicial interpretation—the Fourteenth Amendments of the Constitution.

VENIREMEN   The citizens who are considered for service on a jury.

VERDICT   The decision reached by the jury on the matters presented to it.

VETO POWER   The power of the President to nullify an act passed by Congress, which accomplishes that

purpose unless both Houses repass the measure over his veto by a two-thirds vote.

VIRGINIA PLAN   Authored by James Madison, the first plan considered by the Constitutional Convention called for a radical break from the Articles of Confederation. The plan, which was favored by large wealthy states, provided for a strong national government and a two-house legislature based on state populations or financial contributions to the national government.

"VOTING SPECIALISTS"   The term used by Verba and Nie to describe the persons in their study who voted in presidential elections and always or almost always in local elections, but who did not participate in other forms of political activity.

WAYS AND MEANS COMMITTEE   A standing committee of the House of Representatives in which revenue measures originate and which also has jurisdiction over other vital matters such as health care, welfare, and foreign aid.

WESTERN DEMOCRACY   The form of democracy developed in Western nations like Great Britain, Switzerland, and the United States.

WESTERN REPRESENTATIVE DEMOCRACY   See REPRESENTATIVE DEMOCRACY and WESTERN DEMOCRACY

WHIPS   Assistants to the majority and minority leaders in the Senate and House of Representatives who serve as communications links between the party leaders and rank-and-file members of the party.

"WHIRLPOOLS OF POWER"   See "SUBSYSTEMS"

WHITE HOUSE OFFICE   A unit within the broader structure of the

Executive Office of the President that is populated with the closest aides of the President—those who write his speeches, arrange his appointments, and facilitate his relationships with the media, Congress, other executive officials, and political parties and interest groups.

"WIDE-OPEN" PRIMARY   A system that permits a voter to participate in one party's primary for some officials and in another's for different officials.

WOMEN'S CAUCUS   An unofficial organization of women members of the House of Representatives who confer and plan political strategy on matters of common concern.

"WOMEN'S LIBERATION" BRANCH OF THE FEMINIST MOVEMENT   The part of the women's movement that has sought to alter basic elements of male-female relationships in society, using such methods as "consciousness-raising" through local groups.

"WOMEN'S RIGHTS" BRANCH OF THE FEMINIST MOVEMENT The part of the women's movement that has sought primarily economic and educational equality for women through traditional political and legal channels.

WRIT OF MANDAMUS   A court order requiring a public official to perform an official duty over which he has no discretion.

"ZERO-BASE" BUDGETING   A system under which agencies would be required to justify every dollar they plan to spend during the next fiscal year rather than simply to apply for an increase over their previous year's appropriation, as is presently done.

THE CONSTITUTION OF THE UNITED STATES OF AMERICA

We the People of the United States, in Order to form a more perfect Union, establish Justice, insure domestic Tranquility, provide for the common defence, promote the general Welfare, and secure the Blessings of Liberty to ourselves and our Posterity, do ordain and establish this Constitution for the United States of America.

ARTICLE I

Section 1.   All legislative Powers herein granted shall be vested in a Congress of the United States, which shall consist of a Senate and House of Representatives.

Section 2.   The House of Representatives shall be composed of Members chosen every second Year by the People of the several States, and the Electors in each State shall have the Qualifications requisite for Electors of the most numerous Branch of the State Legislature.

No Person shall be a Representative who shall not have attained to the age of twenty five Years, and been seven Years a Citizen of the United States, and who shall not, when elected, be an Inhabitant of that State in which he shall be chosen.

Representatives and direct Taxes shall be apportioned among the several States which may be included within this Union, according to their respective Numbers, which shall be determined by adding to the whole Number of free Persons, including those bound to Service for a Term of Years, and excluding Indians not taxed, *three fifths of all other persons.** The actual Enumeration shall be made within three Years after the first Meeting of the Congress of the United States, and within every subsequent Term of ten Years, in such Manner as they shall by Law direct. The Number of Representatives shall not exceed one for every thirty Thousand, but each State shall have at Least one Representative; and until such enumeration shall be made, the State of New Hampshire shall be entitled to chuse three, Massachusetts eight, Rhode-Island and Providence Plantations one, Connecticut five, New-York six, New Jersey four, Pennsylvania eight, Delaware one, Maryland six, Virginia ten, North Carolina five, South Carolina five, and Georgia three.

When vacancies happen in the Representation from any State, the Executive Authority thereof shall issue Writs of Election to fill such Vacancies.

The House of Representatives shall chuse their Speaker and other Officers; and shall have the sole Power of Impeachment.

Section 3.   The Senate of the United States shall be composed of two Senators from each State, *chosen by the Legislature thereof,†* for six Years; and each Senator shall have one Vote.

Immediately after they shall be assembled in Consequence of the first Election, they shall be divided as equally as may be into three Classes. The Seats of the Senators of the first Class shall be vacated at the Expiration of the second Year, of the Second Class at the Expiration of the fourth Year, and of the third Class at the Expiration of the sixth Year, so that one third may be chosen every second Year; *and if Vacancies happen by Resignation, or otherwise, during the Recess of the Legislature of any State, the Executive thereof may make temporary Appointments until the next Meeting of the Legislature, which shall then fill such Vacancies.**

No Person shall be a Senator who shall not have attained to the Age of thirty Years, and been nine Years a Citizen of the United States, and who shall not, when elected, be an Inhabitant of the State for which he shall be chosen.

The Vice President of the United States shall be President of the Senate, but shall have no Vote, unless they be equally divided.

The Senate shall chuse their other Officers, and also a President pro tempore, in the Absence of the Vice President, or when he shall exercise the Office of President of the United States.

The Senate shall have the sole Power to try all Impeachments. When sitting for that Purpose, they shall be on Oath or Affirmation. When the President of the United States is tried, the Chief Justice shall preside: And no Person shall be convicted without the Concurrence of two thirds of the Members present.

Judgment in Cases of Impeachment shall not extend further than to removal from Office, and disqualification to hold and enjoy any Office of honor, Trust or Profit under the United States: but the Party convicted shall nevertheless be liable and subject to Indictment, Trial, Judgment and Punishment, according to Law.

Section 4.   The Times, Places and Manner of holding Elections for Senators and Representatives, shall be prescribed in each State by the Legislature thereof; but the

---

* Italics indicate passages altered by subsequent amendments. This was revised by the Sixteenth (apportionment of taxes) and Fourteenth (determination of persons) amendments.

† Revised by Seventeenth Amendment.
* Revised by Seventeenth Amendment.

Congress may at any time by Law make or alter such Regulations, except as to the Places of chusing Senators.

The Congress shall assemble at least once in every Year, and such Meeting shall be *on the first Monday in December,*† unless they shall by Law appoint a different Day.

Section 5. Each House shall be the Judge of the Elections, Returns and Qualifications of its own Members, and a Majority of each shall constitute a Quorum to do Business; but a smaller Number may adjourn from day to day, and may be authorized to compel the Attendance of absent Members, in such Manner, and under such Penalties as each House may provide.

Each House may determine the Rules of its Proceedings, punish its Members for disorderly Behavior, and, with the Concurrence of two thirds, expel a Member.

Each House shall keep a Journal of its Proceedings, and from time to time publish the same, excepting such Parts as may in their Judgment require Secrecy; and the Yeas and Nays of the Members of either House on any question shall, at the Desire of one fifth of those Present, be entered on the Journal.

Neither House, during the Session of Congress, shall, without the Consent of the other, adjourn for more than three days, nor to any other Place than that in which the two Houses shall be sitting.

Section 6. The Senators and Representatives shall receive a Compensation for their Services, to be ascertained by Law, and paid out of the Treasury of the United States. They shall in all Cases, except Treason, Felony and Breach of the Peace, be privileged from Arrest during their Attendance at the Session of their respective Houses, and in going to and returning from the same; and for any Speech or Debate in either House, they shall not be questioned in any other Place.

No Senator or Representative shall, during the Time for which he was elected, be appointed to any civil Office under the Authority of the United States, which shall have been created, or the Emoluments whereof shall have been encreased during such time; and no Person holding any Office under the United States, shall be a Member of either House during his Continuance in Office.

Section 7. All Bills for raising Revenue shall originate in the house of Representatives; but the Senate may propose or concur with Amendments as on other Bills.

Every Bill which shall have passed the House of Representatives and the Senate, shall, before it become a Law, be presented to the President of the United States; if he approve he shall sign it, but if not he shall return it, with his Objections to that House in which it shall have originated, who shall enter the Objections at large on their Journal, and proceed to reconsider it. If after such Reconsideration two thirds of that House shall agree to pass the Bill, it shall be sent, together with the Objections, to the other House, by which it shall likewise be reconsidered, and if approved by two thirds of that House, it shall become a Law. But in all such Cases the Votes of both Houses shall be determined by Yeas and Nays, and the Names of the Persons voting for and against the Bill shall be entered on the Journal of each House respectively. If any Bill shall not be returned by the President within ten Days (Sundays excepted) after it shall have been presented to him, the Same shall be a Law, in like Manner as if he had signed it, unless the Congress by their Adjournment prevent its Return, in which Case it shall not be a Law.

Every Order, Resolution, or Vote to which the Concurrence of the Senate and House of Representatives may be necessary (except on a question of Adjournment) shall be presented to the President of the United States; and before the Same shall take Effect, shall be approved by him, or being disapproved by him, shall be repassed by two thirds of the Senate and House of Representatives, according to the Rules and Limitations prescribed in the Case of a Bill.

Section 8. The Congress shall have Power To lay and collect Taxes, Duties, Imposts and Excises, to pay the Debts and provide for the common Defence and general Welfare of the United States; but all Duties, Imposts and Excises shall be uniform throughout the United States;

To borrow Money on the credit of the United States;

To regulate Commerce with foreign Nations, and among the several States, and with the Indian Tribes;

To establish an uniform Rule of Naturalization, and uniform Laws on the subject of Bankruptcies throughout the United States;

To coin Money, regulate the Value thereof, and of foreign Coin, and fix the Standard of Weights and Measures;

To provide for the Punishment of counterfeiting the Securities and current Coin of the United States;

To establish Post Offices and post Roads;

To promote the Progress of Science and useful Arts, by securing for limited Times to Authors and Inventors the exclusive Right to their respective Writings and Discoveries;

To constitute Tribunals inferior to the Supreme Court;

To define and punish piracies and Felonies committed on the high Seas, and Offences against the Law of Nations;

To declare War, grant Letters of Marque and Reprisal, and make Rules concerning Captures on Land and Water;

To raise and support Armies, but no Appropriation of Money to that Use shall be for a longer Term than two Years;

† Revised by Twentieth Amendment.

To provide and maintain a Navy;

To make Rules for the Government and Regulation of the land and naval Forces;

To provide for calling forth the Militia to execute the Laws of the Union, suppress Insurrections and repel Invasions;

To provide for organizing, arming, and disciplining, the Militia, and for governing such Part of them as may be employed in the Service of the United States, reserving to the States respectively, the Appointment of the Officers, and the Authority of training the Militia according to the discipline prescribed by Congress;

To exercise exclusive Legislation in all Cases whatsoever, over such District (not exceeding ten Miles square) as may, by Cession of particular States, and the Acceptance of Congress, become the Seat of the Government of the United States, and to exercise like Authority over all Places purchased by the Consent of the Legislature of the State in which the Same shall be, for the Erection of Forts, Magazines, Arsenals, dock-Yards, and other needful Buildings;—And

To make all Laws which shall be necessary and proper for carrying into Execution the foregoing Powers, and all other Powers vested by this Constitution in the Government of the United States, or in any Department or Officer thereof.

Section 9. The Migration or Importation of such Persons as any of the States now existing shall think proper to admit, shall not be prohibited by the Congress prior to the Year one thousand eight hundred and eight, but a Tax or duty may be imposed on such Importation, not exceeding ten dollars for each Person.

The Privilege of the Writ of Habeas Corpus shall not be suspended, unless when in Cases of Rebellion or Invasion the public Safety may require it.

No Bill of Attainder or ex post facto Law shall be passed.

No Capitation, or other direct, Tax shall be laid, unless in Proportion to the Census or Enumeration herein before directed to be taken.*

No Tax or Duty shall be laid on Articles exported from any State.

No Preference shall be given by any Regulation of Commerce or Revenue to the Ports of one State over those of another: nor shall Vessels bound to, or from, one State, be obliged to enter, clear, or pay Duties in another.

No Money shall be drawn from the Treasury, but in Consequence of Appropriations made by Law; and a regular Statement and Account of the Receipts and Expenditures of all public Money shall be published from time to time.

No title of Nobility shall be granted by the United States: And no Person holding any Office of Profit or Trust under them, shall, without the Consent of the Congress, accept of any present, Emolument, Office, or Title, of any kind whatever, from any King, Prince, or foreign State.

Section 10. No State shall enter into any Treaty, Alliance, or Confederation; grant Letters of Marque and Reprisal; coin Money; emit Bills of Credit; make any Thing but gold and silver Coin a Tender in Payment of Debts; pass any Bill of Attainder, ex post facto Law, or Law impairing the Obligation of Contracts, or Grant any Title of Nobility.

No State shall, without the Consent of the Congress, lay any Imposts or Duties on Imports or Exports, except what may be absolutely necessary for executing its inspection Laws: and the net Produce of all Duties and Imposts, laid by any State on Imports or Exports, shall be for the Use of the Treasury of the United States; and all such Laws shall be subject to the Revision and Controul of the Congress.

No State shall, without the Consent of Congress, lay any Duty of Tonnage, keep Troops, or Ships of War in time of Peace, enter into any Agreement or Compact with another State, or with a foreign Power, or engage in War, unless actually invaded, or in such imminent Danger as will not admit of delay.

ARTICLE II

Section 1. The executive Power shall be vested in a President of the United States of America. *He shall hold his Office during the Term of four Years,†* and, together with the Vice President, chosen for the same Term be elected as follows:

Each State shall appoint, in such Manner as the Legislature thereof may direct, a Number of Electors, equal to the whole Number of Senators and Representatives to which the State may be entitled in the Congress but no Senator or Representative, or Person holding an Office of Trust or Profit under the United States, shall be appointed an Elector.

The Electors shall meet in their respective States, and vote by Ballot for two Persons, of whom one at least shall not be an Inhabitant of the same State with themselves. And they shall make a List of all the Persons voted for, and of the Number of Votes for each; which List they shall sign and certify, and transmit sealed to the Seat of the Government of the United States, directed to the President of the Senate. The President of the Senate shall, in the Presence of the Senate and House of Representatives, open all the Certificates, and the Votes shall then be counted. The Person having the greatest Number

---

* Revised by Sixteenth Amendment.

† See Twenty-second Amendment.

of Votes shall be the President, if such Number be a Majority of the whole Number of Electors appointed; and if there be more than one who have such Majority, and have an equal Number of Votes, then the House of Representatives shall immediately chuse by Ballot one of them for President; and if no Person have a Majority, then from the five highest on the List the said House shall in like Manner chuse the President. But in chusing the President, the Votes shall be taken by States, the Representation from each State having one Vote; A quorum for this purpose shall consist of a Member or Members from two thirds of the States, and a Majority of all the States shall be necessary to a Choice. In every Case, after the Choice of the President, the Person having the greatest Number of Votes of the Electors shall be the Vice President. But if there should remain two or more who have equal Votes, the Senate shall chuse from them by Ballot the Vice President.*

The Congress may determine the Time of chusing the Electors, and the Day on which they shall give their Votes; which Day shall be the same throughout the United States.

No Person except a natural born Citizen, or a Citizen of the United States, at the time of the Adoption of this Constitution, shall be eligible to the Office of President; neither shall any Person be eligible to that Office who shall not have attained to the Age of thirty five Years, and been fourteen Years a Resident within the United States.

In case of the Removal of the President from Office, or of his Death, Resignation, or Inability to discharge the Powers and Duties of the said Office, the Same shall devolve on the Vice President, and the Congress may by Law provide for the Case of Removal, Death, Resignation or Inability, both of the President and Vice President, declaring what Officer shall then act as President, and such Officer shall act accordingly, until the Disability be removed, or a President shall be elected.†

The President shall, at stated Times, receive for his Services, a Compensation which shall neither be encreased nor diminished during the Period for which he shall have been elected, and he shall not receive within that Period any other Emolument from the United States, or any of them.

Before he enter on the Execution of his Office, he shall take the following Oath or Affirmation:—"I do solemnly swear (or affirm) that I will faithfully execute the Office of President of the United States, and will to the best of my Ability, preserve, protect and defend the Constitution of the United States."

Section 2. The President shall be Commander in Chief of the Army and Navy of the United States, and of the Militia of the several States, when called into the actual service of the United States; he may require the Opinion, in writing, of the principal Officer in each of the executive Departments, upon any Subject relating to the Duties of their respective Offices, and he shall have Power to grant Reprieves and Pardons for Offences against the United States, except in Cases of Impeachment.

He shall have Power, by and with the Advice and Consent of the Senate, to make Treaties, provided two thirds of the Senators present concur; and he shall nominate, and by and with the Advice and Consent of the Senate, shall appoint Ambassadors, and other public Ministers and Consuls, Judges of the supreme Court, and all other Officers of the United States, whose Appointments are not herein otherwise provided for, and which shall be established by Law: but the Congress may by Law vest the Appointment of such inferior Officers, as they think proper, in the President alone, in the Courts of Law, or in the Heads of Departments.

The President shall have Power to fill up all Vacancies that may happen during the Recess of the Senate, by granting Commissions which shall expire at the End of their next Session.

Section 3. He shall from time to time give to the Congress Information of the State of the Union, and recommend to their Consideration such Measures as he shall judge necessary and expedient; he may, on extraordinary Occasions, convene both Houses, or either of them, and in Case of Disagreement between them, with Respect to the Time of Adjournment, he may adjourn them to such Time as he shall think proper; he shall receive Ambassadors and other public Ministers, he shall take Care that the Laws be faithfully executed, and shall Commission all the Officers of the United States.

Section 4. The President, Vice President, and all civil Officers of the United States, shall be removed from Office on Impeachment for, and Conviction of Treason, Bribery, or other high Crimes and Misdemeanors.

ARTICLE III

Section 1. The judicial Power of the United States, shall be vested in one supreme Court and in such inferior Courts as the Congress may from time to time ordain and establish. The Judges, both of the supreme and inferior Courts, shall hold their Offices during good Behavior, and shall, at stated Times, receive for their Services, a Compensation, which shall not be diminished during their Continuance in Office.

Section 2. The judicial Power shall extend to all Cases, in Law and Equity, arising under this Constitution, the Laws of the United States, and Treaties made, or which

---

* Superseded by Twelfth Amendment.
† Revised by Twenty-fifth Amendment.

shall be made, under their Authority;—to all Cases affecting Ambassadors, other public Ministers and Consuls;—to all Cases of admiralty and maritime Jurisdiction;—to Controversies to which the United States shall be a Party;—to Controversies between two or more States;—*between a State and Citizens of another State**;—between Citizens of different States;—between Citizens of the same State claiming Lands under Grants of different States, *and between a State or the Citizens thereof, and foreign States, Citizens, or Subjects.**

In all cases affecting Ambassadors, other public Ministers and Consuls, and those in which a State shall be Party, the supreme Court shall have original Jurisdiction. In all the other Cases before mentioned, the supreme Court shall have appellate Jurisdiction, both as to Law and Fact, with such Exceptions, and under such Regulations as the Congress shall make.

The Trial of all Crimes, except in Cases of Impeachment, shall be by Jury; and such Trial shall be held in the State where the said Crimes shall have been committed; but when not committed within any State, the Trial shall be at such Place or Places as the Congress may by Law have directed.

Section 3.   Treason against the United States, shall consist only in levying War against them, or in adhering to their Enemies, giving them Aid and Comfort. No Person shall be convicted of Treason unless on the Testimony of two Witnesses to the same overt Act, or on Confession in open Court.

The Congress shall have Power to declare the Punishment of Treason, but no Attainder of Treason shall work Corruption of Blood, or Forfeiture except during the Life of the Person attainted.

ARTICLE IV

Section 1.   Full Faith and Credit shall be given in each State to the public Acts, Records, and judicial Proceedings of every other State. And the Congress may by general Laws prescribe the Manner in which such Acts, Records, and Proceedings shall be proved, and the Effect thereof.

Section 2.   The Citizens of each State shall be entitled to all Privileges and Immunities of Citizens in the several States.

A Person charged in any State with Treason, Felony, or other Crime, who shall flee from Justice, and be found in another State, shall on Demand of the executive Authority of the State from which he fled, be delivered up, to be removed to the State having Jurisdiction of the Crime.

No person held to Service or Labour in one State, under the Laws thereof, escaping into another, shall, in Consequence of any Law or Regulation therein, be discharged from such Service or Labour, but shall be delivered up on Claim of the Party to whom such Service or Labour may be due.*

Section 3.   New States may be admitted by the Congress into this Union; but no new State shall be formed or erected within the Jurisdiction of any other State; nor any State be formed by the Junction of two or more States, or Parts of States, without the Consent of the Legislatures of the States concerned as well as of the Congress.

The Congress shall have Power to dispose of and make all needful Rules and Regulations respecting the Territory or other Property belonging to the United States; and nothing in this Constitution shall be so construed as to Prejudice any claims of the United States, or of any particular State.

Section 4.   The United States shall guarantee to every State in this Union a Republican Form of Government, and shall protect each of them against Invasion; and on Application of the Legislature, or of the Executive (when the Legislature cannot be convened) against domestic Violence.

ARTICLE V

The Congress, whenever two thirds of both Houses shall deem it necessary, shall propose Amendments to this Constitution, or, on the Application of the Legislatures of two thirds of the several States, shall call a Convention for proposing Amendments, which, in either Case, shall be valid to all Intents and Purposes, as Part of this Constitution, when ratified by the Legislatures of three fourths of the several States, or by Conventions in three fourths thereof, as the one or the other Mode of Ratification may be proposed by the Congress; Provided that no Amendment which may be made prior to the Year One thousand eight hundred and eight shall in any Manner affect the first and fourth Clauses in the Ninth Section of the first Article; and that no State, without its Consent, shall be deprived of its equal Suffrage in the Senate.

ARTICLE VI

All Debts contracted and Engagements entered into, before the Adoption of this Constitution, shall be as valid against the United States under this Constitution, as under the Confederation.†

This Constitution, and the Laws of the United States which shall be made in Pursuance thereof; and all Treaties

---

* Revised by Eleventh Amendment.

* Superseded by Thirteenth Amendment.
† See Fourteenth Amendment, Section 4.

made, or which shall be made, under the Authority of the United States, shall be the supreme Law of the Land; and the Judges in every State shall be bound thereby, any Thing in the Constitution or Laws of any State to the Contrary notwithstanding.

The Senators and Representatives before mentioned, and the Members of the several State Legislatures, and all executive and judicial Officers, both of the United States and of the several States, shall be bound by Oath or Affirmation, to support this Constitution; but no religious Test shall ever be required as a Qualification to any Office or public Trust under the United States.

ARTICLE VII

The Ratification of the Conventions of nine States, shall be sufficient for the Establishment of this Constitution between the States so ratifying the Same.

Done in Convention by the Unanimous Consent of the States present the Seventeenth Day of September in the Year of our Lord one thousand seven hundred and eighty seven and of the Independence of the United States of America the twelfth. In witness whereof We have hereunto subscribed our Names.

. . .

ARTICLES IN ADDITION TO, AND AMENDMENT OF, THE CONSTITUTION OF THE UNITED STATES OF AMERICA, PROPOSED BY CONGRESS, AND RATIFIED BY THE SEVERAL STATES, PURSUANT TO THE FIFTH ARTICLE OF THE ORIGINAL CONSTITUTION. (Ratification of the first ten amendments was completed December 15, 1791.)

AMENDMENT I

Congress shall make no law respecting an establishment of religion, or prohibiting the free exercise thereof; or abridging the freedom of speech, or of the press; or the right of the people peaceably to assemble, and to petition the Government for a redress of grievances.

AMENDMENT II

A well regulated Militia, being necessary to the security of a free State, the right of the people to keep and bear Arms, shall not be infringed.

AMENDMENT III

No Solider shall, in time of peace be quartered in any house, without the consent of the Owner, nor in time of war, but in a manner to be prescribed by law.

AMENDMENT IV

The right of the people to be secure in their persons, houses, papers, and effects, against unreasonable searches and seizures, shall not be violated, and no Warrants shall issue, but upon probable cause, supported by Oath or affirmation, and particularly describing the place to be searched, and the persons or things to be seized.

AMENDMENT V

No person shall be held to answer for a capital, or other infamous crime, unless on a presentment or indictment of a Grand Jury, except in cases arising in the land or naval forces, or in the Militia, when in actual service in time of War or public danger; nor shall any person be subject for the same offence to be twice put in jeopardy of life or limb; nor shall be compelled in any criminal case to be a witness against himself, nor be deprived of life, liberty, or property, without due process of law; nor shall private property be taken for public use, without just compensation.

AMENDMENT VI

In all criminal prosecutions, the accused shall enjoy the right to a speedy and public trial, by an impartial jury of the State and district wherein the crime shall have been committed, which district shall have been previously ascertained by law, and to be informed of the nature and cause of the accusation; to be confronted with the witnesses against him; to have compulsory process for obtaining witnesses in his favor, and to have the Assistance of Counsel for his defence.

AMENDMENT VII

In Suits at common law, where the value in controversy shall exceed twenty dollars, the right of trial by jury shall be preserved, and no fact tried by a jury, shall be otherwise reexamined in any Court of the United States, than according to the rules of the common law.

AMENDMENT VIII

Excessive bail shall not be required, nor excessive fines imposed, nor cruel and unusual punishments inflicted.

AMENDMENT IX

The enumeration in the Constitution, of certain rights, shall not be construed to deny or disparage others retained by the people.

AMENDMENT X

The powers not delegated to the United States by the Constitution, nor prohibited by it to the States, are reserved to the States respectively, or to the people.

AMENDMENT XI (JANUARY 8, 1798)

The Judicial power of the United States shall not be construed to extend to any suit in law or equity, commenced or prosecuted against one of the United States by Citizens of another State, or by Citizens or Subjects of any Foreign State.

AMENDMENT XII (SEPTEMBER 25, 1804)

The Electors shall meet in their respective states and vote by ballot for President and Vice President, one of whom, at least, shall not be an inhabitant of the same state with themselves; they shall name in their ballots the person voted for as President, and in distinct ballots the person voted for as Vice President, and they shall make distinct lists of all persons voted for as President and of all persons voted for as Vice President, and of the number of votes for each, which lists they shall sign and certify, and transmit sealed to the seat of the government of the United States, directed to the President of the Senate;—The President of the Senate shall, in the presence of Senate and House of Representatives, open all the certificates and the votes shall then be counted;—The person having the greatest number of votes for President, shall be the President, if such number be a majority of the whole number of Electors appointed; and if no person have such majority, then from the persons having the highest numbers not exceeding three on the list of those voted for as President, the House of Representatives shall choose immediately, by ballot, the President. But in choosing the President, the votes shall be taken by states, the representation from each state having one vote; a quorum for this purpose shall consist of a member or members from two-thirds of the states, and a majority of all the states shall be necessary to a choice. And if the House of Representatives shall not choose a President whenever the right of choice shall devolve upon them, *before the fourth day of March next following,** then the Vice President shall act as President, as in the case of the death or other constitutional disability of the President.—The person having the greatest number of votes as Vice President shall be the Vice President, if such number be a majority of the whole number of Electors appointed, and if no person have a majority, then from the two highest numbers on the list, the Senate shall choose the Vice President; a quorum for the purpose shall consist of two-thirds of the whole number of Senators, and a majority of the whole number shall be necessary to a choice. But no person constitutionally ineligible to the office of President shall be eligible to that of Vice President of the United States.

* Revised by the Twentieth Amendment.

AMENDMENT XIII (DECEMBER 18, 1865)

Section 1.   Neither slavery nor involuntary servitude, except as a punishment for crime whereof the party shall have been duly convicted, shall exist within the United States, or any place subject to their jurisdiction.

Section 2.   Congress shall have the power to enforce this article by appropriate legislation.

AMENDMENT XIV (JULY 28, 1869)

Section 1.   All persons born or naturalized in the United States, and subject to the jurisdiction thereof, are citizens of the United States and of the State wherein they reside. No State shall make or enforce any law which shall abridge the privileges or immunities of citizens of the United States; nor shall any State deprive any person of life, liberty, or property, without due process of law; nor deny to any person within its jurisdiction the equal protection of the laws.

Section 2.   Representatives shall be apportioned among the several States according to their respective numbers, counting the whole number of persons in each State, excluding Indians not taxed. But when the right to vote at any election for the choice of electors for President and Vice President of the United States, Representatives in Congress, the Executive and Judicial officers of a State, or the members of the Legislature thereof, is denied to any of the male inhabitants of such State, being twenty-one years of age, and citizens of the United States, or in any way abridged, except for participation in rebellion, or other crime, the basis of representation therein shall be reduced in the proportion which the number of such male citizens shall bear to the whole number of male citizens twenty-one years of age in such State.

Section 3.   No person shall be a Senator or Representative in Congress, or elector of President and Vice President, or hold any office, civil or military, under the United States, or under any State, who, having previously taken an oath, as a member of Congress, or as an officer of the United States, or as a member of any State legislature, or as an executive or judicial officer of any State, to support the Constitution of the United States, shall have engaged in insurrection or rebellion against the same, or given aid or comfort to the enemies thereof. But Congress may by a vote of two thirds of each House, remove such disability.

Section 4.   The validity of the public debt of the United States, authorized by law, including debts incurred for payment of pensions and bounties for services in suppressing insurrection or rebellion, shall not be questioned. But neither the United States nor any State shall assume or pay any debt or obligation incurred in aid of insurrection or rebellion against the United States, or any claim for the loss or emancipation of any slave; but all such debts, obligations, and claims shall be held illegal and void.

Section 5.   The Congress shall have power to enforce, by appropriate legislation, the provisions of this article.

AMENDMENT XV (MARCH 30, 1870)

Section 1.   The right of citizens of the United States to vote shall not be denied or abridged by the United States or by any State on account of race, color, or previous conditions of servitude.

Section 2.   The Congress shall have power to enforce this article by appropriate legislation.

AMENDMENT XVI (FEBRUARY 25, 1913)

The Congress shall have power to lay and collect taxes on incomes, from whatever source derived, without apportionment among the several States, and without regard to any census or enumeration.

AMENDMENT XVII (MAY 31, 1913)

The Senate of the United States shall be composed of two Senators from each State, elected by the people thereof, for six years; and each Senator shall have one vote. The electors in each State shall have the qualifications requisite for electors of the most numerous branch of the State legislatures.

When vacancies happen in the representation of any State in the Senate, the executive authority of such State shall issue writs of election to fill such vacancies: *Provided,* That the legislature of any State may empower the executive thereof to make temporary appointments until the people fill the vacancies by election as the legislature may direct.

This amendment shall not be so construed as to affect the election or term of any Senator chosen before it becomes valid as part of the Constitution.

AMENDMENT XVIII (JANUARY 29, 1919)

Section 1.   After one year from the ratification of this article the manufacture, sale, or transportation of intoxicating liquors within, the importation thereof into, or the exportation thereof from the United States and all territory subject to the jurisdiction thereof for beverage purposes is hereby prohibited.

Section 2.   The Congress and the several States shall have concurrent power to enforce this article by appropriate legislation.

Section 3.   This article shall be inoperative unless it shall have been ratified as an amendment to the Constitution by the legislatures of the several States, as provided in the Constitution within seven years from the date of the submission hereof to the States by the Congress. *

AMENDMENT XIX (AUGUST 26, 1920)

The right of citizens of the United States to vote shall not be denied or abridged by the United States or by any State on account of sex.

Congress shall have power to enforce this article by appropriate legislation.

AMENDMENT XX (FEBRUARY 6, 1933)

Section 1.   The terms of the President and Vice President shall end at noon on the 20th day of January, and the terms of Senators and Representatives at noon on the 3rd day of January, of the years in which such terms would have ended if this article had not been ratified; and the terms of their successors shall then begin.

Section 2.   The Congress shall assemble at least once in every year, and such meeting shall begin at noon on the 3rd day of January, unless they shall by law appoint a different day.

Section 3.   If, at the time fixed for the beginning of the term of the President, the President elect shall have died, the Vice President elect shall become President. If a President shall not have been chosen before the time fixed for the beginning of his term, or if the President elect shall have failed to qualify, then the Vice President elect shall act as President until a President shall have qualified; and the Congress may by law provide for the case wherein neither a President elect nor a Vice President elect shall have qualified, declaring who shall then act as President, or the manner in which one who is to act shall be selected, and such person shall act accordingly until a President or Vice President shall have qualified.

Section 4.   The Congress may by law provide for the case of the death of any of the persons from whom the House of Representatives may choose a President whenever the right of choice shall have devolved upon them, and for the case of the death of any of the persons from whom the Senate may choose a Vice President whenever the right of choice shall have devolved upon them.

Section 5.   Sections 1 and 2 shall take effect on the 15th day of October following the ratification of this article.

Section 6.   This article shall be inoperative unless it shall have been ratified as an amendment to the Constitution by

---

* Repealed by the Twenty-first Amendment.

the legislatures of three-fourths of the several States within seven years from the date of its submission.

AMENDMENT XXI (DECEMBER 5, 1933)

Section 1.   The eighteenth article of amendment to the Constitution of the United States is hereby repealed.

Section 2.   The transportation or importation into any State, Territory, or possession of the United States for delivery or use therein of intoxicating liquors, in violation of the laws thereof, is hereby prohibited.

Section 3.   This article shall be inoperative unless it shall have been ratified as an amendment to the Constitution by conventions in the several States, as provided in the Constitution, within seven years from the date of the submission hereof to the States by the Congress.

AMENDMENT XXII (FEBRUARY 26, 1951)

Section 1.   No person shall be elected to the office of the President more than twice, and no person who has held the office of President, or acted as President, for more than two years of a term to which some other person was elected President shall be elected to the office of President more than once. But this Article shall not apply to any person holding the office of President when this Article was proposed by the Congress, and shall not prevent any person who may be holding the office of President, or acting as President, during the term within which this Article becomes operative from holding the office of President or acting as President during the remainder of such term.

Section 2.   This article shall be inoperative unless it shall have been ratified as an amendment to the Constitution by the legislatures of three-fourths of the several States within seven years from the date of its submission to the States by the Congress.

AMENDMENT XXIII (MARCH 29, 1961)

Section 1.   The District constituting the seat of Government of the United States shall appoint in such manner as the Congress may direct:

A number of electors of President and Vice President equal to the whole number of Senators and Representatives in Congress to which the District would be entitled if it were a State, but in no event more than the least populous State; they shall be in addition to those appointed by the States, but they shall be considered, for the purposes of the election of President and Vice President, to be electors appointed by a State; and they shall meet in the District and perform such duties as provided by the twelfth article of amendment.

Section 2.   The Congress shall have power to enforce this article by appropriate legislation.

AMENDMENT XXIV (JANUARY 23, 1964)

Section 1.   The right of citizens of the United States to vote in any primary or other election for President or Vice President, for electors for President or Vice President, or for Senator or Representative in Congress, shall not be denied or abridged by the United States or any state by reason of failure to pay any poll tax or other tax.

Section 2.   The Congress shall have the power to enforce this article by appropriate legislation.

AMENDMENT XXV (FEBRUARY 10, 1967)

Section 1.   In case of the removal of the President from office or of his death or resignation, the Vice President shall become President.

Section 2.   Whenever there is a vacancy in the office of the Vice President, the President shall nominate a Vice President who shall take office upon confirmation by a majority vote of both Houses of Congress.

Section 3.   Whenever the President transmits to the President pro tempore of the Senate and the Speaker of the House of Representatives his written declaration that he is unable to discharge the powers and duties of his office, and until he transmits to them a written declaration to the contrary, such powers and duties shall be discharged by the Vice President as Acting President.

Section 4.   Whenever the Vice President and a majority of either the principal officers of the executive departments or of such other body as Congress may by law provide, transmit to the President pro tempore of the Senate and the Speaker of the House of Representatives their written declaration that the President is unable to discharge the powers and duties of his office, the Vice President shall immediately assume the powers and duties of the office as Acting President.

Thereafter, when the President transmits to the President pro tempore of the Senate and the Speaker of the House of Representatives his written declaration that no inability exists, he shall resume the powers and duties of his office unless the Vice President and a majority of either the principal officers of the executive departments or of such other body as Congress may by law provide, transmit within four days to the President pro tempore of the Senate and the Speaker of the House of Representatives their written declaration that the President is unable to discharge the powers and duties of his office. Thereupon Congress shall decide the issue, assembling within forty-eight hours for that purpose if not in session. If the Congress, within twenty-one days after receipt of the latter written declaration or, if Congress is not in session, within twenty-one days after Congress is required to assemble, determines by two-thirds vote of both Houses that the President is unable to discharge the powers and duties of his office, the Vice President shall continue to discharge the same as Acting President; otherwise, the President shall resume the powers and duties of his office.

AMENDMENT XXVI (JUNE 30, 1971)

Section 1. The right of citizens of the United States, who are eighteen years of age or older, to vote shall not be denied or abridged by the United States or any state on account of age.

Section 2. The Congress shall have the power to enforce this article by appropriate legislation.

INDEX

Items in **boldface** type indicate that the item is also found in the Glossary.

693

PHOTO CREDITS

Chapter 1

Opener: Courtesy The White House. Page 2: Owen Franken/Sygma. Page 4: Bruce Roberts/Photo Researchers. Page 8: (top) Historical Picture Service; (bottom) Culver Pictures. Page 9: (center) Courtesy Suffolk County Democratic Committee; (bottom) Courtesy Smithsonian Institution. Page 10: (top) Wide World; (bottom) Jeff Albertson/Stock, Boston. Page 11: Historical Picture Service. Page 14: Jan Lukas/Photo Researchers. Page 15: Anestis Diakopoulos/Stock, Boston. Page 18: (bottom) George Hall/Woodfin Camp. Page 19: Lawrence Frank/Photo Researchers. Page 26: (top) J.P. Laffont/Sygma; (bottom) Joel Gordon.

Chapter 2

Opener: Martha Swope. Page 34: (top) Historical Picture Service; (bottom) Courtesy City of Boston. On Fund deposit at the Museum of Fine Arts. Page 35: Emmet Collection, Manuscripts & Archives Division, The New York Public Library, Astor, Lenox and Tilden Foundations. Page 37: New York Public Library Picture Collection. Page 38: (top and center) Courtesy the Free Library of Philadelphia; (bottom) New York Public Library Picture Collection. Page 41: Courtesy the Free Library of Philadelphia. Page 42: (top) Courtesy the Free Library of Philadelphia; (bottom) Courtesy Pennsylvania Academy of Fine Arts, Joseph and Sarah Harrison Collection. Page 45: Historical Picture Service. Page 46: (top and center) Courtesy the Free Library of Philadelphia; (bottom) New York Public Library Picture Collection. Page 48: Sidney Harris. Page 54: (top) Brown Brothers; (bottom) Hugh Rogers/Monkmeyer.

Chapter 3

Opener: New York Daily News Photo. Page 60: Tim Eagen/Woodfin Camp. Page 62: (top) Courtesy the Free Library of Philadelphia; (bottom) Historical Picture Service. Page 66: J.P. Laffont/Sygma. Page 68: Culver Pictures. Page 72: Courtesy the Free Library of Philadelphia. Page 74: Sidney Harris. Page 79: U.P.I. Page 80. George Gardner. Page 82: (top) Burk Uzzle/Magnum. Page 84: New York Public Library Picture Collection. Page 89: Wide World.

Chapter 4

Opener: Joel Gordon. Page 100: Wide World. Page 103: Historical Picture Service. Page 105: Bob Combs/Photo Researchers. Page 110: Jane Latta/Photo Researchers. Page 111: Lawrence Frank/Rapho-Photo Researchers. Page 114: U.P.I. Page 115: New York Public Library Picture Collection. Page 118: George Gardner. Page 121: Bruce Roberts/Rapho-Photo Researchers. Page 125: Sidney Harris. Page 128: Charles Gatewood. Page 129: Joel Gordon. Page 130: Wide World.

Chapter 5

Opener: Jill Freedman/Magnum. Page 140: Mark Godfrey/Magnum. Page 141: Jan Lukas/Photo Researchers. Page 144: Martin Adler Levick/Black Star. Page 143: George Gardner. Page 147: F.B. Grunzweig/Photo Researchers. Page 146: Lawrence Frank/Photo Researchers. Page 155: Tim Kantor/Rapho-Photo Researchers. Page 156: George Gardner.

Chapter 6

Opener: Bettye Lane. Page 171: (top) Courtesy Smithsonian Institution; (center) Rosemary Eakins. Page 173: (top right) Joel Gordon; (top left) Lawrence Frank/Photo Researchers; (center) Charles Gatewood. Page 178: U.P.I. Page 181: (top) New York Public Library Picture Collection; (bottom) Courtesy the Free Library of Philadelphia. Page 182: (top) Dennis Brack/Black Star; (bottom) Wide World. Page 183: (top and bottom) Wide World; (center) U.P.I. Page 184: (top) Courtesy the Free Library of Philadelphia; (bottom) Paul Sequeira/Rapho-Photo Researchers. Page 185: Lawrence Frank/Photo Researchers. Page 186: (top) Fred Ward/Black Star; (bottom) Wide World Page 188: Earl Dotter/Magnum. Page 192: Myron Wood/Photo Researchers. Page 197: Courtesy Mobil Oil. Page 201: Historical Picture Service. Page 203: Bob Adelman/Magnum. Page 205: Stephen Frisch/Photo Researchers. Page 206: Peter Angelo Simon/Photo Researchers. Page 208: Yoichi R. Okamoto/Photo Researchers. Page 210: Ron Sherman/Nancy Palmer. Page 211: Seneca Falls Historical Soceity. Page 212: (top) Historical Picture Service; (bottom) New York Public Library Picture Collection. Page 213: Culver Pictures. Page 215: Vicky Lawrence/Stock, Boston. Page 216 and 218: Bettye Lane/Photo Researchers. Page 219: Diana Mara Henry. Page 220: Lawrence Frank/Photo Researchers.

Chapter 7

Opener: (top) Tony Karody/Sygma; (bottom) Dennis Brack/Black Star. Page 227: Courtesy Smithsonian Institution. Page 230: (left) U.P.I.; (right) Bill Stanton/Magnum. Page 231: U.P.I. Page 232: Diana Mara Henry. Page 234: Courtesy Smithsonian Institution. Page 236: (bottom) New York Public Library Picture Collection. Page 238: Courtesy of Indiana Historical Society Library. Page 239: (top) Courtesy Smithsonian Institution; (bottom) New York Public Library Picture Collection. Page 240: (top) Courtesy Smithsonian Institution; (center) New York Public Library Picture Collection; (bottom) Franklin D. Roosevelt Library. Page 241: (top) Courtesy Smithsonian Institution; (bottom) Manuscripts and University Archives, Cornell University. Page 242 and 243: Courtesy Smithsonian Institution. Page 250: (top) Cooper Union; (bottom) Manuscripts and University Archives, Cornell University. Page 251: Courtesy Smithsonian Institution. Page 252: (top) New York Public Library Picture Collection; (bottom) Courtesy Smithsonian Institution. Page 253: U.P.I. Page 254: Lawrence Frank/Photo Researchers.

Chapter 8

Opener: Andrew Schneider/Black Star. Page 260: (top) Arthur Grace/Sygma; (center) Andrew Schneider/Black Star; (bottom) Arthur Grace/Sygma. Page 261: (top) Wide World; (bottom) Henry Bureau/Sygma. Page 262: (top) Dennis Brack/Black Star; (bottom) Lawrence Frank/Photo Researchers. Page 264: Historical Picture Service. Page 273: Wide World. Page 276: (top) Dennis Brack/Black Star; (bottom) Arthur Grace/Sygma. Page 278: (top) Ken Hawkins/Sygma; (bottom) Arthur Grace/Sygma. Page 284: Wide World. Page 287: Lawrence Frank/Photo Researchers. Page 288: (top) Owen Franken/Stock, Boston; (bottom left) J.P. Laffont/Sygma; (bottom right) Lawrence Frank/Photo Researchers. Page 289: (top) Alex Webb/Magnum; (bottom) Lawrence Frank/Photo Researchers.

Chapter 9

Opener: Dirck Halstead/Contact Press. Page 302: (top) Owen Franken/Stock, Boston;

(bottom) Dennis Brack/Black Star. Page 303: (top) Reproduced by special permission of PLAYBOY Magazine; copyright © 1976 by Playboy; (bottom) Wide World. Page 305: (top) Courtesy of New York Historical Society, New York; (bottom) Historical Picture Service. Page 306: New York Public Library Picture Collection. Page 308: U.P.I. Page 310: Courtesy Smithsonian Institution. Page 314: Andrew Schneider/Black Star. Page 316: Courtesy Smithsonian Institution. Page 317: (bottom) Historical Picture Service. Page 320: Courtesy CBS, Inc. Page 326: (top) Fred Conrad/Sygma; (bottom) Wide World. Page 332 and 333: U.P.I.

Chapter 10

Opener: Paolo Koch/Rapho-Photo Researchers. Page 336: (top) Bruce Roberts/Rapho-Photo Researchers; (bottom) Culver Pictures. Page 338: Lawrence Frank/Photo Researchers. Page 347: (top left) Joel Gordon; (top right) Christa Armstrong/Rapho-Photo Researchers; (center) Charles Gatewood; (bottom left) George Gardner; (bottom right) Daniel Brody/Stock, Boston. Page 357: Richard Kalvar/Magnum. Page 361: Joel Gordon. Page 365: (top) Tony Korody/Sygma; (bottom) Ken Hawkins/Sygma.

Chapter 11

Opener: Dennis Brack/Black Star. Page 374: (top right) M. Brennan/Sygma; (bottom center) Wide World; (bottom right) U.P.I. Page 375: (bottom) U.P.I. Page 376: (top) Robert Siles. Page 379: Sidney Harris. Page 383: (top) J.P. Laffont/Sygma; (bottom) Robert Stiles. Page 386: Robert Stiles. Page 398: U.P.I. Page 401: New York Public Library Picture Collection. Page 404 and 406: Robert Stiles. Page 408: Wide World. Page 412 and 416: Robert Stiles. Page 420: Joel Gordon. Page 421: (top) U.P.I.; (bottom) David Falconer/Black Star. Page 423: Dennis Brack/Black Star.

Chapter 12

Opener: Peter Southwick/Stock, Boston. Page 430: (top) Dennis Brack/Black Star; (bottom) Tim Carlson/Stock, Boston. Page 431: (top, center and bottom left) U.P.I.; (bottom right) J.P. Laffont/Sygma. Page 432: Joseph Kovacs/Stock, Boston. Page 433: Sylvia Johnson/Woodfin Camp. Page 434. and 435: New York Public Library Picture Collection. Page 436 and 437 (top): Courtesy Smithsonian Institution. Page 438: Don Carl Steffen/Photo Researchers. Page 439: Sidney Harris. Page 445: (top left) Wide World; (top right and bottom left) Underwood and Underwood; (bottom right) New York Daily News Photo.

Chapter 13

Opener: Courtesy The White House. Page 456: New York Public Library Picture Collection. Page 460: Sipa/Black Star. Page 462: U.P.I. Page 465: Dennis Brack/Black Star. Page 466: (top) U.P.I.; (bottom) Owen Franken/Sygma. Page 469: Jacques Tiziou/Sygma. Page 471: New York Public Library Picture Collection. Page 477: Owen Franken/Sygma. Page 480: U.P.I. Page 482: (top) Henri Bureau/Sygma; (bottom) Sibo/Sygma. Page 484: (top) Sidney Harris. Page 485: U.P.I. Page 488: Joel Gordon. Page 489: (top) Marion Bernstein; (bottom) Sidney Harris.

Chapter 14

Opener: Arthur Tress/Photo Researchers. Page 498: (top) Dennis Brack/Black Star; (bottom and Page 499 top) From *Memo of the Month Book,* Edited by Charles Peters and

Edward A. O'Neill, copyright © 1973 by The Washington Monthly Co. Page 501: (top) Historical Picture Service. Page 513: Courtesy The White House. Page 515: Courtesy NASA. Page 516: (top) Robert Stiles; (bottom) Courtesy Federal Reserve Board. Page 517: Courtesy U.S. Department of the Interior, Geological Survey. Page 518: (top left) Ian G. MacIntyre, Smithsonian Institution, Museum of Natural History; (top right) Courtesy Smithsonian Institution; (center left) Paul Dix/Refleno/Woodfin Camp; (center right) Photo by Richard Frear/National Park Service; (bottom) Courtesy U.S. Postal Service. Page 520: (top) Fletcher Drake/Braaten Photography. Page 522: Courtesy U.S. Postal Service. Pages 527, 528 and 534: U.P.I.

Chapter 15

Opener: George Gardner. Page 540: Flip Schulke/Black Star. Page 542: George Gardner. Page 543: Daniel S. Brody/Editorial Photocolor Archives. Page 548: George Gardner. Page 555: Cartoon by Conrad, from The Washington Evening Star, Photo from Historical Picture Service. Page 557: (top) Archie Lieberman/Black Star; (bottom) Historical Picture Service. Page 558: U.P.I. Page 559: Fred Ward/Black Star. Page 560: Joel Gordon.

Chapter 16

Opener: Yoichi R. Okamoto/Photo Researchers. Page 568: (top) Dennis Brack/Black Star; (bottom) U.P.I. Page 569: U.P.I. Page 574: Photo by Ron Nelson. Page 575: Yoichi R. Okamoto/Photo Researchers. Page 577: Sidney Harris. Pages 585, 586 and 588: Historical Picture Service. Page 597: (top) U.P.I.; (bottom) Charles Gatewood. Page 599: Sidney Harris.

Chapter 17

Opener: George Gardner. Page 608: (top) George Gardner; (center) Yvonne Freund/ Rapho-Photo Researchers; (bottom) Rosemary Eakins/Research Reports. Page 609: Rosemary Eakins/Research Reports. Page 610: (top) Chie Nishio/Nancy Palmer; (bottom) U.P.I. Page 611 and 612: George Gardner. Page 614: Charles Gatewood. Page 616: (top) Charles Gatewood; (bottom left and right) Mark S. von Wehrden/Uniphoto. Page 621: Courtesy New York State Democratic Committee. Page 624: Daniel S. Brody/ Editorial Photocolor Archives. Page 627: Martin Adler Levick/Black Star. Page 628: Daniel S. Brody/Editorial Photocolor Archives. Page 630: Sidney Harris. Page 631: (top) Charles Gatewood; (bottom) George Gardner. Page 634: (top) U.P.I.; (bottom) Peter Southwick/Stock, Boston. Page 635: Dennis Brock/Black Star. Page 642: Bruce Roberts/Photo Researchers. Page 644 and 645: George Gardner. Page 647: Lawrence Frank/Photo Researchers. Page 649: George Gardner. Page 650: Carl Weese/Photo Researchers. Page 633: Ronald Nelson. Page 654: (top) Eric Kroll/Taurus Photos; (bottom) M.E. Warren/Photo Researchers.